STOCHASTIC MODELS OF
BUYING BEHAVIOR

STOCHASTIC MODELS OF BUYING BEHAVIOR

William F. Massy,

David B. Montgomery,

Donald G. Morrison

THE M.I.T. PRESS
Cambridge, Massachusetts, and London, England

To our parents:
                        Willard Francis Massy
                        Ardys Digman Massy
                        Iva Montgomery Ferrell
                        Roderick Morrison

To the memory of
                        David William Montgomery
                        Ethelyne Murray Morrison

CONTENTS

PREFACE

The use of stochastic models as representations of purchasing processes has been growing in importance during the past ten years. These models provide structural insight into the ways in which consumers regulate their choice of brands and decisions as to purchase timing and amounts for frequently purchased products. In addition, they increase the effectiveness of consumer panels as a source of market research data for these products. Panel data is too complex to be interpreted fully without the use of models, and the models must be stochastic to provide reasonable representations of the purchasing process and to avoid misleading conclusions.

Stochastic models are delicate artifacts. Their assumptions must be specified carefully, and the implications of the assumptions deduced rigorously. This is particularly true when the models are applied to data. To ignore the assumptions of a model or to use faulty statistical tools is likely to produce results that are not only useless but actually misleading. Yet when used properly, the stochastic model provides a powerful tool for the analysis of micro-behavioral data—including that related to purchasing.

This book concentrates on the technology of stochastic models as applied to buying behavior for frequently purchased products. We are concerned with the assumptions and internal consistency of such models and with their implications for purchasing behavior. Methods for mathematically deducing the properties of stochastic models from their underlying assumptions receive extensive treatment. The development of empirical methods for handling stochastic models of buying behavior is our second major theme. Methods of parameter estimation and ways of testing the models' fit to the data are considered in detail. Most of the models discussed are applied to empirical data, and results are reported.

We believe that the major questions in stochastic modeling are currently operational in nature. The difficulties are in the "how to do it" area: that is, how to specify models with reasonable assumptions and rigorously apply them to data. This is our area of concentration.

Interesting and important questions exist at both ends of this subject. Stochastic models should be more closely related to research in the behavioral sciences, on the one hand, and to the detailed needs of

management decision makers, on the other. We do not concern ourselves with these questions directly, though the reader will find many indirect references to both. For example, we deal only with observed purchase behavior and do not concern ourselves with the "causes" of this behavior in the sense of mechanisms for awareness, attitude, or behavior change. We speak of structural insight and prediction in a general sense rather than in connection with a particular management problem such as how much to spend for advertising or what kind of deal to offer.

Our choice of coverage was conscious. It does not represent a downgrading of the inherent importance of behavioral science or problem-oriented research, or the gains to be made by linking these to stochastic modeling. We simply believe that it is necessary to put the technology of stochastic modeling of buying behavior on a firm footing before developing strong links with other fields and detailed applications. We hope that our book will contribute to this objective.

Stochastic Models of Buying Behavior is primarily a report of our own research, as it developed over the years between 1964 and 1968. We have tried to review the literature as it existed during this period, so that credit could be given to our many colleagues who have been active in the field. On the other hand, this book is not a textbook in the usual sense of the word.

Finally, we should say that this book is intended for the serious student of stochastic models of buying behavior. A good background in mathematics, probability theory, and statistics will be required in order to assimilate much of the material. However, prior knowledge of the stochastic models field, as applied in marketing or elsewhere, is not required. (All necessary concepts are developed as we go along.) The reader who wishes to obtain a general overview of the field may wish to read Chapter 1 and then consult a number of the review articles cited in the bibliography.

We wish to acknowledge the assistance of a number of persons. The insightful work and comments of Professors Alfred A. Kuehn and Ronald E. Frank gave us the impetus and direction for our initial efforts. Professors Jerome Herniter, Ronald Howard, Gerald Lieberman, and Timothy McGuire provided helpful inputs at critical stages of our work. Professors Morgan Jones and David Aaker helped us to refine our thinking as they developed their own models during their tenure as doctoral students at Stanford. Particular thanks go to Morgan Jones, who made an important direct contribution to the development

of our models during his term as research assistant to Professor Massy at Carnegie-Mellon University.

Financial support for the development and testing of our models was provided by the Graduate School of Business and the Joint Program in Operations Research (now Department of Operations Research) at Stanford University, and the Sloan School of Management, M.I.T. Computer time at the Stanford Computation Center was subsidized by the National Science Foundation under Grant No. GP948. The Graduate School of Industrial Administration at Carnegie-Mellon University provided research time and financial support for Professor Massy during his tenure as Ford Distinguished Visiting Professor of Research at the School. (The enthusiastic support of Dean Richard M. Cyert is gratefully acknowledged.)

We wish to thank Mrs. Famah Andrew, who typed much of the manuscript. And, last but not least, we are grateful to our wives who put up with some five years of preoccupation and late hours during the course of our research on this project.

Stanford University	WILLIAM F. MASSY
Massachusetts Institute of Technology	DAVID B. MONTGOMERY
Columbia University	DONALD G. MORRISON
September 1969	

PART 1
GENERAL CONSIDERATIONS

CHAPTER 1
APPROACHES TO STOCHASTIC MODELING

The use of mathematical models as aids to the understanding of complex behavioral phenomena is no longer seriously questioned in most scientific circles. When the model-building task is performed well and appropriate data are used to test and revise the model and to obtain information about its parameters for the case or cases in question, such models can yield useful quantitative predictions as well as provide insights into the structure of the behavioral process.

Marketing researchers and practitioners have evidenced increasing interest in mathematical models of behavioral processes in recent years. Of particular importance are models of buying behavior — the subject of this book. Models of the purchasing process are beginning to contribute to our theoretical understanding of the effects of various factors on consumers' purchase timing and brand-choice decisions. In some cases they have become useful adjuncts to the practicing marketing researcher's kit of diagnostic and prediction tools.

1.1 Types of Models

1.1.1 Deterministic vs. Stochastic Models

Models of behavioral phenomena may be either deterministic or probabilistic in character. That is, the model builder may set up a set of equations that either does or does not include probabilistic components. Moreover, the introduction of probabilistic elements may occur as part of the fundamental specification of the model or be added as an afterthought to account for discrepancies between the predictions made by the model and actual behavioral outcomes.

Where and how probabilistic components are introduced into a model, if they are included at all, is more a matter of model-building strategy than an assumption about whether the relevant behavioral process is really stochastic or deterministic in some ultimate sense. The question of whether behavior is ultimately predictable in exact (nonprobabilistic) terms is a moot point given today's theories and technology. What is clear is that any model capable of making exact predictions would have to be incredibly complex. Moreover, the data

3

requirements of such a model would be enormous; at the very least, extensive information on the state of the organism's memory and a detailed picture of the current environment would be necessary. Such a model-building program is beyond our present capabilities.

The use of probabilistic components in a model of behavior serves to formalize the researcher's assumption on the net effect of all the factors not included in the model. Errors of sampling or measurement or a lack of complete understanding of the behavioral process will lead to discrepancies between actual behavior and that predicted by the model. Thus, probabilistic components must be added to the model (at least implicitly) after it has been confronted with data, even if the original theoretical formulation included no such elements.

For example, suppose that two models predicted that half the households in a population would purchase Brand A in a certain period. The probabilistic model would also yield a probability distribution for the deviation of this proportion from its expected value. The deterministic model does not provide such a distribution. This can make it difficult to cipher the degree to which the actual performance of the market (in which the proportion of Brand A buyers would rarely be exactly 0.5) is consistent with the model.

As we understand current terminology, a *stochastic* model is a model in which the probability components are built in at the outset rather than being added ex post facto to accommodate discrepancies between predicted and actual results. That is, the probabilistic components form an important part of the basic structure of the stochastic model.

1.1.2   *Individual vs. Aggregate Models*

A stochastic model may deal with either individual or aggregative behavior. When modeling the decisions of individuals, the predictions of the model are couched in terms of the probability distribution over the set of possible responses. That is, if an individual buyer may buy any one of ten brands, the predictions made by the model would be the probabilities of purchasing Brand 1, Brand 2, Brand 3, etc. The actual outcome on any given trial cannot be predicted exactly; this kind of indeterminacy is known as *response uncertainty*. We argued earlier that there is an irreducible lower limit to the amount of response uncertainty that can be achieved with any model of behavior in sight at the present time.

Stochastic models of aggregate behavior may be constructed in one of two ways. (1) Models of individual behavior, each with response

uncertainty, may be constructed and "added together" to obtain a model of aggregate response. Here the probabilistic properties of the aggregate model, as well as its other properties, are derived from assumptions about individuals' behavior. (2) A model of the aggregate behavior, with its own component of response uncertainty, can be constructed directly and applied to aggregate data. Here the characteristics of the aggregative model are obtained directly. Which one of the two strategies is best depends on what is known about the behavioral process, the nature of the available data, and the purposes for which the model is being constructed.

If we turn back to models of buying behavior, it is clear that aggregate models of the econometric type have much to offer in many circumstances. Many extremely useful models of this type have been constructed, and many more will doubtless be developed in the future. (Consider, for instance, the many models for predicting the aggregate response of sales to advertising and price levels.) These models make effective use of the kind of time series and cross-sectional data often available to marketing researchers.

The field of individual-stochastic model building in marketing is much less populated than that of aggregate econometric-type models (e.g., regression analyses of economic time series). As noted earlier, such models are based on postulates about the behavioral process at the level of the individual. Where aggregation is important, it is accomplished by combining individuals' models according to well-defined rules as opposed to making assumptions about the characteristics of aggregative behavior directly. While a fair variety of individual-stochastic models of buyer behavior have been suggested in the marketing literature (the various types will be reviewed in Section 1.2), there is much less agreement about what kinds of models are "good" than is now the case for econometric models. Nor have models of this type achieved the status of the econometric models as far as their use in applied marketing research and sales forecasting is concerned.

The present state of affairs is probably a result of several causes. (1) In general, individual-stochastic models are more complicated than econometric models. More knowledge of mathematics, probability theory, and statistics is required to construct and understand them, and they usually involve more complex and extensive computations. (2) The whole field is relatively new; fewer researchers are working on the development of these models, and, with few exceptions, not much has been done to try to apply this machinery to the solution of operational

problems of marketing decision makers. (3) Until very recently, these models were not realistic enough or did not include the right variables to serve as a basis for either theory development or applied marketing research. (4) Technical problems connected with the development of the mathematical form of certain important models and efficient computer techniques for estimating their parameters are just now being solved.

Individual-stochastic models appear to offer great promise for our understanding many important aspects of purchase timing and brand switching behavior. Work to date also indicates that when conditions are right and proper data are available such models can produce very good predictions.

1.1.3   *Application of Individual-Stochastic Models*

Most of the accumulated evidence about the performance of in-dividual-stochastic models of buyer behavior is concentrated in the area of frequently purchased food and drug products. This is caused partly by the models' obvious applicability to purchase phenomena in these product classes. An additional impetus has been the availability of combined time series and cross-sectional purchase data from con-tinuous consumer panels. These data are ideally suited to the problem of estimating the parameters and testing the fit of individual-stochastic models. Moreover, commercial suppliers of consumer panel data, such as the Market Research Corporation of America (MRCA) in the United States and the Attwood group in the United Kingdom, have recently become interested in the development and implementation of these models in order to stimulate the demand for their product. Companies that make a business of working with panel data have con-tributed substantial resources to the individual-stochastic model field in recent years. These models have been applied largely to buying decisions for frequently purchased products; however, we must recog-nize that their technology can be applied to a much wider range of products, including consumer durables and even industrial buying. Applications to other marketing phenomena, such as retailers' adver-tising decisions, for example, also provide fruitful opportunities for research.

This book deals with the individual-stochastic class of models. (To avoid tedious repetition, the name "individual-stochastic" will be shortened to be simply "stochastic" in the sequel.) We will investigate the kinds of assumptions that can be used to predict the probability

that an individual will engage in certain aspects of buying behavior. The characteristics of models employing various assumptions will be examined and compared, from both a theoretical and an empirical point of view. Methods for estimating the parameters of these models and assessing their goodness of fit will be presented. Finally, by examining the structure of the various models and considering the methods used to develop them, the reader will be able to formulate strategies to guide his own efforts to create and test stochastic models of buying behavior.

1.2   Characteristics of Stochastic Models of Buying Behavior

In this section we will consider some of the strategic questions involved in constructing and assessing stochastic models of buying behavior. The treatment is sketchy, as these questions will be discussed at length in later chapters. The purpose of this section is to provide a kind of roadway to orient the reader as he examines the assumptions of specific models.

1.2.1   General Considerations

The first step in stochastic model construction is to define the *state space* of possible outcomes of the process under study. For instance, if the process is one of coin flipping, the state space for one trial is (H,T), for two trials it is (HH,HT,TH,TT), etc. An *event* is defined as a single outcome or realization of the process; e.g., H or HT. The state space is the set of mutually extensive and collectively exhaustive events for the process.

Suppose that we are studying buyer behavior in a market consisting of two brands (or one particular brand and one "all other" category). If households are unlikely to purchase more than one brand on a given shopping trip and there is no more than one shopping trip per day, the state space for purchase events on a given day could be represented as follows:

State	Outcome
S_0	No Purchase
S_1	Purchase Brand 1
S_2	Purchase Brand 2

Thus, three states are possible on any given day. The objective of a

stochastic model of this situation would be to predict $\Pr\{S_i(t)\}$ where $i = 0, 1, 2$, for each day (denoted by t).

What is meant by "predict $\Pr\{S_i\}$"? In the simplest possible case this probability would be the same for every day and for all households in the population, just as the probability of obtaining a head by flipping a fair coin does not change from trial to trial or from coin to coin. (This is called a *stationary Bernoulli process:* "stationary" because the probabilities are constant, "Bernoulli" because there are only two states. We shall call a stationary process with more than two states a *multinomial process.*) Unfortunately, purchase behavior processes are not as simple as this. At the very least, $\Pr\{S_i(t)\}$ will depend on the number of days since the last purchase, which is one of many of the "characteristics" of the household as of time t. (Other relevant characteristics might include "brand bought last," "number of members of the family," "exposure to advertising," etc.). Let us denote the household's characteristics, as they exist on day t, by the vector $\mathbf{X}_t$. If these characteristics affect the purchasing process, we should write $\Pr\{S_i(t)\}$ as a conditional probability:

$$\Pr\{S_i(t)|\mathbf{X}_t\} = f(\mathbf{X}_t) \tag{1.1}$$

To set ideas we may note that in the stationary multinomial process mentioned here,

$$\Pr\{S_i(t)|\mathbf{X}_t\} = \text{constant}$$

That is, the purchase probability would be independent of time and household characteristics.

We are now in a position to indicate how one builds a stochastic model. The following steps are important:

1. Determining the state space of purchase events to be considered in the model.
2. Determining which of the many possible components of $\mathbf{X}_t$ are to be included in the model.
3. Determining what functional form should be assigned to $f(\mathbf{X}_t)$, which determines how the included X's affect the probabilities.

After making assumptions 1 to 3, the researcher completes the modeling process by solving whatever mathematical and/or statistical problems are necessary to deduce the properties of the model and provide a method for estimating its parameters from empirical data.

The guidelines for making these assumptions are to be found in the model builder's knowledge of the behavioral process in question and

the purposes to which the model will be put. This must be mediated, of course, by a sense of what kinds of structures can be manipulated mathematically and what type of data will be available to test the model. (In general, it must be possible to obtain data showing which event in the state space occurs on each trial, and what the values of the X's were when the trial was undertaken.) The model should be viewed as a kind of theory of the relevant behavior. The process of model building, as it is viewed in this book, is not an exercise in curve fitting!

1.2.2 Factors Affecting Purchase Probabilities

We feel that the important determinants of purchase probabilities (i.e., the factors to be included as elements of **X**) can be classified under three main headings: (1) feedback from past purchases of the product; (2) the influence of exogenous market forces, and (3) factors indigenous to the household itself, which are not affected in the short run by either of the above. This classification leads us to consider purchase event feedback, time effects, and population heterogeneity as major characteristics of stochastic models of buyer behavior.

1.2.2.1 *Purchase Event Feedback.*   Some models assume that the act of purchasing and using a product has a direct effect on the household's subsequent purchase probabilities. The problem of inventory effects is an obvious example of this phenomenon. In terms of Equation 1.1, if the household purchased Brand 1 or 2 (states S_1 or S_2 were realized) on one day, this would lead directly to an increase in the probability of state S_0 (no purchase) for a number of subsequent days.

The first-order Markov model (see Chapter 4) assumes that the last state to be realized by the process determines the probabilities on the next trial: that is, $\Pr\{S_j(t)\} = f[S(t-1)]$, where $S(t-1)$ is the outcome on the previous day. Furthermore, the *transition probability* of the system, $\Pr\{S_j(t)|S_k(t-1)\}$ is constant for all t, implying that the outcome at $t-1$ is the *only* factor that influences the current purchase probability. The linear learning model for brand choice (see Chapter 5) is another familiar case where the matter of purchase event feedback is paramount.

1.2.2.2 *Time Effects.*   Work to date on stochastic models of buying behavior has rarely considered the effects of market forces, per se.[1] It is

---

[1] For a major exception to this generalization, see the work on variable transition probability Markov processes reported by Telser (1963) and Duhammel (1966).

much more common (and easier) to assume that the net effect of such forces on the purchase probabilities can be summed up by a time trend term in the model (i.e., as an element of **X**). The probability diffusion models considered in Chapters 6 and 7 can be viewed in this light, as can some of the market penetration models treated in Chapters 8 and 9. Chapter 11 presents a frontal attack on the problem of including specific market variables such as advertising and distribution in a stochastic market penetration model, but this model has not yet been applied to empirical data.

From a technical standpoint, there is a great difference between the incorporation of a time trend surrogate for exogenous market forces into a model and the inclusion of purchase event feedback effects. (The latter may also vary with time, as would be the case with inventory effects, for example.) In the former case, the values of the X-variables are independent of previous outcomes of the purchasing process, while in the latter the X's are themselves determined by the random process under study.[2]

1.2.2.3 *Population Heterogeneity.*

Households differ from one another in many ways, and some of these may affect use opportunities or brand preferences for particular products. Households with more members may tend to use more of certain products, for instance, or households where the wife holds certain views may exhibit preferences for one brand over another. The population of potential customers may differ in terms of demographic and socioeconomic factors, awareness, attitudes, and many other characteristics.

Like other models of consumption, many stochastic models of buying behavior attempt to identify, explain, or take account of population heterogeneity. There are at least three ways in which this can be done.
1. Certain specific determinants of the purchase probabilities can be identified and built into the model (i.e., included as elements of **X**). This requires that data on each factor be obtained from each customer in the sample used to estimate the parameters of the model.
2. Household-specific determinants of buying behavior may be identified and data on them collected. The sample is divided into segments on the basis of these variables, and the parameters of the model estimated separately for each segment. We might estimate a model separately for high- and low-income households, for example, or for

---

[2] This distinction is essentially the same as that between experimenter and subject controlled learning in mathematical psychology. See Bush and Mosteller (1955), Chapter III.

heavy- and light-buyer groups. If this approach is used, differences in the parameters estimated for the various segments can be used to make inferences about the effects of the variables used to define the segments. 3. Certain key parameters of the buying process may be assumed to vary from household to household, but no specific factors (such as age or income) are identified with this variation. Instead, we assume simply that the parameter (which might be the purchase probability itself, for instance) has a *distribution of values* in the population under study. (These are often called *prior distributions*.) Each individual in the sample is assumed to represent a random draw from the prior distribution of possible parameter values. The object of the model is more to predict the form and parameters of this distribution than to estimate the value of the parameter for any particular household in the sample.

The prior distribution method for taking account of population heterogeneity is conceptually more difficult than the other two, and it leads to models that may be more complex mathematically. However, it does offer the great advantage of not requiring the researcher to identify and collect data on specific causal factors. Moreover, the use of this procedure is often necessary if unbiased estimates of the effects of purchase event feedback and market forces are to be obtained. (The assumptions and procedures involved in using the distribution-of-parameters approach, and its importance, will be discussed at length in this book, beginning in Chapter 3.)

Often two or more of the methods can be used in combination. This is particularly true of approaches 2 and 3; examples can be found in almost every piece of empirical analysis included in this book. Some theoretical results aimed at the combination of methods 1 and 3 are presented in Chapter 11.

1.2.3 Brand-Choice and Purchase-Incidence Models

It is convenient to subdivide the class of stochastic models of buyer behavior into two additional subclasses: 1 models predicting which of a specified list of brands will be purchased, given that a purchase does occur at a particular point in time; and 2 models that predict when a purchase of a product will occur or (equivalently) how many purchases will occur in a specified interval of time. We will call the former *brand-choice models* and the latter *purchase-incidence models*.

The difference between these two types of models can best be demonstrated with the aid of some additional probabilistic notation. Let the symbol B_j stand for the event "purchase of Brand j," P stand for

"purchase of the product class" (any brand), and $\tilde{P}$ stand for no purchase of the product class. The relation between these event definitions and the ones used in Section 1.2.1 is as follows:

New Event	Old Event	Definition
B_1	S_1	Purchase of Brand 1
B_2	S_2	Purchase of Brand 2
P	S_1 or S_2	Purchase of product class
$\tilde{P}$	S_0	No purchase of product class

The probabilities associated with the new events can be derived easily from those of the old events.

Consider,

$$\Pr\{B_j \in (t, t + h)\}$$

which is the probability that an individual will purchase Brand j in the interval of time between t and $t + h$. We submit that this is the key probability so far as most applications of stochastic models are concerned. In the terms used earlier, it is the probability that Brand j will be purchased during the day defined by the interval $(t, t + h)$. $\Pr\{B_j \in (t, t + h)\}$ is simply another way of writing $\Pr\{S_j(t)\}$, for $j > 0$ (i.e., for those states that do involve a purchase).

For many purposes it is a good model-building strategy to try to separate a decision process into its components. In the present case, this can be accomplished by expanding $\Pr\{B_j \in (t, t + h)\}$ according to the rules of conditional probability:

$$\Pr\{B_j \in (t, t + h)\} = \Pr\{B_j | P \in (t, t + h)\} \Pr\{P \in (t, t + h)\} \quad (1.2)$$

The expanded notation is read as follows: "The probability that Brand j will be purchased between time t and $t + h$ is equal to the conditional probability that Brand j will be purchased between time t and time $t + h$, given that a purchase occurs, times the probability that a purchase will occur during this interval."

It is often convenient to assume that the interval length h is small enough so that at most one purchase of the product class will occur in $(t, t + h)$. (The purchase of multiple units of the same brand — e.g., three packages of Jello — is considered to be a single purchase for purposes of this assumption.) In this case the term $\Pr\{B_j | P \in (t, t + h)\}$ in Equation 1.2 is the probability that Brand j will be chosen on a purchase occasion occurring in the interval $(t, t + h)$, providing of course that a purchase occasion does in fact arise during the interval.

The probability $\Pr\{B_j | P \in (t, t + h)\}$ is a *brand-choice probability*. Similarly, models aimed at predicting this quantity can be termed *brand-choice models*, one of the two subclasses of stochastic models introduced in this section. Note that brand-choice probabilities are defined only for situations where a purchase actually occurs. Furthermore, no attempt is made to predict when a purchase will occur when dealing with a pure brand-choice model.

The second term in Equation 1.2, $\Pr\{P \in (t, t + h)\}$, is the probability that a purchase of the product will occur in the interval between times t and $t + h$. It is a *purchase-incidence probability*, and models aimed at predicting its value are called *purchase-incidence models*. Knowledge of $\Pr\{P \in (t, t + h)\}$ for a range of times permits the calculation of two other important probabilities: 1, the probability that the waiting time between one purchase and the next will be equal to (or less than or greater than) some specified value, and 2, the probability that the number of purchases in a certain time interval (longer than h) will be equal to (or less than or greater than) a given value. Models predicting either of these are members of the purchase incidence class, as both depend ultimately on prediction of $\Pr\{P \in (t, t + h)\}$.

The distinction between brand-choice and purchase-incidence models is important for two reasons. First, models of each type have appeared in the marketing literature: e.g., first-order Markov models and linear learning models on the brand-choice side, and the exponential and logistic market penetration curve models and the negative binomial model on the purchase-incidence side. Considerable confusion about the relation between these two classes of models, and the kinds of situations in which each is applicable, has been generated.

Second, the expansion given in Equation 1.2 often leads to simpler and more tractable models than would be the case if $\Pr\{B_j \in (t, t + h)\}$ were to be predicted directly. It is often a good strategy to construct the brand-choice and purchase-incidence portions of a model separately and then put them together by applying Equation 1.1. As the two parts of the model may make use of rather different behavioral postulates and may differ significantly in mathematical structure, this strategy may result in a clarification of concepts and permit easier manipulation of the probability distributions involved.

The advantages of separating model-building efforts into brand-choice and purchase-incidence components are particularly appealing when there is reason to believe that the behavioral process leading to choice of brand is independent of the time at which the purchase takes place and/or the time since the last purchase of the product: that is,

where

$$\Pr\{B_j | P \in (t, t + h)\} = \Pr\{B_j | P\}$$

In this case, it is possible to work with $\Pr\{B_j | P\}$ without any regard to the timing of purchases. (In dealing with situations of this kind, it is customary to shorten the probability notation of the brand-choice model to $\Pr\{B_j\}$, where the precondition of a purchase event is understood. All the models considered in Part II of this book make use of this simplification.) Then a purchase-incidence model can be constructed without regard to brand-choice considerations. The two models can be tested and their parameters estimated separately, perhaps even by different researchers. Predictions about $\Pr\{B_j \in (t, t + h)\}$ can be obtained by combining the two models at the very last stage of the analysis, if such predictions should turn out to be necessary at all. (For instance, brand-choice probability predictions may serve the model builder's purposes in many situations.)

Having made the distinction between brand-choice and purchase-incidence models, we should also note that it is *not necessary* to expand $\Pr\{B_j \in (t, t + h)\}$ as in Equation 1.2 in order to build useful stochastic models of buying behavior. For example, if a product class is not well defined, it may be best to model the purchase timing of a particular brand without reference to any specific alternative brands. That is, we might construct a model for predicting when Brand j will be purchased but not worry about the probabilities for Brands i, k, or l. (This strategy is explored in Chapter 9.) In this case, the form of the model might look like that of a model for predicting $\Pr\{P \in (t, t + h)\}$, except that P would be assigned the same meaning as B_j. Other situations where the distinction between brand-choice and purchase-incidence models would not be useful are also possible.

In general, however, we will adhere to the strategy of separating brand-choice and purchase-incidence models. Part II of the book will consider the former exclusively, and Part III will deal primarily with the latter.

1.3 Survey of Literature and Plan of the Book

The development of stochastic models of buying behavior, as defined earlier in this chapter, began in 1957 and 1958 with simultaneous work by a number of researchers who were interested in extracting more meaningful information from consumer panel data. The best-known early publications are probably those of Lipstein (1959), Ehrenberg (1959), and a Ph.D. thesis written by Kuehn (1958). Lipstein was one

of the first to apply the first-order Markov model to brand-choice decisions. Kuehn adapted the linear learning model, originally developed by mathematical psychologists,[3] to the same problem. Ehrenberg was the first to present a well-developed stochastic model for purchase incidence — the negative binomial.

Table 1.1 classifies these and other models according to the characteristics developed in Section 1.2, i.e., as to whether they are models for brand choice or purchase incidence, and whether they treat purchase event feedback, time effects, and/or population heterogeneity explicitly. The columns of the table are labeled alphabetically and the rows numerically to provide for easy identification of individual cells in the discussion that follows. Models are given specific names (in some cases fabricated by the present authors) as a further aid to identification. The references cited are those in which the particular model was first applied to purchasing behavior, or in a few cases where it was significantly extended in theory or type of application. No attempt has been made to include works of the many other authors who have made important contributions in the various areas (these are cited in later chapters where appropriate), and the authors admit that some errors in precedence may have been made. Where material on a particular type of model forms a major part of a chapter in this book, the chapter number is also indicated in italics, e.g., *Chapter* 3.

As can be seen from the table, the Markov and linear learning models incorporate assumptions about the effects of purchase-event feed-back on brand choice but do not make provisions for time effects and population heterogeneity (cell B-1). In effect, they are extensions of the stationary, homogeneous Bernoulli model (cell A-1), which seems to have been implied by some early writers on buying behavior but does not enter the literature as a model in its own right.

Kuehn's early work on the linear learning model led Frank (1962) to develop the counterhypothesis that so-called learning effects were really a result of population heterogeneity. His model (cell A-2) postulated a Bernoulli model for each household but assumed that the brand-choice probabilities for different households were likely to differ from one another. His model did not postulate any mechanism for handling population heterogeneity, however; he merely applied the Bernoulli model to each household separately. (This is the extreme form of the segmentation approach to handling population heterogeneity, developed in Section 1.2.2.3: hence the name "Household-Bernoulli model.") Frank found that a substantial part (though not all) of the "learning"

[3] See Bush and Mosteller (1955).

Table 1.1 Stochastic Models of Buying Behavior

	No Time Effects		Time Effects	
	No Purchase Event Feedback (A)	Purchase Event Feedback (B)	No Purchase Event Feedback (C)	Purchase Event Feedback (D)
BRAND–CHOICE MODELS				
(1) Homogeneous Population	Bernoulli	Markov, Lipstein (1959) Linear learning, Kuehn (1958)	Semi-Markov, Howard (1963) Variable Markov, Telser (1963) Dynamic Markov, Lipstein (1965)	Change and response uncertainty, Coleman (1964a) Dynamic inference, Howard (1965) Probability diffusion, Montgomery (1966), Chapters 6 to 7
(2) Heterogeneous Population	Household-Bernoulli, Frank (1962) Compound Bernoulli, Morrison (1965a, b), *Chapter 3*	Household-Markov, Massy (1966) Compound Markov, Morrison (1965a, b), *Chapter 4* Compound learning, Kuehn,* *Chapter 5*	None	Household-variable Markov, Duhammel (1966) Variable learning, Kuehn and Rohloff (1967) Learning-diffusion, Jones (1969)

PURCHASE—INCIDENCE MODELS

(3) Homogeneous Population Poisson Exponential Logistic	None	Variable exponential, Four and Woodlock (1960) Variable logistic, Massy (1960) One-element learning, Haines (1964)	Depth of repeat-penetration, MRCA* Penetration-repeat buyer share, Parfitt and Collins (1968)
(4) Heterogeneous Population Negative binomial (compound Poisson), Ehrenberg (1959) Compound exponential, Anscombe (1961), *Chapter 8*	None	Compound logistic and one-element learning, *Chapter 8*	Two-period negative binomial and logarithmic series distribution, Chatfield et al. (1966) Compound Wiebull, Massy (1967), *Chapters 9 to 11*

* Unpublished research.

effects reported by Kuehn could be accounted for by population heterogeneity.

The cell A-2 line of development was placed on a firm theoretical
footing by Morrison (1965a,b), who developed the compound Bernoulli
model using the approach discussed in Section 1.2.2.3. The term
"Compound" denotes the fact that explicit provision for a distribution
of relevant parameter values (in this case the brand-choice probability
itself) is included in the model. This model and the previous work of
Frank are discussed in detail in Chapter 3.

Massy (1966) applied Frank's approach to testing for population
heterogeneity effects to the Markov model (cell B-2). By estimating this
model for data on individual households, he was able to demonstrate,
at least for his particular sample and the product studied, that much of
the "Markovian" character of the transition probabilities was really
a result of population heterogeneity and that the brand-choice process
was somewhat more Bernoulli than Markov in character. Morrison
(1965a,b) also attacked this problem, developing the compound
Markov process model (see Chapter 4). In addition, Kuehn developed a
compound linear learning model. In unpublished work, he reports that
significant learning tendencies can be identified for many products even
after population heterogeneity is taken into account. (Massy developed
his own version of the compound linear learning model, which is
presented in Chapter 5.)

The basic contributions to stochastic brand-choice models combining
time effects and population heterogeneity (cell C-2) were made by
Coleman (1964a), Howard (1965), and Montgomery (1966). In the work
of the former, the model of change and response uncertainty, households'
purchase probabilities are initially distributed over members of the
population and are then changed according to a time trend function. In
dynamic inference, a household is assumed to draw its probability from
a distribution not once, as in the Coleman model, but again and again
at randomly distributed points in time. In effect, Howard assumes that
households reevaluate the worth of the various brands at discrete points
in time, that the outcomes of the successive evaluations (drawn from the
distribution of probabilities) are independent of one another, and that
the purchase probabilities do not change (i.e., the process is Bernoulli)
between reevaluations. In contrast, Coleman's change and response
uncertainty model and the probability diffusion model postulate that
these "reevaluations" occur continuously and the changes in probabilities per unit time are small and (in some cases) are not independent
of past evaluations. The probability diffusion model is an extension of

Coleman's model. It is developed in Chapter 6, and empirical results are given in Chapter 7.

Models including time effects and purchase event feedback but not population heterogeneity are also available (cell D-1). Howard (1963) postulated a Markov model whose transition probabilities are related to the time since last purchase. Telser (1963) postulates and estimates the parameters of a Markov model in which the parameters are functions of market variables (e.g., advertising). Lipstein (1965) develops a model for the "transition of Markov transition probability matrices." (Markov matrices are estimated from data covering two different time periods, and the relations between them are studied.)

Relatively little has been published on brand-choice models including all four of the characteristics shown in Table 1.1 (see cell D-2). Duhammel (1966) estimated Telser's variable Markov model using individual household data, but his empirical results were not fully satisfactory. Kuehn and Rohloff (1967) discuss a learning model where the learning operators are functions of the time since the last purchase, but details of the model are lacking. Jones (1969) extended Montgomery's probability diffusion model to include learning characteristics. This work is very significant, though some problems remain to be worked out.

Turning to the development of purchase-incidence models, we see from Table 1.1 that Ehrenberg's (1959) model for predicting the number of purchases per unit time (cell A-4) is an extension of the more basic Poisson model for the occurrence of independent events (cell A-3). (Like the Bernoulli model, which plays a similar basic role for brand-choice models, the Poisson model was never used by itself in the context of buying behavior.) Ehrenberg "compounded" the Poisson by introducing a population distribution of purchasing rates, just as Morrison did in the case of the Bernoulli. (Ehrenberg was the first to use compounding in a buying behavior model; his work antedates that of both Morrison and Frank.) Later, he worked with others to extend the model to include other effects [Chatfield et al. (1966), cell D-4].

The exponential model (cell A-3) is the analogue to the Poisson model for cases where a product's percentage penetration of the market or the waiting time to the next purchase is of more interest than the number of purchases per unit time. (See Sections 1.2.3 and 8.1.2.) Fourt and Woodlock (1960) made the exponential "time dependent" in the sense of Section 1.2.2 by making one of its key parameters (the upper asymptote of the process) a function of time (see cell C-3). Massy (1960) used a similar approach on the logistic process, another model that can be used

to describe market penetration. He assumed that certain parameters of the process were functions of market variables. Haines (1964) used linear learning model theory to build a more sophisticated model than that of Massy.

The exponential waiting time or market penetration model was generalized by Anscombe (1961) to include a distribution of purchasing rates among members of the population (cell A-4). His model is the waiting time analogue to Ehrenberg's model for the number of purchases per unit time and in fact either can be derived from the other. Compounding of the Haines one-element learning model for market penetration was performed by Massy, with results presented in Chapter 8.

Shifting to cell D-3 of Table 1.1, we see two references to models combining time and purchase event feedback effects without explicit consideration of population heterogeneity. Both are aimed at predicting the level of demand for new products. The staff of MRCA has for several years been applying the Fourt-Woodlock model to data stratified by whether or not the household had previously tried the new product. In effect, this brings feedback from the first trial into the parameters estimated for the one-time trier group. Parfitt and Collins (1968) report a similar approach, using a somewhat different model, for panel data pertaining to the United Kingdom. Both models do a respectable job in terms of predicting new product demand.

Finally, Massy (1967) generalized the Fourt-Woodlock model by building in compounding using Anscombe's results for the exponential, adding a time trend component (which leads to a compound Wiebull distribution), and developing more refined procedures for parameter estimation and prediction. These results are presented in Chapters 9 and 10. Further generalizations, including the introduction of market variables, specific household characteristics, and information about purchases of other brands, are presented in theoretical terms in Chapter 11.

Chapter 2 of this book presents some general concepts about parameter estimation and statistical inference, as they apply to stochastic models of buying behavior. Part II (Chapters 3 to 7) develops models of the brand-choice class. Part III (Chapters 8 to 11) deals primarily with purchase-incidence models.

CHAPTER 2
ESTIMATING AND TESTING
STOCHASTIC MODELS

2.1 Introductory Comment

This chapter reviews some of the basic elements of statistics used throughout this book. We assume that the reader will be somewhat familiar with these concepts, and therefore this section is a quick review. No attempt is made at a thorough or exhaustive development of statistical inference.

2.2 Estimation

2.2.1 Estimation Criteria

In this section we are concerned with the logic and procedures for obtaining estimates of the unknown parameters in a stochastic model. In particular, we discuss criteria for judging estimators, certain important estimation procedures, the statistical efficiency of these procedures, and certain computational aspects of the estimation problem.

It is appropriate at this juncture to specify what we mean by an *estimator*. An estimator is a function of the sample observations which we will use as an estimate of the true, but unknown, parameter. Since the observations are random variables and since an estimator is a function of these random observations, the estimator itself will be a random variable having some sampling distribution. It is the sampling distribution of the estimator that is our primary concern.

For purposes of discussion, suppose we consider an estimator $\theta_n^*(x_1, \ldots, x_n)$ of the unknown parameter θ. Note that θ_n^* is an explicit function of the vector of sample outcomes denoted by $\mathbf{x} = (x_1, \ldots, x_n)$. Further suppose that we have three alternative functions of the observations that we are considering as estimators for the unknown parameter θ. Dropping the sample size subscript n, we denote these candidate estimators as θ_1^*, θ_2^*, and θ_3^* where we implicitly note the functional dependence upon the vector of sample observations. The sampling distributions of these estimators about the true value θ are illustrated in Figure 2.1. It should be noted that there are an infinite

number of potential estimators for the true parameter θ, since we could propose an infinite number of functions of the sample observations to serve as an estimator of the parameter.

Faced with this infinity of candidate estimators, we must somehow determine what estimator would be best. This then requires us to

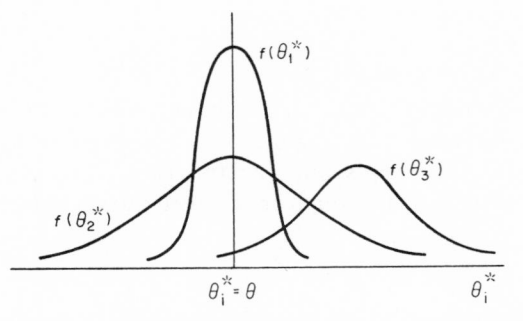

Figure 2.1.   The sampling distributions of three alternative estimators.

specify what we mean by "best." Intuitively, we would like to choose an estimator whose sampling distribution is concentrated about the true value θ. Referring once again to Figure 2.1, we see that we would prefer to use the estimator θ_1^* since its distribution is more closely concentrated about θ than the distribution for either θ_2^* or θ_3^*.

In sum, we need criteria to help us choose estimators that are "best" in some sense, and we use the procedure of restricting the class of estimators in order to avoid obviously bad estimator candidates and to enable us to achieve estimators having properties that are known to be desirable.

2.2.1.1   *Unbiased Estimators.* An estimator $\theta_n^* = \theta_n^*(x_1, \ldots, x_n)$ having the density function $f(\theta_n^*)$ is termed an unbiased estimator of θ if

$$\mathrm{E}(\theta_n^*) = \int_{-\infty}^{\infty} \theta_n^* f(\theta_n^*) \, d\theta^* = \theta$$

That is, an estimator is termed an unbiased estimator of a parameter if the expected value of the estimator is the unknown parameter.[1] Referring again to Figure 2.1, we see that θ_1^* and θ_2^* are unbiased estimators for θ while θ_3^* is a biased estimator.

At first glance it might appear that being unbiased is a necessary

[1] An analogous definition holds for discrete random variables.

property of a good estimator. A simple example shows that this is not the case. Suppose we have the estimators θ_1^* and θ_2^* with their respective sampling densities as shown in Figure 2.2. Although θ_2^* is an unbiased estimator, it is clear from the figure that the biased estimator θ_1^* is more concentrated about the true value θ. Thus, being unbiased is neither a

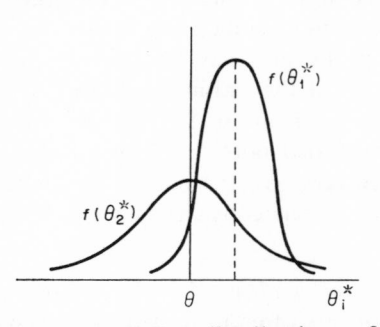

Figure 2.2. Hypothetical sampling distributions of an unbiased and a biased estimator.

necessary nor a sufficient property for a good estimator. Many "good" estimators (in particular maximum likelihood estimators) are often biased.

2.2.1.2 *Consistency.* Consider the sequence of estimators $\{\theta_n^*\}$ for $n = 1, 2, \ldots$, where the estimator θ_n^* is based upon a sample of n observations. The property of consistency relates to the behavior of the sequence $\{\theta_n^*\}$ as $n \to \infty$. That is, consistency refers to an asymptotic property of estimators as the sample size increases without limit.

An estimator is said to be weakly consistent if θ_n^* tends to θ in probability[2] as the sample size increases. In formal terms, an estimator $\theta_n^*(x_1, \ldots, x_n)$ of the parameter θ is said to be weakly consistent if

$$\lim_{n \to \infty} P(|\theta_n^* - \theta| > \epsilon) = 0$$

for every given $\epsilon > 0$. If $E[\theta_n^*] = \theta_n \to \theta$ and the variance $V[\theta_n^*] \to 0$ as $n \to \infty$, then θ_n^* is a weakly consistent estimator for θ.

An estimator is said to be strongly consistent if the probability[3] is one

[2] For convergence in probability see Rao (1965), Chapter 2, or Parzen (1960), Chapter 10.

[3] For strong convergence or convergence with probability one see Rao (1965), Chapter 2, or Parzen (1960), Chapter 10.

that its limit is the true parameter θ as $n \to \infty$. Formally, we have

$$P\left(\lim_{n \to \infty} \theta_n^* = \theta\right) = 1$$

An estimator that is strongly consistent is also weakly consistent since convergence with probability one implies convergence in probability.

Consistency alone is not a sufficient property for a good estimator, as it is only an asymptotic property and says nothing about the small sample characteristics of the estimator. It should be noted, however, that consistency has been one of the most useful criteria for judging estimators. We might also note that being unbiased does not imply consistency and vice versa. In the models developed in this book, we shall generally mean weak consistency when we refer to consistent estimates.

2.2.1.3 *Asymptotic Normality.* In the statistical literature, discussions of estimators are often restricted to the class of estimators that are consistent and asymptotically normal. By asymptotic normality we mean that the distribution of the random variable $\sqrt{n}(\theta_n^*)$ is normal in the limit as $n \to \infty$.[4] One advantage in considering asymptotically normal estimators is that we may then use the normal distribution to draw inferences on θ based upon the estimator θ_n^*.[5]

2.2.1.4 *Efficiency.* The discussion of efficient estimators will be divided into two subsections. In the first, we shall be concerned with the concept of efficiency for a fixed finite sample size. In the second subsection our attention will center on the property of asymptotic efficiency. No proofs of the results will be given. For rigorous developments see Cramer (1946), Chapter 32, and Rao (1961), (1963), and (1965), Chapter 5.

Fixed Finite Samples. Recall in the introductory remarks to Section 2.2 we noted that an.intuitively appealing criterion for a good estimator is that of highest concentration. In formal terms, an estimator θ_n^* has highest concentration about the true parameter θ if for any other estimator $\hat{\theta}_n$ we have

$$P(\theta - \lambda_1 < \theta_n^* < \theta + \lambda_2) \geq P(\theta - \lambda_1 < \hat{\theta}_n < \theta + \lambda_2) \quad (2.1)$$

for all possible λ_1 and λ_2 in a chosen interval $(0,\lambda)$ and for all θ. A

---

[4] For examples of asymptotically normal sample functions see Cramer (1946), Chapter 28.

[5] See Rao (1965), pp. 286–287.

necessary condition for the criterion of highest concentration to be satisfied is that

$$E[(\theta_n^* - \theta)^2] \leq E[(\hat{\theta}_n - \theta)^2] \qquad (2.2)$$

That is, a necessary condition for an estimator θ_n^* to have maximum concentration about the true value θ is that it should have minimum mean square error. Unfortunately, estimators satisfying Equations 2.1 or 2.2 do not exist in general.

Although minimum mean square error estimators do not always exist, the concept is useful and thereby merits further comment. The mean square error of an estimator θ_n^* is defined as the mean square deviation from the true parameter θ. An interesting relationship that reveals some of the nature of the mean square error is

$$E[(\theta_n^* - \theta)^2] = V[\theta_n^*] + b^2 \qquad (2.3)$$

where

$$b = E[\theta_n^*] - \theta \qquad (2.4)$$

We see at once from Equation 2.4 that b is the bias in the estimator. From Equation 2.3 we see that the mean square error is equal to the sum of the variance of the sampling distribution of θ_n^* (for fixed n) and the square of the bias. Note that if θ_n^* is an unbiased estimator of θ, then b is zero, and the mean square error of θ_n^* is simply the sampling variance of that estimator. Thus for the class of unbiased estimators, minimum mean square error and minimum variance are identical.

It can be shown[6] that, under certain general regularity conditions, the mean square error $E[(\theta_n^* - \theta)^2]$ is bounded from below by a positive limit that depends only upon the distribution function from which the sample was generated, the size of the sample n, and the bias of the estimator θ_n^*. For the case of an unbiased estimator, this says that the variance of the estimator can never fall below a certain limit. For a continuous distribution[7] the formal statement is that

$$E[(\theta_n^* - \theta)^2] \geq \frac{(1 + b')^2}{n \int_{-\infty}^{\infty} \left\{ \left[\frac{\partial \log f}{\partial \theta} \right]^2 f(\mathbf{x};\theta) \right\} d\mathbf{x}} \qquad (2.5)$$

where $b' = db/d\theta$, the first derivative of the bias in θ_n^* with respect to the true parameter value θ, where $\mathbf{x}$ is the vector of sample values, and

[6] See Cramer (1946), Chapter 32. For the regularity conditions see p. 479.
[7] For the analogous results for discrete distributions, see Cramer (1946), pp. 486–487.

where $f(\mathbf{x};\theta)$ is the joint distribution of the sample values. For an unbiased estimator the bound is

$$\text{Var}[\theta_n^*] \geq \frac{1}{n\int_{-\infty}^{\infty}\left\{\left[\dfrac{\partial \log f}{\partial \theta}\right]^2 f(\mathbf{x},\theta)\right\} d\mathbf{x}} \tag{2.6}$$

These lower bounds (known as Cramer-Rao lower bounds) for mean square error and variance may serve as the basis for a definition of efficiency of an estimator.

Consider the case where θ_n^* is an unbiased estimate of θ. Then the right-hand side of Equation 2.6 gives the smallest possible value for $\text{Var}[\theta_n^*]$. This lower bound will be denoted Min $\text{Var}[\theta_n^*]$ and will serve as the standard for our definition of efficiency. Among the class of unbiased estimators satisfying certain regularity conditions[8] we shall define efficiency to be

$$e(\theta_n^*) = \frac{\text{Min Var}[\theta_n^*]}{\text{Var}[\theta_n^*]} \tag{2.7}$$

That is, the efficiency[9] of an unbiased estimate is taken to be the ratio of the minimum possible variance to the actual variance of the estimator. This definition of efficiency satisfies the inequality $0 \leq e(\theta^*) \leq 1$. When equality holds in Equation 2.6, we have $\text{Var}[\theta_n^*]$ at its minimum, $e(\theta_n^*) = 1$, and the estimator θ_n^* is said to be efficient.

The definition of efficiency given in Equation 2.7 is for a finite sample size. Efficient estimators for finite samples exist only for a restricted class of populations.[10] The asymptotically efficient estimators discussed later exist under certain general regularity conditions.

Embedded in the expression for the lower bound of either mean square error or variance is Fisher's measure of the information the sample vector $\mathbf{x}$ contains concerning the parameter θ. The information measure $I(\theta)$ may be expressed in any of the following equivalent ways:

$$\begin{aligned}
I(\theta) &= \int_{-\infty}^{\infty}\left[\frac{\partial \log f}{\partial \theta}\right]^2 f(\mathbf{x};\theta)\, d\mathbf{x} \\
&= \int_{-\infty}^{\infty}\left[\frac{1}{f(\mathbf{x};\theta)}\right]\left[\frac{\partial f}{\partial \theta}\right]^2 d\mathbf{x} \\
&= \text{E}\left\{\left[\frac{\partial \log f}{\partial \theta}\right]^2\right\}
\end{aligned} \tag{2.8}$$

[8] See Cramer (1946), p. 479.

[9] For criticism of the minimum variance definition of efficiency for unbiased estimators see Rao (1965), p. 283.

[10] See Cramer (1946), p. 480 and p. 488.

where the multiple integrals and joint density function f are defined as before. We see from Equation 2.8 that the lower bounds for mean square error and variance can be expressed as

$$E[(\theta_n^* - \theta)^2] \geq \frac{(1 + b')^2}{nI(\theta)} \qquad (2.9)$$

and

$$\text{Var}[\theta_n^*] \geq \frac{1}{nI(\theta)} \qquad (2.10)$$

respectively.

Rao[11] has succinctly expressed the intuitive meaning of the information measure in the following statement:

By information on an unknown parameter θ contained in a random variable or in its distribution, we mean the extent to which uncertainty regarding the unknown value of θ is reduced as a consequence of an observed value of the random variable.

Should each value of the parameter be associated with a unique sample value, the random sample value would then contain maximum information since if we know the sample value, we then know the true parameter value. Conversely, if the sample outcomes have the same distribution for all values of the parameter, we then have a case where the sample contains no information about the parameter. In many cases the sensitivity of a random variable with respect to parameter changes may be measured by Fisher's information measure.[12]

Two final comments on the information measure are in order. The definition of information just given relates to the total information with respect to θ contained in the sample. Since an estimator is a function of the sample observations, it is clear that the estimator may contain no more information about θ than is contained in the sample. In general, the information on the parameter θ contained in the estimator θ_n^* will satisfy the inequality.

$$I(\theta) \geq I(\theta_n^*) \qquad (2.11)$$

That is, an estimator can at most contain all the information in the sample. In general, there will be some loss of information for any estimator. We note that for a sufficient estimator,[13] equality holds in

[11] Rao (1965), pp. 270–271.
[12] See Rao (1965), pp. 270–271 and references for details.
[13] For a discussion of sufficient statistics see Hoag and Craig (1959), Chapter 5.

Equation 2.11. We also note that information is additive for independent and identically distributed random variables.

Asymptotic Efficiency.   In this section we shall study the asymptotic efficiency of the estimator θ_n^* as the sample size n goes to infinity. Two formulations of asymptotic efficiency will be considered: v efficiency and Fisher's asymptotic efficiency. A thorough discussion of asymptotic efficiency is beyond the scope of this book. The complete details are given in Rao (1965).

v Efficiency.   A concept of asymptotic efficiency that has been in general use for some time is that based upon the asymptotic variance of an estimator. The class of estimators is restricted to the class of all consistent asymptotically normal (CAN) estimators. An estimator θ_n^* is said to be a CAN estimator of θ if the distribution of $\sqrt{n}[\theta_n^* - \theta]$ becomes normal as the sample size n increases. It was thought that the variance of the limiting distribution of $\sqrt{n}[\theta_n^* - \theta]$ was subject to the lower bound given in Equation 2.10. An estimator θ_n^* that attained this lower bound was then said to be efficient. An efficient CAN estimator has generally been called a best asymptotically normal (BAN) estimator. Rao[14] has shown that this concept of v efficiency is void unless additional restrictions are placed upon the class of estimators. The problem arises from the fact that within the class of *all* CAN estimators we may construct superefficient CAN estimators having no positive lower bound on their asymptotic variance.

Fisher's Asymptotic Efficiency.   Consider a set of n independent and identically distributed observations. Let $i(\theta)$ denote the information on θ in a single observation. Recall from the previous section that information from independent and identically distributed observations is additive. Hence the information in the sample is $ni(\theta)$. Similarly, the information in the estimator θ_n^* will be $ni(\theta_n^*)$ and will satisfy the inequality.

$$i(\theta_n^*) \leq i(\theta) \qquad (2.12)$$

That is, the information on θ per observation in the estimator θ_n^* has as its upper bound the total amount of information on θ per observation that is contained in the sample. An estimator is said to be Fisher efficient if

$$\lim_{n \to \infty} \frac{i(\theta_n^*)}{i(\theta)} = 1 \qquad (2.13)$$

[14] See Rao (1961, 1963).

A rather large class of estimators is Fisher efficient in the sense of Equation 2.13. We might note that as a criterion for judging estimators, Fisher efficiency suggests that we choose an estimator that most nearly has the discriminatory power of the sample values.

2.2.2 Estimation Procedures

In this section we discuss four estimation procedures: minimum chi-square, modified minimum chi-square, maximum likelihood, and the method of moments. The chi-square methods are applicable in what may be termed multinomial situations. A more complete specification of the multinomial situation is given later. The maximum likelihood method is more general and turns out to have many optimal properties.

The chi-square estimation procedures are applicable to situations where the observations are the frequencies of a finite number of mutually exclusive and collectively exhaustive events, or where the observations are continuous but have been grouped into nonoverlapping and exhaustive classes. Let there be k such events or classes. We now obtain a set of observed frequencies $n_1, \ldots, n_k$ for the k classes where an observation falls into class i with probability $\Pi_i(\theta)$, where $i = 1, \ldots, k$. Note that the class or cell probabilities $\Pi_i(\theta), \ldots, \Pi_k(\theta)$ are functions of a q-dimensional vector of unknown parameters θ. The procedures described here begin by defining a measure for the discrepancy between the observed cell frequencies $n_1, \ldots, n_k$ and the expected cell frequencies $n\Pi_1(\theta), \ldots, n\Pi_k(\theta)$ where $n = \sum_{i=1}^{k} n_i$, the total sample size. The estimation method proceeds by finding that parameter vector θ that minimizes the measure of discrepancy which has been defined.

This method is often computationally inconvenient in that it is impossible to solve for explicit functions of the observations that will yield the minimum chi-square estimate of θ. This is especially true when the $\Pi_i(\theta)$ are complicated functions of the parameter vector θ. In these situations we have recourse to numeric procedures on high-speed digital computers.

Several procedures for finding the minimum of chi-square and similar functions are described in the Appendix.

2.2.2.1 *Minimum Chi-Square.*   One measure of discrepancy between observed and expected cell frequencies in the multinomial situation described earlier is given by

$$\chi^2 = \sum_{i=1}^{k} \frac{[n_i - n\Pi_i(\theta)]^2}{n\Pi_i(\theta)} \qquad (2.14)$$

Note that this measure of discrepancy is essentially a weighted sum of squared errors where the weights are the reciprocals of the expected cell frequencies. The expression given in Equation 2.14 is then minimized with respect to the q-dimensional parameter vector $\boldsymbol{\theta}$. The value of $\boldsymbol{\theta}_n^*$ that minimizes Equation 2.14 is the minimum chi-square estimate of the parameter vector $\boldsymbol{\theta}$. In the limit as the sample size n goes to infinity, the statistic χ^2 is asymptotically distributed as a chi-square having $k - q - 1$ degrees of freedom. In Section 2.3 we shall take advantage of this chi-square distribution to test the "goodness of fit" of our theoretical models. The minimum chi-square procedure provides good estimates, since under suitable regularity conditions[15] they are consistent and efficient.

2.2.2.2 *Modified Minimum Chi-Square.*   As the name implies, the modified minimum chi-square procedure involves a modification of the measure of discrepancy used in the chi-square method. Rather than weighting the squared deviations of the observed and expected cell frequencies by the reciprocal of the expected cell frequency, we now weight these squared errors by the reciprocal of the observed cell frequencies. That is, our measure of discrepancy is

$$\chi^2 = \sum_{i=1}^{k} \frac{[n_i - n\Pi_i(\boldsymbol{\theta})]^2}{n_i} \qquad (2.15)$$

Once again we seek that parameter vector $\boldsymbol{\theta}_n^*$ which minimizes the discrepancy measure based on the observed cell frequencies $n_1, \ldots, n_k$. The modified minimum chi-square estimates are consistent and efficient under appropriate regularity conditions.

The asymptotic distribution of χ^2 given in Equation 2.15 is also chi-square having $k - q - 1$ degrees of freedom.[16]

The modified chi-square statistic is somewhat easier to minimize than the regular chi-square statistic, since the denominator is no longer a function of the parameter vector to be estimated. In particular, this statistic will more often yield to analytic minimization procedures than will the minimum chi-square approach.

2.2.2.3 *Other Consistent and Asymptotically Efficient Procedures.* Consistent and asymptotically efficient estimates of the parameter vector $\boldsymbol{\theta}$, for the multinomial case, may also be obtained by minimizing any one of the following three measures of discrepancy between the

---

[15] For details see Rao (1961, 1963).
[16] For the proof see Cramer (1946), pp. 426–434.

observed and the expected cell frequencies:

Hellinger Distance:

$$\text{H.D.} = \cos^{-1} \sqrt{\sum (n_i/n)\Pi_i(\boldsymbol{\theta})} \qquad (2.16)$$

Kullback-Liebler Separator:

$$\text{K.L.S.} = \sum \Pi_i(\boldsymbol{\theta}) \log \left[\frac{\Pi_i(\boldsymbol{\theta})}{(n_i/n)}\right] \qquad (2.17)$$

Haldane's Discrepancy:

$$D_k = \frac{(n+k)!}{n!} \sum \frac{n_i! \, \Pi_i^{k+1}(\boldsymbol{\theta})}{(n_i+k)!} \quad \text{for} \quad k \neq -1 \qquad (2.18)$$

$$D_{-1} = -\frac{1}{n} \sum n_i \log \Pi_i(\boldsymbol{\theta})$$

These methods are discussed by Rao (1965).

It is worth noting that these estimators have many desirable properties, particularly with respect to asymptotic efficiency. We have not used these three estimators in our work, so they will not be discussed further.

2.2.2.4 *Maximum Likelihood.* The maximum likelihood procedure can be used in place of the chi-square methods just described, and also in a much wider range of situations. Let $f(\mathbf{x};\boldsymbol{\theta})$ denote the joint density function of a vector of sample observations.[17] The likelihood of the result $\mathbf{x}$ given the vector of parameters $\boldsymbol{\theta}$ is

$$L(\mathbf{x}|\boldsymbol{\theta}) \propto f(\mathbf{x};\boldsymbol{\theta}) \qquad (2.19)$$

where the symbol $\propto$ denotes "is proportional to." The maximum likelihood estimate $\hat{\boldsymbol{\theta}}$ for $\boldsymbol{\theta}$ is that value for which

$$L(\mathbf{x}|\hat{\boldsymbol{\theta}}) \geq L(\mathbf{x}|\boldsymbol{\theta}')$$

where $\boldsymbol{\theta}'$ is any other admissible value of $\boldsymbol{\theta}$.[18] Under completely general conditions, there may be a set of sample vectors for which $\hat{\boldsymbol{\theta}}$ does not exist, but under regularity conditions on $f(\mathbf{x};\boldsymbol{\theta})$, their occurrence is negligible.

[17] Analogous results hold for discrete distributions. Note that the observations need not be independent.

[18] For a discussion of the maximum likelihood principle in more rigorous terms see Rao (1965), pp. 289–290. He discusses the principle in terms of the supremum of the likelihood function and treats the case of near maximum likelihood estimates when the supremum is not attainable.

In practice, it is generally more convenient to find $\hat{\theta}$ by maximizing $\log L(\mathbf{x}|\theta)$ with respect to θ rather than maximizing $L(\mathbf{x}|\theta)$ itself. Since a log transformation is strictly monotonic, that value $\hat{\theta}$ which maximizes $\log L(\mathbf{x}|\theta)$ will also maximize $L(\mathbf{x}|\theta)$. When $\hat{\theta}$ lies at an interior point in the space of admissible θ values, classical calculus methods may often be used to compute $\hat{\theta}$ as a function of $\mathbf{x}$. If the likelihood function is analytically intractable or if $\hat{\theta}$ lies on a boundary, numerical procedures such as those considered in the Appendix will be required.

Under rather general regularity conditions,[19] maximum likelihood estimates are best asymptotically normal (BAN). That is, they are consistent, asymptotically normal, and asymptotically efficient. Maximum likelihood estimates are also invariant. That is, if $\hat{\theta}$ is the maximum likelihood estimate of θ and if $u(\theta)$ is any single-valued function of θ, then $u(\hat{\theta})$ is the maximum likelihood estimate of $u(\theta)$.[20]

In many situations maximum likelihood estimates are biased, but this fact should not detract from the other "nice" properties that they possess. Also this bias (if it exists) tends to get very small as the sample size increases.

2.2.2.5 *Method of Movements.* Let $\mathbf{x} = (x_1, \ldots, x_n)$ denote a vector of independent and identically distributed observations of a random variable drawn from a population involving the unknown parameter vector $\theta = (\theta_1, \ldots, \theta_q)$. Further suppose that the first of raw moments of the population exists as explicit functions of θ. We denote these theoretical or population moments as $\alpha_1(\theta), \ldots, \alpha_q(\theta)$. The method of moments equates these population moments to the first q sample moments and solves for θ. That is, for the method of moments, we must solve the system

$$\alpha_1(\theta) = \frac{1}{n} \sum_{i=1}^{n} x_i$$

$$\alpha_2(\theta) = \frac{1}{n} \sum_{i=1}^{n} x_i^2$$

$$\cdot \qquad \cdot$$
$$\cdot \qquad \cdot$$
$$\cdot \qquad \cdot$$

$$\alpha_q(\theta) = \frac{1}{n} \sum_{i=1}^{n} x_i^q$$

[19] For details see Rao (1965), pp. 295–302.

[20] If a sufficient statistic exists, $\hat{\theta}$ will be a function of that sufficient statistic. See Hoag and Craig (1959), Chapter 5.

for the parameter vector $\boldsymbol{\theta}$. Estimates obtained by the method of moments are generally consistent but not efficient (and often *very* inefficient).

2.3 Goodness of Fit

A fundamental concern in the empirical application of stochastic models is the question of whether or not a particular model is consistent with a given set of data. That is, is it plausible that the model could have generated the data under consideration? We may take little comfort in having consistent and asymptotically efficient estimates of a model's parameters if, indeed, it is highly unlikely that the model could have generated the data. Unless we have a very strong prior belief that a model is valid, we should test the fit of the model before turning to an interpretation of the model's parameters.

In this section we concentrate upon three important aspects of the goodness of fit of a model to a set of empirical data. The first topic will be the well-known chi-square goodness-of-fit test. In this test the model is essentially the null hypothesis. Since there is often a many-to-one mapping of models into data, the question naturally arises as to the power of the chi-square test to discriminate between alternative models of the same phenomenon. Hence the second topic will relate to the power of the chi-square test in discriminating between competing models. The theory for the power function will be developed for a rather large class of models. The third topic to be considered in this section is that of likelihood ratio tests. These tests permit a direct statistical comparison between two or more models that have been applied to the same set of data. Their use is particularly convenient when the method of maximum likelihood has been used to estimate the parameters of the various models.

2.3.1 The Chi-Square Test with a Model as the Null Hypothesis

We once again find ourselves in the multinomial situation described in Section 2.2.2. We first review the procedure for developing the chi-square test before turning to the interpretation of such tests. The point of departure is one theoretical model that expresses the cell probabilities $\Pi_1(\boldsymbol{\theta}), \ldots, \Pi_k(\boldsymbol{\theta})$ as functions of the parameter vector $\boldsymbol{\theta}$.

Suppose that we have a set of empirical cell frequencies $n_1, \ldots, n_k$ and we wish to determine the extent to which expected cell frequencies $n\Pi_1(\boldsymbol{\theta}), \ldots, n\Pi_k(\boldsymbol{\theta})$ implied by the model are consistent with these data. If we have some means of knowing $\boldsymbol{\theta}$ a priori, we may proceed to

test the model. However, in general we will need to utilize the data in estimating the vector of parameters $\boldsymbol{\theta}$. We may estimate $\boldsymbol{\theta}$ by any of the consistent and asymptotically efficient procedures discussed in Section 2.2.2. It should be noted that we must use a consistent and asymptotically efficient estimation procedure for $\boldsymbol{\theta}$ in order for the test statistic discussed here to be distributed as chi-square.

Once we have estimated $\boldsymbol{\theta}$ by $\boldsymbol{\theta}_n^*$, we may develop the test statistic

$$\chi^2 = \sum_{i=1}^{k} \frac{[n_i - n\Pi_i(\boldsymbol{\theta}_n^*)]^2}{n\Pi_i(\boldsymbol{\theta}_n^*)} \tag{2.20}$$

It has been shown[21] that if $\boldsymbol{\theta}_n^*$ is consistent and asymptotically efficient,[22] the statistic (or discrepancy measure) χ^2 will be asymptotically (as $n \to \infty$) chi-square having $k - q - 1$ degrees of freedom. (Recall that q is the number of parameters we estimated from the data.) If we know $\boldsymbol{\theta}$ a priori, the chi-square statistic will be chi-square with $k - 1$ degrees of freedom. In this case the $\boldsymbol{\theta}_n^*$ in Equation 2.20 would be replaced by $\boldsymbol{\theta}$. We may use the chi-square statistic to test the null hypothesis that the model (with parameter vector $\boldsymbol{\theta}_n^*$ or $\boldsymbol{\theta}$) may have generated the data. In the remainder of this discussion, we shall consider the more usual case where we must use the data to estimate $\boldsymbol{\theta}$.

How do we use the chi-square statistic to test a model? Under the null hypothesis that the model generated the data, we know that the observed value of χ^2 is an outcome of a chi-square random variable having $k - q - 1$ degrees of freedom. We denote the chi-square distribution having $k - q - 1$ degrees of freedom as $f[\chi^2(k - q - 1)]$. Recall that χ^2 is a measure of the discrepancy between observed cell frequencies and the theoretical frequencies implied by the model. We now ask the question, "How likely are we to observe a discrepancy as large or larger than the one we observed, given that the model is correct?" We shall call this probability the "p-level" of the observed χ^2 statistic under the null hypothesis. In formal terms, we have

$$p = \int_{\chi_{\text{obs}}^2}^{\infty} f[\chi^2(k - q - 1)] \, d\chi^2 \tag{2.21}$$

where the χ_{obs}^2 in the lower limit of integration is the minimum value of χ^2 we attained when we estimated θ_n^*. The integral in Equation 2.21 may be evaluated by going to tables of the chi-square distribution for $k - q - 1$ degrees of freedom.

---

[21] Cramer (1946), pp. 424–434 and p. 506.

[22] Again assuming appropriate regularity conditions. See Cramer (1946), pp. 500–501.

Suppose now that we have found a very low *p*-level in fitting a model to a set of data. For purposes of discussion, let this hypothetical value be $p = 0.001$. This result may be interpreted in one of two ways:

1. The model is correct and a rather unlikely event has occurred (in this case an event having probability 0.001),
2. The model is incorrect (i.e., does not fit the data).

We shall generally choose the latter interpretation and say that the model is incorrect. Suppose on the other hand that the *p* level had been 0.20. In this case we would be inclined to say that the model is consistent with the data in that we would expect an observed chi-square this large or larger 20 times out of 100 if the model is, in fact, correct.

It was noted earlier that the model is essentially the null hypothesis. In a test of the null hypothesis, we may more definitively say that the null hypothesis is false then we may say that it is true. What we mean is this: If we reject the model on the basis of its deviation from the data, we may do so with reasonable confidence (depending on the *p*-level). But if we accept the null hypothesis (the model), this simply tells us that the model is consistent with the data. This is a much weaker conclusion than saying that the model is correct. Other models may also be consistent with the same data. Some of the problems that arise in comparing models will be discussed in the next section.

It is necessary at this point to examine a few characteristics of the chi-square test. In the first place, as the sample size *n* becomes very large, the chi-square statistic will also tend to become very large with no increase in its degrees of freedom. This is readily seen if we reexpress Equation 2.20 as

$$\chi^2 = n \sum_{i=1}^{k} \frac{[v_i - \Pi_i(\boldsymbol{\theta}_n^*)]^2}{\Pi_i(\boldsymbol{\theta}_n^*)} \tag{2.22}$$

where v_i is the observed proportion of the sample in cell *i*. That is, $v_i = n_i/n$. This increase in χ^2 as *n* increases with no increase in degrees of freedom means that we will be more likely to reject the null hypothesis (i.e., the model) even though the deviation, of observed from expected cell proportions, remains the same. Thus as *n* increases, the test will become increasingly sensitive to small departures of the model's cell probabilities from the "true" cell probabilities which generated the data. We see from Equation 2.22 that in the limit as $n \to \infty$, we would reject all models except one that yields precisely the true cell probabilities $\Pi_1(\boldsymbol{\theta}), \ldots, \Pi_k(\boldsymbol{\theta})$. Since we really believe that our stochastic models are reasonable first-order approximations rather than

exact processes, we see that any of our approximate models will ultimately be rejected by the chi-square test as the sample size increases. Conversely, if the sample size is too small, the test will lose its power to detect important deviations of the model from the data. Hence, the chi-square statistic may be more useful for comparing the fit of two different models than it is in evaluating the "correctness" of either model. The effect of the sample size on the significance of chi-square statistics should always be remembered when one interprets a chi-square (or any other goodness-of-fit) statistic.

2.3.2   *Comparing Models and the Power of the Chi-Square Test*

In this section we consider in turn the comparison of alternative models, the concept of statistical power, and the power of the chi-square test for a class of models.

2.3.2.1   *Comparison of Models.* Suppose we find that a model which we have formulated is consistent with a set of data — i.e., it passes the chi-square test. Can we now claim that we have the "true" model of the process which generated the response sequence? The answer, of course, is no. All we may say is that we have *a* model that is consistent with the data. Other models, having entirely different structures, may also be consistent with the same data. Consequently, before we conclude that our model is an accurate description of the real world, we should compare its performance to that of some competing models of the same phenomenon.

One approach to the comparison of models is to apply each of the models in turn to the same data. In view of the variation in efficiency between the estimation procedures, it is generally recommended[23] that the same type of estimation procedure (e.g., maximum likelihood, minimum chi-square, etc.) be used for each model under comparison. Once each model has been estimated by the same type of procedure, we compute the chi-square statistic given in Equation 2.20. The models are then compared on the basis of their chi-square statistics or their p-level. If the models each have the same number of degrees of freedom for the data base under consideration, we may compare their chi-square statistics directly. The smaller the chi-square, the better the fit of the model. The logic of this rule becomes clear when we recall that the chi-square statistic is a weighted measure of the squared error between the model and the observations. Hence, the smaller the deviation measure, the better the

---

[23] See Atkinson, Bower, and Crothers (1965), Chapter 9.

fit of the model. If the models have different degrees of freedom, we may compare them on the basis of their p-level which accounts for the differences in degrees of freedom. The higher the p-level, the better the fit of the model.

A residual question is whether an observed difference in the chi-square for two (or more) models is significant. Let χ_i^2 and $df_i(i = 1, 2)$ denote the chi-square statistic and degrees of freedom for two models, 1 and 2. If the chi-squares were independent, we could form the ratio

$$\frac{\chi_1^2/df_1}{\chi_2^2/df_2}$$

and test the significance of this ratio against an F distribution. Since we are using the same set of data to compute the chi-squares for each model, the chi-squares are not independent and the ratio just given is not precisely distributed according to the F distribution. We may still choose to compare the ratio to the F distribution to obtain a rough idea of the significance level, but the violation of the strict independence assumption must be remembered.[24]

2.3.2.2 *The Concept of Statistical Power.* In testing the null hypothesis (our model) with the chi-square statistic, we are looking at only one question: namely, how closely does our model fit the data? The other question is: how well does the test discriminate among competing stochastic models? In other words, we need to consider the power of the chi-square test.

In more formal terms, the test of the null hypothesis yields the following probability, which we have termed the p-level:

$$P[\chi^2 \geq \chi^2 \text{ (observed)}|H_0 \text{ (the model is valid)}]$$

where H_0 denotes the null hypothesis when our model is valid. Now suppose we have a competing model in mind. We shall denote the hypothesis on expected cell frequencies under this alternative model by H_1. The power of the chi-square test of H_0 with respect to H_1 is then given by the following probability:

$$P[\chi^2 < \chi^2 \text{ (observed)}|H_1 \text{ (the alternative model is valid)}]$$

The power gives us the probability of a χ^2 as lower than the observed χ^2 when the alternative hypothesis is true.

[24] See Atkinson, Bower, and Crothers (1965), Chapter 9. They reference a fuller discussion in the 1966 doctoral dissertation at Stanford by Holland entitled "Minimum Chi-Square Procedures." See Holland (1966).

2.3.2.3　*Power of the Chi-Square Test for a Class of Models.*　In this section two methods for calculating the power of certain goodness-of-fit tests will be developed.[25] This approach will be valid in any situation where

1. The population under investigation can be divided into n mutually exclusive and exhaustive subpopulations.
2. Each individual that is observed makes one binary response, and each individual's response is independent of all the other individuals' responses.
3. There is a null hypothesis H_0 that gives the probability p_{0i} of an individual in subpopulation i $(i = 1, \ldots, n)$ making response 1 and a probability $1 - p_{0i}$ of making response 0. There is an alternative hypothesis H_1 that gives the probability p_{1i} of an individual in subpopulation i, $(i = 1, \ldots, n)$ making response 1 and the probability $1 - p_{1i}$ of making response 0.

An example of a situation that meets the three requirements can be found in the analysis of sequential behavior of subjects. In the field of marketing, various models have been presented that attempt to give the probability of buying Brand X, given a family has a certain past history for the purchase of Brand X. Suppose we designate the purchase of Brand X by a 1 and the purchase of any other brand by a 0. Thus Condition 2 is satisfied. If we segment the consumers by, say, their past four purchase decisions, we will have 16 mutually exclusive and exhaustive categories $(0000, 0001, 0010, \ldots, 1011, 0111, 1111)$; Condition 1 is therefore fulfilled. A particular model of consumer behavior (call this model H_0) will predict the probability of a 1 on the next trial given any of the 16 possible past purchase histories. A competing model H_1 may predict 16 different probabilities; thus a set of p_{0i} and p_{1i} exist. Assuming the purchase behavior of one consumer does not effect the behavior of any other consumer in the sample, we have now satisfied all three conditions. See Chapters 3, 4, and 5 for a more complete analysis of consumer behavior via this approach.

The typical learning experiments in mathematical psychology where the binary response can be a correct or an incorrect response also fit into this framework very nicely. In a more general sense, any experimental data that meet the conditions given here can be put in the tabular form exhibited in Table 2.1. The notation in the table has the following

[25] This subsection is based upon Morrison (1965a).

Table 2.1   Tabular Form of Data that Satisfy Conditions 1, 2, and 3.

	Observed Data				
Response	Subpopulation				
	1	2	3 $\cdots$ $n-1$		n
1	O_1	O_2	O_3 $\cdots$ O_{n-1}		O_n
0	O_1'	O_2'	O_3' $\cdots$ O_{n-}'		O_n'
Total	N_1	N_2	N_3 $\cdots$ N_{n-1}		N_n

	Expected Data				
Response	Subpopulation				
	1	2	3 $\cdots$ $n-1$		n
1	E_{01}	E_{02}	E_{03} $\cdots$ E_{0n-1}		E_{0n}
0	E_{01}'	E_{02}'	E_{03}' $\cdots$ E_{0n-1}'		E_{0n}'
Total	N_1	N_2	N_3 $\cdots$ N_{n-1}		N_n

definitions:

n = the number of subpopulations.

N_i = the number of individuals belonging to subpopulation i that were observed.

O_i = the number of individuals in subpopulation i that made response 1.

O_i' = the number of individuals in subpopulation i that made response 0.

$$O_i' = N_i - O_i.$$

p_{ji} = the probability that an individual belonging to subpopulation i will make response 1, given that hypothesis H_j is true, $j = 0, 1$.

E_{ji} = the expected number of individuals in subpopulation i who will make response 1, given that the hypothesis H_j is true. $E_{ji} = p_{ji}N_i$.

E_{ji}' = the expected number of individuals in subpopulation i who make response 0, given that hypothesis H_j is true. $E_{ji}' = (1 - p_{ji})N_i$.

In Table 2.1, the responses that make up O_i (and O_i') must be independent of each other and independent of all the other responses that make up O_j (and O_j'), $j \neq i$. The expected data are with respect to the null hypothesis H_0.

Suppose H_0 and H_1 generate the following sets of probabilities:

$$H_0: \quad p_{01}, p_{02}, \ldots, p_{0i}, \ldots, p_{0n}$$

$$H_1: \quad p_{11}, p_{12}, \ldots, p_{1i}, \ldots, p_{1n}$$

For example, p_{ij} could be the probability of buying Brand X if the model (hypothesis) H_i is true and given that the consumer's past purchase history is j. We will concentrate on finding the distribution of χ^2 under H_1. In so doing, we will obtain the well-known result for the distribution of χ^2 under H_0, where

$$\chi^2 = \sum_{\substack{\text{all} \\ \text{outcomes}}} \frac{(\text{observed} - \text{expected})^2}{\text{expected}} \tag{2.23}$$

Dropping the subscript i for the moment, we have

$$\frac{(O - E)^2}{E}$$

$$= \frac{(O - Np_0)^2}{Np_0} = \frac{[(O - Np_1) + N(p_1 - p_0)]^2}{Np_0}$$

$$= \frac{Np_1}{Np_0} \cdot \frac{[(O - Np_1)^2 + 2N(p_1 - p_0)(O - Np_1) + N^2(p_1 - p_0)^2]}{Np_1}$$

$$\frac{(O - Np_0)^2}{Np_0}$$

$$= \frac{p_1}{p_0} \cdot \frac{(O - Np_1)^2}{Np_1} + \frac{2(p_1 - p_0)}{p_1}(O - Np_1) + \frac{N(p_1 - p_0)^2}{p_1} \tag{2.24}$$

Similarly,

$$\frac{(O' - E')^2}{E'} = \frac{[O' - N(1 - p_0)]^2}{N(1 - p_0)}$$

$$= \frac{1 - p_1}{1 - p_0} \cdot \frac{[O' - N(1 - p_1)]^2}{N(1 - p_1)}$$

$$+ \frac{2(p_1 - p_0)}{1 - p_1}(O - Np_1) + \frac{N(p_1 - p_0)^2}{1 - p_1} \tag{2.25}$$

Adding Equations 2.24 and 2.25 and with a few algebraic manipulations, we get

$$Z = \frac{(O - Np_0)^2}{Np_0} + \frac{[O' - N(1 - p_0)]^2}{N(1 - p_0)^2}$$

$$= \frac{p_1(1 - p_1)}{p_0(1 - p_0)} \left[\frac{O - Np_1}{\sqrt{Np_1(1 - p_1)}} \right]^2$$

$$+ \frac{2(p_1 - p_0)}{\sqrt{\dfrac{p_0(1 - p_0)}{N}}} \times \frac{O - N_{p_1}}{\sqrt{Np_1(1 - p_1)}} + \frac{(p_1 - p_0)^2}{p_0(1 - p_0)/N}$$

We note that Np_1 and $\sqrt{Np_1(1 - p_1)}$ are the mean and variance, respectively, for the binomial random variable O under H_1. Hence, by the central limit theorem, as N increases, the random variable

$$X = \frac{O - Np_1}{\sqrt{Np_1(1 - p_1)}}$$

approaches a normal random variable with mean 0 and variance 1 under the hypothesis H_1. If we let

$$\rho = \frac{\text{Var}[O \text{ under } H_1]}{\text{Var}[O \text{ under } H_0]} = \frac{\sigma_1^2}{\sigma_0^2} = \frac{Np_1(1 - p_1)}{Np_0(1 - p_0)} = \frac{p_1(1 - p_1)}{p_0(1 - p_0)}$$

$$\sigma_{p_0}^2 = \text{Var}\left[\frac{O}{N} \text{ under } H_0 \right] = \frac{p_0(1 - p_0)}{N}$$

and

$$p_1 - p_0 = \epsilon$$

then, the random variable Z becomes

$$Z = \rho X^2 + \frac{2\epsilon}{\sigma_{p_0}} X + \frac{2\epsilon}{\sigma_{p_0}^2} \qquad (2.26)$$

where X is a normal zero mean, unit variance random variable. Now

$$\chi^2 = \sum_{i=1}^{n} Z_i$$

If we consider H_0 as a particular alternative hypothesis H_1, then under this special condition we get $\rho = 1$, $\epsilon = 0$; therefore,

$$\chi^2 = \sum_{i=1}^{n} X_i^2$$

where X_i is $N(0, 1)$ for all i. Hence, X_i^2 is distributed as chi-square with 1 degree of freedom. Now by the additivity property of independent chi-square random variables we have

$$\chi^2 = \sum_{i=1}^{n} Z_i$$

which is distributed as chi-square with n degrees of freedom. This is merely the usual goodness-of-fit result for contingency tables with independent entries.

Under H_1, the ϵ does not equal zero; hence,

$$Z = \rho X^2 + \frac{2\epsilon}{\sigma_{p_0}} X + \frac{\epsilon^2}{\sigma_{p_0}^2}$$

$$E[Z] = \rho\, E[X^2] + \frac{2\epsilon}{\sigma_{p_0}}\, E[X] + \frac{\epsilon^2}{\sigma_{p_0}^2}$$

since expectation is a linear operator.

Since X is $N(0,1)$, $E[X^2] = \text{variance } [X] = 1$
and

$$E[X] = \text{mean } [X] = 0$$

we get

$$E[Z] = \rho + \frac{\epsilon^2}{\sigma_{p_0}^2} \tag{2.27}$$

To calculate the variance of Z, we proceed as follows:

$$\text{Var}[Z] = \text{Var}\left[\rho X^2 + \frac{2\epsilon}{\sigma_{p_0}} X + \frac{\epsilon^2}{\sigma_{p_0}^2} \right]$$

$$= \text{Var}\left[\rho X^2 + \frac{2\epsilon}{\sigma_{p_0}} X \right], \text{ since } \frac{\epsilon^2}{\sigma_{p_0}^2} \text{ is a constant,}$$

$$= \text{Var}[\rho X^2] + \text{Var}\left[\frac{2\epsilon}{\sigma_{p_0}} X \right] + 2\,\text{Cov}\left[\rho X^2, \frac{2\epsilon}{\sigma_{p_0}} X \right]$$

Now

$$\text{Cov}[aX^2, bX] = E[(aX^2)(bX)] - E[aX^2]E[bX]$$

$$= abE[\overset{0}{X^3}] - abE[X^2]E[\overset{0}{X}]$$

$$= 0$$

because all odd central moments of the standardized normal distribution are zero. Hence,

$$\text{Var}[Z] = \rho^2\, \text{Var}[X^2] + \frac{4\epsilon^2}{\sigma_{p_0}^2}\, \text{Var}[X]$$

Since X^2 is a chi-square random variable with 1 degree of freedom,

$$\text{Var}[X^2] = 2$$

Finally,

$$\text{Var}[Z] = \rho^2 \, \text{Var}[X^2] + \frac{4\epsilon^2}{\sigma_{p_0}^2} \, \text{Var}[X]$$

$$\text{Var}[Z] = 2\rho^2 + \frac{4\epsilon^2}{\sigma_{p_0}^2} \tag{2.28}$$

To obtain the mean and variance of χ^2 under H_1, we note that each Z_i is a random variable with

$$\text{mean} = \rho_i + \frac{\epsilon_i^2}{\sigma_{p_{0i}}^2}$$

$$\text{variance} = 2\rho_i^2 + \frac{4\epsilon_i^2}{\sigma_{p_{0i}}^2}$$

Because the Z_i are independent, $\chi^2 = \sum\limits_{i=1}^{n} Z_i$ is a random variable with

$$E[\chi^2] = \sum_{i=1}^{n} \rho_i + \frac{\epsilon_i^2}{\sigma_{p_{0i}}^2} \tag{2.29}$$

$$\text{Var}[\chi^2] = \sum_{i=1}^{n} 2\rho_i^2 + 4 \frac{\epsilon_i^2}{\sigma_{p_{0i}}^2} \tag{2.30}$$

where

$$\epsilon = (p_{01}, p_{02}, \ldots, p_{0n}) - (p_{11}, p_{12}, \ldots, p_{1n}) = (\epsilon_1, \epsilon_2, \ldots, \epsilon_n)$$

$$\sigma_{p_{0i}}^2 = \frac{p_{0i}(1 - p_{0i})}{N_i}$$

Therefore, as N_i increases, $\rho_{p_{0i}}^2$ decreases, and

$$Z_i = \rho_i X^2 + \frac{2\epsilon_i}{\sigma_{p_{0i}}} X + \frac{\epsilon^2}{\sigma_{p_{0i}}^2}$$

becomes dominated by the terms

$$\frac{2\epsilon_i}{\sigma_{p_{0i}}} X + \frac{\epsilon^2}{\sigma_{p_{0i}}^2}$$

Note that ρ_i is a constant independent of the N_i.

Now if X is normal, a constant times X plus another constant is still normal. Hence, as N_i gets large, Z_i becomes normal.

Now $\chi^2 = \sum Z_i$ is a sum of normals, and thus itself is normal. Finally, we conclude that as N_i becomes large $(i = 1, \ldots, n)$, the distribution of $\chi^2 = \sum_{i=1}^{n} Z_i$ under the alternative hypothesis H_1 is approximately normal with mean and variance given by Equations 2.29 and 2.30.

Therefore to find the power of the chi-square test against any alternative hypothesis H_1 we:

1. Determine $p_0 = (p_{01}, p_{02}, \ldots, p_{0n})$ under H_0,
2. Calculate χ_α^2 under H_0 (Thus the probability of a Type I error $= \alpha$),
3. Determine $p_1 = (p_{11}, p_{12}, \ldots, p_{1n})$ under H_1,
4. Find $P(\chi^2 < \chi_\alpha^2)$ under H_1 by the normal approximation. Then $P_{H_1}(\chi^2 < \chi_\alpha^2) =$ probability of a Type II error $=$ the power of the test against $H_1 = \beta$.

An exact density function for each individual Z_j under H_1 can be found, but the expression is very complicated.[26] The distribution of the sum of these n random variables is the n-fold convolution of these density functions, and this expression is completely unwieldy. However, as we have shown, when the N_i became large our approximate distribution will be very good, and for small sample sizes we can always obtain very conservative results by using Chebyshev's inequality.

We now turn our attention to the noncentral chi-square approximation. Under H_1 we see that

$$X_i = \frac{O_i - N p_{0i}}{\sqrt{N_i p_{0i}(1 - p_{0i})}}$$

$$= \frac{(O_i - N_i p_{1i}) + (N_i p_{1i} - N p_{0i})\sqrt{p_{1i}(1 - p_{1i})}}{\sqrt{N_i}\sqrt{p_{0i}(1 - p_{0i})}\sqrt{p_{1i}(1 - p_{1i})}}$$

$$= \frac{(O_i - N_i p_{1i}) + N_i(p_{1i} - p_{0i})}{\sqrt{N_i p_{1i}(1 - p_{1i})}} \cdot \frac{\sqrt{p_{1i}(1 - p_{1i})}}{\sqrt{p_{0i}(1 - p_{0i})}}$$

$$= \frac{\sqrt{p_{1i}(1 - p_{1i})}}{\sqrt{p_{0i}(1 - p_{0i})}} \cdot \frac{O_i - N_i p_{1i}}{\sqrt{N_i p_{1i}(1 - p_{1i})}} + \frac{\sqrt{N_i(p_{1i} - p_{0i})}}{\sqrt{p_{0i}(1 - p_{0i})}}$$

[26] See Morrison (1965a), pp. 129–130.

is approximately normal with

$$\text{mean} = \frac{\sqrt{N_i(p_{1i} - p_{0i})^2}}{\sqrt{p_{0i}(1 - p_{0i})}} = \mu_i$$

$$\text{variance} = \frac{p_{1i}(1 - p_{1i})}{p_{0i}(1 - p_{0i})}$$

If the variance were equal to 1, the X_i^2 would be distributed non-central chi-square[27] with 1 degree of freedom and noncentrality parameter $\frac{1}{2}\mu_i^2$. By the additivity property of noncentral chi-squares,

$$\chi^2 = \sum_{i=1}^{n} X_i^2$$

would be noncentral chi-square with n degrees of freedom and non-centrality parameter[28]

$$\lambda = \frac{1}{2}\sum_{i=1}^{n} \mu_i$$

We now have another method for getting the approximate distribution of χ^2 under H_1, and we calculate the power of the test by the same procedure used with the normal approximation. When p_{0i} is close to p_{1i}, the ratio

$$\frac{p_{1i}(1 - p_{1i})}{p_{0i}(1 - p_{0i})}$$

is very close to 1. Table 2.2 gives a few typical ratios.

For different values of N_i, p_{0i}, $p_{1i}(i = 1, \ldots, n)$ the noncentral chi-square approximation may be better than the normal and vice versa. However, because of the large number of parameters involved, a general rule for determining the better approximation cannot be given. One point worth noting is that when the N_i get large, χ^2 becomes normal; and since we have exact expressions for the mean and variance, we get a very good approximation. Conversely, when N_i get large,

$$\frac{p_{1i}(1 - p_{1i})}{p_{0i}(1 - p_{0i})}$$

is unaffected. Therefore, as the sample size increases, the noncentral approximation does not become exact. As a general statement, we can say that when the N_i are small and p_{0i} is close to p_{1i}, use the noncentral

[27] See Graybill (1961), p. 75.
[28] Graybill (1965), p. 77.

Table 2.2 Typical Values of the
Ratio*

p_{0i}	p_{1i}	$\dfrac{p_{1i}(1 - p_{1i})}{p_{0i}(1 - p_{0i})}$
0.50	0.55	0.99
0.55	0.60	0.97
0.60	0.65	0.95
0.65	0.70	0.92
0.70	0.75	0.89
0.75	0.80	0.85
0.50	0.60	0.96
0.60	0.70	0.88
0.70	0.80	0.76

* Of course, when $p_{0i} = 0.50 + \epsilon$ and
$p_{1i} = 0.50 - \epsilon$, the ratio is 1.0 for all
$0 < \epsilon < 0.50$.

chi-square approximation. When the N_i are large, use the normal approximation.

The method of calculating the power of tests helps us to quantify the following observations. Under a "sharp" null hypothesis (a hypothesis that yields *exact* probabilities) we are sure to

1. Reject the null hypothesis if we have very large sample sizes, and
2. Fail to reject the null hypothesis if we have very small samples.

For a fixed null hypothesis H_0 and a fixed alternative hypothesis H_1, the ρ_i and ϵ_i are also fixed, but $\rho_{p_{0i}}^2$ decreases as N_i increases (see Equations 2.29 and 2.30). As N_i increases, the mean of χ^2 increases as the square of the standard deviation of χ^2; therefore, the probability that $\chi^2 < \chi_\alpha^2$ goes to zero. Hence, regardless of the alternative hypothesis H_1 (as long as it is not *exactly* equal to H_0), we can have complete confidence that we will reject H_0 if H_1 is true and the N_i are sufficiently large. Since no model is an exact description of the real world, H_0 will never be exactly true. Hence, if the sample size is large enough, we will be certain to reject our model H_0, because some alternative model H_1 is really true. Under the more typical circumstance of small sample sizes Equations 2.29 and 2.30 or the noncentral approximation will give us an idea of what competing models can and cannot be rejected by the goodness-of-fit test.

The concept of power is especially important in the area of models of consumer behavior. Very often competing models with grossly different

assumptions yield probabilities (of purchasing a particular brand on the next trial) which are not very different from each other. Before accepting one model as an accurate description of the real world, the researcher would be wise to see what power his test has against some competing models. Under certain conditions, the techniques developed in this section may be used to calculate the desired power.

2.3.3   Comparing Models Using Likelihood Ratio Tests

When we obtain minimum chi-square estimators, we also obtain a chi-square statistic with which to test hypotheses. Similarly, when we obtain maximum likelihood estimators, the maximum value of the likelihood function can be used to test hypotheses. Many times when a parameter is constrained to a particular value the model reduces to another well-known model. For example, when $k = 1$, the Markov model of Chapter 4 reduces to the Bernoulli model of Chapter 3. When $\lambda = 0$, the learning model of Chapter 5 becomes Markovian. In the STEAM model of Chapters 9 and 10, the familiar negative binomial model results when $\gamma = \lambda = 0$.

Let $\boldsymbol{\theta}^0 = (\theta_1, \theta_2, \ldots, \theta_q)$ be the unconstrained vector of parameters. The model described by this parameter vector will be called the null hypotheses. Let $\boldsymbol{\theta}^1 = (\theta_1, \theta_2, \ldots, \theta_r, C_{r+1}, C_{r+2}, \ldots, C_q)$ be a constrained vector when θ_1 through θ_r can take on any value but θ_{r+1} through θ_q must take on the values C_{r+1} through C_q. Let the model described by $\boldsymbol{\theta}^1$ be the alternative hypothesis.

Let $\hat{\boldsymbol{\theta}}^0$ be the maximum likelihood estimate for $\boldsymbol{\theta}^0$, and $\hat{\boldsymbol{\theta}}^1$ be the maximum likelihood estimate for $\boldsymbol{\theta}^1$. Since the alternative hypothesis is a proper subset of the null hypothesis,

$$L(\mathbf{x}|\hat{\boldsymbol{\theta}}^1) \leq L(\mathbf{x}|\hat{\boldsymbol{\theta}}^0)$$

where $\mathbf{x}$ is the vector of sample results.

We can now form the likelihood ratio

$$\lambda = \frac{L(\mathbf{x}|\hat{\boldsymbol{\theta}}^1)}{L(\mathbf{x}|\hat{\boldsymbol{\theta}}^0)} \qquad (2.31)$$

If the likelihood ratio λ is sufficiently small, we see that the null hypothesis is a much more "likely" model than the alternative model. Hence, we would reject the alternative model in favor of the null model. Tests based on the principle of Equation 2.31 are called *likelihood ratio tests*.

It is often useful to test the significance of the difference between the constrained and unconstrained models. That is, we wish to test whether

the sample value of λ is significantly less than one. This can often be done by invoking the fact that, for large samples, $-2 \log_e \lambda$ is distributed as χ^2 with $q - r$ degrees of freedom.[29] Thus, to test the significance between two models, where model 1 is derivable from model 0 by imposing constraints on r of the q parameters of model 0, we

1. Estimate the parameter vector $\boldsymbol{\theta}^0$ by maximum likelihood,
2. Estimate the parameter vector $\boldsymbol{\theta}^1$ by maximum likelihood (setting the appropriate $q - r$ parameters equal to present values),
3. Form the likelihood ratio λ, as given in Equation 2.31,
4. Form the quantity $-2 \log_e \lambda$ and look it up in a table of χ^2 with $q - r$ degrees of freedom, and
5. Base our conclusions on the resulting p value.

Given the sample sizes available for testing most stochastic models of buying behavior, we can ignore the fact that the preceding is a large-sample procedure.

The materials of this chapter provide the theory necessary for estimating the parameters of stochastic models and testing hypotheses relative to goodness of fit and competition among alternative models. By applying these principles, together with the computational procedures described in the Appendix, the researcher will have the basic kit of tools necessary to work in the field.

[29] See Wilks (1962), pp. 419–422.

PART II
BRAND-CHOICE MODELS

CHAPTER 3
ZERO-ORDER MODELS

3.1 · Bernoulli Processes

In this chapter we will discuss the simplest possible stochastic model for consumer behavior; this model is the zero-order process. At any purchase decision in a particular product category, the consumer will have a probability p_i of purchasing Brand i. This probability p_i is constant over time and completely independent of the consumer's actual purchase decisions in the immediate or distant past. In summary, nothing that the consumer does or is exposed to alters the probability p_i that he will purchase Brand i.

Often the researcher is interested in analyzing a particular brand or a family's favorite brands. Then at each trial, or purchase decision, there are only two possible states that the consumer can occupy: He purchased either the particular brand being studied or some brand in the aggregate "all other" class. In any sequential process that can take one of two possible values, 0 or 1 (yes or no, heads or tails, buy or not buy, etc.), the simplest assumption to make is that the process is Bernoulli (a two-state zero-order process). That is, on every trial the process has a constant probability of being in state 1 — *regardless* of the past history of the process. Successive tosses of a fair coin form a Bernoulli process. The probability of a head is always 1/2 irrespective of the outcome of past tosses. Successive rolls of a die form a Bernoulli process; e.g., the probability of getting a "four" is always 1/6, and the probability of a "not four" is always 5/6. An example of a non-Bernoulli process is successively turning over the cards of a bridge deck while looking for the aces. The probability of an ace on the first look is 4/52, but the probability of an ace on the second turn is 4/51 if the first card was not an ace, and 3/51 if the first card was an ace. Hence, the 0-1 process (calling an ace 1 and all other cards 0) is not a Bernoulli process; the past outcomes affect the current probabilities.

Formally, the stochastic process

$$\{X_t, t \in T\} \qquad X_t \in R$$

where $R = \{0,1\}$ and $T = 0, 1, 2, \ldots$ is a Bernoulli process if and only if

$$P[X_t = 1 | x_{t-1}, x_{t-2}, \ldots, x_{t-n}] = p$$

for all

$$(x_{t-1}, \ldots, x_{t-n}) \in R^n \qquad n = 1, 2, 3, \ldots$$

At this point the reader may well ask: Why should we study such naive, obviously incorrect models of consumer behavior? First, the Bernoulli model actually fits some consumer data surprisingly well. More important, however, is that a thorough familiarity of the zero-order models in this chapter is necessary to understand the more complicated (and hopefully much more realistic) models that will be presented in later chapters. The important concepts of interpreting data, estimating parameters, and testing the absolute and relative fits of the models are developed in this chapter. The brief review of the literature that follows will put the Bernoulli model in perspective. We will also witness the phenomenon that seems destined to haunt empirically oriented model builders. It is relatively easy to abstract a stochastic model and deduce its probabilistic properties; it is a much more difficult task to look at empirical data and try to infer the model that produced the data.

3.2 Early Models of Consumer Behavior

Mostly for historical reasons, we will briefly mention the works of Brown and Cunningham. These authors made somewhat implicit use of the Bernoulli model; however, the major contribution made by these men was to focus attention on the concept of brand loyalty and to set the stage for the more sophisticated brand switching models that were to follow.

Brown (1952, 1953) in a series of articles in *Advertising Age* used the purchase records of 100 families for the year of 1951 from the *Chicago Tribune* consumer panel. The products studied were frequently purchased products such as coffee, concentrated orange juice, soap, margarine, and so forth. He classified families as having

> Undivided loyalty,
> Divided loyalty,
> Unstable loyalty, or
> No loyalty.

There were also subclassifications within these categories. Brown's measures of brand loyalty have intuitive appeal, but they lack formal definitions. The main finding of Brown's studies was that consumers concentrate their purchases on fewer brands than marketing men had previously thought.

Cunningham (1956) solved Brown's measurement problem by defining brand loyalty as the proportion of total purchases within a given product category devoted to the most frequently purchased brand (or sets of brands) used by a given family. He classified families as having

Single Brand Loyalty: The percent of purchases devoted to one favorite brand.

Dual Brand Loyalty: The percent of purchases devoted to the first and second favorite brands.

An analogous definition is used for "Triple Brand Loyalty." Cunningham also used the *Chicago Tribune* panel on roughly the same product categories as Brown used. Cunningham (1961) employed definitions analogous to his brand loyalty definitions in investigating store loyalty. His conclusions are based on what brand (or store) loyalty would be under the null hypothesis that all *available* brands (stores) would be purchased (visited) equally often. The number of available choices an individual has uniquely determines loyalty under the null hypothesis. This information was not available. However, even by using unrealistically low numbers of choices available, Cunningham gets significant results. He concludes

1. Significant brand loyalty does exist *within* a product class.
2. Loyalty proneness (or brand loyalty across product classes for an individual family) does not exist.
3. Socioeconomic factors do not help in identifying brand loyal families. Since all products were grouped together to get a measure of family loyalty, this result is really only a corollary of result 2.
4. Store loyalty and brand loyalty are *not* correlated.
5. There is more loyalty toward chain stores than toward independents.

It seems apparent from Cunningham's data that individuals do concentrate their purchases on fewer brands and in fewer stores than would be expected under any reasonable chance model. We will now move on to the first explicit use of the Bernoulli process as applied to consumer behavior.

3.3 Spurious Effects of Heterogeneity

In 1958 Kuehn wrote a Ph.D. dissertation that used linear learning theory as a model for consumer brand choice [Kuehn (1958, 1960)]. This work and its extensions will be thoroughly reviewed in Chapter 5.

Kuehn concluded that consumer brand switching is a high-order process. That is, at least the last four or five purchases affect the current purchase. In 1960 Frank claimed that Kuehn's results were the result of the spurious effects of a heterogeneous population and that the simple Bernoulli model fits quite well, [Frank (1960, 1962)]. The following example will demonstrate the spurious effects of heterogeneity.

3.3.1 Aggregate Probabilities May Be Misleading

Suppose we have 100 urns each containing 60 red balls and 40 white balls (These will be called type I urns), and 500 urns each containing 6 red balls and 94 white balls (These will be called type II urns).

$P(R|I)$ = Probability of drawing a red ball given a type I urn.

$P(W|I)$ = Probability of drawing a white ball given a type I urn.

$P(R|II)$ = Probability of drawing a red ball given a type II urn.

$P(W|II)$ = Probability of drawing a white ball given a type II urn.

$P(R)$ = The unconditional probability of drawing a red ball on the first draw.

$P(RR|R)$ = The probability of drawing a red ball on the second draw given that a red ball was drawn on the first draw (and that the same urn is used, with replacement).

To put this example in a marketing framework, consider the drawing of a red ball to indicate the purchase of a Brand A, the drawing of a white ball to indicate the purchase of a product that competes with Brand B. The market is composed of two types of customers. Type I urns correspond to customers who have a high propensity to buy Brand A. They have a 0.6 probability of buying Brand A on any given trial. Type II urns correspond to customers who have a low propensity to buy Product A on any given purchase trial.

The 600 urns (100 type I and 500 type II) are shuffled. One urn is then picked at random. We do not know which type of urn has been selected. From this urn two balls are drawn sequentially (with replacement). The first ball represents the customer's initial purchase decision, the second ball represents his next purchase decision. Because the draws are independent and with replacement, by continuing to draw from the *same* urn, the probability of drawing a red ball is the same on each trial, regardless of the past history of draws. In fact, in this example, the "true" probability is either 0.6 to 0.06. This is analogous to implying that a given customer has a "true" probability of buying Brand A on any given purchase trial and that this probability is a constant, independent of the past purchase history of this individual.

What, in fact, is the probability of drawing a red ball on the first draw (remember the type of urn is not known)?

$$P(R) = P(R|I)P(I) + P(R|II)P(II)$$
$$= 0.6(100/600) + 0.06(500/600)$$
$$= 0.15$$

Now suppose the first draw is actually a red ball. What is the probability that the second ball will also be red?

$$P(RR|R) = [P(RR|I)P(I) + P(RR|II)P(II)]/P(R)$$
$$= [(0.6)(0.6)(100/600) + (0.06)(0.06)(500/600)]/0.15$$
$$= 0.42$$

The drawing of a red ball on the first draw greatly increases the probability that the second draw will be red. Because the drawing was from the same urn on the second draw, the *actual* probability of drawing a second red ball was not changed. However, having drawn a red ball on the first draw made it more likely that a type I urn was being sampled.

To put these results in a marketing framework, the purchase of Brand A on the initial trial did *not* affect the probability mechanism that determined the purchase on the second trial. But because of the heterogeneous population, the purchase of Brand A on the initial trial *appeared* to have an effect on the purchase decision on the next trial. The fact is that it is just more likely that we have picked a customer with a high propensity to buy Brand A on *any* given trial. This apparent effect is what is sometimes called "contagion." We will refer to this as the spurious effect of heterogeneity.

Let $P(i|jk)$ be the probability that an individual who purchased Brand j at time $t - 1$ and k at time $t - 2$ will purchase Brand i at time t, where $i, j, k = 0, 1$. Kuehn aggregated all people with past histories jk. Of these people, a certain proportion bought Brand i on the next trial. Let p_{jk}^i be this empirical proportion. Kuehn found that

$$p_{11}^1 > p_{00}^1$$

and

$$p_{11}^1 > p_{10}^1$$

He concluded that the first and second most recent purchases had very strong influences on the current purchase. Thus, he rejected the hypothesis of Bernoulli trials. However, as our example showed, this effect could be caused by a group of Bernoulli consumers who had differing probabilities of purchasing Brand 1. More will be said on this

problem of heterogeneity in testing the order of a process in Chapter 4. For this chapter, it will suffice if the reader merely understands that Kuehn-type aggregate probabilities can lead to misinterpretations if heterogeneity is not taken into account.

3.3.2 The Run Test

3.3.2.1 *No Problem with Heterogeneity.*   Frank (1960, 1962) analyzed each consumer's purchase history individually; by doing this he of course eliminated the heterogeneity problem. He used the well-known run test; this test has also been used to test the randomness of fluctuations in stock market prices.

Frank's empirical results are presented in his article. To test these results against a heterogeneous Bernoulli model Frank assumes

> Every purchasing unit has a constant probability of purchasing any given brand on any given purchase trial.

This assumption obviously makes a purchasing unit (with respect to any one brand) behave as a Bernoulli process. For example, if a family was observed for 100 trials and they bought Brand A on 20 of these trials, the hypothesis would be that the family had a probability of $20/100 = 0.2$ of buying Brand A on any given trial. To test this hypothesis the theory of runs is used:

> The number of runs in a sequence of Bernoulli trials is the number of unbroken sequences of successes or failures (purchases or nonpurchases), e.g.,
>
> 0, 111, 00, 1, 0000 contains 5 runs.

3.3.2.2 *The Statistics of the Run Test.*   Notation:

r = number of runs,
n_1 = number of purchases of Brand A,
n_2 = number of purchases of brands other than A,
$n = n_1 + n_2$
$E(r|n_1, n_2)$ = expected number of runs given n_1 purchases and n_2 non-purchases of Brand A.

Derivation of $E(r|n_1, n_2)$: Let

n_1 = number of 0
n_2 = number of 1

and note that

r = (number of transitions from 0 to 1 or from 1 to 0) plus 1,

then

$$E(r|n_1, n_2) = [(n_2/n)(n_1/n) + (n_1/n)(n_2/n)]n + 1$$
$$= [2n_1n_2/n] + 1 = m$$

The variance of the conditional random variable r is difficult to derive; therefore, it is merely stated.

$$\text{Var}(r|n_1,n_2) = \frac{2n_1n_2(2n_1n_2 - n)}{n^2(n - 1)} = \sigma_r^2$$

The normalized deviate from the mean is

$$K = \frac{r + \frac{1}{2} - m}{\sigma_r}$$

For n large, K will be distributed approximately normal (0,1).

Results:

For all purchasing units with at least 20 purchases ($n \geq 20$) and at least 4 purchases of the brand being analyzed ($n_1 \geq 4$), Frank calculated values of K. Under the assumption of independent Bernoulli trials, we would expect K to be approximately normal with zero mean and unit variance. This expectation is compared to the results obtained for Hills Brothers and Chase and Sanborn coffee in Table 3.1.

From the calculated values of K something can be said about the independence of successive purchases. If $K > 2$, it suggests an excessive

Table 3.1   Empirical Values of K for Two Brands of Coffee

K		Exp. % for $N(0,1)$	Hills Brothers	Chase and Sanborn
3		0	0	0
2 to	3	2	6	0
1 to	2	14	9	12
0 to	1	34	25	22
−1 to	0	34	24	34
−2 to	−1	14	29	6
−3 to	−2	2	8	6
−4 to	−3	0	3	8
−5 to	−4	0	4	2
−6 to	−5	0	0	0
(Sample Size)			(71)	(53)

amount of switching; if $K < -2$, it suggests that once a brand is purchased (or rejected), the same decision is more likely on the next trial, e.g.,

$$010101010101010101 \quad K \approx 4$$

$$000000000011111111 \quad K \approx -4$$

Although Frank makes no explicit statistical test of the Bernoulli hypothesis, he concludes:

The model of constant probability of purchase fails in the tails of the distribution. There are too many families with an excess of long runs. On the other hand, there are many families whose behavior is consistent with the hypothesis of constant probability of purchase during the period.[1]

3.3.2.3 The Problem with the Stationarity of p.

A necessary condition for a time series to be stationary is that the mechanism generating the time series does not change over time, e.g., a 0-1 (Bernoulli) process where the probability of a 1 is constant over time. Standard tests exist for examining the assumption of a Bernoulli process. The run test was used by Frank in testing the Bernoulli assumption for coffee purchases. However, these tests are invalid for nonstationary processes. Suppose the researcher is examining an 8-year history of coffee purchases for an individual family. Suppose further that in the first 4 years the family had a constant probability of 0.2 of buying Brand X on any purchase regardless of past history and that during the last 4 years Brand X became the family favorite and had a constant purchase probability of 0.8. The test Frank and others used would estimate the probability of purchase over the entire history and obtain an estimate of $p = 0.5$. The series would then "fail" the run test, and the Bernoulli assumption would be rejected. This would mislead the investigator. The process *is* Bernoulli, but it is nonstationary (probability of purchase had one sudden change). Since people do change their buying habits and favorite brands over the time necessary to generate an individual time series with enough purchases to make valid inferences, tests that do not require long-term stationarity are needed. In the example given here, the hypothesis of Bernoulli trials was correct; one of the underlying assumptions of the test was not fulfilled, and the hypothesis was falsely rejected. Frank's observation of too many families with too few runs may be caused by two factors:

The time series are non-Bernoulli in nature.
They are basically Bernoulli over a short period, but
the overall time series is nonstationary.

[1] Frank (1962), p. 56.

Frank's model attacks only the heterogeneity of the population, but long-run stationarity is implicitly assumed.

3.3.2.4 *Low Power of the Run Test.* As Frank points out, the run test is not very powerful when the sample size is small. However, it is even worse than Frank implies, as shown by the following example: If one observes 20 trials of a 0-1 first-order Markov chain with transition matrix

$$\begin{bmatrix} 0.8 & 0.2 \\ 0.2 & 0.8 \end{bmatrix}$$

the expected value of $|K|$ is less than 2. This particular transition matrix implies that the probability of buying the same brand as purchased on the last trial is 0.8 and the probability of switching brands is 0.2. In other words, for a sample size of 20, this highly non-Bernoulli process would be expected to "pass" the run test. The low power of the run test for processes where 20 to 40 trials are observed may account for the large number of families whose K values ranged between 0 and -2.

In summary, the stationarity assumption of the run test may reject families whose patterns are in fact Bernoulli in nature (recent purchases do not influence future ones, even though p may not be constant over a very long period), but the low power of the run test may accept families whose behavior is highly non-Bernoulli (e.g., first-order Markov with high diagonal entries in the transition matrix).

For runs short enough to be reasonably stationary, we will have low power; i.e., values of K near zero will not imply Bernoulli behavior. In fact, a major disadvantage of this K statistic, which is used to test the sharp null hypothesis of exact Bernoulli behavior, is that it gives no indication of how non-Bernoulli the behavior is. In Chapter 4 we develop a model which quantifies the extent of the influence of the most recent purchase decision. We now go on to develop models for testing the zero-order or Bernoulli hypothesis with respect to consumer behavior. These models will not require a homogeneous population or long-run stationarity, their statistical properties will be known, and they require as inputs data of the form that are readily available.

3.4 Overview of Compound Bernoulli Models

The compound Bernoulli models of this chapter are essentially the same as the model proposed by Frank. Their major advantage is that they lend themselves to statistical analysis much better. We will be using aggregate Kuehn-type probabilities to test the models, but we will

explicitly assume a heterogeneous population. Each consumer's probability p of buying Brand 1 will be unaffected by past purchase decisions (i.e., the zero-order or Bernoulli assumption), but different individuals will be allowed to have different p values. In Section 3.5, we will assume that p has a beta distribution among consumers; this will be called beta heterogeneity. In Section 3.6 we invoke the very powerful likelihood principle to enable us to test the Bernoulli model when p is allowed to have any distribution over consumers; this we call arbitrary heterogeneity.

The techniques used to test the compound Bernoulli models have many advantages over the run test used by Frank. Only short purchase histories of individual consumers will be used; therefore, the stationarity assumption on p is not strained too badly. The types of data that are used to test the models are usually such that we do not have the low power problem encountered in the run test. Finally, virtually all of the conceptual and statistical foundations needed for the models contained in later chapters are developed in the testing of the compound Bernoulli models. Since these models are so simple, the somewhat subtle concepts involved in testing the models can be most clearly explained in conjunction with the compound Bernoulli models. Again we caution the reader that although the Bernoulli model is of some interest in its own right, its major contribution is as a vehicle for understanding the more complex models.

Since *homogeneous* usually means constant over time in most stochastic model contexts, we have decided to call our heterogeneous (in our sense) Bernoulli model the *compound* Bernoulli model to avoid confusion.

3.5 Compound Beta Bernoulli Model

3.5.1 Beta Heterogeneity

Of the consumers in the population being studied, we assume that each one has a probability p of buying Brand 1 and the complementary probability $1 - p$ of buying Brand 0 (usually an aggregated "all other" brand). However, we do not assume that each consumer has the same p. What is assumed is that p has a beta distribution over the individuals in the population. There are two ways to interpret this beta distribution, which has the form

$$b(p) = \frac{\Gamma(\alpha + \beta)}{\Gamma(\alpha)\Gamma(\beta)} \, p^{\alpha-1}(1 - p)^{\beta-1} \qquad \text{for } 0 < p < 1$$

$$\qquad\quad = 0 \qquad\qquad\qquad\qquad\qquad\qquad \text{otherwise}$$

where $\Gamma(\cdot)$ is the gamma function and α, β are > 0. The first interpretation is that if we plotted a histogram of all the consumers' p values, this histogram could be fitted by the two-parameter beta distribution. The second interpretation is that if we pick an individual consumer at random, then our "guessing" distribution for his p value is beta. Note that this guessing distribution has all the earmarks of a Bayesian prior distribution. In fact, we will be updating the guessing distribution on an individual's p value as we observe his purchase decision. But note that this prior or guessing distribution is "objective" in nature. The compound beta Bernoulli model is completely described by the zero-order assumption and the two parameters of the beta distribution α and β. If we use the histogram interpretation, the beta distribution is an objective measure of the heterogeneity in the consumer population. The variance of the beta distribution gives a quantification of the heterogeneity in the population. In our parameterization of the beta distribution the mean and variance of p are

$$E(p) = \frac{\alpha}{\alpha + \beta}$$

$$\mathrm{Var}(p) = \frac{\alpha\beta}{(\alpha + \beta + 1)(\alpha + \beta)^2}$$

More on the interpretation of the beta distribution will be given in Section 3.5.2.

Although many of the mathematical techniques that we use are associated with Bayesian statistics, there is none of the subjective element concerning prior distributions that precipitates the Bayesian versus classical arguments. The "prior" distributions that we use are objective components of the model; they represent the heterogeneity of the consumers with respect to their propensity to purchase Brand 1.

3.5.2 *The Beta Distribution and Consumer Purchase Probabilities*

If we accept the zero-order assumption of the compound Bernoulli models, how realistic is the beta distribution for the heterogeneity of the population? Figure 3.1 shows beta distributions for various values of the parameters α and β. When α and β are less than one, we get "dish-shaped" curves; the majority of the population are concentrated near the $p = 0$ and $p = 1$ extremes. Except for these dish-shaped curves, the beta distribution can take any "reasonable" unimodal shape. Hence, the beta distribution is flexible enough so that it will never give a really bad fit. If Brand 1 represents the family's favorite

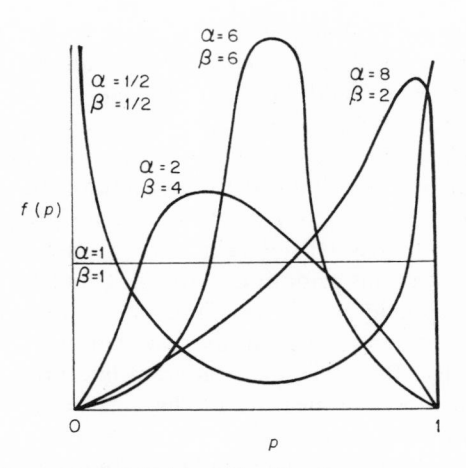

Figure 3.1.   Some possible beta distributions.

brand, the beta distribution has good intuitive appeal. However, if Brand 1 represents a particular brand, there may be a few problems. There will be a group of consumers who never get exposed to the brand, and hence we should have a "spike" at $p = 0$. In a somewhat different context, the STEAM models of Chapters 9, 10, and 11 have possibilities for a spike for representing nonbuyers or equivalently people with probability zero of buying. Figure 3.2 shows this situation for a mixed continuous and discrete probability density.

Assuming Brand 1 is a particular brand, there will be a group of consumers who have Brand 1 as their favorite. There will also be another group of consumers who virtually never buy Brand 1. We would then expect p to be distributed something like the distribution in Figure 3.3. This bimodal distribution cannot be fit very well by a single beta distribution.

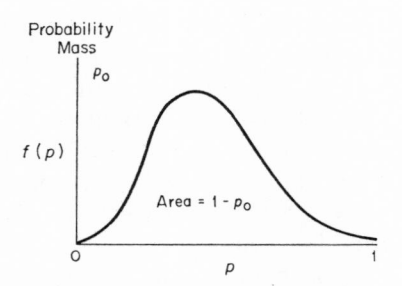

Figure 3.2.   Beta distribution with a spike for nonbuyers.

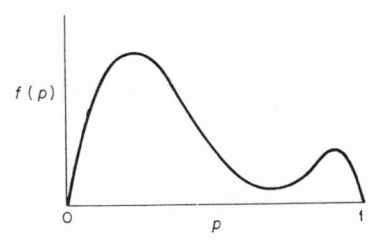

Figure 3.3. Bimodal distribution for p when Brand 1 is a particular brand.

In summary, the beta may be a very realistic distribution for the heterogeneity in some cases but not too good in others. Later we will give a method for assessing how well the beta distribution fits.

3.5.3 The Beta and Binomial as Conjugate Distributions

The results of this section will illustrate the mathematical tractability of using a beta distribution for the heterogeneity in the compound Bernoulli model. First we need to note that Bayes theorem can be expressed as

$$\text{posterior} \propto \text{likelihood} \times \text{prior} \tag{3.1}$$

This means that posterior distribution is proportional to the prior distribution times the likelihood function. Excellent discussions of Equation 3.1 are available in Savage et al. (1962), Raiffa and Schlaifer (1961), and Pratt, Raiffa, and Schlaifer (1965).

Suppose we observe a consumer for n purchases, and he makes r purchases of Brand 1. Let $\ell[(n,r)|p]$ be the likelihood[2] for this observation given that the consumer behavior can be described by a Bernoulli process with probability p of buying Brand 1. Then $\ell[(n,r)|p]$ is merely the binomial probability

$$\ell[(n,r)|p] = \text{constant } p^r (1-p)^{n-r} \tag{3.2}$$

Now before we observed this individual, our guessing distribution on his p-value was beta with parameters α and β. Let the superscript $'$ refer to prior and $''$ refer to posterior. Then

$$b'(p) = \text{constant } p^{\alpha-1}(1-p)^{\beta-1} \tag{3.3}$$

is the prior, or guessing, distribution on p.

[2] The symbols ℓ and L are used interchangeably for "likelihood" throughout this book.

Our observation of r ones in n trials has updated the prior distribution $b'(p)$. Putting Equations 3.2 and 3.3 into 3.1, we get

$$b''(p) = \text{constant } p^{\alpha+r-1}(1 - p)^{\beta+n-r-1} \qquad (3.4)$$

We see that the posterior distribution is still beta but with parameters $\alpha + r$ and $\beta + n - r$. When the prior distribution and the likelihood function combine so as to give a posterior distribution that is of the same form (or family) as the prior, then the distributions involved (in our case the beta and binomial) are said to be conjugate distributions. Letting $E''(p)$ denote the mean of this updated or posterior distribution, we have

$$E''(p) = \frac{\alpha + r}{\alpha + \beta + n} \qquad (3.5)$$

Equation 3.5 is merely a special case of the spurious effects of heterogeneity, which was discussed in Section 3.3. To be specific, let us consider an Individual A with a past history of 1111 for his last four purchases; Individual B has 0000 for his last purchase. Then

$$E''_A(p) = \frac{\alpha + 4}{\alpha + \beta + 4}$$

$$E''_B(p) = \frac{\alpha}{\alpha + \beta + 4}$$

Individual A is much more likely to purchase Brand 1 on the next trial than is B. However, this is not because the past purchases of 1's has influenced A's probability of buying Brand 1 (remember we are assuming each consumer is a zero-order process), but merely by observing 1111 it is much more likely that A is a consumer with a high p and the 0000 past history makes it likely that B is an individual with a low p. The advantage of the tests to be developed in this chapter is that they allow us to separate the nonzero-order effects (the real effects of an individual's past purchases probability) from the spurious effects of heterogeneity. Of course, it is only the former effect that we wish to analyze when we ask if consumers behave like a Bernoulli process.

3.5.4   *Interpretation of Conditional Model Probabilities*

In testing the compound Bernoulli model, we will be segmenting the consumers by their past purchase decisions. In particular all of our examples will be for the case of the last four purchase decisions; however, there is nothing sacred about the last four purchases, and all

of the theoretical results contain the general case of the last n purchases. If n, the number of past purchases, is too small, the tests are hard to interpret; but if n is too large, we will need very large samples (because there will be 2^n possible past histories). Hence, we have somewhat arbitrarily picked a past history of length four as a compromise for the empirical testing of the model.

The notation that will be used is as follows:

N_{ijkl} = the number of consumers whose last four purchases were brands i at time $t - 1$, j at $t - 2$, k at $t - 3$, and l at $t = 4$.

R_{ijkl} = the number of consumers with past history $ijkl$ who purchased Brand 1 at time t.

$\bar{p}_{ijkl}$ = R_{ijkl}/N_{ijkl}, the empirical proportion of consumers with past history $ijkl$ who purchase Brand 1 on the next trial.

$P_M(1|ijkl)$ = the theoretical probability that an individual with past history $ijkl$ will purchase Brand 1 on the next trial when the model of consumer behavior is M. The subscript for the model M will be omitted when it is obvious which model is being discussed. We will call these probabilities *conditional model probabilities*.

(n,r) = any past purchase history of length n that contains r ones and $n - r$ zeros.

p_{ijkl} = the expected value of the individual consumer's parameter p, given that this consumer has past history $ijkl$.

For the models of Chapters 3 and 4, each consumer is completely characterized by a parameter p. This will become clearer in Chapter 4, but note that in the compound Bernoulli model each consumer is completely described (with respect to his purchase behavior toward Brand 1) when we know his value of p, the probability of purchasing Brand 1 on any trial. For the compound Bernoulli models $P(1|ijkl) = p_{ijkl}$, but the distinction between the two concepts will become important in Chapter 4. A very clear understanding of $P(1|ijkl)$ is necessary. To ease notation, let x denote any arbitrary past purchase history; the next three subsections will give three interpretations of $P(1|x)$.

3.5.4.1 $P(1|x)$ *for an Individual Picked at Random.*   For the compound Bernoulli model each individual has a "true" p, his probability of buying Brand 1 on any given trial. Hence, if we somehow know this p value — call it p_{true} — we would know that his probability of buying Brand 1 on the next trial would be p_{true} regardless of his past history x. However, we do not know this consumer's true p value, and if we have observed no past history for this individual, his p value is to us a random

variable with a distribution $b(p)$. For our first examples, $b(p)$ will be beta with parameters α and β, but it will be helpful for later models if the reader considers $b(p)$ as a general probability distribution. Once we observe a past history x, our guessing or prior distribution $b(p)$ gets updated to a posterior distribution $b(p|x)$. Hence, an individual with past history x picked at random will have an expected probability of purchasing Brand 1 of

$$E[P(1|x)] = \int_0^1 pb(p|x)\,dp$$

This is, of course, the mean of the posterior distribution $b(p|x)$.

$$E[P(1|x)] = \text{mean of } b(p|x) \tag{3.6}$$

However, we can also take the expectation operation $E(\cdot)$ from $P(1|x)$ and state that

$$P(1|x) = \text{mean of } b(p|x) \tag{3.7}$$

An individual with past history x that is picked at random from the population of all consumers with the same past history x is a Bernoulli random variable with respect to his next purchase. The outcome of his next purchase is either a 1 (the purchase of Brand 1) or a 0 (the purchase of Brand 0). For an individual picked at random, the probability of a 1 is the possible "true" p values weighted by their likelihood of occurring, i.e., Equation 3.7. If we look at a randomly chosen individual with past history x as a Bernoulli random variable with the probability of a 1 equal to the mean of the posterior distribution $b(p|x)$, we see the underlying concept that allows us to test the models and estimate parameters by use of the chi-square goodness-of-fit statistic.

3.5.4.2 *The Relative Frequency Interpretation for* $P(1|x)$. If we had many individuals with past history x, what proportion of them would purchase Brand 1 on the next trial? Let N_x be the number of individuals with past history x and R_x be the number of those that purchase Brand 1 on the next purchase. Using Equation 3.6 and the fact that the sum of the individual expectations equals the expectation of the sum, we get

$$E[R_x] = N_x\,P(1|x)$$

Here we assume that the N_x are fixed numbers and the R_x are random variables. The R_x is the sum of independent, identically distributed Bernoulli random variables and is thus a binomial random variable. Therefore,

$$\text{Var}[R_x] = N_x\,P(1|x)[1 - P(1|x)]$$

Hence,

$$E\left[\frac{R_x}{N_x}\right] = P(1|x)$$

$$\text{Var}\left[\frac{R_x}{N_x}\right] = \frac{P(1|x)[1 - P(1|x)]}{N_x}$$

Therefore as N_x gets large, we can state that

$$\lim_{N_x \to \infty} \frac{R_x}{N_x} = P(1|x) \qquad (3.8)$$

This last statement gives us the relative frequency interpretation of $P(1|x)$.

3.5.4.3 *Bayesian Minimum Quadratic Loss Interpretation of* $P(1|x)$.
Suppose that we are trying to obtain a point estimate $\hat{p}_x$ for a parameter p which has a posterior distribution $b(p|x)$. Assume that we wish to minimize the expected squared loss

$$L(\hat{p}_x) = E[(\hat{p}_x - p)^2]$$

Here $\hat{p}_x - p$ is the difference between the estimate $\hat{p}_x$ and the true value p.

$$L(\hat{p}_x) = \int (\hat{p}_x - p)^2 b(p|\hat{p}) \, dp$$

$$L(\hat{p}_x) = \hat{p}_x^2 \int b(p|x) \, dp - 2\hat{p}_x \int pb(p|x) \, dp$$

$$+ \int p^2 b(p|x) \, dp$$

To find the value of $\hat{p}_x$ that minimizes the function $L(\hat{p}_x)$, we differentiate $L(\hat{p}_x)$ and find the value of $\hat{p}_x$ such that

$$\frac{\partial L(\hat{p}_x)}{\partial \hat{p}_x} = 0$$

$$\frac{\partial L(\hat{p}_x)}{\partial \hat{p}_x} = 2\hat{p}_x \int b(p|x) \, dp - 2 \int pb(p|x) \, dp$$

$$= 2\hat{p}_x - 2 \int pb(p|x) \, dp = 0$$

$$\hat{p}_x = \int pb(p|x) \, dp = \text{mean of } b(p|x) = P(1|x) \qquad (3.9)$$

Hence, we see that $P(1|x)$ can also be interpreted as the estimate of an individual's true p value which minimizes the expected quadratic loss from misestimating the true p. We are now in a position to restate formally the assumption of the compound beta Bernoulli model plus all of its probabilistic properties.

3.5.5 *Properties of the Compound Beta Bernoulli Model*
The compound beta Bernoulli model is defined by

1. A population of zero-order (Bernoulli) consumers whose probability of purchasing Brand 1 is p regardless of their past purchases,
2. And p is distributed according to a beta distribution with parameters α and β among the consumers in the population.

Table 3.2 summarizes all of the conditional model probabilities for the 16 possible past histories of length four. The likelihood column is merely the result that the probability of any past sequence of length n with r ones is $p^r(1 - p)^{n-r}$. The conditional model probabilities $P(1|\text{Past Sequence})$ were derived in Section 3.5.3, which discussed the beta and binomial as conjugate distributions.

Table 3.2   The Likelihoods and Probabilities Resulting from a Compound Beta Bernoulli Model

Past Sequence	Likelihood of Sequence	P(1|Past Sequence)
1111	p^4	$\dfrac{\alpha + 4}{\alpha + \beta + 4}$
0111 1011 1101 1110	$p^3(1 - p)$	$\dfrac{\alpha + 3}{\alpha + \beta + 4}$
0011 0101 1001 0110 1010 1100	$p^2(1 - p)^2$	$\dfrac{\alpha + 2}{\alpha + \beta + 4}$
0001 0010 0100 1000	$p(1 - p)^3$	$\dfrac{\alpha + 1}{\alpha + \beta + 4}$
0000	$(1 - p)^4$	$\dfrac{\alpha}{\alpha + \beta + 4}$

3.6 Compound Bernoulli Model with Arbitrary Heterogeneity

When researchers asked if the behavior of consumers could be represented as simple Bernoulli processes, they were only interested in the zero-order assumption and not in the form of the heterogeneity. We have developed the beta heterogeneity case first only for pedagogical reasons. However, with the results we now have, we can generalize the compound Bernoulli model to the case where $b(p)$ is any arbitrary distribution.

Recall that in Section 3.5.3, we wrote Bayes theorem in the form of Equation 3.1, "posterior $\propto$ likelihood $\times$ prior." Let the heterogeneity of p, the consumer's probability of buying Brand 1, be represented by the prior or guessing distribution $b'(p)$, and let $b'(p)$ be any arbitrary distribution. Then from Equation 3.1, we immediately see that for any two past histories x^1 and x^2 such that

$$\ell(x^1|p) = \text{constant } \ell(x^2|p)$$

we will have the posterior distributions

$$b''(p|x^1) = b''(p|x^2)$$

We can now formally state one variant of the powerful likelihood principle:

Any two sample outcomes (e.g., past purchase histories) whose likelihood functions differ at most by a constant factor yield the same posterior distribution.

Table 3.3 puts the past histories of length four into groups which yield equal posterior distributions and, hence, equal conditional model probabilities (the means of these posterior distributions). Note that for arbitrary unknown heterogeneity, we do not know the numerical values of the conditional model probabilities. To know these values we would have to evaluate

$$P(1|x) = \int p b''(p|x)\, dp \qquad \text{(See Section 3.5.4.1)}$$

$$= \int p\, \frac{\ell(x|p)b'(p)}{\ell(x)}\, dp \qquad \text{(by Bayes theorem)}$$

$$= \frac{\int p\ell(x|p)b'(p)\, dp}{\ell(x)}$$

$$P(1|x) = \frac{\int p\ell(x|p)b'(p)\, dp}{\int \ell(x|p)b'(p)\, dp} \qquad (3.10)$$

Table 3.3   The Probabilities Resulting from a Compound Bernoulli Model with Arbitrary Heterogeneity

Group	Past Sequence	$P(1\|\text{Past Sequence}) = p_{\text{Past Sequence}}$
4	1111	$P_{4,4}$
3	0111 1011 1101 1110	$P_{3,4}$
2	0011 0101 1001 0110 1010 1100	$P_{2,4}$
1	0001 0010 0100 1000	$P_{1,4}$
0	0000	$P_{0,4}$

Since $b'(p)$ is unknown, we cannot evaluate Equation 3.10, but we do know groups of past histories with the same likelihood function yield the same conditional model probabilities. Equation 3.10 will be developed more thoroughly in Chapter 4 when we explicitly use it.

In Table 3.3, we do not know that value of, say, $P_{2,4}$, but we do know that all the past histories with two 1's and two 0's have the same probability of a 1 on the next purchase. Therefore we are now in a position to examine the zero-order hypothesis free from any restrictions on the heterogeneity $b(p)$. We merely look at the empirical probabilities, say,

$$\frac{R_{0111}}{N_{0111}}, \ \frac{R_{1011}}{N_{1011}}, \ \frac{R_{1101}}{N_{1101}}, \ \text{and} \ \frac{R_{1110}}{N_{1110}}$$

and see if they are sufficiently similar to justify the assumption of zero-order or Bernoulli behavior. Methods for statistically testing this hypothesis will be given in Section 3.7.

3.7   Testing the Goodness of Fit of the Models

The ideas discussed in Sections 3.5.4.1 and 3.5.4.2 are the basis for all of the goodness-of-fit tests for Chapters 3, 4, 6, and 7. Namely, the

sample statistics R_x (the number of people with past history x who purchased Brand 1 on the next trial) are binomial random variables. The central limit theorem will be invoked in order to assume normality of the R_x. From there it will be easy to show that the usual goodness-of-fit statistic

$$\chi^2 = \sum \frac{(\text{observed} - \text{expected})^2}{\text{expected}}$$

is distributed as chi-squares under the null hypothesis that the model being tested is true.

3.7.1 Testing the Compound Beta Bernoulli Model When α and β Are Known

Suppose that we are testing the zero-order hypothesis when we also assume that the heterogeneity of the population is beta with known values for the parameters α and β. Also assume that we have the last four purchase decisions for each consumer and that we then observe the current purchase. It will become obvious how to generalize this result to the case of the last n purchase decisions. Let us index the 16 possible past histories of length four (see Table 3.2 of Section 3.5.5) by the lettter i, $i = 1, \ldots, 16$. Our data will then consist of the sample sizes

$$N_i \qquad i = 1, \ldots, 16$$

and the sample results

$$R_i \qquad i = 1, \ldots, 16$$

From Section 3.5.3, we know that

$$P(1|i) = \frac{\alpha + r_i}{\alpha + \beta + 4}$$

where r_i is the number of 1's in the past history i. Then

$$E_i = N_i\, P(1|i)$$

is the expected number of consumers with past history i who purchase Brand 1 on the current trial. Let

$$R'_i = N_i - R_i$$
$$E'_i = N_i - E_i$$

The usual goodness-of-fit statistic

$$\chi^2_{BB4} = \sum_{i=1}^{16} \frac{(R_i - E_i)^2}{E_i} + \sum_{i=1}^{16} \frac{(R'_i - E'_i)^2}{E'_i} \qquad (3.11)$$

can be formed.

With a few algebraic manipulations, Equation 3.11 can be written as

$$\chi^2_{BB4} = \sum_{i=1}^{16} \frac{[R_i - N_i \, P(1|i)]^2}{N_i \, P(1|i)[1 - P(1|i)]}$$

However, this may be written as

$$\chi^2_{BB4} = \sum_{i=1}^{16} Z_i^2$$

where Z_i has a zero mean and unit variance. By the central limit theorem, Z_i is approximately normal with mean zero and variance one; hence, Z_i^2 is approximately chi-square with one degree of freedom. The additivity property of independent chi-square random variables then makes χ^2_{BB4} have a chi-square distribution with 16 degrees of freedom. For the full details of this derivation, see Section 2.3.2.3 (especially Equation 2.26 when $\rho = 1$ and $\epsilon = 0$). The "$BB4$" subscript on χ^2 indicates the beta Bernoulli model with a past history of length 4 being used. For past histories of length n, there are 2^n possible past histories; hence, the analogous statistic χ^2_{BBn} will be distributed chi-square with 2^n degrees of freedom.

3.7.2 Testing the Compound Beta Bernoulli Model When α and β Are Estimated from the Data

If we are interested in testing the compound beta Bernoulli model, we do not usually have a priori values for α and β. The more usual situation is that we want to test the zero-order assumption of the individual behavior and the assumption of beta heterogeneity. In this case, the values for α and β must be estimated from the sample data. The details of parameter estimation for this model will be given in Section 3.8. The problem is that when we estimate α and β from the data we are partially "fitting" the model to the data. The question is: How does this fitting "contaminate" the distribution of the goodness-of-fit statistic, Equation 3.11?

Fortunately, this contamination is of a very simple form. Let $\hat{\alpha}$ and $\hat{\beta}$ be the estimates for α and β. For many classes of estimators [see Cramer (1946), p. 506], we merely lose one degree of freedom for each parameter that is estimated from the data. In particular, our data are in the contingency table form discussed by Cramer (see Section 2.3.2.3) and the particular class of estimators we finally use (minimum chi-square) meet all the requirements for this simple contamination (alteration) of the sample statistic χ^2.

If we let

$$\hat{P}(1|i) = \frac{\hat{\alpha} + r_i}{\hat{\alpha} + \hat{\beta} + 4}$$

$$\hat{E}_i = N_i \, \hat{P}(1|i)$$

our sample statistic

$$\chi^2_{BB4} = \sum_{i=1}^{16} \frac{(R_i - \hat{E}_i)^2}{\hat{E}_i} + \sum_{i=1}^{16} \frac{(R'_i - \hat{E}'_i)^2}{\hat{E}'_i} \tag{3.12}$$

is distributed as chi-square with 14 degrees of freedom. Of course, χ^2_{BBn} will be distributed chi-square with $(2^n - 2)$ degrees of freedom.

3.7.3 *Testing Only the Zero-Order Hypothesis*

The goodness-of-fit tests that were discussed in the previous two subsections tested both the zero-order and beta heterogeneity assumptions. The more fundamental hypothesis to test is that of zero-order independent of the form of the heterogeneity. Table 3.3 of Section 3.6 gives us the theory needed to perform this desired test. Testing only the zero-order hypothesis is equivalent to testing the following three compound hypotheses:

$$H_0^{3,4}: p_{0111} = p_{1011} = p_{1101} = p_{1110}$$

$$H_0^{2,4}: p_{0011} = p_{0101} = p_{1001} = p_{0110} = p_{1010} = p_{1100}$$

$$H_0^{1,4}: p_{0001} = p_{0010} = p_{0100} = p_{1000}$$

The general hypothesis $H_0^{r,n}$ will mean all past histories of length n with r ones yield the same conditional model probabilities. Note that $H_0^{4,4}$ and $H_0^{0,4}$ are not defined since there is only one past history in each of these groups..

We will now go through a detailed description for the testing of $H_0^{3,4}$. It will then be obvious how to test $H_0^{2,4}$ and $H_0^{1,4}$. Of course in testing the zero-order hypothesis, we will test all three of these hypotheses simultaneously. Let

$$\bar{p}_{3,4} = \frac{R_{0111} + R_{1011} + R_{1101} + R_{1110}}{N_{0111} + N_{1011} + N_{1101} + N_{1110}}$$

Then

$$E_{0111} = \bar{p}_{3,4} N_{0111}$$
$$E_{1011} = \bar{p}_{3,4} N_{1011}$$
$$E_{1101} = \bar{p}_{3,4} N_{1101}$$
$$E_{1110} = \bar{p}_{3,4} N_{1110}$$

Then we let

$$E'_i = N_i - E_i$$
$$R'_i = N_i - R_i$$

We can form the goodness-of-fit statistic

$$\chi^2_{AB3,4} = \sum_i \frac{(R_i - E_i)^2}{E_i} + \sum_i \frac{(R'_i - E'_i)^2}{E'_i}$$

where $i = 0111, 1011, 1101,$ and 1110. The subscript A is for arbitrary heterogeneity, B for Bernoulli behavior, and $3,4$ describes the past histories used.

If $p_{3,4}$ were given a priori (i.e., not determined from the data), $\chi^2_{AB3,4}$ would have a chi-square distribution with 4 degrees of freedom. However, the sample mean $\bar{p}_{3,4}$ is an estimate of the true mean, and we have the same kind of contamination discussed with respect to estimating α and β. Again Cramer (1946), pp. 425, 506, has all the mathematical details. Therefore, since we are partially fitting the sample data when we obtain the parameter estimate $\bar{p}_{3,4}$ of the true mean, $\chi^2_{AB3,4}$ is still distributed as chi-square but with $4 - 1 = 3$ degrees of freedom.

If we let

$$\bar{p}_{2,4} = \frac{R_{0011} + R_{0101} + R_{1001} + R_{0110} + R_{1010} + R_{1100}}{N_{0011} + N_{0101} + N_{1001} + N_{0110} + N_{1010} + N_{1100}}$$

$$\bar{p}_{1,4} = \frac{R_{0001} + R_{0010} + R_{0100} + R_{1000}}{N_{0001} + N_{0010} + N_{0100} + N_{1000}}$$

we can form the analogous sample statistics

$$\chi^2_{AB2,4}$$

$$\chi^2_{AB1,4}$$

These will of course have 5 and 3 degrees of freedom, respectively. Adding the three goodness-of-fit statistics together, we get

$$\chi^2_{AB4} = \chi^2_{AB3,4} + \chi^2_{AB2,4} + \chi^2_{AB1,4} \qquad (3.13)$$

By the additivity property of independent chi-square random variables, Equation 3.13 will be distributed as chi-square with $3 + 5 + 3 = 11$ degrees of freedom. Hence, χ^2_{AB4} can be used to test the null hypothesis of zero-order behavior while allowing any arbitrary form of heterogeneity. For past histories of length n, there will be $n + 1$ groups that yield equal probabilities (counting the one all zero's and one all one's

groups). Therefore,

$$\chi^2_{ABn}$$

will be distributed as chi-square with $2^n - (n + 1)$ degrees of freedom.

Suppose we wish to test the hypothesis of zero-order behavior while assuming a homogeneous population (i.e., assuming everyone has the same p-value). The best method for doing this will be given in Chapter 4 when we discuss Markov models. However, for completeness, we give a chi-square test analogous to Equation 3.13. There is only one probability to be estimated from the data. That is,

$$\bar{p} = \frac{R_{0000} + \cdots + R_{1111}}{N_{0000} + \cdots + N_{1111}}$$

Let

$$E_i = \bar{p}N_i \qquad i = 0000, \ldots, 1111$$

Then

$$\chi^2_{HB4} = \sum_i \frac{(R_i - E_i)^2}{E_i} + \sum_i \frac{(R'_i - E'_i)^2}{E'_i} \qquad (3.14)$$

is distributed chi-square with 15 degrees of freedom (one degree of freedom was lost in obtaining $\bar{p}$). The H is for a homogeneous population. In general χ^2_{HBn} will be distributed as chi-square with $2^n - 1$ degrees of freedom.

This seems to be the test that Kuehn implied when he rejected the Bernoulli hypothesis. However, as we have seen in Section 3.3.1 (which discusses the spurious effects of heterogeneity), Equation 3.14 is completely inapplicable for populations when p is allowed to differ among individuals. We now go on to the problem of interpreting these various chi-square goodness-of-fit statistics.

3.7.4 *Interpreting the Goodness-of-Fit Statistics*

The goodness-of-fit statistics we have just developed can be used to test the null hypothesis of zero-order behavior. Depending on the type of heterogeneity assumed, we will use either Equation 3.11 (beta heterogeneity with α and β known), Equation 3.12 (α and β estimated from the data), or Equation 3.13 (arbitrary heterogeneity). According to the classical theory of hypothesis testing, we pick a critical level (for example, 0.05 or 0.01), and a critical number $\chi^2_{0.05}$ or $\chi^2_{0.01}$ will be determined for each of the three possible null hypotheses. Under the three null hypotheses the sample statistic χ^2 has a chi-square distribution with 16, 14, and 11 degrees of freedom, respectively. Hence, if our data yield a sample statistic $\chi^2 > \chi^2_\alpha$, we will reject the null hypothesis at the α level

(or equivalently with confidence $1 - \alpha$). A practical question is now raised: Is the model no good if we reject the null hypothesis, or, conversely, is it acceptable if we fail to reject the hypothesis? A simple example will convince the reader of the dangers of interpreting statistical significance as practical or managerial significance. We will then relate this result to our goodness-of-fit tests of hypotheses.

Suppose we are sampling from a normal population with known variance σ^2 and unknown mean μ. We wish to test the hypothesis that $\mu = 0$. We observed a sample of size n and calculate the sample mean

$$\bar{x} = \frac{1}{n}\sum_{i=1}^{n} x_i$$

Under the null hypothesis that $\mu = 0$, the sample statistic $\bar{x}$ is normally distributed with mean 0 and variance σ^2/n. The critical level for rejecting the hypothesis $\mu = 0$ is (for a two-sided test) twice the area to the right of the value of the sample statistic $\bar{x}$. The absolute magnitude of $\bar{x}$ is only a partial determinant of the critical level; the sample size also plays a very large role. The problem is that the null hypothesis is that the mean is *exactly* equal to zero. Hence, if the true mean is different from zero (no matter how close to zero), with a large enough sample size we will always reject the null hypothesis.

By the same reasoning the $\bar{p}_1 = R_i/N_i$, the empirical probabilities, may be very close to the conditional model probabilities $P(1|i)$. Yet, if the sample sizes, the N_i, are large enough, χ^2 will be greater than χ^2_α. Hence, we must reject the hypothesis that the Bernoulli model with whatever type of heterogeneity we have assumed is *exactly* correct. Conversely, if the N_i are very small, the $\bar{p}_i$ will probably not differ from the $P(1|i)$ by enough to reject the hypothesis. Therefore, it is very difficult to interpret the absolute values of the sample chi-square statistics or their critical levels. Just as the K statistic for the run test (see Section 3.3.2) does not indicate how far the behavior differs from zero-order, neither do the chi-square statistics.

The chi-square statistics can be interpreted as normalized discrepancies (distances) between the empirical data and the model predictions. When the sample sizes are held constant, the two chi-square statistics resulting when two competing models are applied to the same data give a good indication of the relative fits of the models. This will become very important in Chapter 4. These sample goodness-of-fit statistics will also be very useful in obtaining parameter estimates. In summary, all of the difficulties inherent in testing "sharp" two-sided hypotheses (e.g., the mean is exactly zero, the behavior is exactly

Bernoulli, the distribution is exactly Poisson, etc.) exist for the tests of hypotheses found in Sections 3.7.1, 3.7.2, and 3.7.3.

3.8 Parameter Estimation for the Compound Bernoulli Model

When we allow arbitrary heterogeneity, there are of course no parameters to estimate. We do have to calculate $\bar{p}_{r,n}$ (see Section 3.7.3), but these are estimates of the true probabilities $P[1|(r,n)]$, which in turn are the result of the zero-order behavior and the unknown heterogeneity $b(p)$. It is only when we assume beta heterogeneity that we need to estimate parameters from the data. Then estimates of the two parameters of the beta distribution α and β must be obtained.

Various commonly used classes of estimators and their properties were discussed in Chapter 2. Of these, the method of maximum likelihood had many desirable features. Unfortunately the maximization of the likelihood function for the sample data from this very simple compound beta Bernoulli model proved to be an analytically intractable task. This was true when we used the exact binomial distribution of the R_i and when we used the normal approximation. The main source of difficulty was the fact that the mean and variance, np and $np(1-p)$, of the binomial distribution depend on each other through the value of p. Other analytical methods (notably minimum chi-square and modified minimum chi-square) also proved intractable. In fact, for none of the models contained in this monograph were we able to obtain analytical expressions for parameter values. Hence, we had to use numerical search techniques to maximize likelihood functions or minimize chi-square statistics in order to obtain estimates for the parameters of our models.

A numerical minimum chi-square was used to obtain estimates for α and β in the compound beta Bernoulli model. Complete details of this method will be given in Chapter 4 along with the empirical results. We delay giving the details and results because the compound Bernoulli models are special cases of models developed in Chapter 4. Therefore, the empirical results for the Bernoulli models will be easier to interpret when they are contrasted to the more general Markov models contained in Chapter 4.

3.9 Another Class of Bernoulli Models

Howard has proposed a model for consumer behavior which he calls "Dynamic Inference" [Howard (1965)]. This name is somewhat misleading since he discusses only probabilistic properties of the model; he

states none of the usual "inference" notations of parameter estimation or tests of the model. Howard's model is very similar to our compound Bernoulli model, and he develops conditional model probabilities [e.g., P(1|0110)]. We will present the simplest case of the dynamic inference model. The general model results in a very involved exercise in conditional probabilities and merely involves substituting general probability distributions for the specific ones that we will discuss.

The simplest model is called "The Bernoulli-Beta-Geometric Problem." A two-brand market is assumed, and each consumer buys Brand 1 with a probability p regardless of his past purchase decisions (this is the Bernoulli portion of the model). Each person's p comes from a random draw from a beta distribution (this is the beta component); and at each purchase decision there is a probability λ that the consumer will draw a new p from the beta distribution, and a probability $1 - \lambda$ that he will keep his old p-value (this is the geometric aspect since the number of trials with the same p-value is a random variable with a geometric distribution).

Let p_t be the probability of purchasing Brand 1 at time t. Then

$$b(p_t|\text{new } p \text{ value at time } t) = \text{constant } p^{\alpha-1}(1 - p)^{\beta-1}$$

$$P(\text{new } p \text{ at time } t) = \lambda \quad \text{for all } t$$

If we let c equal the number of trials with the same p, we have

$$f(c) = \lambda(1 - \lambda)^{c-1}$$

This is a three-parameter (α, β, and λ) model. Notice then when $\lambda = 1$, the consumer draws a new p-value at each trial; hence, his past history gives no indication of his current p-value. Then

$$P(1|\text{any past history}) = \frac{\alpha}{\alpha + \beta}$$

Therefore, Howard's model with $\lambda = 1$ is equivalent (in terms of conditional model probabilities) to the Bernoulli model with a homogeneous population. See Equation 3.14.

When $\lambda = 0$ the consumer always keeps the same p. Then when we observe his past history we update our knowledge on his p-value. Hence,

$$P[1|(r,n)] = \frac{\alpha + r}{\alpha + \beta + n}$$

With $\lambda = 0$ Howard's model is equivalent to our compound Bernoulli model and can be tested with Equation 3.11.

When $0 < \lambda < 1$, Howard's conditional model probabilities are difficult to calculate. Although he doesn't mention parameter estimation, it appears that a numerical minmum chi-square procedure could be used to estimate α, β, and λ.

3.10 Concluding Remarks on the Compound Bernoulli Models

As mentioned at the outset, the Bernoulli models are meant to be a vehicle for illustrating some basic ideas and a foundation for building more complex models. The concepts that the reader should grasp before moving on are

1. A heterogeneous population as exemplified by the distribution $b(p)$. See Section 3.5.1.
2. Updating our knowledge on a consumer's p-value. See Section 3.5.3.
3. The concept of conditional model probabilities. See Section 3.5.4.
4. Why the sample statistic χ^2 has a chi-square distribution under the null hypothesis that the model is true. See Section 3.7.
5. The spurious effects of heterogeneity. See Section 3.3.

Much of the work to follow is based on these ideas and concepts. A thorough understanding of these concepts will greatly increase the reader's ability to analyze and interpret models of consumer behavior in particular and stochastic models in general.

CHAPTER 4
TWO-STATE MARKOV MODELS

4.1 Markov Processes

In this chapter, we will discuss models of consumer behavior in which the current brand that is purchased is influenced by only the most recent brand purchased. The order of the process is the number of previous purchases that influence the current purchase. However, before proceeding directly to the marketing models, we will present the basic definitions, concepts, and mathematical properties of Markov processes. This discussion is in no way meant to be complete but will be oriented toward the consumer models that will be developed.

4.1.1 Finite First-Order Markov Chains

In the following subsections, we will deal with processes that have a finite number of states and where the individual's next state is dependent only on his current state. A complete discussion of this subject is not necessary for our purposes. There are many excellent books that deal with Markov chains [e.g., Parzen (1962), Feller (1957) and Kemeny and Snell (1960)].

4.1.1.1 *The States of a Markov Chain.* In this monograph, the state of an individual at time t is the brand he bought at time t. In general, the state of a stochastic process at time t is value of the process at time t. For example, a consumer with a past history of 0111 at times t_1, t_2, t_3, and t_4 respectively bought Brand 0 at time t_1 and bought Brand 1 at times t_2, t_3, and t_4. This idea of state will become clear as we now discuss the fundamental concept of Markov chains, namely, the transition matrix.

4.1.1.2 *The Markov Transition Matrix.* Suppose a Markov chain has m states, which we will label $1, 2, \ldots, m$. Then its transition matrix will be of the following form:

$$
\begin{array}{c}
\text{State at time } t+1 \\
\begin{array}{ccc}
1 & j & m
\end{array}
\end{array}
$$

$$
\text{State at time } t \quad
\begin{array}{c}
1 \\ i \\ m
\end{array}
\begin{bmatrix}
p_{11} & p_{1j} & p_{1m} \\
p_{i1} & p_{ij} & p_{im} \\
p_{m1} & p_{mj} & p_{mm}
\end{bmatrix} = \mathbf{P}(t)
$$

where the transition probability p_{ij} is the *conditional* probability that the individual will be in state j at time $t + 1$, given that he was in state i at time t. The first-order aspect of the Markov chain means that p_{ij} is independent of the individual's state at times $t - 1$, $t - 2, \ldots$ Hence, if we consider time $t + 1$ as the "future," time t as the "present," and times $t - 1$, $t - 2, \ldots$ as the "past," we can say that given the "present" of the process, the "future" is independent of the "past."

For all of the Markov models that we will discuss we will further assume that the Markov chain is stationary; this means that the transition matrix $\mathbf{P}(t)$ is independent of t. The transition probabilities from time 1 to 2 are the same as from 2 to 3 and the same as from t to $t + 1$, etc. In summary, this chapter will deal with stochastic processes that are stationary, have a finite number of states, and for the most part are first-order.

4.1.1.3 *Steady-State Probabilities.* Let $\boldsymbol{\pi} = (\pi_1, \pi_2, \ldots, \pi_m)$ be the m component row vector that is found by solving the system of equations.

$$\boldsymbol{\pi} = \boldsymbol{\pi}\mathbf{P} \tag{4.1}$$

These π_i can be interpreted as the proportion of the time that the Markov chain is in state i when the chain is observed over a long period of time. The probability π_i can also be interpreted as the unconditional probability that the chain will be in state i at time t given that we know nothing of the previous states. This latter interpretation will be used when we form likelihood functions similar to those used in the compound Bernoulli models. The vector $\boldsymbol{\pi}$ is usually referred to as the vector of steady-state probabilities, but it is also called the long-run probabilities and the equilibrium probabilities.

Although there are many other properties of Markov chains (e.g., the expected number of transition to get from state i to state j, classification of states as recurrent or nonrecurrent), the concepts of states, transition matrices, and steady-state probabilities are all that we will need.

4.1.1.4 *Higher Order Markov Chains.* Suppose the probability of an individual buying Brand 1 depends on his last two purchases; we then have a second-order process. However, we can redefine the state space and view this individual as a first-order Markov chain. For simplicity, let us assume a two-brand market, and we will consider his state at time t to be his purchase at time t and also his purchase at time $t - 1$. His

transition matrix is then

State at time $t + 1$

$$
\text{State at time } t \quad
\begin{array}{c}
 \\
(1,1) \\
(0,1) \\
(1,0) \\
(0,0)
\end{array}
\begin{array}{cccc}
(1,1) & (0,1) & (1,0) & (0,0) \\
\left[\begin{array}{cccc}
p_{11} & 0 & 1 - p_{11} & 0 \\
p_{01} & 0 & 1 - p_{01} & 0 \\
0 & p_{10} & 0 & 1 - p_{10} \\
0 & p_{00} & 0 & 1 - p_{00}
\end{array}\right]
\end{array} = \mathbf{P}_2
$$

where $(0,1)$ at time t means a purchase of 0 at $t - 1$ and 1 at t. Hence, the second-order consumer can be treated as a first-order Markov chain with transition matrix $\mathbf{P}_2$. The zero elements represent impossible transitions.

This technique can be generalized such that any nth-order process with m states can be treated as a first-order process with m^n states. Theoretically, then, higher order processes are no different from first-order processes. However, from a practical point of view the number of parameters to estimate and some of the more difficult mathematical properties hamper the application of higher order processes, especially when there are many states.

4.1.2 The No Purchase and Multiple Purchase States

In some of the early work with Markov chains in marketing, the researchers observed all the individuals at the same times. This was fine if from, say, time t_1 to time t_2 an individual made one, and only one, purchase. But what if he made no purchase? The answer was to create an artificial "no purchase" state. If he made more than one purchase, his state was usually considered to be the brand most recently purchased. Howard (1963) raises these issues in condemning the usual application of Markov chains. However, this criticism is really somewhat of a "red herring" for our purposes.

In this book, we do not look at all individuals at the same point in time. We merely record their purchase histories (the brands purchased on consecutive purchase decisions), and hence a consumer's purchase history up through his fifth purchase will be something like 01101. This will be sufficient (as was shown in Chapter 3) to study the aspects of brand switching in which we are interested, namely the influence of past purchases on current purchase probabilities. However, if one is interested in the behavior of a market over a particular interval in time, the no purchase consumer is a problem.

4.2 The Spurious Effects of Heterogeneity Revisited

In Section 3.3.1 we gave a detailed example of the misleading nature of aggregate condition probabilities when they are determined from a heterogeneous population. Therefore, only a short further example using a Markov transition matrix will be given in this chapter.

Assume a population of consumers where half the population consists of individuals with a probability of 0.8 of buying Brand 1 on any trial — regardless of past history of buying. The other half of the population is analogous except the probability of buying Brand 1 is 0.2.

A = individual with p = 0.8.
B = individual with p = 0.2.
$P(1|A)$ = 0.8, the probability that an A buys Brand 1.
$P(1|B)$ = 0.2, the probability that a B buys Brand 1.
$P(1|1)$ = probability of buying Brand 1 given the last purchase was Brand 1.
$P(A|1)$ = probability that an individual is type A given he purchased Brand 1.
$P(1|1) = P(1|A) P(A|1) + P(1|B) P(B|1)$.

By Bayes theorem

$$P(1|1) = 0.8 \frac{P(1|A) P(A)}{P(1|A) P(A) + P(1|B) P(B)} + 0.2 \frac{P(1|B) P(B)}{P(1|A) P(A) + P(1|B) P(B)}$$

$$= 0.8 \frac{(0.8)(0.5)}{(0.8)(0.5) + (0.2)(0.5)} + 0.2 \frac{(0.2)(0.5)}{(0.8)(0.5) + (0.2)(0.5)}$$

$P(1|1) = 0.68$
$P(1|0) = 0.32$

Now a researcher who assumed that he was dealing with a homogeneous population, each obeying a first-order Markov chain, would calculate the following aggregate transition matrix:

Purchase at t

$$\begin{array}{c} \\ \text{Purchase at } t-1 \end{array} \quad \begin{array}{c} 1 \qquad 0 \\ \begin{array}{c} 1 \\ 0 \end{array} \begin{bmatrix} 0.68 & 0.32 \\ 0.32 & 0.68 \end{bmatrix} \end{array}$$

If he then accepted his model without testing its assumptions, he would conclude that the purchase of Brand 1 on the previous trial increases the probability of a subsequent purchase on the next trial.

It is obvious that the transition matrix can tell us only the combined effect of *both* heterogeneity of the population *and* the effect of the past purchase. The true Bernoulli nature of the individual consumers is lost in the aggregate transition matrix. Again we note that if underlying mechanisms of consumer behavior are to be discovered, tests that do not assume homogeneity of the population must be developed.

4.3 Statistical Inference on Homogeneous Populations

4.3.1 Anderson and Goodman Methods and Tests

If we are observing many individuals, all of whom have purchase behaviors that are Markov chains with the *same* transition matrix, then there is a well-developed theory of statistical inference. In their well-known, and by now classic, article Anderson and Goodman (1957) develop maximum likelihood estimates for the transition probabilities p_{ij}; they also give the asymptotic distribution for these estimators. Anderson and Goodman also present likelihood ratio and chi-square tests to test the hypotheses that: (1) the transition matrix **P** is constant over time (stationary hypothesis), (2) the **P** is a given matrix, and (3) the process is nth order versus the alternative hypothesis of rth order. The special case of $n = 0$ and $r = 1$ tests for the independence of observations. We will now give Anderson and Goodman's main results. It will be evident that these procedures are what one would expect on intuitive grounds; their article contains the theoretical justifications.

Assume that we are observing many individuals over $T + 1$ time periods, $t = 0, 1, \ldots, T$, and at each time period they may be in any one of m states. The following definitions are used:

$n_i(t)$ = the number of individuals that are in state i at time t.

$n_{ij}(t)$ = the number of individuals that were in state i at time $t - 1$ and made the transition to state j at time t.

Maximum Likelihood Estimates of Transition Probabilities. Assuming that the chain is stationary, we get

$$\hat{p}_{ij} = \frac{\sum\limits_{t=1}^{T} n_{ij}(t)}{\sum\limits_{t=0}^{T-1} n_i(t)} = \frac{n_{ij}}{n_i^*} \tag{4.2}$$

The equation for $\hat{p}_{ij}$ is simply the proportion of people that were in state i who went to state j in the next time period. When we allow the transition

matrix to change from period to period, we get

$$\hat{p}_{ij}(t) = \frac{n_{ij}(t)}{n_i(t)} \tag{4.3}$$

Testing for Specific Transition Matrices. Suppose we wish to test the hypothesis

$$H_0: p_{ij} = p_{ij}^0 \quad j = 1, 2, \ldots, m \quad \text{for a given } i$$

Then under this null hypothesis

$$\sum_{j=1}^m n_i^* \frac{(\hat{p}_{ij} - p_{ij}^0)^2}{p_{ij}^0} \tag{4.4}$$

is asymptotically distributed as chi-square with $m - 1$ degrees of freedom, where n_i^* (which is defined in Equation 4.2) is the total number of individuals that were in state i from periods 0 through $T - 1$.

Testing the Stationarity of the Transition Matrix. To test whether the transition matrix remains constant over time, we form the statistic

$$\sum_i \sum_j \sum_t \frac{n_i(t-1)[\hat{p}_{ij}(t) - \hat{p}_{ij}]^2}{\hat{p}_{ij}} \tag{4.5}$$

which is asymptotically chi-square with $(T - 1)[m(m - 1)]$ degrees of freedom.

Testing the Order of the Process. Let p_{ijk} be the second-order transition probability of going to state k at time t given that the individual was in state i at time $t - 2$ and j at time $t - 1$. We will write down the chi-square statistic for testing first order versus second order; the general case will then be clear. The maximum likelihood estimate $\hat{p}_{ijk}$ is formed analogously to $\hat{p}_{ij}$.

Under the null hypothesis of first order versus second order we have the statistic

$$\sum_i \sum_j \sum_k \frac{n_{ij}^*(\hat{p}_{ijk} - \hat{p}_{jk})^2}{\hat{p}_{jk}} \tag{4.6}$$

which is asymptotically chi-square with $m(m - 1)^2$ degrees of freedom, where

$$n_{ij}^* = \sum_{t=1}^{T-1} n_{ij}(t)$$

The likelihood ratio tests, corresponding to Equations 4.4, 4.5, and 4.6, are not as intuitive as the chi-square tests. The chi-square tests are

conceptually the same as the goodness-of-fit tests that were developed in Chapter 3.

Homogeneity of the Transition Matrix. Anderson and Goodman briefly discuss a test for determining whether the individuals have the same transition matrix. A goodness-of-fit statistic with the individual's $\hat{p}_{ij}$ and the population $\hat{p}_{ij}$ is used. However, for even moderate sizes of m (the number of states), we need a very large number of time periods.

One Very Long Chain. All of Anderson and Goodman's asymptotic results are for T (the number of time periods) fixed and n (the number of individuals $\rightarrow \infty$. Exactly the same results and tests, except for the stationarity of the transition matrix which must be assumed, hold for $n = 1$ and $T \rightarrow \infty$. This holds because we are dealing with an ergodic process.

Concluding Comments on Anderson and Goodman. Anderson and Goodman have developed a virtually complete theory for inference on homogeneous populations. When the assumption that each individual has the same transition matrix can be accepted, then the problems of estimations and tests of hypotheses have been solved. However, in the area of consumer behavior the homogeneity assumption is almost never true. People have different favorite brands, different stores stock different brands, etc. Hence, the spurious effects of heterogeneity that were discussed in Chapter 3 and in Section 4.2 make the Anderson-Goodman procedures inapplicable for most of the work on consumer behavior. Additional methods of inference on homogeneous Markov chains (from a very mathematical point of view) can be found in Anderson and Darling (1952) and Billingsley (1961a, 1961b).

4.3.2 *Estimation of Transition Probabilities from Market Share Data*

Telser (1963) presents a method for determining transition matrices when only market shares are known. He uses least-square techniques with the constraint that the probabilities must lie between 0 and 1. In his example he gets some negative estimates for variances, and the properties of the estimators are not known. He used the cigarette industry and yearly data. Therefore, the transition probabilities are difficult to interpret. The average cigarette smoker probably makes 50 or more purchases during the course of a year, but only year-to-year transitions can be calculated. Nevertheless, this technique deserves more theoretical and empirical research. It would be of great help to marketing management to be able to infer market dynamics from market

share data; panel data that readily yield transition probabilities are often just not available.

One obvious flaw in Telser's method should be mentioned. The transition probabilities are calculated from the period-to-period changes in market share. If the market is at (or near) equilibrium, these calculations will be based mostly on the random period-to-period fluctuations and measurement errors. This fact would seem to limit the usefullness of this tool in well-established, mature industries where the market shares do not fluctuate very much.

In the last section of Telser's paper, he presents a method for determining the transition probabilities as functions of advertising and promotional variables. Duhamel (1966) employed this technique in his dissertation. However, anyone who uses these methods should do so with care. Although Telser uses least squares for calculating parameters, he points out that these estimates do not have the usual optimal properties of least-square estimates. The error terms in the estimating equations do not have all the desired properties, the independent variables are themselves subject to error, and by the nature of the problem the independent variables are highly collinear. However, there is one big advantage to Telser's methods. They can be applied when little data, all in aggregate form, are available. Market share data are all that is needed. In contrast, the Anderson-Goodman approach requires panel data on individuals.

4.4 Applications of Markov Chains

4.4.1 Homogeneous Chains Applied to Brand Switching

The early work with Markov chains in marketing was mostly descriptions of brand switching viewed as a first-order Markov chain. The brand last purchased was the consumer's state. The homogeneity assumption was usually implicit, and statistical tests on the order of the process were very rarely performed. A few of these studies will be discussed.

Herniter and Magee (1961) were about the first to use Markov analysis of brand switching. Their article is mainly expository, and it contains good discussions on transition probabilities, order, transient and long-run behavior, and the various types of chains. This paper is a well-written and concise description of the basic theory of Markov chains.

Maffei (1961) has done work on the effectiveness of point of sale advertising in supermarkets. He found that he could describe the aggregate market by a first-order transition matrix. This matrix was

also found to remain constant (stationary) during periods when no major promotional activity was underway. Promotional activities substantially altered the matrix in favor of the promoting firm. Maffei concludes that there is no need to identify individual switches (i.e., to estimate transition matrices for the individuals). This is true in one sense; the manufacturer's profit is determined by the aggregate market behavior. However, promotional activities might be made more effective if there were a better understanding of the customers most likely to switch from other brands.

Lipstein (1959) makes an attempt to identify two different segments in his Markov approach. He takes all people who had a loyalty to their first favorite brand of greater than 75% as "hard core." The rest are "switchers." He then calculates the aggregate transition matrix for each of the two groups. He finds that in some product categories "hard core" buyers amount to 70% of the market. This is another indication of brand loyalty in the Cunningham (see Section 3.2) sense. He finds that persons seldom go from hard core for one brand to hard core for another. But even if a consumer were suddenly to switch to another brand, it takes time to balance out his past purchases of the old favorite to get 75% of his last purchases on his new favorite. The results of this type of study will be useful for studying the market, but it provides little understanding of consumer behavior as it is purported to do.

The transition matrices only give conditional probabilities. The fact that these matrices exist has no bearing on the order of the process (recall the discussion in Section 4.2 where aggregate Bernoulli processes gave a highly non-Bernoulli transition matrix). In fact the heterogeneity within the hard core and switcher segments will make the process appear to be of high order; e.g., if Kuehn (see Section 3.3 and Chapter 5) had put his data in transition matrix form, the market he studied would have appeared to be at least a fourth-order process, because $P(S|OSSS) < P(S|SSSS)$. Steady-state probabilities are calculated based on the assumption of a first-order chain. But since the market structure changes too rapidly for anything to resemble a true steady state, these steady-state probabilities are valid only for a basis of determining the general direction of evolution for the market.

Harary and Lipstein (1962) use Markov chains and graph theory to evaluate aggregate performances of brands. Four measurers: brand shares, new triers, repeat-buying rates, and hard-core buyers provide a description of how a new brand evolves in test markets. Their work is useful for predictive and evaluation purposes, especially for non-stationary situations involving new brands and/or changing markets.

Before a new brand gets established, the brand share per se may not be a very good indicator of how well it is doing. The brand share may be rising, but if this rise is due solely to many new buyers while very few of the previous buyers stick with the brand on their next purchase, it is cause for alarm. Markov transition matrices are a very convenient form for displaying this information. However, an objection to using a standard Markov model for describing the innovation of a new brand can be raised. During the course of an introductory campaign, a person's probability of buying the brand (given identical past histories) will most likely change. The learning model to be discussed in Chapter 5 can take this into account (the learning model is Markovian if the state of an individual is his probability of purchase), but a Markov model that uses past purchase decisions as the state space cannot. Harary and Lipstein's Markov approach provides a method for evaluating some important aspects of the performance of a new product. However, a learning approach such as Haines (1964, discussed in Chapter 5) has more appeal as a means for describing market behavior during an introductory campaign. Harary and Lipstein present no evidence to support the contention that consumers behave in a Markov manner with respect to a new product.

There have been other marketing applications of homogeneous Markov chains, but they contain very little that is original and merely show how brand switching can be viewed as a Markov chain. Markov theory has also been used extensively in the physical, biological, and social sciences. We will find that some of the models to be developed in this chapter will have applications in these areas as well as in marketing.

4.4.2 Empirical Results Using Anderson and Goodman Tests

Massy (1966) has examined the order and homogeneity of the brand switching process for specific families. The data base for this study was the *Chicago Tribune* panel purchase records for regular coffee between January 1956 and February 1959.

Since he wanted to study the family specific process, it was necessary to screen the families for purchase frequency. Of the original sample of 800 families, 215 families had purchased regular coffee sufficiently often to be included in the study. Since the inference methods used depended upon stationarity of the process generating the observed time series, it was necessary to screen further the families for stationarity. Massy found that out of the sample of 215 families that had passed the purchase frequency test only 39 could also meet the stationarity requirement.

For this sample of 39 frequent and stationary purchasers of regular coffee, he then computed family specific transition matrices as well as an aggregate transition matrix for all 39 families combined. These transition matrices had three states: favorite brand, second favorite brand, all other brands. Favorite and second favorite brands were defined by purchase frequencies over the entire data period.

Using the appropriate Anderson and Goodman (1957) test on the aggregate matrix, he found that the null hypothesis of a zero-order process could be rejected in favor of a higher order process at the 99% confidence level. Thus, the aggregate switching matrix suggests that the process is of higher order than zero.

Since others [Frank (1962 and Morrison (1965)] had warned of the danger of inferring the order of a process at the individual level from results based upon aggregate transition matrices, Massy then sought to infer the order of the process for each family from its own transition matrix. Based upon this disaggregative data, he found that in only 6 out of the 39 cases would the null hypothesis of a zero-order process be rejected in favor of a higher order process even at the relatively loose 90% confidence level. Recognizing that this doesn't necessarily establish the validity of a zero-order switching process for regular coffee consumption, Massy notes:[1]

... if we had all the data in the world we would be surprised if the probabilities of purchasing different brands are serially independent. The real question at issue is whether the departures from a zero order process are consistently serious enough to warrant using the more complicated first order model to describe brand switching behavior. The results suggest that if we do not have strong a priori views about the matrix for a given family, the size of the departure from a condition of independent trials is probably small relative to the sampling errors that are likely to be obtained when we estimate the relevant parameters.

In summary, Massy's results indicate that stationarity is the exception rather than the rule, that consumers differ markedly in their brand switching transition matrices, that inferences concerning the order of family specific processes from aggregate transition matrices are extremely sensitive to the assumption of homogeneity and stationarity and consequently are very tenuous, and, finally, that for regular coffee a zero-order switching model seems to suffice. This latter point is consistent with Frank's (1962) results for regular coffee as well as the previously discussed Massy and Frank (1964) results.

[1] Massy (1966), p. 51.

Styan and Smith (1964) used Markov chains to analyze product switching behavior for a panel of British housewives. For the 26-week period between January and June 1957, each housewive's purchase behavior in the laundry powder market was classified into one of the following four mutually exclusive and collectively exhaustive categories:

1. Bought detergent only
2. Bought soap powder only
3. Bought both detergent and soap powder
4. Bought no laundry powder at all

These categories define the "state space" of the Markov chain analysis.

The 26-week period enabled them to compute 25 two-period transition matrices for aggregate switching behavior. That is, a transition matrix was computed for times $t - 1$ versus t for $t = 1, 2, \ldots, 25$. It should be emphasized that for any two-period transition matrix, the data for all households were aggregated.

Using the chi-square test developed by Anderson and Goodman (1957), they tested the order of the Markov chain. The null hypothesis and the alternative were:

H_0: the data are from a zero-order Markov chain

H_1: the data are from a first-order chain

Each of the 25 matrices was tested for H_0 versus H_1. It was found that H_0 could be rejected in favor of H_1 at a very high level of significance. Thus, the aggregate data behaved according to a higher than zero-order Markov chain. In this case, there was not sufficient data to test the first-order hypothesis against second- and higher order alternatives. Note, however, that while this aggregate first-order behavior may be useful from a marketing standpoint, it does not establish first-order Markov behavior on the part of the individual households who enter this analysis. Recall Massy's (1966) finding that aggregation led to highly significant inferences of a first-order process whereas disaggregation for the same sample of households tended to support the notion of zero-order or independent trials behavior. Again we see the spurious results of heterogeneity.

The stationarity of the transition matrices over the 26-week period was also tested. In this case, the null hypothesis of stationarity could not be rejected since the significance level of the test was over 24%. Hence, the aggregate data appear to be consistent with a stationary, first-order Markov chain.

Styan and Smith also discuss the use of the limiting distribution of market share for the four alterna'tives. It was found that the market shares for these 26 weeks did not vary much from the equilibrium market shares predicted by the transition matrix formed by aggregating over all 25 of the two-period matrices. Hence, this market was very close to its steady-state condition. Perhaps the most refreshing aspect of this paper is the fact that Styan and Smith *presented their data* and *tested* the *assumptions* of the aggregate Markov model they applied.

4.4.3   A Nonstationary Model

Lipstein (1965) proposed a Markov model in which the transition matrix **P** does not remain constant. Instead there is a change matrix **C** which operates on the transition matrix in each period. $\mathbf{P}(t_{n+1})$ is related to $\mathbf{P}(t_n)$ by the relation

$$\mathbf{P}(t_{n+1}) = \mathbf{P}(t_n)\mathbf{C}$$

Lipstein also breaks up the purchase-to-purchase transition matrix into two matrices: one that takes purchases into attitudes and another that takes attitudes into purchases. The product of these two matrices is then the usual purchase-to-purchase transition matrix. A great deal of work still needs to be done before Lipstein's model is made operational. Nevertheless, he presents some intriguing ideas, and his model is a good starting point for future work on nonstationary marketing models. An updated version of this model appears in Lipstein (1968).

4.4.4   Some Heterogeneous Markov Models

A study from the field of sociology is about the best example of attempting to segment a population into dichotomous groups. Labor mobility was studied by Blueman, Kogan, and McCarthy (1955). They hypothesized that there existed a "stayer" class that always remained in the same job classification. The residual group was "movers," and it moved (or switched job classifications) according to a first-order Markov chain. The transition matrix for the "stayers" would of course be an identity matrix. They tested the mover-stayer hypothesis and calculated the percentage of each present plus the transition probabilities for the movers. The model fits the data surprisingly well. This was a successful attempt to discover an underlying structure of a population. If the total labor force had been analyzed as a homogeneous body, this interesting structure would not have been discovered.

Goodman (1961) showed that the estimates used by Blueman et al.

had bad properties, in fact, they were not even consistent. Goodman developed simpler estimators that were consistent. The mover-stayer model is a natural mechanism for examining hard core loyalty for a brand or product category; the hard core loyal buyers would, of course, be the stayers. Since the statistical theory has been developed, this model should be of great use in many marketing situations.

A model that is a slight simplification of the mover-stayer concept may also be helpful in analyzing brand switching behavior. Here we consider only two classes of consumers: hard-core loyal buyers and potential switchers. All hard-core buyers always buy their favorite brand and all potential switchers buy Brand i with probability π_i, regardless of the brand they last purchased. Recall that in the mover-stayer model a mover's probability of going to occupation j at time $t + 1$ depends on his occupation i at time t.

This hard-core, potential switcher model contains $2n$ parameters, where n is the number of brands. Each Brand i gets a proportion π_i of the potential switcher pool, and of the consumers who stay with the same brand a fraction α_i are hard-core loyal. That is, the transition probability p_{ii} is made up of the hard-core loyal buyers of Brand i plus the potential switchers who came back.

$$p_{ii} = \alpha_i + (1 - \alpha_i)\pi_i$$

Note that all actual switchers were potential switchers, but not all potential switchers switched brands.

Morrison used this hard-core, potential switcher model in analyzing brand switching behavior in the automobile industry. On first looking at transition matrices over a four-year period, it appeared that Company A was losing market share to Company B because of poorer brand loyalty. The transition probability p_{AA} remained roughly constant over the years, but p_{BB} grew over the four years. However, when analyzed as a hard-core, potential switcher model, it was found that the number of hard-core buyers remained the same for both companies, but that B was getting a bigger share of the potential switchers each year.

This study has not yet been published, but it may be in the near future. We mention it only because the hard-core, potential switcher model is a good introduction to the compound Markov model. In the compound Markov model, we will restrict the state space to two brands, but we will expand the two classes of consumers to include a continuum of loyalty. The compound Markov model will be seen to be identical to the compound Bernoulli model, except that now we allow each

consumer to be a first-order instead of a zero-order process. That is the brand last purchased influences the current purchase.

As we have seen, the heterogeneous models give us more insights on brand loyalty than the usual homogeneous Markov approach can. Homogeneous models can give predictions and descriptions of the market; but since consumers are different from each other, some form of a heterogeneous model is needed to get at the underlying behavior of individuals. The compound Markov models will give us a better understanding of the phenomenon of brand loyalty.

Brief, nonmathematical descriptions of compound Markov Models are presented in Morrison (1965a, 1966).

4.5 Compound Markov Models

The compound Markov models differ from the compound Bernoulli models only in terms of the order of the individuals' purchasing process. In the compound Markov model the last purchase, and only the last purchase, influences the current purchase decision. That is, the compound Markov model allows for first-order behavior; the compound Bernoulli models of the last chapter only allowed zero-order behavior. The similarity between the models is that they both allow for a heterogeneous population of consumers. As we have shown in Section 4.2, the spurious effects of heterogeneity also plague the traditional Markov models. Just as the compound Bernoulli models allowed us to test the zero-order assumption independently of the heterogeneity of the population, the compound Markov models will allow us to test independently the first-order assumption.

In addition, the models that are developed in this chapter will yield some new insights into the phenomenon of brand loyalty. As in the Bernoulli models, each consumer's purchase history will consist of a sequence of 0's and 1's, where 1 represents the purchase of a particular brand and a 0 the purchase of one of the aggregated "all other" brands. The two most important compound Markov models have the best marketing interpretation when a 1 represents the purchase of that particular consumer's favorite brand.

The compound Bernoulli model can be viewed as a very special compound Markov model where each consumer is a first-order Markov chain with transition matrix

$$
\begin{array}{cc}
 & t+1 \\
 & \begin{array}{cc} 1 & 0 \end{array}
\end{array}
$$

$$
t\begin{array}{c} 1 \\ 0 \end{array}\begin{bmatrix} p & 1-p \\ p & 1-p \end{bmatrix}
$$

and different consumers are allowed to have different values of p. Hence, we see that the compound Bernoulli model is a special case of the models to be developed in this chapter.

4.6 The Symmetric First-Order Markov Model

This relatively simple model will be used merely to illustrate the important concepts of compound models; it is not a particularly realistic model. The symmetric first-order model is defined as follows:

1. Each individual is a first-order Markov chain with transition matrix

$$
\begin{matrix}
 & 1 & 0 \\
\begin{matrix} 1 \\ 0 \end{matrix} & \begin{bmatrix} p & 1-p \\ 1-p & p \end{bmatrix}
\end{matrix}
$$

2. The probability p is distributed beta among the individuals in the population (i.e., beta heterogeneity; recall Sections 3.5.1 and 3.5.2).

The second point will eventually be relaxed to allow arbitrary heterogeneity.

4.6.1 *Conditional Model Probabilities*

At this point, the reader may wish to review Section 3.5.4. In order to obtain the conditional model probabilities, we must first get the likelihoods for all the past histories of, say, length 4. Take, for example, the past history 1101, at times t_1, t_2, t_3, and t_4. Then the likelihood function is

$$\ell(1101|p) = \pi_1 p(1-p)(1-p)$$

Since we did not observe the consumer before t_1, the probability of a 1 at time t_1 is the steady-state probability π_1 (see Section 4.1.1.3). Solving the steady-state equation

$$\pi = \pi\mathbf{P}$$

we get $\pi_1 = \pi_0 = \frac{1}{2}$. The probability of the 1 at time t_2 is the probability of remaining in 1, which is $p_{11} = p$. The probability of 0 at t_3 is the switching probability $p_{10} = 1 - p$. Similarly, the probability of the 1 at t_4 is $p_{01} = 1 - p$. Hence,

$$\ell(1101|p) = \tfrac{1}{2}p(1-p)^2$$

We see that all the likelihoods will be of the form

$$\tfrac{1}{2}p^a(1-p)^b$$

These binomial likelihoods will update the beta prior distribution to a beta posterior distribution. (Recall that the beta and binomial are conjugate distributions; see Section 3.5.3.) Hence, by the results of the compound Bernoulli model (see Section 3.5.5), the conditional model probability

$$P(1|1101) = \frac{\alpha + 1}{\alpha + \beta + 3}$$

It will now be instructive to calculate a conditional model probability for a sequence that ends with a 0, e.g., 0010. We find that

$$\ell(0010|p) = \tfrac{1}{2}p(1 - p)^2$$

and, therefore, our best estimate (see Section 3.5.4) of that individual's p is $(\alpha + 1)/(\alpha + \beta + 3)$. But because the sequence ends with a 0 his probability of buying Brand 1 on the next trial is $1 - p$. Hence, the conditional model probability

$$P(1|0010) = 1 - \frac{\alpha + 1}{\alpha + \beta + 3}$$

The fact that the steady-state probabilities π_1 and π_0 are constants makes the calculation of the conditional model probabilities very easy. However, this is not the case for the other models of this chapter. (The likelihood functions will not be binomial.) Therefore, it will be helpful to develop the general formula for calculating conditional model probabilities. More precisely, we want to calculate the mean of the posterior distribution on p, the parameter of the transition matrix that is allowed to vary among individuals. For any past history x let p_x be the mean of the posterior distribution; this posterior distribution is the prior distribution on p updated by the past history x. The difference between $P(1|x)$ and p_x was seen in the symmetric compound Markov model where

$$P(1|0010) = 1 - p_{0010}$$

Using Bayes theorem in the form "posterior $\propto$ likelihood $\times$ prior," we get the posterior distribution on p given x in the form

$$b(p|x) = \text{constant } \ell(x|p)b(p)$$

Then utilizing the results of Section 3.5.4.3, we get our fundamental formula

$$p_x = \frac{\int_0^1 pb(p)\,\ell(x|p)\,dp}{\int_0^1 b(p)\,\ell(x|p)\,dp} \tag{4.7}$$

A sample calculation will illustrate this equation. We wish to calculate $P(1|1101) = p_{1101}$ for the symmetric compound Markov model. We have

$$\ell(1101|p) = \tfrac{1}{2}p(1 - p)^2$$

therefore

$$p_{1101} = \frac{\displaystyle\int_0^1 p \, \frac{\Gamma(\alpha + \beta)}{\Gamma(\alpha)\Gamma(\beta)} \, p^{\alpha-1}(1 - p)^{\beta-1} \tfrac{1}{2}p(1 - p)^2 \, dp}{\displaystyle\int_0^1 \frac{\Gamma(\alpha + \beta)}{\Gamma(\alpha)\Gamma(\beta)} \, p^{\alpha-1}(1 - p)^{\beta-1} \tfrac{1}{2}p(1 - p)^2 \, dp}$$

$$\frac{\int_0^1 p^{\alpha+1}(1 - p)^{\beta+1} \, dp}{\int_0^1 p^{\alpha}(1 - p)^{\beta+1} \, dp} = \frac{B(\alpha + 2, \beta + 2)}{B(\alpha + 1, \beta + 1)}$$

where $B(m,n)$ is the beta function, which is equal to $[\Gamma(m)\Gamma(n)]/[\Gamma(m + n)]$. Then using the fact that $\Gamma(n + 1) = n\Gamma(n)$ for $n > 0$, we get

$$P(1|1101) = p_{1101} = \frac{\alpha + 1}{\alpha + \beta + 3}$$

4.6.2 Characterization of Compound Markov Models

Table 4.1 contains all the information that is needed to test the symmetric compound Markov model. We have the conditional model probabilities for all of the 16 past histories of length four, and the past histories with equal likelihoods will allow us to test the model under arbitrary heterogeneity.

4.6.2.1 *The Goodness-of-Fit Test Assuming Beta Heterogeneity.* The ideas here are exactly the same as those developed in Sections 3.7.1 and 3.7.2. The conditional model probability for past history i is multiplied by the number of people with that past history to get $E_i = N_i P(1|i)$, the expected data (the expected number of people with past history i who bought Brand 1 on the next trial). Then letting $E_i' = N_i - E_i$ and R_i equal the observed data and $R_i' = N_i - R_i$, we have the sample statistic

$$\chi^2 = \sum_{i=1}^{16} \frac{(R_i - E_i)^2}{E_i} + \sum_{i=1}^{16} \frac{(R_i' - E_i')^2}{E_i'}$$

distributed as chi-square with 16 degrees of freedom, when the null hypothesis, the symmetric compound Markov model, is true. When α and β, the two parameters of the beta distribution, are estimated from the data, we lose two degrees of freedom (see Section 3.7.2).

Table 4.1 The Probabilities and Likelihoods Resulting from a Symmetric First-Order Markov Population with Beta Heterogeneity

Past Sequence*	Likelihood of Sequence	P(1|Past Sequence)
1111	$1/2\,p^3$	$\dfrac{\alpha + 3}{\alpha + \beta + 3}$
0000		$1 - \dfrac{\alpha + 3}{\alpha + \beta + 3}$
0111 0011 0001	$1/2\,p^2(1-p)$	$\dfrac{\alpha + 2}{\alpha + \beta + 3}$
1000 1100 1110		$1 - \dfrac{\alpha + 2}{\alpha + \beta + 3}$
1001 1101 1011	$1/2\,p(1-p)^2$	$\dfrac{\alpha + 1}{\alpha + \beta + 3}$
0100 0010 0110		$1 - \dfrac{\alpha + 1}{\alpha + \beta + 3}$
0101	$1/2\,(1-p)^3$	$\dfrac{\alpha}{\alpha + \beta + 3}$
1010		$1 - \dfrac{\alpha}{\alpha + \beta + 3}$

* If the past sequence x ends in "0," then the probability of a "1" on the next trial is $1 - p_x$.

4.6.2.2 *The Goodness-of-Fit Test Under Arbitrary Heterogeneity.* When we relax the assumption of a beta distribution on p and allow $b(p)$ to be any arbitrary distribution, we form a goodness-of-fit statistic that is completely analogous to Equation 3.12. From Table 4.1 we see that there are four groups of size 2, 6, 6, and 2 that have equal likelihood functions. Recall the likelihood principle (Section 3.6) that states that sample observations with equal likelihoods yield equal posterior distributions, and hence equal conditional model probabilities. In forming the goodness-of-fit statistic, remember that the proportion of 1's after a past history of, say, 0111 is equal to the proportion of 0's after, say, 1110. This chi-square statistic will be distributed as chi-square with $1 + 5 + 5 + 1 = 12$ degrees of freedom.

4.6.2.3 *The Information Needed to Test Any Compound Model.* It is now evident that a table, such as Table 4.1, that has the likelihoods and conditional model probabilities contains all the information that is needed to test the model. For the remainder of the models in this chapter, we will merely present the likelihoods, conditional probabilities, and the relevant degrees of freedom for the goodness-of-fit tests; the exact details of the tests then will be obvious to the reader.

4.7 The Brand Loyal and Last Purchase Loyal Models

These next two compound Markov models will deal directly with the problem of consumer brand loyalty. They will also demonstrate the calculation difficulties that arise when the steady-state probabilities of the model are functions of the parameter that is allowed to vary among individuals in the population. The two models will be developed together and their marketing implications discussed. Each model assumes that the individuals are 0-1 first-order processs. Given the structure of the transition matrix, each individual is then completely characterized by a single parameter. This parameter has a probability distribution $b(p)$ among the individuals in the population. The only difference between the two models is the structure of the transition matrix that describes the model.

Brand Loyal Model. The brand loyal population is defined as follows:

1. Each individual is a first-order 0-1 process with transition matrix

$$\begin{array}{cc} 1 & 0 \end{array}$$
$$\begin{array}{c} 1 \\ 0 \end{array} \begin{bmatrix} p & 1-p \\ kp & 1-kp \end{bmatrix}$$

2. Where p is distributed beta (α, β) (later $b(p)$ is allowed to be an arbitrary probability density), and k is a constant, the *same* for *each* individual.

$$0 < k < 1$$

Last Purchase Loyal Model. The last purchase loyal population is defined as follows:

1. Each individual is a first-order process with transition matrix

$$\begin{array}{cc} 1 & 0 \end{array}$$
$$\begin{array}{c} 1 \\ 0 \end{array} \begin{bmatrix} p & 1-p \\ 1-kp & kp \end{bmatrix}$$

2. Same as point 2 in the brand loyal population.

4.7.1   Marketing Implications

The brand loyal model says that an individual with a high probability of remaining with Brand 1 will also have a *higher* probability of leaving Brand 0 to buy Brand 1 than an individual with a low probability of remaining with Brand 1. People with high p are more apt to stick with Brand 1 *and* are also more apt to switch to Brand 1 than are people with lower p.

The last purchase loyal population contains the reverse situation. An individual with a high p is more loyal to the brand he last purchased (be it Brand 1 or Brand 0) than a person with a lower p. Here the customer generates loyalty toward the brand he happened to have last purchased.

The two models do *not* say anything about the magnitude of the numbers in the transition matrix. These will depend on k and the value of the individual's p. What they do tell us is something about the structure of the universe of consumers. It will be helpful to consider the following general first-order transition matrix:

$$\begin{array}{cc} & \begin{array}{cc} 1 & 0 \end{array} \\ \begin{array}{c} 1 \\ 0 \end{array} & \begin{bmatrix} p_{11} & p_{10} \\ p_{01} & p_{00} \end{bmatrix} \end{array}$$

In the brand loyal population an individual's p_{11} and p_{00} are negatively correlated. Actually for this idealized model, the correlation is -1.0. In the last purchase loyal population, the correlation is positive, and in fact $+1.0$. Admittedly, these are highly simplified models. However, the concept of brand loyalty will be better understood if we can determine whether the diagonal entries in the transition matrices of a heterogeneous population move together (last purchase loyal model) or in opposite directions (brand loyal model).

It may be helpful for the reader to note that when $k = 1$ in the brand loyal universe, the universe then becomes Bernoulli. When $k = 1$ in the last purchase loyal universe, we then have the first-order symmetric model described for illustrative purposes in the previous section.

The major criticism of these two models is the assumption that the constant k is equal for all individuals. The populations are heterogeneous in that p is allowed to vary, but the relation between the elements of the transition matrix is the same for all individuals. However, the restrictive structure of the proposed models can be justified on two grounds.

1. Testing data against these two simple models promises to yield insight into the phenomenon of consumer "loyalty."
2. More general first-order models are not amenable to valid testing procedures.

Further discussions of the applicability of these models will be presented in Section 4.9, where the models are applied to panel data.

4.7.2 *Mathematical Properties of the Brand Loyal Model*

The transition matrix that describes this model is

$$
\begin{array}{cc}
1 & 0 \\
\begin{array}{c} 1 \\ 0 \end{array}
\begin{bmatrix} p & 1-p \\ kp & 1-kp \end{bmatrix}
\end{array}
$$

Solving the steady-state equations (recall Section 4.1.1.3)

$$ (\pi_1, \pi_0) \begin{bmatrix} p & 1-p \\ kp & 1-kp \end{bmatrix} = (\pi_1, \pi_0) $$

yields the steady-state probabilities

$$ \pi_1 = \frac{kp}{1 - p + kp} $$

$$ \pi_0 = \frac{1 - p}{1 - p + kp} $$

Let $v = 1/(1 - k)$, and we have

$$ \pi_1 = \frac{vkp}{v - p} $$

$$ \pi_0 = \frac{v(1 - p)}{v - p} $$

An example of the method for estimating a conditional model probability will be presented.

Problem: Find $P(1|1011) = p_{1011}$.

Letting $x = 1011$, then we have

$$ \ell(x|p) = \pi_1(1 - p)(kp)p = \frac{vk^2 p^3(1 - p)}{v - p} $$

By the estimation procedure of Equation 4.7,

$$p_x = \frac{\int_0^1 pb(p)\, \ell(x|p)\, dp}{\int_0^1 b(p)\, \ell(x|p)\, dp}$$

$$p_{1011} = \frac{\int_0^1 p\, \dfrac{\Gamma(\alpha+\beta)}{\Gamma(\alpha)\Gamma(\beta)}\, p^{\alpha-1}(1-p)^{\beta-1}\dfrac{v}{v-p}\, k^2 p^3 (1-p)\, dp}{\int_0^1 \dfrac{\Gamma(\alpha+\beta)}{\Gamma(\alpha)\Gamma(\beta)}\, p^{\alpha-1}(1-p)^{\beta-1}\dfrac{v}{v-p}\, k^2 p^3 (1-p)\, dp}$$

$$p_{1011} = \frac{\int_0^1 \dfrac{1}{v-p}\, p^{\alpha+3}(1-p)^{\beta}}{\int_0^1 \dfrac{1}{v-p}\, p^{\alpha+2}(1-p)^{\beta}}$$

Hence, the calculation of p_x is determined by evaluating an integral of the form

$$\int_0^1 \frac{1}{a-p}\, p^{m-1}(1-p)^{n-1}\, dp = \tilde{B}_a(m,n)$$

See the appendix at the end of this chapter (Section 4.12) for the method of evaluating this integral. By the result of that appendix,

$$p_{1011} = \frac{\tilde{B}_v(\alpha+4, \beta+1)}{\tilde{B}_v(\alpha+3, \beta+1)}$$

Define

$$\frac{\tilde{B}_v(m+1, n)}{\tilde{B}_v(m,n)} \equiv P_v(m,n)$$

Then $P(1|1011) = P_v(\alpha+3, \beta+1) = p_{1011}$ (for this particular past history).

Another calculation difficulty arises when the factor $(1-kp)$ enters into the likelihood function $\ell(x|p)$. This will be demonstrated by finding p_{0011} and p_{0001}. Let $x = 0011$,

$$\ell(x|p) = \frac{vkp^2(1-p)(1-kp)}{v-p}$$

$$p_{0011} = \frac{\int_0^1 \dfrac{1}{v-p}\, p^{\alpha+2}(1-p)^{\beta}(1-kp)\, dp}{\int_0^1 \dfrac{1}{v-p}\, p^{\alpha+1}(1-p)^{\beta}(1-kp)\, dp}$$

$$= \frac{\int_0^1 \frac{1}{v-p} p^{\alpha+2}(1-p)^\beta \, dp - k \int_0^1 \frac{1}{v-p} p^{\alpha+3}(1-p)^\beta \, dp}{\int_0^1 \frac{1}{v-p} p^{\alpha+1}(1-p)^\beta \, dp - k \int_0^1 \frac{1}{v-k} p^{\alpha+2}(1-p)^\beta \, dp}$$

$$p_{0011} = \frac{\tilde{B}_v(\alpha+3, \beta+1) - k\tilde{B}_v(\alpha+4, \beta+1)}{\tilde{B}_v(\alpha+2, \beta+1) - k\tilde{B}_v(\alpha+3, \beta+1)}$$

$$p_{0011} \equiv \mathbf{P}_v^k(\alpha+2, \beta+1)$$

Letting $x = 0001$, we have

$$\ell(x|p) = \frac{v}{v-p} \cdot kp(1-p)(1-kp)^2$$

$$p_{0001} = \frac{\tilde{B}_v(\alpha+2, \beta+1) - 2k\tilde{B}_v(\alpha+3, \beta+1) + k^2\tilde{B}_v(\alpha+4, \beta+1)}{\tilde{B}_v(\alpha+1, \beta+1) - 2k\tilde{B}_v(\alpha+2, \beta+1) + k^2\tilde{B}_v(\alpha+3, \beta+1)}$$

$$p_{0001} \equiv \mathbf{P}_v^{k^2}(\alpha+1, \beta+1)$$

In general,

$$\mathbf{P}_v^{k^n}(\alpha, \beta) \equiv \frac{\tilde{B}_v(\alpha+1, \beta) - \binom{n}{1}\tilde{B}_v(\alpha+2, \beta) + \binom{n}{2}\tilde{B}_v(\alpha+3, \beta) - \cdots (-1)^n\tilde{B}_v(\alpha+n+1, \beta)}{\tilde{B}_v(\alpha, \beta) - \binom{n}{1}\tilde{B}_v(\alpha+1, \beta) + \binom{n}{2}\tilde{B}_v(\alpha+2, \beta) - \cdots (-1)^n\tilde{B}_v(\alpha+n, \beta)}$$

Table 4.2 gives the likelihood and probabilities of a purchase of a 1 on the next trial for all past histories of length 4.

4.7.3 *Mathematical Properties of the Last Purchase Loyal Model*

The last purchase loyal model is described by the first-order transition matrix with the following structure:

$$\begin{array}{cc} & \begin{array}{cc} 1 & \quad 0 \end{array} \\ \begin{array}{c} 1 \\ 0 \end{array} & \begin{bmatrix} p & 1-p \\ 1-kp & kp \end{bmatrix} \end{array}$$

Table 4.2 The Likelihoods and Probabilities Resulting from a Brand Loyal Population with Beta Heterogeneity

Past Sequence	Likelihood*	P(1|Past Sequence)
1111	$kp^4 \left/ \dfrac{v}{v-p} \right.$	$P_v(\alpha + 4, \beta)$
0111	$kp^3(1-p) \left/ \dfrac{v}{v-p} \right.$	$P_v(\alpha + 3, \beta + 1)$
1011	$k^2p^3(1-p) \left/ \dfrac{v}{v-p} \right.$	$P_v(\alpha + 3, \beta + 1)$
1101	$k^2p^3(1-p) \left/ \dfrac{v}{v-p} \right.$	$P_v(\alpha + 3, \beta + 1)$
1110	$kp^3(1-p) \left/ \dfrac{v}{v-p} \right.$	$k\,P_v(\alpha + 3, \beta + 1)$
0101	$k^2p^2(1-p)^2 \left/ \dfrac{v}{v-p} \right.$	$P_v(\alpha + 2, \beta + 2)$
1010	$k^2p^2(1-p)^2 \left/ \dfrac{v}{v-p} \right.$	$k\,P_v(\alpha + 2, \beta + 2)$
0110	$kp^2(1-p)^2 \left/ \dfrac{v}{v-p} \right.$	$k\,P_v(\alpha + 2, \beta + 2)$
0011	$kp^2(1-p)(1-kp) \left/ \dfrac{v}{v-p} \right.$	$P_v^k(\alpha + 2, \beta + 1)$
1001	$k^2p^2(1-p)(1-kp) \left/ \dfrac{v}{v-p} \right.$	$P_v^k(\alpha + 2, \beta + 1)$
1100	$kp^2(1-p)(1-kp) \left/ \dfrac{v}{v-p} \right.$	$k\,P_v^k(\alpha + 2, \beta + 1)$
0010	$kp(1-p)^2(1-kp) \left/ \dfrac{v}{v-p} \right.$	$k\,P_v^k(\alpha + 1, \beta + 2)$
0100	$kp(1-p)^2(1-kp) \left/ \dfrac{v}{v-p} \right.$	$k\,P_v^k(\alpha + 1, \beta + 2)$
0001	$kp(1-p)(1-kp)^2 \left/ \dfrac{v}{v-p} \right.$	$P_v^{k^2}(\alpha + 1, \beta + 1)$
1000	$kp(1-p)(1-kp)^2 \left/ \dfrac{v}{v-p} \right.$	$k\,P_v^{k^2}(\alpha + 1, \beta + 1)$
0000	$(1-p)(1-kp)^3 \left/ \dfrac{v}{v-p} \right.$	$k\,P_v^{k^3}(\alpha, \beta + 1)$

* Where $v = 1/(1 - k)$.

The steady-state probabilities are

$$\pi_1 = \frac{u}{2} \cdot \frac{1 - kp}{u - p}$$

$$\pi_0 = \frac{u}{2} \cdot \frac{1 - p}{u - p}$$

where

$$u = \frac{2}{1 + k}$$

The estimation procedure and method of calculation is exactly the same as in the brand loyal model. Table 4.3 of likelihoods and probabilities results.

4.7.4 *Tests for the Brand Loyal and Last Purchase Loyal Models under Beta Heterogeneity*

Each model has three parameters: α, β, and k. When α, β, and k are known (or estimated), $P(1|x)$ is determined for each past sequence x. Therefore, the same chi-square test that was used to test the compound Bernoulli model when α and β are known applies here. Get an observed vector and an expected vector, then calculate χ^2. When only k is known, use the test for arbitrary contagion discussed next. Methods for estimating α, β, and k in particular experimental designs will be given in Section 4.9.

4.7.5 *Tests for the Brand Loyal and Last Purchase Loyal Models under Arbitrary Heterogeneity*

There is now only one parameter k. When k is known (or estimated), obtain groups of past sequences that yield the same probabilities of purchase on the next trial, and perform the same type of chi-square test used for testing the compound Bernoulli model under arbitrary heterogeneity.

Notation: A group

$$1 - \begin{array}{c} 1111 \\ :0000 \\ k:0101 \\ 1 - k:1010 \end{array}$$

would indicate that

$$P(1|1111) = [P(0|0000) = 1 - P(1|0000)] = \frac{1}{k} P(1|0101)$$

$$= \left[\frac{1}{k} P(0|1010) = \frac{1}{k} (1 - P(1|1010)) \right]$$

Table 4.3 The Likelihoods and Probabilities Resulting from a Last Purchase Loyal Population with Beta Heterogeneity

Past Sequence	Likelihood*	P(1|Past Sequence)
0000	$k^3 p^3 (1-p) \Big/ \dfrac{u}{2(u-p)}$	$1 - \mathrm{P}_u(\alpha+3, \beta+1)$
1111	$p^3 (1-kp) \Big/ \dfrac{u}{2(u-p)}$	$\mathrm{P}_u^k(\alpha+3, \beta)$
0111†	$p^2 (1-p)(1-kp) \Big/ \dfrac{u}{2(u-p)}$	$\mathrm{P}_u^k(\alpha+2, \beta+1)$
0011†	$kp^2 (1-p)(1-kp) \Big/ \dfrac{u}{2(u-p)}$	$\mathrm{P}_u^k(\alpha+2, \beta+1)$
0001†	$k^2 p^2 (1-p)(1-kp) \Big/ \dfrac{u}{2(u-p)}$	$\mathrm{P}_u^k(\alpha+2, \beta+1)$
1110	$p^2 (1-p)(1-kp) \Big/ \dfrac{u}{2(u-p)}$	$1 - k\,\mathrm{P}_u^k(\alpha+2, \beta+1)$
1100	$kp^2 (1-p)(1-kp) \Big/ \dfrac{u}{2(u-p)}$	$1 - k\,\mathrm{P}_u^k(\alpha+2, \beta+1)$
1000	$k^2 p^2 (1-p)(1-kp) \Big/ \dfrac{u}{2(u-p)}$	$1 - k\,\mathrm{P}_u^k(\alpha+2, \beta+1)$
0110	$p(1-p)^2(1-kp) \Big/ \dfrac{u}{2(u-p)}$	$1 - k\,\mathrm{P}_u^k(\alpha+1, \beta+2)$
0100	$kp(1-p)^2(1-kp) \Big/ \dfrac{u}{2(u-p)}$	$1 - k\,\mathrm{P}_u^k(\alpha+1, \beta+2)$
0010	$kp(1-p)^2(1-kp) \Big/ \dfrac{u}{2(u-p)}$	$1 - k\,\mathrm{P}_u^k(\alpha+1, \beta+2)$
1011	$p(1-p)(1-kp)^2 \Big/ \dfrac{u}{2(u-p)}$	$\mathrm{P}_n^{k^2}(\alpha+1, \beta+1)$
1101	$p(1-p)(1-kp)^2 \Big/ \dfrac{u}{2(u-p)}$	$\mathrm{P}_u^{k^2}(\alpha+1, \beta+1)$
1001	$kp(1-p)(1-kp)^2 \Big/ \dfrac{u}{2(u-p)}$	$\mathrm{P}_u^{k^2}(\alpha+1, \beta+1)$
0101	$(1-p)^2(1-kp)^2 \Big/ \dfrac{u}{2(u-p)}$	$\mathrm{P}_u^{k^2}(\alpha, \beta+2)$
1010	$(1-p)^2(1-kp)^2 \Big/ \dfrac{u}{2(u-p)}$	$1 - \mathrm{P}_u^{k^2}(\alpha, \beta+2)$

* Where $u = 2/(1+k)$.
† Any two past sequences x^1 and x^2 such that $\ell(x^1|p) = \text{constant} \times \ell(x^2|p)$ yield $p_{x^1} = p_{x^2}$. Recall the likelihood principle of Section 3.6.

Note: The second and fourth probabilities are with respect to a "zero" on the next trial. This notation is used throughout the rest of the chapter. It will be elaborated when the specific probabilities of the brand loyal and last purchase loyal models are explained.

For example, the first group of four past sequences under the Brand Loyal column in Table 4.4 means: Given a brand loyal population with arbitrary heterogeneity,

$$P(1|0111) = P(1|1011) = P(1|1101) = \frac{1}{k} P(1|1110)$$

From Table 4.2 we find $\ell(1101|p) = \text{const} \times \ell(1110|p)$. Hence (by the likelihood principle),

$$p_{1101} = p_{1110}$$

and (from the nature of the brand loyal transition matrix),

$$p_{1101} = P(1|1101)$$
$$kp_{1110} = P(1|1110)$$

Table 4.4 Groups of Past Histories That Yield Equal Probabilities in the Brand Loyal and Last Purchase Loyal Models When k Is Known

Brand Loyal $\begin{bmatrix} p & 1-p \\ kp & 1-kp \end{bmatrix}$	Last Purchase Loyal $\begin{bmatrix} p & 1-p \\ 1-kp & kp \end{bmatrix}$
0111	0111
1011	0011
1101	0001
k:1110	$1-k$:1110
	$1-k$:1100
0101	$1-k$:1000
k:1010	
k:0110	$1-k$:0110
	$1-k$:0100
0011	$1-k$:0010
1001	
k:1100	1011
	1101
k:0010	1001
k:0100	
	0101
0001	$1-k$:1010
k:1000	

Therefore,

$$P(1|1101) = \frac{1}{k} P(1|1110)$$

Recall Section 3.5.4, which discussed the difference between p_x and $P(1|x)$.

Under the last purchase loyal column, the first group of six past sequences means: Given a last purchase loyal population with arbitrary heterogeneity,

$$P(1|0111) = P(1|0011) = P(1|0001) = \frac{1}{k} P(0|1110)$$

$$= \frac{1}{k} P(0|1100) = \frac{1}{k} P(0|1000)$$

Note: The last three probabilities are with respect to "zero."

These equalities result from the fact that

$$\ell(0111|p) = \ell(0011|p) = \cdots = \ell(1000|p)$$

From the structure of the last purchase loyal transition matrix

$$P(1|0111) = p_{0111}$$
$$P(0|1110) = kp_{1110}$$

But by the likelihood principle

$$p_{0111} = p_{1110}$$

Hence,

$$P(1|0111) = \frac{1}{k} P(0|1110), \text{ etc.}$$

For these two models, Table 4.4 gives the groups of sequences which yield empirical probabilities that can be used for the chi-square tests.

The chi-square statistic for the first group under the brand loyal model will be

$$\frac{(R_{0111} - \bar{p}N_{0111})^2}{\bar{p}N_{0111}} + \frac{(R_{1011} - \bar{p}N_{1011})^2}{\bar{p}N_{1011}}$$

$$+ \frac{(R_{1101} - \bar{p}N_{1101})^2}{\bar{p}N_{1101}} + \frac{(R_{1110} - k\bar{p}N_{1110})^2}{k\bar{p}N_{1110}}$$

$$+ \frac{[R'_{0111} - (1 - \bar{p})N_{0111}]^2}{(1 - \bar{p})N_{0111}} + \cdots + \frac{[R'_{1110} - (1 - k\bar{p})N_{1110}]^2}{(1 - k\bar{p})N_{1110}}$$

where

$$\bar{p} = \frac{R_{0111} + R_{1011} + R_{1101} + \frac{1}{k} R_{1110}}{N_{0111} + N_{1011} + N_{1101} + N_{1110}}$$

The chi-square statistic for the first group under the last purchase loyal model will be

$$\frac{(R_{0111} - \bar{p}N_{0111})^2}{\bar{p}N_{0111}} + \cdots + \frac{(R'_{1110} - k\bar{p}N_{1110})^2}{k\bar{p}N_{1110}}$$

$$+ \frac{[R'_{0111} - (1 - \bar{p})N_{0111}]^2}{(1 - \bar{p})N_{0111}} + \cdots + \frac{[R_{1110} - (1 - k\bar{p})N_{1110}]^2}{(1 - k\bar{p})N_{1110}}$$

where

$$\bar{p} = \frac{R_{0111} + \cdots + \frac{1}{k} R'_{1110}}{N_{0111} + \cdots + N_{1110}}$$

The other parts of the chi-square statistics are formed similarly.

Table 4.5 Group of Past Histories That Yield Equal Probabilities in the Brand Loyal and Last Purchase Loyal Models When k Is Unknown

Brand Loyal $\begin{bmatrix} p & 1-p \\ kp & 1-kp \end{bmatrix}$	Last Purchase Loyal $\begin{bmatrix} p & 1-p \\ 1-kp & kp \end{bmatrix}$
0111	0111
1011	0011
1101	0001
1010	1110
0110	1100
	1000
0011	
1001	0110
	0100
0010	0010
0100	
	1011
	1101
	1001

The brand loyal model has five groups of size 4, 3, 3, 2 and 2. Hence, its chi-square test will have $3 + 2 + 2 + 1 + 1 = 9$ degrees of freedom when a past history of four is used: $\chi^2_{ABL4} \sim \chi^2(9)$. "*ABL4*" stands for *a*rbitrary, *b*rand *l*oyal, with past history of *4*.

The last purchase loyal model has four groups of size 6, 3, 3, and 2. Hence, $\chi^2_{ALPL4} \sim \chi^2(10)$. (Note: If k is estimated from the data, one additional degree of freedom is lost.)

In practice k will not be known. Sometimes the data will be in a form such that k can be estimated. If this is so, the preceding method is used. However, when k cannot be estimated from the data, the groups of past sequences given in Table 4.5 can be used to test the hypotheses of brand loyal or last purchase loyal populations.

4.8   General First-Order Compound Models

This section will demonstrate the inapplicability of the methods just developed for testing the more general hypothesis that consumers are merely a general first-order process.

The model is characterized by

1. Each consumer behaves as a first-order Markov chain with transition matrix

$$\begin{bmatrix} p & 1-p \\ 1-q & q \end{bmatrix}$$

2. The parameters p and q are distributed according to the arbitrary joint density $b(p,q)$.

The steady-state probabilities are

$$\pi_1 = \frac{1-q}{(1-p) + (1-q)}$$

$$\pi_0 = \frac{1-p}{(1-p) + (1-q)}$$

Table 4.6 gives the past sequences and likelihoods.

Sequences x^1 and x^2 with equal likelihoods will yield equal values $p_{x^1} = p_{x^2}; q_{x^1} = q_{x^2}$. But, some sequences with equal likelihoods will be of no help:

$$\ell(0111|p,q) = \ell(1110|p,q) = \frac{p^2(1-p)(1-q)}{(1-p) + (1-q)}$$

Table 4.6 The Likelihoods for Past Histories under the General First-Order Model

Group	Sequence	Likelihood of Sequence
I	1011 1101	$p(1-p)(1-q)^2/[(1-p)+(1-q)]$
II	0010 0100	$(1-p)^2q(1-q)/[(1-p)+(1-q)]$
III	0011 1100	$p(1-p)q(1-q)/[(1-p)+(1-q)]$
IV	0101 1010	$(1-p)^2(1-q)^2/[(1-p)+(1-q)]$
V	0111 1110	$p^2(1-p)(1-q)/[(1-p)+(1-q)]$
VI	0001 1000	$(1-p)q^2(1-q)/[(1-p)+(1-q)]$
	1111 1001 0110 0000	$p^3(1-q)/[(1-p)+(1-q)]$ $(1-p)q(1-q)^2/[(1-p)+(1-q)]$ $p(1-p)^2(1-q)/[(1-p)+(1-q)]$ $(1-p)q^3/[(1-p)+(1-q)]$

Hence,

$$p_{0111} = p_{1110}$$
$$q_{0111} = q_{1110}$$

Therefore, the conditional model probabilities are

$$P(1|0111) = p_{0111}$$
$$P(1|1110) = 1 - q_{1110}$$

However, we have no knowledge as to how p_{0111} is related to q_{0111}! The only sequences that yield equal probabilities of purchase on the next trial are Groups I and II of Table 4.6:

$$P(1|1011) = P(1|1101)$$

and

$$P(1|0100) = P(1|0010)$$

This is because Groups I and II of Table 4.6 have sequences that end with the same brand:

$$\begin{matrix} 1 & 0 & 1 \\ 1 & 1 & 0 \end{matrix}\begin{bmatrix} 1 \\ 1 \end{bmatrix}$$

and

$$\begin{array}{ccc} 0 & 0 & 1 \\ 0 & 1 & 0 \end{array}\begin{bmatrix} 1 \\ 0 \end{bmatrix}$$

but for Groups III through VI the reverse holds. For example, Group IV is

$$\begin{array}{ccc} 0 & 1 & 0 \\ 1 & 0 & 1 \end{array}\begin{bmatrix} 1 \\ 0 \end{bmatrix}$$

For this general case we have no way to relate p_{0101} to q_{1010}. It is true that

$$p_{0101} = p_{1010}$$

and

$$q_{0101} = q_{1010}$$

but

$$P(1|0101) = p_{0101}$$

while

$$P(1|1010) = 1 - q_{1010}$$

The resulting chi-square test, which merely tests the first-order behavior, would have only two degrees of freedom. The test would have very little power in rejecting most non-first-order models.

In theory, one could assume the form of the contagion distribution $b(p,q)$, estimate its parameters, and run the same type of chi-square test as for the other models when the form of the contagion was known. In practice this will not be feasible for two reasons:

1. It may be impossible to evaluate the integrals needed to estimate p_x and q_x.
2. Also $b(p,q)$ will have at least five parameters, involving the means and variances of p and q and the correlation between p and q. It will then be impossible to separate the effects because (a) actual deviations from a first-order process, and (b) errors in the estimation of the parameters.

The main conclusion from this section is that by examining aggregate data from a heterogeneous population, it is not possible to either accept or reject the hypothesis of a general first-order process. Kuehn's conclusion on this matter is not valid since he aggregated short histories of many heterogeneous individuals and the form of the contagion was not known or assumed. Long individual time series must be analyzed separately if one is to test general hypotheses on the order of the process, when the individuals do not form a homogeneous population and the

form of the contagion is unknown. Of course, the nonstationary nature of most long individual time series makes this type of analysis very difficult.

4.9 Some Special Second-Order Models

The assumptions made and methods used are exactly the same as for the first-order models. Only the transition matrices are different.

4.9.1 Second-Order Symmetric Model

This model is defined by

1. Each individual is a second-order Markov chain with transition matrix

State at time $t - 1$ and t

$$
\begin{array}{c}
\quad 11 \qquad 01 \qquad\quad 10 \qquad\quad 00 \\
\text{State at time } t - 2 \text{ and } t - 1 \quad
\begin{array}{c} 11 \\ 01 \\ 10 \\ 00 \end{array}
\left[
\begin{array}{cccc}
p & & 1 - p & \\
kp & & 1 - kp & \\
& 1 - kp & & kp \\
& p & & 1 - p
\end{array}
\right]
\end{array}
$$

2. And p is distributed as beta with parameters α and β (the result for arbitrary $b(p)$ is also given), and k is a constant for the population. $0 < k < 1$.

The steady-state probabilities are

$$\pi_{11} = \frac{v}{2} \cdot \frac{kp}{v - p} = \pi_{00}$$

$$\pi_{01} = \frac{v}{2} \cdot \frac{(1 - p)}{v - p} = \pi_{10}$$

where

$$v = \frac{1}{1 - k}$$

See Table 4.7 for the probabilities that result from this model when the heterogeneity is beta and the parameters are known.

When α, β, and k are known (or estimated), the usual chi-square test used when the numerical values of the probabilities are known is run. When only k is known, and when α, β, and k are unknown, the groups of equal probabilities given in Table 4.8 are the basis of the chi-square tests.

Table 4.7 The Likelihoods and Probabilities Resulting from a
Second-Order Symmetric Model

Past Sequence	Likelihood	P(1|Past Sequence)
1111	$kp^3 \Big/ \dfrac{v}{2(v-p)}$	$P_v(\alpha + 3, \beta)$
0000	$kp^3 \Big/ \dfrac{v}{2(v-p)}$	$1 - P_v(\alpha + 3, \beta)$
0111	$kp^2(1-p) \Big/ \dfrac{v}{2(v-p)}$	$P_v(\alpha + 2, \beta + 1)$
0011	$k^2p^2(1-p) \Big/ \dfrac{v}{2(v-p)}$	$P_v(\alpha + 2, \beta + 1)$
0001	$kp^2(1-p) \Big/ \dfrac{v}{2(v-p)}$	$k\, P_v(\alpha + 2, \beta + 1)$
1110	$kp^2(1-p) \Big/ \dfrac{v}{2(v-p)}$	$1 - k\, P_v(\alpha + 2, \beta + 1)$
1100	$k^2p^2(1-p) \Big/ \dfrac{v}{2(v-p)}$	$1 - P_v(\alpha + 2, \beta + 1)$
1000	$kp^2(1-p) \Big/ \dfrac{v}{2(v-p)}$	$1 - P_v(\alpha + 2, \beta + 1)$
1001	$kp(1-p)^2 \Big/ \dfrac{v}{2(v-p)}$	$k\, P_v(\alpha + 1, \beta + 2)$
0110	$kp(1-p)^2 \Big/ \dfrac{v}{2(v-p)}$	$1 - k\, P_v(\alpha + 1, \beta + 2)$
1011	$kp(1-p)(1-kp) \Big/ \dfrac{v}{2(v-p)}$	$P_v^k(\alpha + 1, \beta + 1)$
1101	$kp(1-p)(1-kp) \Big/ \dfrac{v}{2(v-p)}$	$k\, P_v^k(\alpha + 1, \beta + 1)$
0010	$kp(1-p)(1-kp) \Big/ \dfrac{v}{2(v-p)}$	$1 - k\, P_v^k(\alpha + 1, \beta + 1)$
0100	$kp(1-p)(1-kp) \Big/ \dfrac{v}{2(v-p)}$	$1 - P_v^k(\alpha + 1, \beta + 1)$
0101	$(1-p)(1-kp)^2 \Big/ \dfrac{v}{2(v-p)}$	$k\, P_v^{k^2}(\alpha, \beta + 1)$
1010	$(1-p)(1-kp)^2 \Big/ \dfrac{v}{2(v-p)}$	$1 - k\, P_{v_-}^{k^2}(\alpha, \beta + 1)$

Table 4.8   Groups of Past Histories That Yield Equal Probabilities under the Second-Order Symmetric Model

k Known	k Unknown
1111	1111
$1 - :0000$	$1 - :0000$
0111	0111
0011	0011
$k:0001$	$1 - :1100$
$1 - k:1110$	$1 - :1000$
$1 - :1100$	
$1 - :1000$	$1 - :0001$
	$1 - :1110$
$k:1001$	
$1 - k:0110$	1001
	$1 - :0110$
1011	
$k:1101$	1011
$1 - k:0010$	$1 - :0100$
$1 - :0100$	
	1101
$k:0101$	$1 - :0010$
$1 - k:1010$	
	0101
	$1 - :1010$

The degrees of freedom will be 11.	The degrees of freedom will be 9.

4.9.2 Special Second-Order Brand Loyal and Last Purchase Loyal Models

The steady-state probabilities of these models have a denominator of the form $ap^2 + bp + c$. In theory this could be factored into $(h - p) \times (g - p)$. Then the infinite series $(h - p)^{-1}$ and $(g - p)^{-1}$ could be multiplied term by term. For beta heterogeneity, probabilities of the form $P_v^{k^n}(\alpha,\beta)$ could be calculated the same as in previous models (see Section 4.12, the appendix). In fact, these calculations are extremely difficult and messy. Therefore, only the results for arbitrary heterogeneity will be given. The assumptions are the same as in the symmetric

Table 4.9 Groups of Past Histories That Yield Equal Probabilities for the Special Second-Order Brand Loyal and Last Purchase Loyal Models

Brand Loyal		Last Purchase Loyal	
k, c Known	k, c Unknown	k, c Known	k, c Unknown
0111	0111	0111	0111
1011	1011	0011	0011
k:1101		k:0001	
c:1110		$1 - kc$:1110	1100
		$1 - c$:1100	1000
k:1001		$1 - c$:1000	
$1 - kc$:1100			
		1011	
		k:1101	
		k:0101	
		$1 - kc$:1010	
		$1 - kc$:0010	
		$1 - c$:0100	
d.f.* 4	1	8	2

* However, if k and c are estimated from the data, two more degrees of freedom (d.f.) are lost. In particular the brand loyal test would have only two degrees of freedom left.

second-order model. Thus, the models are completely characterized by their respective transition matrices,

$$
\begin{array}{c}
\begin{array}{cccc} 11 & 01 & 10 & 00 \end{array} \\
\begin{array}{c} 11 \\ 01 \\ 10 \\ 00 \end{array}
\left[\begin{array}{cccc}
p & 1-p & & \\
kp & 1-kp & & \\
& cp & & 1-cp \\
& kcp & & 1-kcp
\end{array} \right]
\end{array}
\qquad
\begin{array}{c}
\begin{array}{cccc} 11 & 01 & 10 & 00 \end{array} \\
\begin{array}{c} 11 \\ 01 \\ 10 \\ 00 \end{array}
\left[\begin{array}{cccc}
p & 1-p & & \\
kp & 1-kp & & \\
& & 1-kcp & kcp \\
& & 1-cp & cp
\end{array} \right]
\end{array}
$$

where $0 < c, k < 1$.

The steady-state probabilities are

$$
\pi_{11} = \frac{kp(1 - cp)}{ap^2 + bp + c}
$$

$$
\pi_{01} = \pi_{10} = \frac{(1 - p)(1 - cp)}{ap^2 + bp + c}
$$

$$
\pi_{00} = \frac{kcp(1 - p)}{ap^2 + bp + c}
$$

where $a = 2c(1 - k)$ and $b = (1 + c)(k - 2)$. These steady-state probabilities apply to *both* models.

When $b(p)$ is arbitrary, the sequences given in Table 4.9 yield equal probabilities. Of course, these sequences can then be used in a chi-square goodness-of-fit test.

The last purchase loyal model with k and c known is the only one that yields a good test; but this is a highly structured model. A general second-order model of the form

$$
\begin{array}{c}
\begin{array}{cccc} 11 & 01 & 10 & 00 \end{array} \\
\begin{array}{c} 11 \\ 01 \\ 10 \\ 00 \end{array}
\left[\begin{array}{cccc}
p_1 & & 1 - p_1 & \\
p_2 & & 1 - p_2 & \\
& 1 - q_2 & & q_2 \\
& 1 - q_1 & & q_1
\end{array} \right]
\end{array}
$$

is impossible to analyze by these methods. No two different sequences of length 4 yield the same estimates. In fact, a past history of at least 10 would be needed for an individual to have a chance of making most of the possible transitions (i.e., to be in states $(0,0)$, $(1,0)$, $(0,1)$, and $(1,1)$). There are $2^{10} = 1024$ possible past histories of length 10. And worse yet, a general distribution $b(p_1, p_2, q_1, q_2)$ will involve at least 14 parameters (4 means, 4 variances, and 6 correlations). The conclusions to be reached from the discussion so far are

1. The *aggregate* method of Kuehn can be modified to test hypotheses about *individual* behavior when this behavior is assumed to be Bernoulli or specialized first-, and possibly second-order, and
2. Kuehn's method, and the aggregate Goodman-Anderson tests which assume homogeneous populations, are inadequate for testing hypotheses involving the order of individual processes, when these individuals have obviously different transition matrices.

4.10 Empirical Results

In this chapter the models developed in Chapter 2 are applied to data obtained from the *Chicago Tribune* Consumer Panel. See Boyd and Westfall (1960) for a complete discussion of consumer panels. The product category to be studied here is regular coffee. Coffee was chosen for two reasons. First, the data were readily available; and second, it is a product category that has been studied previously and thus tentative hypotheses on consumer behavior toward coffee have been formulated. Frank (1960) shows some evidence supporting the Bernoulli hypothesis, that is, that past purchase decisions do not alter the probability of

purchasing a particular brand on the current purchase decision. Massy and Frank (1964) used simulation and factor analysis to further substantiate a tentative Bernoulli conclusion.

Massy (1966) used exactly the same data base as the one used in this study. He obtained quite strong evidence in support of the Bernoulli hypothesis. However, Massy's result must be tempered by the fact that only 5% of the eligible families were included in his sample. Only 39 out of 800 families met his long-run stationarity requirement. It is hoped that the empirical results to be reported here will unify some of the competing hypotheses on consumer behavior in general and coffee behavior specifically. Massy's results were reviewed in Section 4.4.2.

4.10.1 Experimental Design

The purchase decisions cover the period January 1956 through February 1959. There were 531 families who met the criterion of having at least 30 purchases of regular coffee during that three-year period. This criterion was set somewhat arbitrarily. However, this was about the minimum number of purchases needed to run the tests, and a higher cutoff would have adversely affected the total sample size.

Each family's purchase history was reduced to a 0-1 process, where a 1 indicated the purchase of that family's favorite brand of coffee; a 0 indicated the purchase of any other brand of coffee. The 0-1 process was defined with 1 representing the family's favorite brand and 0 representing all other brands instead of a particular brand being defined as a 1 for all families for two reasons:

1. It was felt that examining families' behavior toward their favorite brand was the better way to investigate the complex phenomenon of "brand loyalty."
2. For any particular brand there exist a few families who devote virtually all their purchases to this brand, and a sizable portion of the sample that never buy the brand. These two groups of consumers make the beta distribution (a unimodal distribution) a very poor candidate for the heterogeneity in the population of consumers with respect to any particular brand. See Section 3.5.2.

The first 30 purchases of each family were recorded, and this sequence was then broken into two periods. Even if a family had more than 30 purchases, only the first 30 were used. This was to give equal weightings to the purchase histories of light as well as heavy buyers. Period 1 consisted of each family's first 15 purchases and period 2 the last 15

purchases. The brand purchased most often in period 1 was designated the favorite brand for that period, and similarly for period 2. Thus, it became possible to compare the behavior of "switchers" (those whose favorite brand in period 1 was different from their favorite brand in period 2) with the "loyal" consumers who kept the same favorite brand.

Each family yielded two observations, each observation containing a past history of length four and the purchase decision that followed that past history. These ten observations per family were:

	Past History of Length Four		Purchase Decision on the Next Trial
Purchases	4 through 7	and	8
	5 through 8	and	9
	6 through 9	and	10
	7 through 10	and	11
	8 through 11	and	12
	19 through 22	and	23
	20 through 23	and	24
	21 through 24	and	25
	22 through 25	and	26
	23 through 26	and	27

Purchases 14 through 18 were not used because the favorite brand may have switched from period 1 to period 2, thus, the 0-1 process could not be defined. Also purchases 1 through 3 and 28 through 30 were not used in order that the purchase decisions used would be roughly in the middle of the sequence that determined the favorite brand.

Strictly speaking, only two past histories should have been taken (e.g., 6 through 9 and 10 and 21 through 24 and 25). The "overlap" of the past histories makes the past histories within a family dependent. However, when all the $531 \times 10 = 5310$ observations are aggregated, this slight dependence is not harmful to the models. Also, two observations per family would not have been sufficient to test the models adequately.

Market segmentation is a crucial area in market research. The market is not a homogeneous set of people. The company that can identify various segments and appeal directly to these segments has a big advantage. For example, the heaviest buyers in a particular product category may account for only 20% of the families yet generate well over half the sales. Management would like to be able to identify any behavior patterns, socioeconomic characteristics, etc., that set these buyers

apart from the market in general. The firm may then be able to cater to these peculiar characteristics that heavy buyers tend to have. With the concept of market segmentation in mind, the families in this study were segmented by various purchasing characteristics. The segments to be investigated and contrasted were defined as follows:

1. ALL   All 531 families who met the selection criteria.

2. 100 PERCENTERS   The 142 families who bought only one brand of coffee during period 1 or period 2. (128 of them also had only one brand during both period 1 and period 2.)

   EXCEPT 100 PERCENTERS   The remaining 389 families who had one or more zeros.

3. HEAVY   Those families who purchased more than the median amount (for the sample) of coffee. Consumption was measured in number of trips.

   LIGHT   The other half of the sample which purchased less than the median amount.

4. LOYAL   The 360 families whose favorite brand in period 1 was the same as the favorite in period 2.

   NONLOYAL   The remaining 171 families who switched favorite brands.

5. LOYAL, HEAVY   The LOYAL's who consumed more than the median amount.

   LOYAL, LIGHT   Etc.
   NONLOYAL, HEAVY
   NONLOYAL, LIGHT

The rationale for all of the segments apart from the EXCEPT 100 PERCENTERS is obvious. Recall that some of the models assume beta heterogeneity. It was thought that the high percentage of families (over one quarter of the sample) that purchased only one brand during a period would be incompatible with the assumption of beta heterogeneity. These families are termed the 100 percenters. Therefore, it was anticipated that the remaining families — the EXCEPT 100 PERCENTERS — would have a better chance of fitting the beta contagion models.

Since the purchase behavior of the 100 percenters is merely all 1's, it

will not be reported. All the tests developed in Chapters 3 and 4 will now be applied to the remaining ten segments.

The empirical probabilities were calculated for each of the 16 possible past histories of length 4 for each of the market segments. Then the Bernoulli, brand loyal, and last purchase loyal models were fitted to these data. The second-order models were not tried since the parameters of the models would have to be estimated from the data and the resulting degrees of freedom for the second-order brand loyal model would have been only 2 (see Table 4.9, Section 4.9.2).

First, these three models were compared under the assumption of arbitrary contagion. The brand loyal models gave by far the best fit for all the segments; hence, when the assumption of arbitrary heterogeneity was tightened to beta heterogeneity, only the brand loyal model was tested.

The parameters k, α, and β for the brand loyal model (also k for the last purchase loyal model) were estimated by the minimum chi-square method. That is, the three-dimensional parameter space was searched until the combination k^*, α^*, β^* was found that minimized the chi-square goodness-of-fit statistic for the brand loyal model. These estimates have the properties of being asymptotically efficient and asymptotically normal [see Cramer (1946), page 506]. Of course, these estimates also have the property of giving the model the best chance of "fitting" the data, where "fit" is determined by the resulting chi-square statistic. The formulas in the Appendix at the end of this chapter (Section 4.12) were used to calculate the probabilities given the parameter set (k, α, β). After preliminary runs that obtained the general range of the optimum values of these parameters (this took about one minute of IBM-7090 time), the best values of k (within 0.01) and α and β (within 0.1) were found. The FORTRAN program that was written to accomplish this task took only 40 seconds of time on the IBM-7090, for each segment.

An example of the type of output we obtain by this method follows. For the empirical work of this chapter the three-dimensional k, α, and β space was searched. The values of these parameters that minimized the chi-square statistic for a particular segment were

$$k = 0.81$$

$$\alpha = 2.2$$

$$\beta = 0.8$$

$$\chi^2 = 19.0$$

Table 4.10   An Example of a Grid Search Used to Obtain
Minimum Chi-Square Estimates

$\alpha = 2.1$	$\alpha = 2.2$	$\alpha = 2.3$
$\beta = 0.9$	$\beta = 0.9$	$\beta = 0.9$
$\chi^2 = 24.4$	$\chi^2 = 22.3$	$\chi^2 = 20.9$
$\alpha = 2.1$	$\alpha = 2.2$	$\alpha = 2.3$
$\beta = 0.8$	$\beta = 0.8$	$\beta = 0.8$
$\chi^2 = 19.2$	$\chi^2 = 19.0$	$\chi^2 = 19.5$
$\alpha = 2.1$	$\alpha = 2.2$	$\alpha = 2.3$
$\beta = 0.7$	$\beta = 0.7$	$\beta = 0.7$
$\chi^2 = 23.1$	$\chi^2 = 25.0$	$\chi^2 = 27.5$

Fixing k at 0.81, we can show (see Table 4.10) the sensitivity of chi-square to changes in α and β.

This brute force searching technique can be modified by most of the well-known numerical search procedures (Fibonacci, gradient projection, etc.). However, the efficiency of the exhaustive approach for these simple models negates the added sophistication.

Before presenting the chi-square goodness-of-fit statistics for the various models and market segments, the empirical probabilities for these segments will be given. This will enable the reader to get a somewhat better feel for how well or poorly the models fit the data. The two segments ALL and EXCEPT 100 PERCENTERS will first be tabled to best demonstrate the deviations from a compound Bernoulli model with arbitrary heterogeneity (Table 4.11). Later, Tables 4.12, 4.13, and 4.14 will give the data for all segments in a form that shows deviation from the brand loyal model with the beta heterogeneity that best fits the data. The column headings of the tables are to be interpreted as follows:

0   Of those families with the indicated past history, those that followed with a 0.

1   Similarly, except those that followed with a 1.

Total   (1 plus 0)

$\bar{p}$ Empirical probability $= R_i/N_i = 1/\text{Total}$.

p These are the conditional model probabilities given k, α, and β and the appropriate past history.

4.10.2   Deviations form the Compound Bernoulli Model

Table 4.11 is set up so that under the Bernoulli assumption the past histories that are grouped together should yield equal probabilities of purchases on the next trial. The influence of the most recent purchase

Table 4.11 Deviation of the Empirical Probabilities from a Compound Bernoulli Model

Past History	Segment: ALL				Segment: EXCEPT 100 PERCENTERS			
	0	1	Total	$\bar{p}$	0	1	Total	$\bar{p}$
1111	245*	1968*	2213*	0.889	213	759	972	0.781
0111	93	276	369	0.748	89	241	330	0.730
1011	73	222	295	0.753	72	195	267	0.730
1101	84	196	280	0.700	80	177	257	0.689
1110	132	203	335	0.606	121	182	303	0.601
0011	59	128	187	0.684	56	120	176	0.682
0101	62	84	146	0.575	62	81	143	0.566
1001	49	75	124	0.605	49	68	117	0.581
0110	55	79	134	0.590	52	77	129	0.597
1010	72	67	139	0.482	71	65	136	0.478
1100	94	90	184	0.489	90	81	171	0.474
0001	85	105	190	0.553	85	100	185	0.541
0010	68	62	130	0.477	68	61	129	0.473
0100	90	56	146	0.384	90	55	145	0.379
1000	110	64	174	0.368	109	61	170	0.359
0000	156	108	264	0.409	154	106	260	0.408
	$\chi^2 = 58.0$				$\chi^2 = 51.0$			
	$\chi^2_{0.05} = 19.7$				$\chi^2_{0.05} = 19.7$			

* The entries in Tables 4.11 through 4.17 are sample sizes. For example, of the individuals in the segment ALL, 2213 had a past history 1111 and 245 followed this past history with the purchase of Brand 0 and 1968 followed with the purchase of Brand 1.

decision (a deviation from the Bernoulli model) becomes apparent. For example:

$\left.\begin{matrix} 0111 \\ 1011 \\ 1101 \end{matrix}\right\}$ all yield probabilities > 0.70

1110 yields a probability $= 0.61$

0001 yields a probability $= 0.55$

$\left.\begin{matrix} 0010 \\ 0100 \\ 1000 \end{matrix}\right\}$ give an average probability $= 0.41$

$\left.\begin{matrix} 0011 \\ 0101 \\ 1001 \end{matrix}\right\}$ give an average probability $= 0.62$

$\left.\begin{matrix} 0110 \\ 1010 \\ 1100 \end{matrix}\right\}$ give an average probability $= 0.52$

Given these results, it appears that we can find a model that fits the data better than the Bernoulli model. It will also become possible as the brand loyal model results are presented to quantify the deviations from a Bernoulli population.

4.10.3   Deviations from the Brand Loyal Model

The four tables that follow contain the basic results of this study. Tables 4.12 to 4.14 demonstrate how well the brand loyal models with beta heterogeneity fit the data for the various market segments. Recall that this model is characterized as follows:

1. Each individual is a first-order Markov process with the transition matrix

$$
\begin{array}{cc}
1 & 0 \\
\end{array}
$$
$$
\begin{array}{c}
1 \\
0
\end{array}
\begin{bmatrix}
p & 1-p \\
kp & 1-kp
\end{bmatrix}
$$

2. Here p is distributed beta among the individuals, and k is a constant, $0 < k < 1$, the *same* value for *all* the consumers.

In Tables 4.12 to 4.14 the past histories that are grouped together; e.g.,

$$
\begin{array}{l}
0101 \\
k:1010 \\
k:0110
\end{array}
$$

imply that under the brand loyal model

$$
k\, P(1|0101) = P(1|1010) = P(1|0110)
$$

or equivalently

$$
P(1|0101) = \frac{1}{k} P(1|1010) = \frac{1}{k} P(1|0110)
$$

The sample size that is listed at the bottom of the tables is the number of observations in that particular segment. The values of k, α, and β are the minimum chi-square estimates for these three parameters. The chi-square value is the goodness-of-fit statistic

$$
\sum \frac{(\text{observed} - \text{expected})^2}{\text{expected}}
$$

that was described throughout Chapters 3 and 4. In the notation of

Tables 4.12 and 4.14,

$$\chi^2 = \sum_i \frac{(1_i - \text{tot}_i \times p_i)^2}{\text{tot}_i \times p_i} + \frac{[0_i - \text{tot}_i \times (1.0 - p_i)]^2}{\text{tot}_i \times (1.0 - p_i)}$$

where i indexes the past histories.

Table 4.12 gives the results for the segments ALL and EXCEPT 100 PERCENTERS. The only empirical probability that changes much is, of course, $P(1|1111)$. Since this past history contains so many observations, the values of α and β are substantially altered when the 100 PERCENTERS are left out. Recall that only when beta heterogeneity is assumed does the past history 1111 enter into the calculation of the chi-square statistic. Under the assumption of arbitrary heterogeneity neither 1111 nor 0000 enters into the calculations.

The surprising thing to note is the values of the chi-square statistics for the two segments. The EXCEPT 100 PERCENTERS segment was formed explicitly to fit the beta heterogeneity. However, the ALL's fit the model with beta heterogeneity better than the EXCEPT 100 PERCENTERS. More will be said on this fact later. The fact that $\bar{p}_{0000}$ (the empirical probability) is so much higher than p_{0000} (the probability predicted by the brand loyal model with beta heterogeneity) is also related to the beta heterogeneity problem. This too will be discussed in Section 4.10.5.

Heavy vs. Light Consumers. Table 4.13 examines the HEAVY and LIGHT segments. With respect to the parameter values k, α, and β these two segments are virtually identical.

k, α, and β equal (0.82, 2.4, 0.8) for HEAVY's

k, α, and β equal (0.81, 2.1, 0.8) for LIGHT's

However, the LIGHT's do fit the models a little better as evidenced by their lower chi-square statistic.

A major discrepancy between the model and the empirical probabilities occurs at the same point for each segment. This is for the past history 0110. In both segments the empirical probability $\bar{p}_{0110}$ is much higher than the conditional model probability p_{0110}.

Loyal vs. Nonloyal Consumers. Table 4.14 contrasts the LOYAL and NONLOYAL customers. Here there is a decided difference in behavior. The past history 1111 is not a good indication of any basic differences in these segments, because the LOYAL's contain the 128 families whose

Table 4.12 Deviation from Brand Loyal Model

Past History	Segment: ALL					Segment: EXCEPT 100 PERCENTERS				
	0	1	Total	$\bar{p}$	p	0	1	Total	$\bar{p}$	p
1111	245	1968	2213	0.889	0.888	213	759	972	0.781	0.791
0111	93	276	369	0.748	0.748	89	241	330	0.730	0.696
1011	73	222	295	0.753	0.748	72	195	267	0.730	0.696
1101	84	196	280	0.700	0.748	80	177	257	0.689	0.696
k:1110	132	203	335	0.606	0.606	121	182	303	0.601	0.571
0101	62	84	146	0.575	0.606	62	81	143	0.566	0.600
k:1010	72	67	139	0.482	0.491	71	65	136	0.478	0.492
k:0110	55	79	134	0.590	0.491	52	77	129	0.597	0.492
0011	59	128	187	0.684	0.651	56	120	176	0.682	0.626
1001	49	75	124	0.605	0.651	49	68	117	0.581	0.626
k:1100	94	90	184	0.489	0.527	90	81	171	0.474	0.513
0010	68	62	130	0.477	0.397	68	61	129	0.473	0.428
0100	90	56	146	0.384	0.397	90	55	145	0.379	0.428
0001	85	105	190	0.553	0.524	85	100	185	0.541	0.543
k:1000	110	64	174	0.368	0.424	109	61	170	0.359	0.445
0000	156	108	264	0.409	0.134	154	106	260	0.408	0.150

Sample Size	531			Sample Size	389	
$k = 0.81$	$\chi^2 = 19.0$			$k = 0.82$	$\chi^2 = 23.6$	
$\alpha = 2.2$	$\chi^2_{0.05} = 21.0$			$\alpha = 4.2$	$\chi^2_{0.05} = 21.0$	
$\beta = 0.8$				$\beta = 2.2$		

Table 4.13 Deviation from Brand Loyal Model

Past History	Segment: HEAVY					Segment: LIGHT				
	0	1	Total	$\bar{p}$	p	0	1	Total	$\bar{p}$	p
1111	131	1072	1203	0.891	0.891	114	896	1010	0.887	0.887
0111	46	136	182	0.747	0.755	47	140	187	0.749	0.744
1011	33	114	147	0.776	0.755	40	108	148	0.730	0.744
1101	39	95	134	0.709	0.755	45	101	146	0.692	0.744
k:1110	61	108	169	0.639	0.755	71	95	166	0.572	0.744
0101	28	41	69	0.594	0.617	34	43	77	0.558	0.603
k:1010	29	36	65	0.554	0.506	43	31	74	0.419	0.487
k:0110	23	36	59	0.610	0.506	32	43	75	0.573	0.487
0011	27	63	90	0.700	0.660	32	65	97	0.670	0.645
1001	20	33	53	0.623	0.660	29	42	71	0.592	0.645
k:1100	41	36	77	0.468	0.541	53	54	107	0.505	0.522
0010	29	26	55	0.473	0.413	39	36	75	0.480	0.390
0100	35	25	60	0.417	0.413	55	31	86	0.360	0.390
0001	34	53	87	0.609	0.537	51	52	103	0.505	0.515
k:1000	52	23	75	0.307	0.440	58	41	99	0.414	0.417
0000	81	54	135	0.400	0.125	75	54	129	0.419	0.136

Sample Size 266	Sample Size 265
$k = 0.82$	$k = 0.81$
$\alpha = 2.4$ $\quad \chi^2 = 16.2$	$\alpha = 2.1$ $\quad \chi^2 = 11.4$
$\beta = 0.8$ $\quad \chi^2_{0.05} = 21.0$	$\beta = 0.8$ $\quad \chi^2_{0.05} = 21.0$

Table 4.14 Deviation from Brand Loyal Model

Past History	Segment: LOYAL					Segment: NONLOYAL				
	0	1	Total	$\bar{p}$	p	0	1	Total	$\bar{p}$	p
1111	165	1750	1915	0.914	0.912	80	218	298	0.732	0.746
0111	51	181	232	0.780	0.785	42	95	137	0.693	0.654
1011	48	150	198	0.758	0.785	25	72	97	0.742	0.654
1101	49	145	194	0.747	0.785	35	51	86	0.593	0.654
k:1110	64	149	213	0.700	0.683	68	54	122	0.443	0.484
0101	30	45	75	0.600	0.657	32	39	71	0.549	0.562
k:1010	33	45	78	0.577	0.572	39	22	61	0.361	0.416
k:0110	25	44	69	0.638	0.572	30	35	65	0.538	0.416
0011	23	73	96	0.760	0.694	36	55	91	0.604	0.589
1001	14	40	54	0.741	0.694	35	35	70	0.500	0.589
k:1100	46	42	88	0.477	0.603	48	48	96	0.500	0.436
0010	29	23	52	0.442	0.479	39	39	78	0.500	0.362
0100	39	24	63	0.381	0.479	51	32	83	0.386	0.362
0001	35	56	91	0.615	0.578	50	49	99	0.495	0.513
k:1000	44	37	81	0.457	0.503	66	27	93	0.290	0.380
0000	55	46	101	0.455	0.081	101	62	163	0.380	0.200

Sample Size		360		Sample Size		171
$k = 0.87$		$\chi^2 = 17.6$		$k = 0.74$		$\chi^2 = 25.6$
$\alpha = 3.1$		$\chi^2_{0.05} = 21.0$		$\alpha = 4.0$		$\chi^2_{0.05} = 21.0$
$\beta = 0.7$				$\beta = 2.8$		

purchase history was 30 consecutive 1's. For all but three of the remaining 15 past histories (1001, 1100, 0010) the LOYAL's have the
higher empirical probabilities. However, the real difference in their
behavior patterns is in the influence of the most recent purchase. This
is indicated by the parameter k. Recall that when $k = 1$, the brand loyal
model reduces to the compound Bernoulli model.

$$
\begin{array}{cc} 1 & 0 \end{array} \qquad\qquad \begin{array}{cc} 1 & 0 \end{array}
$$

$$
\begin{array}{c} 1 \\ 0 \end{array}
\begin{bmatrix} p & 1-p \\ kp & 1-kp \end{bmatrix}
\xrightarrow{\ k=1.0\ }
\begin{array}{c} 1 \\ 0 \end{array}
\begin{bmatrix} p & 1-p \\ p & 1-p \end{bmatrix}
$$

The *higher* the value of k the *less* effect the last purchase has, or to
put it differently: the higher the value of k, the "more Bernoulli" the
population of consumers becomes. Only in this particular segment
breakdown do we get a substantial difference in the k values.

$$\text{LOYAL: } k = 0.87$$

$$\text{NONLOYAL: } k = 0.74$$

In this sense, the LOYAL's are definitely more Bernoulli than the NON-
LOYAL's. This tends to support Massy's (1966) results. The families
that passed his stationarity test would have almost certainly been
classified as LOYAL'S, and in the small subset of families that he
studied he found essentially Bernoulli behavior. The slight deviations
from strict Bernoulli behavior that Massy observed were in the direction
that could be supported by a brand loyal universe with a high k value.

The fact that the LOYAL's are more Bernoulli than the NON-
LOYAL's is further substantiated by Table 4.15. This table shows that
under the Bernoulli hypothesis the goodness-of-fit statistics are

$$\text{LOYAL: } \chi^2_{\text{Ber}} = 33.4$$

$$\text{NONLOYAL: } \chi^2_{\text{Ber}} = 46.2$$

Also, the number of observations used to calculate χ^2_{Ber} for the LOYAL's
is even greater than the number of observations used for χ^2_{Ber} for the
NONLOYAL's. Recall Section 3.7.4, which discussed the effect of
sample size on the chi-square statistic.

The overall results of this study shown by Tables 4.12 through 4.14
can be summarized as follows:

1. The brand loyal model fits the data for all segments quite well. (A
contrast with the Bernoulli and last purchase loyal models is given next.
Deviations from the brand loyal model are also examined in greater
detail.)

2. LOYAL's are "more Bernoulli" (recent purchase decisions have a smaller effect on the current purchase decision) than the NONLOYAL's.
3. HEAVY and LIGHT buyers are surprisingly similar with respect to all the measures developed in this study.
4. Dropping the 100 PERCENTERS does not better the fit of the beta contagion model as had been expected — in fact, it worsens the fit.

Now that the major results have been presented and structured, a more detailed analysis of the models will be given.

4.10.4 The Superiority of the Brand Loyal Model

Table 4.15 that follows gives the goodness-of-fit statistics for the three competing models: Bernoulli, brand loyal, and last purchase loyal. Here $\chi^2_{\text{B.L.}}$, χ^2_{Ber}, and $\chi^2_{\text{L.P.L.}}$ are the chi-square values for the brand loyal, Bernoulli, and last purchase loyal models with arbitrary heterogeneity. The number of observations used to calculate these statistics is the second figure, under the heading "Sample Size." The effect of sample size on the goodness-of-fit statistics was discussed in Chapter 3 (see Section 3.7.4). For each segment, the three competing models had the same number of observations used for the three statistics $\chi^2_{\text{B.L.}}$, χ^2_{Ber}, and $\chi^2_{\text{L.P.L.}}$. The degrees of freedom for these statistics are 8, 11, and 9, respectively. In all cases the brand loyal model gives a better fit than the last purchase loyal model. (Of course, the brand loyal model gives a better fit than the compound Bernoulli model since the compound Bernoulli model is included as a special case of the brand loyal model with $k = 1.0$.)

The fact that the brand loyal model fits the data so much better than the last purchase loyal model tells us something about the phenomenon of "brand loyalty." Admittedly, these competing modes are highly idealized abstractions of the real world; however, it is apparent that if strong "loyalty" exists, it is generated toward a particular brand — and not toward the most recently purchased brand. Recall that the two models are defined by the following special cases of a general first-order transition matrix:

$$
\begin{array}{ccc}
\text{General} & \begin{array}{c}\text{Brand}\\ \text{Loyal}\end{array} & \begin{array}{c}\text{Last Purchase}\\ \text{Loyal}\end{array}\\[4pt]
\begin{array}{cc} 1 & 0 \end{array} & \begin{array}{cc} 1 & 0 \end{array} & \begin{array}{cc} 1 & 0 \end{array}\\[2pt]
\begin{array}{c} 1 \\ 0 \end{array}\begin{bmatrix} p_{11} & p_{10} \\ p_{01} & p_{00} \end{bmatrix} & \begin{array}{c} 1 \\ 0 \end{array}\begin{bmatrix} p & 1-p \\ kp & 1-kp \end{bmatrix} & \begin{array}{c} 1 \\ 0 \end{array}\begin{bmatrix} p & 1-p \\ 1-kp & kp \end{bmatrix}
\end{array}
$$

A higher repeat purchase probability for the favorite brand (p_{11}) is

Table 4.15 Comparison of the Bernoulli, Brand Loyal, and Last Purchase Loyal Model

Segment	Best k for B.L.*	α	β	$\chi^2_{\alpha,\beta,\text{B.L.}}$	$\chi^2_{\text{B.L.}}$	χ^2_{Ber}	$\chi^2_{\text{L.P.L.}}$	Sample Size for $\chi^2_{\alpha,\beta,\text{B.L.}}$	Other χ^2
All	0.81	2.2	0.8	19.0	16.7	58.0	73.9	5046	2833
Except 100 Percenters	0.82	4.2	2.2	23.6	18.1	51.0	70.7	3630	2658
Heavy	0.82	2.4	0.8	16.2	15.2	33.8	39.3	2525	1322
Light	0.81	2.1	0.8	11.4	9.1	31.8	40.5	2621	1511
Loyal	0.87	3.1	0.7	17.6	14.4	33.4	43.4	3509	1594
Nonloyal	0.74	4.0	2.8	25.6	19.0	46.2	34.8	1547	1249
Loyal-Heavy	0.87	3.2	0.7	9.4	8.9	16.5	18.9	1750	746
Loyal-Light	0.87	2.2	0.6	15.7	8.4	21.3	28.4	1751	840
Nonloyal, Heavy	0.76	4.0	2.8	16.7	12.2	23.6	18.8	777	621
Nonloyal, Light	0.72	3.7	2.6	15.3	11.6	27.0	20.3	770	628
$\chi^2_{0.05}$				21.0	15.5	19.7	16.9		

* B.L. = brand loyal; Ber = Bernoulli; L.P.L. = last purchase loyal.

accompanied by a correspondingly higher probability (p_{01}) of switching back to the favorite brand in the brand loyal model that the data support.

This is perhaps the key result obtained in this study. The direct method of calculating a transition matrix for each family and then observing the correlation between p_{11} and p_{01} is not appropriate. This correlation would be $+1.0$ if the brand loyal model were exactly correct, and it would be -1.0 if the last purchase loyal model were correct. In order to obtain enough purchase histories on each family, it would take from one to five years of data on most families. In this period of time the individual time series are highly nonstationary, and a family may have switched favorite brands many times. Massy's results support this latter fact. Thus, the desired 0-1 process could not be defined.

From a practical point of view, the brand loyal and last purchase loyal models are also better suited to panel data than a model that analyzes long time series of individual consumers. Most panels provide a limited amount of data on many different consumers, rather than extensive data on a few individual families. Therefore, the non-stationarity of individual purchase behavior plus the constraints of most panel data favor the approach taken in this study.

The first three columns of Table 4.15 give the parameters of the brand loyal model that were determined from the data. As remarked earlier, the higher the k, the "more Bernoulli" that particular segment is. Also, the lower the values of α and β, the more heterogeneous is that segment. Thus, these three parameters can provide a quantitative method for segmenting markets according to the influence of recent purchase decisions, and by the homogeneity of purchase probabilities. In this sense the LOYAL, NONLOYAL breakdown provides the best example. The LOYAL's form a more Bernoulli population of customers, and the NONLOYAL's make up a more homogeneous population with respect to the distribution of p.

The $\chi^2_{\text{B.L.},\alpha,\beta}$ is the goodness-of-fit statistic when beta heterogeneity is assumed in the brand loyal model. The $\chi^2_{\text{B.L.}}$ is the corresponding statistic when the heterogeneity can be arbitrary.

4.10.5   *Evidence of Beta Heterogeneity*

From Tables 4.12 to 4.14, it is obvious that p_{0000} is never very close to $\bar{p}_{0000}$. This is not surprising. Recall that only 15 purchase decisions were used to calculate the favorite brand in a given period. If a past history 0000 occurs, there are only 11 other purchases in which the

Table 4.16 Just Significant Levels for the Goodness-of-Fit Statistics for the Brand Loyal Model Under Arbitrary and Beta Heterogeneity

	Arbitrary		Beta	
Segment	$\chi^2_{B.L.}$	Just Significant Level	$\chi^2_{\alpha,\beta,B.L.}$	Just Significant Level
ALL	16.7	0.040	19.0	0.085
EXCEPT 100 percenters	18.1	0.020	23.6	0.023
HEAVY	15.2	0.055	16.2	0.18
LIGHT	9.1	0.33	11.4	0.49
LOYAL	14.4	0.075	17.6	0.13
NONLOYAL	19.0	0.015	25.6	0.013
LOYAL, HEAVY	8.9	0.35	9.4	0.66
LOYAL, LIGHT	8.4	0.39	15.7	0.21
NONLOYAL, HEAVY	12.2	0.15	16.7	0.16
NONLOYAL, LIGHT	11.6	0.18	15.3	0.23

family must make the three to five purchases of 1 necessary to make it that family's favorite brand. Hence, $\bar{p}_{0000}$ takes on a value of approximately 4/11. However, this upward bias caused by the short history used in determining the favorite brand cannot be taken into account by the model. Therefore, the past history 0000 is not used in estimating α and β and the resulting chi-square statistic.

A similar, but less drastic, effect occurs for the past histories 0001, 0010, 0100, 1000. Nevertheless, we decided to use these past histories in estimating α and β. These difficulties, which result from the experimental design, must be kept in mind when interpreting the estimated values of α and β.

A possible remedy would have been to use more purchase decisions for calculating the favorite brands. However, this would result in less stationary time series and in a smaller sample size.

Table 4.16 gives the fit of the brand loyal model with both arbitrary and beta heterogeneity. In general the more restrictive assumption of beta heterogeneity does not worsen the fit of the brand loyal model.

4.10.6 Deviations from a General First-Order Process

Recall that for the general first-order model (see Section 4.8) we only had two groups of size two each that yielded equal probabilities.

$$\begin{bmatrix} 1011 \\ 1101 \end{bmatrix}$$

Table 4.17   Evidence of a Second-Order Effect

Past History	Segment: ALL 1	Total	$\bar{p}$	t
1011	222	295	0.753	1.43
1101	196	280	0.700	
0010	62	130	0.477	1.46
0100	56	146	0.384	

and

$$\begin{bmatrix} 0010 \\ 0100 \end{bmatrix}$$

Table 4.17 gives standard t tests for these two groups. Although the t values are not highly significant, a definite indication of a second-order effect (effect of the second most recent purchase) is seen.

$$P(1|1011) \text{ is higher than } P(1|1101)$$

and

$$P(1|0010) \text{ is higher than } P(1|0100)$$

See Bryant (1960), pp. 90–91, for the t test with unequal sample sizes and unequal variances.

4.10.7   Calculation of the Power of the Chi-Square Tests

In this section the power of the goodness-of-fit test for the brand loyal model (the null hypothesis) versus the compound Bernoulli model (the alternative hypothesis) will be calculated. The market segment used will be the EXCEPT 100 PERCENTERS.

The minimum chi-square estimates, assuming a compound Bernoulli model, were $\alpha = 3.33$ and $\beta = 2.02$. Therefore, under the alternative hypothesis, $\alpha = 3.33$ and $\beta = 2.02$ are our estimates of the beta heterogeneity parameters.

The same data fit to the brand loyal model yielded: $k = 0.82$, $\alpha = 4.2$, $\beta = 2.2$. The two competing hypotheses are

H_0: the population of consumers is brand loyal with $k = 0.82$, $\alpha = 4.2$, $\beta = 2.2$,

H_1: the population is Bernoulli with contagion parameters $\alpha = 3.33$, $\beta = 2.02$.

Table 4.18 gives the resulting probabilities and sample sizes (the N_i) that are necessary to calculate the power of the test.

Table 4.18 The Conditional Model Probabilities and Sample Sizes That Were Used to Calculate the Power of the Chi-Square Test

Past History	P{1|Past History, B.L.}	P{1|Past History, Ber}	N_i
1111	0.791	0.784	972
0111	0.696	0.677	330
1011	0.696	0.677	267
1101	0.696	0.677	257
1110	0.571	0.677	303
0101	0.600	0.570	143
1010	0.492	0.570	136
0110	0.492	0.570	129
0011	0.626	0.570	176
1001	0.626	0.570	117
1100	0.513	0.570	171
0010	0.428	0.463	129
0100	0.428	0.463	145
0001	0.543	0.463	185
1000	0.445	0.463	170

Under H_0: χ^2 is distributed as chi-square with 12 degrees of freedom. Under H_1: χ^2 is distributed approximately normal with mean 52.0 and standard deviation 13.3. See Section 2.3.2.3, Equations 2.29 and 2.30, for the method of arriving at these figures.

Let the probability of a Type I error (α) be 0.05. Then $\chi^2_{0.05} = 21.0$ (there are 12 degrees of freedom). Hence, the probability of a Type II error is

$$\beta \approx \int_{-\infty}^{21.0} \text{normal}(52,13.3) = \int_{-\infty}^{-2.3} N(0,1) = 0.02$$

The power of the χ^2 test of H_0 versus H_1 (with the probability of a Type I error (α) fixed at 0.05) is approximately 0.98; that is, the probability of a type II error (β) is equal to 0.02.

4.10.8 Summary of the Results

The conclusions from the empirical results are now briefly reviewed. These results are only for the coffee data and are not necessarily generalizable.

1. For all ten market segments, the brand loyal model gives by far the best fit when compared to the Bernoulli and last purchase loyal models.
2. The vast superiority of the brand loyal model over the last purchase

loyal model indicates the nature of the heterogeneity among consumers
and sheds light on the whole rather nebulous concept of brand loyalty.
3. When we recall that $k = 1.0$ in the brand loyal model implies a
compound Bernoulli model, the higher the value of k, the "more
Bernoulli" that particular segment is. In this regard only one segmentation (LOYAL, NONLOYAL) resulted in significantly different k
values:

$$\text{LOYAL: } k = 0.87$$

$$\text{NONLOYAL: } k = 0.74$$

In this sense the LOYAL's constitute a more Bernoulli segment than
do the NONLOYAL's.
4. The HEAVY-LIGHT breakdown produced no significant differences. The LIGHT's fit the brand loyal model a little better, but their
parameter values were essentially the same.

	HEAVY	LIGHT
$\chi^2_{\text{B.L.}}$	15.2	9.1
$\chi^2_{\text{B.L.}\alpha,\beta}$	16.2	11.4
α	2.4	2.1
β	0.8	0.8
k	0.82	0.81

5. Table 4.17 shows that the second most recent purchase exerts some
influence on the current purchase decision. However, this effect is not
great enough to invalidate the first-order brand loyal as a good approximate model of consumer behavior.
6. Surprisingly, when the beta heterogeneity assumption is tested, the
segment that includes the 142 LOYAL's (the segment ALL) fits the
data better than when these consumers who concentrate their purchases
on only one brand are excluded (the segment EXCEPT 100 PER-
CENTERS). See Table 4.16. However, since the past history 0000 is
neglected, this whole area of beta heterogeneity is on somewhat shaky
ground.
7. For the sample sizes used in this study, the power of the chi-square
test is quite good.

4.11 Applications of the Compound Models to Other Fields

It was stated at the beginning of Chapter 3 that the compound models
to be developed were of a quite general nature. As concluding remarks,
applications of these models in nonmarketing area will be given.

Sociology

Sociologists conduct opinion polls over time on panels of people. Often the answers to the researcher's questions are dichotomous — yes, no; agree, disagree; etc. The investigator may hypothesize that an individual's opinion at time t depends only on the opinion he held at time $t - 1$ (or perhaps that it is even independent of his opinion at time $t - 1$). The models of this study could be used to test these hypotheses, and the usual assumptions of homogeneity could be dropped.

Mathematical Psychology

In the one-element learning model, it is assumed that all the learning takes place at one point in time (the "a-ha" experience). Hence, for an individual subject, his correct and incorrect answers up until the last error he makes from a Bernoulli process. If he happens to get the correct answer before the last error it is only by guessing correctly. The Bernoulli model developed here can be adapted to test this hypothesis when each subject has a different guessing probability. This can result if the experimental design calls for different subjects to have different numbers of choices of answers available.

Quality Control

Suppose one is interested in determining the failure characteristics of a missile that can be fired, retrieved, reloaded, and fired again. It is hypothesized that each missile has a constant probability p of failing — regardless of its past performance. Further, it is hypothesized that p is distributed beta among the missiles. If only a given number of observations are available, we could fire a few missles very often and apply the run test to these sequences to test the Bernoulli assumption. However, this would give very little indication of the distribution of p. The compound Bernoulli model developed here can test both hypotheses simultaneously.

Given N observations *and assuming Bernoulli behavior*, the problem of how to best allocate the number of observations per missile has been solved by Kullback (1960). However, with the aid of the brand loyal and last purchase loyal models the stringent Bernoulli assumption need not be made. Models of the sort used in this study to analyze consumer purchase behavior appear to be a fruitful starting point for research in certain areas of quality control.

4.12   Appendix: The Evaluation of $\displaystyle\int_0^1 \frac{1}{a-p} p^{m-1}(1-p)^{n-1}\,dp$

When $a^2 > p^2$ (this condition is always satisfied for the models of this study),

$$(a-p)^{-1} = \frac{1}{a}\left(1 + \frac{p}{a} + \frac{p^2}{a^2} + \frac{p^3}{a^3} + \cdots\right)$$

Therefore,

$$\int_0^1 \frac{1}{a-p}\,p^{m-1}(1-p)^{n-1} = \frac{1}{a}\left[\int_0^1 p^{m-1}(1-p)^{n-1}\,dp\right.$$

$$+ \frac{1}{a}\int_0^1 p^m(1-p)^{n-1}\,dp + \cdots$$

$$\left.+ \frac{1}{a^r}\int_0^1 p^{m+r-1}(1-p)^{n-1}\,dp + \cdots\right]$$

which yields

$$\int_0^1 \frac{1}{a-p}\,p^{m-1}(1-p)^{n-1} = \frac{1}{a}\left[B(m,n) + \frac{1}{a}B(m+1,n) + \cdots\right.$$

$$\left.+ \frac{1}{a^r}B(m+r,n) + \cdots\right]$$

where

$$B(m,n) = \int_0^1 p^{m-1}(1-p)^{n-1}\,dp = \frac{(m-1)!\,(n-1)!}{(m+n-1)!} \quad \text{when } m,n \text{ integer}$$

$$= \frac{\Gamma(m)\Gamma(n)}{\Gamma(m+n)} \qquad \text{when } m,n > 0$$

The gamma function has the property that $\Gamma(m+1) = m\Gamma(m)$, for $m > 0$. Using the factorial nature of the B, we can relate them by the formula

$$B(m+r,n) = \frac{(m+r-1)(m+r-2)\cdots(m)}{(m+n+r-1)(m+n+r-2)\cdots(m+n)}\,B(m,n)$$

Letting $1/a = b$, we get the following infinite series expansion for the desired integral:

$$\int_0^1 \frac{1}{a-p}\,p^{m-1}(1-p)^{n-1}\,dp$$

$$= bB(m,n) \times \left[1 + b\,\frac{m}{m+n} + b^2\,\frac{(m+1)(m)}{(m+n+1)(m+n)} + \cdots\right]$$

Define

$$\int_0^1 \frac{1}{a - p} p^{m-1}(1 - p)^{n-1}\, dp \equiv \tilde{B}_a(m,n)$$

Let

$$\frac{m}{m + n} = s$$

Then

$$s^{r+1} < \frac{(m + r)(m + r - 1)\cdots(m)}{(m + n + r)(m + n + r - 1)\cdots(m + n)} < 1$$

$$r = 1, 2, 3 \ldots$$

Hence,

$$bB(m,n)(1 + bs + b^2s^2 + \cdots) < \tilde{B}_a(m,n)$$
$$< bB(m,n)(1 + b + b^2 + \cdots)$$

Therefore, we have upper and lower bounds on $\tilde{B}_a(m,n)$;

$$\underline{\tilde{B}}_a(m,n) = \frac{1}{a} B(m,n)\left[\frac{1}{1 - \dfrac{s}{a}}\right] < \tilde{B}_a(m,n) < \frac{1}{a} B(m,n)\left[\frac{1}{1 - \dfrac{1}{a}}\right]$$
$$= \bar{\bar{B}}_a(m,n)$$

Now $\tilde{B}_a(m,n)$ can be calculated to any desired degree of accuracy by actually calculating the first r terms and then obtaining upper and lower bounds on the remaining terms.

Recalling that

$$\sum_{i=r+1}^\infty b^i = \frac{b^{r+1}}{1 - b}$$

we get

$$\underline{\tilde{B}}_{-a}(m,n) = bB(m,n)\left[1 + b\left(\frac{m}{m + n}\right) + \cdots\right.$$

$$\left. + b^r \frac{(m + r - 1)\cdots(m)}{(m + n + r - 1)\cdots(m + n)} + \left(\frac{b^{r+1}s^{r+1}}{1 - b_s}\right)\right]$$

$$< \tilde{B}_a(m,n) < bB(m,n)\left[1 + b\left(\frac{m}{m + n}\right) + \cdots\right.$$

$$\left. + b^r \frac{(m + r - 1)\cdots(m)}{(m + n + r - 1)\cdots(m + n)} + \left(\frac{b^{r+1}}{1 - b}\right)\right]$$

$$= \bar{\bar{B}}_a(m,n)$$

To determine the accuracy of the approximation

$$\Delta_a^r(m,n) \equiv \bar{\tilde{B}}_a(m,n) - \underline{\tilde{B}}_a(m,n) = \frac{b^{r+1}(1 - s^{r+1}) - b^{r+2}s(1 - s^r)}{(1 - b)(1 - bs)}$$

$$\delta_a^r(m,n) \equiv \frac{\Delta_a^r(m,n)}{\frac{1}{2}[\bar{\tilde{B}}_a(m,n) + \underline{\tilde{B}}_a(m,n)]}$$

gives the approximate percent error by using either the upper or lower bound estimate.

The probabilities that are used in this study are determined by ratios of $\tilde{B}$. For example, suppose $p = \tilde{B}_1/\tilde{B}_2$. Then *very conservative* upper and lower bounds for p would be

$$\underline{p} = \frac{\underline{\tilde{B}}_{-1}}{\bar{\tilde{B}}_2} < p < \frac{\bar{\tilde{B}}_1}{\underline{\tilde{B}}_2} = \bar{p}$$

In practice one would estimate p by

$$\frac{\bar{\tilde{B}}_1}{\bar{\tilde{B}}_2} \quad \text{or} \quad \frac{\underline{\tilde{B}}_{-1}}{\underline{\tilde{B}}_2}$$

so that the errors of approximation will tend to cancel each other.

CHAPTER 5
LINEAR LEARNING MODELS
FOR BRAND CHOICE

5.1 Introduction

Linear learning models have occupied an important position in the literature of brand choice ever since Kuehn (1958) adapted the work of Bush and Mosteller (1955) and applied the model to data on switching patterns for frozen orange juice. The fundamental concept underlying the development of the learning model is that consumers are affected by feedback from past brand choices. That is, the act of purchasing and using a particular brand is assumed to affect the probability that this brand will be selected the next time the product class is to be purchased. The concept of the "purchase event feedback" phenomenon was discussed in Chapter 1.

By *learning*, we do not necessarily mean the acquisition of useful knowledge but rather the concept found in Bush and Mosteller (1958) p. 3,

. . . any systematic change in behavior (is considered) to be learning whether or not the change is adaptive, desirable for certain purposes, or in accordance with any other criterion.

Thus, we leave open the possibility that purchase event feedback may be dysfunctional, even as far as the individual is concerned. Then, too, it may be that "learning" is negative in the sense that increased familiarity with the product may reduce the chances that it will be purchased in the future — such behavior would be dysfunctional from the point of view of the manufacturer while being in the interest of the household decision maker.

The linear learning model was originally developed for the purpose of describing data from laboratory experiments on adaptive behavior by animal and human subjects. Bush and Mosteller (1955) justify the linear learning model in terms of stimulus sampling theory. Miller and Frick (1949) use an information theoretic approach to calculate the effect of past behavior on present behavior, which also amounts to a type of learning model. Recent developments in learning theory are presented in Bush and Estes (1959); a survey chapter by Restle will be of

particular interest to nonmathematical psychologists. Atkinson and Estes (1963) give a review of the class of stimulus sampling learning models. Problems of measurement in the context of learning and other behavioral models are reviewed by Suppes and Zinnes (1963).

The linear learning model represents a highly specific set of hypotheses about the way in which a purchase event feeds back on the post-purchase probabilities. The essential assumption is that the post-purchase probability is always a linear function of the prepurchase probability. That is,

$$p_{t+1} = a + bp_t$$

for all values of p_t and all t. The right-hand side of this equation will be called a *feedback operator*. While linearity is not an unreasonable assumption in many situations, there are times when others might be more appropriate. For instance, we might like to introduce thresholds into the change process which would make it difficult to reduce a large probability through purchase of other brands (e.g., to make it hard to break a "habit"). This would require that p_{t+1} be a nonlinear function of p_t, that is, that the feedback operators be nonlinear.

Certain additional assumptions are implied by this equation as it is embedded in the linear learning model. First, the model assumes quasi-stationarity in the sense that the parameters of the change operators do not change over short periods of time. It does not provide for the effects of marketing variables or other exogenous factors. [Some of Kuehn's later work (1968) incorporates a "forgetting" or "time since last purchase" effect into a hybrid form of the linear learning model. This is an interesting development, but it will not be pursued here.]

Second, the model assumes that all households exhibit adaptive behavior that can be described by feedback operators with at least approximately the same parameters. That is, the parameters in the learning model are assumed to be the same for all families. This is in contrast to the assumptions about heterogeneous Markov models that were introduced in Chapter 4: There the feedback operator was assumed to be independent of the value of p_t but was allowed to vary across families. In this chapter, we will discuss response heterogeneity within the context of linear learning models, but it will refer to differences in the probability levels among families at time t_0 rather than to differences in parameter values. The same strategy will be adopted in connection with the probabilty diffusion models introduced in Chapter 6. In our opinion, the assumption that the learning operator's parameters are the same for all households is not necessarily unreasonable, even though it

is clearly an abstraction. Useful results can probably be obtained from this kind of model. However, homogeneity of parameter values must not be confused with homogeneity of the initial probability levels. We will see that heterogeneity among the p_0 must be considered if meaningful parameter estimates are to be obtained for the linear learning model.

The linear learning model is not the only model of adaptive behavior that can be used to describe brand choice. The various kinds of Markov processes discussed in Chapter 4 all represent a kind of adaptive consumer behavior, in that the purchase event is assumed to feed back on the postpurchase probability vector. (The relation between the linear learning and Markov models will be explored later.) The Stochastic Evolutionary Adoption Model (STEAM) introduced in Chapter 9 is also designed to accommodate learning phenomena with respect to repeated trials of a new brand. In this case, however, the adaptive behavior of consumers is likely to be highly nonlinear. Additional learning assumptions are brought into the extensions to STEAM, developed in Chapter 11.

Outside the particular area of "learning model theory," we have a good example of models incorporating the possibility of adaptive behavior in the many studies of accident statistics that have appeared during the last three decades. In particular, models reported by Arbous and Kerrich (1951) and Bates and Neyman (1952) provide for changes in the probability of having an accident in the future when the subject actually experiences one. This is a good example of "event feedback." It can be termed adaptive, even though it may be dysfunctional depending on the direction of the change. It is also interesting to note that the famous controversy about whether observed accident statistics were the result of "learning" or heterogeneity of initial probabilities (i.e., that some subjects are more prone to accidents than others) has been repeated in the marketing literature. This problem will be considered in Section 5.3 when Kuehn's work is reviewed.

Thus, we see that the linear learning model provides one possible way to accommodate adaptive behavior into stochastic models of consumer brand choice. It is just one of several such possibilities, though it is quite a good one in some situations. On the other hand, it is essential to remember that a model that does not incorporate a linear learning assumption does not necessarily neglect the possibility of adaptive behavior. Nor is it clear that the linear learning assumption should always be adopted even when the adaptive process appears to be linear in the probabilities: the linear learning model is complex, and its use may preclude the consideration of other equally important determinants

of brand-choice behavior. There may be situations where the description of the adaptive part of the process will have to be drastically simplified (e.g., to a simple Markov process) or eliminated entirely so that other important phenomena (e.g., the effects of market variables) can be accommodated effectively.

We have noted that the Markov process provides a rudimentary model of adaptive brand-choice behavior. It is interesting to observe that Kuehn's work on the learning model antedates most of that done on Markov models by other authors. Nevertheless, the simple, homogeneous Markov model grew to surpass the learning model in popularity because its basic simplicity permitted reasonable explanations to nontechnical marketing persons, the kinds of implications that could be derived from it (e.g., switching patterns, loyalty, and equilibrium market shares) were intuitively appealing to managers, many brands could be accommodated simultaneously, and the calculations required to estimate the model's parameters from panel data were simple and understandable.[1] By contrast, the learning model has retained something of an air of mystery, even among professional researchers. It has been discussed extensively in the literature, but very little information about methods by which the model can be put into practical use is available. The same is true with respect to detailed reports of actual applications of the model; with the exception of several theses at Carnegie Institute of Technology, Carman (1966) and McConnell (1968) provide the only example of such a study of which the authors are aware. Thus, the linear learning model has assumed the curious position of being widely discussed and highly revered in some quarters while remaining an unknown quantity and quite remote so far as most empirical applications are concerned.

The purpose of this chapter is to review the theory of the linear learning model, derive methods by which its parameters can be estimated, and report the results of a modest empirical investigation based on the model. We will review the learning model literature only briefly; this has been done elsewhere, and, as already noted, most of the articles are expository rather than substantive in nature.

The formal specifications for the two-brand linear learning model, as it is assumed to apply to individual household behavior, are presented in Section 5.2. Some prior work on learning models will be reviewed in Section 5.3. Parameter estimation methods for the model will be provided in Section 5.4. Some comparisons between the linear

---

[1] The shortcomings of the simple, homogeneous Markov model were discussed in Chapter 4.

learning model and other brand-choice models will be discussed in Section 5.5, and empirical results for the linear learning model will be reported in Section 5.6. Discussion of the application of learning model theory to the analysis of aggregate growth curves will be postponed until Chapter 8.

5.2 Linear Learning Model Microtheory

When dealing with linear learning models, as elsewhere in this book, it is essential to distinguish between the model as it is assumed to apply to an individual decision-making unit (e.g., a household) and its aggregative form, which generates brand switching statistics for the panel population as a whole. For purposes of this chapter, we will refer to the former as the learning model microtheory and the latter as macrotheory. The differences between these two approaches is that in microtheory we regard v_0 as a fixed (though unknown) number while in macrotheory we are forced to view v_0 as being distributed over members of the population. The microtheory is appropriate for discussing the implications of the model and its parameters, while the macrotheory is required if we are to estimate the parameters from panel data.

5.2.1 Description of the Model

We shall deal with the situation where families' purchasing processes can be represented by 0-1 stochastic processes. This is obviously the case when there are only two brands, but multiple-brand processes can be reduced to binary terms subject to the "combining of classes" restrictions developed by Bush and Mosteller (1955), Section 1.8. Given this condition, each family's purchasing history is represented by a series of zeros and ones: a one is recorded if Brand 1 or a member of the set of brands labeled "1" is purchased, and a 0 is recorded otherwise.

Let us represent the probability that a particular family will buy Brand 1 on purchase occasion t by $\Pr[1]_t = v_t$. Then $\Pr[0]_t = 1 - \Pr[1]_t = 1 - v_t$. The linear learning model hypothesis consists of the following recursive relation between $\Pr[1]_t$ and $\Pr[1]_{t+1}$:

$$v_{t+1}^{(1)}\{v_t\} = \alpha + \beta + \lambda v_t \quad \text{if Brand 1 is purchased at } t, \text{ or}$$
$$v_{t+1}^{(0)}\{v_t\} = \alpha + \lambda v_t \quad \text{if Brand 0 is purchased at } t, \tag{5.1}$$

where the functional notation $v_{t+1}^{(i)}\{v_t\}$ reminds us that v_{t+1} depends on v_t and the brand actually purchased at t. The two relations are called

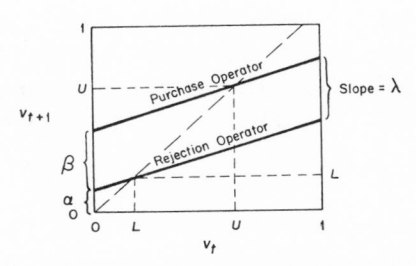

Figure 5.1. Graphical representation of the linear learning model.

the *purchase operator* and *rejection operator*, respectively. All families are assumed to have the same values for the parameters α, β, and λ, though of course the process leads to different values of v_t for different families. (Even if all families started out with the same value of v_t at time 0, variations in realized purchase histories would destroy this homogeneity at times $t > 0$.) The fact that $0 \leq v_t \leq 1$ for all t implies that $\alpha + \beta + \lambda$ must also be constrained to lie in the interval [0,1].

"Learning" takes place because a purchase of Brand 1 leads to a larger value of v_{t+1} than a purchase of Brand 0, for any trial t. The equality of the slope coefficients λ in the purchase and rejection operators is an assumption that might be relaxed in the two-brand case, though it is required if more than two brands are to be considered.[2]

The method by which the purchase probabilities are updated by the purchase and rejection operators is shown graphically in Figure 5.1. Suppose that we start with a household that has initial probability v_0. At time $t = 1$ a purchase decision is made: Brand 1 is purchased with probability v_0 and Brand 0 with probability $1 - v_0$. Then the feedback effect is calculated according to whichever operator is appropriate, given the realized purchase decision. That is, v_0 is entered on the abscissa of Figure 5.1 and the new value v_1 is read off the ordinate opposite one of the two operators. It is obvious from the graph that the value of v_1 must lie between the left-hand intercept of the rejection operator and the right-hand intercept of the purchase operator. Now consider the two points U and L, where the purchase and rejection operators cross the 45° line, respectively. Once the probability is changed so that it lies between these two points, no further application of the operators can cause it to be shifted outside the interval. Thus, it is easy to prove that once the process has been allowed to run long enough to achieve a

[2] If more than two brands are considered, the slopes must be equal in order to assure that the brand-choice probabilities will always lie in the interval [0,1]. See Herniter and Howard (1964). Curiously, this constraint is not required in the two-brand case.

"steady state," v will be between L and U with probability one. This phenomenon has been termed the *incomplete learning–incomplete extinction* property of the linear learning model. For operators with equal slopes, learning is always incomplete unless $\alpha = 0$ and $\beta = 1 - \lambda$.

From Figure 5.1 we can see that the response probability will always be "trapped" inside the interval (L,U) within a finite number of steps unless v_0 is exactly equal to zero or one. (In this case, one or the other brand is always purchased, and there is no real learning.)

5.2.2 The Expectation of v_t for $t > t_0$

Starting with our family's particular value of v_0, successive purchases result in a sequence of applications of the purchase and rejection operators. Each possible sequence of purchases of length N yields a particular value of v_t at the end of the sequence, given v_0 and the parameters of the model. Likewise, the probabilities that each of the sequences will in fact be observed can be obtained by multiplying out the probabilities that the given brand will be purchased at each state of the sequence. These probabilities are given by the sequence v_t, $t = 1$, $2, 3, \ldots, N$, which as noted earlier is known if we know the values of p_0, α, β, and λ.

To set ideas, we denote the 2^t possible sequences of purchases of the two brands on N trials by $S_1, S_2, S_3, \ldots, S_k$, where $k = 2^t$. For example, when $N = 4$, there are 16 possible sequences, ranging from $\{1111\}$ to $\{0000\}$. The probability of a "1" on the $t + 1$ trial will in general be different for each S: it depends on the initial probability v_0 and the parameters of the learning model. We will write this probability as

$$v_{t+1}^{(S_i)}\{v_0\} \quad \text{or} \quad \Pr[1 \text{ at } t + 1 | S_i^{(t)}, v_0]$$

because the purchase probability on a given trial depends on the prior probability and the ensuing sequence of purchases. Each event S also has a certain probability of occurrence, which we shall denote by

$$\Pr[S_i^{(t)} | v_0]$$

(Expressions giving these probabilities for purchase sequences up to length 3 will be developed in Section 5.4.)

Our interpretation of the learning model will be enhanced if we can find an expression for the expected value of $v_{t+1}\{v_0\}$. Following Kuehn and Rohloff (1967), Equation (3), we write

$$E[v_{t+1} | v_t] = v_t(\alpha + \beta + \lambda v_t) + (1 - v_t)(\alpha + \lambda v_t)$$
$$= \alpha + (\beta + \lambda)v_t$$

Their result can be extended by applying the rules of conditional expectation:

$$E[v_{t+1}|v_0] = E_{S^{(t)}}E[v_{t+1}|v_t^{(S_i)}\{v_0\}]$$

$$= \sum_{i=1}^{K} E[v_{t+1}|v_t^{(S_i)}\{v_0\}] \Pr[S_i^{(t)}|v_0]$$

$$= \sum_{i=1}^{K} [\alpha + (\beta + \lambda)v_t^{(S_i)}\{v_0\}] \Pr[S_i^{(t)}|v_0]$$

$$= \alpha + (\beta + \lambda) E[v_t|v_0] \qquad (5.2)$$

The last equality holds because the sum of the probabilities of all the sequences of length t must be one, and the sum of the v_t generated by each sequence times the probability of that sequence is the expectation of v_t.

Equation 5.2 provides a recursive relation for $E[v_{t+1}|v_0]$, which holds for any t. Thus, we can write

$$E[v_1|v_0] = \alpha + (\beta + \lambda)v_0$$

$$E[v_2|v_0] = \alpha + (\beta + \lambda) E[v_1|v_0]$$
$$= \alpha + (\beta + \lambda)[\alpha + (\beta + \lambda)v_0]$$
$$= [\alpha + \alpha(\beta + \lambda)] + (\beta + \lambda)^2 v_0$$

$$E[v_3|v_0] = \alpha + (\beta + \lambda) E[v_2|v_0]$$
$$= [\alpha + \alpha(\beta + \lambda) + \alpha(\beta + \lambda)^2] + (\beta + \lambda)^3 v_0$$

or in general

$$E[v_t|v_0] = [\alpha + \alpha(\beta + \lambda) + \alpha(\beta + \lambda)^2 + \cdots + \alpha(\beta + \lambda)^{t-1}]$$
$$+ (\beta + \lambda)^t v_0 \qquad (5.3)$$

When the model exhibits the incomplete learning–incomplete extinction property discussed in the previous section, $\alpha > 0$ and $0 < (\beta + \lambda) < 1$. Then the first term, which is the sum of the terms of a geometric progression, goes to $\alpha/(1 - \beta - \lambda)$, and the second term goes to zero as N goes to infinity. That is

$$\lim_{t \to \infty} E[v_t|v_0] = \frac{\alpha}{1 - \beta - \lambda} \equiv \bar{v}_{\infty} \qquad (5.4)$$

This expression gives us the equilibrium or long-run purchase probability expectation implied by the learning model. Because $\bar{v}_{\infty}$ is independent of the initial condition we can disregard the unknown v_0 when making equilibrium calculations.

5.2.3   The Distribution of v_t for $t > 0$

Equations 5.2 through 5.4 give us the expected values of v_t for $t > 0$. We now seek a method for finding the distribution of v_t around its expectation. The general expression for the cumulative distribution of v_t is, of course,

$$F(v_t^*|v_0) = \Pr[v_t \leq v_t^*] = \sum_{S_i \in S^*} \Pr[S_i^{(t)}|v_0]$$

where the summation is taken over all those sequences for which $v_t^{(S_i)}\{v_0\} < v_t^*$. This function defines the probability distribution for the family's brand-choice probability v_t. The fact that the sequence of purchases occurs at random (given the sequence of v_t) means that we will be uncertain about what the family's purchase probability will be after N trials, even though we know the value of v_0 and $E[v_t|v_0]$.

While the previous equation can be evaluated from the model's parameters and v_0 for small values of t, the dramatic increase in the number of possible sequences as t becomes large makes this direct method impractical in many situations. Hence, we will set up the problem of finding $F(v_t|v_0)$ in another way, which offers significant computational advantages. The new procedure will also provide a way for evaluating the asymptotic distribution.

The definition of the linear learning operators specifies that v_{t+1} is a function of v_t but not (directly) of any p prior to t. Hence, the model can be regarded as a first-order Markov process, where the probability of purchase determines the state of the system. (In the "ordinary" Markov purchasing model, the purchase decisions defined the states of the process; here the probability of purchase defines the states.) Strictly speaking, we have a first-order Markov process with an infinite number of states, since v can take an infinite number of values between zero and one. Furthermore, the states in the intervals $(0,L)$ and $(U,1)$ are clearly transient, since even if v_0 is outside (L,U), we know the probability will enter this interval at some t and, once there, will remain. To simplify the following discussion, we will deal with a discrete approximation to the continuous state-space Markov process and ignore states outside (L,U).

Let us divide the interval between L and U into g subintervals having midpoints m_i^* $(i = 1, \ldots, g)$ and length ζ. We define ρ_{it} as the probability that v_t falls into subinterval i, as follows:

$$\boldsymbol{\rho}_t(v_0) = \{\rho_{it}(v_0)\} = \left\{ \Pr\left[m_i^* - \frac{\zeta}{2} \leq v_t \leq m_i^* + \frac{\zeta}{2} \middle| v_0 \right] \right\}$$

where $\boldsymbol{\rho}_t(v_0)$ is a column vector whose elements sum to one. This is

really just another way of writing $f(v_t|v_0)$, the mass function corresponding to $F(v_t|v_0)$, if the latter is discrete. For fixed and known v_0 we have $\boldsymbol{\rho}_0' = \{0, 0, \ldots, 1, 0, \ldots, 0\}$, where the "1" corresponds to the subinterval containing v_0.

The Markov process describing the effects of purchases on a household's probability vector is written

$$\boldsymbol{\rho}_{t+1}(v_0)' = \boldsymbol{\rho}_t(v_0)'\mathbf{M} \tag{5.5}$$

where $\mathbf{M}$ is the $g \times g$ matrix of conditional probabilities for transitions of v_t from value (state) i to value j. Here $\mathbf{M}$ is completely determined by the parameters of the learning model, as can be seen from the following expansion of its ith row:

$$\mathbf{m}_{i.} = \{\Pr[v_{t+1} \in j \,|\, v_t \in i], j = 1, \ldots, g\}$$

$$= \{0, \ldots, 1 - m_i^*, 0, \ldots, 0, m_i^*, 0, \ldots, 0\} \tag{5.6}$$

The conditional probability m_i^* is almost equal to v_t for v_t in cell i, providing the cell length is small. The element m_i^* appears in the column corresponding to the cell in which

$$v_{t+1}(v_0) = \alpha + \beta + \lambda v_t(v_0)$$

falls. That is, for v_t in cell i, the v_{t+1} will take on the value given by applying the purchase operator to v_t, with probability $v_t \approx m_i$. Similarly, v_{t+1} will take on the value given by the rejection operator with probability $1 - v_t \approx 1 - m_i$. These arguments hold for all i cells of the transition matrix. Then $\mathbf{M}$ is a nonsymmetric stochastic matrix with two nonzero elements in each row and mostly zeros on the diagonal. (The diagonals will be nonzero only for v_t equal to L or U.) As all the states communicate with one another, we know that $\mathbf{M}$ is ergodic and that the standard theorems for Markov processes apply.

Now it is easy to calculate the probability that v_t will have any particular value, given v_0. Applying Equation 5.5 recursively, starting at v_0, we have

$$\boldsymbol{\rho}_N(v_0)' = \boldsymbol{\rho}_0(v_0)'\mathbf{M}^t \tag{5.7}$$

where $\mathbf{M}^t$ is the t-step transition matrix for the Markov process. Thus, the elements of $\rho_t(v_0)$ and, hence, the values for $f(v_t|v_0)$ can be obtained by raising $\mathbf{M}$ to the proper power and selecting the row corresponding to the value of v_0.

We may also inquire into the distribution of v_t as $t \to \infty$. It has been shown that for a two-event model of the kind considered here that

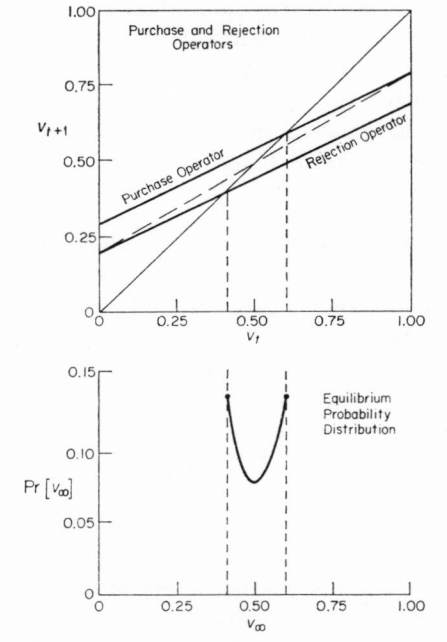

Figure 5.2.   Linear learning model with $\alpha = 0.2$, $\beta = 0.1$, and $\lambda = 0.5$.

$f(v_{t+1}|v_0) \rightarrow f(v_t|v_0)$ as t becomes large.[3] Hence, an asymptotic distribution for v_t exists. It may be approximated by finding the limiting value of $\rho_t(v_0)'$ as $t \rightarrow \infty$. This may be accomplished either by raising $\mathbf{M}$ to successively higher powers until $\mathbf{M}^{t+1} \rightarrow \mathbf{M}^t$ or by solving the determinantal equation implied by

$$\rho_t(v_0)' = \rho_t(v_0)'\mathbf{M}$$
$$0 = \rho_t(v_0)'[\mathbf{M} - \mathbf{I}]$$

The latter method amounts to finding the eigenvector corresponding to the unit eigenvalue of $\mathbf{M}$. Whichever method is chosen, Markov process theory tells us that the asymptotic solution is independent of the initial probability vector $\rho_0(v_0)$, and, hence, it is independent of v_0. (This may be seen by recalling that the rows of $\mathbf{M}^t$ become identical as N becomes large; therefore, all vectors ρ_0 lead to the same limiting ρ_t.) Hence, $f(v_t|v_0) \rightarrow f(v_t)$ as $t \rightarrow \infty$.

An example of limiting learning model distributions, based on hypothetical parameter values, is given in Figure 5.2. (See Figure 5.3

[3] See Bush and Mosteller (1955) p. 99. We have what they call "subject-controlled" events, in that the number of times each operator is applied is determined by purchase events, which in turn are controlled by the decision-making unit.

for a distribution based on real data.) The distribution is constrained between L and U. It is symmetrical because the operators of the model are symmetrical for the given parameters. The distribution is banked up against the two bounds because L and U act as reflecting barriers: Households at U are more likely to repurchase the brand than not, in which case their probability remains at U, and conversely.

5.3   An Early Application of Linear Learning Theory

All of the early empirical work on the linear learning model was performed by Kuehn. In his original study [Kuehn (1958)], he used consumer panel data to test some general hypotheses that, if true, would tend to support the idea that consumer brand choice is an approximately linear adaptive process. As we will see later, these tests did not make direct use of the linear learning model assumptions. Rather, the model was used as a basis for interpreting more general statistical findings. These early findings have been reported in several different articles in which the case for using adaptive models is advanced and the properties of the linear learning model are discussed.[4] In contrast to the published pieces, some of Kuehn's later work has probably been based on methods by which the parameters of the linear learning model are estimated directly from brand switching data, perhaps using methods such as the ones presented in this chapter. Unfortunately, the details of these methods have been a closely guarded secret. Still more recently, some aggregate market share models based in part on linear learning assumptions have been developed and tested.[5] Parameter estimation methods for these models have been provided, but as they utilize time series data on aggregate market shares rather than brand switching statistics, we will not consider them here.

In his original study Kuehn analyzed household brand switching patterns for Snow Crop frozen orange juice. The following discussion provides a summary of his line of reasoning as used in this study.

First, a linear learning model of the type discussed in Section 5.2.1 was postulated. In terms of our notation, the purchase (PO) and rejection (RO) operators are

$$\text{PO}: v_{t+1}^{(1)} = \alpha + \beta + \lambda v_t$$

$$\text{RO}: v_{t+1}^{(0)} = \alpha + \lambda v_t$$

[4] E.g., Kuehn (1962).

[5] See Haines (1964) and others. These aggregate models also incorporate the effects of marketing variables like advertising and promotion.

where v_t is the probability of purchasing Snow Crop on trial t, (1) indicates a purchase of Snow Crop, and (0) is the purchase of another brand. The objective of the analysis was to predict the probability that Snow Crop would be purchased on the $N + 1$ trial from knowledge of the sequence of 1's and 0's on the first N trials. Suppose that $N = 1$ and that the particular sequence (0) has been observed. If the household's v_0 is known, the desired probability is (in terms of the notation in Section 5.2.1)

$$\Pr[1|(0), v_0] = v^{(0)}(v_0) = \alpha + \lambda v_0$$

Similarly,

$$\Pr[1|(00), v_0] = v^{(00)}(v_0) = \alpha + \lambda(\alpha + \lambda v_0) = \alpha + \alpha\lambda + \lambda^2 v_0$$

$$\Pr[1|(01), v_0] = v^{(01)}(v_0) = \alpha + \beta + \lambda(\alpha + \lambda v_0) = \alpha + \beta + \alpha\lambda + \lambda^2 v_0$$

$$\Pr[1|(10), v_0] = v^{(10)}(v_0) = \alpha + \lambda(\alpha + \beta + \lambda v_0) = \alpha + \alpha\lambda + \beta\lambda + \lambda^2 v_0$$

$$\Pr[1|(11), v_0] = v^{(11)}(v_0) = \alpha + \beta + \lambda(\alpha + \beta + \lambda v_0)$$
$$= \alpha + \beta + \alpha\lambda + \beta\lambda + \lambda^2 v_0 \qquad (5.8)$$

The general pattern by which $v^{(S)}(v_0)$ can be computed for any (S) is now clear. For instance,

$$v^{(1101000101)}(v_0) = (\alpha + \beta) + \alpha\lambda + (\alpha + \beta)\lambda^2 + \alpha\lambda^3 + \alpha\lambda^4 + \alpha\lambda^5$$
$$+ (\alpha + \beta)\lambda^6 + \alpha\lambda^7 + (\alpha + \beta)\lambda^8 + (\alpha + \beta)\lambda^9 + \lambda^{10} v_0$$

Consider the case where $N = 3$. Then,

$$v^{(000)}(v_0) = \alpha + \alpha\lambda + \alpha\lambda^2 + \lambda^3 v_0$$

We can use $v^{(000)}(v_0)$ as a base and inquire about how much each purchase of Snow Crop adds to this "complete rejection" probability. By subtracting the expression for $v^{(000)}(v_0)$ from that for each possible sequence involving at least one Snow Crop purchase, we see that the sequence:

001	adds	β
010	adds	$\beta\lambda$
100	adds	$\beta\lambda^2$
011	adds	$\beta + \beta\lambda$
101	adds	$\beta + \beta\lambda^2$
110	adds	$\beta\lambda + \beta\lambda^2$
111	adds	$\beta + \beta\lambda + \beta\lambda^2$

(5.9)

That is, a purchase of Snow Crop in a particular spot in the sequence adds a fixed amount to the probability that Snow Crop will be purchased

at trial $N + 1$. Furthermore:

1. Purchase decisions on previous trials are geometrically weighted by a factor λ. That is, the effects go down by λ^k as k goes $1, 2, \ldots$, units into the past.

2. What happens on trial $t + i$ does not affect the weighting of what happens on trial $t + j$. That is, the weightings are independent.

Recall, however, that these results depend on the fact that all families have the same v_0.

Kuehn uses the factorial analysis of variance technique and was able to isolate the effects of purchase decisions on each trial in the past upon the probability of purchasing Snow Crop on trial $N + 1$. He took $N = 4$ and defined four main effects as purchase on trial k, where $k = 1, \ldots, 4$. The interactions are defined as the influence of trial i on the effect of trial k, where $i \neq k$: By proposition 2, these interaction effects should be negligible.

Kuehn uses the past history of (0000) as a base, and his results showed that

> Trial 4 adds 0.321
> Trial 3 adds 0.198
> Trial 2 adds 0.127, and
> Trial 1 adds 0.141

to the probability as measured on Trial 5. The interactions were in fact negligible, as would be predicted by the theory. Kuehn also gives a plausible explanation why the effect of Trial 1 should be higher than that for Trial 2: In effect, the first trial in the sequence is picking up the cumulative effects of previous trials.

The effects for Trials 2, 3, and 4 follow the predicted geometric pattern quite closely. Following Equation 5.9, we may equate the effects of Trials 3 and 4 to $\beta\lambda$ and β, respectively. (Then α can be approximately estimated from $P^{(0000)}$, given $\hat{\beta}$ and $\hat{\lambda}$.) Thus,

$$\beta = 0.32 \quad \text{and} \quad \lambda = \frac{0.198}{\hat{\beta}} = 0.62$$

Then we would predict an effect of $\beta\lambda^2 = 0.122$ for Trial 2, which is quite close to the observed value of 0.127. These results can be used to predict the probability values, conditional on different sequences of length 4. The empirical proportions, predicted values, and deviations from the predictions are presented in Table 5.1.

Kuehn's main conclusion was that the brand sequence of a customer's past purchases is a good predictor of the brand he is likely to buy in the

Table 5.1 Comparison of Observed and Predicted Probability of Purchasing Snow Crop Given the Four Previous Brand Purchases*

Previous Purchase Pattern (1)	Sample Size (2)	Observed Probability of Purchase (3)	Predicted Probability of Purchase (4)	Deviation of Predictions (5)
SSSS	1047	0.806	0.832	+0.026
OSSS	277	0.690	0.691	+0.001
SOSS	206	0.665	0.705	+0.040
SSOS	222	0.595	0.634	+0.039
SSSO	296	0.486	0.511	+0.025
OOSS	248	0.552	0.564	+0.012
SOOS	138	0.565	0.507	−0.058
OSOS	149	0.497	0.493	−0.004
SOSO	163	0.405	0.384	−0.021
OSSO	181	0.414	0.370	−0.044
SSOO	256	0.305	0.313	+0.008
OOOS	500	0.330	0.366	+0.033
OOSO	404	0.191	0.243	+0.052
OSOO	433	0.129	0.172	+0.043
SOOO	557	0.154	0.186	+0.032
OOOO	8442	0.048	0.045	−0.003

* Ronald E. Frank, Alfred A. Kuehn, and William F. Massy (1962), *Quantitative Techniques in Marketing Analysis*, Richard D. Irwin, Inc., Homewood, Illinois, p. 394.

future. One cannot argue with this conclusion; his figures prove exactly that. (E.g., a person with a history 1111 is much more likely to purchase Snow Crop on the next trial than one with history 0000.) Kuehn applied the methods of Miller and Frick (1949) to determine the quantity of information (in the information theory sense) that is gained by adding each observation to the past history.

One can take exception to Kuehn's conclusions about the efficacy of the linear learning model on at least two counts. First, other models can yield predictions about the probability of a purchase at trial $N + 1$ given outcomes on trials $1, \ldots, N$ that are as good as or perhaps better than the ones given here in Table 5.1. Frank (1962) attempted to show this, although in a rather roundabout way, by postulating that brand choice is a stable (e.g., nonadaptive) probability process at the level of the individual but that individual differences in p produce differential conditional probabilities. (This model is discussed extensively in Chapter 3.) Unfortunately, his methods did not provide an

unambiguous test of the relative merits of the two models. More recently, other models that might explain the trial-ordering effect have been proposed. In addition to the ones discussed elsewhere in this book, Herniter (1965) has given some results from Howard's (1965) dynamic inference model which compare favorably to those given in Table 5.1. While different models may give nearly the same results, there are profound differences in their implications for customer brand-choice behavior.

A second difficulty with Kuehn's conclusion is that there is an error in the procedure he used to assess the efficacy of the model. Recall that Equation 5.9, which is used to justify the learning model interpretations from the analysis of variance, was derived under the assumption that all families have the same value for v_0. We will briefly sketch the situation where this is not true. From the foregoing derivations, we can see that when $N = 4$,

$$\Pr[1|(s), v_0] = \text{(terms involving only } \alpha, \beta, \text{ and } \lambda) + \lambda^4 v_0$$

But the data used to obtain the empirical p in Table 5.1 are not conditioned on v_0. Rather, we must assume that the various people included in the "n" for each row of the table have different v_0. If we regard the people included in the "n" for each row as having come to us by some random process that has $f(v_0|(s))$ as its distribution of v_0 (here (s) denotes the subsample corresponding to the corresponding row of the table), then the probability prediction from the model that is relevant for comparing against the data is

$$\Pr[1|(s)] = \int_0^1 \Pr[1|(s), v_0] f(v_0|(s)) \, dv_0$$

$$= \text{(terms involving only } \alpha, \beta, \lambda) + \lambda^4 \, E[v_0|(s)] \qquad (5.10)$$

where the terms inside the parentheses are the same as in the previous equation.

By the arguments of Chapter 3 as well as by common sense, we would expect that $E[v_0|(0000)] < E[v_0|(1111)]$, and similarly for other pairs of sequences involving grossly different proportions of ones and zeros. In other words, people who bought Snow Crop infrequently are more likely to have had a low initial probability than those who bought it often. It is possible that some of the differences among the $E[v_0|(s)]$ may be relatively large — in fact, all indications point to the truth of this. But, if the differences are important, it is impossible to subtract the values of $\Pr[1|(0000)]$ from the various values of $\Pr[1|(s)]$, as is required to get Equation 5.9, unless λ is small. Thus, we cannot form

predictions about the probabilities on trial $N + 1$ without knowing the value of $E[v_0|(s)]$ for each sequence. It is also clear that estimates of effects based on methods that ignore the influence of $E[v_0|(s)]$ run the risk of being badly biased.

It is hard to say much about how the preceding considerations should affect our assessment of Kuehn's original study. On the one hand, we see that $E[v_0|(s)]$ is multiplied by λ^4, which from his data is about $0.62^4 = 0.15$. Thus, if the differences among the $E[v_0|(s)]$ are only as high as 0.1 or 0.2, the error introduced is of the same order of magnitude as his calculated residuals (column 5 of the table). This might be taken as either positive or negative evidence about the fit of the learning model. On the other hand, as λ gets closer to one, the effect goes up quickly. It is impossible to know what bias is involved in the estimation of λ under the given circumstances.

Our most objective conclusion (pending a reanalysis of his data later in this chapter) is that Kuehn's data do exhibit adaptive properties. However, we cannot trust the specific predictions he obtains or the implied estimates of parameters. The problem boils down to one of handling the heterogeneity of the initial v_0, as correctly suggested by Frank. Methods for handling this problem will be presented later in this chapter.

5.4 Macrotheory and Parameter Estimation

The estimation methods discussed in Chapter 2 and applied to Bernoulli and Markov models in Chapters 3 and 4 can also be used for linear learning models, providing we can develop suitable expressions for the theoretical response probabilities. We recall from our discussion of Kuehn's procedures, in Section 5.3, that these expressions must not depend on the assumption of homogeneous v_0. Thus, we are led to consider a more unified macrotheory for the linear learning model.

5.4.1 *Macrotheory for Response Proportions*

In Section 5.2.2 we considered the conditional probability $\Pr[1|(s), v_0]$, that is, the probability of a "1" given v_0 and a particular purchase sequence (s). However, we found that when we take expectations over v_0, we are left with a different $E[v_0|(s)]$ — one for each (s) — plus α, β, and λ from only k empirical proportions, which is impossible. Thus, we shall have to develop other ways of defining response categories.

Consider the joint probability of observing all the responses in a given sequence of length N. Following a line of reasoning such as that

used in Section 5.2.2, we have for $N = 2$,

$$\Pi_{11}\{v_0\} = v_0 \cdot v_1^{(1)}\{v_0\} = v_0(\alpha + \beta + \lambda v_0) = (\alpha + \beta)v_0 + \lambda v_0^2$$

$$\Pi_{01}\{v_0\} = (1 - v_0) \cdot v_1^{(0)}\{v_0\} = (1 - v_0)(\alpha + \lambda v_0)$$

$$= \alpha + (\lambda - \alpha)v_0 - \lambda v_0^2$$

$$\Pi_{10}\{v_0\} = v_0 \cdot (1 - v_1^{(0)}\{v_0\}) = v_0(1 - \alpha - \beta - \lambda v_0) \qquad (5.11)$$

$$= (1 - \alpha - \beta)v_0 - \lambda v_0^2$$

$$\Pi_{00}\{v_0\} = (1 - v_0)(1 - v_1^{(1)}\{v_0\}) = (1 - v_0)(1 - \alpha - \lambda v_0)$$

$$= (1 - \alpha) + (\alpha - \lambda - 1)v_0 + \lambda v_0^2$$

where $\Pi_{ij}\{v_0\} = \Pr[\text{sequence } ij|v_0]$. It is easily verified that the four probabilities sum to unity regardless of the value of v_0. The expressions for the Π differ from those for the v, given in Equation 5.8, in that the probabilities of the various events in the sequence are multiplied together in addition to introducing the expression for v_t in terms of v_0. The joint probabilities for higher order sequences ($N > 2$), conditional on v_0, can be obtained in a similar manner.

Let us define $f(v_0)$ as the prior distribution of v_0. In this case $f(v_0)$ applies to all families in the panel, as no conditioning in terms of past purchase events has been invoked. The prior distribution $f(v_0)$ is arbitrary: That is, the model can handle any prior distribution, whether generated from the previous action of the linear learning model or induced by changes in market conditions.[6]

The unconditional probability of observing each sequence (assuming a family is sampled at random from the population) is

$$\Pr[\text{sequence } ij] = \Pi_{ij} = \int_0^1 \Pi_{ij}(v_0)f(v_0)\,dv_0$$

[6] If the prior distribution $f(v_0)$ is the steady-state distribution generated by a linear learning model with the same parameters as the current process, μ_1 and μ_2 depend only on α, β, and λ. In Equation 5.4 we showed that

$$\lim_{t \to 0} \mathrm{E}[v_t|v_0] = \frac{\alpha}{1 - \beta - \lambda} = \bar{v}_\infty$$

which in turn is equal to μ_1 under these conditions. A similar expression could be derived for μ_2. Thus, if $f(v_0)$ can be assumed to be the "steady-state" distribution of the process, we have only three parameters to estimate (α, β, and λ), not five as indicated in the text. This assumption requires long-run stationarity of the process, which is very stringent. We prefer to deal with an arbitrary prior distribution.

We will illustrate the result with sequence "01."

$$\Pi_{01} = \int_0^1 [\alpha + (\lambda - \alpha)v_0 - \lambda v_0^2] f(v_0)\, dv_0$$

$$= \alpha + (\lambda - \alpha)E[v_0] - \lambda E[v_0^2]$$

$$= \alpha + (\lambda\mu - \alpha)\mu_1 - \lambda\mu_2 \qquad (5.12)$$

where μ_1 and μ_2 are the first and second raw moments of $f(v_0)$. This procedure is readily applied to the other sequences in Equation 5.11. As noted, μ_1 and μ_2 are moments of the prior distribution for the population as a whole; they are in effect additional parameters of the model. The Π give the theoretical frequencies that we should expect to obtain if the learning model holds exactly and we have parameters α, β, λ, μ_1, and μ_2.

Attempts to estimate the parameters of the linear learning model from purchase sequences of length two must fail. Two purchases generate four response categories, but since the four probabilities must sum to one, there are only three degrees of freedom. However, we must estimate five parameters. The situation becomes better if we consider purchase sequences of length three. Extension of Equations 5.11 and 5.12 shows that the expression for the Π depends on one additional moment of $f(v_0)$. (In general, there are as many moments of $f(v_0)$ in the expressions for the Π as there are terms in the purchase sequence.) The results for the three-purchase case are provided in Table 5.2. For sequences of length three, we have to estimate six parameters from data on seven independent response categories, which leaves one degree of freedom for error. If we use sequences of length four, we have seven parameters (α, β, and λ plus μ_1 through μ_4) and 15 independent response categories. The resulting eight degrees of freedom for error appears to be adequate, though one might like additional power. The methods used to generate the empirical results given later in this chapter are based on purchase sequences of length four.

It is also possible to write expressions for the theoretical probabilities for conditioned purchase history. We have already seen these results for the case where the probability of purchase on the fifth trial was obtained, conditional on the outcomes for Trials 1 to 4 and v_0. (See Equations 5.8 and 5.9.) Other ways of partitioning purchase histories into conditioned sequences and response categories are also possible. The following rather curious method for partitioning histories of length four will be useful in the development of an approximate parameter estimation method:

Let group (ij) include those individuals ($n^{(ij)}$ in all) who purchase

Table 5.2 Expressions for Expected Proportions of Third-Order Purchase Sequences, Given $f(v_0)$

History: $t_0t_1t_2$	Expected Proportion	Term Multiplying:			
		Constant Term	$\mu_1 = \mathrm{E}[v_0]$	$\mu_2 = \mathrm{E}[v_0^2]$	$\mu_3 = \mathrm{E}[v_0^3]$
111	Π_{111}	—	$\alpha^2 + 2\alpha\beta + 2\alpha\beta\lambda + \alpha^2\lambda + \beta^2\lambda + \beta^2$	$2\alpha\lambda^2 + 2\beta\lambda^2 + \alpha\lambda + \beta\lambda$	$+\lambda^3$
011	Π_{011}	$\alpha^2 + \alpha\beta + \alpha^2\lambda$	$-\alpha^2 - \alpha\beta - \alpha^2\lambda + 2\alpha\beta\lambda + \alpha^2\lambda + \beta^2\lambda$	$-2\alpha\lambda^2 - \alpha\lambda - \beta\lambda + \lambda^3$	$-\lambda^3$
101	Π_{101}	—	$-\alpha^2 - \alpha\beta - 2\alpha\beta\lambda - \beta^2\lambda + \alpha\lambda + \beta\lambda$	$-2\alpha\lambda^2 - 2\beta\lambda^2 - \alpha\lambda + \lambda^2$	$+\lambda^3$
001	Π_{001}	$-\alpha^2 - \alpha^2\lambda + \alpha + \alpha\lambda$	$\alpha^2 + \alpha^2\lambda - 2\alpha\beta\lambda - 2\alpha\lambda^2 - \alpha + \lambda^2$	$2\alpha\lambda^2 + \alpha\lambda - \lambda^3 - \lambda^2$	$-\lambda^3$
110	Π_{110}	—	$-\alpha^2 - 2\alpha\beta\lambda - \alpha^2\lambda - \beta^2\lambda + \alpha + \beta$	$-2\alpha\lambda^2 - 2\beta\lambda^2 - \alpha\lambda - \beta\lambda + \lambda$	$-\lambda^3$
010	Π_{010}	$-\alpha^2 - \alpha\beta - \alpha^2\lambda + \alpha$	$\alpha^2 + \alpha\beta + \alpha^2\lambda - 2\alpha\beta\lambda - \alpha^2\lambda - \alpha\lambda + \alpha + \lambda$	$2\alpha\lambda^2 + \alpha\lambda + \beta\lambda - \lambda^3 - \lambda$	$+\lambda^3$
100	Π_{100}	—	$\alpha^2 + \alpha\beta + 2\alpha\beta\lambda + \alpha^2\lambda + \beta^2\lambda - \beta\lambda - \alpha + \beta$	$2\alpha\lambda^2 + 2\beta\lambda^2 + \alpha\lambda - \lambda^3 - \lambda^2 - \lambda$	$+\lambda^3$
000	Π_{000}	$\alpha^2 + \alpha^2\lambda - 2\alpha - \alpha\lambda + 1$	$\alpha^2 - \alpha^2\lambda + 2\alpha\beta\lambda + \alpha^2\lambda + \beta^2\lambda - \alpha\lambda - \beta\lambda - 2\alpha - \beta + 1$	$-2\alpha\lambda^2 - \alpha\lambda + \lambda^3 + \lambda^2 + \lambda$	$-\lambda^3$
Sum	$+1$	$+1$	0	0	0

Brand i at t_1 and j at t_2. Denote $P_{hk}^{(ij)}$ as the proportion of people *in this group* who purchase Brand h at t_0 and k at t_3.

The four groups ($i = 0, 1; j = 0, 1$) and four proportions in each group ($h = 0, 1; k = 0, 1$) make up the necessary 16 combinations of four things taken two at a time. Table 5.3 presents the expected proportions for these 16 sequences, arranged by group. They are obtained by first forming pairs of individual probabilities such as $v_{t_0}v_{t_3}$ (purchase of Brand 1 at t_0 and t_3) and substituting the appropriate combination of purchase and rejection operators for v_3, conditional on the history for t_1 and t_2 specified by the group definition. Integration over $f(v_0|(ij))$ is performed for each group separately. It is important to realize that a different $f(v_0|(ij))$, and hence different values for the $\mu_i^{(ij)}$, must be specified for each group. By and large, people who purchase Brand 1 at t_1 and t_2 will have different initial probabilities than those who purchase 0 on these two occasions. The reasons for this have already been discussed. This case must be carefully distinguished from the one where joint probabilities that are not conditioned on any particular purchase outcomes are obtained (e.g., $\Pi_{1111} = v_{t_0}v_{t_1}v_{t_2}v_{t_3}$).

The only quantities that are directly observable from panel data are the empirical proportions P_{ij} (or $P_{ij}...$ depending on the length of the purchase sequence chosen). Since we have no way of knowing the true v_0 for any individual, we cannot estimate any of the micro $v_{ij}\{v_0\}$ but must restrict ourselves to quantities represented in the aggregate model. In addition to the three basic learning model parameters, these include the raw moments of the distribution of initial probabilities: $\mu_1, \mu_2, \dots$. Therefore, these parameters must also be estimated from the set of sample proportions.

5.4.2 *Maximum Likelihood Estimates*

Suppose that we were to select an individual household at random from the population. Before observing his actual purchase history, we would like to make a priori statements about the probability that this family will turn out to have any particular purchase sequence. If the learning model holds and we know the necessary parameters, the probability statements for sequences of length three are given by the expressions in Table 5.2. Similar though more complicated expressions can be derived for longer sequences.

The expressions in Table 5.2 determine a probability mass function (a discrete "density function") over the set of mutually exclusive and exhaustive events making up the eight response categories. This mass

Table 5.3 Expressions for Expected Proportions of Fourth-Order Purchase Sequences Conditional on the Outcome of the Second and Third Purchases, Given $f(v_0|(ij))$

History: $t_0 t_1 t_2 t_3$	Expected Proportion	Constant Term	Term Multiplying:	
			$\mu_1 = \mathrm{E}[v_0|(ij)]$	$\mu_2 = \mathrm{E}[v_0^2|(ij)]$
1111	$\Pi_{11}^{(11)}$	—	$\alpha + \beta + \alpha\lambda + \beta\lambda + \alpha\lambda^2 + \beta\lambda^2$	λ^3
0111	$\Pi_{01}^{(11)}$	$\alpha + \beta + \alpha\lambda + \beta\lambda + \alpha\lambda^2$	$-\alpha - \beta - \alpha\lambda - \beta\lambda - \alpha\lambda^2 + \lambda^3$	$-\lambda^3$
1110	$\Pi_{10}^{(11)}$	—	$-\alpha - \beta - \alpha\lambda - \beta\lambda - \alpha\lambda^2 - \beta\lambda^2 + 1$	$-\lambda^3$
0110	$\Pi_{00}^{(11)}$	$-\alpha - \beta - \alpha\lambda - \beta\lambda - \alpha\lambda^2 + 1$	$\alpha + \beta + \alpha\lambda + \beta\lambda + \alpha\lambda^2 - \lambda^3 - 1$	λ^3
1011	$\Pi_{11}^{(01)}$	—	$\alpha + \beta + \alpha\lambda + \alpha\lambda^2 + \beta\lambda^2$	λ^3
0011	$\Pi_{01}^{(01)}$	$\alpha + \beta + \alpha\lambda + \alpha\lambda^2$	$-\alpha - \beta - \alpha\lambda - \alpha\lambda^2 + \lambda^3$	$-\lambda^3$
1010	$\Pi_{10}^{(01)}$	—	$-\alpha - \beta - \alpha\lambda - \alpha\lambda^2 - \beta\lambda^2 + 1$	$-\lambda^3$
0010	$\Pi_{00}^{(01)}$	$-\alpha - \beta - \alpha\lambda - \alpha\lambda^2 + 1$	$\alpha + \beta + \alpha\lambda + \alpha\lambda^2 - \lambda^3 - 1$	λ^3
1101	$\Pi_{11}^{(10)}$	—	$\alpha + \alpha\lambda + \beta\lambda + \alpha\lambda^2 + \beta\lambda^2$	λ^3
0101	$\Pi_{01}^{(10)}$	$\alpha + \alpha\lambda + \beta\lambda + \alpha\lambda^2$	$-\alpha - \alpha\lambda - \beta\lambda - \alpha\lambda^2 + \lambda^3$	$-\lambda^3$
1100	$\Pi_{10}^{(10)}$	—	$-\alpha - \alpha\lambda - \beta\lambda - \alpha\lambda^2 - \beta\lambda^2 + 1$	$-\lambda^3$
0100	$\Pi_{00}^{(10)}$	$-\alpha - \alpha\lambda - \beta\lambda - \alpha\lambda^2 + 1$	$\alpha + \alpha\lambda + \beta\lambda + \alpha\lambda^2 - \lambda^3 - 1$	λ^3
1001	$\Pi_{11}^{(00)}$	—	$\alpha + \alpha\lambda + \alpha\lambda^2 + \beta\lambda^2$	λ^3
0001	$\Pi_{01}^{(00)}$	$\alpha + \alpha\lambda + \alpha\lambda^2$	$-\alpha - \alpha\lambda - \alpha\lambda^2 + \lambda^3$	$-\lambda^3$
1000	$\Pi_{10}^{(00)}$	—	$-\alpha - \alpha\lambda - \alpha\lambda^2 - \beta\lambda^2 + 1$	$-\lambda^3$
0000	$\Pi_{00}^{(00)}$	$-\alpha - \alpha\lambda - \alpha\lambda^2 + 1$	$\alpha + \alpha\lambda + \alpha\lambda^2 - \lambda^3 - 1$	λ^3
Sum*	$+1$	$+1$	0	0

* Holds for each group separately.

function applies to all households that might be drawn from the underlying population. Hence, it holds for each and every household represented in our panel (we regard the panel as a "random" sample from some population). It is also reasonable to regard the households as being statistically independent of one another.

Now, the number of households in our sample that will end up in each response category would be a random variable even if v_0 were known for each family. Thus, the determination of the empirical proportions represents a second stage of random sampling, just as was the case in Chapters 3 and 4. In terms of Frank's (1960) original double sampling scheme, we first regard v_0 as having been drawn at random and then draw for the response category. The Π in Table 5.2 have had the condition on v_0 removed by integration over $f(v_0)$. Hence, the draws for the response category can be regarded as being made from independent and identical distributions.

The form of the probability distribution of the empirical P, given the Π, is of course well known. It is the multinomial,

$$f\{\mathbf{P}|\,\mathbf{\Pi}(\boldsymbol{\theta})\} = \text{const} \prod_{g=0}^{k} \Pi_g(\boldsymbol{\theta})^{P_g}$$

where

$$\boldsymbol{\theta} = \{\alpha, \beta, \lambda, \mu_1, \mu_2, \ldots\}$$

and $\mathbf{P}$ and $\mathbf{\Pi}(\boldsymbol{\theta})$ are vectors over the k response categories. (We write $\mathbf{\Pi}(\boldsymbol{\theta})$ as an explicit function of the model's parameters $\boldsymbol{\theta}$.) Once the sample P have been observed, we write the log of the likelihood as

$$\log L = \text{const} + \sum_{g=0}^{k} P_g \log \Pi_g(\boldsymbol{\theta}) \tag{5.13}$$

We may obtain efficient parameter estimates by maximizing Equation 5.13 with respect to the elements of $\boldsymbol{\theta}$. While a glance at Table 5.2 shows that it will be impossible to do this by analytical means (i.e., we cannot find closed-form expressions for $\hat{\boldsymbol{\theta}}$ in terms of $\mathbf{P}$), the numerical procedures discussed in the Appendix can be used to good advantage. Care must be taken, however, because Equation 5.13 will rarely if ever be concave in the parameters.

5.4.3 Minimum Chi-Square Estimates

In practical terms, the procedure for obtaining minimum chi-square estimates is not much different from that for maximum likelihood. Following the methods of Section 2.2.2.1, we write the chi-square function, which is an index of the discrepancy between the respective

elements of **P** and **Π**, as

$$\chi^2 = n \sum_{g=1}^{k} \frac{[P_g - \Pi_g(\mathbf{\theta})]^2}{\Pi_g(\mathbf{\theta})} \qquad (5.14)$$

This must be minimized with respect to $\mathbf{\theta}$. It is clear that analytical solution methods will not work for Equation 5.14 any more than they would for the likelihood function. Nor does replacing $\Pi_g(\mathbf{\theta})$ in the denominator by P_g, which yields a modified minimum chi-square estimator, simplify the expression enough to permit an analytical solution. But once again we can fall back on numerical methods.

5.4.4   A Simple Modified Chi-Square Estimator

While the minimum chi-square and maximum likelihood estimation are practical if fairly large-scale computation facilities are available, it would be desirable to have an easier method by which rough parameter estimates could be obtained. In the particular modified minimum chi-square procedure to be presented here, we simplify the required computations drastically at the expense of the number of degrees of freedom for error and the use of the modified rather than regular chi-square criterion function. Thus, our parameter estimates will be somewhat less efficient (in the second-order sense) and our tests of fit somewhat less powerful than for the methods presented in the previous sections.

Consider the expected proportions of people who purchase Brand h at time t_0 and Brand k at t_3, given that they purchased i at t_1 and j at t_2. The expressions for these expectations were given in Table 5.3. The proportions can be estimated from the relative frequencies in the panel data: In this case,

$$P_{hk}^{(ij)} = \frac{n_{nk}^{(ij)}}{n_{..}^{(ij)}} = \frac{n_{hijk}}{n_{.ij.}}$$

We begin by summing the first and third equations in each of the four groups in Table 5.3. The results give Π that can be compared to the empirical proportions for the following four composite response categories

$$P_{1.}^{(ij)} = P_{11}^{(ij)} + P_{10}^{(ij)} \qquad i, j = 0, 1$$

Addition of these pairs of equations yields the following expressions for the Π:

$$\Pi_{1.}^{(ij)} = \Pi_{11}^{(ij)} + \Pi_{10}^{(ij)} = \mu_1^{(ij)} \qquad i, j = 0, 1$$

That is, the theoretical proportion of people in the (ij)th group who purchase Brand "1" on their first trial (at t_0) is equal to the expected

value of $v_0^{(ij)}$. There is nothing to prevent us from setting up a measure of discrepancy between $\Pi_{1.}^{(ij)}$ and $P_{1.}^{(ij)}$ and minimizing with respect to the only relevant parameter $\mu_1^{(ij)}$. The minimum chi-square formula is

$$\chi^2 = \sum_{ij} n_{.ij.} \left[\frac{(P_{1.}^{(ij)} - \Pi_{1.}^{(ij)})^2}{\Pi_{1.}^{(ij)}} + \frac{(P_{1.}^{(ij)} - \Pi_{1.}^{(ij)})^2}{1 - \Pi_{1.}^{(ij)}} \right]$$

The solution is of course trivial: $\mu_1^{(ij)} = P_{1.}^{(ij)}$ for each i, j. Exactly the same solution would be obtained from the corresponding maximum likelihood procedure.

The fact that these estimators for the μ_1 are BAN (which follows from this) is of great importance, because it allows us to substitute them into new likelihood or chi-square expressions and obtain BAN estimates of the other parameters. In effect, we have shown that the estimating criterion functions are separable in $\mu_1^{(ij)}$ for this model.[7]

To obtain estimates of α, β, and λ, we sum the first two equations in each group of Table 5.3 to obtain:

$$P_{.1}^{(ij)} = P_{11}^{(ij)} + P_{01}^{(ij)} \qquad i, j = 0, 1$$

and
$$\Pi_{.1}^{(11)} = \alpha + \alpha\lambda + \alpha\lambda^2 + \beta + \beta\lambda + (\beta\lambda^2 + \lambda^3)\mu_1^{(11)}$$

$$\Pi_{.1}^{(01)} = \alpha + \alpha\lambda + \alpha\lambda^2 + \beta \qquad\quad + (\beta\lambda^2 + \lambda^3)\mu_1^{(01)}$$

$$\Pi_{.1}^{(10)} = \alpha + \alpha\lambda + \alpha\lambda^2 + \qquad \beta\lambda + (\beta\lambda^2 + \lambda^3)\mu_1^{(01)} \qquad (5.15)$$

$$\Pi_{.1}^{(00)} = \alpha + \alpha\lambda + \alpha\lambda^2 + \qquad\qquad (\beta\lambda^2 + \lambda^3)\mu_1^{(00)}$$

where all the terms involving $\mu_2^{(ij)}$ have dropped out. We can now set up a chi-square function involving the composite response categories corresponding to $P_{.1}^{(ij)}$ and $1 - P_{.1}^{(ij)}$ for each group. For computational purposes, we will use the modified chi-square approximation, wherein the empirical proportions are substituted for the theoretical probabilities in the denominator of each term. (This is acceptable because the sample size for each of the four groups will ordinarily be quite large.) Thus,

$$\text{mod } \chi^2 = \sum_{ij} n_{.ij.} \left[\frac{(P_{.1}^{(ij)} - \Pi_{.1}^{(ij)})^2}{P_{.1}^{(ij)}} + \frac{(P_{.1}^{(ij)} - \Pi_{.1}^{(ij)})^2}{1 - P_{.1}^{(ij)}} \right]$$

$$= \sum_{ij} n_{.ij.} \frac{(P_{.1}^{(ij)} - \Pi_{.1}^{(ij)})^2}{P_{.1}^{(ij)}(1 - P_{.1}^{(ij)})} \qquad (5.16)$$

Each term in the sum over ij contributes one degree of freedom, and so as the groups are independent, there is a total of four degrees of freedom available for estimating α, β, and λ.

---

[7] The same is true for the procedures discussed in Sections 5.4.2 and 5.4.3, if we should care to make use of this fact.

The objective function in Equation 5.16 can be minimized by assuming a series of trial values for λ and solving for α and β, conditional on each λ, by conventional methods. Let us define the following new variables:

$$w^{(ij)} = \sqrt{\frac{n_{.ij.}}{P_{.1}^{(ij)}(1 - P_{.1}^{(ij)})}} \qquad \text{all } ij$$

$$y_\lambda^{(ij)} = P_{.1}^{(ij)} - \lambda^3 P_{1.}^{(ij)} \qquad \text{all } ij$$

$$x_\lambda^{(ij)} = 1 + \lambda + \lambda^2 \qquad \text{all } ij$$

$$z_\lambda^{(11)} = 1 + \lambda + \lambda^2 P_{1.}^{(11)} \qquad (5.17)$$

$$z_\lambda^{(01)} = 1 \qquad\quad + \lambda^2 P_{1.}^{(01)}$$

$$z_\lambda^{(10)} = \qquad \lambda + \lambda^2 P_{1.}^{(10)}$$

$$z_\lambda^{(00)} = \qquad\qquad \lambda^2 P_{1.}^{(00)}$$

Then

$$\operatorname{mod} \chi_\lambda^2 = \sum_{ij} [w^{(ij)} y_\lambda^{(ij)} - \alpha w^{(ij)} x_\lambda^{(ij)} - \beta w^{(ij)} z_\lambda^{(ij)}]^2 \qquad (5.18)$$

as can be seen by substituting Equation 5.17 into Equation 5.15 and comparing the result with Equation 5.16. This is, of course, conditional on a particular value of λ. Minimization of the chi-square conditional on λ is accomplished by minimizing Equation 5.18 with respect to α and β. This can be done by involving standard linear regression theory. The term wy_λ is taken as the dependent variable, and wx_λ and wz_λ are taken as independent variables. (The "regression" is forced through the origin as there is no constant term in Equation 5.18.) The set in ij provides the regression with four independent observations with which to estimate α and β for each λ. Choosing the value of λ, and its associated α and β, for which the χ^2 (sum of squared errors for the regression) is minimum completes the estimation process.

If estimates of the $\mu_2^{(ij)}$ are desired, they can be obtained from this set of relations:

$$\hat{\mu}_2^{(11)} = \frac{P_{1.}^{(11)}}{\lambda^3} [P_{11}^{(11)} - (\alpha + \beta + \alpha\lambda + \beta\lambda + \alpha\lambda^2 + \beta\lambda^2)]$$

$$\hat{\mu}_2^{(01)} = \frac{P_{1.}^{(01)}}{\lambda^3} [P_{11}^{(01)} - (\alpha + \beta + \alpha\lambda \qquad\quad + \alpha\lambda^2 + \beta\lambda^2)]$$

$$\hat{\mu}_2^{(10)} = \frac{P_{1.}^{(10)}}{\lambda^3} [P_{11}^{(10)} - (\alpha \qquad\quad + \alpha\lambda + \beta\lambda + \alpha\lambda^2 + \beta\lambda^2)] \qquad (5.19)$$

$$\hat{\mu}_2^{(00)} = \frac{P_{1.}^{(00)}}{\lambda^3} [P_{11}^{(00)} - (\alpha \qquad\quad + \alpha\lambda \qquad\quad + \alpha\lambda^2 + \beta\lambda^2)]$$

This procedure uses the remaining degree of freedom in each (ij) group to obtain a BAN estimate of $\mu_2^{(ij)}$, given the values of the BAN estimates of the other parameters.

To summarize the results of this section, we have partitioned the chi-square criterion function into the following components, each of which depends on the data vector $\mathbf{P}$:

1. $\chi^2(\mu_1)$
2. $\chi^2(\alpha,\beta|\lambda,\mu_1)$
3. $\chi^2(\alpha,\beta,\lambda|\mu_1)$
4. $\chi^2(\mu_2|\alpha,\beta,\lambda,\mu_1)$

Function 1 is minimized first to obtain μ_1. Then Function 2 is minimized for each of a number of trial values for λ; the value giving the minimum χ^2 here is also the minimum for Function 3. Finally, Function 4 is minimized to obtain $\hat{\mu}_2$. The fact of simple closed form expression for the minima of Functions 1, 2, and 4 makes the short-form estimation procedure easy and practical. On the other hand, the short method provides only one degree of freedom for error, as compared with eight available for the procedures given in Sections 5.4.2 and 5.4.3. (This implies that goodness-of-fit tests based on short-method results will not be as powerful as their long-method counterparts.) Also, the long form provides estimates of μ_3 and μ_4 for the unconditional $f(v_0)$, which may be useful in some studies.

5.5 Comparison with Other Models

In addition to its intrinsic interest, the linear learning model can be viewed as a generalization of both the zero-order Bernoulli and the first-order Markov models. If $\lambda = 0$, Equation 5.1 becomes independent of v_t. This is equivalent to a Markov model with purchase decisions as states having transition matrix:

$$\{Pr[j|i]\} = \begin{matrix} & 1 & 0 \\ 1 \\ 0 \end{matrix} \begin{bmatrix} \alpha + \beta & 1 - \alpha - \beta \\ \alpha & 1 - \alpha \end{bmatrix}$$

All households are assumed to have the same parameters, even though their initial probabilities v_0 may differ, just as in the case of the learning model. Similarly, if $\alpha = \beta = 0$ and $\lambda = 1$, then $v_{t+1} = v_t$ regardless of the outcome at time t, and so we have a zero-order Bernoulli trials model. If the value of v_0 is assumed to vary over the members of the

population, we have a heterogeneous Bernoulli model of the type considered in Chapter 3.

There is no reason why we cannot use learning model theory and estimation procedures in cases where purchase behavior is suspected to be either Bernoulli or Markov in character. If either hypothesis is true, we will find it out from the data. Kuehn (1962) pointed this out in answer to Frank's (1960) doubts about the efficacy of the learning model. We need hardly add, however, that the comparison of models depends on the use of proper estimating procedures.

To push the process of model evaluation further, we may obtain the following three sets of parameter estimates by the maximum likelihood procedure discussed in Section 5.4.2.

$$
\begin{aligned}
&1.\ \ \hat{\theta}_L = \{\hat{\alpha},\hat{\beta},\hat{\lambda},\hat{\mu}_1,\hat{\mu}_2,\hat{\mu}_3,\hat{\mu}_4\} \\
&2.\ \ \hat{\theta}_M = \{\hat{\alpha},\hat{\beta},0,\hat{\mu}_1,\hat{\mu}_2,\hat{\mu}_3,\cdot\} \\
&3.\ \ \hat{\theta}_B = \{0,0,1,\hat{\mu}_1,\hat{\mu}_2,\hat{\mu}_3,\hat{\mu}_4\}
\end{aligned}
\tag{5.20}
$$

(In Case 2 the likelihood is independent of μ_4 because $\lambda = 0$.) Likelihood ratio tests of the type considered in Section 2.3.3 can be used to test the significance of Case 1 vs. Case 2 and Case 3. Thus, the efficacy of the linear learning assumptions can be easily tested against two "extreme" alternatives.[8]

It is important to remember that the Markov model being estimated in Case 2 of Equation 5.20 is homogeneous in the parameters, even though we allow for heterogeneous v_0. (We can think of the Bernoulli model in this way too, although the fact that it has no "parameters" other than those of $f(v_0)$ does breed terminological confusion.) The

---

[8] The beta-Bernoulli assumption used in Section 3.5 serves to set constraints on the μ. If the beta parameters are "a" and "b" ("α" and "β" in the notation of Chapter 3), then

$$
\mu_1 = \frac{a}{a + b}
$$

$$
\mu_2 = \frac{a(a + 1)}{(a + b)(a + b + 1)}
$$

and similar relations hold for μ_3 and μ_4. (Recall that these are moments about the origin.) For the Markov process, the distribution of v_0 may be thought of in at least two different ways. First, if we assume that the process has been going on prior to t_0, we would expect that $f(v_0)$ would be concentrated at $\alpha + \beta$ and α with probabilities equal to the probabilities for purchase of "1" and "0" at time $t - 1$. On the other hand, if the process has just changed, we might expect that the mass of $f(v_0)$ will be more evenly distributed over the $(0,1)$ interval. The estimated values of the μ in $\hat{\theta}_m$ may help shed some light on these questions.

likelihood ratio tests suggested cannot be used to evaluate the heterogeneous Markov models discussed in Chapter 4 (e.g., the "brand loyal" and "last purchase loyal models"). It is interesting to speculate about the possibilities of applying the methods of Chapter 4 to make the linear learning model heterogeneous in the parameters. However, this will not be an easy task, and it is left as a topic for future research.

The linear learning model also bears a relationship to the probability diffusion models to be discussed in Chapter 6 and 7. Consider Equation 5.2 for the expected probability on the $t + 1$ trial:

$$E[v_{t+1}|v_0] = \alpha + (\beta + \lambda) E[v_t|v_0]$$

which may be written as follows:

$$\bar{v}_{t+h} - \bar{v}_t = h[\alpha - (1 - \beta - \lambda)\bar{v}_t] \qquad (5.21)$$

where $\bar{v}_t$ is written instead of $E[v_t|v_0]$ to simplify notation and $h = 1$ stands for the increment to the process provided by one purchase. Now suppose that the "learning" effect does not occur in one big jump after the purchase event at time t but rather is distributed continuously through time between t and $t + 1$. (For instance, product use may produce learning, and use may occur continuously in time.) This fractionalization of the learning effect can be obtained by letting h become small; for $h = 0.1$, say, we have a change in v between t and $t + 0.1$, another between $t + 0.1$ and $t + 0.2$, and so on. By summing Equation 5.21 over h, it is clear that the total change in the expected probability between t and $t + 1$ has not been changed by fractionalizing the effects.

The time path of expected probabilities for the continuous form of the learning model is obtained by letting h go to zero and solving the resulting differential equation:

$$\lim_{h \to 0} \frac{\bar{v}_{t+h} - \bar{v}_t}{h} = \frac{d\bar{v}_t}{d_t} = \alpha - (1 - \beta - \lambda)\bar{v}_t$$

$$\int \frac{d\bar{v}_t}{\alpha - (1 - \beta - \lambda)\bar{v}_t} = \int dt$$

$$\frac{1}{-(1 - \beta - \lambda)} \log [\alpha - (1 - \beta - \lambda)\bar{v}_t] = t + c$$

$$\alpha - (1 - \beta - \lambda)\bar{v}_t = \exp [-(1 - \beta - \lambda)(t + c)]$$

$$\bar{v}_t = \frac{\alpha}{1 - \beta - \lambda} - c' \exp [-(1 - \beta - \lambda)_t]$$

From Equation 5.4 we know that the first term is $\bar{v}_\infty$, the equilibrium probability. The constant of integration can be evaluated from the initial conditions:

$$\bar{v}_0 = \bar{v}_\infty - c' \exp\left[-(1 - \beta - \lambda)0\right]$$

or

$$c' = \bar{v}_\infty - \bar{v}_0$$

Hence,

$$\bar{v}_t = \bar{v}_\infty + (\bar{v}_\infty - \bar{v}_0) \exp\left[-(1 - \beta - \lambda)t\right] \qquad (5.22)$$

This equation is the continuous analogue of Equation 5.3. It is of the same form as equation (3) of Kuehn and Rohloff (1968), who treat it as a variation of the linear learning model. It is also identical to the mean value function derived for the cohesive elements probability diffusion model, derived in Chapter 6.

The identity with the cohesive elements model tells us that Equation 5.22, and its discrete version in Equation 5.3, does not contain any essential *learning* (feedback of a purchase event) elements. By dealing with expected probabilities only, the learning model is emasculated so that it becomes essentially a model for time changes in v: Any process that produces a linear differential equation in v_t meets the requirements of this version of the model. The really interesting properties of the learning model (as a model about purchase event feedback) show up in the deviation of the probabilities about their mean value function. The primary value of Equation 5.3 and 5.22 is that they give us a way of calculating $\bar{v}_\infty$ from the parameters of the underlying learning model.

5.6 Empirical Results

We have estimated the parameters of the linear learning model on some 21 different sets of data, collected from a variety of sources. The results to be reported in this section are divided into the following three sets:

Set 1:

Snow Crop frozen orange juice. These data were first processed by Kuehn (1958) and are reproduced in our Table 5.1. The raw data were originally obtained from the Chicago Tribune Consumer Panel and cover the period from 1950 through 1952.

Folger's coffee. These data cover Chicago Tribune panel households' first four purchases after the introduction of Folger's coffee to Chicago

in 1959. The same raw data have been analyzed by other methods in Frank and Massy (1963) and Frank, Massy, and Morrison (1964).

No-name beer. These data were collected by Douglas McConnell as part of his experimental study of how consumers build up brand loyalties in the absence of product differences, advertising, or promotional effects [McConnell (1968)]. Members of a panel recruited from the married student housing development at Stanford University were allowed to "purchase" one of these bottles of beer on a series of weekly visits by the experimenter. The beers were labeled Brands *L*, *M*, and *P*; actually, they were all from the same brew lot of a given brand. Relative prices were varied during the course of the experiment. Switching statistics were collected for each household, and empirical properties for sequences of length four were compiled by aggregating data for successive groups of four purchases for the various households. Purchases of Brands *L*, *M*, and *P* are treated as "1" in each of three separate runs, with the others treated as "0."

Set 2:

"Favorite-Brand" coffee data. The data on regular coffee purchasing in Chicago, which were used to test the heterogeneous Bernoulli and Markov models in Chapter 3 and 4, are reanalyzed in terms of the learning model. These data treat each household's favorite brand as "1" and all others as "0." The subgroups ALL, EXCEPT 100 PER-CENTERS, HEAVY, LIGHT, LOYAL, and NONLOYAL (see Section 4.10.1 for definitions) are analyzed separately.

Set 3:

Crest dentifrice data. These data cover purchases of Crest toothpaste by members of MRCA's National Consumer Panel. They were originally obtained for purposes of testing the probability diffusion models to be developed in Chapters 6 and 7. Results of estimating the linear learning model are reported here, though most of our discussion of these data appears in Chapter 7. The households in the panel are divided into four groups on the basis of their average frequency of purchasing toothpaste. Sequences of four purchases just before and just after the American Dental Association's endorsement of Crest are analyzed separately. (See Chapter 7 for detailed definitions of these groupings.)

Sections 5.6.1 through 5.6.3 report the results of estimating the linear learning model parameters on the three sets of data, using the full-scale

eight degrees of freedom (d.f.) minimum chi-square procedure given in Section 5.4.3. The nonlinear programming algorithm described in the Appendix was used to minimize the chi-square function with respect to the parameters. The simple (1 degree of freedom) modified minimum chi-square estimation procedure was also tested on most of the data in Sets 1 and 3. Comparisons of the 1 d.f. results with those from the 8 d.f. procedure are discussed in Section 5.6.4.

Several tests can be applied when judging the performance of the learning model. (1) The goodness of fit can be assessed by examining the chi-squares and associated p-values.[9] (2) The estimates of α, β, and λ should be nonnegative and satisfy the constraint

$$0 \leq \alpha + \beta + \lambda \leq 1$$

as required by linear learning model theory. (3) Values of all the μ should lie between zero and one, since all represent raw moments of a distribution defined on $(0,1)$. In addition, the following relations among the μ are implied by their properties as moments of a strictly positive distribution

$$\mu_1 > \mu_2 > \mu_3 > \mu_4$$

$$\sigma_{v_0}^2 = \mu_2 - \mu_1^2 > 0$$

(4) The values of all the parameters should appear to be reasonable, given the nature of the product class. The first three tests will be applied to each set of learning model estimates. (The fourth question is a moot point in many cases, because there is no way of judging reasonableness given the current state of experience about the learning model.) The matter of constraint satisfaction is of major concern because no constraints on parameters were built into the estimation procedures.

5.6.1   Snow Crop, Folger's, and No-Name Beer

Parameter estimates, chi-squares, and p-values for data set 1 are given in Table 5.4. Chi-squares and p-values for testing the heterogeneous Bernoulli model with an arbitrary prior distribution (see Sections 3.6 and 5.5) are also provided.

---

[9] The p-level is defined as

$$p = \int_x^\infty f_{\chi^2}(z)\, dz$$

where $f_{\chi^2}(z)$ is the chi-square density function and x is the chi-square value given in Table 5.4.

Table 5.4 Linear Learning Model Parameter Estimates for Orange Juice, Coffee, and Beer

Product	α	β	$\alpha + \beta$	λ	μ_1	μ_2	μ_3	μ_4	χ^2_{LL} (8 d.f.)	χ^2_{AB} (11 d.f.)	N
Snow Crop Frozen Orange Juice	0.015	0.305	0.320	0.612	0.214	0.108	0.075	0.048	1.16 (>0.99)*	140.04 (<0.001)	13,519
Folger's Coffee	0.057	0.207	0.264	0.502	0.219	0.027	0.056	0.000	36.23	—†	805
Beer Experiment:											
Brand L	−0.019	0.187	0.168	0.862	0.254	0.082	0.049	0.036	16.36 (0.04)	17.84 (0.09)	1202
Brand M	−0.031	0.203	0.172	0.871	0.414	0.212	0.123	0.079	8.44 (0.40)	15.82 (0.18)	1195
Brand P	−0.017	0.171	0.154	0.896	0.340	0.165	0.100	0.051	19.68 (0.01)	17.46 (0.09)	1200

* Probability of getting a larger χ^2 if the data were generated by the model.
† The five-purchase sequence needed for testing the AB hypothesis was not available.

The chi-square value for the linear learning model (χ^2_{LL}) indicates that Kuehn was right in arguing that his Snow Crop frozen orange juice data were consistent with the learning hypothesis. The probability of getting a chi-square of 1.16 or larger (with 8 d.f.), given that the data were generated from the model, is greater than 0.99. (Rarely does a model fit so well.) In contrast, the test of the arbitrary Bernoulli model (χ^2_{AB}) rejects that hypothesis at well beyond the 0.001 level of significance. This is not surprising because the values of β and λ are not even close to 0 and 1, respectively, which would imply Bernoulli behavior. The large sample size makes the power of both the AB and LL tests rather great, so it is not surprising that one hypothesis is sharply rejected.

It is also worth noting that the values of β and λ estimated by our 8 d.f. minimum chi-square procedure are very close to the ones implied by Kuehn's factorial analysis results:

	β	λ
Our estimates (Table 5.4)	0.305	0.612
Kuehn's estimates (Section 5.3)	0.32	0.62

Apparently the existence of v_0 heterogeneity did not cause any difficulty in this particular case. Perhaps Kuehn's procedure is more robust than the theoretical arguments of Section 5.3 would lead us to believe, though it is impossible to draw a conclusion from a single case. At any rate, the properties of the factorial design approximation to the learning model are no longer important now that exact estimation procedures are available.

Figure 5.3 (top) provides a graphical representation of the estimated parameter values for the Snow Crop data. The rejection operator intercept is $\alpha = 0.015$, while $\alpha + \beta = 0.320$ gives the purchase operator intercept. The upper limit on the purchase probability is $U = (\alpha + \beta)/(1 - \lambda) = 0.825$. The lower limit is $L = \alpha/(1 - \lambda) = 0.040$. The equilibrium probability is obtained from Equation 5.4: $\bar{v}_\infty = \alpha/(1 - \beta - \lambda) = 0.181$. An approximation to the equilibrium distribution of purchase probabilities was obtained by using the Markov method developed in Section 5.2.3, with an interval of 0.02. The shape of the distribution is shown in Figure 5.3 (bottom). Most of the probability is banked up against the lower limit L, with a slight bump at U. The mean of the distribution is $\bar{v}_\infty = 0.181$.

We conclude that the linear learning model provides a very good representation of brand switching behavior for frozen orange juice during the period under study. The fit of the model is very good, and

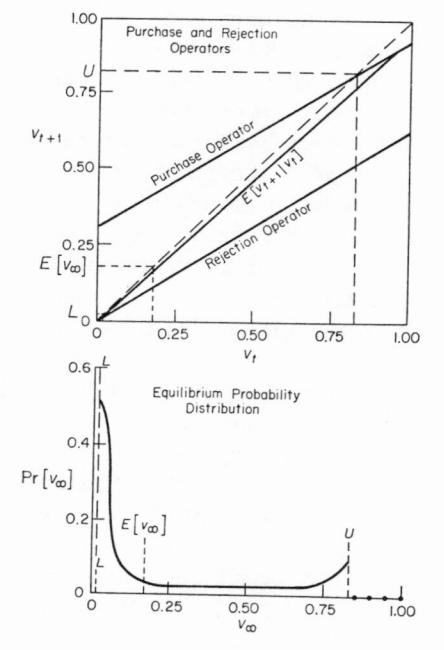

Figure 5.3. Linear learning model as estimated for frozen orange juice.

all the theoretical constraints on the parameters are satisfied. (The only discordant note is that $\bar{v}_\infty < \bar{v}_0 = \mu_1$; thus, the learning model predicts a drop in the market share of Snow Crop which was not borne out by subsequent events.) Kuehn has pointed out (private communication) that the frozen orange juice market did not appear to be highly segmented during the period covered by his study. This implies that, if the learning hypothesis is correct in the first place, most consumers would have the same values of α, β, and λ as assumed by the model. It also seems likely that the orange juice market was relatively free of short-term price fluctuations and deep promotions. Both of these factors would tend to improve the fit of the model.

Our success in applying the linear learning model to the Snow Crop data is highly important. First, it underscores the significance of Kuehn's pioneering work to an extent not possible from previously published empirical results. Second, it gives us confidence in the efficacy of the parameter estimation methods developed earlier in this chapter.

Turning to the other products for which results are presented in

Table 5.4, we see that the learning model does not perform nearly as well for Folger's coffee and the No-name beer experimental data as was the case for frozen orange juice. The chi-square for Folger's rejects the hypothesis that the model fits the data at well beyond the 0.001 level. The learning model is also rejected for beer Brands L and P, at the 0.04 and 0.01 levels, respectively, though the p-level for Brand M is a respectable 0.40. The results for the arbitrary Bernoulli (AB) model are about the same for all three beer brands: with p-levels of 0.09 and 0.18 this model cannot be said to fit the data either. The AB model is a special case of the learning model, and for identical products and a fairly well balanced promotional design there should be no reason to believe that Brand M would perform differently from Brands L and P as far as learning is concerned. Hence, we are forced to conclude that the linear learning model cannot provide a good representation of brand switching behavior in the beer experiment.

This conclusion is reinforced by the fact that the theoretical constraints on the parameters are violated for Folger's coffee and all three brands of beer. For Folger's, $\mu_2 < \mu_3$ and $\sigma_{v_0}^2 < 0$. The variance of v_0 is also negative for all three beer brands. In addition, $\alpha < 0$ (though only slightly), and $\alpha + \beta + \lambda > 1$ for the three beer brands. While the degree of violation of the constraints is small in most cases, which would allow an interpretation and use of the parameters for some purposes, the consistency of the violations casts considerable doubt on the adequacy of the learning model for these data.

We can speculate on some of the reasons for this failure. Folger's was introduced into the Chicago market with a tremendous promotional fanfare, which included both heavy media advertising and very large coupon drops. It is possible that learning occurred very quickly for some families that were "reached" by the promotion: these families quickly became highly loyal to the new brand. Other households returned to their old brands after trying Folger's a few times, while still others were relatively untouched by the promotions. While the basic hypothesis that the purchase event feedback (learning) process was operating strongly during the Folger's postintroductory period is still appealing, it seems unlikely (at least in retrospect) that the various households in the Chicago Tribune panel could have had anywhere nearly the same values of α, β, and λ. Given the probable heterogeneity in the learning operators (as opposed to heterogeneity in v_0, which is included in the model), it is possible that the heterogeneous Markov models of Chapter 4 might find a fruitful application with the Folger's data. (The fact that λ is about 0.5 suggests that the Markov model

might be a good approximation to the adaption process; see Section 5.5.)

In the case of beer, the high values of λ suggest that the purchase process is more Bernoulli than Markov in character. The failure of the AB (Bernoulli) model to fit may be due in part to the variations in relative price introduced for purposes of the experiment (the application of the learning model was not the primary reason for the experiment). In addition, the focus of respondent's attention on "purchases" in the experimental setting was probably greater than is generally the case when buying frequently purchased products. This may have introduced a memory factor that could have caused a randomly fluctuating serial correlation in the purchase probabilities. This kind of behavior lies outside the Bernoulli and linear learning model assumptions.[10]

5.6.2 "Favorite-Brand" Coffee Data

Table 5.5 presents the results when the linear learning model was fitted to the data originally analyzed with the heterogeneous Bernoulli and Markov models, in Chapters 3 and 4. The learning model fits these data quite well, except in the case of "Loyal" buyers. Four of the p-values are greater than 0.5, and a fifth is a still-respectable 0.36. The value for the "Loyal" group is 0.11, which could easily have occurred by chance.

The parameter values meet all the constraints imposed by linear learning model theory. That is, α, β, λ, $\alpha + \beta + \lambda$, and the μ all fall in the (0,1) range, and $\mu_1 > \mu_2 > \mu_3 > \mu_4$ in all cases. The derived quantities $E[v_0]$, $Var[v_0]$, and $E[v_\infty]$ also meet the constraints.

Run	$Var[v_0]$	$E[v_0]$	$E[v_\infty]$
ALL	0.027	0.707	0.728
EXCEPT 100 PERCENTERS	0.014	0.618	0.642
HEAVY	0.033	0.725	0.764
LIGHT	0.016	0.691	0.706
LOYAL	0.025	0.784	0.818
NONLOYAL	0.004	0.544	0.568

These results also indicate that there was a slight tendency toward

[10] It is possible that Howard's "dynamic inference" model might fit the experimental data for beer. This model assumes that consumers' purchase probabilities are changed abruptly at random times, with a new draw being made from the prior distribution each time such a change occurs. This behavior could be consistent with the idea of randomly fluctuating memory influences mentioned earlier.

Table 5.5   Estimates of Learning Model Parameters for Favorite-Brand Coffee Data; By Volume and Loyalty Segments

Run	α	β	$\alpha + \beta$	λ	μ_1	μ_2	μ_3	μ_4	χ^2	p-level*	N
ALL	0.105	0.219	0.324	0.637	0.707	0.527	0.419	0.345	8.90	0.36	5310
EXCEPT 100 PERCENTERS	0.138	0.181	0.319	0.604	0.618	0.396	0.256	0.126	7.13	0.52	3890
HEAVY	0.117	0.220	0.337	0.627	0.725	0.559	0.453	0.377	6.02	0.65	2660
LIGHT	0.091	0.218	0.309	0.653	0.691	0.494	0.382	0.309	5.79	0.67	2650
LOYAL	0.103	0.198	0.301	0.676	0.784	0.639	0.538	0.455	13.21	0.11	3600
NONLOYAL	0.177	0.195	0.372	0.493	0.544	0.300	0.179	0.110	3.80	0.87	1710

* Probability of a larger χ^2 if data were generated by the model.

increasing brand loyalty among coffee buyers during the period under study.

The values of the parameters are also quite reasonable. The value of λ for these data is about the same as that estimated for the Snow Crop frozen orange juice data, and somewhat higher than that for Folger's coffee (see Table 5.4). The value of α is consistently larger than it was for the previous analysis, while β is larger than for Snow Crop but about the same as Folger's. These results suggest that the rejection operator (α) is larger when a household's favorite brand is used as the base for analysis than when a specific brand is used. That is, the negative "learning" effect of other brand purchases is smaller when the household's favorite brand is being analyzed, and this is reasonable. As small differences in α usually lead to large differences in $E[v_\infty]$ — see Equation 5.4, where α appears alone in the numerator of the expression — this observation is of considerable importance. The practical effect can be seen by comparing the equilibrium probability values given earlier with those calculated from the parameters reported in Table 5.4. ($E[v_\infty]$ for Snow Crop is 0.181.)

Comparisons between the fit of the linear learning model and the three models estimated in Chapter 4 are presented in Table 5.6. The linear learning (LL) model fits the data better than the brand loyal (BL) heterogeneous Markov model (which is the best of the earlier models) in every single run. In most cases the fit is far better, as can be seen by comparing the p-values. The fact that the learning model chi-squares include all of the data whereas the alternative models exclude the (0000) and (1111) response categories reinforces this finding. There seems to be little doubt that the linear learning model provides a better representation of the favorite-brand coffee data than the heterogeneous Bernoulli (Ber.) or Markov (CL) models.

5.6.3 *Crest Toothpaste*

The linear learning model was also tried out on the MRCA dentifrice data used to test the probability diffusion models developed in Chapters 6 and 7. Crest toothpaste was the "1" brand, with all others being treated as "0." The results, which are presented in Table 5.7, will be discussed further in Chapter 8. In addition, Carman (1966) used essentially the same set of data to estimate linear learning model parameters. We will compare our results with his later in this section.

The Crest data were divided into the eight groups shown in the table. A total of 751 households purchased toothpaste at intervals averaging

Table 5.6 Comparison of Linear Learning (LL), Brand Loyal (BL), and Customer Loyal (CL) Markov, and Bernoulli Model (Ber.) Goodness of Fit: Favorite-Brand Coffee Data

Run	LL χ^2	LL p	BL* χ^2	BL* p	CL* χ^2	CL* p	Ber.* χ^2	Ber.* p
ALL	8.9	0.36	16.7	0.04	73.9	<0.01	58.0	<0.01
EXCEPT 100 PERCENTERS	7.1	0.52	18.1	0.02	70.7	<0.01	51.0	<0.01
HEAVY	6.0	0.65	15.2	0.06	39.3	<0.01	33.8	<0.01
LIGHT	5.8	0.67	9.1	0.37	40.5	<0.01	31.8	<0.01
LOYAL	13.2	0.11	14.4	0.08	43.4	<0.01	33.4	<0.01
NONLOYAL	3.8	0.87	19.0	0.02	34.8	<0.01	46.2	<0.01
Degrees of freedom	8		8		9		11	

* Chi-square and degrees of freedom exclude the (0000) and (1111) response categories (see Chapter 4).

Table 5.7 Estimates of Learning Model Parameters for Crest Toothpaste; before and after ADA Endorsement, by Average Interpurchase Time

Average Inter-purchase Time (days)	α	β	$\alpha + \beta$	λ	μ_1	μ_2	μ_3	μ_4	χ^2	p-level	N
0 to 30											
1. Before ADA*	0.007	0.359	0.366	0.581	0.158	0.091	0.080	0.020	5.65	0.69	751
2. After ADA	0.019	0.332	0.351	0.662	0.224	0.129	0.082	0.031	3.20	0.92	751
31 to 45											
3. Before ADA	−0.005	0.116	0.111	0.863	0.145	0.075	0.059	0.047	9.26	0.32	618
4. After ADA	0.020	0.332	0.352	0.612	0.242	0.113	0.066	0.039	22.57	0.01	618
46 to 60											
5. Before ADA	0.003	0.106	0.109	0.776	0.131	0.064	0.049	0.037	16.80	0.03	503
6. After ADA	0.043	0.522	0.565	0.336	0.203	0.008	−0.128	−1.917	6.30	0.60	503
> 60											
7. Before ADA	0.007	0.293	0.300	0.643	0.104	0.018	0.019	−0.002	9.21	0.33	1163
8. After ADA	0.033	0.328	0.361	0.604	0.188	0.071	0.026	−0.014	8.30	0.41	1163

* American Dental Association.

between 0 and 30 days. The last four purchases by these households before the American Dental Association (ADA) endorsement of Crest provided the data for the 0 to 30 before ADA run, while the first four after the endorsement from the basis for 0 to 30 after ADA. The same plan was followed for households purchasing at 31 to 45, 46 to 60, and greater than 60-day intervals. (See Chapter 7 for a more detailed discussion of the methods used to process the Crest data.)

By and large, the linear learning model fits fairly well. The null hypothesis that the data were generated by this model is rejected in only two out of the eight cases, at the 10% level. (In fact, the other six p-levels are all 0.3 or greater.)

The constraints on α, β, and λ are violated only once, and that where α is only very slightly negative. The values of the purchase and rejection operator intercepts ($\alpha + \beta$ and α, respectively) average 0.315 and 0.016, which are very close to the values observed for frozen orange juice (see Table 5.4). The average of λ is 0.635, which is also about the same as for the Snow Crop data.

The moments of the prior distribution are also reasonable in most cases. Group 6 is the only one for which pathological results are observed. (Minor violations of constraints also occur in Groups 7 and 8.) The variance of $f(v_0)$ are positive for all the groups except Group 6.

Thus, we can conclude that, with the possible exception of Group 6, the linear learning model provides at least an adequate representation of the Crest dentifrice data. While the fit is not as good as we would like for Groups 4 and 5, the parameter estimates for these groups are nearly the same as those for the other data sets. (Given the average degree of fit for the other groups, these two "extreme" values of chi-square could probably have occurred by chance even if the structure of the purchasing process is the same for all groups.) The parameters of Group 6 are the only ones that seem to be out of line; in addition to the problems with the μ noted earlier, the value of λ is unduly low, and β appears to be too large. A more detailed discussion of the Crest results will be given in Chapter 8, in connection with the cohesive elements probability diffusion model.

Table 5.8 compares our "After ADA" Crest results with those obtained by Carman (1966, Table 1). Carman's parameter estimation method assumes that the population of purchases has homogeneous v_0. He justifies this assumption in terms of the small market share and limited penetration enjoyed by Crest prior to the ADA endorsement. If his assumption is true, then unbiased efficient parameter estimates can be obtained by using a constrained regression analysis, which is described in his paper.

Table 5.8 Comparison of Massy's and Carman's Learning Model Estimates: Crest Toothpaste, after ADA Endorsement, by Average Interpurchase Time

Average Interpurchase Time (days)		α	β	$\alpha + \beta$	λ	$E[v_0]$	N
(Massy)*	(Carman)†						
0–30		0.019	0.332	0.351	0.662	0.224	751
	1–22	0.002	0.413	0.415	0.612	0.228	772
	23–33	0.016	0.418	0.434	0.576	0.218	877
31–45		0.020	0.332	0.352	0.612	0.242	618
	34–44	0.023	0.437	0.460	0.497	0.214	970
46–60		0.043	0.522	0.565	0.336	0.203	503
	45–59	0.032	0.466	0.498	0.482	0.232	734
>60		0.033	0.328	0.361	0.604	0.188	1163
	≥60	0.015	0.439	0.454	0.518	0.243	383

* Source: Table 5.7.
† Source: Carman (1966, Table 1).

The assumption of homogeneous v_0 implies that μ_2, μ_3, and μ_4 are all zero. We have already seen that this is not the case. The estimates of μ_1 and μ_2 given in Table 5.7 yield variances for μ_0 of the order of 0.03 to 0.06, which are the same or slightly smaller than those observed for the frozen orange juice data.

Examination of Table 5.8 shows that there are some systematic differences between our results and those of Carman. In particular, his estimates of λ all tend to be too small, with an average error of about 6%. (The error is 15% if the results for our "pathological" 46 to 60 day group are disregarded.) His β also tend to be somewhat too large, though the two sets of α average out about the same. The same relations show up if we compare Carman's results with our "Before ADA" parameter estimates.

Given that Carman's estimation method is based on an assumption that is known to be somewhat in error, we are forced to conclude that his estimates are the biased ones. The bias is in the direction of finding more purchase event feedback than is really the case (larger β and correspondingly smaller λ). This is a natural result of the effects of v_0 heterogeneity on parameter estimates assuming homogeneous v_0, as was originally pointed out by Frank (1962). Therefore, it appears that while Kuehn's orange juice results were free of the bias discussed in Frank's paper, the problem does exist and can be demonstrated empirically using the work of Carman.

Table 5.9   Estimates of Mean Prior Probabilities by Middle-Purchase-Conditioned Groups

	$\mu_1^{(11)}$	$\mu_1^{(01)}$	$\mu_1^{(10)}$	$\mu_1^{(00)}$
Snow Crop Orange Juice	0.746	0.361	0.451	0.072
Folger's Coffee	0.471	0.152	0.205	0.145
Crest Toothpaste				
Before ADA: 0–30	0.868	0.343	0.485	0.044
After ADA: 0–30	0.741	0.333	0.390	0.045
Before ADA: 31–45	0.755	0.423	0.206	0.055
After ADA: 31–45	0.710	0.377	0.431	0.052
Before ADA: 46–60	0.769	0.363	0.319	0.029
After ADA: 46–60	0.554	0.326	0.552	0.090
Before ADA: >60	0.627	0.311	0.225	0.054
After ADA: >60	0.608	0.350	0.436	0.074

We must hasten to add two additional points in defense of Carman's excellent study. First, while the bias does appear to be reasonably consistent, it is not too large. That is, conclusions based on Carman's parameter estimates would probably be adequate for many purposes. This is particularly true for the comparisons of parameters among population subgroups, all of which would be subject to the same bias, which form the primary focus of Carman's paper.[11] Second, it may well be that the precision of Carman's constrained regression method is what allowed the bias to show up in his results. A less powerful method might have masked the problem altogether.

5.6.4   Comparison of 1 d.f. and 8 d.f. Estimates

The Snow Crop, Folger's coffee, toothpaste, and favorite-brand coffee data were used to provide a test of the simple 1 d.f. modified minimum chi-square estimation method. The conditional purchase proportions defined in Table 5.3 were calculated from the unconditional proportions used as input to the 8 d.f. procedure. Estimates of μ_1 for the four groups were obtained by adding the values of $P_{11}^{(ij)}$ and $P_{10}^{(ij)}$. These are shown in Table 5.9. Then Equation 5.18 was minimized with

[11] Among other things, Carman (1966, p. 28) tests Kuehn's hypothesis that the effects of learning decline with time between purchases. His conclusion that "... the parameters for [households making] frequent purchases are not significantly different from the parameters for infrequent purchases" does not seem to be affected by the v_0 heterogeneity bias. In fact, the same conclusion is suggested by our Crest results.

respect to α and β for each of the following different values of λ: 0, 0.025, 0.050, 0.075, 0.100, . . . , 0.950, 0.975, 1.000. The solution with the minimum chi-square was selected from this set of 21 trials and presented in the "1 d.f." rows in Table 5.10. (The results for the "8 d.f." rows are reproduced from Tables 5.4 and 5.7.)

We turn first to the Snow Crop data, for which the 8 d.f. method provided the best fit. Here the results from the 1 d.f. estimation procedure are very nearly the same as those for the more powerful method. The p-level is not quite as high, but a 0.70 still indicates a very good fit, especially in view of the larger variance of the 1 d.f. chi-square distribution. The values of α, β, and λ are fairly close to one another in the two sets of estimates, and there would seem to be little basis for choosing between them. Thus, we conclude that the very simple 1 d.f. estimation method is adequate for the Snow Crop data.

The situation is quite different when we consider Folger's coffee. While the p-levels attained by the two methods are about the same (neither set of estimates fits the data very well), the parameter values diverge markedly. This is particularly true for λ, which is estimated as 0.125 by the 1 d.f. method and 0.502 by the 8 d.f. program. Could this difference be due to chance, or does it represent a bias in one of the two procedures?

Figure 5.4 shows values of χ^2/N for different values of λ, for both the Folger's and Snow Crop data. The Folger's curve indicates that the χ^2 for $\lambda = 0.502$ (the 8 d.f. result) is almost $2\frac{1}{2}$ times that for $\lambda = 0.125$, the minimum χ^2 value. This difference is rather large, and even though the 8 d.f. λ value could have been higher than the true value (which would inflate the difference between the two values), it does not appear that the observed discrepancy could have occurred by chance. As the 8 d.f. method is an exact chi-square, compared to the modified chi-square used in the 1 d.f. method, and is more powerful because of its larger number of degrees of freedom, we are inclined to believe that the estimates obtained from the 1 d.f. method are wrong rather than the other way around. This inference is reinforced by the fact that the estimates of μ_2 for the 1 d.f. model (not reported) range between -1 and $+5$, with only a few lying in the proper 0 to 1 range. In contrast, the 8 d.f. model yields reasonable results for μ_2.

The λ-discrepancy observed in the Folger's data is not an isolated case, as can be seen by scanning the λ and α columns of Table 5.10. Serious misestimates of λ also occur for the other products. There α is consistently overestimated by the 1 d.f. method, though the small absolute size of this parameter makes these errors less important

Table 5.10 Comparison of Parameter Estimates for 8-df and 1-df Estimation Methods

Run	d.f.	α	β	$\alpha + \beta$	λ	χ^2	p-level*	N
Snow Crop Orange Juice	8	0.015	0.305	0.320	0.612	1.16	>0.99	13,519
	1	0.024	0.300	0.324	0.575	0.15	0.70	13,519
Folger's Coffee	8	0.057	0.207	0.264	0.502	36.23	<0.001	805
	1	0.092	0.249	0.341	0.125	4.99	0.03	805
Crest Toothpaste								
1. B:0–30	8	0.007	0.359	0.366	0.581	5.65	0.69	751
	1	0.016	0.441	0.457	0.475	1.16	0.28	751
2. A:0–30	8	0.019	0.332	0.351	0.662	0.01	0.92	637
	1	0.024	0.309	0.333	0.650	0.01	0.94	637
3. B:31–45	8	−0.005	0.116	0.111	0.863	9.26	0.32	618
	1	0.001	0.094	0.095	0.825	2.89	0.09	618
4. A:31–45	8	0.020	0.332	0.352	0.612	22.57	0.006	556
	1	0.046	0.498	0.544	0.325	11.71	<0.001	556
5. B:46–60	8	0.003	0.106	0.109	0.776	16.80	0.025	503
	1	0.019	0.276	0.295	0.475	0.01	0.91	503
6. A:46–60	8	0.043	0.522	0.565	0.336	6.30	0.61	480
	1	0.048	0.510	0.558	0.325	0.22	0.65	480
7. B:> 60	8	0.007	0.293	0.300	0.643	9.21	0.33	1163
	1	0.031	0.398	0.429	0.350	2.71	0.10	1163
8. A:> 60	8	0.033	0.328	0.361	0.604	8.30	0.41	894
	1	0.049	0.314	0.363	0.575	0.27	0.62	894
Favorite-Brand Coffee								
All	8	0.105	0.219	0.324	0.637	8.90	0.36	5310
	1	0.157	0.209	0.366	0.575	2.335	0.13	5310
Except 100 Percenters	8	0.138	0.181	0.319	0.604	7.13	0.52	3890
	1	0.179	0.168	0.347	0.550	0.144	0.70	3890
Heavy	8	0.117	0.220	0.337	0.627	6.02	0.65	2660
	1	0.151	0.199	0.350	0.600	0.022	0.89	2660
Light	8	0.091	0.218	0.309	0.653	5.79	0.67	2650
	1	0.154	0.205	0.359	0.575	4.300	0.04	2650
Loyal	8	0.103	0.198	0.301	0.676	13.21	0.11	3600
	1	0.144	0.171	0.315	0.650	0.014	0.91	3600
Nonloyal	8	0.177	0.195	0.372	0.493	3.80	0.87	1710
	1	0.213	0.193	0.406	0.425	1.10	0.30	1710

* Probability of getting a larger χ^2 if the data are generated by the model.

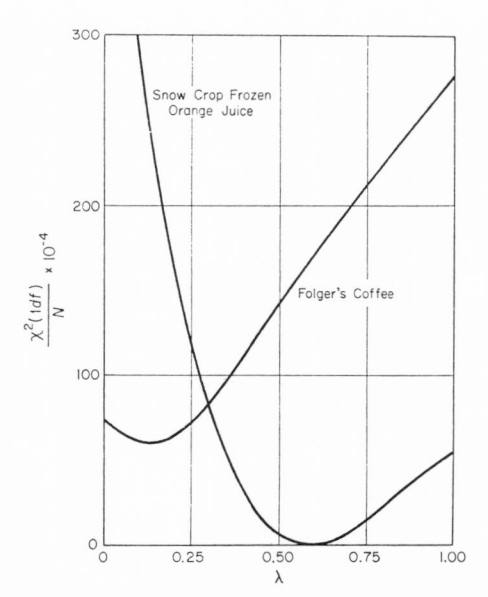

Figure 5.4.   Values of minimum χ^2 given λ for one degree of freedom estimation method: Snow Crop frozen orange juice and Folger's coffee.

than those for λ. The following summary demonstrates the pervasiveness of these discrepancies:

	Number of Cases				
Direction of Difference	α	β	$\alpha + \beta$	λ	p-level
1 d.f. > 8 d.f.	16	5	13	0	8
1 d.f. < 8 d.f.	0	11	3	16	8

This highlights the problem clearly: λ is underestimated and α is over-estimated in all 16 of the cases studied. There is some apparent downward bias in the β parameter. In spite of the difference in power of the 1 d.f. and 8 d.f. tests, the p-levels show no tendency to vary systematically with the method.

Figure 5.5 shows that the size of the bias in λ depends on the fit of the linear learning model. In the Folger's data, where the p-level is less than 0.001, λ is underestimated by a factor of 75% (based on the 8 d.f. results). The next worst fit is for Crest, Group 4; here the underestimate in λ is about 47% of the 8 d.f. value. In contrast, the underestimate falls to only 6% for the Snow Crop data, and 2% for Crest Group 2, where the learning model fits very well.

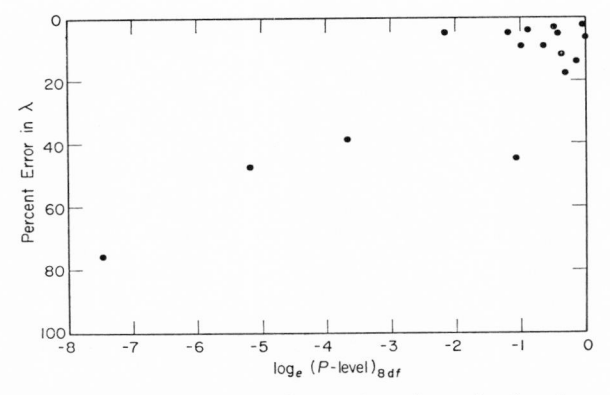

Figure 5.5.   Percentage error in λ as a function of p-level.

We tentatively conclude that the 1 d.f. modified minimum chi-square estimation method is biased with respect to α and λ and to a lesser extent for β. As α is too large and λ is too small, the direction of the bias is in the same direction as that caused by v_0 heterogeneity. While the 1 d.f. estimation method takes v_0 heterogeneity into account, it is possible that similar problems may still be present. The size of the bias appears to increase as the fit of the model declines, which suggests that heterogeneity of the parameters might be causing part of the difficulty. More work, perhaps involving Monte Carlo simulation, is needed on these points.

On balance we recommend that, in spite of its simplicity, the 1 d.f. method be used only in those cases where the learning model is believed likely to provide a good fit to the data. If the fit does not turn out to be very good, the 1 d.f. parameters must be interpreted with great caution. In contrast, the value of the parameters obtained with the 8 d.f. method do not appear to be correlated with goodness of fit. Hence, they can be interpreted even in cases where the learning model is not a particularly good representation of the purchasing process.

5.6.5   *Summary of Empirical Results*

This chapter has developed the theory of the linear learning model, as it is applied to consumer brand switching processes. The model appears to fit a variety of switching data with fairly good accuracy and does very well on some products. If the model were being tested in isolation, on the basis of the chi-square results alone, we would have rejected the hypothesis that the various sets of data analyzed in this

chapter were generated by a linear learning model in 5 out of 13 cases studied. This is not a bad batting average, especially when sample sizes are fairly large and a great variety of exogenous factors are known to be operating in the various markets. Thus, the learning model can be used with confidence as a tool for analyzing brand switching data. Its performance also indicates that the purchase event feedback hypothesis must be taken seriously in many purchasing behavior studies.

CHAPTER 6
A PROBABILITY DIFFUSION MODEL

6.1 Introduction

In this chapter we shall be concerned with the derivation of a zero-order model in which the probability of choosing a particular brand may change between purchases.[1] That is, we shall consider a model that allows nonstationarity in the probability of brand choice but that, in contrast to the linear learning and Markov models, assumes that this nonstationarity is not due to purchase event feedback.

We begin the development of this model with a descriptive overview. The model is then contrasted with the models developed in the previous chapters. The general model (of which the probability diffusion model is the most interesting special case) is then formulated. This is followed by two explicit specifications of the general model. The second specification is shown to have appealing properties as a representation of choice processes and is therefore fully developed as the probability diffusion model. Finally, methods for estimating and testing the model are presented.

6.2 The Probability Diffusion Model: An Overview

In this section we present an overview of the probability diffusion model. This discussion is intended to motivate the more formal development that follows in later sections. We shall also define certain terms that will be used in the model development. Finally, we will indicate the relation of the present model to model developments in mathematical psychology and sociology.

6.2.1 Introduction to the Probability Diffusion Model

In the probability diffusion model, as in all of the previous models considered in this book, what we have termed the response probability or brand-choice probability of an individual is really a conditional probability. It is the choice probability for the response alternatives *given* that a response or purchase is made. In Chapter 8 we shall consider models that explicitly consider the times at which responses are made.

[1] This chapter is based upon D. B. Montgomery (1966) and (1969).

For the present discussion, we simply use the term response probability to represent the probability that one alternative will be chosen over another whenever a choice is made.

In its present form the probability diffusion model applies to a two-response alternative case. Again, this is similar to the previous models developed in this book. As in the other models, we might let one alternative represent a particular brand of interest, while all other brands would represent the remaining alternative. In other cases, the primary alternative of interest might be the individual's favorite brand, with all other brands forming an aggregate "all other" category. Recall for a two-response alternative model that it is sufficient to consider the probability of making one of the responses since this then uniquely determines the probability of the alternative response.

In this introduction to the probability diffusion model we shall focus upon the behavior of an individual's response probability over a sequence of responses (or purchases). For discussion purposes we label the two-response alternatives A and B, respectively; and let $P(A_t)$ denote the individual's probability of choosing A at any point in time t. Recall that this probability is the relevant choice probability for A *if* a choice is made at t.

Perhaps the easiest way to introduce the model is first to consider a model that in the limit becomes the probability diffusion model. Consider a model in which an individual's response probability undergoes a random walk. We see from Figure 6.1 that an individual's response probability is nonstationary, the nonstationarity resulting from the random-walk changes that occur in his response probability. Since the model does not consider the timing of response occasions (i.e.,

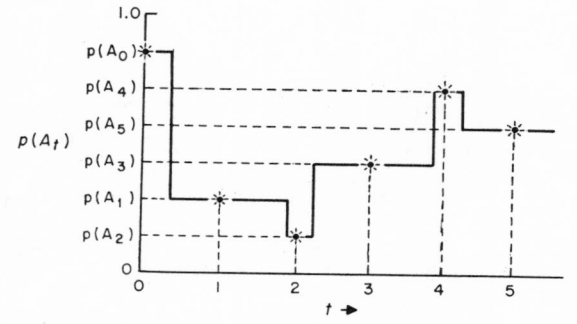

Figure 6.1. A random-walk model. (Asterisk denotes a response occasion.)

the time at which responses occur), responses are taken to occur at integer values of the index t. This representation will be considered at greater length later in this section.

Several salient features of this random-walk model should be noted. First, the individual's response probability changes in discrete jumps. If we suppose that $\Delta P(A)$ represents the minimum jump that may occur in an individual's response probability whenever a change occurs, then each jump (or change) must be an integral multiple of $\Delta P(A)$ in the random-walk model. This fact leads to the second feature that should be noted. In the random-walk model an individual's response probability may only take on one of a finite number of discrete values. The third feature is that an individual's response probability may change in either direction — i.e., it may increase or decrease — from any given value. The only exceptions, of course, are when $P(A_t)$ is equal to one of the extreme values, 0 or 1. Finally, it should be noted that the actual responses made at $t = 0, 1, 2, \ldots$ do not change the response probability. That is, there is no purchase event (or response event) feedback. Thus in this sense the random-walk model is a nonstationary, zero-order model.

In the probability diffusion model, responses are again taken to occur at integer values of the time index t. In Figure 6.2 this relation is denoted by the asterisks indicating responses at $t = 0, 1, 2, 3, 4, 5, \ldots$. At any given response occasion, say $t = 3$, the individual's probability of choosing A is given by $P(A_3)$. In certain applications of the model, this assumption that responses occur at integer valus of t will create no problems. Consider, for example, a multiwave voting intentions panel

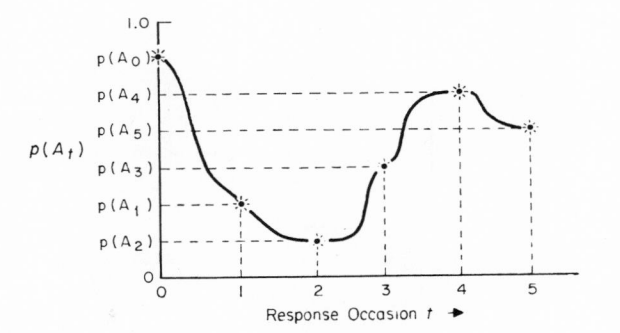

Figure 6.2.   A probability diffusion model.

or a social-psychological experiment.[2] For these cases, responses will occur for each respondent at regular periodic intervals since the time of response is under the control of the researcher. Thus the interresponse interval in the model will correspond to real time (e.g., in a voting intentions panel the responses may be made biweekly, and the interval between $t - 1$ and t will then be two weeks). Furthermore, all respondents will respond at the same periodic intervals. Since the responses of many individuals will have to be aggregated in order to estimate and test the model, the fact that all individuals respond at the same time will enable us to draw real time inferences in applications such as the multiwave voting intentions panel.

When the model is applied to continuous consumer panel data, the assumption is more artificial. Unfortunately, consumers are not so obliging as to all make their purchase decisions in a given product class on identical days, or even with identical time intervals between their purchase decisions. Thus when we apply the model to sequences of choices among brands and make the assumption of equal increments of time between response (or purchase) occasions, the correspondence between model time and real (or calendar) time between purchase events is somewhat elastic. An example will help to clarify this statement. Consider an individual who makes purchases in a given product class on January 2, January 10, and January 29. Thus the calendar (real) time interval between his first and second responses was 8 days, while the calendar time between his second and third purchases was 19 days. As depicted in Figure 6.2, the probability diffusion model considers the interpurchase interval to be of a fixed length. Consequently, the model's time index t will not correspond to calendar time in applications of the model to brand choice. Between the first and second purchases, one unit of model time corresponds to 8 days of calendar time, while between the second and the third purchases it corresponds to 19 days. Thus model time bears an elastic relationship to real time in brand-choice applications. The time problem discussed here will be termed the intrarespondent time problem.

In addition to the intrarespondent time problem, there is also an interrespondent time problem that arises in brand-choice applications. In order to estimate and test the model, we shall find it necessary (as in previous models) to aggregate the responses of individuals who have not all made their first, second, third, etc., purchases at the same time. Yet the estimation and testing of the model requires that we aggregate

[2] See Lazarsfeld (1954) and Coleman (1964b, Chapter 11) for voting studies. See Coleman (1964a) for an application to data from a social-psychological experiment.

these first, second, third, etc., purchases. An operational approach to minimizing the impact of this aspect of the timing problem is to group respondents according to their average interpurchase time. This should bring the purchase cycles of the members of each group somewhat closer together. This approach is taken in the empirical test of the model reported in Chapter 7. Perhaps a better approach would be to group respondents according to both their average interpurchase time and their relative variability of interpurchase time. Relative variability is defined as the variance of the interpurchase time divided by the square of the average interpurchase time. While cross classification on these two dimensions should bring the purchase cycles within each group even closer together, sample size requirements increase very rapidly. This consideration led to the adoption of the simpler classification by average interpurchase time for the purpose of the initial test of the model.

Both the intra- and interrespondent time problems prevent us from using the probability diffusion model to derive real time estimates such as market share at some point in time. This restriction also applies to the previous models, with the exception of a Markov model, which utilizes the rather artificial "no purchase" state. But just as in previous models, the probability diffusion model may be used to examine the structure and dynamics of brand choice. In a brand-choice application, the model considers the time between successive responses to be equal. This implies that the change process for the response probability operates identically between any pair of successive responses, regardless of what calendar time has elapsed. Thus in brand-choice applications, the model represents the change in response probability that occurs between successive responses.

There may be factors that countervail the intra- and interrespondent time problems discussed here. Should response to a marketing stimulus relate more to product use or purchase occasions than to calendar time, the model's equal purchase interval assumption may be more appropriate than calendar time intervals. Response to a consumer product innovation might be an example where the interrespondent and intrarespondent time problems might not be serious. The time scale of the diffusion process for the innovation may well be related to units of product used rather than to calendar time.[3] Even though advertising messages concerning the innovation are received in calendar time, the degree to which they are perceived may be a positive function of usage rates. Thus the diffusion and adoption process may well progress as far

---

[3] See Rogers (1962) for an excellent summary of research on the diffusion and adoption of innovations.

in two weeks for frequent purchasers of the product class as in two months for less frequent purchases.

Whether the elastic nature of the relationship between real (calendar) time and model time is a pitfall or a blessing is likely to depend upon both the specific product class in question and the type of stimulus whose effects are to be measured by the model. In any event, the elastic model time–calendar time relationship should not obviate the use of this model in the continuing attempt to understand the structure and dynamics of consumer brand-choice behavior.

6.2.2 Some Terms Used in the Model Development

To set the stage for the formal model development in later sections, it seems useful to discuss certain terms that will be used. Some of these terms have been defined in the previous discussion, but they will be repeated here for easy reference.

Response. In the binary choice version of the model there are two mutually exclusive and collectively exhaustive responses alternatives, A and B. A response occurs when one of the two response alternatives is chosen. Examples of response alternatives would be an intention to vote Democratic versus Republican or a purchase of the individual's favorite brand rather than some other brand in a given product class.

Response Occasion. A response occasion is the event that one of the two alternative responses is chosen. Response occasions occur at integer values of the index t.

Response Probability. This is the probability that response alternative A will be chosen if a response is made. In the binary response case it is sufficient to consider just $P(A_t)$, the probability of making response A, since $P(B_t) = 1 - P(A_t)$. As a probability measure $P(A_t)$ is bounded by zero and one.

State Space of an Individual. The state of an individual at t is his response probability $P(A_t)$. In the probability diffusion model, there is an infinite number of values in the state space of an individual respondent.

Response Elements. The response elements are hypothetical constructs that are used as a framework for the derivation of the dynamic properties of the model. These response elements are conceptually similar to the stimulus elements of stimulus sampling theory and are used in an analogous manner.[4] As in the stimulus sampling models from mathematical learning theory, there is no need in the present case to

[4] See, for example, Atkinson, Bower, and Crothers (1965).

achieve an isomorphism between these hypothetical response elements and any overt real world phenomena.[5] They simply represent a useful conceptual construct in the model development.

6.2.3   Relation to Models in Mathematical Psychology and Sociology

In this section we shall consider two model types of direct relevance to the model developed in this chapter. The model types are *stimulus sampling models* from mathematical learning theory and the *latent Markov models* developed by James S. Coleman, a mathematical sociologist.

Stimulus sampling theory views behavior as being elicited by stimulus events that are associated with or conditioned to the various responses that may be made in the situation.[6] The basic terms in stimulus sampling models are: *stimulus, response, association,* and *reinforcement.* A given behavioral situation is postulated to present the respondent with a total stimulus that is composed of hypothetical stimulus elements. Each of these stimulus elements is further postulated to be uniquely associated with or conditioned to one of the mutually exclusive and collectively exhaustive response alternatives. When presented with the stimulus situation, the respondent is assumed to sample one of the stimulus elements randomly. He then makes that response to which the sampled stimulus element is associated. Change in the association of the stimulus elements depends upon reinforcement. Once the sampled stimulus has elicited its associated response, the theory postulates a reinforcement mechanism. That is, the response that was made is either rewarding or not rewarding. If the response was rewarding, the sampled stimulus element remains associated with that response. If the response was not rewarding, the sampled stimulus element changes its response associa-tion — i.e., becomes associated with some alternative response. Much work has been done on the noncontingent reinforcement case. Non-contingent reinforcement means that the probability that the current response will be rewarded is independent of which particular response has been made.

The theory remains somewhat vague as to the actual meaning of the hypothetical stimulus elements. Atkinson, Bower, and Crothers make the following comment on this situation:[7]

---

[5] See ibid, p. 346, for a discussion of this point relating to stimulus sampling models.
[6] See ibid., Chapter 8, and Atkinson and Estes (1963) for formal development and discussion of stimulus sampling theory.
[7] See Atkinson, Bower, and Crothers (1965, p. 346).

. . . although stimulus sampling theory has a very precise way of representing the stimulus situation, the theory is vague, in fact noncommitted concerning what is a stimulus. Paradoxically, the flexibility and scope of the theory arises in part because of this lack of commitment regarding how stimulus elements are to be defined.

Thus stimulus sampling models utilize the stimulus element construct in order to generate dynamic response behavior without necessarily establishing an isomorphism between the hypothetical elements and separable portions of the real world stimulus situation. We make use of the analogous concept of response elements in order to model dynamic brand choice behavior in the probability diffusion model.

Stimulus sampling models are generally derived from a precisely stated system of axioms.[8] The probability diffusion model developed in this chapter will also be derived from a set of assumptions (or axioms). These are presented in Section 6.4.

The work of most direct relevance to the present model is that of Coleman.[9] The probability diffusion model derived in this chapter represents a limiting form of the modeling approach taken by Coleman. The relation between Coleman's model and the present model is best understood by reference to the random-walk and diffusion examples in Section 6.2.1. Coleman's model is essentially the random-walk version. The diffusion limit yields a more appealing representation of an individual's response probability. The present chapter also discusses two additional extensions of importance. The first relates to estimation of the model. Methods are presented for estimating the model's parameters from sequences of several responses. Coleman's random-walk model (what he terms a latent Markov model) provided procedures for just identifying the parameters. The present work is concerned with achieving estimates having desirable statistical properties. The second point relates to testing the descriptive adequacy of the model for a set of response data. In Section 6.7.3 we present a minimum chi-square estimation procedure that provides measures of the goodness of fit of the model. In Chapter 7 we present some empirical results using the probability diffusion model.

6.3 Comparison with Previous Models

In this section we shall compare the probability diffusion model with the model types from the previous three chapters. Our comparison

[8] For an example of such a system of axioms see ibid., p. 353.
[9] See Coleman (1964a) and (1964b).

will be based upon how each model represents the response probabilities of individuals.

Before turning to a comparison of the models, it will be useful to discuss the characteristics we shall use to make this comparison. In the discussion to follow, these characteristics are separated into inter-individual and intraindividual characteristics.

Interindividual Representation of Response Probability

Heterogeneity. Heterogeneity in the representation of response probability between individuals means that each individual may have his own individual (perhaps idiosyncratic) response probability. Recall that assuming that a population of individuals all have the same response probability has the danger of leading to a higher order inference of the dependence of response probability upon actual responses than may, in fact, be the case.

Intraindividual Representation of Response Probability

The following characteristics relate to the representation of response probability for any given individual.

Nonstationarity. Nonstationarity refers to whether an individual's response probability may undergo change between response occasions.

Values an Individual's Response Probability May Attain. This characteristic relates to how many distinct values between zero and one a given individual's response probability may attain. This characteristic may vary from a single value to an infinite number of values between zero and one.

Directions in Which an Individual's Response Probability May Change. This characteristic refers to whether an individual's response probability may increase or decrease between response occasions when it starts at any given value. If a model assumes stationarity, then clearly it has a zero value on this characteristic. Nonstationary models may have one or at most two feasible directions of change starting from any given value.

Purchase Event Feedback. This characteristic represents the influence of actual responses in changing response probability. In a zero-order model, there is no purchase event feedback. In a first-order model, the most recent purchase influences the response probability on the next purchase, etc.

We now turn to a discussion of how various models represent

response probability in terms of these characteristics. The models we shall consider are the Bernoulli model, the Markov model, the linear learning model, and the probability diffusion model. In terms of the interindividual representation of response probability, all of the models allow for heterogeneity of the respondents. This characteristic is one of the most important modeling advances provided by the models developed in this book. The issue of the intraindividual representation of response probability is discussed here for each model.

In the Bernoulli model an individual's response probability is considered stationary. Consequently, it exhibits no change and may take on only one value through time. Furthermore, there is no purchase event feedback.

The Markov model allows an individual's response probability to change between response occasions. The particular value it has at response occasion t is dependent upon the response that was made at $t-1$. Thus there is purchase event feedback. In the Markov formulation an individual's response probability may take on only one of two distinct values. The value it takes on depends upon whether the individual made response A or response B on his last response occasion. In addition, from any given value of response probability, an individual's response probability may change in only one direction. For example, consider an individual who has made response B at this most recent response occasion. Now, if he again makes response B, his response probability will not change. However, if he makes response A, his response probability $P(A_t)$ will increase. A similar argument would hold if he started with A as his most recent response.

We now turn to the third basic model type, the linear learning model. Within the upper and lower limits established for response probability in a linear learning model, an individual's response probability is increased whenever he makes response A and is decreased whenever he makes response B. Thus, in the linear learning model, an individual's response probability is nonstationary. As in the Markov model, the nonstationarity is due *entirely* to the individual's responses — i.e., purchase event feedback. The nonstationarity or changes in response probability occur in discrete jumps. Thus from any given initial value of response probability, an individual's response probability may take on only one of a finite set of possible values over a finite number of responses. In contrast to the Markov model, however, the learning model allows for changes in response probability to occur in both directions (i.e., up or down). The direction it changes depends upon which response is made.

Table 6.1   The Representation of Individual's Response Probability

Characteristic of Brand-Choice Probability	Model			
	Bernoulli	Markov	Learning	Diffusion
Interconsumer				
Heterogeneity	yes	yes	yes	yes
Intraconsumer				
Nonstationary	no	yes	yes	yes
Purchase Event Feedback	no	yes	yes	no
Values It May Attain	one	two	several	infinite number
Directions It May Change	no change	one	two	two

The probability diffusion model might be termed a zero-order model in that it does not consider purchase event feedback. Rather, non-stationarity of an individual's response probability is posited to result from events external to the model. In the context of brand choice, changes in response probability would presumably result from market activities and events. The model represents an individual's response probability as having any one of an infinite number of values between zero and one. As in the learning model, the response probability may change either up or down between successive responses. The contrast of the manner in which these models represent individuals' response probabilities is summarized in Table 6.1.

6.4   Assumptions and General Form of the Model

In this section we shall specify the basic assumptions of the model and develop the general set of differential equations that describe it. Explicit specifications of the general model will be developed in the next two sections.

As has been the case with previous models, the present formulation of the model is confined to binary response situations — i.e., to situations in which one of two mutually exclusive and collectively exhaustive responses may be made. Again, in the context of consumer brand choice, the two response alternatives might represent a purchase of a brand of particular interest versus the purchase of some other brand. Alternatively, the two responses might represent a purchase of the consumer's favorite brand versus a purchase of some other brand.

6.4.1   The Model Assumptions

The assumptions underlying the model will be divided into three basic classes: model specification assumptions, response assumptions, and response probability change assumptions. Each of these basic assumption classes are formulated and discussed in the following paragraphs.

6.4.1.1   *Model Specification Assumptions*.   The model specification assumptions are:

S1. Each respondent's response probability is generated by the same basic stochastic process.
S2. At any given response occasion t, different respondents may have different response probabilities.
S3. At any given response occasion t, there are two mutually exclusive and collectively exhaustive responses, A and B.
S4. Each individual respondent possesses N (possibly infinitely many) hypothetical response elements.
S5. At any given response occasion t, each of an individual's response elements is uniquely associated with either response A or B.

By S1 we have assumed that the same basic probability mechanism holds for all respondents. In S2 we have assumed that consumers may differ from one another in terms of their response probabilities even though the same basic process operates on their response probabilities. These two assumptions are analogous to the approaches taken with respect to earlier models. For example, recall in the brand loyal model that each consumer was represented by the same basic transition matrix even though their explicit transition probabilities were allowed to differ. Similarly, the learning model assumed that the same purchase and rejection operators applied to each individual consumer. Heterogeneity of consumers arose in this case because of individual differences in initial response probability as well as individual sequences of brand purchases. The use of S1 and S2 in the present model will become clear in subsequent sections of this chapter.

Assumption S3 indicates that the present model development is restricted to the binary response case. In S4 and S5 we have assumed that an individual respondent may be represented as having a set of hypothetical response elements that form associations with the alternative responses. This response element formulation is similar in form to the stimulus element assumptions used in stimulus sampling models.[10]

---

[10] For a discussion of stimulus sampling models see Atkinson, Bower, and Crothers (1965).

6.4.1.2 *Response Assumptions.* The response assumptions for individual respondents are:

R1. If at response occasion t an individual has i of his elements associated with response A, his probability of making response A at response occasion t will be

$$P\{A \text{ at occasion } t | i \text{ elements associated with } A\} = N$$

where N is the total number of response elements for each individual. R2. For an individual respondent, the actual response he makes at occasion $t - 1$ does not affect the probability that he will make response A at occasion t. That is,

$$P[A \text{ at occasion } t] = P[A \text{ at occasion } t | A \text{ at occasion } t - 1]$$
$$= P[A \text{ at occasion } t | B \text{ at occasion } t - 1]$$

R3. Individuals respond independently of one another.

The role of the hypothetical response elements is indicated by R1. This assumption states that an individual's probability of making response A at any response occasion t is equal to the proportion of his response elements that are associated with response A at occasion t.

Assumption R2 might be termed a pseudo-Bernoulli trial assumption. It is Bernoulli in the sense that the process has two mutually exclusive and collectively exhaustive response alternatives and the probability of the occurrence of these alternatives is independent of the history of responses that have been made by the respondent. Thus R2 assumes that there is no purchase event feedback on the response probability. It is at this point that the current formulation stands in direct contrast to learning and Markov models, which postulate that the particular sampling function observed (i.e., brands chosen) is the *only* factor that causes the probability of choosing Brand A on future trials to change. The adjective "pseudo" is used in recognition of the fact that "true" Bernoulli trials require that the probability of making response A remains stationary between response occasions. As will become evident from the assumptions in the next section, the response probability for any given individual is subject to change between response occasions.

Assumption R3 will prove to be of considerable importance when we consider problems of aggregation and estimation. Perhaps it would be well to state at this point that in applications of these models to consumer panel data this assumption is fulfilled by the nature of the data gathering process. Panel households are sufficiently dispersed geographically to assure us of nearly zero interpersonal interaction.

In summary, R2 assumes that, for any given individual, responses will be independent over time. Assumption R3 assures us that the responses are independent cross-sectionally between individuals. Hence, all responses of all individuals are postulated by the model to be independent.

6.4.1.3 *Response Probability Change Assumptions.* The preceding assumptions have specified a heterogeneous, zero-order response model. In this section we shall specify the assumptions that provide for change (or nonstationarity) in an individual's response probability.

The previous discussion has used t to index response occasions. In the subsequent discussion it will be convenient to view t as a continuous measure having a unit interval between response occasions t and $t + 1$, for all t. This viewpoint will enable us to derive readily relationships for the change in an individual's response probability between response occasion. In certain applications of the model, the index t will represent the actual time between responses.

The state of an individual will be defined as his response probability. Since each individual in the population is assumed to have the same number of response elements N, an equivalent state space would be the number of response elements associated with response A. We shall denote the states of this latter state space by i. In addition, we shall use the symbol $O(\Delta t)$ to denote terms of an order which tend to zero faster than Δt.

The response probability change assumptions then are given by:

C1. If at response occasion t an individual is in state $i(i = 0, 1, \ldots, N - 1)$, the probability of the transition $i \to i + 1$ in the interval $(t, t + \Delta t)$ is $\lambda_i \Delta t + O(\Delta t)$.

C2. If at response occasion t an individual is in state $i(i = 1, 2, \ldots, N)$, the probability of the transition $i \to i - 1$ in the interval $(t, t + \Delta t)$ is $\mu_i \Delta t + O(\Delta t)$.

C3. The probability of a transition to other than a neighboring state is $O(\Delta t)$. Formally, the probability of the transition $i \to j$ for $|i - j| > 1$ is $O(\Delta t)$. Hence,

$$\lim_{\Delta t \to 0} \frac{P\{|i - j| > 0\}}{\Delta t} = 0$$

C4. The process is stationary. That is, λ_i and μ_i are independent of time.

Note that by C1 to C4, we have postulated a general birth-death process on the response elements in terms of their association with

either response A or B. For N (the total number of response elements) finite, the change assumptions specify a birth-death process on a population that has an upper bound N and a potential birth pool constrained to $N - i$ if we consider an element that changes its association from B to A as being "born."

These assumptions specify a latent Markov process that represents the changes in response association of the response elements within any individual. It is Markovian with respect to the state space of response probabilities. The Markov process is latent in that the state space is not directly observable.

6.4.2 The General System of Differential Equations

From the response probability change assumptions, we are able to develop a system of differential equations which express the probability that an individual respondent will occupy a given state (i.e., have some particular response probability) at response occasion t.

Let $p_i(t)$ be the probability that at response occasion t the respondent has i of his response elements associated with response A. To illustrate the derivation of the system of differential equations, we shall examine the probability that a respondent has none of his elements associated with A at $t + \Delta t$, where Δt is taken to be very small. Since Δt is taken to be very small, the change assumptions indicate that at most one of the individual's N response elements could have shifted its association from B to A or from A to B during this interval. Hence, he could be only in state 0 at $t + \Delta t$ if one of two mutually exclusive and collectively exhaustive events has occurred. Either he was in state 0 at t and none of his response elements has shifted its association during Δt, or he was in state 1 at t and the one element that was associated with response A has shifted to an association with response B by $t + \Delta t$. The probability that he was in state 0 and no change occurred is $p_0(t)[1 - \lambda_0 \Delta t - O(\Delta t)]$ where the first factor is the probability that he was in state 0 at t and the second factor is the probability of no change in his state during Δt if he was in state 0 at t. Similarly, the probability that he was in state 1 at t and shifted to state 0 by $t + \Delta t$ is just $p_1(t)[\mu_1 \Delta t + O(\Delta t)]$. Since the two paths to arrive at state 0 by $t + \Delta t$ are mutually exclusive and collectively exhaustive, it is clear that the total probability that this individual respondent is in state 0 at $t + \Delta t$ is given by the sum of the probability of each of these two paths

$$p_0(t + \Delta t) = p_0(t)[1 - \lambda_0 \Delta t] + p_1(t)\mu_1 \Delta t + O(\Delta t) \qquad (6.1)$$

where we have collected all terms of $O(\Delta t)$ in $O(\Delta t)$.

Subtracting $p_0(t)$, dividing through by Δt, and taking the limit as Δt goes to zero yield

$$\lim_{\Delta t \to 0} \frac{p_0(t + \Delta t) - p_0(t)}{\Delta t} = -\lambda_0 p_0(t) + \mu_1 p_1(t) \tag{6.2}$$

where we have used the fact that

$$\lim_{\Delta t \to 0} \frac{O(\Delta t)}{\Delta t} = 0$$

But we note that Equation 6.2 is just the definition of the derivative of the function $p_0(t)$. Hence, we have the following differential equation for the probability of state 0:

$$\frac{dp_0(t)}{dt} = -\lambda_0 p_0(t) + \mu_1 p_1(t) \tag{6.3}$$

By similar reasoning we may complete the system of equations for all $N + 1$ of the possible states of the individual respondent. These equations are

$$\frac{dp_i(t)}{dt} = -(\lambda_i + \mu_i)p_i(t) + \lambda_{i-1}p_{i-1}(t) + \mu_{i+1}p_{i+1}(t) \qquad \text{for } 0 < i < N$$

$$\tag{6.4}$$

$$\frac{dp_N(t)}{dt} = -\mu_N p_N(t) + \lambda_{N-1}p_{N-1}(t) \tag{6.5}$$

Equations 6.3, 6.4, and 6.5 are the general differential equations for the model using arbitrary specifications of λ_i and μ_i. In the models developed in the subsequent two sections of this chapter, we shall further specify λ_i and μ_i. Then we shall examine the steady-state distribution of the response states or, equivalently, the steady-state distribution of response probability.

6.5 The Independent Elements Specification

6.5.1 Formulation of the Independent Elements Specification

We now turn our attention to the development of a special case of the general model which we shall term the independent elements specification (IES). This model specification has been applied by Coleman to consumer behavior (Coleman, 1963) and to voting behavior in small union groups (Coleman, 1964b, Chapter 11). In this section it will be shown

that this specification has serious limitations for a broad class of applications.

In order to analyze this model, we must further specify its properties. In particular, for the IES, we shall assume that

1. The N response elements within an individual behave independently,
2. Each element associated with response B has transition intensity α toward becoming associated with response A,
3. Each element associated with response A has transition intensity β toward becoming associated with response B.

These additional assumptions enable us to specify the λ_i and μ_i of the general model. Thus,

$$\lambda_i = (N - i)\alpha \qquad (6.6)$$

and

$$\mu_i = i\beta \qquad (6.7)$$

Equation 6.6 represents the fact that for Δt, an interval so small that at most one element may change its state, there are $N - i$ elements associated with response B which could shift their association to response A. Hence, in order for the state of an individual to change from i to $i + 1$, one of the $N - i$ elements associated with response B would have to change its association. This can happen in $N - i$ independent ways during the interval Δt. Similarly, one may develop Equation 6.7.

Substituting Equations 6.6 and 6.7 into Equations 6.3, 6.4, and 6.5, we have the following system of differential equations for the independent elements model:[11]

$$\frac{dp_0(t)}{dt} = -N\alpha p_0(t) + \beta p_1(t)$$

$$\frac{dp_i(t)}{dt} = -[(N - i)\alpha + i\beta]p_i(t) + (N - i + 1)\alpha p_{i-1}(t)$$

$$+ (i + 1)\beta p_{i+1}(t) \qquad \text{for } 0 < i < N \quad (6.8)$$

$$\frac{dp_N(t)}{dt} = -N\beta p_N(t) + \alpha p_{N-1}(t)$$

The steady-state distribution of i is given by

$$p_i = \frac{N!}{i!(N - i)!}\left(\frac{\alpha}{\alpha + \beta}\right)^i\left(1 - \frac{\alpha}{\alpha + \beta}\right)^{N-i} \qquad (6.9)$$

[11] It should be noted that this system of differential equations is identical to the one arrived at by Feller (1957, pp. 420–421) in the power supply problem.

Equation 6.9 is simply the binomial distribution. We have dropped the index t, since we are considering the distribution in the steady state. The solution given as Equation 6.9 may be obtained by setting $dp_i(t)/dt = 0$ in Equation 6.8 for $i = 0, 1, \ldots, N$ or by the method of generating functions given in Feller (1957). Now we have the well-known results for the binomial mean and variance

$$E[i] = N\left(\frac{\alpha}{\alpha + \beta}\right) \tag{6.10}$$

$$\text{Var}[i] = N\left(\frac{\alpha}{\alpha + \beta}\right)\left(1 - \frac{\alpha}{\alpha + \beta}\right) \tag{6.11}$$

We shall denote an individual's response probability as $X(t) = i/N$. Then for $X(t)$ in the steady state, we have

$$E[X] = E\left(\frac{i}{N}\right) = \frac{\alpha}{\alpha + \beta} \tag{6.12}$$

$$\text{Var}[X] = \text{Var}\left[\frac{i}{N}\right] = \frac{1}{N^2}\text{Var}[i] = \frac{1}{N}\left(\frac{\alpha}{\alpha + \beta}\right)\left(1 - \frac{\alpha}{\alpha + \beta}\right) \tag{6.13}$$

It remains to examine the behavior of this independent elements specification as a function of N, the number of response elements within an individual. There are two extreme cases of interest: N very small and N very large.

Case 1: N very small. In this case it is clear that an individual's response probability may only take on a few, widely spaced values. If $N = 1$, he may have only the response probability values $X(t) = 0$ or $X(t) = 1$. If $N = 2$, he may have only the values $X(t) = 0$, $X(t) = \frac{1}{2}$, and $X(t) = 1$. In fact, his response probability may take on only $N + 1$ distinct values if there are N elements. It is more intuitively appealing to have a model that allows a response probability continuum. Hence, we shall now turn to the case where the number of response elements increases without limit.

Case 2: N increases without limit. Clearly, in the limit, the values an individual's response probability may take on approach a continuum. This, of course, is a more appealing situation than that of Case 1. But the independent elements specification breaks down in another sense in this case. If we examine Equation 6.13 we see that the variance of response probability in the steady state is inversely related to the

number of response elements. Thus, if we let N increase without limit, we have

$$\lim_{N \to \infty} \text{Var}[X] = \lim_{N \to \infty} \frac{1}{N}\left(\frac{\alpha}{\alpha + \beta}\right)\left(1 - \frac{\alpha}{\alpha + \beta}\right) = 0 \qquad (6.14)$$

This tells us that as $N \to \infty$, an individual described by the independent elements specification will have a response probability in the steady state exactly equal to $\alpha/(\alpha + \beta)$. Since by assumptions S1 and R3, we are assuming that the same process in terms of α and β holds for all the independent members (respondents) of the population, we see that the independent elements specification implies that the entire population of respondents converges to the response probability $\alpha/(\alpha + \beta)$ in the steady state regardless of their individual starting states. Hence the model implies homogeneity of response probability in the steady state. That is, the assumed heterogeneity of individual respondents degenerates in the steady state under this specification. Such a result is no more appealing than the assumption that all individuals start out with the same response probability.

Although these comments indicate why the IES is inappropriate as a model of consumer choice behavior, there are instances in the social sciences where the model may prove useful. For example, Coleman (1964b, pp. 336–343) has applied it to voting behavior in small groups. Our elements correspond to his individuals, and his groups correspond to our individuals. These comments would certainly caution against using this model except for small group analysis and only then if one can assume that individuals make their choices independently.

Fortunately for the utility of the latent Markov models, it is possible to rectify the problems noted here by postulating a process in which there are cohesive forces between the elements. Such a model is studied in detail in Section 6.6.

Although we already know that the IES is unsatisfactory, it nevertheless would prove instructive to examine the evolution of an individual's response probability through time under this model.

6.5.2   *Mean Value Function of the Independent Elements Model Specification*

The mean value function of a stochastic process is defined as $m(t) = \text{E}[X(t)]$ where (t) is the state variable at t.[12] In the models that we are

---

[12] See Parzen (1962, Chapter 3) for a more complete discussion of mean value functions.

considering, $X(t)$ is the probability of making response A at response occasion t. Recall that in terms of the model $X(t)$ is just the proportion of the response elements which are associated with response A at response occasion t.

The development of $m(t)$ requires that we first examine the expected change in response probability during the interval $(t, t + h)$, where h is suitably small. It is notationally convenient to use h in lieu of Δt in the following derivations. Formally, we seek $E[X(t + h) - X(t)]$. It is known from probability theory that

$$E_Y[Y] = E_X\{E_{Y|X}[Y|X]\} \qquad (6.15)$$

where the subscripts denote the random variable with respect to which the expectation is being taken.[13] In the present case, we have

$$E[X(t + h) - X(t)] = E_X\left\{E\left[X(t + h) - X(t)|X(t) = \frac{i}{N}\right]\right\} \qquad (6.16)$$

We have sufficient information to compute $E[X(t + h) - X(t)|X(t) = i/N]$. For h sufficiently small so that the system may change by at most one unit during h, there are three possible values of $X(t + h) - X(t) = \Delta X(t)$. These values and their associated probabilities are given in Table 6.2. From Table 6.2, we have

$$E[\Delta X(t)|X(t) = i/N] = \frac{h}{N}\{(N - i)\alpha - i\beta\}$$
$$= h\{[1 - X(t)]\alpha - \beta X(t)\}$$
$$= h\{\alpha - (\alpha + \beta)X(t)\} \qquad (6.17)$$

Table 6.2 $\Delta X(t)$ Conditional on $X(t)$: Independent Elements Model Specification

$\Delta X(t)$	$P\left[\Delta X(t)|X(t) = \dfrac{i}{N}\right]$
$\dfrac{1}{N}$	$\lambda_i h = (N - i)\alpha h$
0	$1 - (\lambda_i + \mu_i)h$
$\dfrac{-1}{N}$	$\mu_i h = i\beta h$

[13] See Parzen (1960, p. 384).

Substituting Equation 6.17 into Equation 6.16, we have

$$E[X(t + h) - X(t)] = h\{\alpha - (\alpha + \beta) E[X(t)]\} \qquad (6.18)$$

Dividing through by h and taking the limit as $h \to 0$, we find

$$\lim_{h \to 0} \frac{E[X(t + h) - X(t)]}{h} = \lim_{h \to 0} \frac{E[X(t + h)] - E[X(t)]}{h}$$

$$= \frac{d\,E[X(t)]}{dt} = \alpha - (\alpha + \beta) E[X(t)] \qquad (6.19)$$

The first equality follows from the fact that expectation is a linear operator, while the second equality follows by the definition of the derivative of a function.

The solution to Equation 6.19, as may be verified by substitution, is

$$E[X(t)] = E[X(0)] \exp\left[-(\alpha + \beta)t\right] + \frac{\alpha}{\alpha + \beta}\left[1 - \exp\left[-(\alpha + \beta)t\right]\right]$$
$$(6.20)$$

6.5.3   *Variance of the Independent Elements Specification*

It remains to consider the variance of the process. Since

$$\text{Var}[X(t)] = E[X^2(t)] - E^2[X(t)]$$

and since we have $E[X(t)]$ from Equation 6.20, we now seek to develop $E[X^2(t)]$. To do so we first examine $E[X^2(t + h)]$. It is easily seen that

$$E[X^2(t + h)] = E[X^2(t)] + E[\{X(t + h) - X(t)\}^2]$$
$$+ 2\,E[\{X(t + h) - X(t)\}X(t)] \quad (6.21)$$

First, consider

$$E[\{X(t + h) - X(t)\}^2 | X(t)]$$

The possible values of $\{\Delta X(t)\}^2$ and their associated probabilities are given in Table 6.3. From Table 6.3, we have

$$E[\{X(t + h) - X(t)\}^2 | X(t)] = hN^{-2}\{(N - i)\alpha + i\beta\}$$
$$= hN^{-1}\{[1 - X(t)]\alpha + \beta X(t)\}$$
$$= hN^{-1}\{\alpha - (\alpha - \beta)X(t)\}$$

Table 6.3 $\{\Delta X(t)\}^2$ Conditional on $X(t)$:
Independent Elements Model

$\{\Delta X(t)\}^2$	$P\left[\{\Delta X(t)\}^2 \| X(t) = \dfrac{i}{N}\right]$
$\dfrac{1}{N^2}$	$\lambda_i h = (N - i)\alpha h$
0	$1 - (\lambda_i + \mu_i)h$
$\dfrac{1}{N^2}$	$\mu_i h = i\beta h$

Taking the expectation with respect to the distribution of $X(t)$, we have

$$E[\{X(t + h) - X(t)\}^2] = hN^{-1}\{\alpha - (\alpha - \beta)\,E[X(t)]\}$$

It remains to consider

$$E[\{X(t + h) - X(t)\}X(t)]$$

The possible values of $\{\Delta X(t)\}X(t)$ and their associated probabilities are given in Table 6.4. Using the results given in Table 6.4, we find

$$E[\{X(t + h) - X(t)\}X(t)|X(t)] = hX(t)N^{-1}\{(N - i)\alpha - i\beta\}$$
$$= hX(t)\{[1 - X(t)]\alpha - \beta X(t)\}$$
$$= h\{\alpha X(t) - \alpha X^2(t) - \beta X^2(t)\}$$

Table 6.4 $X(t)\{\Delta X(t)\}$ Conditional on $X(t)$:
Independent Elements Model

$X(t)\{\Delta X(t)\}$	$P\left[X(t)\{\Delta X(t)\} \| X(t) = \dfrac{i}{N}\right]$
$\dfrac{X(t)}{N}$	$\lambda_i h = (N - i)\alpha h$
0	$1 - (\lambda_i + \mu_i)h$
$\dfrac{-X(t)}{N}$	$\mu_i h = i\beta h$

Taking the expectation with respect to the distribution of $X(t)$, we have

$$E[\{X(t + h) - X(t)\}X(t)] = h\{\alpha\, E[X(t)] - (\alpha + \beta)\, E[X^2(t)]\}$$

We now may write Equation 6.21 as

$$E[X^2(t + h)] = E[X^2(t)] + hN^{-1}\{\alpha - (\alpha - \beta)\, E[X(t)]\}$$
$$+ 2h\{\alpha\, E[X(t)] - (\alpha + \beta)\, E[X^2(t)]\}$$

Subtracting $E[X^2(t)]$, dividing by h, and taking the limit as $h \to 0$, we find

$$\lim_{h \to 0} \frac{E[X^2(t + h)] - E[X^2(t)]}{h} = \frac{d\, E[X^2(t)]}{dt}$$

$$= \frac{1}{N}\{\alpha - (\alpha - \beta)\, E[X(t)]\} + 2\alpha\, E[X(t)] - 2(\alpha + \beta)\, E[X^2(t)] \quad (6.22)$$

In order to show the degeneracy of this model as $N \to \infty$, we now consider

$$\lim_{N \to \infty} \frac{d\, E[X^2(t)]}{dt}$$

Let a bar over an expectation indicate that the limit as $N \to \infty$ has been taken.

We now have

$$\lim_{N \to \infty} \frac{d\, E[X^2(t)]}{dt} = \frac{d\, \overline{E}[X^2(t)]}{dt} = 2\,\alpha\, \overline{E}[X(t)] - 2(\alpha + \beta)\, \overline{E}[X^2(t)].$$
$$(6.23)$$

In order to find $\overline{\text{Var}}\, X(t)$ we need to solve Equation 6.23 for $\overline{E}[X^2(t)]$.

We shall solve Equation 6.23 by the method of undetermined coefficients. Assume a solution of the form

$$\overline{E}[X^2(t)] = a_0 + a_1 \exp\,[-(\alpha + \beta)t] + a_2 \exp\,[-2(\alpha + \beta)t] \quad (6.24)$$

Differentiating Equation 6.24, we obtain

$$\frac{d\, \overline{E}[X^2(t)]}{dt} = -(\alpha + \beta)a_1 \exp\,[-(\alpha + \beta)t]$$

$$- 2(\alpha + \beta)a_2 \exp\,[-2(\alpha + \beta)t] \quad (6.25)$$

Now we substitute Equations 6.20 and 6.24 into Equation 6.23 noting

that $E[X(t)] = \overline{E}[X(t)]$ as is obvious from Equation 6.20. This yields

$$\frac{d\,\overline{E}[X^2(t)]}{dt} = 2\alpha\{\overline{E}[X(0)]\exp[-(\alpha+\beta)t]$$

$$+ \frac{\alpha}{\alpha+\beta}(1 - \exp[-(\alpha+\beta)t])\} - 2(\alpha+\beta)$$

$$\times \{a_0 + a_1\exp[-(\alpha+\beta)t] + a_2\exp[-2(\alpha+\beta)t]\}$$

$$= \frac{2\alpha^2}{\alpha+\beta} - 2(\alpha+\beta)a_0$$

$$+ \{2\alpha\,\overline{E}[X(0)] - \frac{2\alpha^2}{\alpha+\beta} - 2(\alpha+\beta)a_1\}$$

$$\times \exp[-(\alpha+\beta)t] - 2(\alpha+\beta)a_2 \qquad (6.26)$$

We then denote the initial condition for Equation 6.24 as

$$\overline{E}[X^2(0)] = a_0 + a_1 + a_2 \qquad (6.27)$$

Equating coefficients of similar terms in Equations 6.25 and 6.26 yields two additional equations on the undetermined coefficients.

$$0 = \frac{2\alpha^2}{\alpha+\beta} - 2(\alpha+\beta)a_0$$
$$-(\alpha+\beta)a_1 = 2\alpha\,\overline{E}[X(0)] - \frac{2\alpha^2}{\alpha+\beta} - 2(\alpha+\beta)a_1 \qquad (6.28)$$

Solving Equations 6.27 and 6.28 for a_0, a_1 and a_2, we have

$$a_0 = \frac{\alpha^2}{(\alpha+\beta)^2}$$

$$a_1 = 2\left(\frac{\alpha}{\alpha+\beta}\right)\left\{\overline{E}[X(0)] - \frac{\alpha}{\alpha+\beta}\right\} \qquad (6.29)$$

$$a_2 = \overline{E}[X^2(0)] - a_0 - a_1$$

$$= \overline{E}[X^2(0)] + \frac{\alpha^2}{(\alpha+\beta)^2} - 2\frac{\alpha}{\alpha+\beta}\overline{E}[X(0)]$$

Hence, we have for $\overline{E}[X^2(t)]$ that

$$\overline{E}[X^2(t)] = \left(\frac{\alpha}{\alpha+\beta}\right)^2 + 2\left(\frac{\alpha}{\alpha+\beta}\right)\left\{\overline{E}[X(0)] - \frac{\alpha}{\alpha+\beta}\right\}\exp[-(\alpha+\beta)t]$$

$$+ \left\{\overline{E}[X^2(0)] + \left(\frac{\alpha}{\alpha+\beta}\right)^2 - 2\left(\frac{\alpha}{\alpha+\beta}\right)\overline{E}[X(0)]\right\}$$

$$\times \exp[-2(\alpha+\beta)t] \qquad (6.30)$$

Using the results of Equations 6.30 and 6.20, we now may compute, with a bit of algebra, the variance of the process when the response probability is a continuous random variable (i.e., when $N \to \infty$). The result is

$$\overline{\text{Var}}[X(t)] = \{\overline{\text{E}}[X^2(0)] - \overline{\text{E}}^2[X(0)]\} \exp\left[-2(\alpha + \beta)t\right] \quad (6.31)$$

It might be noted that

$$\overline{\text{Var}}[X(0)] = \overline{\text{E}}[X^2(0)] - \overline{\text{E}}^2[X(0)]$$

and thus

$$\overline{\text{Var}}[X(t)] = \overline{\text{Var}}[X(0)] \exp\left[-2(\alpha + \beta)t\right]$$

From Equation 6.31, we see that the variance tends to zero as the process approaches the steady state. Since the same process applies to each respondent, this means that the only interrespondent variability in the process is caused by the variance in the initial response probability. We have already noted that this is intuitively unappealing.

As a final comment on the IES, suppose we consider an individual with a given initial response probability. Then for this individual $E[X(0)] = X(0)$ and $E[X^2(0)] = X^2(0)$, and hence $\text{Var}[X(0)] = X^2(0) - X^2(0) = 0$. Thus he follows Equation 6.20 deterministically until this response probability equals $\alpha/(\alpha + \beta)$, where it remains forevermore as far as the model is concerned.

6.5.4 Summary of the Independent Elements Specification

The independent elements specification was found to be an unsatisfactory model for consumer choice behavior. This conclusion is based upon the notion that a consumer's brand-choice probability should be a continuous measure. This led us to consider the infinite element case. In the infinite element case, the independent elements model implies that all respondents will have the same response probability in the steady state, even though they initially exhibit heterogeneity. Furthermore, each respondent will deterministically move toward that steady-state response probability.

6.6 The Cohesive Elements Specification

In the previous section the independent elements specification was shown to degenerate when the number of response elements increases without limit — i.e., when an individual's response probability becomes

continuous. The degeneracy is in the sense that all individuals in the population tend deterministically to the same response probability. In the present chapter, this situation is rectified by the development of a birth-death process on the response elements in which the elements are assumed to have a cohesive property. Thus, the present model drops the previous assumption that an individual's response elements behave independently.

In the present section, we first develop the cohesive elements specification and its associated steady-state distribution of response probability for a finite number of elements. If the number of elements is then allowed to increase without limit, the steady-state distribution of response probability is shown to go to a beta distribution. We next consider the mean and variance of the stochastic process that represents response probability changes over a sequence of response occasions. We then examine the diffusion limit of the model. Aggregation and the development of potential estimating equations are the next topics considered. Finally, we examine methods of obtaining information on the cross-sectional distribution of response probability at each response occasion. The general problem of estimating the cohesive elements specification will be reserved for Section 6.7.

6.6.1   Formulation and Steady-State Distribution

Once again, before we may consider the behavior of the model in the steady state, we must further specify its properties. For the present model we shall retain assumptions 2 and 3 of Section 6.5.1 and replace assumption 1 with

1′. The transition intensity of each element is increased by an amount γ for each element associated with the opposite response.

Note that assumption 1′ might be thought of as an assumption of cohesion or attraction between the response elements.

Using 1′, 2, and 3 and the assumptions of Section 6.4, we may examine the process both at the level of the response elements and at the level of the individual respondent.[14] In diagrammatic[15] form the process at the

[14] This section closely follows Coleman's development in Chapters 11, 12, and 13 of *Introduction to Mathematical Sociology*, Coleman (1964b).

[15] The diagrammatic presentation is intended to clarify how the assumed process at the level of the elements induces the $N + 1$ state process at the level of the individual.

level of the response elements is

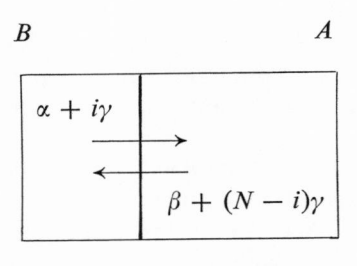

where $i =$ number of elements associated with response A and $N =$ total number of response elements. Since each individual respondent is assumed to have N response elements, the two-state process at the level of the elements induces a $N + 1$ state process at the level of the individual. The transition intensities at the level of the individual respondent are, in the notation of the general model,

$$\lambda_i = \begin{pmatrix} \text{Single-element transition intensity} \\ \text{from } B \text{ to } A \end{pmatrix} \begin{pmatrix} \text{Number of response} \\ \text{elements in state } B \end{pmatrix}$$

$$= (\alpha + i\gamma)(N - i) \qquad\qquad\qquad (6.32)$$

and

$$\mu_i = [\beta + (N - i)\gamma]i \qquad\qquad\qquad\qquad (6.33)$$

In diagram form we have at the level of the individual

B A

$N\alpha$	$(N-1)(\alpha + \gamma)$		$2[\alpha + (N-2)\gamma]$	$\alpha + (N-1)\gamma$	
	$\beta + (N-1)\gamma$	$2[\beta + (N-2)\gamma]$		$(N-1)(\beta + \gamma)$	$N\beta$

where the state space is the number of elements i out of the total of N elements that are associated with response A.

If we substitute Equations 6.32 and 6.33 into the general model

Equations 6.3, 6.4, and 6.5, we have

$$\frac{dp_0(t)}{dt} = -N\alpha p_0(t) + [\beta + (N-1)\gamma]p_1(t)$$

$$\frac{dp_i(t)}{dt} = -\{(N-i)(\alpha + i\gamma) + i[\beta + (N-i)\gamma]\}p_i(t)$$

$$+ (N-i+1)[\alpha + (i-1)\gamma]p_{i-1}(t)$$

$$+ (i+1)[\beta + (N-i-1)\gamma]p_{i+1}(t)$$

$$\text{for } 0 < i < N$$

$$\frac{dp_N(t)}{dt} = -N\beta p_N(t) + [\alpha + (N-1)\gamma]p_{N-1}(t) \tag{6.34}$$

The steady-state solution of this system of differential equations may be obtained by the simultaneous solution of the equations when $[dp_i(t)]/dt = 0$ for $i = 0, 1, \ldots, N$. The steady-state derivation also makes use of the fact that

$$\sum_{i=0}^{N} p_i(t) = 1$$

Coleman[16] reports the solution as

$$p_i = \binom{N}{i} \frac{\Gamma\left(\frac{\alpha}{\gamma} + i\right)\Gamma\left(N + \frac{\beta}{\gamma} - i\right)\Gamma\left(\frac{\alpha + \beta}{\gamma}\right)}{\Gamma\left(\frac{\alpha}{\gamma}\right)\Gamma\left(N + \frac{\alpha + \beta}{\gamma}\right)\Gamma\left(\frac{\beta}{\gamma}\right)} \qquad \text{for } i = 0, 1, \ldots, n \tag{6.35}$$

where

$$\binom{N}{i} = \frac{N!}{i!(N-i)!}$$

and $\Gamma(x)$ represents the gamma function of the argument x. We have dropped t from $p_i(t)$ since we are now considering the steady-state distribution. Coleman termed this distribution the "contagious binomial." In Section 6.6.2, we shall examine the form of the steady-state distribution when the number of elements increases without limit. Coleman has unsuccessfully attempted to take this limit of Equation 6.35 as $N \to \infty$. Recall that the logic behind such a limit process is that when $N \to \infty$ the individual respondent then may be represented by what is essentially a continuous response probability. When N is

[16] Coleman (1964b, p. 345).

finite, the response probability $X(t) = i/N$ clearly takes on only a finite number of discrete values. Hence, letting $N \to \infty$ yields a more satisfying model of an individual's response probability.

6.6.2 The Steady-State Distribution for an Infinite Number of Response Elements

In order to determine the function that will yield a continuous probability density function for an individual's response probability X, in the limit, we first discuss what occurs as $N \to \infty$ in such a way that $X = i/N$ remains constant. The latter restriction is included to ensure that the cumulative probability, $P[X \le C]$ where C is some constant between 0 and 1, remains constant as $N \to \infty$.[17]

Suppose on the interval $(0,1)$ that we have $N + 1$ discrete points at which a probability mass, $p(X = i/N)$, may occur. See Figure 6.3. An alternative representation would be to express the probability mass function $p(X)$ as a histogram in which $h(X)$ denotes the height of the histogram at any point X. See Figure 6.4 for such a histogram. Note that the width of each interval is $1/N$ and the area of the rectangle about X is the probability that the individual respondent has the proportion $X = i/N$ of his N response elements associated with response A.

We have noted that the area of the histogram about any point $X = i/N$ represents the probability that X is the proportion of the N response elements associated with response A. That is,

$$p(X) = \frac{1}{N} h(X)$$

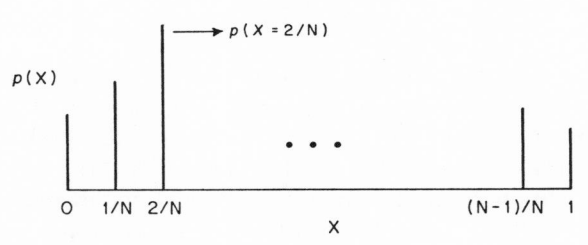

Figure 6.3. A probability mass function.

[17] This restriction is analogous to that used in the development of the Poisson limit of the binomial distribution. See Feller (1957). This section is based upon Montgomery (1968a).

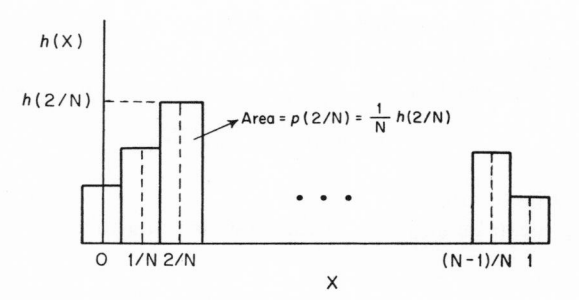

Figure 6.4. A probability histogram.

Hence we may write

$$h(X) = Np(X)$$

Suppose now that in the interval $(0,1)$ we pack in more and more elements, that is, we let N get large. In this case $1/N$ will become very small, and in the limit the $h(X)$ will be so close together that they will trace out a continuous curve. This continuous curve is the continuous probability density function (p.d.f.) of $X = i/N$ when $N \to \infty$ in such a way that $X = i/N$ remains constant. That is, where C indicates that $X = i/N$ remains constant,

$$\lim_{\substack{N \to \infty \\ X=(i/N)=C}} h(X) = \lim_{\substack{N \to \infty \\ X=(i/N)=C}} p(X) = f(X) \tag{6.36}$$

This equation gives us the function that we must take to the limit in order to obtain the probability density function of X, $f(X)$.

For any fixed N, there is a direct equivalence between $p(X)$ in Equation 6.36 and the p_i given by Equation 6.35. Clearly, for some fixed N, the event $X = i/N$ occurs if and only if the event i occurs. Hence, for fixed N the events $X = i/N$ and i are equivalent, and consequently they have the same probability of occurrence. Thus $p(X) = p_i$. Since we have derived the steady-state distribution of i for some fixed N in Equation 6.35, we now may write Equation 6.36 as

$$f(X) = \lim_{\substack{N \to \infty \\ i/N=C}} Np_i = \lim_{\substack{N \to \infty \\ XN=i=NC}} N\binom{N}{i} \frac{\Gamma\left(\dfrac{\alpha}{\gamma} + i\right)\Gamma\left(N + \dfrac{\beta}{\gamma} - i\right)\Gamma\left(\dfrac{\alpha + \beta}{\gamma}\right)}{\Gamma\left(\dfrac{\alpha}{\gamma}\right)\Gamma\left(N + \dfrac{\alpha + \beta}{\gamma}\right)\Gamma\left(\dfrac{\beta}{\gamma}\right)}$$

$$\tag{6.37}$$

A result on the limiting behavior of gamma functions when a term in the gamma argument increases without limit is needed if the limit on the right-hand side of Equation 6.37 is to be found. The result is

$$\lim_{\alpha \to \infty} \Gamma(\alpha + a) = \lim_{\alpha \to \infty} \alpha^a \Gamma(\alpha) \qquad (6.38)$$

where a may be complex.[18]

Using the result given in Equation 6.38 in Equation 6.37, we have

$$f(X) = \lim_{\substack{N \to \infty \\ X = (i/N) = C}} N p_i = \lim_{\substack{N \to \infty \\ NX = i = NC}}$$

$$\times \frac{N\Gamma(N+1)\Gamma\left(NX + \dfrac{\alpha}{\gamma}\right)\Gamma\left(N(1-X) + \dfrac{\beta}{\gamma}\right)\Gamma\left(\dfrac{\alpha+\beta}{\gamma}\right)}{\Gamma(NX+1)\Gamma(N(1-X)+1)\Gamma\left(\dfrac{\alpha}{\gamma}\right)\Gamma\left(\dfrac{\beta}{\gamma}\right)\Gamma\left(N + \dfrac{\alpha+\beta}{\gamma}\right)}$$

$$= \lim_{\substack{N \to \infty \\ NX = i}}$$

$$\times \frac{\Gamma\left(\dfrac{\alpha+\beta}{\gamma}\right)N^2\Gamma(N)N^{\alpha/\gamma}X^{\alpha/\gamma}\Gamma(NX)N^{\beta/\gamma}(1-X)^{\beta/\gamma}\Gamma(N(1-X))}{\Gamma\left(\dfrac{\alpha}{\gamma}\right)\Gamma\left(\dfrac{\beta}{\gamma}\right)NX\Gamma(NX)N(1-X)\Gamma(N(1-X))N^{\alpha/\gamma}N^{\beta/\gamma}\Gamma(N)}$$

$$= \frac{\Gamma\left(\dfrac{\alpha+\beta}{\gamma}\right)}{\Gamma\left(\dfrac{\alpha}{\gamma}\right)\Gamma\left(\dfrac{\beta}{\gamma}\right)} X^{(\alpha/\gamma)-1}(1-X)^{(\beta/\gamma)-1} \qquad (6.39)$$

which is a beta distribution. Hence, the distribution of an individual's response probability X in the steady state and as $N \to \infty$ is the beta distribution. When we consider the diffusion limit in Section 6.6.4, we shall see that Equation 6.39 satisfies the necessary steady-state form of the Fokker-Plank equation.

6.6.3   *Mean Value Function and the Variance of the Change Process*

The next task is to develop relations that describe the evolution of an individual's response probability over a sequence of response occasions. The procedure in this section will be to state the results for the mean-value function and variance of the change process and to comment

[18] See Copson (1935, Chapter 9).

upon their interpretation. It will be seen that the variance of this process does not degenerate as the number of response elements increases without limit. This is in direct contrast to the independent elements specification where the variance tended to zero as the number of response elements increased without limit, as was shown in Section 6.5. For the reader interested in the details the rather lengthy proofs of these results are included at the end of this section.

The cohesive elements specification for λ_i and μ_i may be shown to generate a mean-value function for the change process of the form.[19]

$$\frac{d\,E[X(t)]}{dt} = \alpha - (\alpha + \beta)\,E[X(t)] \tag{6.40}$$

The solution of this equation, as may be readily verified by substitution is

$$E[X(t)] = E[X(0)] \exp\left[-(\alpha + \beta)t\right] + \left(\frac{\alpha}{\alpha + \beta}\right)(1 - \exp\left[-(\alpha + \beta)t\right]) \tag{6.41}$$

where $E[X(0)]$ expresses the initial condition in the equation. That is, $E[X(0)]$ represents the expected initial response probability of an individual respondent drawn at random from the population of respondents represented by the model. Note that the mean-value function for the cohesive elements specification is identical to the mean-value function of the independent element specification given in Equation 6.20.

In our subsequent development of the model, we will be interested in the mean-value function of $X(t)$ for an individual respondent having some specific initial value $X(0)$. That is, we shall be interested in the mean-value function of response probability for an individual respondent conditional upon his initial response probability. In this case

---

[19] Equation 6.40 is identical to Equation 1.2 on page 17 of Coleman (1964a) in the two-response case if one interprets Coleman's v_{1_t} as follows:

$$v_{1_t} = m(t) = E[X(t)]$$

This equation is simply presented in Coleman (1964a); however, it is derived in Coleman (1964b, Chapter 13) by an alternative argument to the one used in this section.

The procedure used here makes it easier to investigate the variance of the process, which Coleman didn't do in either of the works cited here. He did, however, give the variance of the steady-state distribution for the contagious binomial in Chapter 4 of Coleman (1964a).

Equation 6.41 becomes

$$E[X(t)|X(0)] = X(0) \exp[-(\alpha + \beta)t] + \frac{\alpha}{\alpha + \beta}(1 - \exp[-(\alpha + \beta)t])$$

$$(6.42)$$

This result will be particularly useful when we aggregate the responses of individual respondents in order to estimate and test the model.

The variance of $X(t)$ in the infinite element case (which is the one of interest to us) may be shown to be

$$\overline{\mathrm{Var}}[X(t)] = \frac{\alpha\beta\gamma}{(\alpha + \beta)^2(\alpha + \beta + \gamma)} + \frac{2\gamma(\alpha - \beta)}{(\alpha + \beta)(\alpha + \beta + 2\gamma)}$$

$$\times \left\{\frac{\alpha}{\alpha + \beta} - \overline{E}[X(0)]\right\} \exp[-(\alpha + \beta)t]$$

$$+ \left\{\overline{E}[X^2(0)] - \frac{\alpha(\alpha + \gamma)}{(\alpha + \beta)(\alpha + \beta + \gamma)} - \frac{2(\alpha + \gamma)}{\alpha + \beta}\right.$$

$$\times \left.\frac{[(\alpha + \beta)\,\overline{E}[X(0)] - \alpha]}{\alpha + \beta + 2\gamma}\right\} \exp[-2(\alpha + \beta + \gamma)t]$$

$$- \left\{\overline{E}^2[X(0)] - \frac{2\alpha}{\alpha + \beta}\overline{E}[X(0)] + \left(\frac{\alpha}{\alpha + \beta}\right)^2\right\}$$

$$\times \exp[-2(\alpha + \beta)t] \qquad\qquad (6.43)$$

where a bar over a variable again denotes the infinite element case. It is readily seen that $\overline{\mathrm{Var}}[X(t)]$ is greater than zero for all t. Thus the cohesive elements specification provides a true stochastic change process for the response probability in the infinite elements case. This again is in contrast to the independent elements specification for which the change process was deterministic for all t in the infinite elements case. From Equation 6.43 we see that the variance in the change process in the steady state is

$$\overline{\mathrm{Var}}[X] = \frac{\alpha\beta\gamma}{(\alpha + \beta)^2(\alpha + \beta + \gamma)} \qquad\qquad (6.44)$$

which is readily seen to be the variance of the beta distribution given in Equation 6.39. Thus the change process in the present model is truly stochastic over t and in the steady state. Thus the present model is more appealing as a representation of the response process than was the previous model.

The remainder of this section is devoted to the derivation of Equations 6.40 and 6.43. The procedure will be essentially the same as that used in Sections 6.5.2 and 6.5.3. The reader willing to accept the preceding results will probably find it efficient to skip ahead to Section 6.6.4.

Proof of Equation 6.40:

Let h be a small increment such that no more than one transition may occur in the interval from t to $t + h$. Then by assumptions C1 to C5 the only possible values of $X(t + h) - X(t)$ and their associated probabilities of occurrence are those given in Table 6.5. The expectation of $X(t + h) - X(t)$ may be expressed as

$$E[X(t + h) - X(t)] = E_X\left\{E_{\Delta X|X(t)}\left[X(t + h) - X(t)|X(t) = \frac{i}{N}\right]\right\}$$

(6.45)

But notice that $E_{\Delta X|X(t)}[X(t + h) - X(t)|X(t)]$ can be computed from the results for $X(t + h) - X(t)$ and their associated probabilities given in Table 6.5. We have

$$E\left[X(t + h) - X(t)|X(t) = \frac{i}{N}\right]$$

$$= \frac{h}{N}\{(N - i)\alpha + (N - i)i\gamma - i\beta - (N - i)i\gamma\}$$

$$= \frac{h}{N}\{(N - i)\alpha - i\beta\} = h\left\{\left(1 - \frac{i}{N}\right)\alpha - \frac{i}{N}\beta\right\}$$

$$= h\{\alpha - (\alpha + \beta)X(t)\} \qquad (6.46)$$

which is identical to Equation 6.17. Thus the remainder of the proof of Equation 6.40 follows from the derivation given in Section 6.5.

Table 6.5 $\Delta X(t)$ Conditional on $X(t)$: Cohesive Elements Specification

$\Delta X(t)$	$P\left[\Delta X(t)|X(t) = \dfrac{i}{N}\right]$
$X(t + h) - X(t) = \dfrac{1}{N}$	$\lambda_i h = (N - i)(\alpha + i\gamma)h$
$X(t + h) - X(t) = 0$	$1 - (\lambda_i - \mu_i)h$
$X(t + h) - X(t) = \dfrac{-1}{N}$	$\mu_i h = ih[\beta + (N - i)\gamma]$

Proof of Equation 6.43:

An elementary expression for the variance of a random variable is

$$\text{Var}[X(t)] = E[X^2(t)] - E^2[X(t)] \tag{6.47}$$

Since $E[X(t)]$ is given in Equation 6.41, we will be able to compute $\text{Var}[X(t)]$ if we can find $E[X^2(t)]$. Consider

$E[X^2(t + h)]$

$$= E[\{X(t + h) - X(t) + X(t)\}^2]$$

$$= E[X^2(t) + X(t)\{X(t + h) - X(t)\} + \{X(t + h) - X(t)\}^2]$$

$$= E[X^2(t)] + E[\{X(t + h) - X(t)\}^2] + 2\,E[X(t)\{X(t + h) - X(t)\}]$$

$$\tag{6.48}$$

First take

$$E[\{X(t + h) - X(t)\}^2] = E_X\{E_{\Delta X|X}[\{X(t + h) - X(t)\}^2|X(t)]\}$$

$$\tag{6.49}$$

Once again let h be a small increment such that no more than one element may make a transition (i.e., become associated with the opposite state) in the interval t to $t + h$. Then the only possible values of $\{X(t + h) - X(t)\}^2$ given $X(t)$ which may occur with nonzero probability are those given in Table 6.6.

Using the results in Table 6.6 we find

$E[\{X(t + h) - X(t)\}^2|X(t)]$

$$= \frac{h}{N^2}\{(N - i)(\alpha + i\gamma) + i[\beta + (N - i)\gamma]\}$$

$$= h\left\{[1 - X(t)]\left[\frac{\alpha}{N} + \gamma X(t)\right] + X(t)\left[\frac{\beta}{N} + \gamma(1 - X(t))\right]\right\}$$

$$= \frac{h}{N}\{\alpha[1 - X(t)] + \beta X(t)\} + h\gamma\{X(t) - X^2(t) + X(t) - X^2(t)\}$$

$$= \frac{h}{N}\{\alpha - (\alpha - \beta)X(t)\} + 2h\gamma\{X(t) - X^2(t)\} \tag{6.50}$$

Inserting Equation 6.50 into 6.49 yields

$E[\{X(t + h) - X(t)\}^2]$

$$= \frac{h}{N}\{\alpha - (\alpha - \beta)\,E[X(t)]\} + 2h\gamma\{E[X(t)] - E[X^2(t)]\} \tag{6.51}$$

Table 6.6 $[\Delta X(t)]^2$ Conditional on $X(t)$: Cohesive Elements Model

$[\Delta X(t)]^2$	$P\left[\{\Delta X(t)\}^2 \mid X(t) = \dfrac{i}{N}\right]$
$[X(t + h) - X(t)]^2 = \dfrac{1}{N^2}$	$\lambda_i h = (N - i)(\alpha + i\gamma)h$
$[X(t + h) - X(t)]^2 = 0$	$1 - (\lambda_i + \mu_i)h$
$[X(t + h) - X(t)]^2 = \dfrac{1}{N^2}$	$\mu_i h = [\beta + (N - i)\gamma]hi$

Finally, examine the last term on the right-hand side of Equation 6.48, that is, $E\{[X(t + h) - X(t)]X(t)\}$. Consider first $E\{[X(t + h) - X(t)] \times X(t) \mid X(t)]$. The possible values of $X(t)[\Delta X(t)]$ and their associated probabilities conditional upon $X(t) = i/N$ are given in Table 6.7.

Using the results given in Table 6.7, we find

$$E\{[X(t + h) - X(t)]X(t) \mid X(t)\}$$

$$= \frac{hX(t)}{N} \{(N - i)(\alpha + i\gamma) - i[\beta + (N - i)\gamma]\}$$

$$E\{[X(t + h) - X(t)]X(t) \mid X(t)\}$$

$$= hX(t)\{[1 - X(t)](\alpha + i\gamma) - \beta X(t) - [1 - X(t)]i\gamma\}$$

$$= hX(t)\{[1 - X(t)]\alpha + [1 - X(t)]i\gamma - [1 - X(t)]i\gamma - \beta X(t)\}$$

$$= hX(t)[\alpha - (\alpha + \beta)X(t)]$$

$$= h[\alpha X(t) - (\alpha + \beta)X^2(t)]$$

Hence,

$$E\{[X(t + h) - X(t)]X(t)\} = h\{\alpha\, E[X(t)] - (\alpha + \beta)\, E[X^2(t)]\}$$

$$(6.52)$$

Using Equation 6.51 and 6.52, we have for Equation 6.48 that

$$E[X^2(t + h)]$$

$$= E[X^2(t)] + \frac{h}{N} \{\alpha - (\alpha - \beta)\, E[X(t)]\} + 2h\gamma\{E[X(t)] - E[X^2(t)]\}$$

$$+ 2h\{\alpha\, E[X(t)] - (\alpha + \beta)\, E[X^2(t)]\}$$

Table 6.7 $X(t)[\Delta X(t)]$ Conditional on $X(t)$: Cohesive Elements Model

$X(t)[\Delta X(t)]$	$P\left[X(t)[\Delta X(t)] \| X(t) = \dfrac{i}{N}\right]$
$\{X(t + h) - X(t)\}X(t) = \dfrac{X(t)}{N}$	$\lambda_i h = (N - i)(\alpha + i\gamma)h$
$\{X(t + h) - X(t)\}X(t) = 0$	$1 - (\lambda_i + \mu_i)h$
$\{X(t + h) - X(t)\}X(t) = \dfrac{-X(t)}{N}$	$\mu_i h = i[\beta + (N - i)\gamma]h$

Now take

$$\frac{E[X^2(t + h)] - E[X^2(t)]}{h} = \frac{\alpha}{N} - E[X(t)]\left\{\frac{\alpha}{N} - \frac{\beta}{N} - 2\gamma - 2\alpha\right\}$$
$$- E[X^2(t)]\{2\gamma + 2\alpha + 2\beta\}$$

Then,

$$\lim_{h \to 0} \frac{E[X^2(t + h)] - E[X^2(t)]}{h}$$

$$= \frac{d\,E[X^2(t)]}{dt}$$

$$= \frac{\alpha}{N} - \left(\frac{\alpha}{N} - \frac{\beta}{N}\right)E[X(t)] + 2(\alpha + \gamma)\,E[X(t)]$$

$$- 2(\alpha + \beta + \gamma)\,E[X^2(t)]. \tag{6.53}$$

Once again let $\overline{E}[X^2(t)]$ denote $\lim\limits_{N \to \infty} E[X^2(t)]$. Then Equation 6.53 becomes

$$\lim_{N \to \infty} \frac{d\,\overline{E}[X^2(t)]}{dt} = \frac{d\,\overline{E}[X^2(t)]}{dt}$$

$$= 2(\alpha + \gamma)\overline{E}[X(t)] - 2(\alpha + \beta + \gamma)\overline{E}[X^2(t)] \tag{6.54}$$

Equation 6.54 may be solved by the method of undetermined coefficients. Assume the trial solution

$$\overline{E}[X^2(t)] = a_0 + a_1 \exp\left[-(\alpha + \beta)t\right] + a_2 \exp\left[-2(\alpha + \beta + \gamma)t\right] \tag{6.55}$$

where a_0, a_1, and a_2 are arbitrary and as yet undetermined coefficients. Differentiating Equation 6.55, we find

$$\frac{d\,\overline{E}[X^2(t)]}{dt} = -(\alpha + \beta)a_1 \exp\left[-(\alpha + \beta)t\right]$$

$$- 2(\alpha + \beta + \gamma)a_2 \exp\left[-2(\alpha + \beta + \gamma)t\right] \quad (6.56)$$

Then substitute the trial solution in Equation 6.55 into Equation 6.54, in conjunction with Equation 6.41. This yields

$$\frac{d\,\overline{E}[X^2(t)]}{dt}$$

$$= 2(\alpha + \gamma)\left\{\overline{E}[X(0)] \exp\left[-(\alpha + \beta)t\right] + \frac{\alpha}{\alpha + \beta}(1 - \exp\left[-(\alpha + \beta)t\right])\right\}$$

$$- 2(\alpha + \beta + \gamma)\{a_0 + a_1 \exp\left[-(\alpha + \beta)t\right]$$

$$+ a_2 \exp\left[-2(\alpha + \beta + \gamma)t\right]\}$$

$$= \frac{2\alpha(\alpha + \gamma)}{(\alpha + \beta)} + \frac{2(\alpha + \gamma)}{(\alpha + \beta)}\{(\alpha + \beta)\overline{E}[X(0)] - \alpha\} \exp\left[-(\alpha + \beta)t\right]$$

$$- 2(\alpha + \beta + \gamma)a_0 - 2(\alpha + \beta + \gamma)a_1 \exp\left[-(\alpha + \beta)t\right]$$

$$- 2(\alpha + \beta + \gamma)a_2 \exp\left[-2(\alpha + \beta + \gamma)t\right]$$

$$= \frac{2\alpha(\alpha + \gamma)}{(\alpha + \beta)} - 2(\alpha + \beta + \gamma)a_0 + \left\{\frac{2(\alpha + \gamma)}{(\alpha + \beta)}((\alpha + \beta)\overline{E}[X(0)] - \alpha)\right.$$

$$\left. - 2(\alpha + \beta + \gamma)a_1\right\} \exp\left[-(\alpha + \beta)t\right]$$

$$- 2(\alpha + \beta + \gamma)a_2 \exp\left[-2(\alpha + \beta + \gamma)t\right] \quad (6.57)$$

By equating coefficients of similar terms in Equations 6.56 and 6.57 and noting the initial condition $\overline{E}[X^2(0)]$ we have three independent equations for the three unknown coefficients. These equations are

$$0 = \frac{2\alpha(\alpha + \gamma)}{(\alpha + \beta)} - 2(\alpha + \beta + \gamma)a_0$$

$$- (\alpha + \beta)a_1 = \frac{2(\alpha + \gamma)}{(\alpha + \beta)}\{(\alpha + \beta)\,EX(0) - \alpha\} - 2(\alpha + \beta + \gamma)a_1$$

$$\quad (6.58)$$

$$E[X^2(0)] = a_0 + a_1 + a_2$$

The solution of Equation 6.58 is

$$a_0 = \frac{\alpha(\alpha + \gamma)}{(\alpha + \beta)(\alpha + \beta + \gamma)}$$

$$a_1 = \frac{2(\alpha + \gamma)\{(\alpha + \beta)\overline{E}[X(0)] - \alpha\}}{(\alpha + \beta)\{\alpha + \beta + 2\gamma\}} \qquad (6.59)$$

$$a_2 = \overline{E}[X^2(0)] - a_0 - a_1$$

$$= \overline{E}[X^2(0)] - \frac{\alpha(\alpha + \gamma)}{(\alpha + \beta)(\alpha + \beta + \gamma)}$$

$$- \frac{2(\alpha + \gamma)}{(\alpha + \beta)} \frac{\{(\alpha + \beta)\overline{E}[X(0)] - \alpha\}}{\{\alpha + \beta + 2\gamma\}}$$

Hence, we have as the solution of Equation 6.54,

$$\overline{E}[X^2(t)] = \frac{\alpha(\alpha + \gamma)}{(\alpha + \beta)(\alpha + \beta + \gamma)}$$

$$+ \frac{2(\alpha + \gamma)}{(\alpha + \beta)} \frac{\{(\alpha + \beta)\overline{E}[X(0)] - \alpha\}}{\{\alpha + \beta + 2\gamma\}} \exp\left[-(\alpha + \beta)t\right]$$

$$+ \left\{ \overline{E}[X^2(0)] - \frac{\alpha(\alpha + \gamma)}{(\alpha + \beta)(\alpha + \beta + \gamma)} \right.$$

$$\left. - \frac{2(\alpha + \gamma)}{(\alpha + \beta)} \frac{(\alpha + \beta)\overline{E}[X(0)] - \alpha}{[\alpha + \beta + 2\gamma]} \right\} \exp\left[-2(\alpha + \beta + \gamma)t\right]$$

$$(6.60)$$

Now using Equations 6.60 and 6.41 in Equation 6.47, we have, after some tedious algebra, Equation 6.43.

6.6.4   *The Diffusion Limit of the Process*

Suppose that $X(t)$ is a random variable that depends upon the continuous parameter t. Further suppose that this random variable is of the Markov type, that is, future changes depend upon the present state but not upon the realized history of outcomes that led to this state. Now the stochastic process $\{X(t); t > 0\}$ may be of two types: *discontinuous* or *diffusion*. Discontinuous processes are characterized by the fact that the probability of a change in the interval $(t, t + h)$ where h is very small is of the order of magnitude of h (i.e., very small). However, in a discontinuous process, when a change does occur, it is finite

in magnitude. In contrast to processes of the discontinuous type are diffusion processes in which $X(t)$ changes continuously. In diffusion processes, no matter how small the interval $(t, t + h)$, the $X(t)$ will undergo some change. This change is practically certain to be small for small intervals. In formal terms this says that

$$P\{|X(t + h) - X(t)| > \epsilon\} < O(h)$$

where again the symbol $O(h)$ stands for "of the order of the argument," which in this case is h.

For a diffusion process the infinitesimal mean displacement $a(X)$ and the infinitesimal variance $2b(X)$ play a fundamental role. These quantities are defined as

$$\lim_{h \to 0} \frac{E[X(t + h) - X(t)|X(t)]}{h} = a(X) \tag{6.61}$$

$$\lim_{h \to 0} \frac{\mathrm{Var}[X(t + h) - X(t)|X(t)]}{h} = 2b(X) \tag{6.62}$$

Let $f(t,X)$ denote the probability density function of $X(t)$. Kolmogorov has shown that $f(t,X)$ must satisfy the Fokker-Planck diffusion equation

$$\frac{\partial f(t,X)}{\partial t} = \frac{\partial^2 \{b(X)f(t,X)\}}{\partial X^2} - \frac{\partial \{a(X)f(t,X)\}}{\partial X} \tag{6.63}$$

where $a(X)$ and $b(X)$ are as defined earlier.[20]

The cohesive elements specification may be represented as a diffusion process as the number of response elements increases without limit. In this case the change increment $1/N$ becomes infinitesimally small. Thus, an individual's response probability will undergo change in a continuous manner, in contrast to the jump discontinuities in the learning and Markov models. Since our interest has centered upon the infinite element form of the model and since the infinite element form may be represented as a diffusion process on the response probability, we shall hereafter refer to the infinite element form of the cohesive elements specification as the *probability diffusion model*.

The beta distribution derived in Section 6.6.2 as the steady-state distribution of response probability in the infinite element case thus must satisfy the Fokker-Planck diffusion equation (given as Equation

[20] See Feller (1950). For excellent references on diffusion processes and continuous parameter stochastic processes again see Feller (1950) and Bharucha-Reid (1960).

6.63) in the steady state. That is, when

$$\frac{\partial f(t,X)}{\partial t} = 0$$

It can be shown that this indeed is the case.[21]

6.6.5 *Aggregation*

Thus far, consideration has been given to the process at the level of the individual respondent. In order to obtain estimating equations for the model, it is necessary to aggregate a sequence of responses over individual respondents who behave according to the same process — i.e., have the same α, β, and γ. Recall that in assumption S1 we assumed that the same process applies to each respondent. This cross-sectional aggregation procedure will be shown to require only short-run stationarity of the model's parameters, α, β, and γ. That is, the parameters need remain constant over only a relatively short sequence of responses. In a marketing context long-run stationarity of the process is clearly implausible in view of the dynamic nature of most markets.

Perhaps it is well to reiterate just what we mean when we say that all individuals are assumed to behave in accordance with the same process. What we mean by this is that the parameters of the change process — α, β, and γ — are the same for each individual respondent in the population. This is not at all the same thing as saying that all individuals have the same response probability. In fact, the probability diffusion model allows for heterogeneity among respondents with respect to their response probabilities $X(t)$ even after the process has reached statistical equilibrium or the steady state. This point follows from the development in Section 6.6.3.

In the remainder of this section we shall utilize the following notation:

$M = $ Number of individual respondents.

$N = $ Number of response elements within *each* individual respondent.

$N_k = $ The number of response elements within individual k which are associated with response A, $k = 1, 2, \ldots, M$.

$X_k(t) = \dfrac{N_k}{N} = $ The probability that individual k having N_k elements out of N associated with response A at time t will make response A at time t.

---

[21] For a proof of this assertion and for the derivation of $a(X)$ and $b(X)$ for the probability diffusion model see Montgomery (1966).

$f[X(t)] =$ The probability density function of the population of individuals with respect to their response probability $X(t)$, at time t. That is, $f[X(t)]$ is just the distribution of the response probability in the population.

The heterogeneity of respondents may be represented by a probability density function $f[X(t)]$. That is, $f[X(t)]$ is the distribution of response probability in the population of respondents at response occasion t. In this section we shall have no need to consider further the specific form of $f[X(t)]$. When we turn to the problem of estimating $f[X(t)]$ in Section 6.6.6, we shall then examine the beta form mentioned in earlier sections. In any case, the results of this section are free of any assumption as to the form of $f[X(t)]$.

From response data for M individual respondents, we may tabulate the proportion of individuals who made response A at t and the proportion of individuals who, having made response A at 0, again make response A at t. These empirical proportions will be denoted by $Q(t)$ and $Q(0,t)$, respectively. In Lemma 1 and Lemma 2 it will be shown that $Q(t)$ and $Q(0,t)$ are unbiased estimates of $P(t)$ and $P(0,t)$, which are the theoretical expected response proportions. The objective at this point is to see whether or not it might be possible to relate the observed proportions to the postulated underlying process in such a way as to obtain estimates of the parameters of the probability diffusion model. The relations established in the two lemmas proved here will provide the foundation for the derivation of estimating equations.

LEMMA 1. *If* $P(t)$ *denotes the expected proportion of the M respondents making response A at t, then*

$$P(t) = E[X(t)] = \int_0^1 E[X(t)|X(0)]f[X(0)]\,dX(0) \qquad (6.64)$$

and the observed proportion $Q(t)$ *is an unbiased estimate of* $P(t) = E[X(t)]$.

Proof:
From probability theory we know that Equation 6.64 holds.[22] What needs to be shown is that $E[Q(t)] = P(t) = E[X(t)]$. Consider any individual respondent k. At t he has probability $X_k(t)$ of making response A if he makes a response at t. Let $r_k(t) = 0$ if individual k makes response B at response occasion t. Let $r_k(t) = 1$ if individual k makes response A at response occasion t. Now

$$E[r_k(t)|X_k(t)] = X_k(t)$$

[22] See Parzen (1960, p. 384).

and thus $\qquad E[r_k(t)] = E\{E[r_k(t)|X_k(t)]\} = E[X_k(t)]$

Hence, summing across all M respondents, we have

$$E[Q(t)] = E\left[\frac{\sum\limits_{k=1}^{M} r_k(t)}{M}\right] = \frac{1}{M}\sum\limits_{k=1}^{M} E[r_k(t)] = E[X(t)]$$

The proof is now complete.

LEMMA 2. *If* $P(0,t)$ *denotes the expected proportion of the* M *respondents making response* A *at* 0 *and* A *again at* t *then*

$$P(0,t) = E[X(0,t)] = \int_0^1 E[X(t)|X(0)]X(0)f\,[X(0)]\,dX(0) \quad (6.65)$$

and the observed proportion $Q(0,t)$ *is an unbiased estimate of* $P(0,t) =$ $E[X(0,t)]$.

Proof:
Consider any individual respondent k. His probabilities of making response A at 0 and A at t are $X_k(0)$ and $X_k(t)$, respectively. Recall that under assumption $R2$ of the model, successive responses by a given respondent are independent. Hence, the probability of the compound event $r_k(0)r_k(t) = 1$ is just $X_k(0,t) = X_k(0)X_k(t)$.

Then
$$E[r_k(0)r_k(t)|X_k(0,t)] = X_k(0,t) = X_k(0)X_k(t)$$

Hence the unconditional probability is

$$\begin{aligned}E[r_k(0)r_k(t)] &= E\{E[r_k(0)r_k(t)|X_k(0,t)]\}\\ &= E[X_k(0)X_k(t)] = E[X_k(0,t)]\end{aligned}$$

Now summing across all M respondents, we have

$$\begin{aligned}E[Q(0,t)] &= E\left[\frac{\sum\limits_{k=1}^{M} r_k(0)r_k(t)}{M}\right] = \frac{1}{M}\sum\limits_{k=1}^{M} E[r_k(0)r_k(t)]\\[2mm] &= \frac{M}{M}\,E[X_k(0,t)] = E[X_k(0)X_k(t)]\\[2mm] &= \int_0^1 E[X(0)X(t)|X(0)]f\,[X(0)]\,dX(0)\\[2mm] &= \int_0^1 E[X(t)|X(0)]X(0)f\,[X(0)]\,dX(0)\end{aligned}$$

and the proof is complete.

6.7 Estimating and Testing the Probability Diffusion Model

A requisite for an empirically useful model of choice behavior is the ability to estimate and test the model based upon actual respondent choices.[23] Accordingly, in this section we shall develop methods for estimating and testing the probability diffusion model.

Two alternative estimation procedures will be discussed. The recursive regression method has the virtue of being computationally convenient. However, the asymptotic properties of the estimators and the measures of fit of the model which may be obtained from the regression procedure are less clear than for the minimum chi-square method. The minimum chi-square estimation procedure yields parameter estimates with desirable asymptotic properties. Unfortunately, there does not appear to be any hope of obtaining an analytic solution to minimum chi-square estimates of the model's parameters. However, given the present state of computer technology, numerical minimization is a viable computational procedure.

In this section we shall first analyze some general considerations in the development of estimation procedures for the probability diffusion model. Then the recursive regression and minimum chi-square procedure will be presented. Finally, we shall develop a method for estimating the cross-sectional distribution of response probability $f[X(t)]$.

6.7.1 General Estimation Considerations

In this section we shall use the results of Section 6.6 to develop two general equations that will be used as the basis of our estimation procedures. We shall then develop certain bounds on the model's parameters which will prove useful in our numerical minimization of chi-square. Finally, we note certain properties of the empirical response proportions $Q(t)$ and $Q(0,t)$.

6.7.1.1 *General Equations for Estimation.* Recall that in Lemma 1 (Equation 6.64) we found that

$$P(t) = E[X(t)] = \int_0^1 E[X(t)|X(0)]f[X(0)]\,dX(0) \qquad (6.66)$$

---

[23] In his use of the finite number of elements form of the model, Coleman (1964a, pp. 96–97) recognized the need for better estimation procedures and for methods of testing the model. However, he left the development of these methods and procedures to future research. In most instances he seemed content with methods which would just identify the parameters. In no case did he consider the properties of the estimates or the adequacy of the fit of the model to empirical data.

Substituting Equation 6.41 into Equation 6.66, we have

$$P(t) = \int_0^1 \left\{ X(0) \exp\left[-(\alpha + \beta)t\right] \right.$$

$$\left. + \frac{\alpha}{\alpha + \beta} (1 - \exp\left[-(\alpha + \beta)t\right]) \right\} f[X(0)] \, dX(0)$$

$$= \exp\left[-(\alpha + \beta)t\right] \int_0^1 X(0) f[X(0)] \, dX(0)$$

$$+ \frac{\alpha}{\alpha + \beta} (1 - \exp\left[-(\alpha + \beta)t\right]) \int_0^1 f[X(0)] \, dX(0)$$

$$= P(0) \exp\left[-(\alpha + \beta)t\right] + \frac{\alpha}{\alpha + \beta} \{1 - \exp\left[-(\alpha + \beta)t\right]\} \quad (6.67)$$

Similarly, if we use Equation 6.41 in the result of Lemma 2 (Equation 6.65), we have

$$P(0,t) = P(0,0) \exp\left[-(\alpha + \beta)t\right] + P(0) \frac{\alpha}{\alpha + \beta} \{1 - \exp\left[-(\alpha + \beta)t\right]\}$$

$$(6.68)$$

It is necessary at this point to consider what we mean by $P(0,0)$. It may be thought of in two ways. The first is to note that by reasoning analogous to the proofs of the previous lemmas, we have $P(0,0) = E[X^2(0)]$. Hence, it may be considered the second raw moment of the initial distribution of response probability across the population. An alternative, but related, view is to consider $P(0,0)$ as the expected proportion making response A on two successive occasions when there is no change in probability on the part of any of the M individuals between these two response occasions.

A sequence of two responses in a situation in which the response probabilities do not change enables one to obtain information relative to the distribution of response probability in the population.[24] In terms of the present model, $P(0,0)$ represents a hypothetical replication of the responses at $t = 0$ when there has been no intervening change in response probabilities. Clearly, this is not an observable outcome in this case since the response probabilities are assumed to change between successive responses. Fortunately $P(0,0)$ may be estimated from the data. Since $P(0,0)$ may be considered the raw second moment of the initial distribution of response probability in the population, having estimates

[24] See Coleman (1964b, Chapter 13).

of P(0) and P(0,0) will enable us to estimate the mean and variance of the initial distribution of response probability irrespective of the functional form of this distribution.

From Equation 6.67, we see that $\alpha/(\alpha + \beta)$ is the equilibrium or steady-state choice share of response A (i.e., we let $t \to \infty$). Also from Equations 6.67 and 6.68, we see that $\alpha + \beta$ represents the rate at which the model approaches its steady state. To capture these notions in our estimating procedure and also for reasons of notational convenience, we reparameterize Equations 6.67 and 6.68 using

$$a = \frac{\alpha}{\alpha + \beta} \tag{6.69}$$

and

$$k = \alpha + \beta \tag{6.70}$$

We now have in place of Equations 6.67 and 6.68

$$P(t) = P(0) \exp(-kt) + a[1 - \exp(-kt)] \tag{6.71}$$

and

$$P(0,t) = P(0,0) \exp(-kt) + a\,P(0)[1 - \exp(-kt)] \tag{6.72}$$

These two equations will provide the foundation for our estimation procedures.

6.7.1.2 *Parameter Bounds.* Prior to developing the regression and the minimum chi-square estimation procedures, we must first consider the inherent constraints on the parameters themselves. Recall from assumptions 2 and 3 in Section 6.5.1 that α and β represent transition intensities in opposite directions. We suffer no loss of generality if we require that

$$\alpha \geq 0 \quad \text{and} \quad \beta \geq 0 \tag{6.73}$$

Naturally this implies that

$$k = \alpha + \beta \geq 0 \tag{6.74}$$

It is interesting to note the implications of $k = 0$. In this case no elements change their response association over a sequence of responses. Hence, in this case the model is stationary with respect to the response probabilities. Chapter 3 has presented methods for estimating and testing the assumption of just such a heterogeneous, stationary Bernoulli process as is represented by the probability diffusion model with $k = 0$. In simple English, $k = 0$ means that an individual respondent (consumer) does not change his response probability over a sequence of responses.

The equilibrium choice share of response A (i.e., "a") is also bounded. Recalling that $a = \alpha/(\alpha + \beta)$, it is clear that

$$0 \le a \le 1 \qquad (6.75)$$

It remains now to establish bounds for $P(0,0)$. Since $P(0,0) = E[X^2(0)]$ and $\text{Var}[X(0)] \ge 0$, it is clear that

$$P(0,0) \ge P^2(0) \ge 0 \qquad (6.76)$$

It is interesting to note that if $P(0,0) = P^2(0)$, then $\text{Var}[X(0)] = 0$, and all individuals in the population have the same initial probability of making response A. An upper bound for $P(0,0)$ given $P(0)$ can also be formulated. This result is stated as Lemma 3.

LEMMA 3. *Given a particular* $P(0) = E[X(0)]$ *where* $0 \le P(0) \le 1$, *the upper bound for* $P(0,0) = E[X^2(0)]$ *is*

$$P(0,0) \le P(0) \qquad (6.77)$$

Proof:
Suppose for the purpose of argument, and in this case without loss of generality, that $X(0)$ may take on only two values, $X_1(0)$ and $X_2(0)$. Let the proportions of the respondents having $X_1(0)$ and $X_2(0)$ be m_1 and m_2, respectively. Clearly $m_2 = 1 - m_1$. Now we have

$$P(0) = E[X(0)] = X_1 m_1 + X_2 m_2 \qquad (6.78)$$

and

$$P(0,0) = E[X^2(0)] = X_1^2 m_1 + X_2^2 m_2 \qquad (6.79)$$

Hence, after some algebra,

$$\begin{aligned} \text{Var}[X(0)] &= E[X^2(0)] - E^2[X(0)] \\ &= X_1^2 m_1 + X_2^2 m_2 - (X_1 m_1 + X_2 m_2)^2 \\ &= (m_1 - m_1^2)(X_1 - X_2)^2 \end{aligned} \qquad (6.80)$$

For given m_1 and $P(0)$, $\text{Var}[X(0)]$ and hence $P(0,0)$ are maximized when $|X_1 - X_2| = 1$. But since $0 \le X(0) \le 1$, the only case for which the absolute difference between the two values of $X(0)$ may equal one is for one of the values to be one and the other zero. Letting a "$\frown$" denote the maximum variance case we have

$$\widehat{\text{Var}[X(0)]} = \hat{P}(0,0) - P^2(0) = m_1 - m_1^2 \qquad (6.81)$$

But now since $X_1 = 1$ and $X_2 = 0$, we have from Equation 6.78

$$P(0) = m_1 \qquad (6.82)$$

Hence from Equations 6.81 and 6.82 we have

$$\hat{P}(0,0) = m_1 - m_1^2 + P^2(0) = m_1 = P(0) \qquad (6.83)$$

Since $\hat{P}(0,0)$ is the maximum value of $P(0,0)$ given $P(0)$, Equation 6.83 establishes the upper bound stated as Lemma 3.

Note that if $P(0,0) = P(0)$, then all respondents are clustered at the two extreme initial response probabilities $X(0) = 0$ and $X(0) = 1$. The proportion of the respondents having $X(0) = 1$ is just $P(0)$. For the strict inequalities

$$P^2(0) < P(0,0) < P(0)$$

the individual respondents are distributed across the response probability continuum.

6.7.1.3 *Properties of the Empirical Response Proportions.* Before turning to the development of the estimation procedures, it is well to consider the properties of the sample estimates $Q(t)$ and $Q(0,t)$ of the population moments $P(t)$ and $P(0,t)$, respectively. Recall that in Section 6.6.5 Lemma 1 and Lemma 2 demonstrated that

$$E[Q(t)] = P(t) = E[X(t)]$$

and

$$E[Q(0,t)] = P(0,t) = E[X(0)X(t)] = E[X(0,t)]$$

where $Q(t)$ is the sample proportion (moment) making response A at t, where $E[X(t)]$ is the average probability of making response A in the population at t, where $Q(0,t)$ is the sample proportion making response A at zero and again at t, and where $E[X(0,t)] = E[X(0)X(t)]$ is the average probability in the population of making response A at time 0 and again at time t.

Thus the lemmas proved that $Q(t)$ and $Q(0,t)$ are unbiased estimates of $P(t)$ and $P(0,t)$, respectively.

It has been shown that the variance of the sample proportion $Q(t)$ in a heterogeneous Bernoulli population is just

$$\text{Var}[Q(t)] = \frac{P(t)\{1 - P(t)\} - \text{Var}[X(t)]}{M}$$

$$= \frac{E[X(t)] - E^2[X(t)] - \text{Var}[X(t)]}{M}$$

$$= \frac{E[X(t)] - E[X^2(t)]}{M} \qquad (6.84)$$

where M is the number of respondents entering into the proportions.[25] Since $E[X(t)]$ and $E[X^2(t)]$ are independent of M, we see that

$$\lim_{M \to \infty} \text{Var}[X(t)] = 0$$

The sample proportions $Q(t)$ and $Q(0,t)$ have also been shown to converge in probability to the population values.[26] That is,

$$\lim_{M \to \infty} P\{|Q(t) - P(t)| \geq e\} = 0$$

and

$$\lim_{M \to \infty} P\{|Q(0,t) - P(0,t)| \geq e\} = 0$$

where e is an arbitrarily small real number.

Finally, it can be shown under certain rather general conditions that $Q(t)$ is asymptotically normal with mean $P(t)$ and variance

$$\frac{P(t)\{1 - P(t)\} - \text{Var}[X(t)]}{M}$$

For a heterogeneous population the central limit theorem holds when Liapounoff's conditions are satisfied.[27] Cramer has shown that a sufficient condition for the sample proportion of a heterogeneous Bernoulli population to be asymptotically normal is that no member of the population has a probability of exactly 0 or exactly 1 of making response A.[28] This condition, while only sufficient and not necessary for asymptotic normality of $Q(t)$, would not be restrictive in applications of the probability diffusion model to human populations, particularly consumer populations. Intuitively it seems very unlikely that any brand is so overwhelmingly superior that it will be chosen with certainty or so inferior that it would be chosen under no circumstances on a particular occasion by a consumer. It seems very reasonable to assume that the probability of making response A never gets to precisely 0 or precisely 1. Note that this view is consistent with Kuehn's argument for incomplete learning in the consumer brand-choice situation.[29] In summary, the sample proportion $Q(t)$:

1. Is an unbiased estimate of $P(t)$,
2. Converges in probability to $P(t)$, and

[25] See Cramer (1946, p. 207) and Kendall and Stuart (1958, p. 126–27).

[26] Cramer (1946, p. 207).

[27] See Cramer (1946, pp. 215–216). There are more general cases of the central limit theorem. See Parzen (1960, Chapter 10).

[28] Cramer (1946, pp. 217–218).

[29] Kuehn (1962).

3. Is asymptotically normal with mean $P(t) = E[X(t)]$ and variance

$$\frac{E[X(t)] - E[X^2(t)]}{M}$$

under certain seemingly reasonable conditions.

Similar results hold for $Q(0,t)$.

6.7.2 Regression Estimation Procedure

In this section we shall develop a regression or least-squares procedure for estimating the parameters of the probability diffusion model. The fundamental regression relations will first be derived. Then consideration will be given to sources of error in the regression relations. Attention will next focus upon the regression procedure, its properties, and its pitfalls.

6.7.2.1 *The Fundamental Regression Relations.* We first rearrange Equation 6.71 as

$$P(t) - P(0) \exp(-kt) = a[1 - \exp(-kt)] \qquad (6.85)$$

Substituting Equation 6.85 into 6.72 then yields

$$P(0,t) = P(0,0) \exp(-kt) + P(0) P(t) - P^2(0) \exp(-kt) \qquad (6.86)$$

which may be written as

$$P(0,t) - P(0) P(t) = \{P(0,0) - P^2(0)\} \exp(-kt) \qquad (6.87)$$

Taking natural logarithms of this equation, we find

$$\ln\{P(0,t) - P(0) P(t)\} = \ln\{P(0,0) - P^2(0)\} - kt \qquad (6.88)$$

which is the first of our basic regression relations.

Rearranging Equation 6.71 in yet another way leads to

$$P(t) - a = \exp(-kt)[P(0) - a] \qquad (6.89)$$

Similarly, rearranging Equation 6.72, we have

$$P(0,t) - a P(0) = \exp(-kt)[P(0,0) - a P(0)] \qquad (6.90)$$

It is easy to see from Equations 6.89 and 6.90 that we now have

$$\frac{P(t) - a}{P(0) - a} = \frac{P(0,t) - a P(0)}{P(0,0) - a P(0)} \qquad (6.91)$$

Equation 6.91 may be written as

$$[P(t) - a][P(0,0) - a\,P(0)] = [P(0) - a][P(0,t) - a\,P(0)] \quad (6.92)$$

With a bit of algebra, we find

$$P(0)\,P(0,t) = P(t)\,P(0,0) - a\,P(0,0) + a[P(0,t) + P^2(0) - P(0)\,P(t)] \quad (6.93)$$

Equations 6.88 and 6.93 form the basis for the regression estimation procedure. For convenience of discussion, these equations are now restated:

$$\ln\{P(0,t) - P(0)\,P(t)\} = \ln\{P(0,0) - P^2(0)\} - kt \quad \text{(6.88 restated)}$$

$$P(0)\,P(0,t) = -a\,P(0,0) + P(0,0)\,P(t) + a[P(0,t) - P(0)\,P(t) + P^2(0)] \quad \text{(6.93 restated)}$$

for $t = 1, 2, \ldots, T$. The parameters of these two equations are a, k, and $P(0,0)$. The variables are t, which indexes response occasions, and $P(t)$ and $P(0,t)$, which are expected response proportions that may be directly estimated by the sample proportions $Q(t)$ and $Q(0,t)$.

In the discussion to follow, it will be helpful to let $B = P(0,0)$ and $Y_t = P(0,t) - P(0)\,P(t)$ in Equations 6.88 and 6.93. These equations then become

$$\ln Y_t = \ln\{B - P^2(0)\} - kt \quad (6.94)$$

and

$$P(0)\,P(0,t) = -aB + B\,P(t) + a[Y_t + P^2(0)] \quad (6.95)$$

It is important to recall that in these equations $P(t)$ and $P(0,t)$ represent *expected* response proportions. That is, the probability diffusion model implies these exact linear relations on functions of the expected response proportions.

6.7.2.2 *Sources of Error.* Thus far the fundamental regression equations contain no error. The equations express exact linear relationships that would hold if the model were a completely accurate description of the process and the variables were measured without error. It would be most surprising if the probability diffusion model were actually a complete and accurate description of such a complex process as the dynamics of response in the binary choice case. Rather, it seems more reasonable to consider the model as a first-order approximation to the true process.

In recognition of the fact that the probability diffusion model is not an exact description but rather an approximate model, the fundamental relations may be revised in order to reflect this fact. We now have

$$\ln Y_t = \ln \{B - P^2(0)\} - kt + U_{1t} \tag{6.96}$$

and

$$P(0)\,P(0,t) = -aB + B\,P(t) + a[Y_t + P^2(0)] + U_{2t} \tag{6.97}$$

where U_{1t} and U_{2t} represent the true errors at t in the first and second equations, respectively. The errors that we have been considering thus far are termed errors in equations or specification errors in the econometric literature. It should be noted that we have assumed additive specification errors.[30] Errors of this type are easily handled by least-squares procedures in most cases.[31] The formulation given in Equations 6.96 and 6.97 treats the model relations on the variables as linear approximations to the true relations.

A far more serious source of error arises because we must use observed response proportions as estimates of the expected response proportions. That is, we are faced with an error in variables situation.[32] Standard least squares will yield biased estimates of the regression coefficients in the presence of errors in the independent variables. Errors in the dependent variable are indistinguishable from specification errors from the standpoint of the estimation procedure.[33] Hence Equation 6.96 has no errors in variables problem since the variables error is entirely in the dependent variable Y_t, while the independent variable t is nonstochastic. Note, however, that in the intercept term of Equation 6.96 the estimate $Q^2(0)$ of $P^2(0)$ is subject to error. Since this error occurs in the intercept term, we do not face an error in variables situation when we apply least squares. However, when we use the estimate of the intercept and the estimate of $P(0)$ to estimate B, we will have the error in the estimate of B perfectly negatively correlated with the error in $P(0)$.

For Equation 6.97, however, the errors in variables problem may be serious. Fortunately, as the number of respondents included in the analysis increases, the variances of the observed proportions $Q(t)$ and

---

[30] This assumption of additive specification errors is made for convenience and is not implied by the theory.

[31] See Johnston (1963). See especially Chapter 7 and 8 for problems of autocorrelation, heteroscedasticity, and lagged variables.

[32] For a treatment of errors in variables and the problems that they generate see Klein (1953, pp. 282–305), Johnston (1963, Chapter 6), or Goldberger (1964, Chapter 6).

[33] See Massy in Frank, Kuehn, and Massy (1962, pp. 83–85).

$Q(0,t)$ about $P(t)$ and $P(0,t)$ decrease. Thus the errors in variables problem encountered in Equation 6.97 may be overcome by increasing the number of individual respondents. Similarly, in Equation 6.96 the error in the estimate of B due to the error in the estimate of $P(0)$ will decrease as the number of respondents increases. We will then be left with only specification error, which is considerably easier to deal with.

6.7.2.3 *Estimating the Simultaneous Equations.*

In this two-equation system Y_t is an endogenous variable. That is, Y_t is the dependent variable in Equation 6.96 and an independent variable in 6.97. Consequently, we must treat these equations as a simultaneous system.[34]

Simultaneous equations often lead to very formidable estimation problems. In the present case the problem is greatly simplified by the fact that Equations 6.96 and 6.97 form a recursive system.[35] A two-equation recursive system has the following general form

$$-y_1(t) \qquad + b_{11}X_1(t) + \cdots + b_{k1}X_k(t) + u_1(t) = 0$$

$$a_{12}y_1(t) - y_2(t) + b_{12}X_1(t) + \cdots + b_{k2}X_2(t) + u_2(t) = 0$$

where t indexes observations, y_1 and y_2 are endogenous variables, and X_i for $i = 1, \ldots, k$, are predetermined variables. If we examine the matrix of coefficients of the endogenous variables y_1 and y_2, we see that we have the following triangular matrix

$$\begin{bmatrix} -1 & 0 \\ a_{12} & -1 \end{bmatrix}$$

The triangularity of the matrix of coefficients of the endogenous variables distinguishes a recursive system. It further indicates that y_1 should be the dependent variable in the first equation while y_2 should be the dependent variable in the second.[36] It is easily seen that Equations 6.96 and 6.97 form a recursive system. The implications of Equation 6.96 being log linear are discussed later. For a more systematic development of recursive systems and their properties see Klein (1953, Chapter 3).

For a recursive system, if the errors between the equations of the system are independent (i.e., if U_{1t} and $U_{2t'}$ are independent for all t

---

[34] It is well known that simultaneous equations cannot be treated as separate regressions without subjecting the results of the analysis to considerable error. See, for example, Johnson (1963) and Goldberger (1964).

[35] See Klein (1953, pp. 80–92 and 100–122) and Johnson (1963, pp. 265–266), and Goldberger (1964, pp. 354–356) for further information regarding recursive systems of equations.

[36] Thus, in a recursive system the direction in which to minimize the sum of the squared errors is clear in each equation of the system.

and t'), then single-equation least squares applied to each equation *in turn* will be identical to maximum likelihood estimates.[37] If the errors are not independent, then single-equation least squares applied to each equation *in turn* are no longer identical to maximum likelihood procedures. The equations may still be estimated sequentially, however. In this case the estimates will maintain the property of consistency even though they may no longer be fully efficient.[38] Thus as the correlation between the errors of the two equations goes to zero, the estimates obtained by the recursive single-equation procedure will tend toward maximum likelihood estimates.

At this point, it is necessary to clarify what is meant by applying single-equation procedures *in turn* to each equation. In the present case, this means that we first estimate Equation 6.96 by standard least squares. We then use the values of Y_t estimated by this equation as our endogenous variable in Equation 6.97. The recursive nature of the system enables us first to estimate the endogenous variable as the dependent variable of one equation and then to use the estimated values of this variable as an independent variable in the second equation.[39]

Before presenting a summary statement of the procedure for estimating the two recursive equations, it is useful to express Equation 6.97 in an alternative form:

$$P(0) \, P(0,t) - B \, P(t) = a[Y_t - B + P^2(0)] + U_{2t} \qquad (6.98)$$

Equation 6.98 is a regression constrained to pass through the origin, given that we know B as well as $P(0)$, $P(0,t)$, $P(t)$, and Y_t. But recall that the recursive procedure discussed in the preceding paragraph requires that we first estimate Equation 6.96. The estimated intercept of this equation is just

$$\ln [P(0,0) - P^2(0)] = \ln [B - P^2(0)]$$

Thus we shall have an estimate of $B = P(0,0)$ to use in Equation 6.98 as a result of estimating Equation 6.96.

The question remains as to what statistical properties this estimate of $P(0,0) = B$ will possess. Recall that if the errors in the two equations of the system are uncorrelated and if we make the standard regression assumptions with normally distributed errors, then the estimate of the

[37] Provided, of course, that the standard regression assumptions — including the assumption of normally distributed errors — are made.

[38] See Klein (1953, pp. 112–113).

[39] See Klein (1953, Chapter 3, Section 2) for the logic of this procedure in a recursive system of this nature.

intercept in Equation 6.96 will be the maximum likelihood estimate[40] of

$$\ln [B - P^2(0)] = \ln [P(0,0) - P^2(0)]$$

The operation of taking a logarithm is a strictly monotonic or one-to-one transformation of its argument. Since maximum likelihood estimates are invariant under one-to-one transformations, we will have a maximum likelihood estimate of $P(0,0)$ in this case.[41] If the errors between the equations are not independent, then the estimate of $\ln [P(0,0) - P^2(0)]$ will be consistent but not maximum likelihood. But consistent estimates are invariant under continuous transformations,[42] and the operation of taking a logarithm is also a continuous transformation. Hence, in this case we will have a consistent estimate of $P(0,0)$ to use in Equation 6.98. Thus at worst we will be substituting a consistent estimate of $B = P(0,0)$ into Equation 6.98 while at best this estimate will be maximum likelihood.

The advantage of this recursive procedure is further underscored when one considers the problems inherent in Equation 6.97 because the intercept term of this equation is $-aB$ while the regression coefficients of the independent variables are a and B. Fortunately the estimation of Equation 6.96 prior to Equation 6.97 yields an estimate of B having desirable statistical properties. Using this estimate of B, we are then able to use Equation 6.98 rather than Equation 6.97 to estimate the parameter a. If this recursive procedure were not available, the problem of estimating the equations would be extremely complex. This becomes clear when we note that the intercept of Equation 6.96 contains $\ln (B - P^2(0))$ while Equation 6.97 is subject to the nonlinear constraint that its intercept equals $-aB$. The B must be the same in both equations. While it is possible to speculate about iterative procedures to satisfy the relations between and within these equations, the statistical properties of such estimates would be most difficult, if not impossible, to obtain. All this has been by way of underscoring our good fortune that the simultaneous regression relations for the cohesive elements model form a recursive system.

At this point it seems appropriate to summarize the three-step regression procedure to follow in estimating the two recursive simultaneous equations of the probability diffusion model.[43]

---

[40] See Johnston (1963, Chapter 1).
[41] See Mood (1950, Chapter 8).
[42] See Goldberger (1964, p. 130).
[43] This estimation procedure is patterned after that given by Klein (1953, Chapter 3, Sections 2 and 4) for recursive systems.

Recursive Regression Procedure

Step 1. Estimate Equation 6.96 by classical least squares to obtain estimates of k and $\ln [P(0,0 - P^2(0)]$. Be certain that the number of respondents included in the analysis is sufficiently large so that the errors in variables problem may be safely neglected.

Step 2. From the estimate of the intercept, $\ln [P(0,0) - P^2(0)]$, and from $Q(0)$, the observed proportion which is the sample estimate of $P(0)$, solve for $B = P(0,0)$. Denote this estimate by $\hat{B}$.

Step 3. From the estimated relation in Step 1, compute the values of Y_t which would be estimated at each value of t given the estimated parameters. Denote this estimate by $\hat{Y}_t$. Then using $\hat{Y}_t$ and $\hat{B}$ estimate Equation 6.98 in the following manner

$$Q(0)Q(0,t) - \hat{B}Q(t) = a[\hat{Y}_t - \hat{B} + Q^2(0)] + e_{2t}$$

where now e_{2t} is the sample estimate of the error measured from the "true" relation and $Q(t)$ and $Q(0,t)$ are sample estimates of $P(t)$ and $P(0,t)$, respectively. This final equation is simply a regression through the origin.

6.7.2.4 *Problems in the Regression Procedure.* Recall that we noted in Section 6.7.1.2 certain inherent theoretical constraints on the parameter values. The estimation procedure recommended in Section 6.7.2.3 does not incorporate these constraints. Should any of these constraints be *significantly* violated by the unconstrained estimates, the model itself would be called into question. For example, data could yield an estimate of $a > 1$, which is theoretically impossible. Such a value implies an equilibrium or steady-state choice share for response A versus response B of over one hundred percent. By a significant violation of a theoretical constraint, we shall mean an over- or underestimate of a parameter the order of magnitude of which would be very unlikely to result from sampling fluctuations about a true parameter value which, in fact, satisfies the constraint.

We could, of course, seek to resolve this problem by attempting to solve the quadratic programming problem that will result if we should seek to minimize the squared error subject to these theoretical constraints. Goldberger refers to some results by Zellner relating to this problem.[44] Goldberger does not present Zellner's results on the sampling distribution of such estimates, but he does give Zellner's recommendation to set the estimated parameter equal to the constraining value

---

[44] This procedure is termed restricted least squares in the econometrics literature. See Goldberger (1964, pp. 261–262).

it has violated whenever unconstrained least squares yield an infeasible estimate.

Another problem in the regression procedure is the measure of goodness of fit of the probability diffusion model to data. At first glance, it seems natural to use the square of the correlation coefficient as the measure of the fit of the model to the data in each equation. However, there are pitfalls in this approach.

For the "k" estimating Equation 6.96 the correlation coefficient measure is rather ambiguous. In this case, it measures whether k is significantly different from zero, but this is not identical to a test of the model. An example will illustrate this point. Suppose that the probability diffusion model really is the model that generates a particular set of observations. Further, suppose that in this case we are dealing with a group of individual respondents each of whom experiences no change in his response probability between successive responses. That is, we now have a group of respondents who are stationary with respect to their response probabilities. This coincides with the quasi-stationary Bernoulli universe discussed in Chapter 3. In terms of the probability diffusion model this is the degenerate case where $k = \alpha + \beta = 0$. But note that if the true value of k is zero, the regression given as Equation 6.96 should yield an estimated correlation coefficient very close to zero. If this correlation coefficient were to be taken as a measure of the fit of the model, the conclusion in this case would be the erroneous one that the probability diffusion model does not fit the data. The correct conclusion would be that the model is valid with $k = 0$. Hence, the correlation coefficient in Equation 6.96 or a test of the significance of the estimated slope k does not necessarily measure the veracity of the probability diffusion model in an empirical situation.

A similar problem occurs in Equation 6.98. Since $a = 0$ is a legitimate parameter value, the square of the regression coefficient again does not provide a useful measure of the descriptive adequacy of the model for a set of data.

In summary, then, we see that the recursive regression estimation procedure does not yield any clear-cut measure of the goodness of fit of the model to a set of data. Fortunately, the minimum chi-square procedure that is developed in the next section does yield measures of the overall fit of the model to a set of data.

Furthermore, the regression procedure places rather stringent demands upon a data base in order for the estimators to have desirable statistical properties. In the first place, a large number of individual respondents must be available in order to diminish the errors in variables problem to negligible proportions. Second, the asymptotic

property of consistency holds as the number of responses per respondent increases. This requirement is troublesome in terms of both data availability and possible nonstationarity in the change process itself. Thus the regression procedure requires both a large sample of respondents and a large number of responses per respondent in order for the asymptotic properties of the estimators to hold. In any empirical situation where we have available only a few responses per respondent, the "nice" *asymptotic* properties of the regression estimates are of little comfort.

Finally, estimation of Equation 6.96 will degenerate if $P(0,t) - P(0)P(t) = Y_t \leq 0$ since the natural logarithm of such an argument is not defined. A negative value for Y_t may result for one of two reasons:

1. Sampling error in the estimators of $P(0)$, $P(t)$, and $P(0,t)$.
2. The model doesn't describe the data very well.

As the number of respondents increases, the sampling errors in the estimates of $P(0)$, $P(t)$, and $P(0,t)$ decrease. Thus the likelihood of degeneracy resulting from sampling error diminishes as the sample size increases. Preliminary empirical experience with MRCA dentifrice data suggests that degeneracy is likely to occur when the number of respondents is less than fifty. But with a sample as small as this, the errors in variables problem is itself sufficiently serious to invalidate the use of the recursive regression procedure. The second source of degeneracy may result if extreme changes in response probability are common or if $P(0,t)$ is very small.

In conclusion, the recursive regression procedure may be useful and convenient for developing estimates of $P(0,0)$, a, and k when a test of the model is not required. This conclusion is, of course, subject to an adequate number of respondents and attention to the theoretical constraints on the estimates.

6.7.3 Minimum Chi-Square Estimation Procedure

Our objective in this section is to formulate a variant of the minimum chi-square procedure in order to be able to estimate and test the probability diffusion model (PDM). This procedure will provide a test of the model in the goodness of-fit sense as well as parameter estimates that have desirable asymptotic properties as the number of respondents increases.

We first consider the proportion of the total of M respondents who make each of the four possible response combinations of A or B at zero and A or B at t. These observed proportions are arranged in Table 6.8.

Table 6.8   Observed Response Proportions

		Time t		
		A	B	
Time 0	A	$Q(0,t)$	$Q(0) - Q(0,t)$	$Q(0)$
	B	$Q(t) - Q(0,t)$	$1 - Q(0) - Q(t) + Q(0,t)$	$1 - Q(0)$
		$Q(t)$	$1 - Q(t)$	1.0

If the PDM generated these responses, then the corresponding expected response proportions may be determined from Equations 6.67 and 6.68. The expected response proportions corresponding to the cells in Table 6.8 are arrayed in Table 6.9.

The expected response proportions for $t = 1, 2, \ldots$ are functions of four parameters, a, k, P(0), and P(0,0). A direct estimate of P(0) is available from the corresponding observed response proportion $Q(0)$. As M, the number of independent respondents, increases, it is known that $Q(0)$ is asymptotically normally distributed with mean P(0) and variance $\{P(0)[1 - P(0)] - \text{Var}[X(0)]\}/M$.[45] For sufficiently large M, our observed $Q(0)$ is a sample of size one from a normal distribution with the mean and variance given here. Since the sample mean from a normal distribution is a maximum likelihood estimator of the population mean, $Q(0)$ will asymptotically be a maximum likelihood estimator of P(0). Estimates of a, k, and P(0,0) are obtained from the minimum chi-square procedures.

Now consider only those respondents who made response A on the initial response occasion (i.e., $t = 0$). The proportion of the M respondents falling in this category is just $Q(0)$. If we knew the values of

Table 6.9   Expected Response Proportions

		Time t		
		A	B	
Time 0	A	$P(0,t)$	$P(0) - P(0,t)$	$P(0)$
	B	$P(t) - P(0,t)$	$1 - P(0) - P(t) + P(0,t)$	$1 - P(0)$
		$P(t)$	$1 - P(t)$	1.0

[45] See Cramer (1946, p. 207) and Kendall and Stuart (1958, pp. 126–127) as well as the references for Section 6.2.

the parameters a, k, and $P(0,0)$, and since the PDM assumes that individuals respond independently from one another, we could then formulate the chi-square statistic for the deviation of the observed from the expected response proportions for 0 and t as

$$\chi^2_A(0,t) = M\left[\frac{\{Q(0,t) - P(0,t)\}^2}{P(0,t)} + \frac{\{Q(0) - Q(0,t) - P(0) + P(0,t)\}^2}{P(0) - P(0,t)}\right]$$

(6.99)

with one degree of freedom. Since the PDM assumes that the successive responses of each individual are independent, $\chi^2_A(0,t)$ and $\chi^2_A(0,t')$ are independent chi-square random variables when $t \neq t'$. By the additivity property of independent chi-square random variables, we have

$$\chi^2_A(0,T) = \sum_{t=1}^{T} \chi^2_A(0,t)$$

(6.100)

which is chi-square distributed with T degrees of freedom.

In a similar manner we could consider only those respondents who made response B on the initial response occasion. That is, we are now considering the fraction $1 - Q(0)$ out of the total of M respondents. For this case the appropriate chi-square goodness of fit statistic for zero and t is

$$\chi^2_B(0,t) = M\left[\frac{Q(t) - Q(0,t) - P(t) + P(0,t)^2}{P(t) - P(0,t)}\right.$$
$$\left. + \frac{1 - Q(0) - Q(t) + Q(0,t) - 1 + P(0) + P(t) - P(0,t)^2}{1 - P(0) - P(t) + P(0,t)}\right]$$

(6.101)

with one degree of freedom. Again, since the PDM assumes that the successive responses of an individual are independent, we have

$$\chi^2_B(0,T) = \sum_{t=1}^{T} \chi^2_B(0,t)$$

(6.102)

which is chi-square distributed with T degrees of freedom.

Now, if $\chi^2_A(0,T)$ and $\chi^2_B(0,T)$ were independent, we could form

$$\chi^2(0,T) = \chi^2_A(0,T) + \chi^2_B(0,T)$$

(6.103)

which again, by the additivity of independent chi-square random variables, would be chi-square distributed having $2T$ degrees of freedom. Since we also need to estimate the parameters a, k, and $P(0,0)$, we would then minimize Equation 6.103 with respect to a, k, and $P(0,0)$.

The resulting minimum value of $\chi^2(0,T)$ would be chi-square distributed with $2T - 3$ degrees of freedom. The parameter estimates for a, k, and $P(0,0)$ which minimize Equation 6.103 will be best asymptotically normal estimates of the parameters.

Since the partitioning between $\chi_A^2(0,T)$ and $\chi_B^2(0,T)$ depends upon $Q(0)$, a random variable, there will be some dependence between those two chi-square random variables. The question arises as to how we should evaluate and estimate the model under these conditions. We shall continue to minimize the $\chi^2(0,T)$ statistic given in Equation 6.103 with respect to a, k, and $P(0,0)$. As we indicated earlier, the minimized $\chi^2(0,T)$ will be chi-square distributed with $2T - 3$ degrees of freedom if $\chi_A^2(0,T)$ and $\chi_B^2(0,T)$ are independent. This independence case will establish an upper bound on the "fit" (or p-level) of the model.[46] Now we ask what would be the distribution of the minimum $\chi^2(0,T)$ if $\chi_A^2(0,T)$ and $\chi_B^2(0,T)$ were *totally* dependent. Clearly, this is the other extreme from independence. With three parameters to estimate from the data, Holland has shown that for the case of *complete* dependence between the partitions, minimum $\chi^2(0,T)$ will be distributed as twice a chi-square random variable having $T - 3$ degrees of freedom.[47] This establishes a lower bound for the p-level of the PDM. The case of partial dependence between $\chi_A^2(0,T)$ and $\chi_B^2(0,T)$ will lie between these extremes.

Under the conditions of partial or total dependency between $\chi_A^2(0,T)$ and $\chi_B^2(0,T)$, the minimizing estimates of a, k, and $P(0,0)$ will be consistent asymptotically normal (CAN) estimates.[48] They will not necessarily be fully efficient. However, as the dependency between the two component chi-squares diminishes, the estimators approach full efficiency (i.e., become BAN).

The total dependence case is a very crude lower bound for the p-level of the PDM since total dependence can never occur for this model. In fact, the p-level of the PDM will always tend to lie near the p-level of the independence case. Thus the lower bound established by the total dependence case provides a *very conservative* test of the PDM — i.e., it is biased against the model.

---

[46] If X^2 denotes an observed value of a chi-square random variable, then the p-level will be given by the tail of the distribution for values of χ^2 which exceed X^2. Formally,

$$p\text{-level} = \int_{X^2}^{\infty} f(\chi^2)\, d\chi^2$$

[47] See Holland ([1966], Chapter 4).

[48] Ibid.

In most cases, there will be only a very modest amount of dependence between $\chi_A^2(0,T)$ and $\chi_B^2(0,T)$ in the PDM. The dependency will diminish as:

1. The number of individual respondents M increases.
2. The population of respondents becomes more heterogeneous with respect to their response probabilities.

Fortunately, both of these conditions tend to be present in applications of the PDM to consumer brand choice. Consequently, we will err very little if we use $\chi^2(0,T)$ to test the model assuming independence.

6.7.4 Estimating the Cross-Sectional Distribution of Response Probability

In this section we shall develop a procedure for estimating the distribution of response probability across individual respondents $f[X(t)]$, at any response occasion t. That is, our interest will center upon ascertaining certain characteristics of the distribution in our population of respondents of their probability of making response A at t. We develop estimates for the mean and variance of this distribution without any assumption as to its form. If we wish to specify its form, the mean and variance may be used to identify any two-parameter form of $f[X(t)]$. In many cases it would seem reasonable to use the steady-state form of $f[X(t)]$, the beta distribution, as a reasonable approximation at t.

The first two raw moments of $f[X(t)]$ are

$$P(t) = E[X(t)] = \int_0^1 X(t)f[X(t)]\,dX(t) \qquad (6.104)$$

and

$$P(t,t) = E[X^2(t)] = \int_0^1 X^2(t)f[X(t)]\,dX(t) \qquad (6.105)$$

Now $P(t)$ may be directly estimated by $Q(t)$, which will be a maximum likelihood estimate by the same reasoning that was applied to $Q(0)$ as an estimate of $P(0)$. However, as was true for $P(0,0)$, there is no direct estimate of $P(t,t)$. Thus we must develop an estimation method.

In a manner analogous to Lemma 2 (Equation 6.65), we could show that

$$P(t, t + 1) = E[X(t)X(t + 1)]$$
$$= \int_0^1 E[X(t + 1)|X(t)]f[X(t)]\,dX(t) \qquad (6.106)$$

Since we have assumed that the process is stationary with respect to the parameters α and β, the choice of the time origin is essentially arbitrary. That is, only the elapsed time is important in terms of the change process. Thus we have, with a change in time origin in Equation 6.42,

$$E[X(t + 1)|X(t)] = X(t) \exp(-k) + a[1 - \exp(-k)] \quad (6.107)$$

since $t + 1 - t = 1$. Substituting Equation 6.107 into Equation 6.106 we have

$$P(t, t + 1) = \int_0^1 \{X(t) \exp(-k) + a[1 - \exp(-k)]\}X(t)f[X(t)]\,dX(t)$$

$$= E[X^2(t)] \exp(-k) + a\,E[X(t)][1 - \exp(-k)]$$

$$= P(t,t) \exp(-k) + a\,P(t)[1 - \exp(-k)] \quad (6.108)$$

We now solve Equation 6.108 for $P(t,t)$ to find

$$P(t,t) = a\,P(t) + \exp(k)[P(t, t + 1) - a\,P(t)] \quad (6.109)$$

Since $P(t)$ and $P(t, t + 1)$ are estimable by $Q(t)$ and $Q(t, t + 1)$, respectively, and since a and k may be estimated by one of the methods discussed in Sections 6.7.2 and 6.7.3, we are able to estimate $P(t,t)$ when these estimates are substituted into Equation 6.109. If $\hat{P}(t,t)$ and $\hat{P}(t)$ denote the estimates of $P(t,t)$ and $P(t)$ obtained by the methods described earlier, our estimate of the variance of the distribution of response probability at t will be given by

$$\text{Var}[X(t)] = \hat{P}(t,t) - [\hat{P}(t)]^2 \quad (6.110)$$

Thus we are able to obtain estimates of the mean, second raw moment, and variance of the cross-sectional distribution of response probability at t without making any assumptions as to the form of the distribution.

Recall in Section 6.6.2 we found that the steady-state distribution for the PDM is a beta distribution. Suppose we now decide to use the beta form as an approximation to the functional form of $f[X(t)]$ in a non-equilibrium situation. Two factors would seem to make this a reasonable approximation:

1. The beta distribution is the natural conjugate of Bernoulli trials, and for a given t, the PDM implies a Bernoulli process.[49]
2. The beta is rather rich in its ability to represent the distribution of response probability, as was noted in Chapter 3.

[49] See Raiffa and Schlaifer (1961).

If we use the beta form where $n > r > 0$,

$$f_{\beta_t}(X(t)|r,n) \equiv \frac{\Gamma(n)}{\Gamma(r)\Gamma(n-r)}\{X(t)\}^{r-1}\{1 - X(t)\}^{n-r-1} \quad (6.111)$$

we then have that the first two raw moments are

$$\mu_1 = \frac{r}{n} \quad (6.112)$$

and

$$\mu'_2 = \frac{r(r+1)}{n(n+1)} \quad (6.113)$$

We thus may obtain moment estimates of the beta parameters by equating Equation 6.112 to 6.104 and Equation 6.113 to 6.109 and solving for r and n, the two beta parameters. While moment estimators are generally somewhat inefficient, the complexity of the development of just the moment estimators makes it doubtful that more efficient procedures will prove to be tractable for this model.

CHAPTER 7
APPLICATION OF THE PROBABILITY DIFFUSION MODEL

7.1 Introduction

In this chapter we apply the probability diffusion model (PDM) developed in the previous chapter to brand-choice data from a consumer panel. Our objective is to ascertain whether the model is empirically viable as a model of consumer choice processes. We begin with a discussion of certain empirical considerations of importance in understanding this application. We first consider the empirical situation to which the model will be applied. Certain operational issues are then discussed. We then turn to the minimum chi-square results for the probability diffusion model. The chapter concludes with an empirical comparison of the four basic model types considered thus far in this book.

7.2 Empirical Considerations

This section will develop certain empirical issues of relevance to this application. It begins with a discussion of the market environment in which the application is made. Then certain issues in operationalizing the model are discussed.

7.2.1 A Dynamic Market: The ADA Endorsement of Crest Toothpaste

The data which will be utilized to test the PDM are the Market Research Corporation of America's (MRCA) National Consumer Panel records of dentifrice purchases for the period subsequent to the American Dental Association (A.D.A.) endorsement of Crest as a decay preventive dentifrice.[1] In this section discussion will center on this dynamic market situation and the reasons why it is of interest as a first test of the PDM.

The unprededecented American Dental Association endorsement of Crest toothpast on August 1, 1960, gave Crest an unusual differentiating appeal in the dentifrice market. Prior to this endorsement, Crest had obtained a respectable but unspectacular share of the dentifrice market

---

[1] See Boyd and Westfall (1960) for an evaluation of consumer panel as a source of marketing data.

since its introduction in the mid-1950s.[2] While a portion of the market prior to this endorsement had undoubtedly been aware of the potential benefit of a fluoride toothpaste, the endorsement by a noncommercial, professional group gave Crest a legitimated differential appeal. This legitimated appeal, coupled with an intensive promotional campaign, swept Crest to the forefront in the dentifrice market in a matter of a few months.[3] Hence, the dentifrice market was in a state of considerable transition in the period immediately following the ADA endorsement.

There are several reasons for choosing this market situation as an initial test of the PDM. First, the ADA endorsement of Crest allows us to segment the response data into before and after periods which are meaningful in terms of the behavior respresented by the model. The before period represents a relatively normal market situation where the dynamics of response probability exhibit no particularly strong trend. On the other hand, the significant market impact of the ADA endorsement of Crest gives us an after period in which the market was in a rapid state of transition. In the latter case, the response probability of many individuals was undergoing very rapid and significant change. Thus, the dentifrice market in the periods just before and just after the Crest endorsement affords us the opportunity to test the PDM in both a "normal" and a "transient" period.

The behavior of the model in each of these periods is of considerable interest from the standpoint of testing its empirical viability. It might turn out that the model breaks down in either the transient or the normal market case for reasons which are not clear a priori. The MRCA dentifrice data have two principal advantages from the standpoint of examining the model's performance in these contrasting market situations. In the first place, the dentifrice data for both time periods are for the same product class and the same set of brands. If the normal period were for one product classification and set of brands and the transient period were for yet another, the behavior of the model in each of these contrasting market situations would be confounded with the question of the behavior of the model in different product classes.[4] Hence, if the model fits well in one period but not in the other, this failure may more reasonably be attributed to a breakdown of the model in that

---

[2] Crest's market share was on the order of 10% prior to the ADA endorsement.

[3] The post-ADA market share of Crest was in excess of 30%.

[4] Naturally, the behavior of the PDM in various product classes is of considerable interest and needs to be explored in future research. The important point about the dentifrice market at the time we are considering it is that it provides us with an opportunity to analyze the transient and normal market behavior without the confounding problem of different products.

type of market situation since we have used the same product in both cases. Secondly, the MRCA data provide continuous purchasing records for the same group of households in the transient as in the normal period. Should the model perform poorly in one of the two cases, this control of respondent-to-respondent variability should once again enable us to more reasonably suspect the model's appropriateness in the type of market situation where it broke down. Thus, the use of the dentifrice data centered about the ADA endorsement provides a bonus opportunity to study the performance of the model under two contrasting market conditions for the same product class and the same sample of respondents.

The second major advantage of using the MRCA dentifrice data to test the PDM is that the brand of interest, Crest, was already an established brand at the time of the ADA endorsement in August 1960. Hence, in both the before and after periods Crest was available on a fully distributed basis.[5] Thus, lack of availability should not be a reason for a consumer choosing some brand other than Crest.[6]

Third, dentifrice is purchased frequently enough to provide sequences of brand choices which are long enough to provide ample degrees of freedom for testing the model.

Fourth, MRCA's National Consumer Panel has several thousand member households. Such a large sample of households will enable us to segment the sample into meaningful groups and still have enough respondents in each group to have confidence that the asymptotic properties of the estimates hold.

Finally, the Market Research Corporation of America agreed to make its dentifrice data from the National Consumer Panel available for use in this study.[7]

7.2.2   Some Operational Considerations

7.2.2.1   *Definition of Brand-Choice Events.*   In empirical applications of the PDM to consumer brand choice, it is necessary to have an unambiguous definition of a purchase decision or brand-choice event.

---

[5] The problem of having the product or brand available to consumers in the distribution system is particularly acute when one attempts to analyze new product or new brand introductions.

[6] To be sure, some stockouts occurred in the rush to try Crest after the ADA endorsement. This, however, is unlikely to have had any but a minor influence on brand choice and that over a very short interval of time.

[7] The authors are particularly indebted to Dr. I. J. Abrams, Vice President — Technology, of MRCA for generously supplying the data at nominal cost.

The fact that consumers may and do make multiple purchases of the same or different brands on the same day makes it necessary to consider a reasonable and precise operational rule for determining brand choice events.

After the two operational decision rules for the multiple purchase case are presented, consideration will be given to the justification for using these rules and to illustrative examples. The operational rules for multiple purchases of the same or different brands on the same day are:

Rule 1: Multiple purchase of the same brand on the same day will be considered to be a single brand-choice decision for the purpose of estimating the model.

Rule 2: Multiple purchases of different brands on the same day will be considered to be separate brand-choice decisions for each brand.

The first rule is justifiable in terms of the process which the PDM purports to represent. The model seeks to describe the dynamics of brand choice behavior independent of the amount purchased on any given purchase occasion. If a consumer purchases several packages of a single brand on a given shopping trip, this behavior most likely represents a single brand decision followed by an inventory decision — i.e., the decision to purchase more than one package of the chosen brand. While there may be a few cases where the purchase of several packages of the same brand represents a series of brand decisions, it seems more likely that it is an inventory decision once the brand of purchase has been chosen.

The second rule follows the same type of logic. The fact that a consumer purchased more than one brand on a particular shopping trip makes it obvious that more than one brand decision has been made. However, if the consumer purchases two packages of one of the brands purchased on a given day, these two packages simply count as a single brand decision consistent with the logic of Rule 1.[8]

It should be pointed out that the operational rules defined here were applied prior to the recoding of the brands into a 0–1 process. The recoding step codes a "brand decision" to purchase Crest as a 1 while

---

[8] The order of purchase of the brands for those days on which multiple purchases of brands occurs is taken as the order in which the brand purchases in question appear on the MRCA data tape. While this does some violence to the model in terms of perhaps introducing a spurious order of purchase effect, for practical purposes the incidence of this problem is quite infrequent and consequently it does not create any significant problems in the present empirical application. This is fortunate since the manner in which the data are recorded and presented would make adjustments difficult and somewhat arbitrary.

a "brand decision" to purchase some other brand is coded as 0. Since the operational rules are applied prior to this recoding, the purchase of one unit of Stripe and one unit of Dr. Lyons on the same day would be coded 00. If the recoding were done first, the operational rules would then record this as a single brand decision 0, which clearly would violate the notion we wished to capture in developing our operational rules.

Perhaps the application of these rules is best clarified by a consideration of some hypothetical examples. Three illustrative cases are given in Table 7.1.

Consumer 1 illustrates the application of Rule 1. We see that the multiple purchase of Colgate on 8/7/60 is simply coded as a 0 while the multiple purchase of Crest on 9/25/60 is recoded as a 1.

Consumer 2 illustrates Rule 2. Here we see that he purchased both Stripe and Crest on 9/30/60. Rule 2 tells us to recode this as 01.

Finally, Consumer 3 illustrates the notion that Rule 1 and Rule 2 are to be applied prior to the recoding of the "brand decision" sequence into a 0–1 vector. Here we see that a purchase of both Stripe and Dr. Lyons on 10/30/60 is recoded as two "non-Crest" purchase events — i.e., as 00.

In any empirical application of the PDM, a decision must be made as to how many successive responses are to be included in the analysis. The greater the number of responses from each respondent, the greater

Table 7.1   Hypothetical Purchase Sequences

Consumer	Date	Brand Purchased	Quantity	0–1 Vector*
1	8/7/60	Colgate	2	
	8/22/60	Crest	1	
	9/25/60	Crest	2	
	10/31/60	Ipana	1	0110
2	8/25/60	Colgate	1	
	9/30/60	Stripe	1	
	9/30/60	Crest	1	
	11/14/60	Crest	1	0011
3	8/15/60	Crest	1	
	10/30/60	Stripe	1	
	10/30/60	Dr. Lyons	1	
	11/3/60	Ipana	1	1000

* A Crest "brand decision" is coded as a 1. A "brand decision" involving the purchase of some brand other than Crest is coded as 0. In the notation of Chapter 6, response A is coded as a 1, while response B is coded as a 0.

the number of degrees of freedom for error in both the regression and the chi-square estimation procedures. In the minimum chi-square method, in particular, the greater the number of degrees of freedom the more rigorous is the test of the model since, in classical statistical terms, the model is a null hypothesis in this procedure.[9] In operational terms, this means that if data having nine degrees of freedom are consistent with the model this is stronger evidence in favor of the model than if the data had only had five degrees of freedom. Thus the desire to apply a rigorous test to the model suggests that a long sequence of successive responses for each respondent be included in the analysis.

There are two major countervailing forces that encourage restraint in the number of responses per respondent to be included in the analysis. Since all respondents must contribute the same number of responses to the analysis, an excessively long response sequence criterion would tend to decrease the number of respondents who can meet the criterion and consequently reduce the total sample size. A bias may also result because only very heavy purchases of the product class in question may be able to meet the frequency criterion. The second major reason for restraint is the fact that while the model attempts to describe the dynamics of response probabilities, the process which is postulated to determine these dynamics is itself assumed to be constant or stationary over the period of interest. Since α, β, and γ may change from time to time, the longer the sequence of responses that is used, the more likely it is that these parameters of the process itself may change. Hence sample size considerations and nonstationarity of the change process countervail the tendency to require long purchase sequences.

In this study an appropriate compromise purchase (or response) sequence length was deemed to be seven consecutive purchases in any period under study. This decision will provide nine degrees of freedom in the estimation procedures without unduly restricting the number of households able to qualify for analysis or running a great risk of nonstationarity in the change process. It should be pointed out that this was a judgmental resolution of the problem and that no precise decision rules are available.

In order for a household to enter the sample for this analysis, it had to meet the twin criteria of having reported seven purchases of dentifrice in both the period immediately preceding and immediately subsequent to the ADA endorsement of Crest. Within each of these groups the empirical proportions needed to estimate and test the probability diffusion

[9] The statistical notion involved here is that of the power of the test to reject the model. See Chapter 2 for a discussion of statistical power.

model were developed for both the before and the after ADA periods. This before–after analysis will enable us to test the model in a relatively normal period as well as in the transient market of the post-ADA period. In addition, the estimates obtained in the after period may be contrasted to the estimates obtained in the before period in order to ascertain the impact of the ADA endorsement and its accompanying promotional effort.

7.2.2.2 *Stratification by Average Interpurchase Time.* Recall that in Section 6.2.1 the time problems which arise when the PDM is applied to consumer brand-choice behavior were discussed. A natural method to

Table 7.2   Groups Stratified by Average Interpurchase Time in the pre-ADA Period

Group	No. of Households in Group	Average Interpurchase Time
1	637	0–30 Days
2	556	31–45 Days
3	480	46–60 Days
4	894	Over 60 Days

use to reduce the magnitude of this problem is to stratify the sample of consumers according to their average interpurchase time. Such a strategy is followed in the present case. Those households that met the twin criteria of seven before ADA and seven after ADA purchases were subdivided according to their average interpurchase time in the pre-ADA period. The sample size of the groups thus formed and the range of their average interpurchase times is given in Table 7.2.

7.3   Minimum Chi-Square Estimation for the Crest Case

In this section we examine the application of the probability diffusion model to the Crest case. We first examine the goodness of fit of the model to the data from each of the cases specified in Section 7.2.2.2. The estimated parameter values are then presented along with comments upon their interpretation.

The estimation procedure minimized Equation 6.103 with respect to a, k, and $P(0,0)$. The minimization was implemented numerically via a three-dimensional grid search.[10] The direct maximum likelihood

[10] Each parameter to be estimated specifies one dimension of the grid to be searched. Since we have three parameters to estimate via the grid search, the search occurs in three dimensions.

estimate of $P(0)$ — i.e., $Q(0)$ — was used. This ability to estimate $P(0)$, directly, reduces the computational burden of the numeric minimization of the chi square statistic.

7.3.1 Goodness-of-Fit Results

In Section 7.2.2.2 we defined four groups (or strata) each having a before ADA and an after ADA sequence of seven purchases. Thus we will have a total of eight goodness-of-fit statistics with which to evaluate the probability diffusion model in this case.

The goodness-of-fit results are presented in Table 7.3. The minimum χ^2 value represents the value of $\chi^2(0,T)$ when it is minimized with respect to a, k, and $P(0,0)$. In order to assess the fit of the probability diffusion model to these data, we examine the p-level of the observed minimum χ^2. Recall that the p-level represents the probability of observing a χ^2 value as large or larger than the one that was observed, under the hypothesis that the model generated the observed responses.

We first examine the p-level when $\chi^2_A(0,T)$ and $\chi^2_B(0,T)$ are independent. Since we have sequences of seven purchases and estimate three parameters in the numeric minimization, the minimum chi-square statistic under independence will have $2T - 3 = 2 \cdot 6 - 3 = 9$ degrees of freedom.[11] The independent p-levels reported in Table 7.3 were computed by comparing the observed minimum χ^2 to a chi-square random variable having nine degrees of freedom. From the large p-levels exhibited in Table 7.3, we see that the probability diffusion model provides an excellent fit to the dentifrice data in both the stable before period and the transient after period.

While we have good reason, as noted later, to believe that the independence case is closely approached, we now examine the *very conservative* case of total dependence between $\chi^2_A(0,T)$ and $\chi^2_B(0,T)$. In this case we compare the statistic $\chi^2(0,T)/2$ to a chi-square random variable having $T - 3 = 6 - 3 = 3$ degrees of freedom. The resulting p-levels are reported in Table 7.3. We see from these results, which are biased against the model (i.e., the test is conservative), that even in this case the probability diffusion model is found to yield an excellent fit to the dentifrice data in both periods.

In summary, then, the probability diffusion model provides an

---

[11] A fourth parameter $P(0)$ is estimated directly. The degree of freedom which is used to make this estimate was accounted for when we established the $2T - 3$ formula for determining degrees of freedom.

Table 7.3 Goodness of Fit for the Probability Diffusion Model (Crest Case, Seven Purchase Sequences)

Group	Sample Size	Minimum χ^2	Independent	Dependent	$E[X(0)] = P(0)$	$\mathrm{Var}[X(0)]$	Standard Deviation of $X(0)$
Before 1	637	2.07	>0.990	0.800	0.1617	0.0840	0.289
Before 2	556	12.60	0.185	0.098	0.1331	0.0693	0.263
Before 3	480	12.28	0.197	0.107	0.1313	0.0524	0.229
Before 4	894	5.11	0.822	0.471	0.0973	0.0430	0.207
After 1	637	6.73	0.665	0.346	0.2355	0.1166	0.342
After 2	556	5.48	0.790	0.443	0.2230	0.1017	0.320
After 3	480	3.89	0.917	0.588	0.2063	0.0679	0.261
After 4	894	4.71	0.855	0.502	0.1957	0.0758	0.275

Table 7.4 Probability Diffusion Model Parameter Estimates for the Crest Case

Group	$P(0)$	a	Δa^*	k	Δk^*	α	$\Delta \alpha^*$	β	$\Delta \beta^*$
B-1 0–30 Days	0.1617	0.1446		0.0070		0.0010		0.0060	
B-2 31–45 Days	0.1331	0.1076		0.0584		0.0063		0.0521	
B-3 46–60 Days	0.1313	0.0688		0.1025		0.0071		0.0954	
B-4 Over 60 Days	0.0973	0.1160		0.1203		0.0140		0.1063	
A-1 0–30 Days	0.2355	0.7875	0.6429	0.0219	0.0147	0.0172	0.0162	0.0047	−0.0013
A-2 31–45 Days	0.2230	0.5097	0.4021	0.0450	−0.0134	0.0229	0.0166	0.0221	−0.0300
A-3 46–60 Days	0.2063	0.7181	0.6493	0.0259	−0.0766	0.0186	0.0115	0.0073	−0.0881
A-4 Over 60 Days	0.1957	0.4743	0.3583	0.0519	−0.0684	0.0246	0.0106	0.0273	−0.0790

* For any parameter r ($r = a, k, \alpha, \beta$) the Δ measure is determined as $\Delta r = r_{\mathrm{after}} - r_{\mathrm{before}}$.

excellent fit to the dentifrice date. The independent p-level is the more appropriate p-level to use in this case since:

1. The sample sizes are large (i.e., several hundred), and
2. $\text{Var}[X(0)]$ for each group indicates considerable interrespondent heterogeneity with respect to response probability.

These three factors will tend to make $\chi_A^2(0,T)$ and $\chi_B^2(0,T)$ independent. Consequently, we will err but little if we use the independent p-levels to assess the model's fit to the data.

7.3.2 Parameter Estimates

We turn now to the parameter estimates and their interpretation when the PDM is applied to the Crest data. The parameter estimates of interest are presented in Tables 7.3 and 7.4.

The first parameters we discuss are the mean, $E[X(0)]$, and variance, $\text{Var}[X(0)]$, of the cross-sectional distribution of response probability at the first response in each sequence of responses. It is useful to examine a diagram of the response sequences and note the points at which $E[X(0)]$ and $\text{Var}[X(0)]$ are measured for each of these periods. See Figure 7.1. Since sequences of seven consecutive purchases are being used in both the before and the after periods, each respondent must contribute a sequence of fourteen consecutive responses to the analysis. Recall the criteria for inclusion of a respondent in the sample given in Section 7.2.2.1. These fourteen responses are broken into two sequences of seven responses in Figure 7.1. The initial cross-sectional distributions of response probability are given at $t = 0$ in both the before and the after periods. That is, in the before period the initial distribution of response probability is measured as of the seventh purchase of dentifrice prior to the ADA endorsement while in the after period the distribution is measured as of the first purchase after the endorsement.

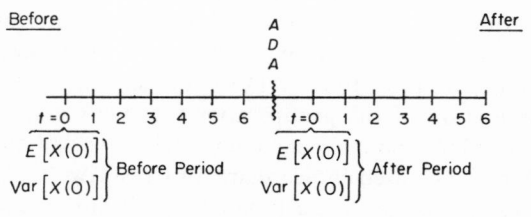

Figure 7.1. Response sequences and initial distributions. Responses occur at $t = 0, 1, 2, \ldots, 6$.

From Table 7.3 we see that in both the before and the after periods, the expected initial probability of purchasing Crest $E[X(0)]$ is inversely related to the average interpurchase time. The interpretation of $E[X(0)]$ is as the expected probability of purchasing Crest on the initial trial for an individual selected at random from a particular group. A post hoc argument for the reasonableness of these results is as follows:

Before Period. Purchase frequency may be considered a surrogate measure of interest in the product class of dentifrice. To the extent that this relationship is reasonable one might expect frequent (more interested) consumers to have noted and perhaps reacted to the potential benefits of stannous flouride even prior to the ADA legitimation of this belief. That is, it is suggested that purchase frequency is related to product class interest which in turn is related to perception of the relatively weak stimulus of the potential benefit of stannous fluoride prior to the endorsement.

After Period. The intergroup differences in $E[X(0)]$ are smaller in the after period than they are in the before period. If we assume that frequency of purchase is related to interest which in turn is related to the perception of relatively weak stimuli in the before period, then we would expect the massive stimulus of the ADA endorsement to bring the groups closer together with respect to their expected response probabilities in the after period.

An examination of $\text{Var}[X(0)]$ and the corresponding standard deviations of $X(0)$ in Table 7.3 indicates that each group exhibits considerable heterogeneity in terms of the response probabilities of the group members. This result reinforces the argument for the near independence of $\chi^2_A(0,T)$ and $\chi^2_B(0,T)$.

We now examine the parameter estimates presented in Table 7.4. First consider a, which is the expected proportion of Crest purchases we would anticipate in the steady state (or at equilibrium). If we compare $P(0)$, the initial choice share for Crest, to the estimate of a for the groups in the before period, we see that for three of the four groups in the before period the model indicates a long-term deterioration in the market for Crest. This implication is consistent with the deterioration of Crest's market share prior to the ADA endorsement reported by Bliven (1963). Examination of the groups after the ADA endorsement indicates that the ADA endorsement completely reversed this trend. All groups exhibit an increased choice share for Crest ($\Delta a > 0$) immediately after the endorsement and the estimated equilibrium choice shares are very high in all cases.

The estimates of the equilibrium choice share a in the after period

would seem unduly high if we really believed that the process itself (i.e., α and β) would remain stationary into the indefinite future. It is to be expected, however, that these early results will be dampened by strong competitive retaliation in the form of dealing and increased advertising. Thus these results are merely an estimate of what Crest's equilibrium choice share would be in each of these segments if the process did not change but were to be allowed to run to equilibrium.

We see from Table 7.4 that in the before period k is directly related to the average interpurchase time. The greater the average interpurchase time, the more exogenous market stimuli (such as competitive advertising) are likely to impinge on the consumer between purchases. Thus we would expect less frequent purchasers to be somewhat more volatile with respect to their brand response probabilities from purchase to purchase. Since k is a measure of the extent to which individuals shift their response probabilities between trials, we would expect the relation between k and average interpurchase time which was observed. While we would expect this time effect on a priori grounds, nevertheless it is surprising that Group 1, the most frequent purchasers of dentifrice, is so much more stable with respect to its members' response probabilities than any of the other three groups in the before ADA period.

When we examine the change in k as we go from the before period to the after period, we see that for all but the most frequent purchasers (Group 1) the overall propensity to change response probability decreases (i.e., $\Delta k < 0$). A mechanism which accounts for this result will be discussed when we consider the parameters α and β. For the most frequent purchasers $\Delta k > 0$, which indicates that for this group the overall propensity to change response probability between purchases increased.

It is of interest to examine the change in α as we pass from the before period into the after period. In all cases α increased markedly. Recalling that α represents the propensity for an individual's response probability to increase, we may interpret this as an indication that the ADA endorsement and the resulting promotional campaign made it quite likely that an individual's probability of purchasing Crest would increase. Note that the greatest increases in α were in the two most active groups, Group 1 and Group 2. They may well reflect the interest factor which was previously postulated. Thus the most frequent purchasers of dentifrice were the most likely to have their probability of purchasing Crest enhanced.

The results on β are particularly interesting. Recall that β measures

the propensity for an individual's probability of purchasing Crest to decrease between purchases. Table 7.4 reveals that in all groups β decreased in the after period from what it had been in the before period. In fact, β decreased so sharply for Groups 2, 3, and 4 that the total amount of shifting in individuals' probabilities (measured by k) decreases as we move from the before period to the after period. In these three cases the decrease in β (the likelihood that an individual's probability of purchasing Crest will decrease) was several times the increase in α (the likelihood that an individual's probability of purchasing Crest will increase). Thus, while the endorsement made it much more likely that an individual's probability of purchasing Crest would increase, for Groups 2, 3, and 4 the impact of the endorsement was even more striking in the manner in which β decreased.

The absolute changes in α and β for Groups 2, 3, and 4 could be interpreted in terms of a probabilistic ratchet effect on an individual's probability of purchasing Crest. That is, the endorsement enhanced the likelihood that this probability would, in fact, increase and if it did increase, it would be very unlikely that it would subsequently decrease from its new high level. Even for those individuals experiencing no increase in their probability of purchasing Crest, the magnitude of β in the after period indicates that the likelihood is small that these individuals will experience a decrease in their probability of purchasing Crest. It might be said that this sharp decline in β markedly increased the loyalty of Crest consumers. Another way of saying this is that the ADA endorsement enhanced the retentive power of Crest as a brand in the dentifrice market even more than it increased its attractive power.

For Group 1 the change in α was of the same order of magnitude as the change in α for other groups. The overall amount of change, $k = \alpha + \beta$, increased since β started from such a low value in the before ADA period that it couldn't fall as sharply in absolute terms as it could for the other three groups.

To summarize briefly, the probability diffusion model suggests that the impact of the American Dental Association's endorsement of Crest and the subsequent promotional campaign to capitalize on this legitimate appeal increased both Crest's attractiveness and its retentive capacity.

The fact that the increase in retentive capacity was considerably greater than the increase in attractiveness is somewhat of a surprising result. This is an example of a stochastic model, which fits a set of data very well, yielding an unexpected inference. Without the model, we probably would have given more serious consideration to the alternative

hypothesis that the attractive properties of the brand were the ones most enhanced by the endorsement.

7.4 Empical Comparison of Four Stochastic Models

Thus far in this book we have presented four basic types of stochastic models of choice behavior: Bernoulli models, Markov models, the linear learning model, and the probability diffusion model. How can we evaluate these models in terms of their ability to describe data — i.e., in terms of goodness of fit? In this section we provide an initial empirical comparison of four stochastic models developed in previous chapters.[12] The first two are Markov models — the brand loyal model (BL) and the last purchase loyal model (LPL). The third is the generalized linear learning model (LL) which allows for consumer heterogeneity. The final model is the probability diffusion model (PDM). It should be noted that the Bernoulli model occurs as a special case of each of the models compared in this section.

7.4.1 The Chi-Square, Goodness-of-Fit Measure

Each of the models are fitted to consumer brand-choice data using minimum chi-square procedures. The BL and LPL models are fitted for the case of an arbitrary distribution of p in the consumer population. Fitting these models under an arbitrary distribution as opposed a specific distribution of p enhances their comparison to the LL and the PD models in terms of their relative goodness of fit.

The chi-square, goodness-of-fit procedures yield a chi-square statistic from which we may assess the fit of a model to the data. Recall that in general terms, the chi-square statistic arises from a function of the form

$$\chi^2 = \sum_{i=1}^{I} \frac{[O_i - E_i(\Delta)]^2}{E_i(\Delta)} \tag{7.1}$$

where $i = 1, \ldots, I$ indexes a set of mutually exlcusive and collectively exhaustive categories of brand-choice responses. Also,

O_i = Observed number of consumers purchasing Brand A in brand-choice response category i.

$E_i(\Delta)$ = The (model generated) expected number of consumers purchasing Brand A in brand-choice category i. Note that this expected number depends upon the parameter vector Δ.

Δ = Vector of parameters in the model. The vector will have d elements.

---

[12] This section is based upon Montgomery (1968b).

The chi-square statistic is distributed as a chi-square random variable having l-d-1 degrees of freedom under the hypothesis that the model generated the O_i. It should be noted that the brand-choice categories i, the parameter vector Δ, and the expected number $E_i(\Delta)$ are all specific to a particular model. Thus we see that χ^2 is the weighted squared deviations of the model's predictions from the actual data, the weights being the reciprocals of the model's predictions.

Since the chi-square statistic has a different number of degrees of freedom for each model, we shall base our comparison upon the p-level of the statistic. The p-level is given by

$$p\text{-level} = \int_{\hat{\chi}^2}^{\infty} f[\chi^2(df \text{ for the model})] \, d\chi^2 \qquad (7.2)$$

where $\hat{\chi}^2$ is the observed value of the statistic for a particular model. Thus the p-level tells us the probability of observing deviations of the model from the data at least as large as the ones we have observed under the hypothesis that the model generated the data. Thus, the closer the p-level is to 1.0, the better the fit of the model. The closer the p-level is to 0.0, the worse the fit of the model. Since the p-level adjusts for different degrees of freedom for each of the models, it may be used directly in the comparison.

Strictly speaking, the p-levels reported later for the PD model represent upper bounds on the p-level. (See Chapter 6.) While a lower bound may also be established, the large sample size and the degree of consumer heterogeneity in the empirical case reported later make the upper bound representative of the fit of the PDM in this case.

7.4.2 The Empirical Case

The MRCA dentifrice purchase records from the National Consumer panel provide the data base for this empirical comparison. The data used to compare the models consists of the five brand purchases prior to the endorsement and the five brand purchases subsequent to the endorsement. Thus by using the relatively stable preendorsement period and the very unstable postendorsement period, we shall have an opportunity to assess the models in two markedly different market situations.

The population of consumer households was segmented into four groups by average interpurchase time in the before ADA period. Thus we have eight sets of brand choice data (four before and four after) on which to compare the results.

At this point it should be noted that the data used in this comparison are not identical to the data use in Section 7.3. In Section 7.3 a household had to report fourteen consecutive purchases spanning the ADA endorsement in order to be included in the analysis. In this section a household need have reported only ten consecutive purchases spanning the endorsement. A total of 2567 households qualified for the analysis in Section 7.3 as may be seen from Table 7.3. The data used in this section came from 3035 households which met the ten purchase criterion. Thus there are 468 households included in this section which were not used in Section 7.3.

It should also be noted that the purchase sequences differ between the two sections. In Section 7.3, the PDM was estimated using sequences of seven purchases per household. In this section we estimated the models using sequences of only five purchases. The reason we used seven purchases in Section 7.3 was to apply a more stringent test to the PDM. In this section we must use the shorter sequence because longer sequences would greatly complicate the estimation procedure and strain the size of the data base for all but the PDM.[13]

7.4.3   The Empirical Results

The results from fitting each model to each of the eight sets of data are reported in Table 7.5. The BL model provides a reasonably good fit in four cases, a moderately good fit in one case, and a very poor fit in three cases. The LPL model, with one exception, provides a very poor fit. Thus, the BL model would appear to be the better of the two Markov models in this case. It should be noted that this is similar to the Chapter 4 conclusions using coffee purchasing data. The LL model provides a good fit in all but two of the cases, while the PDM provides a good fit in all but one case. Examination of the p-levels in Table 7.5 suggest that the LL and PDM perform the best with respect to our goodness-of-fit criterion.

One method of summary comparison of the models is to examine the number of times each model provided the best fit to the data. This result is presented in Table 7.6 for the before period, the after period, and overall. From the table we see that in terms of providing the best fit among the four models, the LL model is best in the relatively stable before period, while the PDM is best in the unstable after period.

---

[13] The notion of obtaining a bound on the p-level via the independent and dependent chi-square procedure used in Chapter 6 may be applied to these other models. See Holland (1966).

Table 7.5   Comparison of *p*-Levels: MRCA Dentifrice Data

Group*	Sample Size	*p*-Level of Model			
		BL	LPL	LL	PDM
Before 0–30 Days	751	0.37	0.00	0.69	0.54
31–45 Days	618	0.13	0.01	0.32	0.28
46–60 Days	503	0.30	0.00	0.03	0.04
Over 60 Days	1163	0.00	0.00	0.33	0.61
Sum of Before		0.01	0.00	0.13	0.17
After 0–30 Days	751	0.01	0.25	0.92	0.76
31–45 Days	618	0.04	0.00	0.00	0.66
46–60 Days	503	0.33	0.00	0.60	0.94
Over 60 Days	1163	0.32	0.01	0.41	0.63
Sum of After		0.00	0.00	0.15	0.95

* The Before and After designates brand purchasing data before and after the ADA endorsement of Crest. The range of days given represents the range of average interpurchase times for households included in each of these groups.

Another method of overall comparison of the models is to develop summary measures of their performance in both the before and after periods. To illustrate the development of such a measure, consider the groups in the before period. The chi-square statistic developed for each of these groups will be independent of all the others. Thus, we may form an overall chi-square statistic for the before period by summing the chi-square statistics for each of the before groups. The degrees of freedom for this overall chi-square statistic will just be the sum of the degrees of freedom from each group. A similar procedure was used to develop an overall measure of fit for the after groups. These results are reported in Table 7.5 as "Sum of Before" and "Sum of After." We see from the table that on this criterion, the PDM provides the best overall

Table 7.6   Best Fitting Model: MRCA Dentifrice Data

Period	Model			
	BL	LPL	LL	PDM
Before	1	0	2	1
After	0	0	1	3
Overall	1	0	3	4

fit in both the before and after periods. Note the remarkably good overall fit of the PDM in the unstable after period and the fact that by the present criterion it provides the best overall fit in the before period. The difference between this result and the result in Table 7.6 for the before period is because the overall measures take account of the magnitudes of the deviations of the model from the data, whereas the Table 7.6 method only uses an ordinal property of the data.

While we must be careful not to overgeneralize our results from this one comparative study, the following would seem to be justified conclusions in the present case:

1. Both the LL model and the PDM provided reasonably good fits to the data.
2. The LPL model did not provide an adequate fit to the data. The alternative Markov model (BL) was found to be much better.
3. The BL model was generally dominated by the LL model and the PDM. The more flexible representation of brand-choice probability in the LL and PDM probably accounts for this.
4. The PDM clearly dominated the other models in the transient after period.

Much more needs to be done by way of comparing models before we will have confidence in our ability to generalize.

In conclusion, we note that even though the LL model and the PDM differ significantly in their representation of the mechanism whereby a consumer's brand-choice probability may change between purchase occasions, both models provide rather good fits to the data. This suggests that both the learning and the diffusion phenomena are important aspects of the brand-choice process. What seems needed is a model that incorporates both phenomena.[14]

[14] See Jones (1969).

PART III
PURCHASE INCIDENCE MODELS

CHAPTER 8
MODELS FOR PURCHASE TIMING
AND MARKET PENETRATION

The previous chapters have been devoted to models that aim to predict what brand will be selected on a particular purchase occasion, given that a purchase event will in fact occur at that time. Now we turn to models for predicting when purchase events will occur or, equivalently, how many such events will occur in a specified interval of time. The models in Chapters 3 through 7 have been termed "brand-choice" models. Models for purchase timing and amount, which provide the subject matter for Chapters 8 through 11, are called "purchase-incidence" models. Within this class we will consider (1) *purchase timing* and *market penetration* models, on the one hand, and (2) *total demand* models on the other.

The fundamental characteristics of purchase-incidence models were discussed in Section 1.2. There we considered the differences between the purchase-incidence and brand-choice approaches, as well as the relation between purchase timing and total demand models within the purchase incidence model class. A general approach to combining all of these model types into a single representation of all aspects of purchasing behavior was also explored.

The reader is already familiar with our fundamental approach to modeling buying behavior. We postulate a stochastic process which we think will provide an adequate representation of response uncertainty connected with a particular aspect of buyer behavior. The key attribute of this stochastic process is the probability that particular types of behavior will occur at particular times. The process of model construction involves working out the relations between this probability and the effects of three main classes of determinants: (1) heterogeneity of initial conditions or parameters among members of the relevant population; (2) changes in the probability over time, perhaps as the result of firms' marketing efforts; and (3) effects of actual responses upon the probabilities that will determine future responses. Brand-choice and purchase-incidence models differ in terms of the type of behavior to which the probabilities in the stochastic process applies; that is, in terms of the definition of events or states in the models.

Within a given class of models, further differentiation is possible in terms of the types of influences that are allowed to affect the probabilities and the exact way in which certain influences are represented. All of these considerations affect purchase-incidence models as much as they did the models of brand choice presented in earlier chapters. A variety of purchase incidence models, each differing somewhat in terms of the way population heterogeneity, time change, and event feedback are handled will be presented in this and the following chapters.

The present chapter will begin with the fundamentals of purchase-incidence model construction and testing. This will be followed by an examination of certain well-known models for purchase incidence, some of which have been used with good success in marketing applications. We will seek to show the relations among, for instance, the negative binomial, mixed exponential, logistic, and one-event linear learning models. Some original extensions to several of these models will be developed later in this chapter. Chapter 9 will present our Stochastic Evolutionary Adoption Model (STEAM), which was developed in order to describe the new product adoption process but also turns out to represent a reasonable and simplified approximation to most of the models considered in Chapter 8. A full-scale comparison of all the models for market penetration and a discussion of parameter estimation and methods by which complex penetration models can be used to provide explicit forecasts of future demand for a new product will be given in Chapters 9 and 10. Since STEAM can be viewed as providing an approximation to many other penetration models, these latter, more practical, points will be considered in the STEAM context. Some empirical results from STEAM will be given in Chapter 10. Chapter 11 deals with some generalizations of STEAM, which bring in a considerably richer set of demand determinants than has heretofore been possible. While extended STEAM involves some difficult computational problems, the basic ideas appear to be feasible. These extensions also suggest some directions in which future research on purchase incidence models can fruitfully be undertaken.

8.1 Fundamentals

8.1.1 Uses of Purchase Incidence Models

Perhaps the most obvious use of purchase-incidence models is in predicting the total demand for a new or established product. Consider

the situation with respect to established products, where the process that generates purchase events may be fairly stable over time. In this case a model for purchase incidence can be applied to the population as a whole, without regard for how many times each member has purchased the product in the past. (We may still want to keep track of the last few purchases, in order to consider purchase event feedback.) The most useful form for such a model would be to predict the total number of purchases that would be made by members of the population during some specified time interval; that is, we would want a "total demand" type of purchase incidence model. Such a model would be useful for a company that was trying to determine how much inventory to carry, for example. The advantage of a stochastic demand model in this context is that it provides the whole probability distribution for total demand, rather than just an average or expected value. Those who are familiar with inventory theory know that the spread of the demand distribution is as an important determinant of the risk of stockout as is the mean or expected value of the distribution.

Purchase-incidence models can also be useful in cases where a brand-choice model might seem to be called for at first glance. The successful application of a brand-choice model depends upon the researcher's ability to define the product class that is relevant to purchases of the various brands of interest. It is essential that, by and large, customers tend to place all the brands covered by the analysis in the same product class. Likewise, households should be reasonably consistent in their product class definitions over time. Violation of these conditions will reduce the degree to which the brand-choice model fits the data and may lead to faulty interpretation of parameters. The simple Markov model provides a case in point. For instance, suppose that preference patterns for detergents depend on the type of use involved: e.g., high suds products may be preferred for dishwashing and low suds for laundry applications. Suppose that households keep a separate inventory of detergents for each end use, and that brand choice follows a first-order Markov process for each use. If we observe only the time series for purchases, without knowledge of which inventory each purchase is intended to replenish, it is unlikely that we will see a first-order Markov process, even though the real activity is a combination of such processes — perhaps operating in different phase relationships. Clearly, such a situation would require a fairly complex model for brand choice, such as Howard's (1965) semi-Markov process, for example. On the other hand, for some purposes it may be possible to turn away from the brand-choice problem and attempt to predict only the total number of

purchases of each type or brand of detergent during fixed intervals of time. This would be, in effect, a purchase incidence model.

Common sense suggests that the homogeneous product class assumption may not be unreasonable for many groups of established products, and experience with brand-choice models tends to bear this out. Toothpaste and coffee, for which brand-choice data were examined in earlier chapters, are good cases in point. For other products, such as detergents, it may be possible to generalize existing brand-choice models to take account of heterogeneous but still fairly well-defined groupings within the same product class. If we consider the case of new products, however, the situation is likely to be quite different. We submit that "product classes" for innovations tend to be less well defined than those for established products. This occurs for at least two reasons: (1) consumers have less information about new products and, hence, more difficulty in relating them to patterns of needs and the products that can be used to satisfy them; and (2) new products are often deliberately placed in an ambiguous position vis-á-vis established product classes. The first point should be self-explanatory, but the second deserves some additional comment.

Consider the process by which a manager chooses from among alternative new product ideas. According to the textbooks, he should generally seek to find a product that fills some combination of consumer needs that is not already being strongly exploited by competitors. While comparative advantages in production or marketing may sometimes lead a firm to enter a large market in which substantial competition already exists, there can be no doubt that the lucrative but sparsely populated cells of the "market grid" usually offer the best opportunities for new product success.

One of the attributes of the sparsely populated market-grid cell is that there are no close substitutes for the new product. This means that it will be difficult or impossible to define a neat "product class" into which the product falls — in the sense that all members of the class are freely substitutable for one another. Are pop tarts in the bread, jam, breakfast food, or still another product class, for example? How can one use a probability vector that is defined over all of these possibilities? Many similar examples could be given, and the authors are impressed by the proportion of cases in which the new product problem is defined in these terms by experienced market research people. Finally, we should note that it is precisely in the cases where the product fits between product classes that management's information needs are greatest, since these products represent the greatest innovative effort

and involve the most uncertainty. Therefore, we would do well to design our new product demand models with these situations in mind.

The answer to this problem seems to lie in the adoption of a strategy that limits, so far as possible, the need for rigorously defining the product class prior to an empirical analysis. This means, of course, that we will want to consider purchase-incidence models when we try to represent the growth of demand for many new products. Modeling strategies appropriate to the new product situation will be discussed in detail in Section 9.1.

8.1.2 General Properties of Purchase Incidence Models

The fundamental objective of purchase-incidence models is to define, determine, and predict the probability distribution of some measure of purchase incidence. The two main measures that are used for this purpose are (1) the number of purchases in a fixed time interval and (2) the waiting time between purchases. We will discuss the relations between these measures before going on to consider specific models.

Purchases are discrete events that occur in time. Therefore, models aimed at determining the probability distribution of the number of purchases observed during an interval of time must take the form of a stochastic counting process. The general class of processes of this type is discussed by Parzen (1962, p. 117). The stochastic counting model defines the probability that the number of events that will be counted is N_1 (say) at time t, given that it was N_0 at time t_0. The probability mass function, over all the possible values of N_1, is the probability law of the counting process, given the initial condition.

Application of stochastic counting process theory to purchasing behavior for a brand or product class results in a model that is very closely allied with those that attempt to predict the time of the next purchase. Suppose that the time interval in question is of length t. Then the probability that there will be no purchases by an individual household during the interval is equal to[1]

$$\Pr(N_t = 0) = \Pr[\mathscr{P} \in (t_0, t)]$$

We may write the probability of the event that no purchase occurs in the interval (t_0, t) in terms of the probability that a purchase does occur in

---

[1] The symbol $\mathscr{P}$ is used to denote the event "purchase." The symbol $\bar{\mathscr{P}}$ denotes the event "no purchase." The symbol $\in$ can be read as "in" (e.g., "in the interval from t_0 to t").

the particular interval $(t, t + h)$.

$$\Pr[\tilde{\mathscr{P}} \in (t_0,t)] = \Pr[\tilde{\mathscr{P}} \in (t_0,t_1)]$$

$$\Pr[\tilde{\mathscr{P}} \in (t_1,t_2)|\tilde{\mathscr{P}} \in (t_0,t_1)]$$

$$\cdot$$
$$\cdot$$
$$\cdot$$

$$\Pr[\tilde{\mathscr{P}} \in (t_h,t)|\tilde{\mathscr{P}} \in (t_0,t_h)] \qquad (8.1)$$

where t_i and t_j are separated by h, and

$$\Pr[\tilde{\mathscr{P}} \in (t, t + h)] = 1 - \Pr[\mathscr{P} \in (t, t + h)]$$

A major simplification is available when

$$\Pr[\tilde{\mathscr{P}} \in (t_j, t_j + h)|\tilde{\mathscr{P}} \in (t_0,t_j)] = \Pr[\tilde{\mathscr{P}} \in (t_j, t_j + h)]$$

for all values of j. This means that we can make statements about the likelihood that a purchase will be observed during a particular time interval without regard for the household's past history. This is called the property of *independent increments*.

The probability that $N_t = 1, 2, 3, \ldots$ can also be built up from the fundamental expressions $\Pr[\mathscr{P} \in (t,t + h)]$. It will be easier, however, to consider the random variable "waiting time to the next purchase." Define t^* as the time between t_0 and the first purchase after t_0. Clearly, the distribution of t^* is a function of the $\Pr[\mathscr{P} \in (t,t + h)]$. In particular,

$$\Pr[t \leq t^* \leq t + h] = \Pr[\mathscr{P} \in (t, t + h)|\tilde{\mathscr{P}} \in (t_0,t)]$$
$$\times \Pr[\tilde{\mathscr{P}} \in (t_0,t)]$$

and $$= F(t + h) - F(t) \qquad (8.2)$$

$$\lim_{h \to 0} \frac{F(t + h) - F(t)}{h} = \frac{dF(t)}{dt} = f(t)$$

where $F(t)$ is the probability distribution function for t. (A main task in the development of most purchase-incidence models is to find the expression for $F(t)$.) Now, the probability that no purchases are observed during the interval (t_0,t^*) can be written as

$$\Pr[N_t = 0] = \Pr[t^* > t]$$

which is equivalent to the expression given earlier. Similarly, we may define t^{**} as the waiting time between the first and the second purchase after t_0. Then

$$\Pr[N_t = 1] = \Pr[t^* \leq t, t^* + t^{**} > t]$$

That is, the probability of observing exactly one purchase is equal to the joint probability of the events, "the waiting time to the first purchase is less than t," and "the total waiting to the second purchase is greater than t." Expressions for the probability that $N_t = 2, 3, 4, \ldots$ are easily obtained by extending the above to include the waiting times to later purchases. We must emphasize the fact that the random variables N_t and t^* provide two different ways of representing the *same* purchase incidence process. It is impossible to say that one is better than the other purely on the basis of some model criterion, because any model can be used to develop the distribution of either measure. Rather, the choice between them must be based on the nature of the problem being studied and the form of the available data. Sometimes it will be convenient to use one measure during part of the analysis (e.g., parameter estimation) and the other during another part (e.g., the derivation of forecasts of future purchasing rates). In fact, this is exactly what is done in Chapters 9 and 10.

The parameters of $\Pr[\mathscr{P} \in (t, t + h)]$ may be functions of time, marketing variables, previous purchase events, and household descriptors. For new product penetration models, we must keep track of the number of previous times the household has tried the innovation. Therefore, we are led to write

$$\Pr[\mathscr{P} \in (t, t + h)| \tilde{\mathscr{P}} \in (t_0, t)]$$

$$= f(t; \text{household descriptors}; \text{marketing variables}) \quad (8.3)$$

as our fundamental description of the adoption process for new products.

Here the symbol $\mathscr{P}$ refers to a particular trial number. When Equation 8.3 applies to an individual household, it will be given the name *propensity function*, and written as

$$\mu(t)_i = \frac{\Pr[\mathscr{P} \in (t, t + h)| \tilde{\mathscr{P}} \in (t_0, t)]_i}{h} \quad (8.4)$$

where the subscript i refers to a particular household. (The subscript will usually be omitted in the sequel; $\mu(t)$ always applies to a particular household or, equivalently, to a group of perfectly homogeneous households.) The exact dimension of $\mu(t)$ depends on the time interval h. In most of the applications we will consider that $\mu(t)$ represents the limiting value of the ratio on the right side of Equation 8.4, as $h \to 0$. That is, $\mu(t)$ will be regarded as an "instantaneous purchase rate," applicable to a continuous time stochastic process of the kind considered in Chapter 6. While ordinary probabilities are constrained between zero

and one, the only requirement on the limiting value of Equation 8.4 is that $\mu(t)$ be nonnegative; of course, if $\mu(t) = 0$, the probabilities are strictly zero for all values of h. Many comparisons among purchase-incidence models will be couched in terms of the way in which $\mu(t)$ depends upon marketing variables and other factors.

The conditional purchase probability given in Equation 8.3 may also depend on household descriptor variables. That is, the parameters of the propensity function $\mu(t)$ may vary over members of the population. In applying the models, however, it is still necessary to deal with "aggregate" data of the type obtained from consumer panels. While we know the historical and descriptor variables for individual households to some extent, we still do not know all we would need to specify all the parameters for an individual a priori. Nor do we know enough to classify panel households into groups that are homogeneous on the relevant purchase-incidence parameters. Purchase-incidence models must include provision for response heterogeneity, just as was the case for the models of brand-choice behavior discussed in Chapters 3 through 7. The general procedure is to assume that certain relevant parameters of $\mu(t)$ are distributed among members of the population according to some specified density function and then attempt to estimate the parameters of this distribution, along with any other parameters of the individual purchase incidence model, from the empirical data. Once this has been done, the distributions of N_t and/or t^* for the market as a whole can be obtained.

These considerations imply that we cannot observe the parameters of $\mu(t)$ for any particular household but rather must regard each household as a sample from the prior distribution of $\mu(t)$. This changes the interpretation of Equation 8.4 enough to warrant making a new definition. Let

$$R(t) = \frac{\Pr[\mathscr{P} \in (t, t + h) | \tilde{\mathscr{P}} \in (t_0, t)]}{h} \qquad (8.5)$$

where this time the probability refers to a household with unknown purchase propensity, which is assumed to have been randomly selected from the prior distribution on $\mu(t)$. The $R(t)$ is known as the *hazard function* in reliability engineering.[2] In the present context we will call it the *purchase contingency function*, to indicate that $R(t)$ represents the contingent likelihood of purchasing at time t, given that there has been no previous purchase by the household.

[2] See Barlow and Proschan (1965).

The difference between the propensity and contingency functions can be seen in the following way. We have already defined $F(t)$ as the probability that a household's first purchase will occur in (t_0, t). Its derivative, the density function of t, will be denoted by $f(t)$. Now let us write $F(t|i)$ as the probability distribution of waiting times for households with a particular purchase propensity function i and $F(t)$ as the distribution for households randomly sampled from the population. Clearly,

$$F(t) = \int_0^\infty F(t|i)g(i)\, di$$

where $g(i)$ is the prior density on i. By the definitions of the quantities involved and the rules of conditional probability, we can write

$$\mu(t)_i = \frac{f(t|i)}{1 - F(t|i)}$$

$$R(t) = \frac{f(t)}{1 - F(t)}$$

$$(8.6)$$

In the context of particular models we will see that the forms of $\mu(t)$ and $R(t)$ vary considerably when population heterogeneity assumptions are invoked.

Equation 8.6 also shows that, in general,

$$R(t) \neq E_i[\mu(t)_i] = \int_0^\infty \mu(t)_i g(i)\, di$$

except in the trivial case where the μ for all households are identical. The expectation of $\mu(t)$ refers to the average instantaneous purchase propensity at t, among the original members of the population. On the other hand, $R(t)$ depends on the whole history of the process, beginning at time t_0. The effect of this difference can be seen by means of a simple example. Suppose that $\mu(t)_i = \mu_i$ is constant over time but that μ_i varies over the population. (This is the mixed exponential model discussed in Section 8.2.2.) The contingency function refers in effect to the average μ of those people in the population who have not purchased at time t. As people with high μ would be likely to purchase first, $R(t)$ will decline over time as the mix of μ in the remaining population changes, even though the μ for individual families are constant.

The quantity $R(t)$ is useful for several reasons. Its definition reminds us that we cannot judge the fit of a model by comparing empirical penetration curves with an assumed time path for purchase propensity. Even conditional penetration increments, which represent the empirical

analogue to $R(t)$, may not resemble the time path of $\mu(t)$ if there is heterogeneity among members of the population. Some hypothetical curves showing this situation are given in Figure 8.1. However, it is often useful to calculate the time path for $R(t)$ for the model in question and compare it with data when evaluating a model.

Another set of advantages for $R(t)$ stems from the fact that it is sometimes possible to infer some of the characteristics of $f(t)$ from $R(t)$ and, as will be seen later, the expression for $R(t)$ is usually much simpler than that for $f(t)$. We are often interested in whether or not $F(t)$ can assume an "s-shape" for certain values of parameters in a specific model. This occurs only if $f(t)$ reaches a maximum at some $t > 0$; that is, if $F(t)$ has an inflection point. It is often difficult to examine the conditions under which $df(t)/dt > 0$ at $t = 0$, which is required for a maximum. However, $dR(t)/dt$ can often be evaluated nicely. Now, from Equation 8.6 we know that

$$f'(t) = \frac{df(t)}{dt} = R'(t)[1 - F(t)] - R(t)f(t)$$

where $1 - F(t)$, $R(t)$, and $f(t)$ are nonnegative. From this we see that $f'(0)$ is negative if $R'(0) < 0$. If $R'(0) > 0$, we cannot infer the sign of $f'(0)$ directly, but we do know that if $f'(t)$ is initially positive it must turn around before $R'(t) = 0$. Also, we know that $f(0) = R(0)$, since

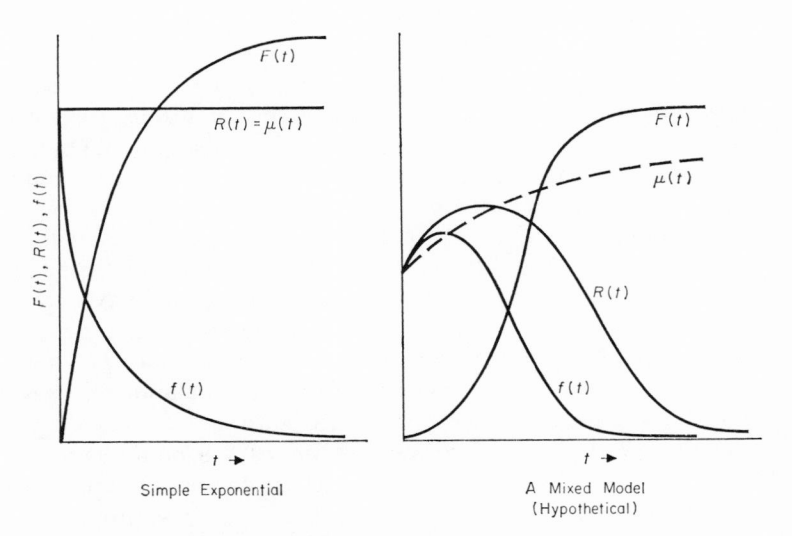

Figure 8.1.   Some relations between $F(t)$, $f(t)$, and $R(t)$.

$1 - F(0) = 1$. Hence $R'(t)$ and $R(t)$ give us some qualitative information about $f(t)$ and $F(t)$.[3]

8.1.3 Parameter Estimation for Purchase Incidence Models

The problem of parameter estimation for purchase-incidence models does not differ from that for brand-choice models in any important respect. The main question is in how to arrange the sample data so as to apply the methods of Chapter 2 in the most convenient way. If anything, there are more estimation options available when dealing with purchase incidence models than was the case for brand choice.

If we are dealing with stationary total demand models, we form statistics giving either the frequency distribution of households making $0, 1, 2, \ldots$ purchases per unit time or a similar frequency distribution for different levels of total market demand in different periods. These may be related to the measures $\Pr[N_t = k]$, as derived from the postulated purchase counting process, by methods discussed in the previous section. The discrepancy between the actual and theoretical frequencies can be minimized with respect to the model's parameters, using the method of maximum likelihood or minimum chi-square, as discussed in Chapter 2. Other methods, such as the method of moments, are also available if "quick and dirty" procedures are desired.

Parameter estimates for market penetration models may be based on $F(t)$, $R(t)$, or sometimes $f(t)$. The first two measures yield theoretical frequencies which can form the basis for either maximum likelihood or minimum chi-square estimates. If $F(t)$ is used, we construct the unconditional frequency distribution of households who purchase in each of a number of discrete time intervals. The total number of people in all these cells, plus the number who do not purchase, add up to the population size. If there are k purchase time intervals, plus one nonpurchase cell, the frequency distribution yields a single chi-square variable with k degrees of freedom. The theoretical frequencies (π) are set equal to $\Pr[\mathscr{P} \in (t, t + h)] = F(t + h) - F(t)$, as given in Equation 8.2. Estimates based on $R(t)$ use the conditional frequency of people who purchase in interval $(t, t + h)$, among those who did not purchase prior to t. This yields a total of k chi-squares, each with one degree of freedom, where the π are equal to $R(t)$. If the model fits exactly, these chi-squares will be independent and the result will be equivalent to that using $F(t)$. Finally, maximum likelihood estimates based on very small

[3] Barlow and Proschan (1965) present interesting theorems on the relation of various waiting time models to the Polya class of distributions. The hazard function $R(t)$ plays a key role in these theorems.

intervals of time can be obtained by using $f(t)$. This latter method is discussed in detail by Anscombe (1961).

The best procedure to use depends on computational considerations and the properties of the specific model in question. In particular, the choice of estimator may depend on the manner in which we think that the data might depart from the model and the kind of tests that are to be made on the model. We will go into all these matters more deeply in Chapter 10, when we develop estimation methods for STEAM and consider their empirical properties.

Finally, we must note that, in cases where population heterogeneity is not a problem, the value of the purchase propensity function $\mu(t)$ may sometimes be used to estimate the parameters of a market penetration model. This method will be demonstrated in connection with the logistic model, in Section 8.3, and mentioned again in Section 8.4.1. Most existing "econometric" studies of new product demand are in effect based on $\mu(t)$. We must remember, however, that $\mu(t)$ is not identified in cases where population heterogeneity is involved. (The only exception to this is the extreme case where we assume binary heterogeneity — that is, where some households are assumed to have $\mu(t) = 0$ and the others form a homogeneous group. Then *any* household that purchases is known to have belonged to the homogeneous $\mu > 0$ group.)

8.2   Poisson-Exponential Models

8.2.1   The Negative Binomial Model

A. S. C. Ehrenberg was probably the first to derive an explicit heterogeneous purchasing behavior model and apply it to data.[4] In an early paper [Ehrenberg (1959)], he presents results showing that the negative binomial distribution tends to fit the frequency histogram for the total number of units bought by members of a consumer panel during a fixed time interval. Of equal significance is the fact that he justified the model on theoretical grounds in terms of: (1) a basic model for the incidence of purchase events and (2) a hypothesis about the way in which the parameters of the basic model vary over members of the population.

The negative binomial is a discrete distribution of nonnegative integer random variables. As such, it can be used as a distribution for N_t, the total number of purchases observed during a fixed interval of time.

---

[4] Frank's (1960) paper was based on the idea that consumer populations are heterogeneous, but he did not develop an integrated stochastic model for which parameters could be estimated. See Chapter 3 of this book.

Ehrenberg points out that the negative binomial distribution can be derived by assuming that the process which generates purchases at the level of the individual household is Poisson, and that the parameters of these processes are distributed over members of the population according to a gamma distribution. That is,

$$\Pr\{N_t = k|\mu\} = f(N_t|\mu) = \frac{\exp{(-\mu)\mu^k}}{k!} \qquad k \geq 0 \qquad (8.7)$$

which is the Poisson assumption, and

$$f(\mu) = \frac{\beta \exp{(-\beta\mu)(\beta\mu)^{\alpha-1}}}{\Gamma(\alpha)} \qquad \mu > 0 \qquad (8.8)$$

which assumes that the "contagion" is gamma distributed with parameters α and β. This version of the gamma distribution is parameterized so that[5]

$$E[\mu] = \frac{\alpha}{\beta} \qquad \text{Var}[\mu] = \frac{\alpha}{\beta^2}$$

Ehrenberg's justification for these assumptions is best expressed in his own words. The following quotation also establishes that Ehrenberg had developed a genuine heterogeneous consumer behavior model before 1959.

Poisson Distribution in Time. For the purchases of any particular consumer in successive periods of time, e.g., purchases of 2, 0, 3, 1, 1 units and so on, the model requires that these purchases behave like random samples from a Poisson distribution. This is plausible under two conditions which should normally be more or less fulfilled, namely
(a) That the successive periods of time are not only of equal length but also similar to each other, e.g., weeks or longer periods measured in weeks, rather than days.
(b) That the periods are not too short, so that purchases made in one period do not directly affect those made in the next. Periods of one week for instance may be too short for some products: e.g., if a tin of cocoa is bought in one week, no such purchase is likely to be made in the following week.
The Poisson distribution has one parameter, the mean μ, i.e., the average rate of purchasing "in the long run."

A χ^2-Distribution of Consumers. The second part of the model then specifies that the distribution of the average rates of purchasing μ of different consumers should be proportional to a χ^2 or [Pearson] Type III distribution [a Gamma distribution] with α degrees of freedom. This is also plausible, since such a distribution is fairly flexible (having two adjustable parameters) and

[5] See Raiffa and Schlaifer (19 61) p. 225.

of the right shape (i.e., a continuous distribution for nonnegative values, reversed-J-shaped or hump-backed and always positively skewed).[6]

The Poisson distribution has the property of independent increments discussed in the previous section. That is, the probability that a consumer will purchase in a particular time interval is independent of whether or not he purchased in the previous time period, or any period before that. This is quite a strong assumption, which requires (among other things) the justification presented in point b in the Ehrenberg quote: if a purchase in one period produces a "dead time" due to inventory, which reduces the probability that the product will be purchased in the next period, the independent increments assumption is violated and the Poisson model cannot apply without modification. Similarly, Ehrenberg assumed that the Poisson process that generates individual household purchases is stationary over the fixed time interval during which purchases are to be counted ("quasi-stationary" in the language of this book). Hence the probability cannot be different for different Δt within this interval. Now this condition cannot strictly hold, because the probability time series will vary with the hour of the day, the day of the week, the week of the month, the season, etc. A nonstationary Poisson model with a mean value function that could track all of these factors would be required to fit this aspect of purchasing behavior exactly. Nevertheless, Ehrenberg is correct in pointing out that these effects will be minimized if the fixed report period is set in such a way that most of these effects cancel out (e.g., daily fluctuations average out over weeks). This is the sense of his point b. Assessment of the assumption that the prior distribution of μ is gamma is more a matter of empirical investigation than a priori reasoning. It is clear that there is some distribution on μ in the population, and there may be no reason to think that it is not unimodal and asymmetric. If the gamma distribution appears to fit the data, it should be used, especially since it leads to relatively simple analytical results for a variety of different purchase timing models.

Application of the methods of the previous chapters yields the aggregate distribution of purchase events for the population:

$$f(N_t) = \int_0^\infty f(N_t|\mu) f(\mu) \, d\mu$$

$$= \left[\frac{\beta}{1+\beta}\right]^\alpha \left[\frac{\Gamma(N_t+\alpha)}{N_t \cdot \Gamma(\alpha)}\right] \left[\frac{1}{1+\beta}\right]^{N_t} \qquad (8.9)$$

[6] A. S. C. Ehrenberg (1959, p. 35) with minor changes in notation.

The last expression is that of the negative binomial mass function, with moments:

$$E[N_t] = \frac{\alpha}{\beta}$$

$$Var[N_t] = \frac{\alpha(\beta + 1)}{\beta^2}$$

It is also of interest to note that

$$Pr[N_t = 0] = \left(1 + \frac{1}{\beta}\right)^{-\alpha}$$

The fact that Poisson events with gamma contagion lead to a negative binomial mass function is well known, particularly in the context of accident proneness studies. The incidence of accidents is assumed to be Poisson and the possibility that different people may have different susceptibilities or environments may have different hazards is represented by a gamma prior distribution on μ. The negative binomial distribution was observed to fit the empirical frequency distributions of accidents quite well. Unfortunately, however, the negative binomial distribution can be derived in more than one way, which prevented researchers from concluding that accident proneness did in fact vary over the population. One important contrary hypothesis involved the idea that the event of having one accident increased (or decreased) the probability that the same person would have another in a subsequent period. That is, the probability of an accident might depend on the individual's accident history before time t, which would destroy the independent increments property of the model. This amounts to a learning assumption, and, as mentioned earlier, plausible assumptions about the form of the learning operator lead to a negative binomial distribution for aggregate accident statistics. The argument about whether the observed data supported the hypothesis of learning or that of population heterogeneity raged in the accident literature for some years — the whole situation was analogous to the exchange between Kuehn (1958, 1962) and Frank (1960) on the same subject in the brand-choice context. The reader who is interested in the application of accident incidence models should consult Arbous and Kerrich (1951), Bates and Neyman (1952), Edwards and Gurland (1961), Bhattacharya and Holla (1965), and the references cited therein. The beginnings of this line of development, and also of the development of our own models of purchase behavior which are the descendents of those for accident incidence, can be found in a paper by Greenwood and Yule (1920).

A recent paper by Chatfield, Ehrenberg, and Goodhardt (1966) extends the negative binomial model in some very important ways. First, they show that the distribution of the total number of purchases (in a fixed time interval) for those members of the population who do in fact purchase the product at least once during the interval can be closely approximated by a *logarithmic series distribution*. The mass function for this distribution can be written in terms of N_t:

$$f(N_t|N_t > 0) = \frac{-q^{N_t}}{N_t \log_e (1 - q)} \qquad N_t > 0$$

for which

$$E[N_t|N_t > 0] = \frac{-q}{(1 - q) \log_e (1 - q)}$$

where q is the single parameter of the distribution. This distribution provides an approximation to the distribution of N_t for those members of a panel who are known to have purchased the product (i.e., with the zero-buyer subpopulation excluded). It has two main advantages: (1) it does not require that the population of relevant purchasers be defined a priori — this may not be easy for some products such as cigarettes or dietary aids; and (2) it is much simpler to handle than the negative binomial or the distribution obtained by truncating it to eliminate the "0" cell.[7]

The second new development is the introduction of the concept of the joint distribution of N_t for different values of t. Consider the joint probability,

$$\Pr[N(t_0,t_1) = k_1, N(t_1,t_2) = k_2, \ldots, N(t_{h-1},t_h) = k_h]$$

where we have written $N(t_i,t_j)$ instead to N_t in order to keep track of the various time intervals. Chatfield et al. show that the multivariate negative binomial distribution comes about as a logical extension of the heterogeneous Poisson process theory discussed earlier in this section. The multivariate negative binomial gives the necessary expressions for the joint probabilities given earlier. It has the important property that

[7] The parameter of the logarithmic series distribution can be estimated — although inefficiently — by equating the mean purchase rate for households that do purchase in the time period under study with the theoretical expression for $E[N_t|N_t > 0]$ and solving iteratively for q. In contrast, the negative binomial distribution parameters are estimated as functions of the mean purchase rate for all the households in the population — with 0 averaged in for those that do not purchase — and the proportion of nonbuyers. As Chatfield et al. point out, the first statistic is usually much easier to obtain than the second two, even in situations where there is no ambiguity in the definition of the relevant population.

the marginal and conditional distributions for all the N are univariate negative binomial. The question of conditional distributions deserves some comment. Suppose that we separate all the families that made exactly N_{t_1} purchases in period t_1 into a separate subpopulation. Then the result states that the distribution of purchases among members of this subpopulation in period t_2 will be (univariate) negative binomial, regardless of the value of N_{t_1} used for conditioning purposes. (Of course the parameters of the conditional distributions will be different for different values of N_{t_1}.) This is quite important and by no means obvious from the form of the various distributions.

There is also a multivariate analogue to the logarithmic series distribution. In this case, however, the conditional distributions are not of the same form as the univariate logarithmic series distribution. In fact, the conditional distributions approximate the negative binomial. This important result lends support to the idea that the negative binomial is a basic and powerful distribution for describing stationary purchase incidence processes.

Ehrenberg and his colleagues also present data which indicate that the negative binomial fails to fit the tails of the empirical distribution of purchases. These results are apparently based on the application of the model to a wide variety of different frequently purchased products. The logarithmic series distribution seems to do better. In interpreting these results, they indicate that the failure of the negative binomial to fit exactly appears to come from a breakdown of the assumption that the prior distribution of purchasing rates is gamma. The gamma distribution would appear to fail to fit in the tails, which is not an uncommon situation in statistical investigations. In contrast, they conclude that the evidence indicates that the stationary Poisson assumption is adequate, at least when dealing with established products. These points will be taken up again in Section 9.1.5.

Space will not permit further discussion of the Ehrenberg models. The reader is urged to read the original papers, and especially the most recent ones on the subject. We now turn to models that concentrate on the time at which purchases occur rather than on the number of purchases in a fixed time interval.

8.2.2 *The Mixed Exponential Model*

Fourt and Woodlock (1960) and Woodlock (1963) consider the cumulative penetration curves for frequently purchased products. These curves represent the time series for the proportion of people in a given

population who have engaged in the activity of interest at least once during the interval of time (t_0, t). The "relevant activity" may at various times be making the first purchase of a product, making the second purchase of the product, and so on. Alternatively, it may be desirable in the context of the analysis to discard the first purchase if it occurs as the result of a free sample or introductory offer. Then the relevant activities might be labeled "first purchase not on a deal," "second purchase not on a deal," etc. Strata generated in this way are usually called "depth of trial classes." The penetration curves are defined in terms of the cumulative proportion of people who have so far entered the first depth of trial class, the second, and so on. Thus we may well deal with a family of cumulative penetration curves, each one lying below the other.

According to Fourt and Woodlock (1960, p. 32),

Observation of numerous annual cumulative penetration curves shows that (1) successive increments to these curves decline, and that (2) the cumulative curves seem to approach a limiting penetration of less than 100% of households — frequently far less.

Therefore, Fourt and Woodlock are led to postulate a model in which

. . . increments in penetration for equal time periods are proportional to the remaining distance to the limiting "ceiling" penetration. In other words, each period the ceiling is approached by a constant fraction of the remaining distance.

They express their model in terms of finite time intervals. The equation for the value of the ith increment is

$$\Delta_i = rM(1 - r)^i \qquad\qquad (8.10)$$

That is, each increment is just $(1 - r)$ times the preceding increment. They call this the "$M - r$ penetration model," where M is the ceiling and r is the proportional increment that occurs in each period.[8]

Fourt and Woodlock note that if Equation 8.10 is fitted to data for the early part of a penetration process the predictions made for the later part of the sequence will tend to be too low. In their words, there is a "stretch-out" effect in the decline of the penetration increments. They handle this by modifying Equation 8.10 to allow the ceiling to be a linear function of time. That is,

$$M(t) = M(0) + kt$$

---

[8] Fourt and Woodlock denote the "ceiling" by X instead of M.

or equivalently:

$$\Delta_i = rM_0(1 - r)^i + k$$

This "M_0,r,k" model provides a better empirical fit to penetration data for frequently purchased products than does the simpler "M,r" model.

The Fourt-Woodlock "M,r" model can be developed in a slightly different way, which will be valuable for comparing it with the other models to be discussed later in this chapter. We consider the development in some detail because the same ideas will be used in the sequel.

Suppose that we postulate the following expression for the conditional probability of purchasing in a particular time interval (for those households in the population who may be regarded as susceptible to the product).

$$\Pr[\mathscr{P} \in (t, t + h)|\tilde{\mathscr{P}} \in (t_0,t)] = \mu(t) = \mu h \qquad (8.11)$$

where $\mu h = r$, the discrete rate of change used in Equation 8.10. This means that the "purchase propensity function," defined in Section 8.1.2, is independent of time. The distribution of the waiting time to the next purchase is given by the product of Equation 8.11 and the probability that a randomly chosen customer in the available population will not purchase in (t_0,t). The existence of a ceiling (M) complicates the derivation somewhat. As this will be discussed in connection with Anscombe's work, and again in Section 9.1.5, we will simply write the probability of finding a customer who might purchase but does not do so in (t_0,t) as $M - F(t)$. Then

$$\Pr[\mathscr{P} \in (t, t + h)] = \mu h[M - F(t)]$$

where M is the constant ceiling factor introduced in Equation 8.10. Now this probability is by definition the difference between $F(t + h)$ and $F(t)$, so after dividing by the interval length h we have

$$\frac{F(t + h) - F(t)}{h} = \mu[M - F(t)]$$

Taking the limit as $h \to 0$

$$\lim_{h \to 0} \frac{F(t + h) - F(t)}{h} = \frac{dF(t)}{dt} = f(t)$$

by the definitions of derivatives and probability distribution and density functions.

The form of $F(t)$ can be obtained by solving the following differential equation:

$$\frac{dF(t)}{dt} = \mu[M - F(t)]$$

This is easily handled by separation of variables:

$$\int \frac{dF(t)}{[M - F(t)]} = \mu \int dt$$

$$-\log[M - F(t)] = \mu t + \text{const}$$

$$M - F(t) = \exp(-\mu t)\,\text{const}$$

$$F(t) = M - \exp(-\mu t)\,\text{const}$$

The initial condition for the system is $F(0) = 0$. Hence

$$0 = M - \text{const}$$

so const $= M$. Thus the distribution and density functions for the waiting time to the next purchase are

$$F(t) = [1 - \exp(-\mu t)]M$$
$$f(t) = M\mu \exp(-\mu t) \tag{8.12}$$

This is a continuous version of the Fourt-Woodlock model, with $f(t)$ being analogous to Δ_i in Equation 8.10 and $F(t)$ to the expected value of the cumulative penetration at time t. Also note that by the operations made on the model we can see that

$$\mu = \lim_{h \to 0} r(h), \quad \text{given that } r(h)h = r \text{ for all } h$$

That is, if $r(h)h$ is viewed as the probability of making a response in a particular (finite) time interval of length h, then μ is the limiting value of the response probability that would describe the process as the time interval goes to zero, providing that the response probability in the original time interval remains unchanged.

At this point it will be well to discuss the relations between the Fourt-Woodlock model and that of Ehrenberg. As pointed out in the previous section, Ehrenberg assumes that purchase incidence can be described by a Poisson process. His model is aimed at determining the distribution of the number of purchases that will be made in a fixed time interval. As already noted, however, the same assumptions may be used to

determine the distribution of the time between purchases. In particular, we may start our time index at t_0 — the time of introduction of a new product — and investigate the distribution of the time to the first purchase under Ehrenberg's assumption that the incidence of purchase events at the level of the individual household is a Poisson process.

The fact that the interarrival times for Poisson events are exponentially distributed is well known.[9] Suppose for a moment that the mean purchase rate for the product in question — the μ of the Poisson distribution — is the same for all members of the population. Then the waiting time to the next purchase for each member of the population will follow the exponential density function

$$f(t) = \mu \exp(-\mu t) \tag{8.13}$$

which is the same as the second part of Equation 8.12 except for the ceiling factor M.

Anscombe (1961) pointed out that the introduction of a constant ceiling factor M is equivalent to assuming that a proportion M of the population have purchase rate $\mu = \mu^*$ and a proportion $(1 - M)$ have $\mu = 0$. In terms of the notation of Section 8.1.2, the prior distribution on μ is assumed to be

$$\begin{aligned} f(\mu) &= M \qquad \text{for } \mu = \mu^* \\ f(\mu) &= (1 - M) \qquad \text{for } \mu = 0 \end{aligned} \tag{8.14}$$

The fact that the simple M,r model with constant ceiling factor fails to fit the data is now easily understood. It is very unlikely that the population consists of only two homogeneous groups, as implied by Equation 8.14.

The way around this difficulty is to assume some continuous form for $f(\mu)$ that will spread purchase rates more evenly over members of the population. The Pearson type III or gamma distribution works well for this purpose, which should be no surprise in view of its performance for Ehrenberg. The resulting model, which will be reviewed later, yields a "mixed exponential" response law. That is, the aggregate cumulative penetration curve can be regarded as having been derived by taking a mixture of exponential laws in proportions given by $f(\mu)$.[10]

[9] See, for example, Parzen (1962).
[10] Anscombe (1961) suggests that the approach taken here will be useful for analyzing purchasing behavior. This apparently occurred independently of the work of Ehrenberg, though Anscombe includes results referenced by Ehrenberg's 1959 paper.

The mixed exponential distribution with parameters α and β is derived as follows:

$$f(t) = \int_0^\infty f(t|\mu)f(\mu|\alpha,\beta)\,d\mu$$

where $f(t|\mu)$ is exponential as in Equation 8.13 and $f(\mu|\alpha,\beta)$ is gamma with parameters α and β, as given by Equation 8.1. This yields

$$f(t) = \alpha\beta^\alpha \frac{1}{(t+\beta)^{\alpha+1}}$$

$$F(t) = 1 - \left(\frac{\beta}{t+\beta}\right)^\alpha \quad t \geq 0 \tag{8.15}$$

which is the distribution of waiting times between "negative binomial" events. If $f(\mu|\cdot)$ is given by Equation 8.14 — with parameters M,λ^* — the mixed exponential reduces to Equation 8.12.

To set ideas, we recall the arguments of Section 8.1.2 and present the "purchase propensity" and "purchase contingency" functions for the mixed exponential model. From Equation 8.6, and the fact that it is μ which varies over families, we have

$$\mu(t) = \frac{f(t|\mu)}{1 - F(t|\mu)} = \frac{\mu\exp(-\mu t)}{\exp(-\mu t)} = \mu$$

$$R(t) = \frac{f(t)}{1 - F(t)} = \frac{\alpha\beta^\alpha(t+\beta)^{-\alpha-1}}{\beta^\alpha(t+\beta)^{-\alpha}} = \frac{\alpha}{(t+\beta)} \tag{8.16}$$

Note that $\mu(t)$ is constant, as we originally assumed in this model, but that $R(t)$ declines with time. In particular, when $t = 0$, $R(t) = \alpha/\beta$, which is the mean of the prior distribution for μ: this makes sense because at $t = 0$ no one has yet been eliminated from the population by purchasing the new product. Finally, as $t \to \infty$, $R(t) \to 0$; that is, if a household has not purchased in a very long interval of time, it must have a very small μ-value, and hence is unlikely to purchase in the future.

The "gamma-exponential" penetration law given by Equation 8.15 can produce the "stretchout" effect noted by Fourt and Woodlock. The stretchout occurs because households with large values of μ tend to purchase quickly and hence leave the relevant population. This produces large initial increments that are not representative of those generated by persons with smaller μ who tend to make up the available relevant population in later time periods. The gamma-exponential law takes these factors into account and provides a better fit than the

simple two-population mixed exponential with constant ceiling. Thus, the need to provide for a variable ceiling, as in the Fourt-Woodlock "M_0,r,k" model, would seem to be eliminated. In fact, one might question the need for a ceiling at all; because while the penetration described by Equation 8.15 always goes to one eventually it is possible to set α and β so that the stretchout is prolonged. In this case Equation 8.15 might approximate the variable upper asymptote observed by Fourt and Woodlock without in fact limiting $F(t)$ to values less than one (100% penetration).

The proper method for handling the "no purchase" problem is not obvious. Nor is the question confined to the exponential class of models. We will see that $F(t) \to 1$ in any model in which $\Pr\{\mathcal{P} \in (t, t + h) | \tilde{\mathcal{P}} \in (t_0,t)\}$ is not zero for some households or does not go strictly to zero as t increases. This occurs because any household with a nonzero purchase probability is bound to purchase eventually, though if its probability is small the event may be long delayed.

8.2.3 *Parameter Estimation for the Gamma-Exponential Model*

At this point we will digress slightly to present an improvement on the parameter estimation methods for the mixed exponential that were provided by Anscombe in his original article (1961). The method to be presented is also illustrative of the general class of procedures that may be applied to heterogeneous waiting time models.

We shall revert to Anscombe's original notation (1961, p. 500) for this analysis. He defines the gamma-exponential model as

$$F(t) = \int_0^\infty [1 - \exp(-\alpha t)]\, dW(\alpha)$$

$$dW(\alpha) = \frac{\alpha^{\nu-1} \exp(-\alpha/\lambda)\, d\alpha}{\Gamma(\nu)\lambda^\nu}$$

This leads to a reparameterization of our Equation 8.15. Of course, $F(t)$ is the proportion of people who have purchased the new product at least once by time t.

The sample data will consist of m individuals who first purchased at time $t_1, t_2, \ldots, t_m$ and $n - m$ individuals who did not purchase from time 0 through time T. Anscombe showed how to obtain approximate maximum likelihood estimates of λ and ν by doing a two-dimensional search on an approximate likelihood function. His approximate likelihood function has the nice property that the sufficient statistics are the sample moments of the t_i. We will now show how to find the maximum

likelihood estimators of λ and ν by performing a search on the exact likelihood function in λ space.

The likelihood function for our sample data is

$$\ell = (\lambda\nu)^m (1 + \lambda T)^{-(n-m)\nu} \prod_{i=1}^{m} (1 + \lambda t_i)^{-(\nu+1)}$$

Letting $L = \log_e \ell$, we get

$$L = m \log_e \lambda + m \log_e \nu - (n - m)\nu \log_e (1 + \lambda T)$$
$$- (\nu + 1) \sum_{i=1}^{m} \log_e (1 + \lambda t_i) \quad (8.17)$$

$$\frac{\partial L}{\partial \nu} = \frac{m}{\nu} - (n - m) \log_e (1 + \lambda T) - \sum_{i=1}^{m} \log_e (1 + \lambda t_i) \quad (8.18)$$

$$\frac{\partial^2 L}{\partial \nu^2} = -\frac{m}{\nu^2} < 0 \qquad \text{since } m, \nu > 0$$
$$\qquad\qquad\qquad\qquad\qquad\qquad\qquad (8.19)$$
$$\frac{\partial^2 L}{\partial \nu^2} = -\frac{m}{\nu^2} < 0 \qquad \text{since } m, \nu > 0$$

$$\frac{\partial L}{\partial \lambda} = \frac{m}{\lambda} - (n - m)\nu \left(\frac{1}{1 + \lambda T}\right) T - (\nu + 1) \sum_{i=1}^{m} \left(\frac{t_i^2}{1 + \lambda t_i}\right) \quad (8.20)$$

$$\frac{\partial^2 L}{\partial \nu^2} = -\frac{m}{\lambda^2} + (n - m)\lambda \frac{T^2}{(1 + \lambda T^2)} + (\nu + 1) \sum_{i=1}^{m} t_i^2 (1 + \lambda t_i)^{-2} \quad (8.21)$$

Equation 8.19 shows that L is convex in ν; unfortunately Equation 8.21 shows that L is not convex in λ.

To solve for the maximum likelihood estimates for λ and ν we set Equation 8.18 and 8.20 equal to zero. Setting Equation 8.18 equal to zero, we have

$$\nu = \frac{m}{(n - m) \log_e (1 + \lambda T) + \sum_{i=1}^{m} \log_e (1 + \lambda t_i)} \quad (8.22)$$

Putting Equation 8.22 into 8.20, we obtain

$$\frac{\partial L}{\partial \lambda} = \frac{m}{\lambda} - \left[\frac{m(n - m)}{(n - m) \log_e (1 + \lambda T) + \sum_{i=1}^{m} \log_e (1 + \lambda t_i)}\right] \frac{T}{1 + \lambda T}$$
$$- \left[\frac{m}{(n - m) \log_e (1 + \lambda T) + \sum_{i=1}^{m} \log_e (1 + \lambda t_i)} + 1\right] \sum_{i=1}^{m} \frac{t_i}{1 + \lambda t_i}$$
$$(8.23)$$

Using a one-dimensional search on Equation 8.23 we find the value(s) of λ that makes Equation 8.23 equal zero. We use the results in Equation 8.22 to get the corresponding value(s) for ν. If we have more than one (λ, ν) pair, we put these into Equation 8.16 to see which pair gives the largest value for L. This pair, call it $(\hat{\lambda}, \hat{\nu})$, will be the maximum likelihood estimates. Since there exist many efficient search techniques for obtaining roots of equations, this one-dimensional procedure using the exact likelihood function should be a substantial improvement on Anscombe's two-dimensional method on an approximate likelihood function.

8.3 Logistic Models

The best-known growth curve besides the exponential is probably the logistic. The logistic equation specifies that the cumulative proportion of people who have engaged in the activity of interest is given by

$$F(t) = \frac{M}{1 + \exp(-\mu t + c)} \quad \text{with derivative}$$

$$f(t) = \mu F(t)[M - F(t)] \tag{8.24}$$

where M is a ceiling level for penetration. As we will see, the basic assumptions underlying the logistic are that the rate of increase of penetration varies:[11]

1. Proportionately to the level [of penetration] in a given year; the rate of increase therefore rises as the value of the series rises.
2. Proportionately to the difference between the variable itself [i.e., penetration] and its maximum value; i.e., saturation level. Hence, the rate of increase declines as this difference decreases.

The effects of these two assumptions can be seen in the expression for $f(t)$. The logistic generates an S-shaped penetration curve as first $F(t)$ and then $[1 - F(t)]$ dominate the rate of increase. The logistic is similar in shape to the *Gompertz curve*, which is also used to describe market growth.[12]

The logistic curve has been used extensively by investigators studying

[11] Ferber and Verdoorn (1961, p. 334).
[12] The equation for the Gompertz curve is

$$F(t) = Ma^{\mu^t}$$

See Ferber and Verdoorn (1962, p. 335). Note, however, that this $F(t)$ cannot be interpreted as a probability distribution function.

the growth of demand for durable goods.[13] The fact that its *S*-curve shape resembles that of the cumulative normal distribution has made it attractive as a way to describe the progression of adoption from one subpopulation to another.[14] Another, more basic, way of looking at the logistic assumptions is to assume that other people's consumption enters an individual's utility function.[15] The assumption that the degree to which other people consume the new product at time t can be taken as proportional to $F(t)$ leads directly to Equation 8.24. This can be regarded as a form of "learning"; i.e., other people's purchase events feed back on the purchase probability for a given household. (This effect has also been called the "diffusion of an innovation," though in this case diffusion is used in a different sense than in Chapters 6 and 7.) We will explore the logistic process in some detail.

8.3.1   The Basic Logistic Process

Yance (1955) developed a model in which the probability that a certain number of decision-making units will have adopted a new product at time t is described by a nonstationary Markov chain. The mathematics of his approach were developed from those of stochastic simple birth processes, which result from assumptions relating the probability of an increase in a population to its current level, with no reductions in population size being possible. He applied his model to data on the time pattern of adoption of diesel engines by the American railroads.

The following is a short description of the Yance model. First, assume that the rate at which replacements are made (either diesel or steam) is constant. Hence, the cumulative number of possible change points for the process can be represented by a time index. Then let

$P_n(t)$ be the probability that exactly n diesels will be in use at time t. This can be termed a state of the system.

t_0 be the time at which diesels were first introduced.

M be the total number of engines being used in the railroad system. It represents the natural ceiling on the number of diesel units in use.

---

[13] See for example, DeWolff (1938), Roos and von Szeliski (1939), Griliches (1957), and Dernberg (1958).

[14] There has been a tendency to classify people into groups based on their propensity to accept innovations (e.g., innovators, early adopters, early majority, late majority, and diehards). At least one set of authors, Foundation for Research on Consumer Behavior (1959), indicate that membership in these categories tends to be normally distributed in the population. See also Coleman, Katz, and Menzel (1950).

[15] See James S. Duesenberry (1949).

$\mu(n)h$ be the probability that the system will move from state n to state $n + 1$ in a small time interval h. (Since h is arbitrarily small, the probability that the system will move from n to $n + k$ can be neglected for $k > 1$.)

The probability $\mu(n)h$ is really a composite of the probabilities that a replacement will be needed in time interval h and that the available slot will be filled by a diesel. Given these definitions, Yance writes the following stochastic birth process equations:

$$P_n(t + h) = [1 - \mu(n)h] P_n(t) + [\mu(n - 1)h] P_{n-1}(t)$$

That is, the probability that the system will have generated n adoptions at time $t + h$ is equal to the sum of the probabilities that it had generated n at t and did not change and that it was at $n - 1$ in t and did change. The reader can verify that this amounts to an infinite state Markov process with values of $P_n(t)$ as states, with transition probabilities $[1 - \mu(n)h]$, $[\mu(n - 1)h]$, and zero.[16] Rewriting the birth process equation yields

$$\frac{P_n(t + h) - P_n(t)}{h} = \mu(n - 1)P_{n-1}(t) - \mu(n)P_n(t)$$

which of course yields a differential equation in $P'_n(t)$ as $h \to 0$.

To complete the argument, Yance specified that the transition probability $\mu(n)$ should exhibit "learning" in the sense that a railroad manager's propensity to fill a vacant slot with a diesel is a positive function of the number of diesel units already in operation — both on his line and others. The transition probability must also include a saturation component, because replacement slots can represent conversions to diesel only if they are not already filled by a diesel unit. Yance represents the probability that a replacement can generate a changeover to diesel in terms of the factor $M - n$, where M is the total number of engines in use. Combining these conditions into a simple functional form yields

$$\mu(n) = \mu(0)n(M - n)$$

Substitution of this into the differential equation for growth yields

$$P'_n(t) = \frac{d\,P_n(t)}{dt} = \mu(0)n_{t-1}(M - n_{t-1})P_{n-1}(t)$$

$$- \mu(0)n_t(M - n_t)P_n(t)$$

[16] For the development of a similar process see Chapter 6.

Yance does not obtain an analytical solution for this equation, but rather derives its form by Monte Carlo simulation. The results indicate that the time series for n is logistic in shape. This is not surprising, since the change process for μ is assumed to be like Equation 8.24. The value of Yance's theoretical work is that it suggests how the logistic (and indeed other growth functions) can be obtained from the stochastic theory of epidemics.

8.3.2 The Semilogistic Process

The logistic function can also be derived in terms of the more familiar approach used in this chapter. Rather than cover this ground, however, let us define the following *semilogistic process*. Suppose that the conditional probability of purchase is

$$\Pr[\mathscr{P} \in (t, t + h) | \tilde{\mathscr{P}} \in (t_0, t)]$$
$$= h\mu(t) = h[\mu F(t) + \mu_0] \qquad \mu_0 > 0,\ \mu + \mu_0 > 0 \quad (8.25)$$

The initial probability μ_0 is not included in the specification which leads to the basic logistic function given in Equation 8.24. We have added it in order to obtain a probability distribution that is well behaved at t_0 and to provide for a comparison between the logistic and the other models discussed in this chapter. Equation 8.25 can be interpreted as an assumption that an individual's purchase propensity $\mu(t)$ starts at μ_0 and then changes with $F(t)$. The model allows the effect of $F(t)$ to be negative. This occurs when $\mu < 0$; but because $F(t) \rightarrow 1$ at t increases, the condition that the contingent purchase probability be nonnegative implies that, if μ is negative, its absolute value must be less than μ_0. This accounts for the constraints on the admissible values of the coefficients that are included in Equation 8.25.

Proceeding as in Section 8.2.2, we have[17]

$$\Pr[\mathscr{P} \in (t, t + h)] = F(t + h) - F(t)$$
$$= \Pr[\mathscr{P} \in (t, t + h) | \tilde{\mathscr{P}} \in (t_0, t)]\, \Pr[\tilde{\mathscr{P}} \in (t_0, t)]$$

$$\frac{F(t + h) - F(t)}{h} = [\mu F(t) + \mu_0][1 - F(t)]$$

$$\frac{dF(t)}{dt} = [\mu F(t) + \mu_0][1 - F(t)]$$

---

[17] A ceiling $M < 1$ could be introduced into this model if desired, in which case the last term would be $[M - F(t)]$.

The solution is again obtained by separation of variables.

$$\int \frac{dF(t)}{[\mu F(t) + \mu_0][1 - F(t)]} = \int dt$$

$$-\frac{1}{(\mu + \mu_0)} \log \left[\frac{1 - F(t)}{\mu F(t) + \mu_0} \right] = t + \text{const}$$

After applying the initial condition $F(0) = 0$, we have

$$F(t) = \frac{1 - \exp[-(\mu + \mu_0)t]}{1 + \frac{\mu}{\mu_0} \exp[-(\mu + \mu_0)t]} \qquad (8.26)$$

with density function

$$f(t) = \frac{(\mu + \mu_0)^2}{\mu_0} \exp[-(\mu + \mu_0)t] \left[1 + \frac{\mu}{\mu_0} \exp[-(\mu + \mu_0)t] \right]^{-2} \quad (8.27)$$

The reader can verify that

$$\frac{f(t)}{1 - F(t)} = \mu F(t) + \mu_0$$

as postulated in Equation 8.25.

Let us examine the characteristics of this version of the logistic. First, $F(t)$ will have the logistical S-shaped character if $f(t)$ reaches a maximum at some $t^* > 0$. That is, under this condition $F(t)$ will rise at an increasing rate until t^* and then continue upward at a decreasing rate. The derivative of $f(t)$ has the form:

$$f'(t) = Q(t) \left\{ \frac{\mu}{\mu_0} \exp[-(\mu + \mu_0)t] - 1 \right\}$$

where $Q(t)$ is strictly positive for all $t \geq 0$ and all admissible values of μ and μ_0. The inflection point in $F(t)$ occurs when $f'(t) = 0$, that is, at

$$t = \frac{1}{\mu + \mu_0} \log \left(\frac{\mu}{\mu_0} \right)$$

Thus, $F(t)$ will take on an S-shape only when $\mu > \mu_0$ and the greater μ is relative to μ_0 the greater the amount of time before the inflection point. Conversely, as μ becomes small relative to μ_0, Equation 8.26 becomes more and more like an exponential. When $\mu = 0$, the semilogistic

distribution is exponential with parameter μ_0. Of course this also can be seen immediately from the propensity function, Equation 8.25.

Second, we can see that $\mu_0 > 0$ is what differentiates the basic and semilogistic functions. In the limit, as $\mu_0 \to 0$, the denominator of Equation 8.26 comes to dominate $F(t)$ and the semilogistic approaches the basic logistic given by Equation 8.24. The basic logistic, like the normal distribution, is defined on the interval $t \in (-\infty, +\infty)$. Then $F(t)$ cannot be zero in Equation 8.24 unless $t = -\infty$, no matter what parameters are chosen. In contrast, $F(0) = 0$ in Equation 8.25: the semilogistic is defined on $t \in (0, +\infty)$, which is more appropriate for a penetration curve.

Third, $F(t)$ goes to $+1$ at $t \to \infty$, according to Equation 8.26, whereas Equation 8.24 allows for an upper asymptote $M < 1$. This difference is not relevant to a comparison of the two models. An upper asymptote could easily be added to the semilogistic. The result is

$$F(t) = \frac{\{1 - \exp[-(\mu M + \mu_0)t]\}M}{1 + \dfrac{\mu M}{\mu_0} \exp[-(\mu M + \mu_0)t]} \tag{8.28}$$

The analogy of this to both Equations 8.24, for the basic logistic, and Equation 8.12, for the Fourt-Woodlock version of the mixed exponential should be obvious. In fact, we are justified in regarding Equation 8.24 and 8.28 as the "mixed logistic" and "mixed semilogistic" distributions respectively, with prior distribution:

Logistic	Semilogistic
$\Pr[\mu^* = \mu > 0] = M$	$\Pr[\mu^* = \mu, \mu_0^* = \mu_0, \mu_0 + \mu > 0] = M$
$\Pr[\mu^* = 0] = 1 - M$	$\Pr[\mu^* = \mu_0^* = 0] = 1 - M$

This is analogous to Equation 8.14 for the mixed exponential.

Finally, it does not appear to be practical to use continuous prior distributions to represent heterogeneity on μ and μ_0, as we did in the development of the gamma exponential presented in Equation 8.15. While gamma prior densities would appear to be reasonable representations of heterogeneity for the logistic parameters, the integration of either μ or μ_0 from Equation 8.28 is not attractive.

The semilogistic function can be estimated by the methods discussed in Section 8.1.3, though the relative complexity of the expression for $F(t)$ may be something of a handicap. However, a shortcut procedure is available. This procedure yields consistent parameter estimates, but it is likely that they will be biased for small sample sizes.

In Section 8.3 we found that if the population in question is homogeneous, we can write

$$\frac{Y(t+h) - Y(t)}{1 - Y(t)} = \mu(t) + e(t)$$

where $Y(t)$ is the level of penetration reached as of time t. Then, under certain conditions on $\mu(t)$, minimization of the sum of $e(t)$ with respect to the parameters, over the range of t for which data are available, provides consistent parameter estimates. If both sides of this equation are weighted by the factor $1/\sqrt{Y(t)[1 - Y(t)]}$, the e are made homoscedastic and the estimates are asymptotically efficient — in fact, they are modified minimum chi-square estimates.

In the present case, we have

$$\frac{Y(t+h) - Y(t)}{1 - Y(t)} = \mu_0 + \mu F(t) + e(t) \approx \mu_0 + \mu Y(t) + e(t) \quad (8.29)$$

from which estimates of μ_0 and μ can be obtained by weighted linear regression. The basic logistic admits the same procedure, except that μ_0 is constrained at zero. Unfortunately, however, we know that the empirical $Y(t)$ will not generally be equal to its expectation $F(t)$. Hence, Equation 8.29 is an *errors in variable* equation, and the simple regression estimates will be biased.[18] As the relative variances of the dependent variable and $Y(t)$ cannot be determined easily and since the $[Y(t) - F(t)]$ will be correlated for adjacent t, it does not seem practical to try to eliminate the bias by standard econometric techniques. We do know, however, that the errors in $Y(t)$ will go to zero as the number of people in the population increases, so the shortcut procedure is consistent.

If the model is assumed to have an upper asymptote $M < 1$, the following estimating equation may be effective:

$$Y(t+h) - Y(t) = b_0 + b_1 Y(t) + b_2 Y(t)^2 + e(t)$$
$$b_0 = \mu_0 M, \qquad b_1 = \mu M - \mu_0, \qquad b_2 = \mu \quad (8.30)$$

After estimating the b, $\hat{\mu}$ is determined from b_2, $\hat{M}$ by solving the quadratic,

$$\hat{\mu}\hat{M}^2 + b_1\hat{M} + b_0 = 0$$

and $\hat{\mu}_0$ is calculated from b_0 once $\hat{M}$ is known. These estimates are consistent, but they also suffer from small-sample bias because of errors in $Y(t)$. The precision of the estimates of μ_0 and μ will also be

---

[18] See Johnston (1963, Chapter 6).

lower than for the case when M is known. This can best be seen by noting the probable collinearity of $Y(t)$ and $Y(t)^2$ in Equation 8.30 and considering its effect on the standard errors of the b.

8.3.3   The Nonstationary Logistic Model

As noted earlier, the parameter of both the basic and semilogistic function can be considered as a measure of the diffusion rate of the new product, i.e., the extent to which other people's purchases affect the purchase propensity of the household in question. Suppose that this rate depends on the extent to which the product is advertised, the amount of its distribution, etc. In this section we will extend the basic logistic process to provide for some of these effects.

Suppose that the propensity change parameter μ in Equation 8.25 is modified to include the effects of marketing variables $Z_1(t), Z_2(t), \ldots,$ $Z_k(t)$ — where $Z_1(t)$ might be the advertising level, $Z_2(t)$ the distribution level, etc. (For the basic logistic process μ_0 is assumed to be zero.) Two hypotheses about the form of the change process suggest themselves:

$$\text{a.} \qquad \mu(t) = \mu^* Z_1(t)^{\epsilon_1} Z_2(t)^{\epsilon_2} \ldots Z_k(t)^{\epsilon_k} \tag{8.31}$$

$$\text{b.} \qquad \mu(t) = \mu^* + \epsilon_1 Z_1(t) + \epsilon_2 Z_2(t) + \cdots + \epsilon_k Z_k(t)$$

The first formulation has been widely used by authors who have applied econometric techniques to the basic logistic models.[19] If $M = 1$, the parameters of Equation 8.31a can be estimated by substituting the expression for $\mu(t)$ into the propensity function $R(t)$. This leads to the following estimating equation

$$\frac{Y(t + h) - Y(t)}{1 - Y(t)} = \mu^* Z_1(t)^{\epsilon_1} Z_2(t)^{\epsilon_2}, \ldots, Z_k(t)^{\epsilon_t} Y(t) \exp\left[e(t)\right]$$

This admits the linear transform

$$\log Y^*(t) = \log \mu^* + \epsilon_1 \log Z_1(t) + \cdots + \epsilon_k \log Z_k(t) + e(t)$$

$$Y^*(t) = \frac{Y(t + h) - Y(t)}{Y(t)[1 - Y(t)]} \tag{8.32}$$

Least squares will yield consistent unbiased estimates of the parameters. Note that this formulation depends on the absence of μ_0 from the basic logistic.

[19] See for example DeWolff (1938), Roos and von Szeliski (1939), and Dernberg (1958).

Hypothesis 8.31b seems to be of greater interest so far as the stochastic theory of buyer behavior is concerned. We shall continue to deal with the basic logistic and assume that $M = 1$. Substitution of the linear expression for $\mu(t)$ in Equation 8.31 yields

$$\frac{dF(t)/dt}{1 - F(t)} = \mu(t)F(t) = [\mu^* + \epsilon_1 Z_1(t) + \cdots + \epsilon_k Z_k(t)]F(t)$$

This also yields the simple estimating equation

$$Y^*(t) = \mu^* + \epsilon_1 Z_1(t) + \epsilon_2 Z_2(t) + \cdots + \epsilon_k Z_k(t) + e(t) \quad (8.33)$$

which can be solved by least squares to give consistent unbiased estimates of the ϵ. (We must note, however, that if some ϵ are negative then certain combinations of the $Z(t)$ could yield negative values for $\mu(t)$, which would cause a breakdown in the model. Hence Equation 8.33 must be regarded as holding only for reasonably small ranges of the $Z(t)$.)

The advantage of the linear form for $\mu(t)$ is that it allows us to make closed-form predictions about $Y(t)$, given certain assumptions about the time series of the $Z_i(t)$. Suppose that the time series for each marketing variable can be described by a polynomial in t,

$$Z_i(t) = a_{i0} + a_{i1}t + a_{i2}t^2 + a_{i3}t^3 + \cdots + a_{in}t^n \quad (8.34)$$

As many terms can be added to Equation 8.34 as are needed to represent either the actual or planned time series for the ith marketing variable. The coefficients a_{ij} are determined from the $Z_i(t)$ series only, and are known constants so far as the estimation of the nonstationary logistic is concerned.[20] Substitution of Equation 8.34 into Equation 8.33 yields the following differential equation, which must be solved in order to obtain the expression for $F(t)$:

$$\frac{dF(t)/dt}{(1 - F(t))} = \left(\mu^* + \sum_{i=1}^{K} \epsilon_i \sum_{j=0}^{n} a_{ij}t^j \right) F(t)$$

Separating the variables and collecting terms, we have

$$\frac{dF(t)}{F(t)(1 - F(t))} = \left[\left(\mu^* + \sum_i \epsilon_i a_{i0} \right) + \sum_{j=1}^{n} t^j \sum_i \epsilon_i a_{ij} \right] dt$$

[20] See Section 11.3 for a further development of these ideas.

The solution is

$$\log\left[\frac{F(t)}{1-F(t)}\right] = \left(\mu^* + \sum_i \epsilon_i a_{i0}\right)t + \sum_{j=1}^{n} \frac{t^{j+1}}{j+1}\sum_i \epsilon_i a_{ij} + \text{const}$$

$$F(t) = \cfrac{1}{1 + \text{const}\cdot\exp\left\{-\left[\left(\mu^* + \sum_i \epsilon_i a_{i0}\right)t + \sum_{j=1}^{n} \frac{t^{j+1}}{j+1}\sum_i \epsilon_i a_{ij}\right]\right\}} \quad (8.35)$$

where exp is the exponential function and const is the constant of integration which must be determined from the initial conditions. (Recall that $F(0) \neq 0$ for the basic logistic.) Equation 8.35 gives $F(t)$ as an explicit function of the parameters of the marketing variables' time series and the assumed model of buyer behavior.

An approximation to Equation 8.35 in terms of the actual values of the marketing variables, without reducing them to polynomial form through (8.34), can also be obtained. Write

$$F(t) = \cfrac{1}{1 + \text{const}\cdot\exp\left\{-\left[\mu^* + \sum_i \epsilon_i \sum_{j=0}^{t} Z_i(j)\right]\right\}} \quad (8.36)$$

This representation amounts to a numerical integration of Equation 8.33. If the ϵ are estimated from Equation 8.33 either Equation 8.35 or 8.36 can be used to project $F(t)$ beyond the limits of the available data. Alternatively, either equation can be used as a basis for maximum likelihood or minimum chi-square estimates of the kind discussed in Section 8.1.3. An upper asymptote $M < 1$ can be added to either equation by the methods of Section 8.3.2. Finally, we should note that the procedures of this section will not work on the semilogistic process, because the existence of μ_0 prevents separation of the F and t variables in the differential equation leading to Equation 8.35.

Finally, we should try to relate our work on the nonstationary logistic to previous results. Dernberg (1958), estimated the parameters of

$$\log\left[\frac{Y(t)}{1-Y(t)}\right] = b_0 + b_1 Z_1(t) + \cdots + b_k Z_k(t)$$

which he calls a "logit" equation, by using least squares procedures on cross-sectional census tract data. His Y were the proportion of homes in a tract who owned TV receivers as of the 1950 census, while his Z were primarily socioeconomic and demographic variables. The Dernberg model is appropriate for cross-sectional analysis, at least under certain

reasonable conditions,[21] but it is important to note that it will not work properly in time series applications where the Z vary over time. According to Equation 8.36 the time series version of the "logit" estimating equation should be:

$$\log \left[\frac{Y(t)}{1 - Y(t)} \right] = b_0 + \mu^* t + b_1 \sum_{j=0}^{t} Z_1(j) + \cdots + b_k \sum_{j=0}^{t} Z_k(j)$$

On the other hand, we have seen that in this case it would be better to estimate the propensity function according to Equation 8.33 than to try to deal with the distribution function directly as in time series "logit" analysis.

Massy (1960) developed another variant of the nonstationary logistic Process. He argued that the coefficients of sensitivity of $\mu(t)$ to marketing variables ought themselves to be functions of $F(t)$. Adopting Hypothesis 8.31a he writes (in our present notation):

$$\frac{dF(t)/dt}{1 - F(t)} = \mu(t)F(t) = \mu^* F(t) Z_1(t)^{\epsilon_{10} + \epsilon_{11} F(t)} Z_2(t)^{\epsilon_{20} + \epsilon_{21} F(t)} \cdots$$

and calls it the "modified logistic." An asymptote $M < 1$ can be added to the modified logistic if desired. Integration of the modified logistic is tricky, because of the presence of $F(t)$ in the right-hand exponents. An infinite series approximation to the integral, under the assumption that all the Z are constant over time, is provided, and the results plotted for various values of the parameters.[22] The curve for $F(t)$ can be quite asymmetric — involving either a sharp "knee" or a long "stretchout" near the upper asymptote — depending on the signs of the ϵ_{i1}. Massy estimates the parameters of the modified logistic with asymptote M using an obvious variation of Equation 8.32.

Finally, Haines (1963, 1964) points out that in nonstationary models where an upper asymptote $M < 1$ is assumed it may be as reasonable to make M a function of marketing variables as it is to assume that $\mu(t)$ is such a function. In criticizing Massy (1960), he justly points out that failure to make M a function of the Z can lead to bias in the estimates of the ϵ. The same criticism's could be applied to all the penetration models discussed in this book, if there is reason to believe that M is a function of the Z.

---

[21] See the original arguments by Dernberg (1958) and comments by Massy (1960, pp. 55–61).

[22] Massy (1960, pp. 68–79).

8.4 Learning Models

Linear learning assumptions of the type discussed in Chapter 5 can also be used to generate growth curves for percentage market penetration and models yielding certain characteristics of the distribution of the number of purchases of a given product or brand during a fixed interval of time. Haines (1963, 1964) was the first to consider these ideas. We will briefly review his work and then develop some new linear learning models for the time path of market penetration. All of these models are based on the "one-event" learning assumption described in the next section.

8.4.1 A One-Event Learning Model for Purchase Propensity

Haines (1963, 1964) describes the basic assumptions underlying one-event learning models. Suppose that potential customers for a new product are "exposed" to it at frequent intervals, beginning at the time of introduction t_0. These exposures may take the form of shopping trips where the new product may be seen on the supermarket shelf, receipt of advertising messages, conversations with other exposees, etc. Let us define each exposure as an "event," and assume that each event causes learning in the sense of the Bush-Mosteller model described in Chapter 5.

Following the notation used earlier in this chapter, we define the probability that an individual will purchase the new product in a small interval of time, given that he has not previously purchased it, as

$$\Pr[\mathscr{P} \in (t, t+h)|\tilde{\mathscr{P}} \in (t_0,t)] = h\mu(t) \qquad (8.37)$$

Now suppose that exposure events occur at the rate of approximately one per unit time interval, and that "learning" takes place after each event. As there is only one kind of event, the learning operator is of only one type — that is, only one line of Equation 5.1 is needed to describe the learning phenomenon. Thus we can write the following recursive relation describing the learning process caused by successive exposures to the new product.

$$\mu(t+1) = Q\mu(t) = \lambda\mu(t) + (1-\lambda)\mu_* \qquad (8.38)$$

where Q can be termed the "event operator." (Equation 8.38 is a reparametrization of the top line of Equation 5.1.) Successive applications of the event operator yield the following expression for $\mu(t)$ as a function of the initial purchase propensity μ_0:

$$\mu(t) = Q^t\mu_0 = \lambda^t\mu_0 + (1-\lambda^t)\mu_* \qquad (8.39)$$

As can easily be seen, $\mu(t) \to \mu_*$ as t becomes large so long as $0 < \lambda < 1$ as required by the basic learning model assumptions. Thus μ^* is the equilibrium or long-run value of the purchase propensity $\mu(t)$.

Haines also considers the differential equation analog to the solution for the time path of $\mu(t)$ given by Equation 8.39. He writes:

$$\mu(t + 1) - \mu(t) = Q\mu(t) - \mu(t)$$
$$= (1 - \lambda)[\mu_* - \mu(t)]$$

where the last equality is obtained by applying Equation 8.38. The solution to this difference equation is approximated by the differential equation

$$\frac{d\mu(t)}{dt} = (1 - \lambda)[\mu_* - \mu(t)]$$

which can be solved by separation of variables. Invoking the initial condition that $\mu(0) = \mu_0$, this yields

$$\mu(t) = \mu_0 \exp\left[-(1 - \lambda)t\right] + \mu_*(1 - \exp\left[-(1 - \lambda)t\right])$$

(8.40)

This has the same properties as Equation 8.39.

Now, Haines (1964, p. 640) compares Equation 8.40 with the two-population exponential process investigated by Fourt and Woodlock and Anscombe.[23] While it is true that for $\mu_0 = 0$ (which is a reasonable assumption where new products are concerned) Equation 8.40 is the same as 8.12, the two models represent quite different aspects of behavior. The exponential model assumes that the purchase propensity function is constant, in which case we derive Equation 8.12 from the relation

$$\Pr[\mathscr{P} \in (t, t + h)] = \Pr[\mathscr{P} \in (t, t + h) | \tilde{\mathscr{P}} \in (t_0, t)] \Pr[\tilde{\mathscr{P}} \in (t_0, t)]$$

or equivalently

$$F(t + h) - F(t) = \mu(t)(M - F(t)) \qquad \mu(t) = \mu$$

where $F(t)$ is the expected proportion of the population who have purchased the product (the height of the penetration curve) and M is the proportion of people who might buy it sometime. In contrast, Haines' Equation 8.40 refers to the time path of $\mu(t)$ itself. Thus the learning model cannot be used to justify the Fourt-Woodlock-Anscombe model, which explicitly assumes that $\mu(t) = $ constant, on

---

[23] See Section 8.2.2.

the one hand, and accounts for removal of purchasers from the pool of potential triers on the other.

To see what Haines has really done we must make the additional assumption that an individual's $\mu(t)$ is independent of whether or not he has already purchased the product and, indeed, how many times he has purchased it in the past. That is, we assume that learning *only* occurs as a result of exposure events and *not* as a function of actual product trial. This assumption implies that

$$\Pr[\mathscr{P} \in (t, t + h) | \tilde{\mathscr{P}} \in (t_0, t)] = \Pr[\mathscr{P} \in (t, t + h)] = h\mu(t) \quad (8.41)$$

which in turn allows us to think of $\mu(t)$ as applying to all members of the population at time t, regardless of their purchase history.

What the assumption in Equation 8.41 does, in effect, is to transform the thrust of Haines' model from a "waiting time to next purchase" model, which is what Fourt and Woodlock are talking about, to a "number of purchases in the population during a fixed time interval" model of the general type developed by Ehrenberg. Indeed, Haines uses the model in exactly this latter sense when he applies it to data. After extending his equation to take account of the fact that different people in the population may have different exposure histories and hence different values of $\mu(t)$ at any t, he applies it to time series data for total market sales.[24] The validity of this procedure can be seen by supposing that there are N people in the population, and that each of them purchases once during interval $(t, t + h)$ with probability $\mu(t)$; we assume that h is small enough so that the probability of two or more purchases is negligible. Then:

$$E[\text{no. of purchases} \in (t, t + h)] = Nh\mu(t)$$

If N is large, total sales of the product will of course approximate the expectation (Haines also allows for variations in package size) and so bears a direct relation to $\mu(t)$.

The fact that Haines' model does not lead to market penetration curves need not detract from its usefulness in particular contexts. If we are willing to accept the idea that the act of purchasing and using the

[24] The derivation of Haines' "average probability" or "total market" model is quite interesting and does lead to an equation that is, in effect, more like a logistic equation than 8.40. See Haines (1964), pp. 640–641 and 654–657. This extension does not affect the necessity for assuming 8.41 nor change the fact that it is essentially $\mu(t)$ that is being related to empirical data, however. Thus Haines' "average purchase propensity" model bears no more relation to the assumptions underlying the logistic, as developed in Section 3, than his homogeneous model does to the Fourt-Woodlock-Anscombe model.

product does not effect purchasing propensities any more than any other kind of exposure event, the model can be used to track the expected number of purchases in successive time intervals for a growing product. While this particular assumption would seem to be untenable in many new product situations, there are doubtless cases where it would be likely to apply. In addition, other interesting models can be built around the idea of one-event learning. Some of these will be explored in Sections 8.4.2 and 8.4.3.

8.4.2 A One-Event Learning Model for Market Penetration

The one-event linear learning model can easily be modified to provide a representation of the time path of market penetration; that is, for $F(t)$. In this section, we will briefly present our results for homogeneous purchase propensities. The problem of heterogeneous $\mu(t)$ will be explored in Section 8.4.3.

The one-event linear learning operator is applied to the purchase propensity function $\mu(t)$, as shown in Equation 8.38. By the definition of the propensity function,[25] we can write

$$\frac{F(t + h) - F(t)}{h} = \mu(t)[1 - F(t)]$$

$$= Q^t \mu_0 [1 - F(t)]$$

$$= [\lambda^t \mu_0 + (1 - \lambda^t)\mu_*][1 - F(t)] \qquad (8.42)$$

where the last relation is obtained from Equation 8.39. The time path of $F(t)$ is obtained by letting $h \to 0$ and solving the resulting differential equation:

$$\int \frac{df(t)}{1 - F(t)} = \int [\lambda^t \mu_0 + (1 - \lambda^t)\mu_*] \, dt$$

$$- \log [1 - F(t)] = \mu_* t - \frac{\lambda^t}{\log (1/\lambda)} (\mu_0 - \mu_*) + \text{const}$$

Solving for $F(t)$ and invoking the initial condition $F(0) = 0$ to evaluate the constant yields:

$$F(t) = 1 - \exp \left\{ -\left[\mu_* t - \frac{1}{\log (1/\lambda)} (1 - \lambda^t)(\mu_* - \mu_0) \right] \right\} \qquad (8.43)$$

Equation 8.43 is the equation that should be compared to the Fourt-Woodlock model, not Equation 8.40. As can easily be seen,

[25] See Equation 8.4.

Equation 8.43 does not, by itself, yield an upper asymptote less than one. In fact, the one-event learning model approaches the exponential as t becomes large and $\mu_* t$ comes to dominate the exponent.

What are the properties of the homogeneous one-event linear learning model? First, the expression for the time path of purchase propensity $\mu(t)$ has already been given in Equations 8.39 and 8.40. As no population heterogeneity is assumed, $R(T)$ is the same as $\mu(t)$. The true shape of $F(t)$ can be examined in terms of the derivatives:

$$f(t) = [\mu_* - (\mu_* - \mu_0)\lambda^t]$$

$$\times \exp\left\{-\left[\mu_* t - \frac{1}{\log(1/\lambda)}(1 - \lambda^t)(\mu_* - \mu_0)\right]\right\}$$

$$f'(t) = \left[\log\left(\frac{1}{\lambda}\right)(\mu_* - \mu_0)\lambda^t - \mu_* - (\mu_* - \mu_0)\lambda^t\right]$$

$$\times \exp\left\{-\left[\mu_* t - \frac{1}{\log(1/\lambda)}(1 - \lambda^t)(\mu_* - \mu_0)\right]\right\}$$

As $\log(1/\lambda)$ and the exponential function are always nonnegative, the expression for $f'(t)$ shows that the one-event linear learning model can produce an S-shaped time path for $F(t)$ for some parameter values. This will occur if $f(t)$ is rising, that is if $f'(t) > 0$, for small values of t. At $t = 0$ the sign of $f'(t)$ is determined by the sign of

$$\log\frac{1}{\lambda}(\mu_* - \mu_0) - \mu_0$$

which will be positive if λ is near zero, μ_0 is small, and $\mu_* > \mu_0$. In other words, this means that if the initial purchase propensity (μ_0) and the learning factor (λ) are both small, the process will start slowly and then accelerate, providing that the equilibrium propensity (μ_*) is larger than μ_0. If $\mu_0 > \mu_*$, then the purchase propensity must decline and $F(t)$ cannot have an inflection point. We can also see that as $t \to \infty$, $\lambda^t \to 0$, and the expression for $f'(t)$ takes the sign of $-\mu_*^2$, which of course is always negative. Thus $f(t)$ must always turn down and approach the zero axis, as befits a proper density function.

Thus we see that the homogeneous one-event linear learning assumption yields a market penetration model that can approximate, at least in gross terms, the characteristic S-shape of the familiar logistic model. This approximation is best when $\mu_0 = 0$, which would not be an unreasonable assumption if we are considering the penetration of a new product among potential first-time triers. Moreover, the expression for

$F(t)$ in the one-event learning model is easier to work with than the ones derived for the basic and semilogistic models.

8.4.3 Heterogeneous One-Event Learning Models

In Chapter 5 we argued that it is usually necessary to assume that the initial purchase probability varies over members of the population. The present situation is easier because only one learning operator is involved, and its application does not depend upon any purchase events during the period of time covered by the data (e.g., the waiting time to the next trial). Therefore, we will be able to develop one-event models where either μ_0 or μ_*, or both, are assumed to vary over members of the population.

Model 1: Heterogeneous μ_0. Suppose that a population is believed to be heterogeneous in μ_0 but that all members have the same long-run purchase propensity μ_*. (The learning rate parameter λ is assumed to be homogeneous in all these models.) This assumption might be reasonable in situations where all people are believed to have similar tastes, but different people have been exposed to different kinds of experiences (e.g., advertising or promotion) that are relevant to making an initial assessment of the new product's merit. Thus people might start the process with different purchase propensities, but a common series of subsequent learning experiences would be expected to bring them together.

Following the ideas presented in Section 8.2, we will assume that the frequency function of μ_0 in the population can be approximated by a gamma distribution with parameters α and β. That is,

$$f(\mu_0|\alpha,\beta) = \frac{\beta \exp{(-\beta\mu_0)}(\beta\mu_0)^{\alpha-1}}{\Gamma(\alpha)} \qquad \alpha, \beta > 0$$

as presented originally in Equation 8.8. The distribution function for time to trial under the one-event learning assumption, given in Equation 8.43, must now be regarded as conditional on μ_0. To remove the condition, we write

$$F(t) = \int_0^\infty F(t|\mu_0)f(\mu_0|\alpha,\beta)\,d\mu_0$$

$$= 1 - \exp\left[-\mu_*t\,\frac{1}{\log{(1/\lambda)}}\,(1 - \lambda^t)\mu_*\right]\frac{\beta^\alpha}{\Gamma(\alpha)}$$

$$\times \int_0^\infty \exp\left[-\frac{1}{\log{(1/\lambda)}}\,(1 - \lambda^t)\mu_0\right]\exp{(-\beta\mu_0)}\mu_0^{\alpha-1}\,d\mu_0$$

Except for constants, the quantity inside the integral has the form of a gamma distribution with parameters α and $\beta + [1/\log (1/\lambda)](1 - \lambda^t)$, which of course integrates to one. This leads to the solution

$$F(t) = 1 - \frac{\beta^\alpha}{\left[\beta + \dfrac{1}{\log 1/\lambda}(1 - \lambda^t)\right]^\alpha} \exp\left\{-\mu_*\left[t - \frac{(1 - \lambda^t)}{\log 1/\lambda}\right]\right\} \quad (8.44)$$

To check ourselves, we can note that $F(0) = 0$ and $F(t) \to 1$ as $t \to \infty$, regardless of the values of the parameters. As $0 < \lambda < 1$ by the assumptions of the basic learning model, the quantity that is raised to the α power in the denominator is always positive and so the distribution is defined for all parameter values.

The density function for time to trial is obtained by differentiating $F(t)$ with respect to t. As the development is tedious, we merely state the result:

$$f(t) = \beta^\alpha\left[\beta + \frac{(1 - \lambda^t)}{\log 1/\lambda}\right]^{-(\alpha+1)}\left[\alpha + (\mu_*\beta - \alpha)(1 - \lambda^t) + \frac{(1 - \lambda^t)^2}{\log 1/\lambda}\right]$$

$$\times \exp\left\{-\mu_*\left[t + \frac{(1 - \lambda^t)}{\log \lambda}\right]\right\}$$

While the analysis of the derivative of $f(t)$ would be difficult, we would expect that $F(t)$ would exhibit S-shaped behavior, just as in the homogeneous model.

We can also obtain the following expression for the purchase contingency function:

$$R(t) = \frac{f(t)}{1 - F(t)} = \frac{\left[\alpha + (\mu_*\beta - \alpha)(1 - \lambda^t) + \dfrac{(1 - \lambda^t)^2}{\log 1/\lambda}\right]}{\left[\beta + \dfrac{(1 - \lambda^t)}{\log 1/\lambda}\right]} \quad (8.45)$$

The form of the purchase contingency function can be inferred from the time derivative of $R(t)$:

$$R'(t) = \frac{\lambda^t\beta^2}{\left[\beta + \dfrac{(1 - \lambda^t)}{\log (1/\lambda)}\right]^2}\left[\left(\mu_* - \frac{\alpha}{\beta}\right)\log\frac{1}{\lambda} + 2\frac{(1 - \lambda^t)}{\beta} + \frac{(1 - \lambda^t)^2}{2\log\dfrac{1}{\lambda}}\right]$$

$$(8.46)$$

where of course $\log 1/\lambda > 0$. As the terms outside the brackets are always nonnegative, we can see that at $t = 0$, the $R'(t)$ takes on the sign of

$$\mu_* - \frac{\alpha}{\beta} = \mu_* - \mathrm{E}[\mu_0]$$

That is, $R(t)$ will be dropping at t_0 if the expected value of the initial purchase propensity is greater than the long-run equilibrium propensity. Whether $R(t)$ will eventually begin to rise in this case depends primarily on the value of β; if β is small (which implies that the variance of $f(\mu_0)$ is large relative to its mean) the purchase contingency function may not be monotonically decreasing, even if $\mu_* < \mathrm{E}[\mu_0]$. On the other hand, if $\mu_* > \mathrm{E}[\mu_0]$ then $R'(t) \geq 0$ for all t and the purchase contingency function will rise monotonically. Finally, as $t \to \infty$, the lead term λ^t will come to dominate $R'(t)$, which means that $R'(t)$ will eventually vanish and $R(t)$ will flatten out. From Equation 8.45 we see that

$$\lim_{t \to \infty} R(t) = \frac{\mu_* \beta \log 1/\lambda + 1}{\beta \log 1/\lambda + 1}$$

Our development of the properties of $R(t)$ is useful, because it indicates what type of market penetration curves may be fit by the model. The fact that $R(t)$ may or may not be monotonic stands in contrast to the known monotonicity of the individual household purchase propensity function $\mu(t)$, given by Equation 8.40. Once again, the addition of heterogeneity leads to a much richer set of properties for the aggregate market penetration process than could be obtained from an equivalent homogeneous model. We may also compare Equation 8.45 with the expression for $R(t)$ obtained for the heterogeneous exponential model in Equation 8.16. There we found that $R(t) = \alpha/(t + \beta)$, which decreases monotonically toward zero with t as the result of the heterogeneity in the population. In the one-event learning model with heterogeneous μ_0, the effects of learning may or may not dominate the effects of heterogeneity. This comes about because the effects of heterogeneity die out as the population is exposed to common learning experiences: for those that may be left in the population of nontriers, $\mu(t)_i$ goes to the homogeneous value μ_* with the passage of time. The effect of this assumption can be further demonstrated by the fact that $R(t)$ goes to a positive limit as $t \to \infty$, rather than to zero as is the case with the heterogeneous exponential.

Model 2: Heterogeneous μ_*. The obvious analogue to the heterogeneous μ_0 model is the case where the equilibrium purchase

propensity is different for different members of the population. If anything, this situation should be more common than the one envisioned in Model 1, especially where new products are concerned. It may be reasonable to assume, for example, that $\mu_0 = 0$ for all members of the population (as might be the case where the product is totally new to everyone) but that "learning" may lead to a variety of different values for μ_*.

We will again assume that the prior distribution is gamma with parameters α and β. Now we have to integrate μ_* from the homogeneous model, as given in Equation 8.43. We have

$$F(t) = \int_0^\infty F(t|\mu_*) f(\mu_* | \alpha, \beta) \, d\mu_*$$

$$= 1 - \exp\left\{ -\mu_0 \left[\frac{1 - \lambda^t}{\log 1/\lambda} \right] \right\} \frac{\beta^\alpha}{\Gamma(\alpha)} \int_0^\infty \exp\left\{ -\left[t - \frac{1 - \lambda^t}{\log 1/\lambda} \right] \mu_* \right\}$$

$$\times \exp\left(-\beta \mu_* \right)(\mu_*)^{\alpha - 1} \, d\mu_*$$

Proceeding as we did in the development of Equation 8.44 for Model 1, we have the solution

$$F(t) = 1 - \frac{\beta^\alpha}{\left[\beta + t - \dfrac{1 - \lambda^t}{\log 1/\lambda} \right]^\alpha} \exp\left\{ -\mu_0 \left[\frac{1 - \lambda^t}{\log 1/\lambda} \right] \right\} \qquad (8.47)$$

Once again we see that $F(0) = 0$ and $F(t) \to 1$ as $t \to \infty$. This time, however, the time term in the denominator comes to dominate $F(t)$ as t gets large.

It is also possible to verify that the term raised to the power α in the denominator is always positive, as is required if $F(t)$ is to be defined for all t. We know that $\beta > 0$, so the result hinges on the condition

$$t - \frac{1 - \lambda^t}{\log 1/\lambda} \geq 0$$

or

$$Q = t \log \frac{1}{\lambda} + \lambda^t \geq 1$$

$$\frac{dQ}{dt} = \log \frac{1}{\lambda} - \lambda^t \log \frac{1}{\lambda} = (1 - \lambda^t) \log \frac{1}{\lambda} \geq 0 \qquad (8.48)$$

Now, Q is equal to one when $t = 0$, and, since the derivative of Q is nonnegative, Q must be greater than one for all $t > 0$, which proves the point.

The density function for Model 2 is

$$f(t) = \beta^\alpha \left[\beta + t - \frac{1 - \lambda^t}{\log 1/\lambda} \right]^{-(\alpha+1)}$$

$$\times \left[\left(\beta + t - \frac{1 - \lambda^t}{\log 1/\lambda} \right) \mu_0 \lambda^t + \alpha(1 - \lambda^t) \right] \exp \left\{ -\mu_0 \left[\frac{1 - \lambda^t}{\log 1/\lambda} \right] \right\}$$

which is easily seen to be nonnegative for all t. The purchase contingency function is then

$$R(t) = \frac{f(t)}{1 - F(t)} = \mu_0 \lambda^t + \frac{\alpha(1 - \lambda^t)}{\beta + t \dfrac{1 - \lambda^t}{\log 1/\lambda}} \tag{8.49}$$

which has the derivative

$$R'(t) = -\mu_0 \lambda^t \log \frac{1}{\lambda} + \frac{\alpha \left(\beta + t - \dfrac{1 - \lambda^t}{\log 1/\lambda} \right) \lambda^t \log 1/\lambda - \alpha(1 - \lambda^t)^2}{\left(\beta + t - \dfrac{1 - \lambda^t}{\log 1/\lambda} \right)^2}$$

At $t = 0$, $R(t) = \mu_0$ and $R'(t)$ takes the sign of

$$\frac{\alpha}{\beta} - \mu_0 = E[\mu_*] - \mu_0$$

Thus the purchase contingency function for Model 2 takes off positively from $t = 0$ if the expected value of the equilibrium purchase propensity is greater than μ_0. This will always be the case if $\mu_0 = 0$, as suggested earlier. Equation 8.49 also shows that

$$\lim_{t \to \infty} R(t) = 0$$

Hence the purchase contingency function must turn down eventually, and so $R'(t) < 0$ for large t. It seems likely that, if $\mu_0 > E[\mu_*]$, then $R(t)$ will be monotonic decreasing just as was the case for the heterogeneous exponential.

Model 3: Heterogeneous μ_0 and μ_*. We now consider the case where both μ_0 and μ_* are to be regarded as varying over the population and only the learning rate parameter λ is regarded as homogeneous. This is the most realistic set of assumptions we have made with respect to the one-event learning model. It would be applicable to the analysis of cumulative penetration curves for second and subsequent triers of a

new product, for instance, even in cases where the assumption of homogeneous μ_0 would be appropriate for developing the distribution of time to first trial. In general, we would like to use Model 3 whenever the population has been exposed to heterogeneous stimuli prior to t_0 and we believe that all households may not react the same way to subsequent learning experiences. Unfortunately, however, our efforts to develop this doubly heterogeneous model have not led to a completely satisfactory representation of $F(t)$. The results to be presented here are acceptable on theoretical grounds but would appear to be too unwieldy to allow the efficient estimation of parameters.

We begin by rewriting our original Equation 8.43 for the waiting time distribution, given particular values for the initial and equilibrium purchase propensities

$$F(t|\mu_0,\mu_*) = 1 - \exp\left[-\left(\frac{1-\lambda^t}{\log 1/\lambda}\right)\mu_0\right]\exp\left\{-\left[t - \frac{(1-\lambda^t)}{\log 1/\lambda}\right]\mu_*\right\}$$

(8.50)

We will suppose that the distribution of μ_0 in the population is gamma with parameters α and β:

$$f(\mu_0|\alpha,\beta) = \frac{\beta^\alpha}{\Gamma(\alpha)}\exp(-\beta\mu_0)\mu_0^{\alpha-1}$$

(8.51)

just as in Model 1.

What assumptions about the distribution of μ_* are likely to be realistic? Clearly the distribution must cover only positive values, and we would like it to be able to assume a variety of shapes. This suggests that μ_* should be gamma distributed, as in Model 2. But there is one major complication. If we could pick one individual from the population and somehow observe his μ_0 value, this would certainly be expected to give us some information about his μ_*: people with high initial purchase propensities might be expected to have relatively high equilibrium propensities and conversely. Thus the distribution of μ_0 and μ_* should not be independent of each other.

There are many ways in which the distribution of μ_* can be made to depend on μ_0. We have chosen to assume that μ_* is gamma with parameters $(a + c\mu_0)$ and b. That is,

$$f(\mu_*|a,b,c,\mu_0) = \frac{b^{a+c\mu_0}}{\Gamma(a + c\mu_0)}\exp(-b\mu_*)\mu_*^{a+c\mu_0-1}$$

(8.52)

for which

$$E[\mu_*|\mu_0] = \frac{a + c\mu_0}{b}$$

and

$$\text{Var}[\mu_*|\mu_0] = \frac{a + c\mu_0}{b^2}$$

The parameter c is obviously a measure of the covariation of μ_0 and μ_*. This formulation has a measure of logic behind it, aside from the fact that the mean of μ_* varies linearly with the mean of μ_0. The parameter α of the gamma distribution, as written in Equation 8.51, represents the number of degrees of freedom of the distribution. That is, any gamma distribution for which α is integer can be derived by finding the sum of α independent and identically distributed exponential random variables; gammas with noninteger α are in effect interpolations between these successive sums. It seems to make sense to assume that the number of degrees of freedom for $f(\mu_*)$, and hence the general shape of the distribution should vary with the value of μ_0 associated with that member of the population. In contrast, β is essentially a scale parameter of the distribution. We are assuming that the scale of μ_*, that is, the units in which μ_* is measured, does not depend upon the household's initial purchase propensity.

To form the unconditional waiting time distribution we integrate μ_* and μ_0 from the conditional distribution, given by Equation 8.50. Starting with μ_*, we have

$$F(t|\mu_0) = \int_0^\infty F(t|\mu_0,\mu_*)f(\mu_*|a,b,c,\mu_0)\,d\mu_*$$

$$= 1 - \exp\left[-\left(\frac{1-\lambda^t}{\log 1/\lambda}\right)\mu_0\right]\frac{b^{a+c\mu_0}}{\Gamma(a+b\mu_0)}$$

$$\times \int_0^\infty \exp\left\{-\left[b+t-\frac{(1-\lambda^t)}{\log 1/\lambda}\right]\mu_*\right\}\mu_*^{a+c\mu_0-1}\,d\mu_*$$

$$= 1 - \exp\left[-\left(\frac{1-\lambda^t}{\log 1/\lambda}\right)\mu_0\right]b^{a+c\mu_0}\left[b+t-\frac{1-\lambda^t}{\log 1/\lambda}\right]$$

where the integration is the same as for Equation 8.47 in Model 2 and 8.44 in Model 1. Let

$$Q(t) = \frac{b}{b+t-\dfrac{1-\lambda^t}{\log 1/\lambda}} \tag{8.53}$$

Then the removal of the condition on μ_0 proceeds as follows:

$$F(t) = \int_0^\infty F(t|\mu_0)f(\mu_0|\alpha,\beta)\, d\mu_0$$

$$= 1 - \frac{\beta^\alpha}{\Gamma(\alpha)} \int_0^\infty Q(t)^{a+c\mu_0} \exp\left\{-\left[\beta + \frac{1-\lambda^t}{\log 1/\lambda}\right]\mu_0\right\}\mu_0^{\alpha-1}\, d\mu_0$$

$$= 1 - \frac{\beta^\alpha Q(t)^a}{\left[\beta + \dfrac{1-\lambda^t}{\log 1/\lambda}\right]^\alpha} \frac{\left[\beta + \dfrac{1-\lambda^t}{\log 1/\lambda}\right]^\alpha}{\Gamma(\alpha)} \int_0^\infty Q(t)^{c\mu_0}$$

$$\times \exp\left\{-\left[\beta + \frac{1-\lambda^t}{\log 1/\lambda}\right]\mu_0\right\}\mu_0^{\alpha-1}\, d\mu_0$$

where the last line is obtained by separating out $Q(t)^a$ and multiplying numerator and denominator by the factor raised to α. The term inside the brackets has the form of a gamma distribution with parameters α and $\beta + [(1-\lambda^t)/\log 1/\lambda]$, multiplied by $Q(t)^{c\mu_0}$. The integration can be performed by substituting the series expansion for $Q(t)^{c\mu_0}$:

$$Q(t)^{c\mu_0} = 1 + c\log Q(t)\mu_0 + \frac{[c\log Q(t)]^2}{2!}\mu_0^2 + \frac{[c\log Q(t)]^3}{3!}\mu_0^3 + \cdots$$

Except for constants, integration of the terms of the expansion yield the successive raw moments of the gamma distribution. That is,

$$F(t) = 1 - \frac{\beta^\alpha Q(t)^a}{\left[\beta + \dfrac{1-\lambda^t}{\log 1/\lambda}\right]^\alpha} \sum_{i=0}^\infty \frac{[c\log Q(t)]^i}{i!} \mathrm{E}_\gamma\left[\mu_0^i \Big| \alpha, \beta + \frac{1-\lambda^t}{\log 1/\lambda}\right]$$

For a gamma with parameters (u,v) the raw moments are[26]

$$\mathrm{E}_\gamma[\mu^0|u,v] = .1 \qquad \mathrm{E}_\gamma[\mu^2|u,v] = \frac{u(u+1)}{v^2}$$

$$\mathrm{E}_\gamma[\mu^1|u,v] = \frac{u}{v} \qquad \mathrm{E}_\gamma[\mu^3|u,v] = \frac{u(u+1)(u+2)}{v^3}$$

and so on. By invoking the relation $\Gamma(n+1) = n\Gamma(n)$, for $n > 0$, we have

$$F(t) = 1 - \frac{\beta^\alpha Q(t)^a}{\left[\beta + \dfrac{1-\lambda^t}{\log 1/\lambda}\right]^\alpha} \sum_{i=0}^\infty \frac{\Gamma(\alpha+i)}{i!\Gamma(\alpha)}\left[\frac{c\log Q(t)}{\beta + \dfrac{1-\lambda^t}{\log 1/\lambda}}\right]^i \qquad (8.54)$$

where $Q(t)$ is defined by Equation 8.53. Since $Q(t) \to 0$ as $t \to \infty$, it

[26] See Raiffa and Schlaifer (1961, Section 7.6.2).

appears that $F(t) \to 1$ with large t. At $t = 0$, the $Q(t) = 1$. Thus the first term in the sum is 1, all the others are zero, and the term outside the sum is $1.$[27] Hence $F(0) = 0$.

Analysis of the purchase contingency function (not given) shows that

$$R(0) = \frac{\alpha}{\beta}$$

$$\lim_{t \to \infty} R(t) = 0$$

as would be expected from our work with Models 1 and 2. While the exact conditions have not been worked out, it would appear that $R(t)$ might rise for a while given some parameter values and be monotonically decreasing for others. We conjecture that the relevant condition is the sign of:

$$E[\mu_*] - E[\mu_0], \quad \text{that is,} \quad \frac{a}{b} + \frac{c}{b}\frac{\alpha}{\beta} - \frac{\alpha}{\beta}$$

By analogy with Models 1 and 2, we would expect $R(t)$ to be rising at zero if the expected equilibrium purchase propensity is greater than the expected initial purchase propensity and conversely.

8.5 Summary

In this chapter we have discussed a variety of models that have been or might be used to describe the purchase incidence process. Most of our stress has been on purchase timing models that are couched in terms of the waiting time to the next purchase rather than number of purchases or total demand in a fixed time interval. There were two reasons for this.

(1) Purchase timing models can be translated into total demand models by applying the methods of Section 8.1.2. While these procedures would be somewhat unwieldly for the more complex models considered in this chapter, it is often possible to obtain the distribution of the number of purchases in a fixed time interval by Monte Carlo simulation. In addition, the theory of stochastic renewal processes can sometimes be used to get the approximate distribution of total demand during a long time interval from the parameters of a waiting time model. The calculations involved are quite simple where these methods can be used. This theory is reviewed and an example of the type of calculations required will be provided in Section 9.4.

(2) Purchase timing models can be used in situations where a total demand model would not be appropriate. The prime example of this

[27] There is some ambiguity in Equation 8.54 when $t = 0$. To avoid this we define $0^0 = 1$ so that the first term in the sum is unity regardless of t, as required by the expansion of $Q(t)$.

occurs in the case of new products. If we believe that usage of the new product is likely to have a great influence on the probability of making a subsequent purchase, we may wish to model behavior in each depth of repeat class separately. That is, we may wish to estimate parameters for nontriers separately from first-time triers, etc. A purchase timing model can easily be applied to such situations. In effect, the purchase timing model becomes a model of market penetration so far as these applications are concerned.[28]

In this chapter, we have reviewed the gamma-Poisson model, first considered by Ehrenberg (1959), the exponential and mixed exponential models, Fourt-Woodlock (1960) and Anscombe (1961), stationary and nonstationary homogeneous logistic models, Yance (1955), Massy (1960), and others, and various types of one-event linear learning models, first introduced by Haines (1964). We have interpreted these authors' works freely and offered numerous extensions to the basic models, particularly in the learning theory case.

Our efforts in this chapter have concentrated largely on developing expressions for: $\mu(t)$, the time path of an individual household's propensity to purchase; $F[t|\mu(t)]$, the conditional distribution of waiting time to next purchase given a particular purchase propensity function; $F(t)$, the unconditional distribution of waiting times for population members with unknown μ; and $R(t)$, the purchase contingency function, which represents the unconditional purchase likelihood for population members who have not purchased prior to time t. (All of these measures were defined In Section 8.1.2.) In addition, we have had occasion to consider various prior distributions for the parameters of $\mu(t)$ — primarily the initial and/or equilibrium purchase propensities. The prior distributions for the models of this chapter have either been binary (purchase-nonpurchase) distributions or, if μ is assumed to vary continuously over the population, a gamma distribution has been used. As noted earlier, our efforts have been devoted to developing the properties of the various models. Problems of parameter estimation were dealt with briefly in Section 8.1.3, pending a more complete discussion in the context of the STEAM model in Chapter 10. The properties of all of the models discussed in this chapter will be summarized again in Section 9.3.

---

[28] Two very interesting papers by Tarow Indow (1970a, b) have come to our attention. Both use what we have called purchase timing models to measure warranty card returns. Two models are given: one a negative exponential and one a Weibull, of the type to be discussed in Chapter 10. Some very useful results involving cascaded processes and Laplace transforms are presented.

CHAPTER 9
A STOCHASTIC MODEL FOR MONITORING
NEW PRODUCT ADOPTION

The number of new products introduced to the market each year is large and growing. Thousands of items have been added to the class of frequently purchased products alone during the past few years. While many of these newcomers represent modifications of products or brands already on the market, many of them are true innovations. Our notions about the definitions of certain product classes have had to undergo some revisions because of the large number of new product offerings that cannot be forced into one of the established molds.

Managers of new product introduction campaigns need information about how their product is doing in test markets and during the critical months after the beginning of national or regional distribution. Their needs are often greater than those of managers responsible for marketing established products because of the dynamic nature of the new product adoption process, the difficulty of obtaining reliable information from nonmarket sources, and the tremendous risks that are often connected with bringing out a new product.

The factors that increase the information needs of new product managers also make it difficult to provide such information. Workers in the field are familiar with the "humped" nature of the sales curves for many new products, for example. Sales rise as more and more consumers try the product (perhaps in response to an introductory offer) but then often taper off as repeat purchases become more and more scattered in time. This phenomenon is accentuated because of the effects of pipeline filling if factory rather than retail sales are monitored. Given that early sales trends are often poor predictors of eventual product performance, it has been necessary to develop methods for decomposing the aggregate sales curve by means of stochastic models describing the behavior of customers exposed to the new product during its introductory period.

The purpose of this chapter is to present another stochastic model that can be used to provide a practical description of the adoption process for new products. The output of the model is designed to provide forecasts of future purchase rates for the new product and statistics that can be used to diagnose the character of its demand trends. Like the

325

other models discussed in this book, this one is "data rich" in the sense that it is designed to exploit consumer panel data. These data are often collected as a normal part of the procedure by which test markets and new product introduction are monitored, so the model provides a very direct extension of current methods. However, we must not lose sight of the fact that stochastic models can be used to evaluate the implications of managers' "subjective beliefs" about the structure of demand. It is likely that market researchers will want to modify the parameter estimates obtained from data before committing them to a forecasting program. These possibilities were discussed at length in Chapter 1 and will not be repeated here, except to note that dynamic interaction between the manager, the researcher, the model, and the data will probably be particularly important in the context of the new product adoption process.

This chapter will present the intuitive justification and mathematical development for what we call our basic "*S*tochastic *E*volutionary *A*doption *M*odel" (hereafter denoted by the achronym "STEAM"). STEAM is very much like the evolutionary market penetration models discussed in Chapter 8. We use the nonstationary Poisson process to generate waiting times conditional on purchase propensity, involve a modified version of the familiar gamma prior distribution, and develop the usual kinds of expressions for $F(t)$, $f(t)$, and $R(t)$. While the assumptions leading to the time path for $\mu(t)$ are somewhat arbitrary compared to the diffusion and one-element learning assumption explored in Chapter 8, a great advantage of STEAM is that with certain parameter values it can approximate some of the characteristics of the Chapter 8 models at a considerable gain in simplicity. A second advantage is that certain calculations can be performed on the STEAM model that would be difficult or impossible with the more complex models (e.g., the determination of $F^{-1}(t)$ so that random purchase time can be calculated easily in a simulation and the fact that prior-posterior analysis on $\mu(t)$ is easily performed).[1] Third, we have succeeded in generalizing STEAM to include effects of advertising and promotion and purchases of other brands (see Chapter 11). While some of these extensions could be applied to the simpler Chapter 8 models, this has not yet been worked out. Finally, except for the Fourt-Woodlock model, STEAM is the only true stochastic model that seems likely to be put to use in practical business situations in the near future, and it is the only one for which the authors have developed substantial empirical experience.

[1] See Sections 9.2.5 and 9.2.6.

Section 9.1 will be devoted to a largely verbal description and justification of the assumptions that went into the STEAM model. This discussion will be in the context of what we know about the new product adoption process itself, rather than continuing in the more technical vernacular of Chapter 8. This will necessitate a restatement of some of our earlier results. A mathematical summary of the derivation and properties of the STEAM model will be given in Section 9.2. Section 9.3 will pick up the threads of Chapter 8 by providing a detailed comparison between STEAM and the purchase timing models considered previously. Chapter 10 gives a description of the sample likelihood and chi-square functions for STEAM and discusses some problems of parameter estimation. There we will outline a simulation procedure designed to provide forecasts of market penetration, based on STEAM. Empirical results obtained by applying this machinery to several new product introduction situations are also provided in Chapter 10. In Chapter 11 the mathematics of STEAM will be extended to allow consideration of purchases of compliment and substitute products during the adoption period; advertising, price, and other time-varying marketing variables; and descriptor variables such as socioeconomic and demographic factors or the results from preintroduction attitude and awareness studies on members of the test panel.

9.1 Introduction to STEAM

Specification of a stochastic model requires explicit hypotheses about the probability law that is believed to describe the behavioral process under study. A number of different laws, some stochastic and some not, will have to be specified in order to provide a reasonable model for the process of new product adoption. First, we introduce a primary model, representing the purchasing decisions of individual families in particular time intervals. Second, we develop a series of secondary models that describe the ways in which the parameters of the primary model vary from individual to individual, over time, and in response to certain classes of events. In combination, the primary and secondary models define a composite probability law for the new product adoption process, as seen in the aggregate. The latter is the most relevant for the business firm, at least from the forecasting point of view, since the firm is concerned with the total number of purchases made by all consumers. Nevertheless, the underlying primary and secondary models are important because they determine the properties of the composite probability law, provide means for judging its validity, and allow the use of

certain types of diagnostic procedures that are not available at the aggregate level.

9.1.1   Incidence of Purchase Events

Purchases are discrete events that occur in time. As such, they may be described in terms of a stochastic counting process of the type discussed by Parzen (1962, p. 117). The purpose of the model is to predict the number of events that will occur in a fixed time interval. More precisely, the stochastic process model defines the probability that the number of events which have been counted will be X_1 (say) at time t_1, given that it was X_0 at time t_0. The probability mass function over all possible values of X_1 is the probability law of the counting process, given the initial condition.

Our primary model for the occurrence of events will take the form of a stochastic counting process of the type discussed in Section 8.1.2. An *event* is defined as the occurrence of a purchase, regardless of the size of the purchase. That is, a *purchase* may involve one small package of the product or several large ones: it is always counted the same as far as STEAM is concerned. This treatment leads to significant simplifications in the mathematics of the probability model. Some reasons why it is appropriate for the new product adoption process are presented later.

The simplest and best known representation of a counting process is provided by the Poisson distribution:

$$P\{N(t) = x|\mu\} = \exp(-\mu t)\frac{(\mu t)^x}{x!} \qquad x \geq 0 \qquad (9.1)$$

The random variable $N(t)$ is defined as the number of counts and the parameter μ is the mean rate of occurrence of the counts in the interval $[0,t]$. Note that the Poisson probability function does not depend on the number of counts that have been observed prior to t_0.

The Poisson distribution is known to be appropriate for describing a stochastic process with the following general characteristics. See Parzen (1962, p. 118).

1. Since we begin counting events at time 0, we define $N(0) = 0$.
2. The process has independent increments; that is, the random variable $N(t)$ is independent of $N(t + h) - N(t)$ for all values of t and h.
3. For any $t > 0$, $0 < P[N(t) > 0] < 1$; that is, in any interval (no

matter how small), there is a positive probability that an event will occur, but it is not certain that an event will occur.

4. For any time $t \geq 0$

$$\lim_{h \to 0} \frac{P[N(t + h) - N(t) \geq 2]}{P[N(t + h) - N(t) \geq 1]} = 0$$

that is, at most one event can occur in sufficiently small intervals.

The Poisson process formed the basis for the negative binomial and mixed exponential models that were considered in Section 8.2. We agree with Ehrenberg (1959), who argues that the process provides a reasonable first approximation to the counting process for many kinds of purchase events. To fix ideas, let us examine the specific characteristics given earlier in the context of purchasing behavior.

Suppose that the product in question is a new variety of TV dinner, for example. Many families tend to use TV dinners on certain types of occasions, as when some members of the family are absent and it is not convenient to cook a regular meal for the rest. Suppose that these use opportunities occur relatively infrequently and at irregular intervals. Each time one does occur the housewife chooses from among the available selection of TV dinners on a shopping trip just prior to the anticipated event. We will ignore the possibility that she will "stock up" periodically and maintain her own freezer inventories for a considerable period of time before use. The number of opportunities for using TV dinners is very large — in a sense the family is "exposed" to the possibility of eating them almost every day. Yet the actual number of days on which this particular delicacy is served will usually be small. Hence the probability of purchasing TV dinners on any given shopping trip is also small.

The axioms of the Poisson process are fulfilled in this example. The number of opportunities for purchase is large and the probability of making a purchase on any given exposure is small. Thus there is a chance of making a purchase any time, but there is no certainty of making one in any finite time interval. Furthermore, the nature of the process that generates use opportunities suggests that the occurrences of consumption events are stochastically independent. That is, the fact that TV dinners are served on Monday may neither enhance nor inhibit the chances that they will be served again on Tuesday or Wednesday, at least to a first approximation. Neglecting the problem of "stocking up," this implies that purchase decisions for TV dinners are also stochastically independent and that a consumer is equally likely

to make a purchase on a given shopping trip whether or not she made one on the previous trip or any trip before that. This meets the independent increments requirement of the Poisson process. Even when consumers normally hold some inventories of a product, the assumption of stochastic independence tends to become more and more appropriate as the mean interval between purchases increases relative to the average length of the inventory holding period. For example, suppose that a family purchases cream cheese at irregular intervals, on the average of four times a year. Since cream cheese must be used up within about a week, the fact that further purchases of the product will be inhibited during the time it takes to consume the quantity bought on the last occasion is not likely to affect seriously the purchase probabilities on subsequent trips. (The Poisson model might also be modified to allow a fixed "dead time" between purchases, as will be suggested later.)

The last requirement of the Poisson model is easily accommodated. Since we define a purchase to include any quantity of the product or brand in question bought on a given shopping trip, it is not hard to accept the idea that two such events cannot occur simultaneously. A method for reintroducing the amount purchased into the analysis for purposes of making forecasts of sales volumes will be presented in Section 10.2, but the problem will not be considered further here.

Let us return to the problem of representing the occurrence of purchases of a new variety of TV dinner by means of a stochastic process. We have argued that the counting process for purchases of TV dinners meet the conditions of the Poisson process but have not linked this with the new brand taken by itself. Suppose that the housewife's preferences for different kinds of TV dinners can be represented by a vector of probabilities. If the probability that she will choose our particular brand, given that she has decided to buy TV dinners in general, remains constant over the interval from t_0 to t, then the occurrence of purchases of our brand can also be described by a Poisson process. It can be shown that:

$$P\{N(t) = x | v, \eta\} = \exp{(-v\eta t)} \frac{(v\eta t)^x}{x!} \qquad (9.2)$$

where $N(t)$ = number of purchases of Brand A in $(0,t)$, and η = mean purchase rate for TV dinners, and v = probability of purchase Brand A, given that some brand is going to be bought.

The composite parameter $(v\eta)$ thus represents the mean purchase rate for Brand A and is equivalent to the "μ" of Equation 9.1. It is worth

noting that an assumption of stability for the probability element v denies the existence of either learning or evolutionary effects. That is, relative preferences for Brand A are not affected by product usage or exposure to promotion. The same assumptions apply to the process that generates use opportunities for TV dinners in general, as summed up by the mean use rate η. (The introduction of secondary models will relax these restrictions.)

The user of panel data will not be able to observe the incidence of *use opportunities* directly. However, if the product class in question is well defined, one may count all purchases of any brand or variety of product and thus produce estimates of the mean realized usage rate parameter η. The share of these purchases devoted to Brand A then provides an estimate of the choice probability v. Often brand share figures suffice for the purposes of analyzing consumer preferences, in which case there is no need to consider the counting process at all. On the other hand, the methods discussed in this paper are designed to apply to situations where the class of use opportunities is not well enough defined to permit observation of total usage through panel data. One advantage of our approach is that even where the boundaries of the product class are not clear, it is still possible to deal with models couched in terms of the composite parameter μ. Since this represents the use rate for the new product or variety directly, it is possible to proceed without depending upon any notion of product class. (Of course it is not possible to obtain separate estimates of v and η in this case.) We have argued in Section 8.1.1 that this last situation tends to be the rule rather than the exception where new products are concerned.

9.1.2 Distribution of Interpurchase Times

The primary model given above represents the probability law for the number of purchases made by a given family in a particular interval of time. As is apparent from Chapter 8, however, it will be more convenient to consider the distribution of the length of time between one purchase and the next rather than the distribution of the number of purchases occurring during a fixed time interval.

In order to develop an expression for the distribution of waiting times to the next trial, we will have to take into account the fact that an individual's purchase propensity will in general change over time. Using the notation of Chapter 8, we write the time path of purchase propensity as $\mu(t)$; the form of this function will be made explicit in Section 9.1.3. Thus we have what is known as a *nonhomogeneous Poisson process*.

(In the present context, nonhomogeneous refers to time. Our model is also nonhomogeneous over families because of the mixed population assumption to be introduced later.) The distribution of waiting times for the nonhomogeneous Poisson process can be written as follows [e.g., Parzen (1962), p. 125].

$$F(t) = 1 - \exp[-m(t)]$$
$$f(t) = \exp[-m(t)]\mu(t) \qquad (9.3)$$

where t is the waiting time to the next purchase. The expression $m(t)$ is called the *mean value function* of the nonhomogeneous Poisson process; it is defined as

$$m(t) = \int_0^t \mu(x)\, dx$$

Equation 9.3 can be derived by means of the methods of Chapter 8. Write

$$\Pr[\mathscr{P} \in (t, t+h)|\tilde{\mathscr{P}} \in (t_0, t)] = \frac{F(t+h) - F(t)}{1 - F(t)} = h\mu(t)$$

$$\frac{F(t+h) - F(t)}{h} \cdot \frac{1}{1 - F(t)} = \frac{dF(t)}{dt}\frac{1}{1 - F(t)} = \mu(t)$$

This differential equation may be solved by separation of variables

$$\int \frac{dF(t)}{1 - F(t)} = \int \mu(t)\, dt$$
$$-\log[1 - F(t)] = m(t)$$
$$F(t) = 1 - \exp[-m(t)]$$

where the last result is obtained by applying the initial condition $F(0) = 0$ and noting that $m(0) = 0$. This is the same as Equation 9.3.

9.1.3 Time Path of Purchase Propensity

The idea that the purchase propensity function $\mu(t)$ may vary during the interval prior to a household's next purchase is already familiar. The logistic and one-event linear learning models developed in Chapter 8 were based on particular assumptions about the forces that lead to changes in $\mu(t)$. The "independent elements" and "contagious elements" probability diffusion models of Chapter 6 represent another set of possible assumptions. Still other relations are clearly possible, and it is likely that a variety of forces will be operating on a given consumer during any time interval.

It would appear that most of these forces would be included in the following list of determinants of the time change process for purchase propensity:

1. Learning to like or dislike the product through cumulative exposures to advertising, distribution, and word of mouth. The logistic process of Section 8.3 provides one representation for the word of mouth effect, while the one-event linear learning model of Section 8.4 is relevant for other types of exposure-based driving forces.

2. Attitude change because of internal processes as well as external influences. The probability diffusion models of Chapter 6 are relevant here. Also included in this category would be loss of saliency with respect to the product as the time since the last purchase increases. This has been called a "forgetting effect." It has been investigated empirically by Kuehn (1962), Herniter (1965), and Morrison (1966a).

3. Changes in the market environment, which directly affect the possibility or ease of purchasing the product. An example of this would be a loss of distribution for the product at the customer's favorite store. Positive effects caused by special promotions or deals could be included in the category, as they affect the short run market environment rather than contributing only to the general or long-run learning effect envisaged in Item 1 above.

4. Effects due to competition, including special promotion and consumer learning caused by actual purchase of competitive products.

5. Seasonal and other exogeneous factors that affect use opportunity for the new product.

Items 1 and 2 normally lead to fairly smooth shifts in purchase propensities over time. We shall attempt to represent them in the STEAM model. The effects of Items 3 and 4 may be fairly sharp in that they can cause a notable short run shift or even a discontinuity in the time path for $\mu(t)$. We will neglect the problem of sharp shifts here but take them up in Chapter 11. Item 5 will not be important for most products where the expected growth in demand is large compared to the seasonal. Where significant, a seasonal can be handled by preliminary operations on the data, or else included in the model by the methods developed for advertising and promotion effects in Chapter 11.

Our specific assumption is that $\mu(t)$ varies geometrically with the time since the last purchase of the new product. That is,

$$\mu(t) = \mu_0 t^\lambda \qquad \text{for } t \geq t_0 = 1 \tag{9.4}$$

The adoption of this relation requires us to set our time origin at one

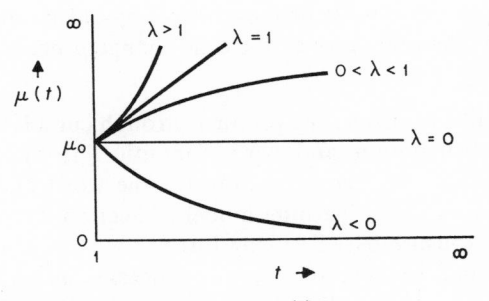

Figure 9.1.   Possible time paths for $\mu(t)$.

rather than 0, as has been done in all the models so far. Given this restriction, $\mu(t)$ takes on one of the family of paths shown in Figure 9.1. At $t = 1$, $\mu(t) = \mu_0$; then $\mu(t)$ rises or falls depending on the value of λ. If we had not started t at one, there would be no common origin μ_0.

If λ is fairly close to zero (either positive or negative), Equation 9.4 can approximate the time paths of $\mu(t)$ for the semilogistic process, given by Equation 8.25, and the one-element learning model given by Equation 8.40. Both functions have a fixed asymptote; but for small λ, Equation 9.4 will produce enough "stretchout" to provide a fairly good fit for reasonable values of t. At small values of t, Equation 9.4 would seem to stand somewhere between the semilogistic, for which the degree of initial curvature of $\mu(t)$ is usually small, and the one-element learning model, for which it is fairly large.

Equation 9.4 can also be viewed as a representation of the "forgetting function" noted in Item 2. We have argued that consumers have relative preference for different ways of satisfying their needs and that the new product represents one way of responding to these needs when they arise. As noted in connection with Equation 9.2, the needs are considered to be use opportunities which may arise more or less at random with rate η, while the families relative preferences are summed up by the probability element v. It is reasonable to assume that the latter variable will change as the period since the last time a similar use opportunity was satisfied increases. Since we cannot observe the timing of use opportunities that do not elicit purchases of the new product, however, we have to assume that the relevant time interval is the time since the last purchase of the new product itself. The latter assumes that the probability of choosing the new product when a use opportunity arises declines as the length of time since the last trial of the new product increases. Since the probability element v is not observable in the

absence of methods for defining use opportunities, our model must be framed in terms of the composite measure μ. This will also allow for interactions between time since trial of the new product and the process that generates use opportunities, if any should exist. These assumptions lead to Equation 9.4, but this time with $\lambda < 0$. While the lower asymptote of the forgetting process is zero, compared to the market and advertising share asymptotes reported for established products by Kuehn (1962) and Herniter (1965), respectively, this may not be inappropriate in the case of new products where total rejection is a possibility.

9.1.4 Purchase Event Feedback

The act of purchasing and using any item in the product class is likely to affect the family's assessment of relative preference for the various brands (leading to change in ν), the mean rate at which the product class is consumed (leading to a change in η), or both. Representations of this kind of learning for established products were discussed in Chapter 5, where the two-element linear learning model was developed. We believe that learning is likely to be an important component in the process of new product adoption but doubt that the linear model is applicable to the situation where both ν and η are subject to change.

A major simplification is available when we consider learning in the context of the adoption of really new products. It seems plausible to assume that the largest learning effect occurs in connection with the purchase and use of the new member of the product class. While use of older alternatives may continue to affect subsequent purchasing behavior, it seems likely that the impact of new experience with respect to the innovation will swamp the learning effects due to using the older products, at least for awhile. Thus we are justified in neglecting learning effects due to purchases of other items in the product class. Indeed, this course of action may be required when we deal with product classes that are not well defined, since in that case it is difficult to monitor purchases besides those of the particular new product under study.

It is difficult to formulate a reasonable model for representing the effect of purchases of the new product on the parameter of the primary counting model. It seems likely that trial will tend to increase usage rates if consumers like the product. On the other hand, the possibility of trial followed by rejection is much more likely in the new product context than in the case of many of the established products studied by Kuehn; this

would imply that μ could decline with use. Finally, the effects of increased experience are not necessarily monotonic. Cases where several trials are required before the consumer accepts or rejects the product are quite common. It is not unusual to find that μ will increase after the first four or five purchases and then decrease. In fact, this is the rule rather than the exception with "fad" products. Unfortunately, it is often very difficult to determine the extent to which early acceptance of new products is "fadish." This often represents one of the primary purposes of consumer research in the new product context. The considerations given here imply that the effect of learning on μ will not always be linear or exponential. A quadratic form is the minimum for describing fadishness, and even that would seem to be rather restrictive.

We shall handle the problem of learning by assuming that a different prior distribution of μ exists for families who have made different numbers of purchases of the new product. The panel data can be stratified by depth of trial class, and the values of α and β in Equation 9.6 estimated separately for each stratum. Thus the form of the learning effect can be inferred after the fact from the series of $E(\mu)$ and $Var(\mu)$ for the various depth of trial groups. The fact that stratification by depth of trial class is a familiar device to workers in the new product research field makes the above procedure particularly attractive.

Effects of learning have been considered in connection with the mixed Poisson models of accident occurrences mentioned earlier. Workers in this field use the term *contagion* as synonomous with learning, implying that the occurrence of one accident changes the probability that the individual in question will have more accidents. This terminology is confusing, because Frank (1962), adopting the language of the mathematical sociologists, has used contagion in a very different sense when attacking Kuehn's models. Bates and Neyman (1952), Arbous and Kerrich (1951) and others discuss the possibility of positive, negative, and irregular contagion. Models for monotonic contagion have been discussed in the accident literature, e.g., models based on the Polya scheme, but no operational methods for dealing with the problem of irregular contagion have been presented. In the previous paragraph we argued that, in the context of new product adoption at least, consumer learning is likely to be a process of irregular contagion.

9.1.5   Population Heterogeneity

Purchase rates have been assumed to occur at random according to a nonstationary Poisson counting process, but so far nothing has been

specified about how the process varies across members of the population. The time path of purchase propensity for a given household, as given in Equation 9.4 depends upon two parameters. We will assume that the initial conditions in each depth of repeat class, the μ_0, are subject to population heterogeniety but that the time change parameter λ is not. This is in the same spirit as the various heterogeneous linear learning models discussed in Section 8.4.

From Chapter 8 it is apparent that the gamma distribution provides a convenient representation of the prior probability density for the parameter μ of a Poisson process. Anscombe (1961) and Ehrenberg (1959) use the gamma to obtain the gamma-exponential distribution of interpurchase time and the negative binomial distribution for numbers of purchases, respectively. We will also use the gamma density as part of our population heterogeneity assumption in STEAM.

Chatfield, Ehrenberg, and Goodhardt (1966) point out that the negative binomial fails to fit the tails of the empirical frequency function for numbers of purchases in a fixed time interval for many populations.[2] The main problem seems to be with the class of nonpurchasers or, in other words, the determination of the "relevant population" which represents the purchasing potential for the product in question.

We believe that these empirical difficulties stem from the fact that the gamma is a unimodal distribution. If there is a large group of households with purchase propensities at or near zero, the gamma will tend to take an exponential form with a large tail at zero. This will prevent the distribution of μ from having another peak at some $\mu > 0$, which may not represent the real situation. If the "zero group" is large enough, it will dominate the fitted gamma, which will go to zero very fast as μ increases. Thus the proportion of the population with large μ will probably be underestimated, which tends to account for the "variance discrepancy" noted by Chatfield et al. (1966).

These difficulties would likely disappear (or at least be greatly reduced in significance) if we could apply our gamma heterogeneity assumption only to the "relevant population." Those in the population who are strictly nonsmokers would be eliminated from a study of cigarette purchase incidence, for instance. The problem is, how can we determine the "relevant population?" Surely all those that do in fact purchase are members, but so are some of those who do not purchase in a particular interval. The latter condition occurs because purchase incidence is assumed to be a random process; even households with fairly large μ

---

[2] See Section 8.2.1.

can be expected to fail to purchase some fraction of the time. Thus we must find a way to partition the nonpurchasing groups.[3]

Therefore, we are led to make the following assumption about the distribution of initial purchase propensities:

$$\Pr[\mu_0 > 0] = M$$
$$f(\mu_0|\mu > 0) = \text{gamma } (\alpha, \beta)$$
(9.5)

This asserts that a proportion $1 - M$ of the population have $\mu_0 = 0$ and hence are to be excluded from the "relevant population," while the remaining members have μ distributed according to a gamma distribution with parameters α and β. One possible form for this compound distribution is shown in Figure 9.2, along with the form that would probably be fitted if M were to be left out of the model.

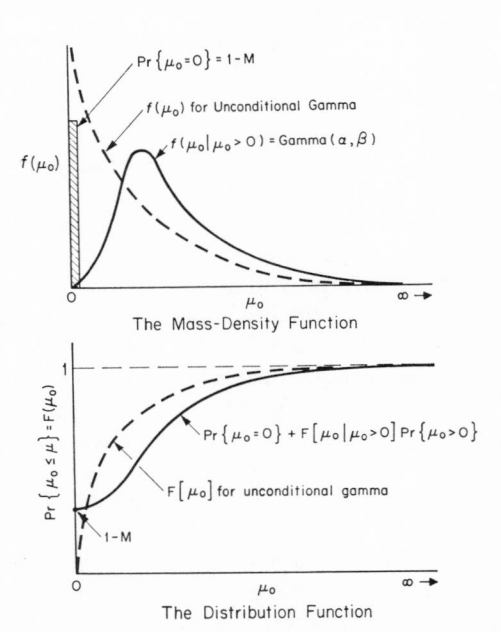

Figure 9.2. Hypothetical density and distribution functions for conditional and unconditional gamma heterogeneity assumptions.

[3] Chatfield, Ehrenberg, and Goodhardt (1966) report that the negative binomial seriously underestimates the proportion of households making no purchases, when it is fit to data on the purchasing population only. This phenomenon is a direct result of the fact that the relevant population does include some nonpurchasers.

The mean and variance of the gamma distribution parameterized as in Equation 8.9 have already been given. Hence,[4]

$$E[\mu_0|\mu_0 > 0] = \frac{\alpha}{\beta} \qquad E[\mu_0] = M\frac{\alpha}{\beta}$$

$$\text{Var}[\mu_0|\mu_0 > 0] = \frac{\alpha}{\beta^2} \qquad \text{Var}[\mu_0] = \frac{\alpha M}{\beta^2}[1 + \alpha - \alpha M] \tag{9.6}$$

The parameters α, β, and M are to be estimated from the data.

This set of assumptions amounts to combining the two mixed exponential models discussed by Anscombe (1961) and reviewed in Section 8.2.2. We will see that the provision of an $M < 1$ introduces an upper asymptote on the new product penetration curve; that is, the proportion $1 - M$ of households with $\mu_0 = 0$ never purchase the product. Equation 9.5 could be applied to any of the models of Chapter 8 with similar results.

9.1.6 Time of Conversion Effects

By estimating the parameters of the prior distribution of μ_0 separately for each depth of trial class, we are assuming that purchase propensities are likely to be systematically related to the number of previous purchases of the new product made by the household in question. We may also inquire as to whether the timing of the previous purchases might have an effect on μ_0. The answer to this question is "yes," as can been seen from the following example.

Suppose that we have only two groups of families in the population: one group with high initial purchase rates for the new product and one with low initial rates. We begin observing the population at the time the new product is introduced and find that some families make their first purchase early, others make theirs late, and still others never purchase the new product at all. Given the Poisson model, it can be shown that while it is possible for a family with a small value of μ to be among the early adopters, the majority of members of this group will have the higher initial purchase rates. The converse is true for members of the late adopter and diehard (disinterested) groups. We now inquire about the probable distribution of μ after one trial of the product. If a family's assessment of the product's attributes after use is positively correlated

---

[4] $\text{Var}[\mu_0] = E[\mu_0^2] - E[\mu_0]^2 = E[\mu_0|\mu_0 > 0]M - E[\mu_0|\mu_0 > 0]M^2$

$$= \frac{\alpha(\alpha + 1)M}{\beta^2} - \frac{\alpha^2}{\beta^2}M^2 = \frac{\alpha M}{\beta^2}[1 + \alpha - \alpha M]$$

with his prior assessment, as seems likely for many products, we should expect to find that the mean of the distribution describing post-trial preferences would be larger for people who converted from the "0" to the "1" depth of trial class soon after the product was introduced than for those who waited for a considerable period of time. This would be true because members of the former group would tend to have had larger initial μ than members of the latter. The process just described is related to the one discussed by Frank (1962), who demonstrated the results of self-selection on the interpretation of brand loyalty behavior. However, we must not forget that in the present case the effects of self-selection are moderated by the existence of the learning phenomenon.

It is possible to allow for the effect of conversion time in at least two ways. First, we could adopt the same procedure we used in the case of learning — that is, to stratify the members of each depth of trial class according to the time at which they entered the class (time of last conversion) and make separate estimates of α, β, and M for each stratum. The cross-classification scheme would be set up as shown in Figure 9.3.

Membership in class a_{ij} Implies that the family entered the ith depth of trial class (i.e., made his ith purchase of the product) in the jth time interval. The same family can be a member of different cells of the table during the new product adoption process. For example, Family A in the figure is represented as being exposed to the new product for the first time in January, making its first purchase in February, and its second and third purchases in March and April, respectively. Family B was also exposed in January but did not make its first purchases until March; then it made two more purchases in March and entered the "four purchase" class in April. Finally, Family C was not exposed to

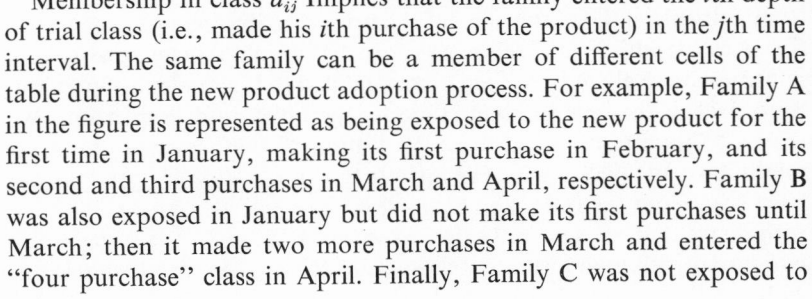

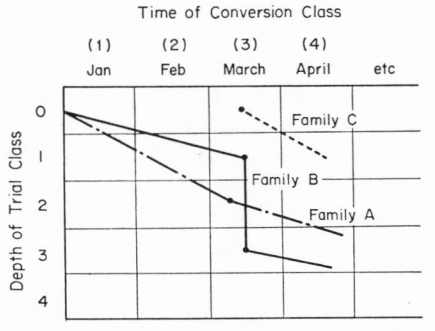

Figure 9.3.   Cross-classification format for representing the effects of conversion time.

the product until March; this might be a case where the family moved into the territory or where the brand was introduced into a new market area at that time. The general rule for tracing families through the table is that any cell can be entered from a cell in the next higher row that is either above or to the left of the cell in question. The relevant classification criterion is the time at which the family *entered* the depth of trial class; once in a class the family stays in the given cell (and does not move to the right) until the next purchase is recorded.

The approach described here will be called the *cross-classification procedure* for handling the effects of conversion time. It is completely flexible in the sense of allowing all types of relations between learning and time effects to be represented, subject to the restriction that the conversion times be grouped into discrete classes. Of course the classes can be defined as desired (months would probably be too short for many products). An additional restriction is implied by the fact that only the time of *last* repeat is considered in the analysis, though it seems likely that this is sufficient for most problems. The main problems of the cross-classification method is that it requires large quantities of data and necessitates many separate estimations of parameters. Given that the same family enters many cells and the class widths can be adjusted to alter the total number of cells, these problems are not necessarily insurmountable.

Another method for handling time of conversion effects is to incorporate them directly into our mathematical structure by means of another secondary model. Suppose that the ith family in our sample makes his kth purchase at time t. Let us represent this family's "time of conversion" to the kth depth of trial class by τ_{ki}, which will be defined as

$$\tau_{ki} = t - \tau_{k0} + 1$$

where τ_{k0} represents data on the "time origin" of the kth depth of trial class as will be discussed later. Recall that we are concerned with the prior distribution of purchase probabilities for each depth of trial class. (These probabilities apply to households in the kth class, though they actually refer to the upcoming $k + 1$ purchase.)

Effect on the parameters of $f(\mu_0|\mu_0 > 0)$. We shall assume that the parameter of the conditional gamma prior distribution depends on τ in the following manner:

$$\alpha(\tau) = \alpha_0 \tau^\gamma \qquad \tau \geq 1 \tag{9.7}$$

where α_0 and γ are new parameters to be estimated from the data. The initial condition parameter α_0 (the value of $\alpha(\tau)$ when $\gamma = 1$) will be

written simply as α to simplify notation in the sequel, and the indices k and i are to be understood wherever this or similar expressions are used. The restriction on τ is implied by the definition given here; it is required in order to provide a fixed initial condition for $\alpha(\tau)$. Equation 9.7 is of the same form as Equation 9.4, which was plotted in Figure 9.1.

This formulation provides a flexible monotonic representation for the effect of conversion time (τ) on the conditional prior distribution that is to be applied to families in a given depth of repeat class. The mean of this distribution is assumed to be α_0/β for households that enter the class at the earliest possible time; then it changes with $\alpha(\tau)/\beta$, proportional to one of the paths given in Figure 9.1. The arguments given earlier suggest that $\alpha > 0$ if the correlation between purchase propensities before and after the kth trial is positive. If using the product produces some kind of disappointment, however, α might be negative. In any event, we would expect $-1 < \alpha < 1$ to avoid explosive behavior. Finally, we should note that there is no strong reason for assuming that it is α, not β, that depends on τ. Some properties of the converse assumption will be explored in Chapter 11.

We now consider the "time origin" parameter. The value of τ_{k0} will determine how much Equation 9.7 departs from linearity, given the actual conversion times for households in the kth depth of trial class. If τ_{k0} is very small relative to the actual conversion times, for instance, the differences between the computed τ for different households will be small and the function $\alpha(\tau)$ will tend to be fairly linear for $-1 < \alpha < 1$. As can be seen from Figure 9.1, the maximum curvature $\alpha(\tau)$ occurs for small values of τ.

The determination of τ_{00} is generally no problem, because the date of introduction for the new product is known.[5] For higher depth of trial classes, however, the determination of τ_{k0} involves some ambiguity. One possibility is to set τ_{k0} equal to t_0, the time of introduction for the new product. Another is to set it at the time at which the first few households enter the kth class. If the potential usage rate for the product is known, a third possibility is to set τ_{k0} at t_0 plus k times this rate. For example, a product that would usually be used up in a week might be expected to

---

[5] If all households are in the same market area τ_{00} will be the same for everyone and Equation 9.7 will drop out of the model. If different markets are opened at different times, as would be the case in a "rollout" operation, τ_{00} can be taken as the starting date in the area in which the household resides. Here the effect of Equation 9.7 would have to be interpreted in terms of roll out time rather than time of conversion. In other applications, τ_{00} might be taken as the time at which the household receives an introductory offer, its favorite store first stocks the product, or other kinds of starting dates.

be repurchased once in two weeks, twice in three weeks, etc. — assuming that a household "adopts" the product immediately. Actual conversion times could then be taken as differences from this norm. (Households that convert prior to τ_{k0} would have their τ set to one arbitrarily.) Alternative three is probably the best from a theoretical standpoint, since alternative one may produce τ_{k0} that are very small relative to the actual conversion times while alternative two tends to place too great a reliance on what may be a few relatively unstable random variables — the actual conversion times of the first few households to enter the depth of trial class. If the pace of the initial conversions to the higher depth of trial classes is fairly rapid, however, the particular method used to determine τ_{k0} will be relatively unimportant. This does appear to be the case for the general class of new grocery products.

Effect on $\Pr[\mu_0 > 0]$. The mathematics of the STEAM model produce much more stringent constraints on the admissible form of the relation between the probability that $\mu_0 > 0$ and time of conversion than was the case for the parameters of $f(\mu_0|\mu_0 > 0)$. For instance, the obvious (and apparently trivial) relation

$$M_\tau = M \qquad \text{for all } \tau$$

does not lead to simple estimation procedures. (This will be shown in Section 10.1, where maximum likelihood estimators are discussed.) Thus our freedom of choice is reduced considerably. The formulations to be discussed here are members of what appears to be a fairly small class of admissible relations. Fortunately, both lead to identical estimates for the other parameters of the model, so it is not too important to distinguish between them.

To set ideas, let us write the following expression for the probability of purchase during the interval (t_0, T) where T is the maximum time covered by the available data. For each value of τ we have,

$$\Pr[\mathscr{P} \in (t_0, T)|\tau] = \Pr[\mathscr{P} \in (t_0, T)|\mu_0 > 0, \tau]\Pr[\mu_0 > 0|\tau]$$

$$+ \Pr[\mathscr{P} \in (t_0, T)|\mu_0 = 0, T]\Pr[\mu_0 = 0]$$

$$= F[T|\mu_0 > 0, \tau]M_\tau \qquad (9.8)$$

where $F[T|\mu_0 > 0]$ is the value of the distribution function for the waiting time to the next purchase, given that $\mu_0 > 0$. (Of course $\Pr[\mathscr{P} \in (t_0, T)|\mu_0 = 0] = 0$.) The expression for $F[T|\mu_0 > 0]$ will be developed in Section 9.2; it depends on α, β, λ, and γ, as well as the value of τ, for the depth of repeat class in question.

Now, it is possible to allow M_τ to be estimated separately for each

value of τ by equating 9.8 to the empirical proportion of purchasers for the τ class. That is, we set

$$E[\text{proportion of purchasers}] = F[T|\mu_0 > 0; \tau]M_\tau \to P_\tau \quad (9.9)$$

for each τ class. In effect, this allows each M_τ to be determined by P_τ and τ once α, β, λ, and γ have been estimated — that is, M is a free parameter in each τ class. (In Section 10.1, we will show that under this assumption the likelihood for the whole parameter vector $\theta = [\alpha, \beta, \lambda, \gamma, M_1, M_2, \ldots]$ is separable and that the above procedure permits maximum likelihood estimates for all parameters, including the M.)

The above setup can be generalized. Indeed, any formulation in which $F[T|\mu_0 > 0, \tau]M_\tau$ is equal to an expression where α, β, λ, and γ do not interact with the particular τ class will lead to a tractable likelihood function. Equation 9.9 meets this requirement since P_τ does not involve any parameters. Other possibilities are

$$F[T|\mu_0 > 0; \tau]M_\tau = \bar{P}$$

where $\bar{P}$ is the overall empirical proportion of purchasers for the population as a whole (i.e., aggregated over τ classes), and

$$F[T|\mu_0 > 0; \tau]M_\tau = M \sum_\tau \omega_\tau F[T|\mu_0 > 0, \tau] \quad (9.10)$$

where ω_τ is the proportion of sample households in the τ class. The summation over τ on the right side of Equation 9.10 can be viewed as removing the τ condition in F, which yields

$$F[T|\mu_0 > 0; \tau]M_\tau = F[T|\mu_0 > 0]M \approx \bar{P}$$

This suggests that the two possibilities given earlier are equivalent. (This will be proved in Section 10.1.2.) Equation 9.10 assumes, in effect, that the probability of finding a purchaser in the interval (t_0, T) is the same for all τ classes. This assumption is not particularly realistic but, as noted, it leads to exactly the same estimate for α, β, λ, and γ as are obtained from Equation 9.9. We take these results as indicating that a wide range of assumptions about the relations of the M_τ to one another are possible without upsetting the basic characteristics of the STEAM model.

For purposes of empirical analysis, we will adopt the free parameter assumption, Equation 9.9. Where appropriate, we will report "average" values of M, which will be calculated according to

$$\bar{M} = \sum_\tau \omega_\tau M_\tau = \sum_\tau \frac{\omega_\tau P_\tau}{F[T|\mu_0 > 0, \tau]} \quad (9.11)$$

9.2 Properties of STEAM

9.2.1 Review of Specifications

Let us review the specifications of the STEAM model, as given in Sections 9.1.1 through 9.1.6, in terms of a consistent set of notation.
For each depth of trial class, we have

Primary model for interpurchase times:

$$f[t|\mu(\cdot)] = \exp\,[-m(t)]\mu(t) \tag{9.12}$$

where

$$m(t) = \int_1^t \mu(x)\,dx$$

Secondary model for time changes in purchase propensity:

$$\mu(t) = \mu_0 t^\lambda \qquad t \geq 1 \tag{9.13}$$

Secondary model for population heterogeneity:

$$\Pr[\mu_0 > 0|\tau] = M_r$$
$$f(\mu_0|\mu_0 > 0, \tau) = \frac{\beta\,\exp\,(-\beta\mu_0)(\beta\mu_0)^{\alpha(\tau)-1}}{\Gamma[\alpha(\tau)]} \tag{9.14}$$

Secondary model for time of conversion:

$$\alpha(\tau) = \alpha_0 \tau^\gamma \qquad \tau \geq 1$$
$$\bar{M} = \sum_\tau \frac{P_r \omega_r}{F[T|\mu_0 > 0, \tau]} \tag{9.15}$$

Effects of purchase event feedback are taken care of by applying the model to data for each depth of trial class separately.

The STEAM model is built around two random variables, which are defined as follows:

$t =$ The time between a household's entry in a given depth of trial class and its conversion to the next class: that is, an interpurchase time.

$\mu_0 =$ The initial purchase propensity for a given household. Once determined, the value of μ_0 determines the entire time path of purchase propensities $\mu(t)$.

The model contains five or more free parameters, depending upon whether or not the constraint given in Equation 9.10 is applied to the M_r. Alternatively, we may report $\bar{M}$ as a parameter of the process, even where the individual M_r are allowed to float free. In the latter case we

have the parameter vector:

$$\boldsymbol{\theta}_k = \{\alpha, \beta, \lambda, \gamma, \overline{M}\}_k \qquad (9.16)$$

for the kth depth of trial class. This will be taken as the parameter vector for STEAM, unless otherwise noted. We recall that the parameters are defined as follows:

$\lambda = $ The rate at which a household's purchase propensity changes with time since its last purchase. The model requires $-1 < \lambda$. For $\lambda < 0$ the expected purchase rate declines with time, and conversely. In any case $\lambda < 1$ to avoid explosive behavior.

$\beta = $ The scale factor in the conditional distribution of initial purchase propensities. The model requires $\beta > 0$.

α_0 or $\alpha = $ The number of degrees of freedom in the conditional distribution of expected purchase rates for the first families to enter a given depth of trial class. This parameter is proportional to the mean of the distribution. The model requires $\alpha > 0$.

$\gamma = $ The rate which the mean of the conditional prior distribution of expected rates changes with respect to the period of time since the first family entered the given depth of trial class. We should expect that $-1 < \gamma < +1$ in order to avoid explosive behavior.

$M_\tau = $ The probability that a household which entered the depth of trial class at time τ will have a purchase rate greater than zero. This is the probability that is applicable to the "conditions" in the prior distribution of purchase rates that is defined by α, β, and γ.

$\overline{M} = $ The average value of M_τ over all households in a given depth of trial class.

The following fixed variables used in the model are defined by the general characteristics of the data:

$k = $ An index used to designate depth of trial classes (this index is always implied for all variables and parameters, though it is usually not written explicitly).

$\tau = $ The time at which a given household enters the current depth of trial class; it is usually taken relative to a "time origin" defined later.

$\tau_{k0} = $ The "time origin" for the kth depth of trial class; it may be roughly defined as the earliest time at which the kth purchase is feasible.

t_0 = The time at which the new product is introduced.

T = The maximum time period covered by the available data.

P_τ = The proportion of households with a given value of τ who convert from the kth to the $k + 1$ depth of trial class during the interval (t_0, T).

ω_τ = the proportion of households in the kth depth of trial class who have the given value of τ.

The nature of the various time indices can be clarified by reference to Figure 9.4, where the purchase histories for two hypothetical households are presented. Both households are assumed to have been exposed to the new product at time t_0. Household 1 makes its first purchase at time $P_1^{(1)}$, where the subscript represents k and the superscript is the household number. Thus the waiting time to the first purchase is $t_0^{(1)}$ (i.e., waiting time in the 0th depth of trial class). Its first purchase is also represented as being $\tau_1^{(1)}$ time units after the "time origin" for the first depth of trial class; i.e., $P_1^{(1)} - \tau_{10} = \tau_1^{(1)}$. This establishes the time of conversion or τ class for the first household, in the first depth of trial class. (The τ class for the 0th depth of trial class is identically 1 for all households in this example.) The waiting time to the second purchase is $t_1^{(1)}$, which puts the family in the $\tau_2^{(1)}$ τ class for the second depth of trial class, and so on. A similar chain of indices can be traced out for the second household.

We will now develop the properties of the STEAM model. First, the conditional density and distribution functions for interpurchase times (conditional on a fixed value for μ_0) will be derived. Then we consider the unconditional density and distribution, and the purchase contingency function; these are the $f(t)$, $F(t)$, and $R(t)$ functions defined in Chapter

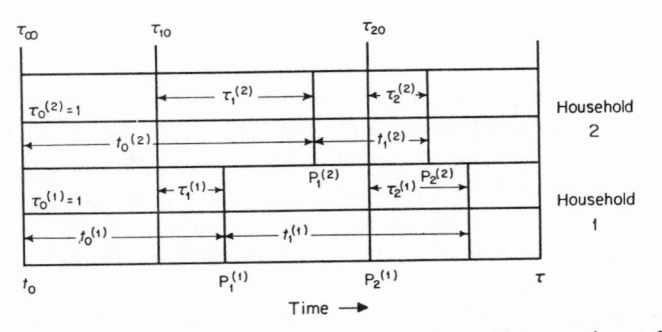

Figure 9.4. Time indices for first two purchases by two hypothetical households.

8. Finally, we will develop a new set of "posterior" density functions which indicate our probability assessments on what μ_0 must have been for a given household, given the parameter of the prior distribution and the household's actual purchase history in the depth of trial class under study. (This history takes the form of a statement that the household did convert to the $k + 1$ class at time $P_k^{(i)}$, or did not convert during the period covered by the data.) These properties will be used to compare STEAM with other market penetration models (Section 9.3), and lay out methods for applying the model in business situations (Section 9.4).

9.2.2   The Conditional Distribution of t

Suppose that $\mu_0 > 0$. Then the distribution of interpurchase times, conditional on a fixed value of μ_0, is obtained by combining Equation 9.12 and 9.13. First the purchase propensity function is integrated to yield:

$$m(t) = \int_1^t \mu(x)\, dx = \mu_0 \int_1^t x^\lambda\, dx = \frac{\mu_0}{\lambda + 1}\, (t^{\lambda+1} - 1)$$

Substitution of this into the density function yields:

$$f(t|\mu_0, \mu_0 > 0) = \mu_0 t^\lambda \exp\left[-\frac{\mu_0}{\lambda + 1}\, (t^{\lambda+1} - 1)\right] \qquad t \geq 1 \quad (9.17)$$

The conditional distribution function is obtained by integrating Equation 9.17. The integration is easy if the change of variable $x = t^{\lambda+1}$ is employed.

$$F(t|\mu_0, \mu_0 > 0) = \frac{\mu_0 \exp\left[\mu_0/(\lambda + 1)\right]}{(\lambda + 1)} \int_1^t x^\lambda \exp\left[\frac{-\mu_0}{(\lambda + 1)}\, x\right] dx \quad (9.18)$$

$$= 1 - \exp\left[-\frac{\mu_0}{\lambda + 1}\, (t^{\lambda+1} - 1)\right]$$

It is apparent that the parameter λ must be constrained to the range of values greater than -1 in order for the conditional density and distribution functions to be properly defined. If $\lambda = -1$ the ratio $\mu/(\lambda + 1)$ is infinite, while if $\lambda < -1$ the ratio is negative and the probability mass does not converge to one as t becomes large.

Equation 9.17 is a form of the Weibull distribution, which is used extensively in reliability engineering. The Weibull is itself a member of the broader class of Polya frequency densities of order 2. [See Barlow, Marshall and Proschan (1963).] Given these facts, we can use propositions proved by Barlow and Proschan (1965, p. 25) to assert that

the conditional distribution of interpurchase time has the following properties, any one of which implies the others and conversely:[6]
    If $0 < \lambda < 1$ (or $-1 < \lambda < 0$), then

a. $\log [1 - F(t)]$ is concave (convex) in t,

b. $\dfrac{F(t + h) - F(t)}{1 - F(t)}$ is monotonically increasing (decreasing) in t, and

c. $R(t) = \dfrac{f(t)}{1 - F(t)}$ is monotonically increasing (decreasing) in t.

The quantity given in (b) represents the conditional probability that a consumer will purchase in the interval $(t, t + h)$, given that he has not purchased in the prior period $(1,t)$. The quantity $R(t)$ defined in (c) is found by taking the limit of $1/h$ times the conditional probability as h goes to zero. We have called it the purchase contingency function of the process (the *hazard rate* in reliability or accident studies) and represents the instantaneous likelihood that an event will occur, given that it has not occurred previously. The reader may verify that the expression for $R(t)$ has already been given in Equation 9.13: that is, $R(t)$ is the same as $\mu(t)$, the purchase propensity function for this homogeneous purchasing process.
    If $\mu_0 = 0$, of course the conditional density and distribution functions are uniformly zero.

9.2.3 Unconditional Distribution of t

The unconditional density of the interpurchase times is obtained by integrating μ_0 from the conditional density function. Equation 9.14 defined the prior distribution of μ_0 as gamma $[\alpha(\tau),\beta]$ with a jump of size $1 - M$ at $\mu_0 = 0$, while the definition of $\alpha(\tau)$ was given in Equation 9.15. Combining these relations gives us the following results:

$$f(t|\tau) = f(t|\tau, \mu_0 = 0) \Pr[\mu_0 = 0] + f(t|\tau, \mu_0 > 0) \Pr[\mu_0 > 0]$$

$$f(t|\tau, \mu_0 = 0) = 0 \qquad \text{all } t \text{ and } \tau$$

$$f(t|\tau, \mu_0 > 0) = \int_0^\infty f(t|\mu_0) f(\mu_0|\tau, \mu_0 > 0) \, d\mu_0$$

$$= \frac{\beta^{\alpha\tau^\gamma} t^\lambda}{\Gamma(\alpha\tau^\gamma)} \int_0^\infty \left(\exp \left\{ -\mu_0 \left[\frac{t^{\lambda+1} - 1}{\lambda + 1} + \beta \right] \right\} \right) \mu_0^{\alpha\tau^\gamma} \, d\mu_0$$

[6] Our distribution differs from the Wiebull in that its time origin is one rather than zero. Therefore, standard expression for the moments of the Wiebull do not apply. The results given above are valid because they depend only on the kernel of the density.

The quantity to be integrated has the form of a gamma distribution, which can be handled by well-known rules:

$$f(t|\tau, \mu_0 > 0) = \frac{\beta^{\alpha\tau^\gamma} t^\lambda}{\Gamma(\alpha\tau^\gamma)} \frac{\Gamma(\alpha\tau^\gamma + 1)}{\left(\dfrac{t^{\lambda+1} - 1}{\lambda + 1} + \beta\right)^{\alpha\tau^\gamma+1}}$$

Simplifying the above and introducing M_τ for $\Pr\{\mu_0 > 0\}$, we have

$$f(t|\tau) = M_\tau \alpha\tau^\gamma \beta^{\alpha\tau^\gamma} \frac{t^\lambda}{\left(\dfrac{t^{\lambda+1} - 1}{\lambda + 1} + \beta\right)^{\alpha\tau^\gamma+1}} \tag{9.19}$$

The unconditional distribution function for interpurchase times may be obtained by integrating Equation 9.19. The result can be verified by differentiation:

$$F(t|\tau) = M_\tau \alpha\tau^\gamma \beta^{\alpha\tau^\gamma} \int_1^t \frac{t^\lambda \, dt}{\left(\dfrac{t^{\lambda+1} - 1}{\lambda + 1} + \beta\right)^{\alpha\tau^\gamma+1}}$$

$$= M_\tau \alpha\tau^\gamma \beta^{\alpha\tau^\gamma} \left[\frac{\left(\dfrac{t^{\lambda+1} - 1}{\lambda + 1} + \beta\right)^{-\alpha\tau^\gamma}}{-\alpha\tau^\gamma} \right]_1^t$$

$$= M_\tau \left\{ 1 - \left(\frac{\beta}{\dfrac{t^{\lambda+1}}{\lambda + 1} + \beta} \right)^{\alpha\tau^\gamma} \right\}$$

$$= M_\tau - M_\tau \left[\frac{\beta(\lambda + 1)}{t^{\lambda+1} + \beta(\lambda + 1) - 1} \right]^{\alpha\tau^\gamma} \quad \text{for } t \geq 1 \tag{9.20}$$

It is easy to see that $F(t|\tau) \to M_\tau$ ad $t \to \infty$ and that $F(0|\tau) = 0$ for all τ. Of course,

$$F(t|\tau, \mu_0 > 0) = 1 - \left[\frac{\beta(\lambda + 1)}{t^{\lambda+1} + \beta(\lambda + 1) - 1} \right]^{\alpha\tau\gamma} \tag{9.21}$$

is a proper distribution function, converging to 1 as t becomes large.

The unconditional purchase contingency function is easily obtained from Equations 9.19 and 9.20. We have

$$
R(t|\tau) = \frac{f(t|\tau)}{1 - F(t|\tau)} = \frac{M_r \alpha \tau^\gamma \beta^{\alpha\tau^\gamma} \dfrac{t^\lambda}{\left(\dfrac{t^{\lambda+1} - 1}{\lambda + 1} + \beta\right)^{\alpha\tau^\gamma+1}}}{1 - M_r + M_r \left(\dfrac{\beta}{\dfrac{t^{\lambda+1} - 1}{\lambda + 1} + \beta}\right)^{\alpha\tau^\gamma+1}}
$$

$$
= \frac{M_r \alpha \tau^\gamma \beta^{\alpha\tau^\gamma} t^\lambda}{(1 - M_r)\left(\dfrac{t^{\lambda+1} - 1}{\lambda + 1} + \beta\right)^{\alpha\tau^\gamma+1} + M_r \beta^{\alpha\tau^\gamma}\left(\dfrac{t^{\lambda+1}}{\lambda + 1} + \beta\right)} \tag{9.22}
$$

In contrast, the purchase contingency function for the subpopulation with nonzero purchase propensity is much simpler:

$$
R(t|\tau, \mu_0 > 0) = \frac{f(t|\tau, \mu_0 > 0)}{1 - F(t|\tau, \mu_0 > 0)} = \frac{\alpha \tau^\gamma \beta^{\alpha\tau^\gamma} \dfrac{t^\lambda}{\left(\dfrac{t^{\lambda+1} - 1}{\lambda + 1} + \beta\right)^{\alpha\tau^\gamma+1}}}{\left(\dfrac{\beta}{\dfrac{t^{\lambda+1} - 1}{\lambda + 1} + \beta}\right)^{\alpha\tau^\gamma}}
$$

$$
= \frac{\alpha \tau^\gamma t^\lambda}{t^{\lambda+1} + \beta(\lambda + 1) - 1} \tag{9.23}
$$

The difference between the two contingency functions stems from the fact that the proportion of households in the population of non-purchasers in (t_0, t) who have $\mu_0 > 0$ declines as t grows. In the limit, $\Pr[\mu_0 > 0 | \tilde{\mathscr{P}} \in (t_0, t)] \to 0$ as $t \to \infty$. Comparison of $R(t|\tau)$ and $R(t|\tau, \mu_0 > 0)$ demonstrates that the addition of M_r to the model represents more than a trivial change.

It is possible to infer some general characteristics of the distribution of interpurchase times for STEAM by examining the derivatives of the purchase contingency function, just as we did for the several models discussed in Chapter 8. First, we note that $R(t)$ is in reality a conditional probability density and use the rules of conditional probability to write the unconditional contingency function as

$$
R(t|\tau) = R(t|\tau, \mu_0 > 0) \Pr[\mu_0 > 0 | \tilde{\mathscr{P}} \in (t_0, t)]
$$

Thus the time derivative of R is

$$R'(t|\tau) = R'(t|\tau, \mu_0 > 0) \Pr[\mu_0 > 0 | \tilde{\mathscr{P}} \in (t_0,t)]$$

$$+ R(t|\tau, \mu_0 > 0) \frac{d \Pr[\mu_0 > 0 | \tilde{\mathscr{P}} \in (t_0,t)]}{dt}$$

Now, we have already argued that the probability that $\mu_0 > 0$ in the subpopulation of nonpurchasers at time t declines with time; hence the last element of the second term is negative for all t. As $R(t|\tau, \mu_0 > 0)$ and $\Pr[\mu_0 > 0 | \tilde{\mathscr{P}} \in (t_0,t)]$ are always nonnegative, the sign of $R'(t|\tau)$ will surely be negative if $R'(t|\tau, \mu_0 > 0) < 0$. (Of course, the converse is not necessarily true.)

Differentiation of Equation 9.23 yields

$$R'(t|\tau, \mu_0 > 0) = \frac{\alpha\tau^\gamma t^{\lambda-1}}{(t^{\lambda+1} + \beta(\lambda + 1) - 1)^2} [\lambda^2\beta + \lambda(\beta - 1) - t^{\lambda+1}]$$

where the ratio in front of the brackets is necessarily positive. Two cases may now be distinguished:

    1. For $\lambda = 0$:

$$R'(t|\tau, \mu_0 > 0) = - \frac{\alpha\tau^\gamma}{(t + \beta - 1)^2} < 0 \text{ for all } t$$

    2. For $\lambda \neq 0$:

$$R'(t|\tau, \mu_0 > 0) > 0 \text{ when } t \text{ is small if } \beta \text{ is not too small}$$

and

$$R'(t|\tau, \mu_0 > 0) < 0 \text{ when } t \text{ is large}$$

From Case 1 and the considerations given above we see that $R'(t|\tau)$ is always declining with time, even when there is no trend in the purchase propensities for individual households (i.e., $\lambda = 0$). From Case 2 it appears that $R'(t|\tau)$ may increase for a while, though it eventually becomes constantly decreasing for large t. In particular, $R'(t|\tau, \mu_0 > 0) > 0$, and hence $R'(t|\tau)$ may be positive, when $t \approx 1$ and $\lambda > 0$, $\beta > 1$, or $\lambda < 0, \beta < 1$. It appears that $R(t|\tau)$ will have only one extreme point, and this a relative maximum, which will occur at a fairly small value of t if it exists at all.

9.2.4 *The Mean and Variance of t*

For some purposes, it may be useful to consider the expected waiting time to the next purchase and/or the variance of the interpurchase times. However, it is clear that the jump in $F(t|\tau)$ at the origin implies

that the mean and variance of the waiting times for the population as a whole will always be infinite, as long as $M_r < 1$. (This occurs because households with $\mu_0 = 0$ will never purchase; hence their waiting times are always infinitely long.) However, it may still be useful to determine the mean and variance of the interpurchase times for the subpopulation with $\mu_0 > 0$.

The unconditional density of waiting times for households with $\mu_0 > 0$ is obtained from the second part of Equation 9.19:

$$f(t|\tau, \mu_0 > 0) = \alpha\beta^\alpha(\lambda + 1)^{\alpha+1} \frac{t^\lambda}{(t^{\lambda+1} + \beta(\lambda + 1) - 1)^{\alpha+1}}, \quad t \geq 1,$$

where the terms have been rearranged slightly and $\alpha\tau^\gamma$ has been written simply as α to simplify the notation. We seek to find

$$E[t|\tau, \mu_0 > 0]$$
$$\text{Var}[t|\tau, \mu_0 > 0] = E[t^2|\tau, \mu_0 > 0] - E[t|\tau, \mu_0 > 0]^2$$

The conditioning factors τ and $\mu_0 > 0$ will be dropped from the notation for the remainder of this section, but they are implied throughout.

Let $b = \beta(\lambda + 1) - 1$. Two cases must be considered separately: one for $b < 0$ and one for $b > 0$.

Case 1. *For* $b < 0$:

$$E[t] = \alpha\beta^\alpha(\lambda + 1)^{\alpha+1} \int_1^\infty \frac{t^{\lambda+1}}{(t^{\lambda+1} + b)^{\alpha+1}} \, dt$$

Let[7]

$$y = \frac{1}{t^{\lambda+1}} \Rightarrow t^{\lambda+1} = \frac{1}{y} \Rightarrow (\lambda + 1)t^\lambda \, dt = -\frac{1}{y^2} \, dy$$

$$\Rightarrow t = \left(\frac{1}{y}\right)^{1/(\lambda+1)}$$

therefore

$$E[t] = \alpha\beta^\alpha(\lambda + 1)^\alpha \int_1^0 \frac{1}{\left(\frac{1}{y} + \gamma\right)^{\alpha+1}} \left(\frac{1}{y}\right)^{1/(\lambda+1)} \left(-\frac{1}{y^2}\right) dy$$

$$= \alpha\beta^\alpha(\lambda + 1)^\alpha \int_0^1 \frac{y^{\left(-\frac{1}{\gamma+1}-2\right)}}{\left(\frac{1 + by}{y}\right)^{(\alpha+1)}} \, dy$$

$$= \alpha\beta^\alpha(\lambda + 1) \int_0^1 \frac{y^{\left(\alpha - \frac{1}{\lambda+1}-1\right)}}{(1 + by)^{(\alpha+1)}} \, dy$$

[7] The symbol $\Rightarrow$ is read "implies."

Now, let

$$z = -by \Rightarrow y = -\frac{z}{b} \Rightarrow dy = -\frac{dz}{b}$$

$$E[t] = \alpha\beta^{\alpha}(\lambda + 1)^{\alpha} \int_0^{-b} (1 - z)^{-(\alpha+1)} \left(-\frac{z}{b}\right)^{\left(\alpha - \frac{1}{\lambda+1} - 1\right)} \left(-\frac{dz}{b}\right)$$

$$= \frac{\alpha\beta^{\alpha}(\lambda + 1)}{(-b)^{\left(\alpha - \frac{1}{\lambda+1}\right)}} \int_0^{-b} (1 - z)^{-(\alpha+1)} z^{\left(\alpha - \frac{1}{\lambda+1} - 1\right)} \, dz \qquad (9.24)$$

which is a form of the incomplete beta function. Note that $b < 0$, so that $-b > 0$. Also, by an exactly similar procedure,

$$E[t^2] = \frac{\alpha\beta^{\alpha}(\lambda + 1)^{\alpha}}{(-b)^{\left(\alpha - \frac{2}{\lambda+1}\right)}} \int_0^{-b} (1 - z)^{-(\alpha+1)} z^{\left(\alpha - \frac{2}{\lambda+1} - 1\right)} \, dz \quad (9.25)$$

Case 2. For $b > 0$:

$$E[t] = \alpha\beta^{\alpha}(\lambda + 1)^{\alpha+1} \int_1^{\infty} \frac{t^{\lambda+1}}{(t^{\lambda+1} + b)^{\alpha+1}} \, dt$$

Let

$$y = \frac{1}{t^{\lambda+1} + b} \Rightarrow t^{\lambda+1} + b = \frac{1}{y} \Rightarrow (\lambda + 1)t^{\lambda} \, dt = -\frac{1}{y^2} \, dy$$

$$\Rightarrow t = \left(\frac{1 - by}{y}\right)^{\frac{1}{\lambda+1}}$$

Therefore,

$$E[t] = \alpha\beta^{\alpha}(\lambda + 1)^{\alpha} \int_{\frac{1}{b+1}}^0 \left(\frac{1 - by}{y}\right)^{\frac{1}{\lambda+1}} y^{\alpha+1} \left(-\frac{1}{y^2} \, dy\right)$$

$$= \alpha\beta^{\alpha}(\lambda + 1)^{\alpha} \int_0^{\frac{1}{b+1}} (1 - by)^{\frac{1}{\lambda+1}} y^{\left(\alpha - \frac{1}{\lambda+1} - 1\right)} dy$$

Let

$$z = by \Rightarrow y = \frac{z}{b} \Rightarrow dy = \frac{dz}{b}$$

$$E[t] = \alpha\beta^{\alpha}(\lambda + 1)^{\alpha} \int_0^{\frac{b}{b+1}} (1 - z)^{\frac{1}{\lambda+1}} \left(\frac{z}{b}\right)^{\left(\alpha - \frac{1}{\lambda+1} - 1\right)} \left(\frac{dz}{b}\right)$$

$$= \frac{\alpha\beta^{\alpha}(\lambda + 1)^{\alpha}}{b^{\left(\alpha - \frac{1}{\lambda+1}\right)}} \int_0^{\frac{b}{b+1}} (1 - z)^{\frac{1}{\lambda+1}} z^{\left(\alpha - \frac{1}{\lambda+1} - 1\right)} dz \qquad (9.26)$$

which is also an incomplete beta function. Similarly,

$$E[t^2] = \frac{\alpha\beta^{\alpha}(\lambda + 1)^{\alpha}}{b^{\left(\alpha - \frac{2}{\lambda+1}\right)}} \int_0^{\frac{b}{b+1}} (1 - z)^{\frac{2}{\lambda+1}} z^{\left(\alpha - \frac{2}{\lambda+1} - 1\right)} dz \qquad (9.27)$$

These expressions allow us to determine $E[t]$ and $Var[t]$ from knowledge of the parameter values and a table of the incomplete beta function,[8] providing that certain conditions on the values of α and λ hold.

The incomplete beta function may be parameterized as

$$f(x) \propto \int_0^x (1 - z)^{c_1-1} z^{c_2-1} dz \qquad 0 \le x \le 1$$

It is defined only for c_1 and $c_2 > 0$. In Equations 9.24 and 9.25, for the mean waiting time, we have

$$c_1 = \frac{1}{\lambda + 1} + 1 > 0$$

$$c_2 = \alpha - \frac{1}{\lambda + 1} \gtrless 0$$

That is, c_2 may be negative for small values of α, especially if $\lambda < 0$. If c_2 is negative we conclude that the mean waiting time is infinite, even for the subpopulation with $\mu_0 > 0$. This is easy to understand. If α is small, many households in the $\mu_0 > 0$ group will have small values of

[8] See Pearson (1934).

μ_0. Furthermore, negative λ implies that $\mu(t)$ declines with time (or, a small positive λ implies that $\mu(t)$ will only increase slowly), which means that the purchase propensity for these households will remain small or get even smaller through time. Hence there may be a relatively large probability mass for very large values of t. In the extreme, the density will not go to zero fast enough for the waiting time expectation integral to converge, and the mean will be infinite.

The situation is slightly more critical when we consider the variance. From Equations 9.25 and 9.27, we have

$$c_2 = \alpha - \frac{2}{\lambda + 1}$$

which will go negative before c_2 in the expression for the mean. Hence we may find situations where the variance of the unconditional waiting time distribution for households with $\mu_0 > 0$ is infinite while the mean is finite.

9.2.5   *The Inverse Distribution Function for t*

The fact that the mean and variance of $F(t|\mu_0 > 0)$ may be infinite suggests that it may be necessary to use Monte Carlo simulation methods to make forecasts about future penetration rates. To this end, we will develop an expression for the inverse of $F(t)$. The inverse function is necessary to convert a rectangularly distributed random number in the $(0,1)$ range, which can easily be generated on a computer, to a random waiting time distributed as $F(t)$. (Of course, this waiting time may be infinite.)

The solution for $F^{-1}(t)$ is obtained as follows. From Equation 9.20, we have

$$F(t|\tau) \equiv y = M - M\left(\frac{\beta(\lambda + 1)}{t^{\lambda+1} + \beta(\lambda + 1) - 1}\right)^{\alpha}$$

where y is the rectangularly distributed random variable and references to τ have been dropped temporarily to simplify the notation. Then

$$\left(\frac{\beta(\lambda + 1)}{t^{\lambda+1} + \beta(\lambda + 1) - 1}\right)^{\alpha} = \frac{M - y}{M}$$

If the quantity on the right is negative, i.e., if $y > M$, we take the household's μ-value as zero and set its waiting time to infinity (i.e., we do

not report back any simulated purchase for this household). Otherwise,

$$[t^{\lambda+1} + \beta(\lambda + 1) - 1]^\alpha = [\beta(\lambda + 1)]^\alpha \frac{M}{M - y}$$

$$t^{\lambda+1} + \beta(\lambda + 1) - 1 = \exp\left\{\frac{1}{\alpha} \log\left[\beta^\alpha(\lambda + 1)\frac{M}{M - y}\right]\right\}$$

$$t = \exp\left\{\frac{\log\left\{\exp\left[\dfrac{\log\left[\beta^\alpha(1 + \lambda)^\alpha M/(M - y)\right]}{\alpha}\right] - \beta(\lambda + 1) + 1\right\}}{\lambda + 1}\right\}$$

(9.28)

where exp stands for the exponential or antilogarithmic function. While the evaluation of this expression takes some time, even on a large-scale computer, it does provide a practical way for determining STEAM distributed interpurchase times. This facility will prove to be essential in the development of a forecasting system.

9.2.6 *Posterior Distribution for μ_0*

In some cases it will also be useful to evaluate the posterior distribution of μ_0 for a given household, after its purchase history is known. Consider a household that makes its first two purchases after waiting times t_0 and t_1 but does not make a third purchase during the period covered by the data. Suppose that the parameters of the STEAM model have been evaluated for depth of trial classes 0, 1, and 2. In particular, we require that the following parameters are available for the ith household.

Depth of trial class	0	1	2
α parameter	$\alpha_0(\tau^{(\alpha)})$	$\alpha_1(\tau^{(\alpha)})$	$\alpha_2(\tau^{(\alpha)})$
β parameter	β_0	β_1	β_2
M parameter	M_{0r}	M_{1r}	M_{2r}

The α parameters are assumed to be adjusted to take account of the time of conversion of the household into the kth depth of trial class according to the expression for $\alpha_k(\tau^{(\gamma)})$ given in Equation 9.15, while M_{kr} is specific to the family's τ class. These parameters define the prior distributions of initial purchase propensitites:

$$\Pr[\mu_0 > 0] = M'_r$$

$$f(\mu_0 | \mu_0 > 0, \tau) = \frac{\beta' \exp(-\beta'\mu_0)(\beta'\mu_0)^{\alpha'(\tau)-4}}{\Gamma[\alpha'(\tau)]}$$

for each depth of trial class. These distributions apply to all households in the given trial class, including the ith household.

We seek to find the posterior distribution of μ_0 for the ith household. That is, for the three relevant depth of trial classes:

$$k = 0: \quad f(\mu_0|\tau, \mathscr{P} @ t_0)$$
$$k = 1: \quad f(\mu_0|\tau, \mathscr{P} @ t_1)$$
$$k = 2: \quad f[\mu_0|\tau, \mathscr{P} \in (1, t_2^*)]$$

where t_2^* represents the number of time periods during which we observed that the household did leave the second depth of trial class. The distribution for $k = 0$ and $k = 1$ are of the same form; they will be developed first.

Posterior distribution given a purchase. In most cases a prior-posterior analysis of the type considered here can be handled by a direct application of Bayes' theorem. That is, the posterior density is proportional to the product of the prior density and the sample likelihood.[9] However, our situation is complicated by the fact that the prior and likelihood functions depend on whether μ_0 is zero or positive. Hence, we must proceed in two stages.

First, we must find the posterior probability that $\mu > 0$, given that a purchase does occur at time t. By Bayes' theorem,[10]

$$\Pr[\mu_0 > 0|\mathscr{P} @ t] = \frac{\Pr[\mathscr{P} @ t|\mu_0 > 0]\,\Pr[\mu_0 > 0]}{\Pr[\mathscr{P} @ t]}$$

where, of course, $\Pr[\mu_0 > 0]$ is the prior value of M. The denominator can be expanded as follows:

$$\Pr[\mathscr{P} @ t]$$
$$= \Pr[\mathscr{P} @ t|\mu_0 > 0]\,\Pr[\mu_0 > 0] + \Pr[\mathscr{P} @ t|\mu_0 = 0]\,\Pr[\mu_0 = 0]$$

As the probability of making a purchase is zero when $\mu_0 = 0$, the second term vanishes. Hence,

$$\Pr[\mu_0 > 0|\mathscr{P} @ t] \equiv M_{\mathscr{P}}'' = 1$$

(The result that the posterior value of M, given a purchase, equals one is, of course, trivial; however, the same method is used to advantage for the "no purchase" case.)

Second, we must find an expression for the posterior density of μ_0, given that $\mu_0 > 0$ and that a purchase did occur at a certain time t.

---

[9] See Raiffa and Schlaifer (1961, Sections 9.1 and 10.1).
[10] References to τ are deleted to simplify the notation.

The posterior density is, of course, proportional to the sample likelihood (conditional on μ_0) times the prior density:

$$f(\mu_0 | \mathscr{P} @ t, \mu_0 > 0) \propto f(t | \mu_0, \mu_0 > 0) f(\mu_0 | \mu_0 > 0)$$

The first term is given by Equation 9.17, while the second is given by Equation 9.14. Making these substitutions, we have

$$f(\mu_0 | \mathscr{P} @ t) \propto M\mu_0 t^\lambda \exp\left[\frac{\mu_0}{\lambda + 1}(t^{\lambda+1} - 1)\right] \frac{\beta' \exp(-\beta'\mu_0)(\beta'\mu_0)^{\alpha'-1}}{\Gamma(\alpha')}$$

or after neglecting terms not involving μ_0 and collecting terms,

$$f(\mu_0 | \mathscr{P} @ t) \propto \exp\left\{-\mu_0\left[\frac{t^{\lambda+1} - 1}{\lambda + 1} + \beta'\right]\right\}\mu_0^{\alpha'}$$

The right-hand side is the kernel of a gamma density function with parameters

$$\alpha'' = \alpha' + 1$$
$$\beta'' = \frac{t^{\lambda+1} - 1}{\lambda + 1} + \beta' \qquad (9.29)$$

The constants are evaluated by setting the integral of $f(\mu_0 | \mathscr{P} @ t)$ to one. Summarizing these results, we have

$$\Pr[\mu_0 > 0 | \mathscr{P} @ t] \equiv M''_{\mathscr{P}} = 1$$
$$f(\mu_0 | \mu_0 > 0, \mathscr{P} @ t) = \frac{\beta'' \exp(-\beta''\mu_0)(\beta''\mu_0)^{\alpha''-1}}{\Gamma(\alpha'')} \qquad (9.30)$$

Note that the prior value of the asymptote M' drops out of this expression, which is to be expected given that a purchase does in fact occur.

Posterior distribution given no purchases. To evaluate the posterior distribution of μ_0, given no purchase in the interval $(1,t)$, we must find the posterior value of M. By Bayes' theorem:

$$\Pr[\mu_0 > 0 | \tilde{\mathscr{P}} \in (1,t)] = \frac{\Pr[\tilde{\mathscr{P}} \in (1,t) | \mu_0 > 0] \Pr[\mu_0 > 0]}{\Pr[\tilde{\mathscr{P}} \in (1,t)]}$$

$$= \frac{\Pr[\tilde{\mathscr{P}} \in (1, t) | \mu_0 > 0] \Pr[\mu_0 > 0]}{\Pr[\tilde{\mathscr{P}} \in (1,t) | \mu_0 > 0] \Pr[\mu_0 > 0]}$$
$$+ \Pr[\tilde{\mathscr{P}} \in (1,t) | \mu_0 = 0)] \Pr[\mu_0 = 0]$$

The probability that there is no purchase in the interval $(1,t)$, given $\mu_0 > 0$, is equal to one minus the distribution function for t given

$\mu_0 > 0$. For $\mu_0 = 0$, this probability is, of course, one. Making these substitutions and changing notation, we have

$$\Pr[\mu_0 > 0 | \tilde{\mathscr{P}} \in (1,t)] = \frac{[1 - F(t|\mu_0 > 0)]M'}{[1 - F(t|\mu_0 > 0)]M' + 1(1 - M')}$$

$$= \frac{[1 - F(t|\mu_0 > 0)]M'}{1 - M'F(t|\mu_0 > 0)}$$

$$= 1 - \frac{1 - M'}{1 - M'F(t|\mu_0 > 0)} \equiv M''_{\tilde{\mathscr{P}}}$$

Note that at $t = 1$, $F(t|\mu_0 > 0) = 0$ and $M'' = M'$; and that as $t \to \infty$, $F(t|\mu > 0) \to 1$ so $M'' \to 0$. (At $t = 1$ the population of nonpurchasers is the same as the original population, while at $t = \infty$ the nonpurchaser population must be made up entirely of households with $\mu_0 = 0$.)

The second stage is again to evaluate the posterior density of μ_0, given that $\mu_0 > 0$ and that no purchases occurred in $(1,t)$. The sample likelihood is one minus the distribution function for t conditional on μ_0 (for $\mu_0 > 0$), as given by Equation 9.18. The prior density for $\mu_0(\mu_0 > 0)$ is again given by Equation 9.14. Thus,

$$f(\mu_0|\mu_0 > 0, \tilde{\mathscr{P}} \in (1,t)) \propto [1 - F(t|\mu_0, \mu_0 > 0)]f(\mu_0|\mu_0 > 0)$$

$$= \left\{ 1 - \left[1 - \exp\left(-\frac{\mu_0}{\lambda + 1}(t^{\lambda+1} - 1) \right) \right] \right\} \left\{ \frac{\beta' \exp(-\beta'\mu_0)(\beta'\mu_0)^{\alpha'-1}}{\Gamma(\alpha')} \right\}$$

$$= \frac{\beta'}{\Gamma(\alpha')} \left\{ \exp\left[-\mu_0\left(\frac{t^{\lambda+1} - 1}{\lambda + 1} + \beta' \right) \right](\beta'\mu_0)^{\alpha'-1} \right\}$$

Once again, the quantity within the brackets has the form of a gamma density function, this time with parameters

$$\alpha'' = \alpha'$$

$$\beta'' = \frac{t^{\lambda+1} - 1}{\lambda + 1} + \beta' \tag{9.31}$$

Summarizing, we have for the posterior distribution on μ_0 for a household with no purchases in an interval $(1,t)$:

$$\Pr[\mu_0 > 0 | \tilde{\mathscr{P}} \in (1,t)] \equiv M''_{\tilde{\mathscr{P}}} = 1 - \frac{1 - M'}{1 - M'F(t|\mu_0 > 0)}$$

$$f(\mu_0|\mu_0 > 0, \tilde{\mathscr{P}} \in (1,t)) = \frac{\beta'' \exp(-\beta''\mu_0)(\beta''\mu_0)^{\alpha''-1}}{\Gamma(\alpha'')}$$

Table 9.1   Prior and Posterior Mean Purchase Propensities

Sample Result	$E'[\mu_0\|\mu_0 > 0]$	$E'[\mu_0]$	$E''[\mu_0\|\mu_0 > 0]$	$E''[\mu_0]$
$\mathscr{P} @ t$	$\dfrac{\alpha}{\beta}$	$M'\dfrac{\alpha}{\beta}$	$\dfrac{\alpha + 1}{\beta + \dfrac{t^{\lambda+1} - 1}{\lambda + 1}}$	$\dfrac{\alpha + 1}{\beta + \dfrac{t^{\lambda+1} - 1}{\lambda + 1}}$
$\tilde{\mathscr{P}} \in (1,t)$	$\dfrac{\alpha}{\beta}$	$M'\dfrac{\alpha}{\beta}$	$\dfrac{\alpha}{\beta + \dfrac{t^{\lambda+1} - 1}{\lambda + 1}}$	$M''_{\mathscr{P}}\dfrac{\alpha}{\beta + \dfrac{t^{\lambda+1} - 1}{\lambda + 1}}$

It is useful to compare the mean of the prior and posterior distribution for the purchase and no purchase cases. Table 9.1 gives these expressions in terms of the prior values of α and β. As the quantity $(t^{\lambda=1} - 1)/(\lambda + 1)$ is nonnegative and $M''_{\mathscr{P}} \leq M'$, we see that the posterior means are always smaller than the prior means when there is no purchase in $(1,t)$. If there is a purchase at t, the posterior conditional mean may be either larger or smaller than its prior counterpart: if t is small the unit increment in the numerator will dominate, making the posterior mean larger, and conversely. That is, if a household purchases quickly, we tend to upgrade our assessment of μ_0 while if the household waits a long time we tend to downgrade it. As M' does not carry over to the posterior unconditional mean, we would expect it to be larger than its prior counterpart, at least when M' is small. Finally, we can see that the posterior means for a purchase at time t are always greater than the ones for no purchase in $(1,t)$.

9.3   Comparison of Models

Four main types of models that can be used to describe market penetration processes have been discussed in this and the preceding chapter. They are the: (1) mixed exponential, (2) logistic, (3) one-event linear learning, and (4) heterogeneous Wiebull or STEAM models. At this point it will be well to pause briefly and compare some of the characteristics of these models.

Elsewhere in this book, we have focused on three basic behavioral postulates upon which stochastic models of buyer behavior may be based. They are: (1) that purchase events feed back on future purchase propensities, (2) that time-varying exogenous variables affect purchase propensities; and (3) that propensities differ for different members of the population.

Table 9.2 Comparison of Purchase Propensity, Heterogeneity, and Distribution Functions for Alternative Penetration Models

Model	Propensity Function $\mu(t)$	Parameters Subject to Heterogeneity	Distribution Function,† $F(t)$
1. STEAM§ (9.4)‡	$\mu_0 t^\lambda$	μ_0	(9.21) $1 - \left\{ \dfrac{\beta(\lambda+1)}{t^{\lambda+1} + \beta(\lambda+1) - 1} \right\}^\alpha$, $t \geq 1$
2. Mixed Exponential (8.14)	μ_0	μ_0	(8.15) $1 - \left\{ \dfrac{\beta}{t+\beta} \right\}^\alpha$
3. Semilogistic (8.25)	$\mu_0 + \lambda F(t)$	none	(8.26) $\dfrac{1 - \exp[-(\lambda + \mu_0)t]}{1 + \dfrac{\lambda}{\mu_0}\exp[-(\lambda+\mu_0)t]}$
4. Heterogeneous One-Event Linear Learning Models	(8.40) $\mu_0 \exp[-(1-\lambda)t]$ $\quad + \mu_*\{1 - \exp[-(1-\lambda)t]\}$	μ_0	(8.44) $1 - \left[\dfrac{\beta}{\beta + \dfrac{1 - \lambda^t}{\log 1/\lambda}} \right]^\alpha \exp\left\{ -\mu_*\left[t - \dfrac{1 - \lambda^t}{\log 1/\lambda} \right] \right\}$
		μ_*	(8.47) $1 - \dfrac{\beta^\alpha}{\left[\beta + t - \dfrac{1 - \lambda^t}{\log 1/\lambda} \right]^\alpha} \exp\left\{ -\mu_0\left[\dfrac{1 - \lambda^t}{\log 1/\lambda} \right] \right\}$
		μ_0 and μ_*	(8.54) $1 - \dfrac{\beta^\alpha Q(t)^\alpha}{\left[\beta + \dfrac{1 - \lambda^t}{\log 1/\lambda} \right]^\alpha} \sum_{i=0}^{\infty} \dfrac{\Gamma(\alpha + i)}{i!\,\Gamma(\alpha)} \left[\dfrac{c \log Q(t)}{\beta + \dfrac{1 - \lambda^t}{\log 1/\lambda}} \right]^i$

† Possible upper asymptotes M are neglected to simplify notation.
‡ References to equation numbers are given in parentheses.
§ The time of conversion effect is neglected for purposes of comparing STEAM to alternative models.
‖ The $Q(t)$ is given by Equation 8.53.

All four of the models mentioned here can be used in a way such that purchase event feedback is taken into account. This is accomplished by estimating the parameters separately for each depth of trial class; that is for nontriers, one-time triers, two-time triers, etc. Variation in parameters from trial class to trial class permit inferences about the effects of feedback.

The differences between the four types of models depend in part on their assumptions about the effects of time and exogenous variables. The assumptions about the time shape of individuals' propensity functions are given in the first column of Table 9.2. The mixed exponential model assumes that purchase propensities are constant within any depth of trial class, at least in the short run. The logistic model essentially treats the proportion of other people who have converted out of the current depth of trial class into the next one as an exogenous variable as far as an individual household (that has not yet converted) is concerned. Hence $\mu(t)$ is assumed to depend linearly on $F(t)$, the expected proportion of households that will have converted as of time t.[11] The one-element linear learning models assume that propensity changes through time as the result of cascading a series of identical linear learning operators with parameters μ_* and λ. (Recall, however, that here "learning" is not synonomous with "feedback.") The STEAM model makes a direct assumption about the time path of $\mu(t)$; the assumption is not derived from any underlying theory about the process which induces time change. (The extended STEAM model, developed in Chapter 11, postulates that $\mu(t)$ depends on purchases of competitive or complimentary products and on market variables like price, advertising, and retail distribution levels.)

All the models postulate that the process of time change in purchase propensities begins at some initial condition, which we have denoted by μ_0. The population heterogeneity postulate is usually applied to these

---

[11] An interesting variation on the logistic model would be to make $\mu(t)$ a function of $F(t)$ for subsequent depth of trial groups as well as its own group. For example, where working with depth of trial class k we might modify Equation 8.25 to read as follows:

$$\mu_k(t) = \sum_{i=k}^{n} \mu_i F_i(t) + \mu_0$$

where n is the maximum depth of trial class that we are willing to consider. This would extend the dependence on other people's purchasing and allow the growth of multiple trier groups to exert disproportionate influence on the purchase propensities of members of low depth of trial classes. As the value of $F_i(t)$ for $i \neq k$ can be treated as exogenous during the parameter estimation process this approach does not introduce any new theoretical complications. This model will not be followed up here, however.

initial purchase propensities, as indicated in the second column of Table 9.2. For example, the mixed exponential assumes that μ_0 varies over members of the population. The same assumption might be made with respect to the μ_0 of the semilogistic model, but here difficult mathematical problems are encountered. The one-event linear learning model offers two opportunities to apply the heterogeneity postulate: one on μ_0 and one on the equilibrium propensity μ_*. The STEAM model reverts to the idea of heterogeneity on μ_0.

While it is also possible to postulate that the parameter describing the *rate* of time change of purchase propensity (as opposed to the initial condition) is subject to heterogeneity, this procedure appears to lead to intractable mathematics. Hence λ is assumed to be the same for all households. While this assumption is dictated by mathematical convenience, there appears to be some justification for believing that the incremental effects of time and exogenous variables on purchase propensities will be more homogeneous among households in a given depth of trial class than the cross section of purchase propensity values at a point in time.

Two of the four models incorporate both time and heterogeneity effects. They are STEAM and the one-event linear learning model. Let us examine the nature of the interaction between the two effects in these models. Figure 9.5 shows some possible time paths of individual household purchase propensities for each of the three heterogeneous one-event linear learning models and STEAM. Each of the diagrams gives the $\mu(t)$ for households with different values of μ_0 (or μ_*), which we may imagine were drawn from an appropriate prior distribution. In all cases we have assumed that the other parameters of the model are such that the rate of change of purchase propensity is positive for these households. (The opposite condition could of course be postulated without changing the following discussion.)

The top two diagrams show that for the two learning models with one-dimensional heterogeneity, the purchase propensities converge toward a fixed equilibrium condition or away from a fixed initial condition, respectively. At any given time there is a distribution of current purchase propensities, $f[\mu(t)]$, which describes the population heterogeneity as it exists at that time. We do not directly assume anything about the characteristics of these distributions as part of our specification of the model. Rather, they are determined by the shape of $f(\mu_0)$ or $f(\mu_*)$ and values of the other parameters. However, it is easy to see that the variance of $f[\mu(t)]$ decreases to zero with t in the heterogeneous μ_0 model and increases from zero when μ_* varies over the population.

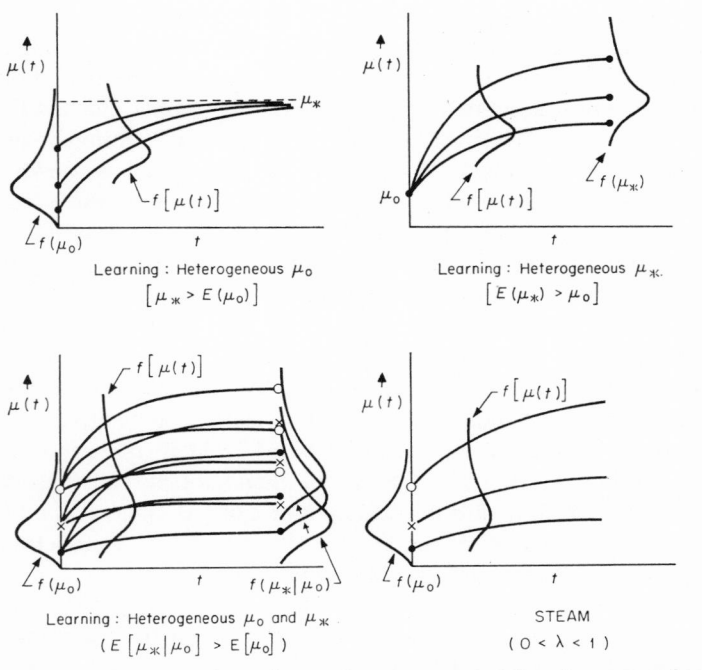

Figure 9.5. Time paths of purchase propensities for one-element learning and STEAM models.

(We assume for this argument that all households remain in the relevant population.)

The third diagram depicts the double sampling process described by the heterogeneous $\mu_0 - \mu_*$ learning model. Many values of μ_* may be generated from $f(\mu_*|\mu_0)$, given a particular draw from $f(\mu_0)$. We have shown three μ_* for each μ_0, for a total of nine hypothetical households. One important characteristic of this model is that the variance of $f[\mu(t)]$ is nonzero initially and does not converge to zero with the passage of time. (It tends to rise or fall to some extent, however, depending on the parameters.) Thus the population is assumed to be heterogeneous with respect to purchase propensity initially and remain so through time. This general characteristic is shared by the STEAM model, as can be seen from the bottom right diagram in Figure 9.5. We believe that it will generally provide a more reasonable representation of real-world conditions than either of the other two learning models.

The purchase propensity patterns for STEAM and the doubly

heterogeneous learning models differ in three main respects. First, the $\mu(t)$ in STEAM do not ever level out, while those for the learning model approach an asymptote. While it is hard to evaluate the relative merits of these two postulates definitively on a priori grounds, the fact that the purchase propensities in STEAM are unbounded from above (and bounded from below only by zero if λ is negative) is somewhat disquieting. Second, the single draw from $f(\mu_0)$ determines the entire time path of $\mu(t)$ in the STEAM model: households who start with a given propensity level travel exactly the same road, at least until their next purchase. This is roughly equivalent to a condition where the parameters are such that $\text{Var}[\mu_* | \mu_0] \approx 0$ in the doubly heterogeneous learning model. Third, the doubly heterogeneous learning model allows the purchase propensities for different households to move in opposite directions, provided there is appreciable density in some $f(\mu_* | \mu_0)$ below their corresponding μ_0. In contrast, the STEAM formulation requires that both the direction and the rate of change of purchase propensity be the same for all members of the population.

The comparisons given here suggest that the STEAM model will not generally provide as accurate a representation of the market penetration process as the doubly heterogeneous learning model. However, it does have the advantage of allowing for the continued heterogeneity of purchase propensities through time. As such, it would seem to be better than either of the singly heterogeneous learning models.[12]

The main advantage of STEAM compared to the doubly heterogeneous learning model lies in the tractability of its distribution function for interpurchase times. The forms of $F(t)$ for the various models are given in the last column of Table 9.2. We do not have a closed form expression for the doubly heterogeneous learning model, and even the $F(t)$ for the singly heterogeneous models are more complicated than that for STEAM. They also involve more parameters. These considerations imply that it will be easier to estimate the STEAM parameters from data than would be the case for the other models. Indeed, estimation of the parameters of the doubly heterogeneous learning model may be impossible, even with powerful numerical methods.

We think that these conditions provide some additional justification for trying to apply the STEAM model. While any final conclusions about

---

[12] A one-event linear learning model with the postulated relation

$$\mu_* = k\mu_0$$

where μ_0 is heterogeneous provides an approximation to the characteristic of STEAM discussed above, though at the cost of an additional parameter.

the relative efficacy of the alternative models must depend on confrontations with real data, a priori arguments can, and indeed must, be used to filter alternative possibilities and assign priorities before engaging in the substantial investments required for empirical testing.

9.4 Forecasts Based on Penetration Models

Market penetration models are interesting because they can be used to make quantitative projections about the number of purchases that will be observed in future time periods. (They are also useful for diagnostic purposes.) These projections can be obtained in several ways, depending on the purposes of the analysis and the assumptions the researcher is willing to make. We will discuss the main approaches briefly in this section, and develop some analytical results that may be useful in particular situations. This material is applicable to any of the four classes of penetration models discussed in this book.

It will be well to keep two points in mind as we approach the subject of forecasting. First, the processes of parameter estimation and forecasting represent two distinct phases in the application of penetration models. Parameters are estimated from available past data and, after this has been done, the model (with estimates of parameters embedded) is "turned around" and used to predict the future. Second, the new product evaluation process will almost never be based on a single forecast. Rather, there will usually be a whole sequence of forecasts, each of which incorporates new information and represents a change or refinement of previous forecasts. A possible forecasting sequence for a new product is shown in Figure 9.6. Forecasts B, C, and D are based on 2, 4, and 6 months of data, respectively. Forecast A is not based on data, and indeed would probably be made well before the date of introduction. Forecast A might be based on a stochastic penetration model

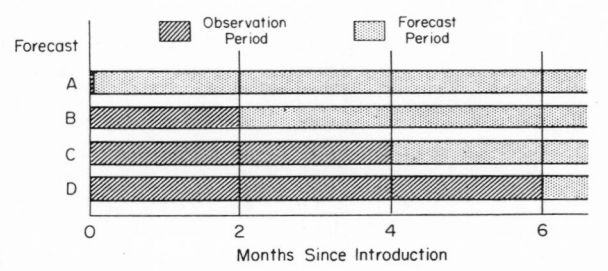

Figure 9.6. Forecasting sequence for a hypothetical new product.

whose parameters were set on the basis of analysis of similar products, modified by managerial judgment.

Requirements for forecasts may come in either of the following two forms:

1. Forecasts of the number of purchases per unit time or, equivalently, the growth of the various depth of trial classes over time, or
2. Forecasts of the total volume of purchases per unit time (cans or ounces or dollar sales, for instance).

These forecasts can be prepared for either:

i. Specific future time periods (such as the last quarter of 1970), which would normally include the transition of the product from the "new" to "established" category, or
ii. Equilibrium or asymptotic conditions (e.g., average quarterly volume when the market has had a chance to stabilize).

Finally, we may try to make forecasts for either:

a. Particular depth of trial classes (e.g., the growth the cumulative percentage of two-time triers in the population or the average quarterly volume from the class of households that have purchased seven or more times), or
b. The market as a whole, where the purchase processes in all the depth of trial groups are aggregated.

To set ideas we will consider how a forecast of type (1,i,a) is constructed, once the parameters of an appropriate stochastic penetration model have been estimated. Suppose we want an estimate of the proportion of households who will have tried the product at least once as of a particular future period of time. The required estimate is given simply by $F(t)$ for the 0th depth of trial group, where t is the particular time point in question. (That is, $F(t)$ is the expected proportion of households who will have made at least one purchase by time t.) Similarly, an estimate of the asymptotic penetration level for one-time triers is the M parameter (using STEAM notation) for depth of trial class 0. This is a forecast of type (1,ii,a). A forecast of the asymptotic penetration level for the kth depth of trial class is given by:

$$\hat{P} = \prod_{i=0}^{k-1} M_i$$

It is easy to see that the M parameter, or probability that a household's purchase propensity is greater than zero, is of key importance for asymptotic type forecasts.

Some other types of forecasts are best obtained by simulation methods. This is particularly true when specific time period forecasts for the total market — types (1,i,b) and (2,i,b) — are required. Here it is necessary to keep track of membership in each depth of trial class continually through time, since movements out of each class affect both the total market and the subsequent behavior of higher depth of trial classes. A detailed discussion of how Monte Carlo simulation can be used to obtain forecasts based on the STEAM model, together with empirical results, will be given in Chapter 10.

In the following sections, we will develop some analytical results that can be used to make forecasts of types (1,ii,a) and (2,ii,a) when we are willing to assume that the process of purchase event feedback has ceased and the effects of exogeneous variables are stationary. Suppose that we believe the following:

The kth depth of trial class (e.g., those households who have purchased seven or more times) represents "hard core" customers, whose distribution of purchase propensities is not going to be affected very much by subsequent usage of the product, and
The effects of "exogenous" factors (e.g., inventory effects or forces leading to "forgetting" about the product as the time since the last purchase increases) start anew after each purchase occasion.

In more technical terms, the assumption is that each household in the kth class makes a draw from the prior distribution $f(\mu_0)$ after each purchase and that the parameters of $f(\mu_0)$ and the purchase propensity function $\mu(t)$ are stationary in time and unaffected by additional purchases. (Note that the assumption of independent draws from $f(\mu_0)$ implies that there is no correlation among a given household's μ_0 after successive purchase events.[13])

9.4.1 Forecasts of Equilibrium Numbers of Purchases

Suppose that there are a total of n_k households in the kth depth of repeat class (or, equivalently, we predict that there will be N_k at some time in the future). If we have estimated the parameter $\bar{M}_k = \Pr[\mu_0 > 0]$ for the kth class, we may say without loss of generality that there are a total of $\bar{M}_k n_k$ households available to make purchases. By the assumptions given above we suppose that each of these households will

---

[13] An alternative assumption is to imagine that a household makes *one* draw from $f(\mu_0)$ and then makes successive purchases with waiting time distributed according to a conditional density $f(t|\mu_0)$, as given in Equation 9.17 for the STEAM model. While this process could be simulated an analytical solution along the lines given in this section does not appear to be possible.

make a series of purchases, with waiting times that are generated by the distribution function $F(t|\mu_0 > 0)$.

This representation can be regarded as a renewal counting process. Exact expressions for the probability distribution of the number of events in particular (short) intervals of time may be very difficult to obtain. (The exception, of course, is the gamma-exponential waiting time model, which yields the negative binomial distribution — see Section 8.2.1.) However, the asymptotic properties of such processes are well known.

The following limit theorems for renewal counting processes may be found in Parzen (1962, p. 180). Let $N_i(T)$ be the total number of purchases made by the ith household between the beginning of the forecast period and some future time T. Then,

$$\text{(a)} \qquad \lim_{T \to \infty} \frac{E[N_i(T)]}{T} = \frac{1}{E(t)}$$

$$\text{(b)} \qquad \lim_{T \to \infty} \frac{\text{Var}[N_i(T)]}{T} = \frac{\text{Var}(t)}{E(t)^3} \qquad (9.32)$$

$$\text{(c)} \qquad \lim_{T \to \infty} f \left\{ \frac{N_i(t) - \dfrac{T}{E(t)}}{\dfrac{T \, \text{Var}(t)}{E(t)^3}} \right\} = N(0,1)$$

where $E(t)$ and $\text{Var}(t)$ are the mean and variance of $F(t|\mu_0 > 0)$ for the kth depth of trial class. The last theorem implies that if a long enough forecasting period is provided, the total number of purchases made by a given household will be normally distributed with mean $T/E(t)$ and variance $T \, \text{Var}(t)/E(t)^3$. The mean and variance of the average number of purchases per unit time (averaged over the forecasting period as a whole) are given by Expressions a and b of Equation 9.32.

These results apply to each household separately, but if the households are assumed to be independent we know by the reproductive property of the normal distributions that:

$$N(T) = \sum_i N_i(t)$$

$$E[N(T)] = \sum_i E[N_i(t)] = \frac{n\bar{M}}{E(t)} T \qquad (9.33)$$

$$\text{Var}[N(T)] = \sum_i \text{Var}[N_i(t)] = \frac{n\bar{M} \, \text{Var}(t)}{E(t)^3} T$$

for large T. The mean and variance for the average number of purchases are obtained through division by T.

Equations 9.33 are readily applied providing: (1) we know the mean and variance of $F(t|\mu_0 > 0)$; and (2) these moments are finite. A table lookup procedure for finding $E(t)$ and $Var(t)$ from the parameters of the STEAM model was given in Section 9.2.4. Unfortunately, the mean and variance are infinite for some combinations of parameter values, in which case the distribution in Equation 9.32 is not defined. (An approximation can be obtained by simulation, however.) The mean and variance of interpurchase time for the semilogistic and linear learning models are not available.

9.4.2 Forecasts of Equilibrium Sales Volume

Given suitable assumptions, penetration models can be extended to provide forecasts of the total sales volume to be expected during fixed intervals of time. These forecasts of sales volume will differ from the ones for number of purchases that were developed earlier because of the existence of different package sizes and the possibility that a consumer will buy more than one package on a given shopping trip.

Let us assume that, to a first order of approximation, *the volume of product purchased on a given trip is stochastically independent of the factors that induce the household to make a purchase in the first place.* In other words, we assume that: (1) the size of the kth purchase (the number and size of packages bought) is independent of the waiting time to the kth purchase; and (2) the waiting time to the $k + 1$ purchase is independent of the size of the kth purchase. This assumption can be rationalized by the idea that the decision to use the product is to some extent separate from decisions about family requirements, given that the product will be used.

Consider the case of frozen TV dinners, for instance. The decision to adopt is presumably based on the family's style of life and general tastes in food. On the other hand, requirements are determined by the size of the family. The same would be true of other products such as pop tarts, low-sudsing detergents, buffered aspirin, and so forth. While it is possible that preferences and requirements are related — as where the decision to adopt TV dinners depends on the number of children, for example — there is no clear evidence as to the magnitude or even the direction of these effects for most products. (Even in the TV dinner case, it is not clear whether large families would tend to adopt the product for economy or time saving reasons or whether they would be purchased by small or single member households for purposes of convenience.)

The assumption introduced above should not be regarded as a "good" one, in spite of the arguments supporting it. It is intended as a working hypothesis that would be used only until more general methods become available. Models that take interdependences between the incidence and size of purchases into account can probably be built: the generalized and filtered Poisson processes and models for the occurrence of light and heavy accidents are cases in point. We regard the development of such models as being highly desirable.

The independence assumption allows us to analyze the distribution of purchase values, given that a purchase occurs, separately from the process that generates purchases. The simplest purchase size distribution is clearly the multinomial, where we define states in terms of package size units or ranges of total weight of product. Let there be a total of $r + 1$ separate size classifications. Then the amount bought on any given purchase occasion can be regarded as a random variable obtained by taking one draw from a multinomial distribution with parameters $p_0, p_1, \ldots, p_r$, where of course

$$p_0 = 1 - p_1 - p_2 - \ldots - p_r$$

Now consider the total volume of product purchases during the interval from t_0 to T, for the market as a whole, which we shall denote by $Q(T)$. Given our assumptions about independence of waiting time and volume and the independence of different households, the above can be represented as the sum of $N(t)$ multinomial random variables, where $N(t)$ itself is random with mean and variance given by Equation 9.33. That is,

$$Q(t) = Y_1 + Y_2 + \cdots + Y_{N(t)}$$

where $Y_k = X_i$ with probability p_i. We must find the mean and variance of this sum in order to make forecasts of the total quantity purchased $Q(t)$.

The distribution of $Q(t)$ can be characterized by its moment generating function, which is defined as $h(s) = E\{\exp [sQ(t)]\}$. Consider the case where the number of purchases is set at some fixed number z. Then the moment generating function of total quantity is equal to the z-fold product of the moment generating functions of the individual Y, since the Y have been assumed to be independent. The moment generating function (m.g.f.) of an $r + 1$ dimensioned multinomial random variable with "sample size" 1 is a function of r arguments, as follows:

$$\text{m.g.f.}(Y) = g(\mathbf{s}) = [p_0 + p_1 \exp (s_1) + p_2 \exp (s_2) + \cdots + p_r \exp (s_r)]$$

The m.g.f. of the convolution of exactly z multinomial variables is therefore given by the quantity in the brackets raised to the zth power. It is now necessary to remove the condition on z. By the rules of conditional expectation we have the following:

$$\text{m.g.f.}[Q(t)] = h(\mathbf{s}) = \int_{-\infty}^{\infty} \text{m.g.f.}[Q(t)N(t) = z]f(z)\,dz$$

The density of $N(t)$ can be approximated by the normal function, as shown in the last section. Therefore, we have

$$h(\mathbf{s}) = \int_{-\infty}^{\infty} (p_0 + p_1 \exp(s_1) + p_2 \exp(s_2) + \cdots + p_r \exp(s_r))^z$$

$$\times \frac{1}{\sqrt{\pi 2\sigma^2}} \exp\left[-\frac{1}{2}\left(\frac{z-\mu}{\sigma}\right)^2\right] dz \qquad (9.34)$$

While the process is really defined only for discrete positive values of z, the nature of the approximation is such that we are justified in using continuous methods. Likewise, the density of z in the negative range will be so small that we can integrate over both positive and negative values without introducing substantial error.

Since $p_0 + p_1 \exp(s_1) + p_2 \exp(s_2) + \cdots + p_r \exp(s_r) > 0$, we can write the sum as a constant a and expand a^z in the exponential series:

$$a^z = 1 + z \log a + z^2 \frac{\log^2 a}{2!} + z^3 \frac{\log^3 a}{3!} + \cdots$$

Applying this to Equation 9.34, we see immediately that $h(\mathbf{s})$ is given by a weighted sum of the raw moments of the normal distribution.

$$h(\mathbf{s}) = 1 + E[z] \log a + \frac{E[z^2]}{2!} \log^2 a + \frac{E[z^3]}{3!} \log^3 a + \cdots \qquad (9.35)$$

where

$$E[z] = \mu, \qquad E[z^2] = \mu^2 + \sigma^2, \qquad E[z^3] = \mu^3 - 3\mu\sigma^2, \ldots$$

and a is a function of $\mathbf{s}$. (It is possible that more than four terms will be required for convergence of the series.)

Evaluation of the derivatives of Equation 9.35 with respect to s_i at $\mathbf{s} = \mathbf{0}$ yields the expected number of purchases of size i, and the expected value for the total quantity purchased is given by the sum of these

expectations weighted by the amounts in their respective size classes. The derivative of s_i at $\mathbf{s} = \mathbf{0}$ is

$$E[N(t)_i] = \frac{dh(\mathbf{s})}{ds_i}\bigg|_{s=0}$$

$$= \frac{p_i}{p_0 + p_1 \exp(s_1) + p_2 \exp(s_2) + \cdots} \\ \times [E[z_1] \exp(s_i) + E[z_2] \exp(s_i) \\ \times \log(p_0 + p_1 \exp(s_1) + \cdots)]$$

$$= p_i E[z_i] \qquad i = 1, \ldots, r \tag{9.36}$$

Also,

$$E[N(t)_0] = p_0 E[z_i]$$

because the probabilities sum to one. Thus the expected value of the total quantity purchased can be determined by evaluating the following in terms of Equation 9.36 and the well-known expressions for the raw moments of a normal distribution.

$$E[Q(t)] = \sum_{i=0}^{r} X_i E[N(t)_i] \tag{9.37}$$

While the mean of this distribution turns out to be the obvious weighted sum of products of p_i times $E[z]$, the distribution itself is not a simple multinomial. Its variance must be determined by evaluating the cross partial derivatives of $h(\mathbf{s})$, at $\mathbf{s} = \mathbf{0}$, in order to find the variances and covariances of the $N(t)_i$. Then the usual formula for finding the variance of a sum of correlated random variables can be applied to find the variance of $Q(t)$. While this procedure is straightforward, it is too tedious to warrant presentation here.

The approach to finding the moments of the distribution of total sales given above is not the only possible one. A different distribution of purchase quantities could be used, for example. If purchase quantities are taken relative to some origin X_0 and restricted to equal increments the Poisson distribution might be used. [See Massy and Frank (1964) for an example of this application of the Poisson distribution.] The multinomial assumption seems to be the most flexible in terms of obtaining a fit to the data, though the only essential idea is that of obtaining the moments of a distribution of a random number of purchase quantity variables by the use of generating functions and conditional expectation.

CHAPTER 10
PARAMETER ESTIMATION AND SOME
EMPIRICAL RESULTS FOR STEAM

We now turn to the application of the STEAM model to empirical data. First we shall discuss methods of parameter estimation for STEAM. Then a simulation procedure for projecting new product demand, as represented by the STEAM model, will be described. The last two sections of this chapter report the results obtained by applying STEAM to empirical data on two new products.

10.1 Methods of Parameter Estimation

10.1.1 Statistics of the Adoption Process

Before considering methods of estimation, it will be well to describe a set of sample statistics relevant to penetration models. We define a time interval of length h (one or more weeks, biweekly, months, etc.). The time interval is chosen on the basis of computer memory space and run time consideration: longer intervals mean faster computer runs but fewer degrees of freedom in the analysis.

Let,

$n_{\tau,t}^{(k)}$ Be the number of households that enter the kth depth of trial class between τ and $\tau + h$ who make their $k + 1$ purchase between t and $t + h$ periods later, and

$\tilde{n}_{\tau,T}^{(k)}$ Be the number of households that enter the kth depth of trial class between τ and $\tau + h$ who do not make their $k + 1$ purchase in the T periods remaining before the end of the observation period.

The k index runs from 0 for households who have yet to make their first trial to K for households who have tried the new product K or more times. These statistics are calculated from the raw panel data, and provide the input to the parameter estimation process.[1] Each household is counted once in each depth of trial (DOT) class it reaches during the observation period. It appears in the $\tilde{n}$ matrix for the last DOT class

---

[1] The program that computes these summary statistics can be embedded in the generalized panel data processing system described in Frank and Massy (1968).

reached (the one that the household is in at the end of the observation period) and in the n matrices for all previous DOT classes.

Figure 10.1 shows the configuration of the n and $\tilde{n}$ data matrices for a hypothetical case where the h interval is equal to one week and the observation period is six weeks. The entry n_{11} gives the number of households that entered the kth DOT class in the first week after the product was introduced (i.e., in τ interval 1) and who made their $k + 1$ purchase within seven days of their kth purchase. The n matrix is always upward triangular because (for example) it is impossible to observe a household that enters the kth DOT class in week 4 and makes its $k + 1$ purchase between 3 and 4 weeks later, all within a six week observation period. The $\tilde{n}$ matrix is diagonal for the same reason. If a household enters the kth DOT class in week 3 and does not purchase again before the end of the observation period, it must have waited between 3 and 4 weeks without buying.

The τ intervals are always based on calendar time with origin either at the date of introduction of the new product or a special date judged to be appropriate for the particular time of conversion class. (See the discussion of τ_{k0} in Section 9.1.6.) The new product's introductory date

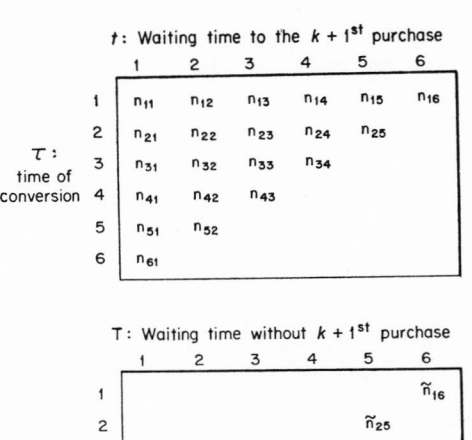

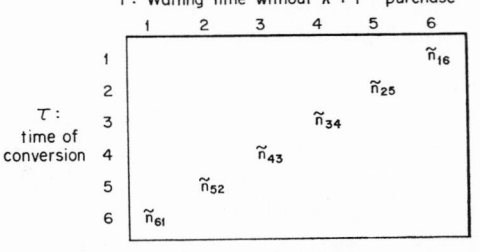

Figure 10.1. Hypothetical data matrices for six weeks of data and $h = 1$ week: kth depth of trial class.

can be specified separately for different geographic areas; this is important if the introduction takes the form of a national roll out.

The n and $\tilde{n}$ statistics include all the information provided by the cumulative penetration curves for various depth of trial classes that are familiar to users of the Fourt-Woodlock (1960) and related models. For example, the proportion of households who have made k or more purchases as of the end of week t is given by the sum of all the elements through column t in the n and $\tilde{n}$ matrices, given in Figure 10.1, divided by the total number of households in the panel. The same figure can be obtained by dividing the sum of the appropriate n elements (not $\tilde{n}$) for the $k - 1$ DOT class (not shown in the figure) by the total panel size. (The equivalence of the two methods is based on the obvious identity that, as of a given time, the sum of all the purchasers and non-purchasers in a given depth of trial class is equal to the sum of all the purchasers in the previous class.) Thus, the statistics used in STEAM are merely a disaggregation of those used to estimate the Fourt-Woodlock and other penetration models.

The computer program that computes the n and $\tilde{n}$ statistics should also provide output records giving the status of each panel household as of the end of the observation period. In addition to the household's serial number and socioeconomic-demographic description, each record should contain the current depth of trial class, time since conversion to that DOT, and time of conversion to the DOT. This information provides the initial conditions for the STEAM prediction simulation to be described in Section 10.2.

10.1.2 Maximum Likelihood Estimation

The parameters of the STEAM model are estimated by the method of discreet maximum likelihood, following the procedure suggested by Anscombe (1961, p. 146). Consider a household that enters DOT (k) in a given τ interval and makes its $k + 1$ purchase a certain number of t intervals later. The probability that this event will occur depends on the values of the STEAM parameters for the kth DOT class. In particular, the probability of purchase in the interval $(t, t + h)$ is

$$\Pr\{\mathscr{P} \in (t, t + h)|\tau, \boldsymbol{\theta}\} = F(t + h|\tau, \boldsymbol{\theta}) - F(t|\tau,\boldsymbol{\theta})$$

where $\boldsymbol{\theta} = \{\alpha,\beta,\lambda,\gamma,M_r\}$ is the parameter vector and $F(t|\tau,\boldsymbol{\theta})$ is the distribution function for interpurchase time given by Equation 9.20. Similarly, the probability that a household which enters DOT (k) at

time τ will not purchase again in the T time intervals remaining is

$$\Pr\{\tilde{\mathscr{P}} \in (t_0,T)|\tau,\boldsymbol{\theta}\} = 1 - F(T|\tau,\boldsymbol{\theta})$$

where we define t_0 as the time of entry to DOT (k) — that is, the time of the kth purchase. (Recall that T is defined as units of waiting time without a purchase, which of course depends on τ and the length of the observation period.)

The sample likelihood function is obtained by taking the product of these probabilities over all the households that have entered the kth depth of trial class during the observation period. Thus, the logarithm of the likelihood function is given by the weighted sum

$$L = \sum_{\tau} \{ \sum_{t} n_{\tau,t} \log [F(t + h) - F(t)] + \tilde{n}_{\tau,T} \log [1 - F(T)]\} \quad (10.1)$$

where references to DOT, τ, and $\boldsymbol{\theta}$ have left out of $F(t)$ to simplify the notation.[2]

It will be easier to work with Equation 10.1 if we simplify the distribution function by introducing the following quantity:

$$Q(t) = \frac{\beta(\lambda + 1)}{t^{\lambda+1} + \beta(\lambda + 1) - 1} \quad (10.2)$$

If we substitute Equations 9.20 and 10.2 into 10.1 and simplify, we have

$$L = \sum_{\tau} \{ \sum_{t} n_{\tau t} \log [M_{\tau} - M_{\tau}Q(t + h)^{\alpha\tau^{\gamma}} - M_{\tau} + M_{\tau}Q(t)^{\alpha\tau^{\gamma}}]$$

$$+ \tilde{n}_{\tau T} \log [1 - M_{\tau} + M_{\tau}Q(T)^{\alpha\tau^{\gamma}}]\}$$

$$(10.3)$$

$$L = \sum_{\tau} \{ n_{\tau.} \log M_{\tau} + \sum_{t} n_{\tau t} \log [Q(t)^{\alpha\tau^{\gamma}} - Q(t + h)^{\alpha\tau^{\gamma}}]$$

$$+ \tilde{n}_{\tau T} \log [1 - M_{\tau} + M_{\tau}Q(T)^{\alpha\tau^{\gamma}}]\}$$

where

$$n_{\tau.} = \sum_{t} n_{\tau t}$$

the total number of households in the τ class that make a subsequent purchase.

---

[2] From Figure 10.1 we can see that the n will be zero for many combinations of t and τ in the first term of Equation 10.1. This fact is important for the design of efficient schemes for calculating values of L, but we shall not complicate the notation by introducing it here.

A major simplification is provided by the fact that the likelihood function is separable in M_τ. We differentiate Equation 10.3 with respect to M_τ and set the result equal to zero to obtain a maximum.

$$\frac{\partial L}{\partial M_\tau} = \frac{n_{\tau.}}{M_\tau} + \frac{\tilde{n}_{\tau T}[Q(T)^{\alpha\tau^\gamma} - 1]}{1 - M_\tau + M_\tau Q(T)^{\alpha\tau^\gamma}} = 0 \qquad \text{all } \tau \qquad (10.4)$$

Hence we can obtain a solution for $\hat{M}_\tau$ in terms of the other parameters:

$$\hat{M}_\tau = \frac{n_{\tau.}}{(n_{\tau.} + \tilde{n}_{\tau T})(1 - Q(T))^{\alpha\tau^\gamma}} = \frac{P_\tau}{F(T|\tau, \mu_0 > 0)} \qquad (10.5)$$

where P_τ is the proportion of households in the τ class that purchased during the observation period and $F(T|\tau, \mu_0 > 0)$ is the conditional waiting time distribution function given by Equation 9.21, evaluated at T and τ. We may note in passing that the solution given by Equation 10.5 is indeed a maximum, since

$$\frac{\partial^2 L}{\partial M_\tau^2} = -\frac{n_{\tau.}}{M_\tau^2} - \frac{\tilde{n}_{\tau T}(Q(T)^{\alpha\tau^\gamma} - 1)^2}{(1 - M_\tau + M_\tau Q(T)^{\alpha\tau^\gamma})^2} < 0$$

for all possible values of the data and parameters.

Substitution of Equation 10.5 into 10.3 yields the following reduced likelihood function

$$L = \sum_\tau \left\{ n_{\tau.} \log \left[\frac{P_\tau}{F(T|\tau, \mu_0 > 0)} \right] + \sum_t n_{\tau t} \log [Q(t)^{\alpha\tau^\gamma} - Q(t + h)^{\alpha\tau^\gamma}] \right.$$
$$\left. + \tilde{n}_\tau \log \left[\frac{(1 - P_\tau)(1 - Q(T)^{\alpha\tau^\gamma})}{F(T|\tau, \mu_0 > 0)} \right] \right\}$$

or

$$L = \text{const} + \sum_\tau \sum_t n_{\tau t} \log \left[\frac{F(t + h|\tau, \mu_0 > 0) - F(t|\tau, \mu_0 > 0)}{F(T|\tau, \mu_0 > 0)} \right] \qquad (10.6)$$

This expression must be maximized with respect to α, β, λ, and γ. As it cannot be solved explicitly this must be done by numerical means; the methods discussed in the Appendix have been used effectively.

The expression within the log function in Equation 10.6 is the conditional probability that a purchase will take place in the interval $(t, t + h)$, given that one does in fact occur during the interval (t_0, T). This fact leads to the following intuitive explanation of the likelihood maximizing procedure.

The sample data consist of the following three subpopulations:

(i) Households with $\mu_0 > 0$ who do purchase during the observation period.
(ii) Households with $\mu_0 > 0$ who do not purchase during the observation period.
(iii) Households with $\mu_0 = 0$ who do not purchase during the observation period or at any other time.

The members of subgroup (i) can be unambiguously identified, but the data alone are not sufficient to distinguish between members of groups (ii) and (iii).

Separation of the likelihood function reflects the fact that the inter-purchase times for group (i) do not depend on $\Pr[\mu_0 > 0] = M$. Hence, we can

a. Estimate α, β, λ, and γ from the data on members of subpopulation (i) by maximizing the likelihood given by Equation 10.6. [The likelihood is explicitly conditioned on $\mathscr{P} \in (t_0, T)$.]
b. Estimate $\hat{M}_r$ by comparing the actual proportion of purchasers (P_r) with the predicted proportion of purchasers in subpopulations (i) and (ii) combined, given the parameter values obtained in a, as shown in Equation 10.5.
Equation 10.5 equates the theoretical and empirical proportion of purchasers for the population of the τ class taken as a whole:

$$F(T|\tau, \mu_0 > 0)M_r = \Pr[\mathscr{P} \in (t_0, T)|\tau, \mu_0 > 0]\Pr[\mu_0 > 0|\tau] = P_r$$

The value of $\hat{M}_r$ is the equilibrating factor. In effect, it provides an estimator of the relative sizes of subpopulations (ii) and (iii), though the group membership of individual nonpurchasing households is not determined.

These relations are illustrated in Figure 10.2, where the solid points indicate hypothetical data points and the curve the fitted function for $F(t)$. The left-hand scale indicates proportions in the total population, while the right-hand one is based on the subpopulation of potential purchasers. The figure highlights two essential features of the parameter estimation process: First, the fitted function for $F(t|\mu_0 > 0)$ is constrained to pass through points 0 and X because $F(1) \equiv 0$ and $F(T|\mathscr{P} \in (t_0, T)) \equiv 1$ regardless of the parameters. Thus, the estimation process can be compared to the problem of fitting a string through the data points where the string must pass through two end points. (At the end of Section 9.2.3 we also argued that $F(t)$ can have at

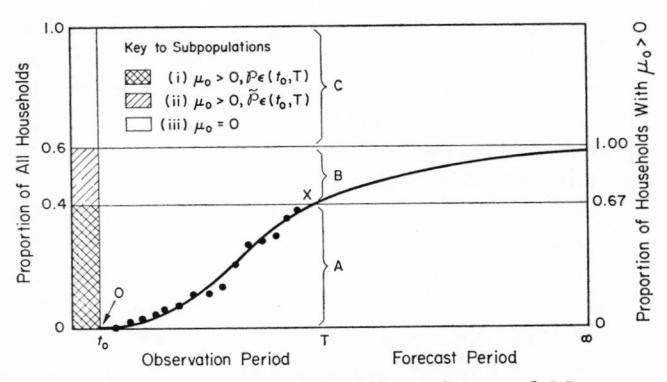

Figure 10.2.   Hypothetical data showing estimate of M.

most one inflection point.) Second, the quantity $F(T|\mu_0 > 0)$ used in the estimation of M is the proportion of households who will eventually purchase (i.e., with $\mu_0 > 0$) who have done so by time t. This proportion is given by

$$F(T|\mu_0 > 0) = \frac{A}{A + B}$$

where A and B are identified as line segments in the figure. Similarly, the empirical proportion of purchasers in the population as a whole is

$$P = \frac{A}{A + B + C}$$

Therefore, by Equation 10.5,

$$M = \frac{P}{F(T|\mu_0 > 0)} = \frac{A/(A + B + C)}{A/(A + B)} = \frac{A + B}{A + B + C}$$

In effect, the numerator of this ratio is obtained by extrapolating the estimated value of $F(t|\mu_0 > 0)$ to infinity.

In the above discussion, the P are obtained for each τ class separately, while the F are fit to the pooled data for all the classes. While the M are estimated separately for each τ class, we will usually report the average M for all time of conversion groups. The calculation of $\bar{M}$ was given in Equation 9.11 and again in 9.15.

10.1.3   Discussion of Parameter Estimation

The preceding section outlined the method used to estimate the parameter of the STEAM model. Here we will briefly discuss some general

considerations that arose during the development and testing of the discreet maximum likelihood procedure. First, we will deal with problems of theoretical constraints on the parameters, especially $\hat{M}$, and what to do if the estimates violate the constraints. Then we will discuss a number of miscellaneous questions, including concavity, bias, and some alternative estimation approaches.

The parameters of STEAM are subject to two types of constraints. The first represents conditions that are necessary if the various probability functions used in the model are to be defined; the constraints $\alpha > 0$, $\beta > 0$ and $\lambda > -1$ are of this type. Members of the second type are based on a priori beliefs about the range of plausible values for each parameter, as where we expect λ and γ to be less than one, for example.[3] The numerical procedure that maximizes the likelihood in Equation 10.6 has the "necessary" constraints built in: if the search algorithm selects a negative value for α or β or a $\lambda \leq -1$ the likelihood is arbitrarily set to $-\infty$. (The likelihood function is meaningless for infeasible parameter sets.) Constraints of the second or "plausible" type are not built into the program; the data are free to produce implausible values. The meaningfulness of the model is judged in part on whether plausible parameters are in fact obtained for most data.

The parameter M requires special handling. As it is interpreted as $\Pr[\mu_0 > 0]$ it is necessarily between 0 and 1. The conditional likelihood in Equation 10.6 does not depend on M, so it is impossible to apply a "necessary" constraint of the type discussed in the previous paragraph. As both P_r and $F(T|\tau, \mu_0 > 0)$ in Equation 10.5 are always nonnegative, $\hat{M}_r$ must satisfy the lower constraint, but what should be done if the empirical proportion of purchases in the whole population is larger than the proportion predicted for the $\mu_0 > 0$ groups alone?

A value of $\hat{M} > 1$ will occur if segment B is greater than one minus segment A in Figure 10.2. While A is given by the data, B is obtained by free extrapolation of $F(t|\mu_0 > 0)$; nothing in the structure of the model requires B to bear any particular relation to A. Pathological situations can occur for a variety of reasons, including sparseness of data and misspecification of the model. For instance, if the data fall in a straight line between the points 0 and X in Figure 10.2, the fitted $F(t|\mu_0 > 0)$ may well project this trend to values that far exceed the size of the total population. Where the data do not begin to "flatten out" during the obervations period the extrapolation of $F(t|\mu_0 > 0)$ will be unstable and may result in inadmissible values of M. This problem is common to

[3] See Section 9.2.1 for a review of constraints on the STEAM parameters.

all models that attempt to estimate asymptotic conditions from early data.

When unreasonable M estimates occur, we have assumed trial values of M and maximized the unconditional likelihood given in Equation 10.3 with respect to the other parameters. This produces a set of estimated parameter vectors, each conditional on a value of M that is judged to be "reasonable" on a priori grounds. The set whose $F(t)$ provides the closest fit to the aggregative penetration curve is chosen. While this procedure cannot be justified on theoretical grounds, it does work out in practice. Fortunately, we have had to apply it in only a relatively few situations.

The matter of concavity of the likelihood function can be handled with a relatively few words. It is impossible to prove that Equation 10.6 is concave with respect to α, β, λ, and γ, but the large number of parameter estimation runs that yielded good results suggests that there is no serious problem here. Moreover, different starting values for the parameters were used in maximization runs on the same data during the early tests of the model, and essentially the same estimates were obtained each time.[4]

There is some evidence that the maximum likelihood procedure may be biased, especially with respect to the parameter λ. Previous work on the Wiebull distribution has shown that maximum likelihood estimates of λ are biased, and it is possible that this carries over to the heterogeneous Wiebull used in STEAM. It would be worthwhile to perform experiments in which the estimation process is tried out on simulated data (for which the model fits exactly and parameter values are known), but this experiment has not been performed. When the sample sizes used in the estimation process are large the problem may not be serious. Also, the errors introduced by the effects of exogenous variables (which are not at present included in the model) are likely to swamp the bias problem.[5]

Two other efficient estimation procedures could perhaps be applied to STEAM. They are the minimum chi-square procedure and the continuous version of the maximum likelihood method. The chi-square

[4] It is worth noting that the unconditional likelihood function given in Equation 10.3 can be quite unstable when M is free to vary. In particular, the search process seems to find a ridge moving toward large values of M (often greater than one). Apparently, the first term of the likelihood tends to dominate the search rules, especially when α is small. This problem does not occur when fixed values of M are assumed, and of course the conditional likelihood in Equation 10.6 is free of it also.
[5] If we adhere to the "likelihood principle," the matter of bias becomes irrelevant in any case.

method would be applied in much the same manner as discrete maximum likelihood. However, the separate solution for M attained in Equation 10.5 is not possible with a chi-square objective function. In addition, the sample sizes in the various time cells (the n in Figure 10.1) are likely to be rather small for some depth of trial classes. This would adversely affect the efficiency of the minimum chi-square procedure. (The problem would be acute when the extensions to STEAM developed in Chapter 11 are added to the model; minimum chi-square is precluded for extended STEAM.)

The continuous maximum likelihood approach deserves some comment since it illustrates a potential problem in the estimation of other interpurchase time models by continuous likelihood methods. The form of the continuous likelihood function was given by Anscombe (1961, p. 495) in his study of the mixed exponential model. In our notation (neglecting τ),

$$L = \left[\prod_{t=1}^{T} f(t) \right] [1 - F(T)]$$

The density function for the STEAM model was given in Equation 9.19 and the distribution function by Equation 9.20. Substituting (again neglecting τ), taking the logarithm of the likelihood, and collecting terms, we have

$$\log L = n \cdot \log \left(M \frac{\alpha}{\beta} \right) + \sum_t n_t [\lambda \log t + (\alpha + 1) \log Q(t)]$$

$$+ \tilde{n} \log [1 - M + MQ(T)^\alpha] \qquad (10.7)$$

where $Q(t)$ was given by Equation 10.2. Now,

$$\lim_{\lambda \to -1} Q(t) = \lim_{\lambda \to -1} \left[\frac{\beta(\lambda + 1)}{t^{\lambda+1} + \beta(\lambda + 1) - 1} \right] = 1$$

for all β and t. Hence the terms in Equation 10.7 involving $Q(t)$ become negligible as λ goes to -1. But in this case the likelihood is dominated by the first term, which is unbounded in α. The continuous maximum likelihood function has a global maximum at $\alpha = +\infty$, $\lambda = -1$ regardless of the data.[6] The numerical search routines found this path to infinity during early attempts to maximize a version of Equation 10.7, thus making this method of estimation infeasible.

[6] This state of affairs is not unusual. See, for example, the comments by Harter and Moore (1966, p. 848) in connection with maximum likelihood estimates of the lognormal distribution from sample order statistics. Anscombe is not troubled by the problem because λ is fixed at 0 in his model.

10.2 The STEAM Projection Simulation

The general problem of making forecasts of future purchasing rates, based on stochastic penetration models, was discussed at length in Section 9.4. There we indicated that it might be desirable to obtain forecasts of both the total number of purchases and the volume of purchases, for the population as a whole, for various time periods in the future. While it was possible to derive some analytical results covering asymptotic purchasing rates for particular depth of trial classes, we concluded that the more general forecasts could only be obtained by simulation. We will now describe such a simulation. Based on the STEAM model, it is used to develop empirical results presented in the later sections of this chapter.

The STEAM projection simulation is microanalytic in the sense of Orcutt, Greenberger, Korbel, and Rivlin (1961). That is, the actions of individual behavioral unit are simulated separately. The output of the simulation is obtained by summarizing these microbehavior patterns, in much the same way as we would summarize real-world data on the same kinds of behavioral units for purposes of analysis.

Orcutt et al. specify two kinds of behavioral units in their models of economic systems: decision making units (DMU), and markets. DMU are the actors of the process while markets are treated as black boxes relating the behavior of the various DMU to one another. As each DMU is assumed to operate in isolation from other DMU in our models of new product penetration, we will have no need to consider markets in our simulations.

DMU are assumed to have two classes of attributes: status variables and operating characteristics. In our models a household is taken as the basic DMU. A household's status, as it exists at any point in time, includes its depth of trial level, its time of conversion to that DOT (its τ value) and the time since it entered that DOT. The household's socioeconomic and demographic descriptors could also be included as status variables if desired. Operating characteristics give the probabilities that a DMU status at one point in time will change to each of the possible status conditions available at a future time. The simulation is stochastic, because the operating characteristics are probabilistic rather than deterministic in nature. In our case, $F(t)$ which gives the probability of making a purchase before time t, is an operating characteristic. Operating characteristics may be assumed to depend on status variables, as where we make $F(t)$ a function of τ and the household's current DOT, for example. The stochastic microanalytic simulation begins with a population of DMU, each with a specified initial status

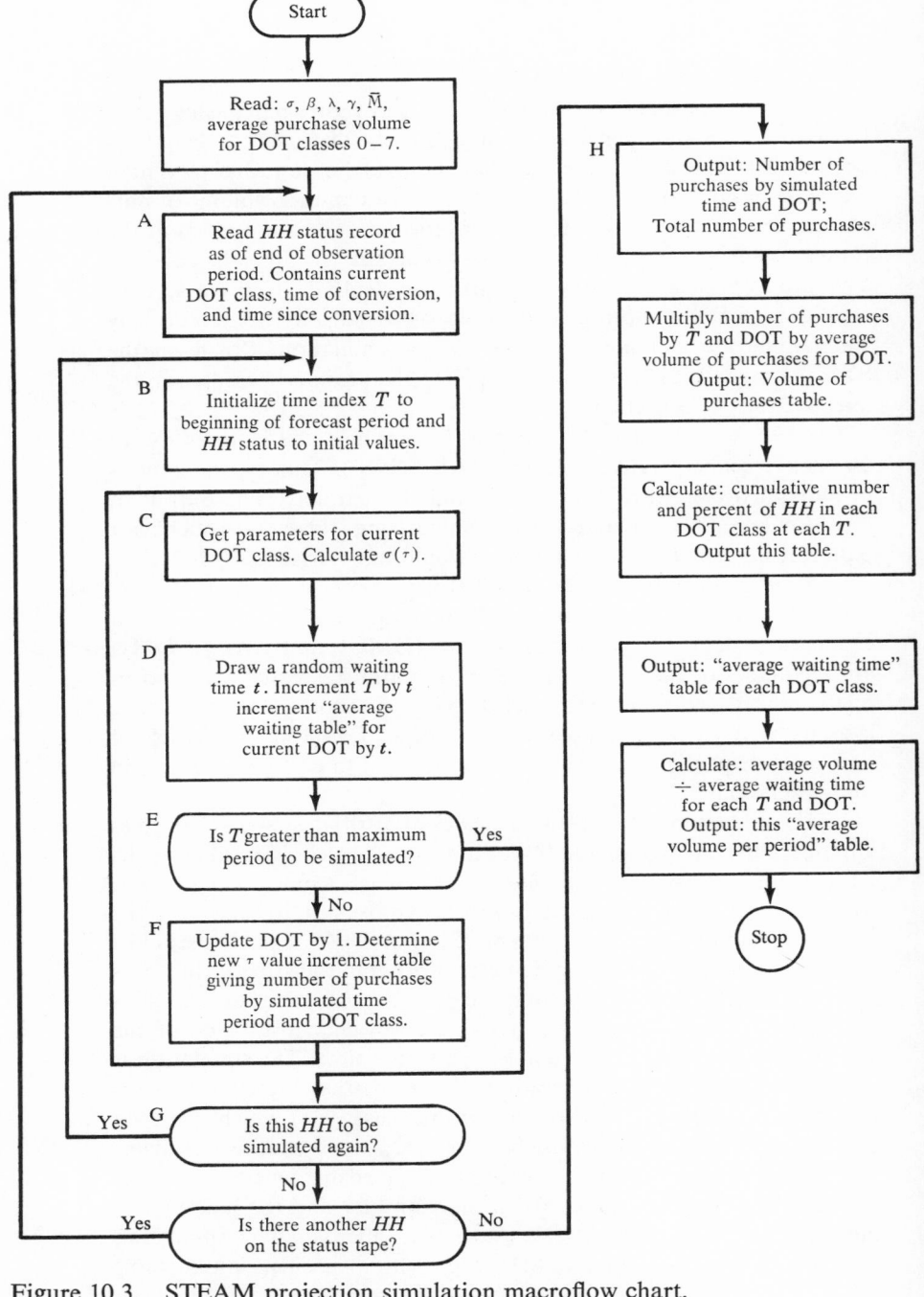

Figure 10.3. STEAM projection simulation macroflow chart.

variable vector, and traces out the changes in the status variables implied by the probabilistic application of the operating characteristics.

The macro flow chart of the STEAM projection simulation is given in Figure 10.3. The program starts by reading in the five STEAM parameters for each of the eight DOT classes considered in the model. (The last DOT class is assumed to be open ended; it is handled using special rules to be discussed below.) The input parameters would normally be based on estimates obtained from observation period data, though the raw estimates can be modified by judgment prior to use in the simulation.

The panel used to estimate the STEAM parameters also sets the initial conditions of the population to be simulated. A tape containing the status vector for each household as of time T (the end of the observation period) is prepared as a by product of the estimation program. The actual panel population is used as the basis for the simulation because it automatically provides the proper distribution of initial conditions on the status variables. The initial status vector for each household is read at point A, at the beginning of the household processing loop of the macro flow chart.

At point B the simulated time index is set to the beginning of the forecast period and the status for the simulated DMU is set to the initial status vector for the current household. (The t and τ intervals are the same as used to estimate the STEAM parameters — e.g., weeks, biweekly, etc.) Then the parameters of the operating characteristic that will apply to the next purchase by the DMU are determined. They depend on the household's current DOT and τ — where $\alpha(\tau)$ is calculated from Equation 9.15 and $\bar{M}$ is used in place of M_r.

Application of the operating characteristic occurs at point C. A rectangularly distributed random number between 0 and 1 is obtained from a standard psuedorandom number generator. If this number is greater than $\bar{M}$, the household is placed in the $\mu_0 = 0$ group and the "waiting time to next purchase" is set to $+\infty$. If not, the number is used as the argument of $F^{-1}(t)$, given by Equation 9.28.[7] This yields a random value of t, distributed as $F(t)$. If $t < \infty$ its value is added to a table which will be used to calculate the mean interpurchase time for households

---

[7] A slightly revised version of $F^{-1}(t)$ is used to get the waiting time to the first simulated purchase for each DMU. Suppose that a household entered its current DOT class at time t^*, during the observation period. Then it has already been "waiting" $T - t^*$ periods, and this fact must be taken into account when estimating the remaining time to next trial. (The machinery for doing this is developed in Section 11.2.2.1.)

with $\mu_0 > 0$, for households in the given DOT class during each simulated time period. (This and the other output tables will be discussed later.) Then the current waiting time is added to the simulated time index. If the new T is less than the maximum time interval to be simulated (e.g., two years) the purchase is entered in an accumulations table for period T and the DOT classes (point F in the flow chart). Then the depth of trial and time of conversion status variables are updated and the program returns to point C to process another purchase for the DMU. If T exceeds the upper limit, simulation of the current DMU is terminated and the program proceeds to point G and attempts to process another household.

Provision is made to simulate the purchase history of each panel household more than once. This is desirable if the number of households that are initially in certain DOT classes is small. (The expansion factor may be different for different DOT classes.) Replication helps to eliminate the variance caused by the stochastic character of the simulation. If replication is used, each pass for a given household is treated as a completely separate DMU, as indicated by the loop leading from the "yes" branch of point G in the flow chart. Results for multiple simulated households are weighted down so that the output is always comparable to the actual panel population.

Summarization of the simulated data begins at point H, when all the households in the panel have been processed. Five different output tables are provided, as shown in the flow chart. Each table presents $K + 1$ time series for the relevant statistic: one for each of the K DOT classes considered separately and one for the market as a whole.

Two special procedures for handling the M parameter are included in the simulation program. First, there is the possibility that the results of the parameter estimation process will show that M depends strongly on the τ class. In this case it would probably be a mistake to base the simulation only on $\bar{M}$; that is, to make $\Pr[\mathscr{P} \in (1, \infty)]$ independent of τ. On the other hand, we do not wish to use the empirical estimate of M_τ for each τ class, because these individual estimates will doubtless be subject to relatively large sampling fluctuations. To handle this case the following option was built into the simulation program:

Input: $M_1 =$ the estimated M at $\tau = 1$

$M_\infty =$ the estimated M at $\tau = \infty$

these values would normally be selected judgmentally after viewing the estimated M_τ array. Then the following formula is used to calculate

specific values of M_r:

$$M_r^* = M_1 + (M_\infty - M_1)[1 - \exp(-a\tau)]$$

where a is either supplied directly as an input parameter or calculated by the program according to

$$a = -\frac{\log[(M_\infty - \bar{M})/(M_\infty - M_1)]}{(T/2) + 1}$$

Here T is the length of the data period used in estimating parameters and $\bar{M}$ is the average value of M_r defined earlier. This procedure allows M_r^* to approach M_∞ exponentially at a rate determined by a. If a is calculated by the program, the rate is set so that M_r reaches $\bar{M}$ halfway through the initial data period.

The second option with respect to M concerns the open-ended DOT class. Three options are built into the simulation:

1. The parameters of the Kth DOT class are used to generate the waiting time between the Kth and $K + 1$ purchase, and for all subsequent purchases.
2. The $\bar{M}_k$ parameter is adjusted according to the formula

$$\bar{M}_{k+1} \leftarrow \bar{M}_k + \tfrac{1}{2}(1 - \bar{M}_k)$$

after the $K + 1$ and all subsequent purchases, and the other DOT(K) parameters are not changed.
3. After the $K + 1$ purchase, $\bar{M}$ is set to one, and the α and β parameters are set to their "posterior" values — given by Equation 9.29 — based on the random waiting time obtained after the Kth trial. In this fashion α and β are updated after each subsequent purchase.

The need for careful handling of the open-ended DOT class was discussed in Section 9.4. Option (1) represents the extreme case where μ_0 is selected independently from the prior distribution for DOT(K) after each purchase. Option (2) softens this assumption by reducing the amount of "leakage" in the population of frequent purchasers. The probability that a household will totally reject the product ($\mu_0 = 0$) is reduced by half after each trial, but the rest of the prior remains unchanged. Option (3) builds in correlation with respect to successive (nonzero) values of μ_0 through the use of the posterior distribution on μ_0. While this procedure is strictly heuristic, it does have the advantage of convenience. Option (2) is the standard one; the empirical results reported in this chapter are based on it.

Table 10.1 Percent Distribution of Purchasers and Nonpurchasers by Time of Conversion Group Within Depth of Trial Class: 13 Biweekly Periods for Product A

Time of Conversion Group		Depth of Trial Class											
		0		1		2		3		4		5	
t	τ	n_τ	$\bar{n}_\tau$	n_τ	$\bar{n}_\tau$	n_τ	$\bar{n}_\tau$	n_τ	$\bar{n}_\tau$	n_τ	$\bar{n}_\tau$	n_τ	$\bar{n}_\tau$
1–2	1.5	8	92	9*	7	5	1	6	2	7	0	10	0
3–4	3.5	—	—	8	9	12	5	13	2	10	0	12	4
5–6	5.5	—	—	6	8	12	3	13	1	14	1	23	2
7–8	7.5	—	—	7	13	11	10	14	4	13	4	14	0
9–10	9.5	—	—	5	13	7	12	11	7	15	8	10	0
11–12	11.5	—	—	5	11	10	12	15	13	14	10	10	17
Total		8	92	39	61	57	43	71	29	72	28	77	23
Approx. Base		5–6000		4–500		150–200		100–150		75–100		50–75	

* Read: 9% of the 4–500 households available for analysis in the first depth of trial class entered the class in the first or second t interval and made their next purchase before the end of the data period.

10.3   Empirical Results for Product A

The results to be reported in this section are for the first product to be tested on the STEAM model.[8] We will call this "Product A" in order to protect the interests of the company in question. Product A is a fairly typical frequently purchased food item that was introduced into national distribution a few years ago. It does not initially appear to have strong seasonal variations in demand, nor did it suffer major problems of retail distribution during its introductory period. While the levels of price and promotional support during the introductory period were not as constant as we would have liked, our judgment was that the assumptions of the STEAM model would not be grossly violated. The product caught on quickly, but its later sales history proved to be something of a disappointment. Taken together, these characteristics make Product A a reasonably good example with which to test STEAM under field conditions.

The STEAM model was first applied to an observation period consisting of 13 biweekly periods, using data from the Market Research Corporation of America's National Consumer Panel.[9] Pairs of τ classes were pooled during the data reduction phase of the analysis of Product A. That is, the product for $\tau = 1$ and $\tau = 2$ were combined into a single class with τ set at 1.5, $\tau = 3$ and $\tau = 4$ were pooled into one group with $\tau = 3.5$, and so on. This introduces a certain amount of noise into the parameter estimation process, especially with respect to the M_τ, but the effects should not be serious.

Table 10.1 shows how members of the panel were divided among depth of trial and time of conversion classes during the six months covered by the data. The table indicates the approximate sample sizes that were available for analyzing the various DOT classes for product A, though a percentage representation on approximate bases is required for coding purposes. Samples n were adequate through Depth of Trial Class (3) and marginal for DOT (4) and DOT (5). The data were insufficient to estimate higher depth of trial classes.[10] The table indicates that the respondents are spread fairly evenly among τ groups and also shows that except for DOT (5) there is a tendency for higher proportions

[8] The material in this section is adapted from Massy (1967).
[9] Thanks are due to Dr. I. J. Abrams of MRCA for making the data available for analysis.
[10] The choice of data period for these runs turned out to be somewhat unfortunate. Most of the sample was purchased in a relatively few periods, thus effectively reducing the amount of information provided per respondent. A shorter data period was possible and would have "stretched" the sample. Also, it is possible to pool the data for two or more depth of trial classes.

of those who enter a given depth of trial class early to make a subsequent purchase than is the case for those who enter late. This indication must be interpreted with caution, however, because the later a household enters a DOT class the less time is available for the subsequent purchase prior to the end of the 13 data periods.

10.3.1   Estimated Parameters

The STEAM parameters were estimated by the methods developed in Section 10.1.1, with results as shown in Table 10.2. The initial value of $\hat{M}$ for DOT (0) was much greater than one, so the procedure discussed in Section 10.1.2 was invoked. In Figure 10.4 M values of 0.15, 0.25, and 0.35 were tried and the resulting $F(t)$ curves were compared with the actual penetration series for the proportion of first-time triers. The three fitted curves are quite close together, but when the sums of squares of the deviations between each change in $F(t)$ and the actual data were computed, the curve with $M = 0.15$ was found to give the best fit.

M	ϕ	
0.15	1.45×10^{-4}	
0.25	3.40×10^{-4}	$\phi = \sum_{t} [\Delta P_t - \Delta F(t)]^2$
0.35	1.94×10^{-4}	

The failure of the M estimation procedure in this case seems to be the result of the relative linearity of the empirical penetration curve. As noted in Section 10.1.2, without curvature in the data the model has no basis for predicting anything other than a steady rise in F when M is free to vary without constraint. It is interesting to note that while α and β vary strongly as functions of M, the unconditional mean purchase propensities remain almost the same.

M	$(\alpha/\beta)M$	$E[\mu_0]$
0.35	$(0.859/35.95)0.35 = 0.0083$	
0.25	$(38.48/1155.)0.25 = 0.0082$	
0.15	$(5592/118358)0.15 = 0.0071$	

Except for DOT (0), the estimated values of $\bar{M}$ appear to be satisfactory. There is a steady rise in the mean asymptotic proportions through DOT (3), after which they stabilize at a little over 0.8. (Recall

Table 10.2 Parameter Estimates by Depth of Trial Class: 13 Data Periods for Product A

Depth of Trial Class	α	β	λ	γ	$\bar{M}$
	0.859	35.95	+0.201	n.a.†	0.35
0*	38.48	1155.79	+0.159	n.a.	0.25
	5592.7	118358.6	+0.320	n.a.	0.15
1	2.76	4.01	−0.332	+0.170	0.417
2	14.35	1.75	−0.526	−0.526	0.633
3	3.64	1.65	−0.469	−0.369	0.840
4	1.63	1.23	+1.405	−0.198	0.766
5	1.00	0.29	+0.695	−0.234	0.845

* M estimation failed for 0th DOT class. Parameters estimated for three fixed values of M as shown. Underlined values are estimates of best fit. See text and Figure 10.4.
† Not applicable.

that the data for the various depth of trial classes are completely independent.) The individual M_r values tend to decline with time of conversion, as shown in Figure 10.5. This is plausible in terms of the assumptions of the model (i.e., households who reach a given trial level later are less likely to remain in the market), but it could also be an artifact of the estimation process.

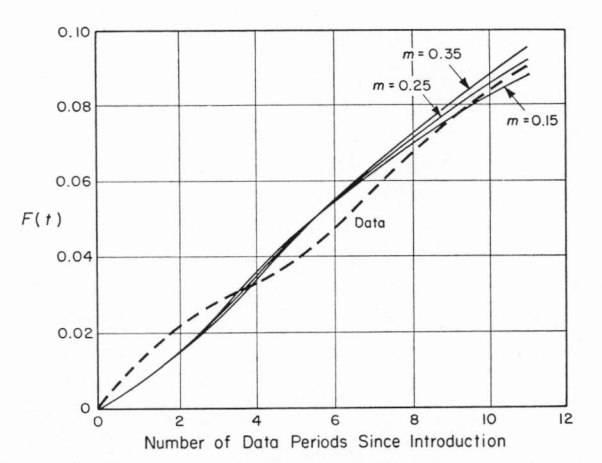

Figure 10.4. Estimated and actual distributions of waiting time to first trial: Product A.

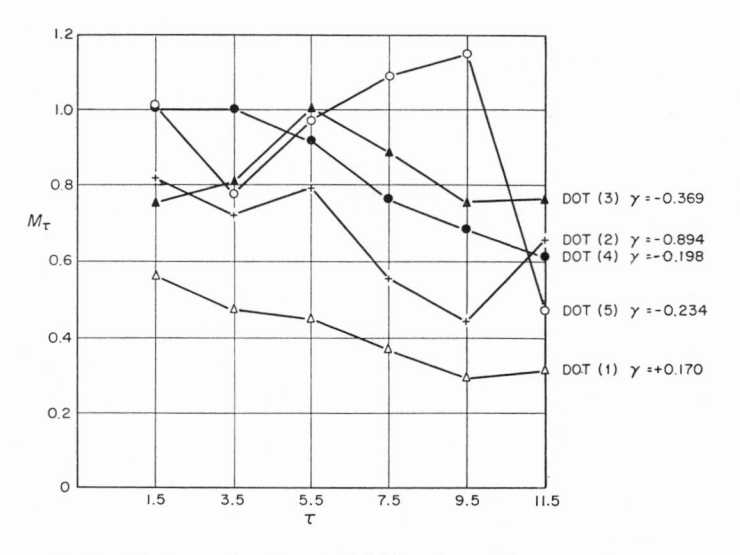

Figure 10.5.   Estimated values of M by time of conversion group and depth of trial class; based on 13 data periods for Product A.

The estimated values of γ are also fairly satisfactory on a priori grounds. One would expect that the effect of conversion time on the distribution of purchase propensities would be greater for the lower depth of trial classes where a good deal of learning about product attributes is taking place. The large negative value of γ for DOT (2) can be interpreted as implying that households which reach the second DOT level during the first few data periods are (1) more likely to "adopt" the product and (2) use more of the product (e.g., have larger families) than those who delay longer. The very small value of γ for DOT (1) could well be the result of the compounding of percent distribution changes and start up sampling or promotional effects with those indicated earlier. The time of first trial is more a function of these extraneous factors than the time of second and subsequent trials. Finally, the fact that γ is less negative for DOT (3–5) than for DOT (2) can be explained by the decline in the learning effect, as noted earlier, and by the fact that larger quantities of product are purchased per buying occasion on the later trials. This is shown by the following table of relative purchase volumes (the trial 1 volume is pegged at 100 for purposes of coding). The sharp rise after trial 2 would tend to counteract the usage effect noted as point (2) in our discussion of DOT (2), above.

DOT Class	Relative Mean Purchase Amount
0	100
1	105
2	145
3	153
4	122
5	160
≥ 6	165

The time since conversion parameter, λ, is satisfactory for DOT (0–3). For DOT (0), $\lambda > 0$ implies that the likelihood of purchasing increases as a function of the time since the new product is introduced. This is doubtless caused by the combined effects of distribution improvements, cumulative promotion, and positive word of mouth. The negative λ for DOT (1–3) imply that these effects are more than offset by "forgetting" or loss of saliency, as the time since the last trial increases, once the household has some experience with the product. The estimated λ for DOT (4–5) appear to be pathological — this needs more study but it is probably due in part to the thinness of the data for these depth of trial classes coupled with the inventory effects to be discussed below.

The estimated values of α and β must be interpreted in the context of their associated γ because α represents an extreme point of the $\alpha(\tau)$ function. Table 10.3 provides some statistics based on $\tau = 7.5$, which is roughly in the middle of the range of relevant sample values. The first column of the table gives values of $\alpha(\tau)$. There is a clear tendency for $\alpha(7.5)$ to decline with DOT. As the α parameter represents the number

Table 10.3   Characteristics of the Distribution of Initial Purchase Propensities for $\tau = 7.5$ by Depth of Trial Class: Based on 13 Data Periods for Product A*

Depth of Trial Class	$\alpha\tau^\gamma$	$E[\mu_0|\mu_0 > 0]$	$\sigma[\mu_0|\mu_0 > 0]$	$E[\mu_0]$
0	38.43	0.033	0.07	0.01
1	3.887	0.965	0.49	0.40
2	2.313	1.320	0.87	0.84
3	1.731	1.050	0.80	0.88
4	1.092	0.887	0.85	0.68
5	0.622	2.120	2.69	1.79

* One data period = 2 weeks.

of degrees of freedom of the gamma prior distribution (e.g., the number of exponential distributions that must be combined to yield the gamma), we see that the prior becomes less and less "humped" as the number of trials increases. The next two columns give the mean and variance of the prior (conditional on $\mu_0 > 0$). Except for DOT (0) and DOT (5), the means appear to be fairly constant across DOT classes, which indicates that households which are in the market and enter the DOT at the same time do not differ in their average purchase propensities. (Recall, however, that $\bar{M}$ increases with DOT.) But these figures must be interpreted with caution: for instance, comparison of the means for DOT (1) and DOT (3) suggests that households who make their first trial at about data period 7 have the same mean initial purchase propensity as those which make their third trial in period 7, providing that they remain in the market. At the same time, the variance of purchase propensities tends to rise through the first two trials. Taken together, these results imply that trial produces positive feedback on the part of some households but that other households react negatively to product use. Coupled with the fact that $\bar{M}$ stabilizes at about 0.80 to 0.85, which indicates that there is still a substantial "leakage" of customers after 4 or 5 trials, this would seem to be a danger signal for the marketers of Product A. The prior distribution for DOT (5) is almost rectangular: this may be an extension of the effects noted here or an artifact of the thinness of the data for that depth of trial class.

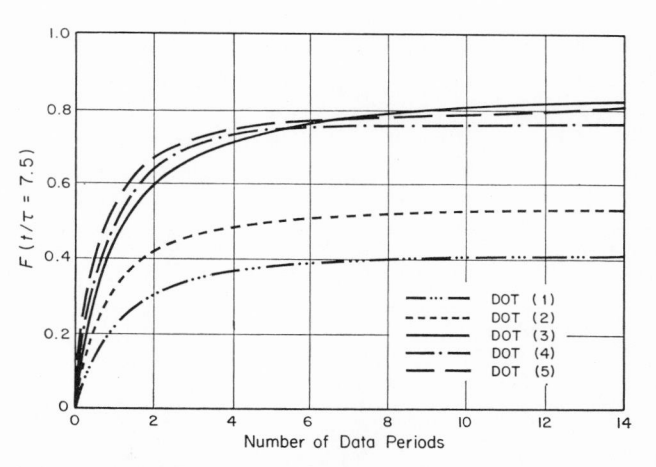

Figure 10.6. Estimated interpurchase time distribution by depth of trial group; based on 13 data periods for Product A.

Figure 10.6 shows the general shapes of the cumulative penetration curves, $F(t)$, implied by the parameters given in Table 10.2. The curves are also based on a τ value of 7.5. The $F(t)$ for other τ values lie somewhat above or below the plotted curves, depending on the sign and magnitude of γ.

One of the most striking characteristics of the curves in Figure 10.6 is the fact that they rise very rapidly during the first few data periods and are strictly monotonically decreasing in slope. Except for the case of DOT (0), this does not quite fit the data, which tend to be slightly S shaped near the origin. The nature of this effect is clarified in Figure 10.7, which plots the actual and estimated probability increments (the first differences of the cumulative curves in Figure 10.6) for $\tau = 3.5$,

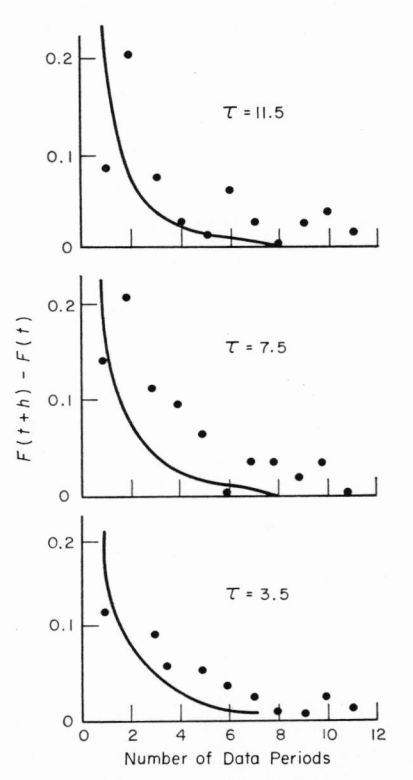

Figure 10.7.   Actual and estimated probability increments for depth of trial class 1 and selected τ-values; based on 13 data periods for Product *A*.

7.5, and 11.5 in depth of trial class 1. The S-shaped characteristics of the data can be seen by noting that the empirical scatter tends to have a mode at $t = 2$ rather than being generally exponential in form as in the case for the fitted distribution. One possible cause of the small empirical proportion of purchases in the first t interval is that some households do not use up their inventory of the product within one period after purchase. This hypothesis is supported by the fact that the relative discrepancy in $\Delta p(t = 1)$ increases with τ: if the arguments given here are correct, early purchases tend to be those who are likely to use more of the product and, hence, would exhaust a given inventory faster.[11]

If λ is strongly positive and α/β is small, the model is capable of fitting an S-shaped penetration curve, but this may be detrimental to the degree of fit in the right-hand tail. (Inventory effects, as such, are not built into the model.) There appear to be four ways of handling the problem. First, we may be justified in ignoring the initial S-shaped phenomenon on the grounds that it is not important for purposes of forecasting. Second, we may average the purchase proportions in the first two data periods or collapse periods 1 and 2 entirely in order to reduce the effect of the inventory problem on the fit of the model elsewhere in the penetration time series. Third, we may try to build inventory effects into the model directly. (It appears that inventory effects can be included by using the methods developed for the purpose of adding distribution and promotion to the basic STEAM model (see Section 11.3.2), but this matter is beyond the scope of our current program of empirical analysis.)

Our objectives in the development of STEAM were to produce a model that could provide useful diagnostic information about the market penetration of the new product and could be used to make quantitative predictions. The foregoing discussion has provided some illustration of the kind of diagnostic information that can be obtained. While the interrelations of these findings are necessarily rather speculative, we feel that for an initial set of empirical results they are promising.

10.3.2 Predictions

We now turn to the matter of predictive efficacy. One set of predictions were prepared for Product A, based on the 13 biweekly periods of data analyzed earlier. The first is based on the $\bar{M}$ values given in Table 10.2.

---

[11] This argument has more force for DOT (2) than for DOT (1), where the effects of distribution are likely to confound inventory usage. The phenomenon noted here is also noticeable for DOT (2), however.

They can be used to make predictions of the asymptotic levels of penetration to be expected in each depth of trial class.

Table 10.4 compares the predicted asymptotic penetration values (the $\bar{M}$ values estimated from the 13 data periods) with actual penetration figures observed after 46 periods.[12] The length of time included in the 46 period data is long enough so that the penetrations should be very nearly at their asymptotic values — the product ceased to be considered "new" well before the end of the 46 periods.

By and large the model does fairly well in terms of its penetration predictions. The major discrepancy occurs in DOT (1), where there is a significant underpredication. The 46 period data indicate that there was a spurt of new triers around period 30, apparently as the result of changed market conditions or a special promotion. This brought "new blood" into DOT (1), which could well have changed the repeat characteristics of that population. The only other discrepancy is the reversal of errors in DOT (3) and DOT (4), but this is of relatively minor importance. Comparison of the predicted penetration proportions with the actual proportions for 13 data periods indicates that in most cases the model is projecting larger asymptotic values than would be predicted by using a simple naïve model.[13] These predictions could possibly be improved by fitting a relation between M_r and τ, a shown in Figure 10.5, and forecasting for each time of conversion group separately.

The figures at the left of the table give penetration predictions for each depth of trial class: that is, the proportion of people in a given DOT class who will make another purchase. The three right-most columns give cumulative percent trial predictions for the population as a whole. Thus, we would predict that between 2.2 and 3.6% of the households will make 6 purchases. (The actual figure is 4.2%, which is fairly close.) When we recognize that we are losing about 15% of households at the 5 trial level and make some guesses about the leakage at higher levels (remember that the $\bar{M}$ for the last 3 DOT are fairly stable), we would be likely to conclude on the basis of the $\bar{M}$ that the future is not bright for Product A.

10.4 Empirical Analysis for Product B

Product B is a frequently purchased food item, the same as Product A.[14] Data from MRCA National Consumer Panel (NCP) were available

[12] Raw panel data for Product A were available for all 46 biweekly periods, which permitted calculation of the actual penetration figures used in Table 10.4.
[13] There does appear to be a fairly constant ratio between the values of $p(46)$ and $p(13)$. But this fact could not be used for making predictions because the value of the ratio cannot be determined from the 13 period data alone.
[14] The material in this section is adapted from Massy (1968).

Table 10.4 Actual and Predicted Penetration Levels Based on $\bar{M}$ Calculations; by Depth of Trial Class, 13 and 46 Data Periods for Product A

Depth of Trial Class	$p(46\|13) = M(13)$	$p(46)$	$p(13)$	Cumulative % of Triers (46)	Estimated Cumulative % of Triers (46|13)	
					$M = 0.15$	$M = 0.25$
0	0.15	0.22	0.08	1.000	1.000	1.000
1	0.42	0.52	0.39*	0.220	0.150	0.250
2	0.63	0.69	0.57	0.114†	0.063	0.105
3	0.84	0.76	0.61	0.079	0.040	0.066
4	0.77	0.82	0.62	0.060	0.033	0.055
5	0.85	0.85	0.67	0.050	0.026	0.043
6	—‡	0.86	0.75	0.042	0.022	0.036

* Read: 39% of one time triers make a second purchase during the first 13 data periods.
† Read: 11.4% of the total population tried the product twice in the 46 periods.
‡ Insufficient data.

for one year, beginning with the date at which the product was introduced into national distribution. Aggregate sales data covering additional periods were culled from reports of projected volume.

The product took hold rapidly and reached a respectable sales level
within the first six months after introduction. Distribution did not prove
to be a problem either during the introductory period or later. Substantial advertising support was provided throughout the period covered
by the data. To the knowledge of the authors, the product was not
subject to heavy dealing, except for one promotion that occurred
during the first six months after introduction. (This will be discussed
later.)

The STEAM model was estimated twice for Product B: once 13
weeks and once 26 weeks from the date of introduction. Tables 10.5 and
10.6 show how members of the NCP divided themselves among depth of
trial and time of conversion classes for the three and six month data
periods. The tables show that there are data for a reasonable range of
time of conversion groups in all but the highest two depth of trial
classes in the three-month case. (These tables must be interpreted with
care, because they do not show either the time to next trial or the time to
end of data, which are the essential ingredients for estimating any
penetration model.)

The relative mean number weight of product purchased per buying
occasions are presented in Table 10.7. As was the case for product A,
the quantities are normalized with depth of trial class 0 taken as numeraire; this is necessary to protect the company involved. The results
show that while there is a slight tendency for purchase volume to increase with depth to trial class, the trend is not nearly as great as was the
case for Product A.

Sample sizes were judged to be adequate for parameter estimation for
depth of trial classes 0–3 for the 3 month data and 0–4 for the 6 month
case. The remaining DOT were pooled to make an additional parameter estimation pass for each set of data (i.e., for DOT 4–7 and 5–7).

10.4.1 Estimated Parameters

The STEAM parameters were estimated by the maximum likelihood
method described earlier, with results as reported in Table 10.8 and 10.9.
Some difficulty in estimating the model for DOT (0) was encountered
for both the 3 month and 6 month data. Values of M had to be assumed
a priori and the other parameters estimated conditionally for each value.
M was started at 0.15 and incremented in steps of 0.10 in each case.

Table 10.5 Percent Distribution of Purchasers and Nonpurchasers by Time of Conversion Group Within Depth of Trial Class; 3 Months Data for Product B

Time of Conversion Group		Depth of Trial Class											
		0		1		2		3		4		≥5	
t	τ	n_t	$\tilde{n}_t$	n_t	$\tilde{n}_t$	n_t	$\tilde{n}_t$	n_t	$\tilde{n}_t$	n_t	$\tilde{n}_t$	n_t	$\tilde{n}_t$
1–2	1.5	19	81	4†	4	1	0	0	0	0	0	0	0
3–5	4.0	—	—	8	12	9	4	6	3	0	2	0	0
6–8	7.0	—	—	11	13	9	13	12	1	12	2	16	0
9–11	10.0	—	—	8	23	13	23	15	20	13	24	26	13
12–13	12.5	—	—	1	17	5	24	10	34	8	39	6	39
Total*		19	81	32	69	37	64	43	58	33	67	48	52
Approx. Base		5–6000		10–1100		3–400		100–150		50–75		30–40	

* Totals may not add to 1.0 because of rounding errors.
† Read: 4% of the 1000–1100 households trying the product at least once did so in the first or second week *and* made a second purchase before the end of the data period.

Table 10.6 Percent Distribution of Purchasers and Nonpurchasers by Time of Conversion Group Within Depth of Trial Class; 6 Months Data for Product B

Time of Conversion Group			Depth of Trial Class												
			0		1		2		3		4		5		≥ 6	
t	τ		n_t	$\tilde{n}_t$	n_t	$\tilde{n}_t$	n_t	$\tilde{n}_t$	n_t	$\tilde{n}_t$	n_t	$\tilde{n}_t$	n_t	$\tilde{n}_t$	n_t	$\tilde{n}_t$
1–2	1.5		30	70	4†	2	0	0	0	0	0	0	0	0	0	0
3–5	4.0		—	—	6	7	5	1	2	1	1	0	0	0	0	0
6–8	7.0		—	—	7	7	7	4	5	0	4	0	3	0	1	0
9–11	10.0		—	—	9	12	11	7	10	3	7	4	6	3	4	1
12–14	13.0		—	—	4	8	8	7	13	5	11	4	6	1	4	1
15–17	16.0		—	—	5	6	7	6	12	5	13	3	14	2	14	1
18–20	19.0		—	—	2	5	5	5	7	7	11	2	2	2	14	6
21–23	22.0		—	—	1	5	2	7	7	8	6	9	11	14	13	13
24–26	25.0		—	—	1	6	2	9	1	8	4	18	10	12	7	9
27	27.0		—	—	0	3	0	6	0	5	0	5	0	5	0	13
Total*			30	70	39	61	47	52	57	42	57	44	63	36	56	44
Approx. Base			5–6000		1500–2000		6–700		2–300		150–200		75–100		100–150	

* Totals may not add to 1.0 because of rounding errors.

† Read: 4% of the 1000–1100 households trying the product at least once did so in the first or second week *and* made a second purchase before the end of the data period.

Table 10.7   Relative Mean Purchase Amount by Depth of Trial Class; 3 and 6 Month Data for Product *B*

DOT Class	3 Month	6 Month
0	1.00	1.00
1	1.08	1.03
2	1.17	1.05
3	1.01	1.11
4	1.01	1.07
5	1.12	1.09
6	0.84	1.33
≥ 7	1.12	1.13

Table 10.8   Parameter Estimates by Depth of Trial Class: 3 Month Data for Product *B*

Depth of Trial Class	Parameters				
	α	β	λ	γ	$\bar{M}$
0*	4380.90	239,201.0	1.14	—	0.15
	2.64	207.7	1.14	—	0.25
	0.62	65.2	1.15	—	0.35
	0.33	48.1	1.14	—	0.45
1	1044.60	2571.7	−0.93	0.05	0.55
2	3.02	174.7	0.27	1.55	0.46
3	2.49	103.5	0.52	1.29	0.59
4–7	1.33	136.1	0.82	1.67	0.58

* Regular *M* estimation failed for DOT (0). Parameters estimated for four fixed values of *M* as shown. Underlined values produced the best likelihood (see text and Figure 10.8).

Table 10.9 Parameter Estimates by Depth of Trial Class; 6 Months Data for Product *B*

Depth of Trial Class	Parameters				
	α	β	λ	γ	$\bar{M}$
0*	32.25	2470.0	0.85	—	0.15
	3.90	425.4	1.05	—	0.15
	3.29	234.0	0.74	—	0.35
	0.71	73.1	0.89	—	0.45
	$\overline{0.55}$	$\overline{41.4}$	$\overline{0.63}$	—	$\overline{0.55}$
1	0.34	1.7	1.16	0.01	0.50
2	0.56	2.2	0.60	0.08	0.57
3	1.98	7.7	0.47	−0.04	0.67
4	1.34	7.0	0.27	0.18	0.67
5–7	3.10	8.1	0.38	0.02	0.72

* Regular M estimation failed for DOT (0). Parameters estimated for five fixed values of M as shown. Underlined values produced the best likelihood (see text and Figure 10.9).

Figure 10.8 and 10.9 show the loci of $F(t)$ for each value of M superimposed on the actual data.

The likelihood attained a maximum for an interior value of M (i.e., for M not equal to 0 or 1) in both the 3 and 6 month cases, as shown below:

Trial M Value	Log Likelihood	
	3 Month	6 Month
0.15	−5528.5	−8988.6
0.25	−5478.6*	−8609.3
0.35	−5488.9	−8514.9
0.45	−5492.4	−8510.1*
0.55	—	−8519.8

* Maximum likelihood.

This meant that an estimate of M could be obtained directly from the likelihood function, without resorting to the θ criterion used in connection with Product A. The best values of M are 0.25 for 3 months data and 0.45 for the 6 month run. The parameters corresponding to these values are underlined in Tables 10.8 and 10.9, and they are the ones

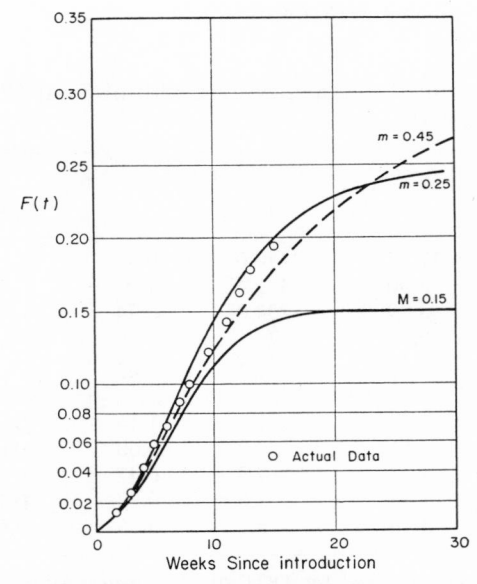

Figure 10.8. Estimated and actual distributions of waiting time to first trial; 3 months data for Product *B*.

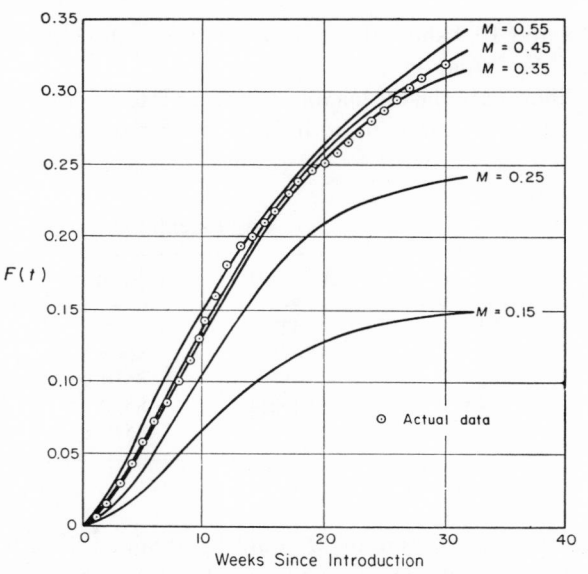

Figure 10.9. Estimated and actual distributions of waiting time to first trial; 6 months data for Product *B*.

used throughout the remainder of this section. (A finer search in the vicinity of the optimal M value would have been desirable, but this was not possible given the resources available for the study.)

Comparison of the estimated $\bar{M}$ values for the 3 and 6 month runs shows that the latter are somewhat larger in all except the first depth of trial class. The largest change is in the estimated asymptotic proportion of new triers [M for DOT (0)], which rises from 0.25 to 0.45. One possible reason for this change is that a substantial deal was offered on Product B, beginning during the third month after introduction. This doubtless had the effect of raising the rate of trial. As the deal was continued for some time it could also have influenced the repurchase rates for Product B, thus raising the M for the later depth of trial classes.

The values of M show a steadily rising trend for the 6 month data and trend in the same direction for the 3 month runs. This phenomenon was also observed for Product A (see Table 10.2). The only real outlier is DOT (1) for 3 months; as it is also the only case to show a decline between 3 and 6 months one is tempted to attribute the large value to chance. In general, the data for both time periods show that the "leaky-bucket" principle is operating to the detriment of Product B: it appears that between $\frac{1}{4}$ and $\frac{1}{3}$ of households who have tried the brand as many as four or five times reject it at that point. This is worse than was observed for Product A, where the equivalent figure was 15–20%.

Table 10.10 compares the predicted asymptotic penetration levels (the M) with actual penetration levels as of 3, 6, and 12 months after the introduction of Product B. As was the case for Product A (see Table 10.4), the agreement between the actual and predicted figures is fairly close. This is particularly true for the 6 month results, which take advantage of data covering the deal period. Note in each case that the values of $\bar{M}$ are significantly higher (and much closer to the actual penetrations after 12 months) then the actual levels as of the time the estimates were made. The main difficulty occurs in predicting the number of initial triers, just as for Product A, though it is likely that some additional triers will eventually come into the market as predicted by $\hat{p}(\infty|6 \text{ mo.})$ for DOT (0).

Turning to the other parameters, we see by comparing Tables 10.8 and 10.9 that the estimated values of γ show some significant changes between the 3 and 6 month runs. The time of conversion effects (γ) are negligible for all depth of trial classes over 6 months, but this is not so for 6 months where large positive values are observed for DOT (2) and above.

Table 10.10 Actual and Predicted Penetration Levels Based on $\bar{M}$ Calculations 13, 26, and 52 Data Periods, by Depth of Trial Class, for Product B

DOT Class	Proportion Converting Out of DOT					Cumulative Proportion Reaching DOT		
	$P(13)$	$P(26)$	$P(52)$	$P(\infty|13)$	$P(\infty|26)$	$CP(52)$	$CP(\infty|13)$	$CP(\infty|26)$
0	0.19	0.30	0.38	0.25	0.45	1.00	1.00	1.00
1	0.30	0.38	0.48	0.55	0.50	0.38	0.25	0.45
2	0.36	0.46	0.56	0.46	0.57	0.18	0.14	0.22
3	0.43	0.58	0.63	0.59	0.67	0.10	0.06	0.13
4	0.33	0.57	0.66	0.58	0.67	0.06	0.04	0.09
5	0.56	0.65	0.67	0.58	0.72	0.04	0.02	0.06

The differences in γ are associated with large differences in the ratio of α/β for the two time periods. (Recall that $\alpha/\beta = \mathrm{E}[\mu_0|\mu_0 > 0]$ for the first time of conversion class.) The nature of these effects is highlighted in Table 10.11, which gives the characteristics of the distribution of μ_0 for $\tau = 7$. This is the middle time of conversion for the 3 month data, which provides a reasonable basis for comparing the two sets of runs. Except for DOT (1), the estimated values of $\mathrm{E}[\mu_0|\mu_0 > 0]$ and $\mathrm{E}[\mu_0]$ are remarkably similar for the two time periods. This indicates that the differences in the estimated values of γ are compensated for by the estimates of α and β. The table also shows that the estimated standard deviations (SD) of the prior distributions are greater by a factor of 5 or more for the 6 month data. There does not seem to be any reason why this should be so apart from the γ effects mentioned earlier. Sensitivity analysis of the likelihood functions (not shown here) shows that the covariances between these parameters are probably very great. This fact casts some doubt on the efficacy of trying to estimate time of conversion effects when short time periods are under study.

Tables 10.8 and 10.9 also show a certain amount of change in the values of λ as the time period is lengthened. The largest change occurs in DOT (1), where λ goes from -0.93 to $+1.16$. One possible explanation for this can be found in the deal mentioned earlier. During the first three months after Product B's introduction it appears that the likelihood of making a second trial declined markedly as time since trial increased. That is, Product B seems to have been a product for which one-time triers' purchase propensities declined rapidly in the absence of reinforcement. After the third month the deal doubtless drew many households who had previously "rejected" the product after the first trial back into the market. In fitting itself to the 6 month data, the model seems to have downgraded $\mathrm{E}[\mu_0|\mu_0 > 0]$ from 0.45 to 0.20 and compensated for the delayed second trial with a large value of λ.

The nature of this possibility is illustrated in Figure 10.10, which gives a reasonably plausible time path for a "typical" household's purchase propensity and superimposes a time path that might be estimated by the STEAM model. The first segment of the solid curve is consistent with $\lambda < 0$ and the second corresponds to $0 < \lambda < 1$. As the STEAM model is incapable of fitting a curve that changes its characteristics in this way, it might well approximate it with the dashed curve (which implies $\lambda > 1$).

The large values of λ observed for DOT (3) and above in the 3 month data might also be explained in terms of the effects of the deal, because most households entered that class close to the time when it was introduced. The same general line of reasoning can also be used to explain

Table 10.11 Characteristics of the Distribution of Initial Purchase Propensities for $\tau = 7.0$; by Depth of Trial Class; 3 and 6 Months Data for Product B

Depth of Trial Class	3 Months Data				6 Months Data			
	$\alpha \cdot \tau'$	$E[\mu_0 \mid \mu_0 > 0]$	$SD[\mu_0 \mid \mu_0 > 0]$*	$E[\mu_0]$	$\alpha \cdot \tau'$	$E[\mu_0 \mid \mu_0 > 0]$	$SD[\mu_0 \mid \mu_0 > 0]$†	$E[\mu_0]$
0	2.64	0.13	0.025	0.03	0.71	0.10	0.12	0.05
1	1155.60	0.45	0.013	0.25	0.34	0.20	0.34	0.10
2	60.40	0.35	0.045	0.16	0.57	0.26	0.34	0.15
3	30.60	0.30	0.540	0.18	1.83	0.24	0.18	0.16
4–7	34.60	0.25	0.043	0.15	1.90	0.27	0.20	0.18

* Standard deviation (SD) of μ_0 for $\mu_0 > 0$.

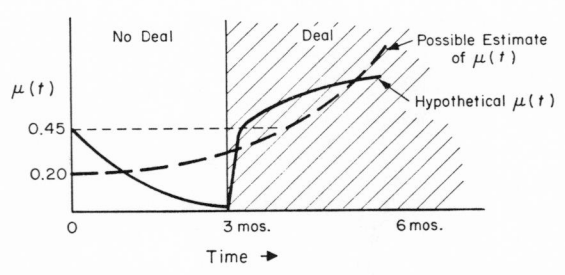

Figure 10.10.   Hypothetical $\mu(t)$ and estimated $\mu(t)$; given introduction of a deal.

the decline in λ with depth of trial class in the 6 month data. Indeed, even the large values of γ noted in connection with the 3 month run could be caused in part by the deal. Households who reached a given level of trial during the third month could take advantage of it when re-purchasing and, hence, would be expected to have higher average purchase propensities than those entering the depth of trial class earlier.

In summary, it appears that the estimated values of λ (and also per-haps of γ) are highly sensitive to the timing of promotional efforts for the new product. The evidence seems to indicate that the purchase pro-pensity of one-time triers, at least, tended to decline with time prior to the introduction of the deal. The deal reversed this trend and probably elicited a rising (but at a decreasing rate) trend with λ in the 0.2 to 0.4 range as estimated for DOT (4) and above in the 6 month data. The λ estimate for DOT (3) and above for 3 months and DOT (1) and (2) for 6 months seem to be caused by the transient effects illustrated in Figure 10.10.

10.4.2 Simulation Results

The parameters estimated from the six months of panel data were used as input to the STEAM projection simulation described in Section 10.2.[15] Figure 10.11 compares the results of the simulation with the actual sales performance of Product B. The simulation was begun in the 27th week after the product's introduction — following the close of the six month data period. It was continued out to week 156, three full years after the launch. (A total of some 10,000 individual purchase events were simulated.)

[15] A simulation based on the three month STEAM parameter estimates was also run, with about the same results as those to be reported for six months.

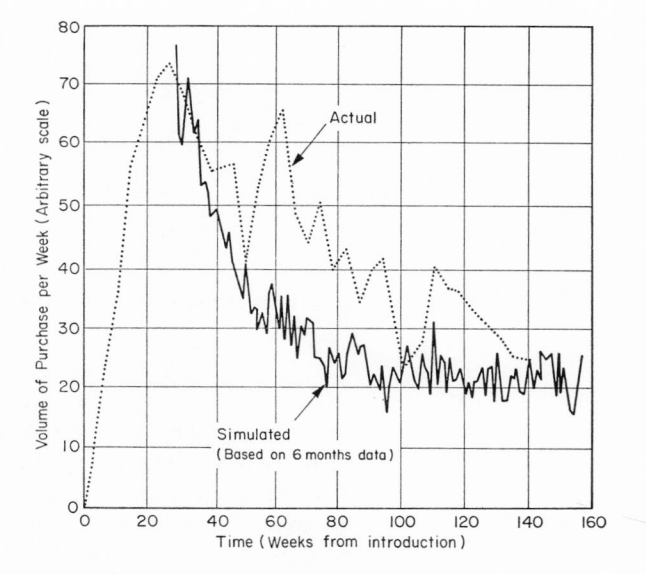

Figure 10.11.   Actual versus simulated sales; Product *B*.

The actual sales data were obtained from reports given to the company by MRCA, based on its National Consumer Panel. These figures were reported monthly but have been adjusted to a weekly basis to maintain comparability with the simulation output. The actual data are carried out to week 140, the last period for which the source reports were available to the author at the time of this research.

As can be seen from the figure, the simulation began at the product's sales peak. It tracks the actual sales rather closely until week 40, and fairly well until week 50. (The jitter in the predicted time series is because of the random character of the simulation; this could be stabilized by adding replications if desired.) At week 50 the sales of Product *B* begin a sharp upward recovery that lasted about three months, after which they began declining again at approximately the old rate. The simulation fails to track this upward shift; rather, it continues downward and eventually stabilizes at a level of about 22 (disguised figure). On the other hand, the actual series also appears to be bottoming out in the vicinity of 20–30, very close to the equilibrium value predicted by the simulation.[16]

[16] The three-month simulation stabilized at a level of about three-fourths of that for the six-month simulation.

The existence of the sharp increase in sales at around week 50 led us to question the company's management about the promotional history of the product. They replied that they had introduced a moderate amount of dealing at around week 15–18, and then had *really poured it on in the vicinity of weeks 40–60.*

As these deals were undoubtedly aimed at obtaining new trials and early repeats, it is tempting to conclude that the spurt in sales came as a result of this special promotion — an event that could hardly have been predicted by any simulation. Once the promotional effort slackened, however, the market reverted to its original structure and the process of decline continued. Thus, it appears the deal served only to delay the inevitable, a view that is more or less shared by the company involved.

As near as we can determine, the company's original forecasts of the equilibrium were in the 40 range or even higher. In contrast, the simulation seems to have predicted the equilibrium sales level more or less correctly, though (possibly because of the deal) it underestimated the time that would elapse before reaching the equilibrium.

It is obvious that additional research will be required before we can say with certainty that a combination of STEAM and its stochastic simulation will produce good new product forecasts. Other products need to be examined and doubtless changes will have to be made in the detailed formulations used in the model and simulation. We hope to continue our program of testing when additional resources become available.

On balance, we feel safe in concluding that a reasonably close prediction of a sales rate three years out, on the basis of only six months of data and in the face of the dynamics of the new product adoption process, is not an insignificant result. We have high hopes for this type of diagnostic and prediction method.

CHAPTER 11
EXTENSIONS TO STEAM

In this chapter, we develop some extensions to our stochastic evolutionary adoption model (STEAM). The model is designed as a descriptive-analytical tool to be used in research performed for managers of new product marketing activities. The mathematical specifications of the basic model were developed and justified in Chapter 9 and some empirical results were given in Chapter 10.

Our present task is to provide the theoretical basis for incorporating the effects of the following three classes of variables upon households' purchasing propensitites with respect to the new product into the basic STEAM model.

1. Purchase of specified substitute or compliment products during the new product introduction period.
2. Changes in the levels of certain types of advertising and distribution variables during the introductory period.
3. Differences in specified descriptor variables among households in the sample. (E.g., purchase rates of certain products prior to the introduction, socioeconomic variables, or whether or not the household received a free sample at introduction time.)

All of the extensions appear to be practical from an operational point of view, but in view of the extensive computer programming that will be required to implement them no attempt has been made to derive empirical results. However, some general considerations involved in the design of the necessary programming system are discussed in Section 11.5.

11.1 Review of Basic STEAM

The specifications for the basic STEAM model were developed in Chapter 9. The model consists of a representation of the purchasing mechanism in terms of a nonhomogeneous Poisson process. This, in turn, leads to a variable exponential distribution for the elapsed time between two purchases of the new product by a given household (or the time between the introduction of the new product and its initial purchase by a household). This "primary model for interpurchase times" is modified by secondary models for, (1) the effect of the time that has

414

elapsed since the last purchase of the product by a household upon the density function for time to the next purchase ("forgetting"); (2) the variation of propensities to purchase among members of the population being considered ("heterogeneity of tastes"); and (3) the effect of the time at which a given family made its last purchase upon the probability density for time to its next purchase. The entire STEAM machinery is applied to data for each depth of trial class separately (i.e., for the waiting time data for purchase k to $k + 1$, separately for each k beginning at zero). This allows for the effect of learning or, more generally, feedback of a new product purchase (and usage) event upon tastes.

In this chapter we will begin with a slightly reduced form of the basic STEAM model. Specifically, the provision for the effects of *time of conversion*, which are discussed in Section 9.1.6, will not be treated explicitly. Rather the time of conversion (τ) for a given household will be considered as one of the household's descriptor variables and treated in Section 11.4.1. This more uniform approach seems to have good properties and yields a simpler model. (We emphasize that time of conversion effects are not deleted from the model but only changed slightly in form and notation.)

Likewise, we will not carry the probability that a household's $\mu_0 > 0$ through the mathematical derivations in this chapter. Parameters M_r can easily be added to the model to accommodate this effect, and indeed they will have to be incorporated when the new model is made operational. For the present, however, they would only complicate an already difficult discussion.

The model that provides the starting point for this chapter is as follows:

Primary model for interpurchase times:

$$f\{t|\mu(t)\} = \exp\left[-m(t)\right]\mu(t) \quad t \geq 1 \tag{11.1a}$$

where

$$m(t) = \int_1^t \mu(x)\, dx$$

Secondary model for the effect of time since conversion:

$$\mu(t) = \mu t^\lambda \quad \text{where } t \geq 1 \tag{11.1b}$$

Secondary model for mixed populations, given $\mu_0 > 0$:

$$f(\mu|\alpha,\beta) = \frac{\beta \exp\left(-\beta\mu\right)(\beta\mu)^{\alpha-1}}{\Gamma(\alpha)} \tag{11.1c}$$

The indices for household and depth of trial class have been deleted in order to simplify the notation.

This basic model contains three free parameters which, as the reader will recall, are estimated from consumer panel data and interpreted as follows:

$\lambda =$ The rate at which the family's purchase propensity changes with time since the last purchase (sometimes termed *forgetting*, though other factors may also be important).

$\alpha,\beta =$ The parameters of the prior distribution of purchase propensities.

The model requires that $\lambda > -1$ and $\alpha,\beta > 0$. When $\lambda = 0$ this model reduces to the negative binomial discussed by Ehrenberg (1959).

The reader is referred to Chapters 9 and 10 for a more detailed discussion of the STEAM model, its justification and uses, and methods for estimating its parameters. We will assume familiarity with that material throughout the present chapter.

11.2 Purchases of Other Products or Brands

In our introduction of basic STEAM we argued that new product adoption models should not place great reliance upon the researcher's ability to define the product class in which the new offering is imbedded. This implies, in turn, that models for predicting choice among a fixed set of brands, given that a purchase occurs in the first place, are likely to be of limited usefulness in the new product context. The reasons for this view were (1) many new products are positioned between the currently defined product categories, and (2) in most new product research studies it is as important to predict usage rate as it is to predict brand choice. The basic STEAM model neglected purchases of other brands and related products entirely.

We are now in a position to relax the rigid assumption that other brand purchases have no effect on a household's propensity to purchase the new product, while still retaining our original position as described in the last paragraph. The hypothesis which provides the basis for this extension of STEAM is:

Purchases of certain substitute or complimentary products or brands during the time the household is in the kth depth of trial class lead to a revaluation of the worth of the new product and hence a change in the time path of the purchase propensity μ. However, changes in the propensity to

purchase the new product exert only a negligible effect on the purchase rates for the other products, at least during the introductory period.

This phenomenon is another example of the "purchase event feedback" or learning concept; it is analogous to but not necessarily identical with the feedback that is assumed to take place when the new product itself is purchased.

11.2.1 Basic Assumptions

Suppose we observe the purchase sequence given in Figure 11.1 as part of the data collected for a particular panel household. That is, the household entered the kth depth of trial class at time t_0, made a purchase of a substitute product in the interval between t_p and $t_p + h$ and made his $k + 1$ new product purchase in the interval following t_q.

In the basic STEAM model, we assumed that the household evaluated the new product shortly after the kth purchase and came up with a particular value of μ at t_0, denoted by $\mu(t_0)$ or just μ. Our knowledge about $\mu(t_0)$ for a given depth of repeat class was summed up by the "prior" distribution $f(\mu|\alpha,\beta)$, as shown in Equation 11.1c. Starting at the value of $\mu(t_0)$ obtained by the "draw" from $f(\mu|\alpha,\beta)$, we assumed in Equation 11.1b that the household's μ would evolve through time according to the relation $\mu(t) = t^\lambda \mu(t_0)$.

We now extend the model to allow the household to change its μ-value as the result of purchasing other products. Let us define

$w_s = i + 1$, where i is the number of purchases of substitute products since entering the current depth of trial class;

$w_c = j + 1$, where j is the number of purchases of compliment products since entering the current depth of trial class; and

v_s, v_c = new parameters.

Equation 11.1b must be changed to make μ a function of w_c and w_s. It will be convenient to assume that all these transformations are made at

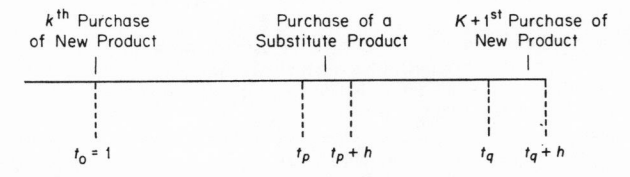

Figure 11.1.   A purchase sequence for a hypothetical household.

time t_0, and updated to t_p later. (This will be discussed later in connection with Figure 11.2.) We assume that

$$\mu(t_0, w_s, w_c) = w_s^{v_s} w_c^{v_c} \mu(t_0, 1, 1) \qquad (11.2a)$$

where $\mu(t_0, 1, 1) = \mu(t_0) = \mu$, as given in Equation 11.1b. It will also be
useful to express μ as a recursive function of the w as follows:

$$\mu(t_0, w_s + \Delta w_s, w_c + \Delta w_c)$$

$$= \left(\frac{w_s + \Delta w_s}{w_s}\right)^{v_s} \cdot \left(\frac{w_c + \Delta w_c}{w_c}\right)^{v_c} \cdot \mu(t_0, w_s, w_c) \quad (11.2b)$$

for $w_s, w_c \geq 1$.

The new parameters v_s and v_c may be interpreted in the same manner
as λ and γ, which is shown in Figure 9.1 of Chapter 9. If their absolute
values are less than one, the incremental effects of additional "other
product" purchases will decline. That is, in this case the most damage
done by substitutes or assistance given by compliments will occur during
the first few such purchases in a given depth of trial class. This seems
reasonable. We would expect purchases of the substitute brand to
decrease μ, so v_s should normally be negative. By the same argument v_c should be positive. Of course either w_s or w_c could be left out of
the model without affecting the interpretation of its counterpart.[1]

The extended STEAM model does not attempt to predict when the
purchases of other products will occur. Our approach is to wait passively
until such a purchase is made (if indeed it is made at all) and then modify
the household's propensity to purchase the new product accordingly.
More precisely, we change the appropriate w-value in Equation 11.2a
whenever an "other product" purchase occurs, thus causing a jump in
the time series for μ. Multiple purchases of other products will be
handled by cascading the change process through further increments to
w, as in Equation 11.2b.

Our assumptions about purchase event feedback can be regarded as a
variant on the linear learning model discussed in Chapter 5. We regard
learning as taking place through a change in the household's purchase
propensity parameter μ rather than via a brand-choice probability.

---

[1] A revision of the definition of w_c and w_s to include the *total* number of purchases of
other products since the introduction of the new product (rather than just the number
in the current depth of trial class) is also intuitively appealing. For $v < 1$ this
definition implies that the effect of other product purchases is likely to be smaller in
higher depth of repeat classes, which is reasonable. However, the biggest advantage
of this approach is that the probable strong relation between w and τ might allow us to
drop the τ effect given in Section 9.2.4 of Chapter 9, thus saving one parameter and
simplifying the estimation procedure.

The "gain operator," that specifies the change in μ as the result of purchasing the new product, is left unspecified; we estimate parameters for each depth of repeat class separately. The "loss operator" is introduced by our current extension to basic STEAM; at each transition it is essentially a linear learning assumption with the intercept term fixed at zero.

The main limitation to our treatment of "other product" purchases lies in the fact that we must assume that their incidence is independent of the factors included in the model; that is, that the w-value conditions μ but that μ has no effect on the incidence or timing of other product purchases. This assumption is clearly false if the other products are really close compliments or substitutes to the new product; in this case a brand-choice model like those discussed in Chapters 3 through 7 might provide a better starting point for a new product evaluation model. (It would still be necessary to build purchase timing into these models, however.) The justification of our assumption lies in the fact that few new products bear a one-to-one relation with a product that is already on the market. We feel that it is much better not to have to commit ourselves as to product class in new product evaluation work. The extended STEAM model discussed here seems to represent a reasonable compromise on this question precisely because it allows for other product purchase effects to be incorporated without making the fundamental properties of the model depend on the correct determination of product class prior to the analysis of empirical data.

11.2.2 Mathematical Specification

In order to make our model of other purchase effects operational, we must find a closed form expression for the probability of getting any sequence of purchases, given a particular set of parameter values. Consider the sequence given in Figure 11.1, where we have a purchase of the new product in the interval $(t_q, t_q + h)$ and an other product purchase in $(t_p, t_p + h)$. Let us denote a new product purchase event by $\mathscr{P} \in (t_q, t_q + h)$, and its compliment (i.e., the event that no purchase takes place in an interval) by $\tilde{\mathscr{P}} \in (t_0, t_q)$. Then the likelihood of observing the event given in Figure 11.1 is $\Pr[\mathscr{P} \in (t_q, t_q + h)]$. Anticipating the need to provide for a change in μ at t_p, and recalling that the purchase of the other product is to be regarded as an act of God, we can write the sample likelihood for this household as

$$\Pr[\mathscr{P} \in (t_q, t_q + h)] = \Pr[\mathscr{P} \in (t_q, t_q + h) | \tilde{\mathscr{P}} \in (t_0, t_p)] \Pr[\tilde{\mathscr{P}} \in (t_0, t_p)]$$

$$(11.3)$$

The second term does not pose any problem, but we must establish the results shown in Section 11.2.2.1 and 11.2.2.2 before we can adequately specify the conditional probability needed for the first term.

11.2.2.1 The Distribution of t, Starting at t_p Rather than t_0. Equation 11.1a specifies that the primary model for interpurchase times is nonstationary Poisson, with intensity function $\mu(t)$. This is a stochastic counting process where the counts are assumed to begin at $t = t_0 = 1$, which is defined as the time of the last purchase of the new product. (We shall only be concerned with the waiting time to the first count — the next purchase of the new product.) In dealing with purchases of other brands, however, we will have occasion to begin counting at t_p rather t_0, because the process is assumed to change at t_p. But in doing this we must remember that the origin of $\mu(t)$ remains fixed at t_0, in order that the *forgetting curve*[2] be keyed to the last purchase of the new product. Therefore, we must consider the following generalization of Equation 11.1a:

$$\mu(t) = \mu t^\lambda$$

$$m(t|t_p) = \int_{t_p}^{t} \mu(x)\,dx = \frac{\mu}{\lambda + 1}\,(t^{\lambda+1} - t_p^{\lambda+1})$$

for $t > t_p \geq 1$. All t are measured relative to $t_0 = 1$. The fact that the fixed origin of $\mu(t)$ makes this more than a simple translation of the Poisson process is emphasized by writing the mean value function as $m(t|t_p)$ rather than $m(t - t_p)$.

Hence the conditional density for the time to the next new product purchase, given that we start counting at t_p, is

$$f(t|\mu,\lambda,t_p) = \mu(t)\exp\left[-m(t|t_p)\right]$$

$$= \mu t^\lambda \exp\left[-\frac{\mu}{\lambda+1}\,(t^{\lambda+1} - t_p^{\lambda+1})\right] \qquad (11.4)$$

Easy integration shows that the conditional distribution function is

$$F(t|\mu,\lambda,t_p) = 1 - \exp\left[-\frac{\mu}{\lambda+1}\,(t^{\lambda+1} - t_p^{\lambda+1})\right] \qquad (11.5)$$

---

[2] The *forgetting curve* is shorthand for the time-change process that applies to μ as given in Equation 11.1b. It is something of a misnomer, as "forgetting" can lead to positive increments to μ if λ is positive, and in any case other things can enter besides loss of awareness. Nevertheless, it is a fairly good description of what we assume to be the basic process in purchasing behavior that is described by this function. Also, we ignore the extension to Equation 11.1b given by Equation 11.2a for purposes of the argument stated above.

The relation of Equations 11.4 and 11.5 to 9.17 and 9.18 of Chapter 9 is obvious: the fixed value "1" in all terms of the form $t^{\lambda+1} - 1$ is replaced by $t_p^{\lambda+1}$ to yield $t^{\lambda+1} - t_p^{\lambda+1}$ throughout, while terms of the form t^λ are unchanged. The same relations hold up when μ is integrated out to obtain the unconditional density and distribution functions for inter-purchase times given in Equations 9.19 and 9.20. We restate the results here mainly to provide a point of reference for the sequel.

$$f(t|\alpha,\beta,\lambda; t_p) = \alpha\beta^\alpha(\lambda + 1)^\alpha \frac{t^\lambda}{[t^{\lambda+1} - t_p^{\lambda+1} + \beta(\lambda + 1)]} \quad (11.6)$$

$$F(t|\alpha,\beta,\lambda; t_p) = 1 - \left[\frac{\beta(\lambda + 1)}{t^{\lambda+1} - t_p^{\lambda+1} + \beta(\lambda + 1)}\right]^\alpha \quad (11.7)$$

The notation of Equation 11.6 and 11.7 may be shortened by specification of a parameter vector $\boldsymbol{\theta} = \{\alpha,\beta,\lambda\}$.

11.2.2.2 *The likelihood as a function of $F(t|\boldsymbol{\theta},t_p)$.* Let us examine the first term of Equation 11.3:

$$\Pr[\mathscr{P} \in (t_q, t_q + h)|\mathscr{P} \in (t_0,t_p)] = \frac{F(t_q + h|\boldsymbol{\theta}', t_0) - F(t_q|\boldsymbol{\theta}',t_0)}{1 - F(t_p|\boldsymbol{\theta}',t_0)} \quad (11.8)$$

where $\boldsymbol{\theta}'$ is the vector of original or "prior" parameter values, in contrast to the "posterior" values to be discussed later. While Equation 11.8 is clearly correct, it seems reasonable to expect that the conditional probability can also be expressed as a function of $F(t|\boldsymbol{\theta},t_p)$, the waiting time distribution starting at t_p rather than t_0. This leads us to the following proposition, which we will now prove.

PROPOSITION

$$\Pr[\mathscr{P} \in (t_q, t_q + h)|\tilde{\mathscr{P}} \in (t_0,t_p)] = F(t_q + h|\boldsymbol{\theta}'',t_p) - F(t_q|\boldsymbol{\theta}'',t_p),$$
$$(11.9)$$

where $\boldsymbol{\theta}'' = (\alpha'',\beta'',\lambda)$ and

$$\alpha'' = \alpha' \equiv \alpha \qquad \beta'' = \frac{t_p^{\lambda+1} - t_0^{\lambda+1}}{\lambda + 1} + \beta' \qquad \beta' \equiv \beta$$

Here β'' is the β-value of the posterior distribution of $\mu(t_0)$, given that no new product purchase has occurred in the interval (t_0,t_p). (See Equation 9.31 of Chapter 9, which also shows that $\alpha'' = \alpha'$.)

To prove the proposition we need to show that the right side of Equation 11.9 is equal to the right side of Equation 11.8.

Proof:

Starting with the last term of Equation 11.9, we have

$$F(t_q|\theta'',t_p) = \int_{t_p}^{t_q} f(t|\theta'',t_p)\, dt$$

$$f(t|\theta'',t_p) = \int_0^\infty f(t|\lambda,\mu,t_p)f''(\mu|\alpha'',\beta'')\, d\mu$$

where the first term is given by Equation 11.4. The second term is the posterior density of μ; by Bayes' theorem it can be written as a function of the prior distribution and the conditional likelihood of observing no new product purchase during the interval (t_0,t_p), given μ:

$$f''(\mu|\alpha'',\beta'') = \frac{1}{K}\,[1 - F(t_p|\mu,\lambda,t_0)]f'(\mu|\alpha',\beta')$$

where

$$K = \int_0^\infty [1 - F(t_p|\mu,\lambda,t_0)]f'(\mu|\alpha',\beta')\, d\mu = 1 - F(t_p|\theta',t_0)$$

By Equation 9.31, we know that $f''(\mu|\alpha'',\beta'')$ is a gamma distribution. Substitution into the preceding expression yields

$$f(t|\theta'',t_p) = \frac{1}{1 - F(t_p|\theta',t_0)} \int_0^\infty f(t|\lambda,\mu,t_p)[1 - F(t_p|\mu,\lambda,t_0)]$$

$$\times f'(\mu|\alpha',\beta')\, d\mu$$

$$= \frac{1}{1 - F(t_p|\theta',t_0)} \int_0^\infty \mu t^\lambda$$

$$\times \exp\left[-\frac{\mu}{\lambda+1}\,(t^{\lambda+1} - t_p^{\lambda+1} + t_p^{\lambda+1} - t_0^{\lambda+1})\right]$$

$$\times f'(\mu|\alpha',\beta')\, d\mu$$

$$= \frac{f(t|\theta',t_0)}{1 - F(t_p|\theta',t_0)}$$

Hence,

$$F(t_q|\theta'',t_p) = \frac{1}{1 - F(t_p|\theta',t_0)}\,\{F(t_q|\theta',t_0) - F(t_p|\theta', t_0)\}$$

and

$$F(t_q + h|\theta'', t_p) = \frac{1}{1 - F(t_p|\theta',t_0)}\,\{F(t_q + h|\theta', t_0) - F(t_p|\theta',t_p)\}$$

Subtracting the first of this pair of equations from the second yields Equation 11.9, which is now seen to be identical to 11.8. Hence we can "break" the purchasing behavior process at t_p, using $F(t|\boldsymbol{\theta}',t_0)$ before the break and $F(t|\boldsymbol{\theta}'',t_p)$ after the break, without changing the likelihood function.

11.2.2.3 *The Case of an "Other Product" Purchase.*

The independent increments property of the Poisson process, which provides our basic model of purchasing behavior, allows us to think of the terms of Equation 11.3 as representing two separate processes. The first process begins at t_0 with the "prior" parameter vector $\boldsymbol{\theta}'$. It will be regarded as having ended at t_p. The second process comes into play at $t_p + h$, with parameters $\boldsymbol{\theta}''$, which are of course linked at $\boldsymbol{\theta}'$. (The interval during which the other product is purchased — t_p to $t_p + h$ — will be regarded as "dead" so far as the model is concerned; this involves the small change in notation to be shown below.)

We are assuming that the household's μ-value has been changed just prior to the application of the second process at t_p. However, the multiplicative property of Equation 11.2, which gives μ as a function of w_s, w_c, and t, allows us to, (1) represent the change as occurring at the origin (t_0) and then, (2) update μ by $t_p^{\lambda+1}$. The fact that the second process does not become operative until t_p ensures that this fiction will not effect the sample likelihood function. The situation is depicted graphically in Figure 11.2, where the solid curves indicate the time periods in which each μ-series is operative and the w are specified at their initial values of "1" before the purchase of the substitute. We need to find the distribution of $\mu(t_0,w_s,w_c)$, which determines the intercept of the lower curve at $t = t_0$.

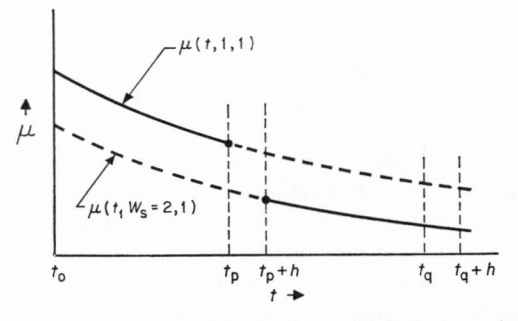

Figure 11.2. Time path of μ before and after the purchase of a substitute product.

We have already shown that as of t_p the relevant distribution of $\mu(t_0,1,1)$ — the intercept of the upper curve — is $f''(\mu|\alpha'',\beta'')$. By Equation 11.2, the $\mu(t_0,w_s,w_c)$ is a transformation of $\mu(t_0,1,1)$. That is,

$$f''\{\mu(t_0,w_c,w_s)\} = f''\{w_c^{v_c}w_s^{v_s}\mu|\alpha'',\beta''\}$$

The Jacobian of the transformation is $1/w_s^{v_s} w_c^{v_c}$ so it is obvious from the form of the gamma distribution given in Equation 11.1c that $f''\{\mu(t_0,w_s, w_c)\}$ is gamma with parameters α'' and

$$\beta''(w_s,w_c) = \frac{\beta''}{w_s^{v_s}w_c^{v_c}} = \frac{1}{w_s^{v_s}w_c^{v_c}}\left\{\frac{t_p^{\lambda+1} - t_0^{\lambda+1}}{\lambda + 1} + \beta'\right\} \qquad (11.10)$$

We must recall, however, that Equation 11.10 applies only to the case where *either* w_c or w_s is equal to two, and the other is unity (i.e., only one other product purchase has occurred).

11.2.2.4   *The Case of Multiple Other Product Purchases.*   Only minor modifications are required in order to apply this machinery to multiple other product purchases in the same depth of trial class. We will present a set of recursive relations by which each such purchase may be handled in turn.

Suppose we observe that a household makes other product purchases in $(t_p, t_p + h)$, $(t_r, t_r + h)$, and $(t_s, t_s + h)$, and finally purchases the new product in the interval $(t_q, t_q + h)$. We first consider the other product purchase made at t_r. By Equation 11.2b and the arguments given in Section 11.2.2.3, we have

$$\beta'''(w_s + \Delta w_s, w_c + \Delta w_c) = \frac{\beta'''(w_s,w_c)}{\left(\dfrac{w_s + \Delta w_s}{w_s}\right)^{v_s}\left(\dfrac{w_c + \Delta w_c}{w_c}\right)^{v_c}} \qquad (11.11)$$

where $\beta'''(w_s,w_c)$ is the parameter of the distribution of μ posterior to observing no new product purchases in $(t_p + h, t_r)$, given that there were none in (t_0,t_p).

To get the posterior distribution of μ as of t_r, we multiply the prior of μ as of $t_p + h$ by the likelihood of observing no purchases in $(t_p + h, t_r)$. The prior as of $t_p + h$ is given by Equation 11.10, which incorporates information on both the fact that there was no new product purchase in the interval (t_0,t_p) and that there was an other product purchase, and hence a change in μ, just before $t_p + h$. The likelihood of $\tilde{\mathscr{P}} \in (t_p + h, t_r)$ is a function of $F(t|\mu, \lambda, t_p + h)$ as given by Equation

11.5. Therefore, the arguments given in connection with Equation 9.31 of Chapter 9 and above imply that

$$f'''\{\mu(t_0, w_s, w_c)\} = \frac{1}{K}[1 - F(t_r | \mu, \lambda, t_p + h)]f''\{\mu(t_0, w_c, w_s)\}$$

is gamma distributed (the same as f'') and $\alpha''' = \alpha'' = \alpha$ and

$$\beta'''(w_s, w_c) = \frac{t_r^{\lambda+1} - (t_p + h)^{\lambda+1}}{\lambda + 1} + \beta''(w_s, w_c)$$

$$= \frac{t_r^{\lambda+1} - (t_p + h)^{\lambda+1}}{\lambda + 1} + \frac{1}{w_s^{v_s} w_c^{v_c}} \left\{ \frac{t_p^{\lambda+1} - t_0^{\lambda+1}}{\lambda + 1} + \beta' \right\} \quad (11.12)$$

The substitution for β'' is obtained from Equation 11.10. The transformation to the new value of μ given the increments Δw_s and Δw_c (one of which will be one and the other zero) is then obtained by applying Equation 11.11.

By the same set of arguments, we have for the other product purchase after t_s,

$$\beta^{(4)}(w_s + \Delta w_s, w_c + \Delta w_c) = \frac{\beta^{(4)}(w_s, w_c)}{\left(\dfrac{w_s + \Delta w_s}{w_s}\right)^{v_s} \left(\dfrac{w_c + \Delta w_c}{w_c}\right)^{v_c}}$$

where

$$\beta^{(4)}(w_s, w_c) = \frac{t_s^{\lambda+1} - (t_r + h)^{\lambda+1}}{\lambda + 1} + \beta'''(w_s, w_c)$$

The values of w_s and w_c are of course taken at time $t_r + h$, just after the second other product purchase. Similar relations would hold for any subsequent other product purchases. These results will be summarized in the next section.

11.2.3 The Likelihood Function

In Chapter 10 we discussed several methods for estimating the parameters of basic STEAM: i.e., continuous and discreet maximum likelihood and minimum chi-square. However, a discussion of estimation procedures for extended STEAM will be limited to the discreet maximum likelihood case. This is because difficulties were encountered when using continuous maximum likelihood, on the one hand, and the fact that the larger number of variables required for extended STEAM will reduce cell sample sizes below the level needed for effective use of chi-square on the other. (See Section 11.5.)

A general expression for the discreet time likelihood function for one other brand purchase was given in Equation 11.3. This can be extended to cover the multiple purchase case. A slightly more expressive notation will also be provided.

Suppose that a household is observed to have the following purchase sequence

> Enters Kth depth of trial class at t_0,
> Purchases another product in $(t_1, t_1 + h)$,
> Purchases another product in $(t_2, t_2 + h)$,
> Purchases the new product again in $(t_3, t_3 + h)$.

The likelihood of this event is

$$
\begin{aligned}
\Pr[\mathscr{P} \in (t_3, t_3 + h)] &= \Pr[\mathscr{P} \in (t_3, t_3 + h) | \tilde{\mathscr{P}} \in (t_2 + h, t_3)] \\
&\times \Pr[\tilde{\mathscr{P}} \in (t_2 + h, t_3) | \tilde{\mathscr{P}} \in (t_1 + h, t_2)] \\
&\times \Pr[\tilde{\mathscr{P}} \in (t_1 + h, t_2) | \tilde{\mathscr{P}} \in (t_0, t_1)] \\
&\times \Pr[\tilde{\mathscr{P}} \in (t_0, t_1)]
\end{aligned}
\qquad
\begin{aligned}
&(3)\\
&(2)\\
&(1)
\end{aligned}
$$

where we have numbered the terms for easy identification.

Each term will depend on a particular set of parameters which will be denoted by $\theta^{(i)}$. We also define the vector giving the number of substitute and compliment products purchased so far in terms of i:

$$
\mathbf{w}^{(i)} = \{w_s^{(i)}, w_c^{(i)}\} \quad \text{where} \quad w_s^{(1)} = w_c^{(1)} = 1
$$

Using this notation and the results leading to Equation 11.9, we can write the logarithm of the likelihood as:[3]

$$
\begin{aligned}
&\log \Pr[\mathscr{P} \in (t_3, t_3 + h)] \\
&\quad = \log \left[\frac{F(t_3 + h|\theta^{(3)}, t_2 + h) - F(t_3|\theta^{(3)}, t_2 + h)}{1 - F(t_3|\theta^{(3)}, t_2 + h)} \right] \Bigg\} \quad (3) \\
&\quad + \log [1 - F(t_3|\theta^{(3)}, t_2 + h)] \\
&\quad + \log [1 - F(t_2|\theta^{(2)}, t_1 + h)] \qquad\qquad\qquad (2) \\
&\quad + \log [1 - F(t_1|\theta^{(1)}, t_0)] \qquad\qquad\qquad (1) \quad (11.13)
\end{aligned}
$$

where $\theta^{(i)} = \{\alpha, \beta^{(i)}, \lambda\}$.

---

[3] The denominator of second part of term (3) can be canceled against the first part of term (3) in Equation 11.13. However, the evaluation of

$$
F(t_3 + h|\theta^{(3)}, t_2 + h) - F(t_3|\theta^{(3)}, t_2 + h)
$$

requires taking the difference between two terms which are each raised to the α power. As the two terms will be nearly equal for h small relative to t_3, this will lead to serious problems of numerical accuracy. It is easier to work with the two terms of (3) separately in this case, as can be seen from Equation 11.16.

The values of $\beta^{(1)}$ are defined recursively by Equation 11.10 to 11.12:

$$\beta^{(1)} = [w_s^{(1)v_c} w_c^{(1)v_c}]^{-1}\beta = \beta$$

$$\beta^{(2)} = \left[\left(\frac{w_s^{(2)}}{w_s^{(1)}}\right)^{v_s}\left(\frac{w_c^{(2)}}{w_c^{(1)}}\right)^{v_c}\right]^{-1}\left[\frac{t_1^{\lambda+1} - t_0^{\lambda+1}}{\lambda + 1} + \beta^{(1)}\right] \qquad (11.14)$$

$$\beta^{(3)} = \left[\left(\frac{w_s^{(3)}}{w_s^{(2)}}\right)^{v_s}\left(\frac{w_c^{(3)}}{w_c^{(2)}}\right)^{v_c}\right]^{-1}\left[\frac{t_2^{\lambda+1} - (t_1 + h)^{\lambda+1}}{\lambda + 1} + \beta^{(2)}\right]$$

Hence the likelihood function is completely defined by the parameters α, β, λ, v_s, and v_c, and the known values of the $\mathbf{w}^{(i)}$ and the t. In general, the function will consist of $m + 1$ terms, where m is the total number of purchases observed including the new product purchase which terminates the sequence.

We can get some idea about the form of the likelihood function by substituting Equation 11.7 for the F in 11.13. To simplify notation we shall define a new function,

$$G(t|\boldsymbol{\theta}^{(i)}, t_k) = \frac{t^{\lambda+1} - t_k^{\lambda+1} + \beta^{(i)}(\lambda + 1)}{\lambda + 1} \qquad (11.15)$$

which is the inverse of the denominator of the kernel of Equation 11.7. Then the likelihood can be written as

$$\log \Pr[\mathscr{P} \in (t_3, t_3 + h)] = \log\left[1 - \left(\frac{G(t_3|\boldsymbol{\theta}^{(3)}, t_2 + h)}{G(t_3 + h|\boldsymbol{\theta}^{(3)}, t_2 + h)}\right)^{\alpha}\right]$$

$$+ \alpha \log\left[\frac{G(t_3|\boldsymbol{\theta}^{(3)}, t_2 + h)}{\beta^{(3)}}\right]$$

$$+ \alpha \log\left[\frac{G(t_2|\boldsymbol{\theta}^{(2)}, t_1 + h)}{\beta^{(2)}}\right]$$

$$+ \alpha \log\left[\frac{G(t_1|\boldsymbol{\theta}^{(1)}, t_0)}{\beta^{(1)}}\right] \qquad (11.16)$$

The equations defining $\beta^{(1)}$ can also be recast in terms of the G functions.

$$\beta^{(i)} = \left[\left(\frac{w_s^{(i)}}{w_s^{(i-1)}}\right)^{v_s}\left(\frac{w_c^{(i)}}{w_c^{(i-1)}}\right)^{v_c}\right]^{-1} G(t_{i-1}|\boldsymbol{\theta}^{(i-1)}, t_{i-2}) \qquad (11.17)$$

for $i > 1$, and $\beta^{(1)} = \beta$. Hence the problem of evaluating the likelihood for the purchase sequence of any family is reduced to a matter of evaluating the G functions given in Equation 11.15, for $i = 1, \ldots, m$, and substituting into Equations 11.16 and 11.17.

The likelihood for the total sample is obtained by performing these

operations for each household and summing. Thus the total sample likelihood function would consist of a sum of $N(\bar{m} + 1)$ terms, where N is the number of families in the depth of repeat class and $\bar{m}$ is the average number of purchases per family. We will have more to say about the implementation of these procedures in Section 11.5.

11.3 Effects of Marketing Variables

Basic STEAM neglects the effects of advertising, price, distribution and other marketing variables, both for the new product and its competitors. More precisely, our interpretation of Equation 11.1b and its parameter λ in terms of forgetting implies that we assume such effects to be negligible or the variables themselves to be constant during the new product introduction period. As neither assumption may be tenable in certain cases, we seek to incorporate the effects of marketing variables directly into the STEAM model.

11.3.1 Basic Assumptions

Let $Z_i(t)$ be the value of the ith marketing variable at time t, where $i = 1, \ldots, m$ (the number of marketing variables being considered). These variables might represent the level of advertising support during week (or month) t in a test market, the average price of the new product, its percent distribution, or other data that are commonly available as time series during a market test, roll out, or new product launch. Measures of competitive marketing efforts could also be included among the Z, or composite variables like price or advertising ratios could be used if desired.

The analogue of the classical economic concept of demand in the STEAM model is the purchase propensity parameter μ. Variations in marketing variables should induce changes in μ; these changes should be in addition to the ones related to the forces generated internally by the household which we have characterized by *forgetting*. Thus the *demand function* analog in STEAM is

$$\mu(t|t_0) = f\{\mu(t_0),t^{\lambda},\mathbf{Z}(t)\} \tag{11.18}$$

where $\mathbf{Z}(t)$ is the vector of current marketing variables, $\mu(t_0)$ is the family-specific parameter representing basic preferences, and t^{λ} is the forgetting relation.

A variety of assumptions about the form of Equation 11.18 yield tractable extensions of STEAM. The choice between them will depend partly on a priori considerations (i.e., what seems to be the most reasonable representation) and partly on goodness of fit, just as with

any empirical study of demand relations.[4] For instance, we might specify a demand function that is strictly additive in the effects of forgetting and the marketing variables,

$$\mu(t|t_0) = \mu(t_0)\{t^\lambda + \epsilon_1 Z_1(t) + \epsilon_2 Z_2(t) + \cdots\} \qquad (11.19)$$

This implies that while the effects of t^λ and Z depend on the household's basic preference structure represented by $\mu(t_0)$, they are independent of each other. The situation is illustrated in Figure 11.3, where we assume that $\lambda < 0$ and that advertising support (for instance) builds up to a peak a short time after the introduction of the new product and then is allowed to taper off to zero. The net value of $\mu(t)$, which determines the distribution of waiting times to the next purchase, is given by the sum of the two lower curves in Figure 11.3.

Equation 11.20 seems to provide a more reasonable representation of the demand relation:

$$\mu(t|t_0) = \mu(t_0)t^\lambda\{\epsilon_0 + \epsilon_1 Z_1(t) + \epsilon_2 Z_2(t) + \cdots\} \qquad (11.20)$$

Here the marginal effects of marketing variables are assumed to depend on the household's basic purchase propensity at time t, rather than at t_0 as in Equation 11.19. This implies that it will be harder for advertising (or other marketing variables) to influence a consumer that has "forgotten" about the new product than one whose current μ-value is large. We will develop our extension to STEAM in terms of Equation 11.20. However, the same procedures could be applied to Equation 11.19 without difficulty.

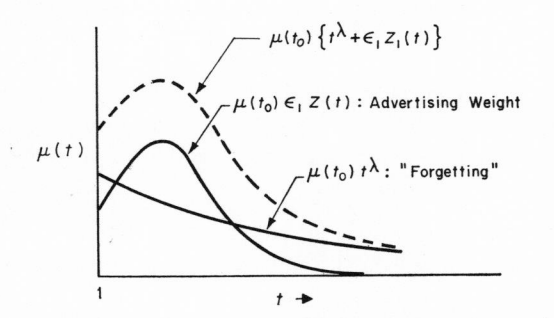

Figure 11.3.   Effects of advertising and forgetting on the time path of purchase propensity for a hypothetical household.

[4] It is much more difficult to estimate the STEAM parameters than (say) regression coefficients. This implies that fewer alternatives can be investigated empirically and hence that a priori consideration will receive relatively greater weight in the choice of STEAM-type demand functions than has become common in other types of demand studies.

11.3.2 Mathematical Specifications

The main task of this section is to incorporate the demand relation 11.20 into the likelihood function for waiting time to the next purchase. We will keep the notation as simple as possible by dealing only with the situation where there are no purchases of other products. An extension of these results to include other product purchases will be given later. Before proceeding to the likelihood function, however, we will have to deal with the relations between the parameters and find a way of representing the time series for the marketing variables by an appropriate algebraic expression.

11.3.2.1 *Scaling the Parameters.* The STEAM model permits $\mu(t_0)$, the basic preference parameter in Equation 11.20, to be different for different households in the population. The distribution of $\mu(t_0)$ is assumed to be gamma with parameters α and β, as given by Equation 11.1c. We have already noted that β is the scale parameter of this distribution.

These considerations imply that the ϵ parameters on the right side of Equation 11.20 depend on β up to a multiplicative transformation. Multiplying Equation 11.20 by a positive constant will serve only to change the scaling of $\mu(t_0)$ and hence the value of β will be changed in exactly the same proportion. (We considered such transformations in connection with Equation 11.10 earlier in this chapter.) Thus β and all of the ϵ cannot be estimated separately. We must fix the value of one parameter, which will be regarded as a kind of Numeraire, and estimate all the other parameters in relation to it. Let us arbitrarily set

$$\epsilon_0 = 1$$

so that the t^λ term in the demand function will be regarded as having unit weight. The parameters ϵ_1, ϵ_2, etc., may now be interpreted as reflecting the *relative effects* of their associated Z variables.

11.3.2.2 *The Time Paths of the Marketing Variables.* Suppose that the time path of each Z variable can be represented by a polynomial with origin at t_0, which we will define temporarily as the date of introduction of the new product.

$$Z_i(t - t_0) = a_{i0}^{(0)} + a_{i1}^{(0)}(t - t_0) + a_{i2}^{(0)}(t - t_0)^2 + a_{i2}^{(0)}(t - t_0)^3 + \cdots \tag{11.21}$$

for $i = 1, 2, \ldots, m$. The a parameters are written with superscripts (0) to indicate that the polynomial has origin at t_0. They can be determined from the time series of the Z by using a standard polynomial fitting

program. (The method of orthogonal polynomials could be used if convenient, but this is not a necessary part of the model.) The polynomials can be carried to as many terms as needed to provide an adequate fit to the time series of the Z: additional terms add to the scale of the calculations required to estimate STEAM but do not otherwise affect the model. This operation would be performed before the application of, and quite apart from, the STEAM model. Hence the a are regarded as known numbers as far as STEAM is concerned.

Substitution of the polynomials into the demand function, which is assumed to be of the form of Equation 11.20, yields:

$$\mu(t|t_0) = \mu t^\lambda \left\{ \epsilon_0 + \epsilon_1 \sum_{r \geq 0} a_{1k}^{(0)} t^k + \epsilon_2 \sum_{k > 0} a_{2k}^{(0)} t^k + \cdots \right\}$$

where the sum in k runs over the terms included in the polynomials. (Some references to t_0 have been dropped to simplify the notation.) Multiplying through by t^λ and collecting terms in the powers of t, we have

$$\mu(t|t_0) = \mu \{ [\epsilon_0 + \epsilon_1 a_{10}^{(0)} + \cdots] t^\lambda + [\epsilon_1 a_{11}^{(0)} + \epsilon_2 a_{21}^{(0)} + \cdots] t^{\lambda+1} + \cdots \}$$

$$= \mu \sum_{k \geq 0} \left\{ \delta_k + \sum_{i=1}^{m} \epsilon_i a_{ik}^{(0)} \right\} t^{\lambda+k}$$

$$= \mu k_0(t|t_0)$$

where $\delta_0 = \epsilon_0 = 1$, and $\delta_k = 0$ for $k > 0$.

11.3.2.3 *The Distribution of Interpurchase Times.* Incorporation of the demand relation given the time paths of the marketing variables into STEAM requires that we generalize the distributions given in Equation 11.4 through 11.7 to take account of Equation 11.21.

We begin by substituting 11.21 into the mean value function of the purchasing process, conditional on a given value of $\mu(t_0)$, as given in Equation 11.1a and extended in connection with Equation 11.4.

$$m(t|t_0) = \int_{t_0}^{t} \mu(x)\,dx$$

$$= \mu \int_{t_0}^{t} \sum_{k \geq 0} \left\{ \delta_k + \sum_i \epsilon_i a_{ik}^{(0)} \right\} x^{\lambda+k}\,dx$$

$$= \mu \left[\sum_{k \geq 0} \left\{ \delta_k + \sum_i \epsilon_i a_{ik}^{(0)} \right\} \frac{x^{\lambda+k+1}}{\lambda + k + 1} \right]_{t_0}^{t}$$

$$= \mu \sum_{k \geq 0} \left\{ \delta_k + \sum_i \epsilon_i a_{ik}^{(0)} \right\} \frac{t^{\lambda+k+1} - t_0^{\lambda+k+1}}{\lambda + k + 1}$$

$$= \mu k_1(t|t_0) \tag{11.22}$$

The probability density of the time to the next purchase, conditional on μ, is given by

$$f(t|\mu,\lambda,\epsilon,\mathbf{A}^{(0)},t_0) = \mu(t|t_0) \exp\left[-m(t|t_0)\right] = \mu k_0(t|t_0) \exp\left[-\mu k_1(t|t_0)\right]$$

(11.23)

where $\mathbf{A}^{(0)}$ is the matrix of known polynomial coefficients based on t_0. The functions $k_0(t|t_0)$ and $k_1(t|t_0)$ are defined implicitly by Equation 11.22. Note that

$$\frac{dk_1(t|t_0)}{dt} = k_0(t|t_0)$$

by virtue of Equation 11.22.

The conditional distribution function is obtained by integrating Equation 11.23. The result

$$F(t|\mu,\lambda,\epsilon,\mathbf{A}^{(0)},t_0) = 1 - \exp\left[-\mu k_1(t|t_0)\right]$$

(11.24)

is easily verified by differentiation.

The unconditional density of t is obtained by integrating μ from the conditional density. Except for the fact that μ is now multiplied by $k_0(t|t_0)$ and $k_1(t|t_0)$ the integration proceeds as for Equation 9.9 of Chapter 9. The result is

$$\begin{aligned}
f(t|\alpha,\beta,\lambda,\epsilon,\mathbf{A},t_0) &= \int_0^\infty f(t|\mu, \lambda,\epsilon,\mathbf{A},t_0) f(\mu|\alpha,\beta)\, d\mu \\
&= \frac{\beta^\alpha k_0(t|t_0)}{\Gamma(\alpha)} \int_0^\infty \exp\left\{-\mu[k_1(t|t_0) + \beta]\right\} \mu^\alpha\, d\mu \\
&= \alpha\beta^\alpha \frac{k_0(t|t_0)}{[k_1(t|t_0) + \beta]^{\alpha+1}}
\end{aligned}$$

which is analogous to Equation 11.6. The distribution function of waiting times is obtained by integrating $f(t|\alpha,\beta,\lambda,\epsilon,\mathbf{A},t_0)$. We assume the result

$$\alpha\beta^\alpha \int \frac{k_0(t|t_0)}{[k_1(t|t_0) + \beta]^{\alpha+1}}\, dt = -\left(\frac{\beta}{[k_1(t|t_0) + \beta]}\right)^\alpha$$

This is easily verified by differentiation, since

$$\frac{d}{dt} - \left(\frac{\beta}{[k_1(t|t_0) + \beta]}\right)^\alpha = \frac{\alpha\beta^\alpha}{[k_1(t|t_0) + \beta]^{\alpha+1}} \cdot \frac{dk_1(t|t_0)}{dt}$$

and $k_1'(t|t_0) = k_0(t|t_0)$. Hence the distribution of waiting times to the next purchase is given by

$$F(t|\alpha,\beta,\lambda,\boldsymbol{\epsilon},\mathbf{A}^{(0)},t_0) = \left[-\left\{ \frac{\beta}{[k_1(x|t_0) + \beta]} \right\}^{\alpha} \right]^t_{t_0}$$

$$= 1 - \left\{ \frac{\beta}{\beta + \sum_{k \geq 0} \left\{ \delta_k + \sum_i \epsilon_i a_{ik}^{(0)} \right\} \dfrac{t^{\lambda+k+1} - t_0^{\lambda+k+1}}{\lambda + k + 1}} \right\}^{\alpha}$$

(11.25)

Except for the fact that $k_1(x|t_0)$ is somewhat complicated, this is identical to Equation 11.7.

11.3.2.4 *The Posterior Distribution of μ Given $\tilde{\mathscr{P}} \in (t_0,t)$.* The posterior distribution of μ is obtained by multiplying the prior density by the conditional likelihood of observing no purchases in the interval (t_0,t). The derivation is a routine extension of the work leading to Equation 9.31.

$$f''(\mu|\alpha'',\beta'') = \text{const} \, [1 - F(t|\mu,\lambda,\boldsymbol{\epsilon},\mathbf{A}^{(0)},t_0)] f'(\mu|\alpha',\beta')$$

$$= \text{const} \, e^{-\mu[k_1(t|t_0)+\beta']} \mu^{\alpha'-1} \qquad (11.26a)$$

which is the kernel of a gamma distribution with parameters

$$\alpha'' = \alpha' \quad \text{and} \quad \beta'' = k_1(t|t_0) + \beta' \qquad (11.26b)$$

11.3.3 The Likelihood Function

Suppose that a particular household enters the kth depth of trial class at time t_0 and make its next new product purchase during the interval $(t_q, t_q + h)$. Following the general approach used earlier in this chapter, we can write the discreet time likelihood of this event as

$$\Pr[\mathscr{P} \in (t_q, t_q + h)] = \Pr[\mathscr{P} \in (t_q, t_q + h) | \tilde{\mathscr{P}} \in (t_0,t_q)] \Pr[\tilde{\mathscr{P}} \in (t_0,t_q)]$$

Hence the logarithm of the likelihood function is

$$\log \Pr[\mathscr{P} \in (t_q, t_q + h)] = \log \left[\frac{F(t_q + h|\boldsymbol{\theta},\mathbf{A}^{(0)},t_0) - F(t_q|\boldsymbol{\theta},\mathbf{A}^{(0)},t_0)}{1 - F(t_q|\boldsymbol{\theta},\mathbf{A}^{(0)},t_0)} \right]$$

$$+ \log \, [1 - F(t_q|\boldsymbol{\theta},\mathbf{A}^{(0)},t_0)]$$

where

$$\boldsymbol{\theta} = \{\alpha,\beta,\lambda,\epsilon_1,\epsilon_2,...\}$$

is the vector of parameters. This reduces to

$$\log \Pr[\mathscr{P} \in (t_q, t_q + h)] = \log \left[1 - \left(\frac{k_1(t_q|t_0) + \beta}{k_1(t_q + h|t_0) + \beta} \right)^\alpha \right]$$

$$+ \alpha \log \left[\frac{\beta}{k_1(t_q|t_0) + \beta} \right] \qquad (11.27)$$

This is summed over all the households in the panel to yield the overall sample likelihood which will then be maximized with respect to the elements of θ by numerical methods.

One additional complication is involved in the specification of the likelihood: different households may have different values of t_0 for all but the 0th depth of trial class. The value of t_0 is known for each household, because that is the time at which it entered the current depth of trial class. It is necessary to translate the a so that the $Z(t)$ polynomials have origin at each household's t_0 when evaluating its part of the likelihood.

The best procedure will be to evaluate the elements of a basic matrix $\mathbf{A}^{(t*)}$, where t_* is the time of introduction for the new product, from the empirical time series for the marketing variables. This need only be done once. Then $\mathbf{A}^{(t*)}$ can be transformed to $\mathbf{A}^{(t_0)}$, for the various values of t_0, by means of one of the standard routines for translating the origin of a polynomial. This may have to be done once for each household in each depth of repeat class (except perhaps the 0th, where all t_0 will probably coincide with t^*). Once these translations are made, however, the likelihood can be evaluated as many times as necessary without repeating this part of the work. (We do *not* have to maximize the likelihood with respect to the elements of $\mathbf{A}$.) These procedures can be easily extended to cover situations where the time series of the marketing variables are different for different metropolitan areas.

11.3.4   Adding "Other Product" Effects

The likelihood for the fully extended STEAM model can be obtained without difficulty from Equations 11.16 and 11.27. This model includes the effects of both "other product" purchases and marketing variables, as well as the representations of response heterogeneity, "forgetting," and prior conditioning that were a part of basic STEAM.

First, we note that if the marketing variables are removed from Equation 11.22 — that is, if the elements of the $\mathbf{A}$ matrix or ϵ vector

are set to zero — then the k_1 function reduces to the following familiar quantity

$$k_1(t|t_0) \equiv k_1(t|\lambda,\epsilon,\mathbf{A}^{(0)},t_0) = \frac{t^{\lambda+1} - t_0^{\lambda+1}}{\lambda + 1}$$

for

$$\epsilon \quad \text{or} \quad \mathbf{A}^{(0)} = 0$$

The parameters of the k_1 function are written out explicitly in the notation used here, but the function itself is the same as that given in Equation 11.22.

The above suggests that we can express the G function defined in Equation 11.15 in terms of the k_1 function:

$$G(t|\boldsymbol{\theta}^{(i)},\mathbf{A}^{(0)},t_k) = k_1(t|\lambda,\epsilon,\mathbf{A}^{(0)},t_k) + \beta^{(i)} \qquad (11.28)$$

where the parameter vector $\boldsymbol{\theta}^{(i)}$ now includes ϵ and the known polynomial coefficient matrix $\mathbf{A}^{(0)}$ has been added to the argument list of G. The parameter $\beta^{(i)}$ in $\boldsymbol{\theta}^{(i)}$ is updated to i, the time of the last purchase of any product, by Equation 11.17; Equations 11.26b and 11.28 indicate that 11.17 is valid given the new definition of G.

The likelihood function for the combined model is still given by Equation 11.16, but now using the new definition of the G function provided by 11.28. This formulation offers considerable flexibility to the model. Indeed, the machinery developed in this chapter will hold for any k_1 function one wishes to select, provided only that it is differentiable with respect to t and meets certain general requirements about the nature of its time origins. The demand relation (i.e., the relation giving a household's purchase propensity as a function of the marketing variables and the time trend or "forgetting" term) is equal to k_0, which is the time derivative of k_1. Hence a wide variety of demand relations can be included in the model with a minimum of effort, once the basic system has been set up.

11.4 Effects of Household Descriptor Variables

Suppose that each household in the sample can be described in terms of a set of attributes $X = \{X_1, X_2, \ldots\}'$. The elements of X might be derived from

1. Socioeconomic and demographic variables,
2. Attitudes or other psychological variables,
3. Media viewing habits,
4. Shopping habits,

5. Usage patterns for suspected substitutes or compliments to the new product, measured before the date of introduction,
6. Attitudes toward or awareness of new product preadvertising,
7. Whether or not the household recieved a free sample of the new product at introduction time.

The time at which the household entered the current depth of repeat class could also be included in X and handled like any other descriptor variable, instead of being introduced separately as in Chapter 9.

The elements of X are called "descriptors" to emphasize the fact that any variable which can be measured quantitatively and used to differentiate households can be included in the analysis. The only requirements are that the measurements be taken on each family in the panel, that they do not involve purchasing behavior during the introductory period, and that they can be regarded as remaining constant during the period covered by the model.[5] The procedures to be discussed seek the same type of results as the many cross sectional studies which have attempted to relate purchasing behavior to descriptor information. Indeed, this extension of STEAM can be regarded as an attack on the general problem of using cross-sectional and time series data in a single model, which has received considerable attention in the econometric literature.

We will consider two ways of analyzing the effects of descriptor variables on purchasing behavior. In the *prior analysis* approach, we condition our prior distribution for the household's μ-value on the values of its descriptors. In *posterior analysis*, we attempt to relate our posterior distribution for the household's μ, given his observed purchasing behavior in a given depth of trial class, to the descriptors. The prior method is more comprehensive in that all the relations in the model are estimated simultaneously, but this requires that the form of the relations be specified a priori, more parameters are involved, and more extensive calculations are needed. The posterior analysis is less elegant but much more flexible; it is analogous to the process of analyzing the residuals of an estimated regression relation against variables not included in the original model. Of course the two modes of

---

[5] Purchasing behavior during the introductory period is covered elsewhere in the model; to include it in the descriptor set would be circular. Variables whose values change with time would have to be handled in the same way as the "marketing variables" considered earlier. That is, their time paths would have to be reduced to algebraic expressions and included in $k_0(t|t_0)$. We do not expect that it will ever be necessary to deal with time-varying descriptors for individual households, though this is theoretically possible.

analysis can be combined in a single study: a subset of descriptors can be incorporated in a prior analysis with the remainder being handled a posteriori.

11.4.1 Prior Analysis of Descriptors

We assume that the μ-value for a given household at time t_0 can be expressed as the following function of its descriptors:

$$\mu(t_0|X) = \mu X_1^{\gamma_1} X_2^{\gamma_2} X_3^{\gamma_3} \cdots \qquad (11.29)$$

where $X > 0$ and μ is drawn from the prior distribution $f(\mu|\alpha,\beta)$ as in earlier versions of the model. The γ-parameters reflect the relative effects of the various descriptors on the household's purchasing propensity.[6]

The work leading up to Equation 11.10 shows that if $f\{\mu(t_0)|\alpha,\beta\}$ is gamma distributed with parameters α and β, as assumed in basic STEAM and throughout this chapter, then $f\{\mu(t_0|X)|\alpha(X),\beta(X)\}$ is also gamma with parameters:

$$\alpha(X) = \alpha$$

and

$$\beta(X) = \beta/X_1^{\gamma_1} X_2^{\gamma_2} \cdots = \beta X_1^{-\gamma_1} X_2^{-\gamma_2} \cdots \qquad (11.30)$$

Thus the only change required in the machinery provided earlier in this chapter is to substitute $\beta(X)$ for β wherever it appears. Note, however, that $\beta(X)$ is *not* substituted for $\beta^{(i)}$, where $i > 1$. This is taken care of automatically by the substitution in the last line of Equation 11.17. Once these substitutions are made, the likelihood is maximized with respect to $\theta = \{\alpha,\beta,\lambda,\epsilon,\gamma\}$.

11.4.2 Posterior Analysis of Descriptors

In this mode of analysis our strategy is to: (1) estimate the parameters of either the basic or extended STEAM models by the methods discussed in Chapter 9 and earlier in this chapter, neglecting the effects of some or all of the descriptor variables; and then (2) relate the parameters of the posterior distribution of $\mu(t_0)$, as they are calculated for

---

[6] Many alternative specifications of the relation of μ to X are possible, just as was the case for the relation of purchasing propensity to marketing variables. The present one was chosen for the same reasons as led to the relation of $\alpha(\tau)$ to τ, given in Chapter 9: it offers a flexible method of representation while insuring that $\mu(t|X)$ is always positive. The constraint $X > 0$ implies that some descriptors may have to be scaled, but this is not a serious drawback. Note that this formulation could not have been adopted for the relation of μ to the marketing variables without seriously complicating the integration of $k_0(t|t_0)$.

each household in the panel for each depth of trial class, to the household's descriptor variables. The reader will recall that the parameter vector $\theta = \{\alpha, \beta, \lambda, \epsilon\}'$, is estimated for all the households in a given depth of trial class taken as a group. After this has been done, it is possible to assess a posterior distribution of the purchase propensity parameter μ for each household individually: the posterior parameters α'' and β'' are calculated from the prior parameters α and β and the households purchasing history in the depth of trial class under study.

Two separate cases must be considered when evaluating the posterior distribution of μ for a household in a given depth of trial class for purposes of descriptor analysis.

Case 1.   A household that entered the kth class at time t_0 and did not make its $k + 1$ purchase during the remainder of the time period covered by the data.

Case 2.   A household that entered the kth class at time t_0 and made its $k + 1$ purchase at time t.

Households who have not made their kth purchases of the new product during the period covered by the data are considered not to have entered the kth depth of trial class and so are not included in the analysis for that class. Purchases of other products will be ignored in our initial discussion and then added later.

The method for assessing the posterior distribution of μ for households who do not purchase in the interval (t_0, t) — that is, case one households — was given in Equation 9.31 for basic STEAM and generalized to include the effects of advertising and promotion in Equation 11.26. The latter result is

$$f''\{\mu | \theta, \mathbf{A}^{(0)}, t_0, \tilde{\mathscr{P}} \in (t_0, t)\} = \text{gamma}(\alpha'', \beta'') \qquad (11.31)$$

where

$$\alpha'' = \alpha \quad \text{and} \quad \beta'' = k_1(t|t_0) + \beta$$

and the k_1 function is defined by Equation 11.22. If the effects of marketing variables are excluded from the model, the expression for β'' reduces to

$$\beta'' = \frac{t^{\lambda+1} - t_0^{\lambda+1}}{\lambda + 1} + \beta$$

which is only a slight generalization of Equation 9.31.

In dealing with Case 2 households we know that a purchase was made at time t. The posterior distribution for the household is proportional to the product of the likelihood of this event, conditional on μ,

and the prior density of μ. It is convenient to represent the likelihood by $f(t|\mu,\lambda,\boldsymbol{\epsilon},\mathbf{A}^{(0)},t_0)$, which is the conditional density of interpurchase times (including the effects of marketing variables) as given by Equation 11.23. Since the prior is a gamma distribution (see Equation 11.1c) the posterior density is proportional to

$$f''\{\mu|\boldsymbol{\theta},\mathbf{A}^{(0)},t_0,\mathscr{P} \text{ at } t\} \propto f(t|\mu,\lambda,\boldsymbol{\epsilon},\mathbf{A}^{(0)},t_0)f(\mu|\alpha,\beta)$$

$$= \mu k_0(t|t_0) \exp\left[-\mu k_1(t|t_0)\right] \cdot \beta \exp\left(-\beta\mu\right)(\beta\mu)^{\alpha-1}$$

$$= \text{const} \exp\{-\mu[k_1(t|t_0) + \beta]\}\mu^{\alpha}$$

which is the kernel of a gamma distribution with parameters $\alpha'' = \alpha + 1$ and $\beta'' = k_1(t|t_0) + \beta$. This implies that

$$f''\{\mu|\boldsymbol{\theta},\mathbf{A}^{(0)},t_0,\mathscr{P} \text{ at } t\} = \text{gamma}(\alpha'',\beta'') \tag{11.32}$$

where

$$\alpha'' = \alpha + 1 \quad \text{and} \quad \beta'' = k_1(t|t_0) + \beta$$

The addition of other product purchases requires only a slight modification in the above. Suppose that a certain "Case 2" household made a total of i other product purchases, with the last one occurring at t_k (prior to the next purchase of the new product). The kernel of the posterior for this household can be written as follows

$$\text{likelihood } \{\mathscr{P} \text{ at } t|\mu, \ \tilde{\mathscr{P}} \in (t_0,t_k)\} \cdot \text{density}\{\mu|\tilde{\mathscr{P}} \in (t_0,t_k)\}$$

where the prior density of μ is already posterior to the fact that no new product purchase was observed up to t_k. By Equation 11.9 we know that the likelihood can be obtained by simply shifting the time origin in Equations 11.22 and 11.23 from t_0 to t_k. From the results of Equations 11.12 to 11.15, we can write the prior density conditional on a sequence of i other product purchases, simply as a gamma distribution with parameters α and $\beta^{(i)}$. Hence the results given above are unchanged except that we write

$$\beta'' = k_1(t|t_k) + \beta^{(i)} \tag{11.33}$$

and make appropriate notational changes in the arguments of f'' in Equations 11.31 and 11.32.

We are now in a position to obtain the parameters of the posterior distribution of μ for each household in each depth of trial class (providing of course that we have estimates of $\boldsymbol{\theta}$ for that class). Suppose that for each such household we calculate

$$E''_{jc}[\mu] = \left\{\frac{\alpha''}{\beta''}\right\}_{jc} \tag{11.34}$$

This is of course the expected value of household j purchasing propensity in depth of trial class c, given the model's parameters and this particular household's purchase history in the cth class.

The new statistic $E''_{jc}[\mu]$ can be used as a dependent variable in regression or cross-classification analyses aimed at getting at the effects of descriptors on purchasing behavior. In fact, it can be used for almost any purpose for which the more familiar "direct" measures of purchasing behavior (e.g., waiting times or total number of purchases in an interval) would be appropriate. Its advantages are that: (1) it has a natural interpretation in terms of the STEAM model; (2) it reduces all the data for a given j-c combination to a single number (this may represent a considerable degree of summarization especially if other product purchases are considered); and (3) it nets out population heterogeneity, forgetting, effects of marketing variables and other product purchases, etc. before the analysis of descriptors begins. One of the main purposes of a descriptive model is to transform data into a more usable form, and that is what is done when $E''[\mu]$ is used as a dependent variable in a posterior analysis of descriptors.

11.5 Computational Considerations

The extensions to STEAM developed in this chapter require modification of the parameter estimation procedures developed in Chapter 10. There we proceeded by aggregating the data for individual households into cells representing the cross classification of waiting time to the next purchase or the end of the data, tau class (time of conversion), and depth of trial class. Each cell of this table contained the number of families meeting the criteria of the cell. The cells formed the basis for the discreet maximum likelihood or minimum chi-square procedures used to estimate the parameters of basic STEAM. In the latter, for instance, each cell contributed one degree of freedom to the chi-square.

This cellular approach will not work for extended STEAM because the process of conditioning on other purchases and possible descriptor variables blows up the number of cells to an unmanageable level. Consider the situation where: (1) there are 5 descriptor variables (excluding time of conversion) each with two possible levels; (2) other purchases are neglected; and (3) twenty time intervals are covered by the data — this is of course a relatively small problem. There are $2^5 = 32$ possible combinations of descriptors, each of which would have to be broken out separately in our tables. The possible values for time of conversion run from $\tau = 1, \ldots, 20$ and for each such value

there are τ possible intervals in which the next new produce purchase may ocur, and one more representing its nonoccurrence. Thus a total of $32 \times (20 \times 21)/2 = 6720$ cells would be required for each depth of trial class. If the descriptors were each allowed to take on 4 values instead of 2, the total number of cells would be 215,040 per depth of trial class! The addition of other product purchases would multiply these totals many times.

Not only would tables like these exhaust the capacity of almost any computer, but it is easy to see that most of their cells would be empty. The number of new product purchases reported by households in a typical study runs from 15,000 to 20,000 for MRCA's National Consumer Panel down to 3000 to 5000 for the smaller test panels. As each purchase contributes to one cell the above totals represent the maximum number of cells that could be filled, even if no two households had the same descriptors or purchased at the same time. For a single depth of trial class the numbers are more likely to be in the low thousands or even the hundreds.

The way around this difficulty is to abandon the cellular structure altogether and simply maintain the data for individual households in the computer memory. A program to accomplish results would include at least three main parts:

1. *Preprocessor.* As data for each household enters the processing unit the values of its descriptors would be encoded into a compact bit pattern, which would be stored at the beginning of a memory buffer. Purchases would be processed in order, with interpurchase time, value of t_0, t_k, $\mathbf{A}^{(0)}$ and other statistics necessary for extended STEAM being calculated and encoded in the buffer. At the end of the data for each family, the portion of the buffer used for the family's history would be transferred to secondary storage (disc or binary tape). The preprocessed record for each family would be compact relative to the original purchase records and it would contain information in the form required for the STEAM likelihood function. It would be of variable length, depending on the number of depth of trial classes and other product purchases observed for the household in question. As new data became available the preprocessor would simply extend the length of the household's logical record. All the information available for a given household would always be stored in a single logical record in secondary storage.

2. *Parameter estimator.* An instruction to estimate the model's parameters for a given depth of trial class would cause the machine to search the records for each family in secondary storage and bring all the information relevant to that class into core. The information would be

arranged so that the Equations 11.12 to 11.16, 11.22, and 11.28 could be applied with a minimum of calculation once specific values for the parameters are assumed. Given the typical number of purchases present in a single depth of trial class, all this information should fit easily into the core storage of a large machine. The estimation procedure itself would consist of maximizing the sum of the logs of the likelihoods for each household, as given in Equation 11.16, by numerical methods like those discussed in Chapter 10.[7]

3. *Postprocessor.* After the parameters for all relevant depth of repeat classes have been estimated, the postprocessing program would use the household-specific logical records (which remain in secondary storage during the estimation process) to calculate summary statistics for the run. These would include: (a) predictions as to purchase rates and/or quantities, as discussed in Chapter 9; and (b) the mean of the posterior distribution of μ for each household, according to the methods developed in Section 11.4. It would probably be convenient to output a summary tape containing descriptor information and the posterior means, which could then be used for separate regression or cross-classification analyses.

The programming required to accomplish this is within the capabilities of today's practice, given a large-scale computer. On the other hand, it will have to be undertaken by experts and is likely to be rather expensive.

The main problem from the standpoint of operating the finished program is that the number of terms that have to be calculated for each evaluation of the likelihood function will run into the hundreds or even thousands, compared to the much smaller number involved when working with the cellular configuration of basic STEAM. This does not cause any particular programming problem but since the likelihood function must be evaluated many times during the estimation process it can add substantially to the program's running time, and hence to the cost of operating the system. On the other hand, this is entirely central processing unit time — no input or output is involved — so with present cost trends this problem should not be unsurmountable.

It is also interesting to speculate on the impact that time-shared computer systems with remote access consoles will have on the operation of STEAM-type models, or indeed on any of the models discussed in this book. It will be possible for the researcher to use panel data to estimate the parameters of the STEAM model, make purchase rate

---

[7] Minimum chi-square methods cannot be used here because in the absence of cellular aggregation the sample size in each cell will always be one.

and/or volume predictions based on these empirical parameters, and then "interact" with the system by affecting changes in parameters based on intuition or historical experience in order to observe their effects on the predictions. If the parameter values are assumed without the use of data, application of the STEAM model amounts to a kind of Bayesian analysis. [Howard's appliation of his dynamic inference model (1965) is of this type.] With time-shared computer systems and "classical" estimation methods such as the ones discussed here it will be possible for the researcher to freely interact with his data as he develops diagnostic statistics and sales predictions.

APPENDIX:
ON NUMERICAL METHODS FOR
PARAMETER ESTIMATION

In Chapter 2 we discussed the maximum likelihood and minimum chi-square methods for estimating the parameters of stochastic models of buying behavior. We noted that it is rarely if ever possible to minimize these functions by analytical methods; that is, one usually cannot obtain closed-form expressions giving the parameter estimates as functions of the sample statistics.

The purpose of this Appendix is to sketch two procedures for finding the maximum or minimum of the objective function used in parameter estimation, and to indicate how they may be combined to form a reasonably powerful estimation program. We do not discuss the program itself for two reasons: (1) such a discussion would be very tedious, and beyond the scope of this book; and (2) given the rate of development of nonlinear programming it is likely that our program will be obsolete long before this book sees print. However, the basic principles will endure and this appendix may help the reader to consult with experts or develop his own routine.

The basic problem in parameter estimation is to find the extremum of a function of the unknown parameter vector, say $f(\theta)$. If the estimation is minimum chi-square, for example, the function would be

$$f(\theta) = \sum_i \frac{[n_i - n\Pi_i(\theta)]^2}{n\Pi_i(\theta)} \tag{A.1}$$

In this case we would want to minimize $f(\theta)$, perhaps subject to some constraints on the elements of θ (e.g., that $\theta_j \geq 0$). We will take this minimization problem as our prototype in the following discussion. If maximization is desired, as is the case with maximum likelihood estimation, all we will need to do is substitute $-f(\theta)$ for $f(\theta)$ throughout.

One way to minimize Equation A.1 is to try to break up the feasible (and reasonable) range of θ into cells and evaluate $f(\theta)$ for one value of θ in each cell. If a certain point is found to have the smallest value the cell size may be decreased and a subinterval around this point searched. This procedure can be continued until an acceptable level of accuracy (determined by the cell size) is obtained.

445

This grid search procedure is simple to implement but it suffers from two major drawbacks. First, it is not very efficient in terms of its use of computer time. This problem becomes serious enough to make it infeasible for problems with more than a few variables.[1] Second, for many objective functions encountered in parameter estimation, the global minimum may not turn out to be anywhere near the minimum obtained with a "coarse" grid. This may occur either because of the problem of local minimum, or because the variables in the objective are highly interactive — which can lead to "valleys with steep sides which can wind between the points in the coarse grid. (The latter situation would yield a minimum at a boundary point when the finer grid is used at the next stage, requiring another fine grid search and, thus, more usage of computer time.)

It is clear that a more systematic way for deciding what values of θ to use at each stage of the searching process is needed. The two methods described below represent rather different approaches to solving this problem.[2]

The first technique is a modified, second-order Newton's method.[3] Basically, the technique consists of two stages.[4] The first stage establishes a "direction" in the parameter space such that movement in this direction will cause a decrease in $f(\theta)$. The second stage then searches for the "best" (lowest) point in the established direction.

To find the direction, the nonlinear function $f(\theta)$ is expanded through a Taylor series to terms of second order

$$f(\theta) = f(\theta_0) + \nabla f(\theta_0)(\theta - \theta_0) + \tfrac{1}{2}(\theta - \theta_0)' H(\theta_0)(\theta - \theta_0) + R$$

where θ is an arbitrary point in the parameter space, θ_0 is the "starting point," $\nabla f(\theta_0)$ is the vector

$$\left(\frac{\partial f}{\partial x_1}, \frac{\partial f}{\partial x_2}, \dots, \frac{\partial f}{\partial x_k} \right)$$

[1] The number of objective function evaluations at each "level" of the grid search is equal to K^v, where K is the number of points to be evaluated for each variable and v is the number of variables. For 7 variables and 10 points (as might be required as a bare minimum for the linear learning model discussed in Chapter 5, for example), this is equal to 10^7. If we can make 100 evaluations per second, we will have to use 10^5 seconds of machine time, which is obviously unrealistic.

[2] The description of the two methods is adapted with permission from Jones (1969, Section 5.3). The authors further acknowledge Professor Jones' assistance in developing the programs used to implement these methods.

[3] This technique has been proposed by Fiacco and McCormick (1964) to solve a wider class of problems.

[4] See Crockett and Chernoff (1955).

evaluated at $\theta = \theta_0$, $H(\theta_0)$ is the Hessian matrix,

$$H = \begin{bmatrix} \dfrac{\partial^2 f}{\partial x_1^2} & \dfrac{\partial^2 f}{\partial x_1 \partial x_2} & \cdots & \dfrac{\partial^2 f}{\partial x_1 \partial x_k} \\[2ex] \dfrac{\partial^2 f}{\partial x_1 \partial x_2} & \dfrac{\partial^2 f}{\partial x_2^2} & \cdots & \dfrac{\partial^2 f}{\partial x_2 \partial x_k} \\[1ex] \cdot & & & \cdot \\ \cdot & & & \cdot \\ \cdot & & & \cdot \\[1ex] \dfrac{\partial^2 f}{\partial x_1 \partial x_k} & & \cdots & \dfrac{\partial^2 f}{\partial x_k^2} \end{bmatrix}$$

evaluated at $\theta = \theta_0$, and R is a remainder term.

With this Taylor series, and ignoring the remainder, we have

$$\nabla f(\theta) \cong \nabla f(\theta_0) + H(\theta_0)(\theta - \theta_0)$$

and, using the necessary condition for optimality

$$\nabla f(\theta) = 0$$

we have

$$\nabla f(\theta_0) + H(\theta_0)(\theta - \theta_0) = 0$$

or, rearranging, we have

$$\theta = \theta_0 - H^{-1}(\theta_0)\,\nabla f(\theta_0) \tag{A.2}$$

which would give the optimum parameter vector θ, if $f(\theta)$ were a quadratic function. However, since $f(\theta)$ is not quadratic, we modify Equation A.2 to provide a direction along which to search

$$\theta = \theta_0 - qH^{-1}(\theta_0)\,\nabla f(\theta_0)$$

where q is an arbitrary scalar. That is, if $q = 0$, $\theta = \theta_0$, and the point θ is the starting point θ_0. As q changes from zero (either positive or negative), θ will change in a specified way. We say that $H^{-1}(\theta_0)\,\nabla f(\theta_0)$ is a direction because an arbitrary multiple of it is added to θ_0 to create θ.

Once the direction has been established, the variable q must be determined. An obvious criterion would be that of finding q such that $f(\theta)$ is a minimum in the established direction. To achieve this while allowing for nonconcavity, our procedure employs a Fibonacci search on an interval centered about θ_0. A Fibonacci search procedure has

been shown to be optimum in a minimax sense,[5] and can be applied to any unimodal function.

This procedure thus performs the optimization in the following sequence:

1. From a feasible starting point θ_0, find a direction by calculating $\mathbf{H}(\theta_0)$ and $\nabla \mathbf{f}(\theta_0)$. Let $i = 1$.
2. Using a Fibonacci search on an interval centered about θ_{i-1}, find the value of $q = q^*$ for which $f(\theta)$ is a minimum.
3. Let $\theta_i = \theta_{i-1} - q^*\mathbf{H}^{-1}(\theta_{i-1}) \nabla \mathbf{f}(\theta_{i-1})$, and find a direction from θ_i by calculating $\mathbf{H}(\theta_i)$ and $\nabla \mathbf{f}(\theta_i)$.
4. Continue steps 2 and 3 until an optimum is achieved, incrementing i on each iteration.

The second nonlinear procedure which we have used is a technique called *pattern search*.[6] Pattern search is again a method which finds a direction and then moves in that direction. However, unlike the modified Newton's method, the "best" point in the indicated direction is not found. Rather, the distance between the original point θ_0, and the new point θ is determined by the parameters of the search and its recent history of success.

To find a direction, pattern search evaluates $f(\theta_0 + \epsilon_1 \mathbf{e}_1)$, where $\mathbf{e}_1 = (1, 0, 0, \ldots, 0)'$, and ϵ_1 is a scalar whose value is small relative to x_1. (The ϵ_i are the "step sizes" for the algorithm.) If $f(\theta_0 + \epsilon_1 \mathbf{e}_1) < f(\theta_0)$, then $\theta_1 = \theta_0 + \epsilon_1 \mathbf{e}_1$, and $f(\theta_1 + \epsilon_2 \mathbf{e}_2)$ is compared with $f(\theta_1)$. Generally, if $f(\theta_{i-1} + \epsilon_1 \mathbf{e}_1) < f(\theta_{i-1})$, then $\theta_i = \theta_{i-1} + \epsilon_i \mathbf{e}_i$, and $f(\theta_i + \epsilon_{i+1} \mathbf{e}_{i+1})$ is compared with $f(\theta_i)$. If however, $f(\theta_{i-1} + \epsilon_i \mathbf{e}_i) \geq f(\theta_{i-1})$, $f(\theta_{i-1} - \epsilon_i \mathbf{e}_i)$ is compared with $f(\theta_{i-1})$. In summary, a (positive, then perhaps negative) step is attempted in each variable of θ sequentially, *with any point at which success occurs* $[f(\theta_{i-1} + \epsilon_i \mathbf{e}_i) < f(\theta_{i-1})]$ *becoming the base point for the search in the next variable.* Hence, $\theta_k = \theta_0$ if and only if $f(\theta_{i-1} + \epsilon_i \mathbf{e}_i) \geq f(\theta_0)$ for $i = 1, 2, \ldots, k$.

Let us assume that $\theta_k \neq \theta_0$. Then the line connecting θ_0 and θ_k, $q\theta_0 + (1 - q)\theta_k$, becomes the "direction" for pattern search. Rather than finding the "best" point in this direction, however, pattern search assumes that if $f(\theta_k) < f(\theta_0)$, it can be expected that $f(2\theta_k - \theta_0) < f(\theta_k)$. That is, $f(\cdot)$ is evaluated at a distance from θ_k equal to the distance between θ_k and θ_0.

---

[5] For an excellent discussion of the Fibonacci procedure, see Wilde (1964), pp. 24–32.
[6] We are grateful to Professor Timothy McGuire of Carnegie-Mellon University for providing a computer program for pattern search.

If $f(2\theta_k - \theta_0) < f(\theta_k)$, the process is accelerated. This acceleration can take place either by conducting another direction finding excursion from $2\theta_k - \theta_0$,[7] or by simply comparing $f(q\theta_0 + (1-q)\theta_k)$ with $f(2\theta_k - \theta_0)$ for some $q < -1$. For instance, if $f(4\theta_k - 3\theta_0) < f(2\theta_k - \theta_0)$, then compare $f(8\theta_k - 7\theta_0)$ with $f(4\theta_k - 3\theta_0)$, etc. Many other acceleration schemes can be proposed, of course. The major point is that success breeds confidence. That is, for every point which is lower than the previous point, the distance between trial points increases.

Let us now return to the point where we compared θ_k with θ_0, and let us suppose that $\theta_k = \theta_0$. This implies $f(\theta_{i-1} + \epsilon_i e_i) \geq f(\theta_0)$ for $i = 1, 2, \ldots, k$, or that, for steps (from θ_0) of sizes $\epsilon_1, f(\theta_0)$ is a minimum. To test this, pattern search decreases the values of the ϵ_i, and tries to establish a new direction with the smaller step sizes. If a new direction can be found, the search proceeds as above using the new ϵ_i. If no new direction can be found, the ϵ_i are again decreased in value. This process is continued until the ϵ_i are smaller than some lower bound, at which point the routine terminates.

The pattern search procedure can accommodate simple constraints under favorable conditions. Because the derivatives of $f(\theta)$ are not calculated, an inequality constraint involving one variable (e.g., $\theta_i \geq 0$) is inserted by merely setting $f(\theta)$ to $+\infty$ (or some large number) if θ strays into the nonfeasible range. While the use of constraints increases the potential difficulty with local minima (the procedure may get "trapped" against a boundary) our experience with them has been good. More complex inequality constraints of the type $g(\theta) \geq K$ can also be handled in the same way, though our experience with them is minimal. Equality constraints cannot be handled efficiently, as there is no way of insuring that a very high proportion of the values of θ generated in the search will meet the constraint.

The two techniques discussed here have been used in estimating the parameters for many of the models discussed in this book. Each has its advantages, so in many cases each was partially used to find the optimum. Pattern search has the advantage of not requiring too many function evaluations per iteration. The modified Newton procedure has the advantage of taking fewer iterations per comparable decrease in $f(\theta)$, but at the expense of requiring more function evaluations per iteration. Since the function evaluation for the cases studied is quite complicated, each routine was used in the exploloration for minimum

[7] This type of acceleration, as well as a complete description of pattern search, can be found in Wilde (1964, pp. 145–150).

values. The main program alternated a few iterations of pattern search with a few (usually fewer) iterations of modified Newton.

The parameters of the linear learning model, some variants of the probability diffusion models,[8] and the STEAM model have all been estimated many times using the above procedures. Computer running times are in the order of one-half to two minutes of execution on the IBM 360-65. Experiments utilizing widely separated starting values of θ indicate that, for these models at least, the problems of local minima are not severe. The combination of the modified Newton and pattern search procedures seems to be quite powerful for estimating the parameters of stochastic buying behavior models.

[8] See Jones (1969).

REFERENCES

Anderson, T. W., and D. A. Darling (1952), "Asymptotic Theory of Certain Goodness of Fit Criteria Based on Stochastic Processes." *Annals of Mathematical Statistics*, Vol. 23, No. 1, pp. 193–212.

Anderson, T. W., and L. A. Goodman (1957), "Statistical Inference about Markov Chains." *Annals of Mathematical Statistics*, Vol. 28, No. 1, pp. 89–109.

Anscombe, F. J. (1961), "Estimating a Mixed-Exponential Response Law." *Journal of the American Statistical Association*, Vol. 56, pp. 493–502.

Arbous, A. G., and J. E. Kerrich (1951), "Accident Statistics and the Concept of Accident Proneness. Part I: A Critical Evaluation, Part II: The Mathematical Background." *Biometrics*, Vol. 7, pp. 340–429.

Atkinson, Richard C., and William K. Estes (1963), "Stimulus Sampling Theory," Chapter 10 in Luce, Bush and Galanter, *Handbook of Mathematical Psychology*, Vol. II, New York: John Wiley & Sons, Inc.

Atkinson, R. C., G. H. Bower, and E. J. Crothers (1965), *An Introduction to Mathematical Learning Theory*, New York: John Wiley & Sons, Inc.

Barlow, R. E., A. W. Marshall, and F. Proschan (1963), "Properties of Probability Distributions with Monotone Hazard Rates." *Annals of Mathematical Statistics*, Vol. 34, pp. 375–389.

Barlow, R. E., and F. Proschan (1965), *Mathematical Theory of Reliability*, New York: John Wiley & Sons, Inc.

Bartlett, M. S. (1962), *An Introduction to Stochastic Processes*, Cambridge: Cambridge University Press.

Bass, F. M. et al. (1961), *Mathematical Models and Methods in Marketing*, Homewood, Illinois: Richard D. Irwin, Inc.

Bates, G. E., and J. Neyman (1952), "Contributions to the Theory of Accident Proneness. I. An Optimistic Model of the Correlation Between Light and Severe Accidents. II. True or False Contagion." *University of California Publications in Statistics*, pp. 215–76.

Bharucha-Reid, A. T. (1960), *Elements of the Theory of Markov Processes and Their Applications*, New York: McGraw-Hill Book Company, Inc.

Bhattacharya, S. K., and M. S. Holla (1965), "On a Discrete Distribution with Special Reference to the Theory of Accident Proneness." *Journal of the American Statistical Association*, Vol. 60, pp. 1060–1066.

Billingsley, Patrick (1961), "Statistical Methods in Markov Chains." *Annals of Mathematical Statistics*, Vol. 32, No. 1, pp. 12–40.

Billingsley, Patrick (1961), *Statistical Inference for Markov Processes*, Chicago: University of Chicago Press.

Bliven, B., Jr. (1963), "And Now a Word from Our Sponsor." *New Yorker*, March 23, 1963.

Blueman, Isadore, Kogan, Marvin, and Phillip J. McCarthy (1955), *The Industrial Mobility of Labor as a Probability Process*, Cornell Studies in Industrial and Labor Relations, Vol. 6.

Boyd, H. W., Jr., and R. L. Westfall (1960), "An Evaluation of Continuous Consumer Panels as a Source of Marketing Information," Chicago: American Marketing Association, *Marketing Research Techniques*, Series A, No. 4.

Brown, George (1952–53), "Brand Loyalty — Fact or Fiction?" *Advertising Age*, Vol. 23, Jun. 9, Jun. 30, Oct. 6, Dec. 1, 1952; Vol. 24, Jan. 25, 1953.

Brownlee, K. A. (1960), *Statistical Theory and Methodology in Science and Engineering*, New York: John Wiley & Sons, Inc.

Bush, Robert R. (1963), "Estimation and Evaluation," in *Handbook of Mathematical Psychology*, Vol. I, Luce, Bush and Galanter (eds.), New York: John Wiley & Sons, Inc., pp. 429–469.

Bush, Robert R., and Frederick Mosteller (1955), *Stochastic Models for Learning*. New York, John Wiley & Sons, Inc.

Bush, Robert R., and William K. Estes (1959), *Studies in Mathematical Learning Theory*, Stanford, California: Stanford University Press.

Carman, J. (1965), "Brand Switching and Linear Learning Models: Some Empirical Results," Working Paper No. 20, Research Program in Marketing, Graduate School of Business Administration, University of California, Berkeley.

Carman, James M. (1966), "Brand Switching and Linear Learning Models." *Journal of Advertising Research*, Vol. 6, No. 2, pp. 23–31.

Chatfield, C., A. S. C. Ehrenberg, and G. J. Goodhardt (1966), "Progress on a Simplified Model of Stationary Purchasing Behavior." Read before the Royal Statistical Society on March 16, 1966.

Chatfield, C., and G. J. Goodhardt (1969), "The Beta-Binomial Distribution for Consumer Purchasing Behavior." (In process of publication.)

Coleman, J. S. (1963), "The Study of Consumer Behavior in Repetitive Purchases with Consumer Diary Panels," paper presented to the Research Workshop in Marketing, Graduate School of Business Administration, University of California, Berkeley, on July 30, 1963.

Coleman, J. S. (1964a), *Models of Change and Response Uncertainty*, Englewood Cliffs, New Jersey: Prentice-Hall, Inc.

Coleman, J. S. (1964b), *Introduction to Mathematical Sociology*, New York: The Free Press of Glencoe.

Coleman, J., E. Katz, and J. Menzel (1950), "The Diffusion of a New Product Among Physicians." *Sociometry*, January, 1950, p. 253.

Copson, E. T. (1935), *An Introduction to the Theory of Functions of a Complex Variable*, London: Oxford University Press.

Cramér, Harald (1946), *Mathematical Methods of Statistics*, Princeton, New Jersey: Princeton University Press.

Crockett, J., and H. Chernoff (1955), "Gradient Methods of Maximization." *Pacific Journal of Mathematics*, Vol. 5, pp. 33–50.

Cunningham, R. M. (1956), "Brand Loyalty — What, Where, How Much?" *Harvard Business Review*, Vol. XXXIV, No. 1, pp. 116–128.

Cunningham, R. M. (1961), "Customer Loyalty to Store and Brand," *Harvard Business Review*, Vol. XXXIX, No. 6, pp. 127–137.

Dernberg, R. F. (1958), "Consumer Response to Innovation: Television." In Dernberg, Rosett, and Watts, *Studies in Household Economic Behavior* (Volume 9 of Yale Studies in Economics). New Haven, Conn.: Yale University Press.

DeWolff, P. (1938), "The Demand for Passenger Cars in the United States." *Econometrica*, Vol. 6, No. 2, pp. 113–129.

Duesenberry, J. S. (1949), *Income, Saving, and the Theory of Consumer Behavior*, Cambridge: Harvard University Press.

Duhammel, William F. (1966), "The Use of Variable Markov Processes as a Partial Basis for the Determination and Analysis of Market Segments." Unpublished Ph.D. dissertation at the Graduate School of Business, Stanford University.

Edwards, C. B., and J. Gurland (1961), "A Class of Distributions Applicable to Accidents." *Journal of the American Statistical Association*, Vol. 56, pp. 502–517.

Ehrenberg, A. S. C. (1959), "The Pattern of Consumer Purchases." *Applied Statistics*, Vol. VIII, pp. 26–41.

Ehrenberg, A. S. C. (1965), "An Appraisal of Markov Brand-Switching Models," *Journal of Marketing Research*, Vol. 2, 347–362.

Ehrenberg, A. S. C. (1968), "On Clarifying M and M." *Journal of Marketing Research*, Vol. 5, 228–229.

Farley, J. U. (1964), "Why Does Brand Loyalty Vary over Products?" *Journal of Marketing Research*, Vol. I, No. 4, pp. 9–14.

Feller, W. (1950), "Diffusion Processes in Genetics," in *Second Berkeley Symposium on Mathematical Statistics and Probability*, Berkeley: University of California Press, pp. 227–246.

Feller, W. (1957), *An Introduction to Probability Theory and Its Applications*, Vol. I, Second Edition, New York: John Wiley & Sons, Inc.

Ferber, R., and P. J. Verdoorn (1962), *Research Methods in Economics and Business*. New York: The Macmillan Company.

Fiacco, Anthony V., and Garth P. McCormick (1964), "Computational Algorithm for the Sequential Unconstrained Minimization Technique for Non-Linear Programming." *Management Science*, Vol. 10, pp. 601–617.

Foundation for Research on Consumer Behavior (1959), *The Adoption of New Products, Process and Influence*, Ann Arbor, Michigan.

Fourt, L. A., and J. W. Woodlock (1960), "Early Prediction of Market Success for New Grocery Products." *Journal of Marketing*, Vol. XXV, pp. 31–38.

Frank, Ronald E. (1960), "Prediction and Brand Choice." Unpublished Ph.D. Dissertation, University of Chicago.

Frank, Ronald E. (1962), "Brand Choice as a Probability Process." *Journal of Business*, Vol. XXXV, pp. 43–56.

Frank, Ronald E., A. A. Kuehn, and W. F. Massy (1962), *Quantitative Techniques in Marketing Analysis*, Homewood, Illinois: Richard D. Irwin, Inc.

Frank, Ronald E., and William F. Massy (1963), "Innovation and Brand Choice: The Folger's Invasion," in Stephen Grayser (ed.), *Toward Scientific Marketing*, Proceedings of the 1963 Educators Conference of the American Marketing Association, pp. 96–107.

Frank, Ronald E., William F. Massy, and Donald G. Morrison (1964), "The Determinants of Innovative Behavior with Respect to a Branded, Frequently Purchased Food Product," in George Smith (ed.), *Reflections on Progress in Marketing*, Proceedings of the 1964 Educators Conference of the American Marketing Association, pp. 312–323.

Frank, Ronald E. and William F. Massy (1968), "Computer Programs for the Analysis of Consumer Panel Data." *Journal of Marketing Research*, Vol. V, 210–17.

Gani, J. (1961), "On the Stochastic Matrix in a Genetic Model of Moran." *Biometrika*, Vol. XLVIII, pp. 203–206.

Goldberger, A. S. (1964), *Econometric Theory*, New York: John Wiley & Sons, Inc.

Goodhardt (1968), "A Comparison of American and British Repeat-Buying Habits." *Journal of Marketing Research*, Vol. 5, 15–18.

Goodhardt (1968), "Pack-Size Rates of Purchasing." *Proceedings XXI ESOMAR Congress*, Opatija. Brussels: ESOMAR.

Goodhardt (1968), "The Incidence of Brand-Switching." *Nature*, Vol. 220, 5764, 394.

Goodhardt (1968), "The Empirical Approach to Brand-Switching." *Proceedings ESOMAR Seminar on 'OR in Marketing.'* Frankfurt. Brussels: ESOMAR.

Goodhardt (1968), "Repeat-Buying of a New Brand." *British Journal of Marketing*, Vol. 2, 200–205.

Goodhardt and A. S. C. Ehrenberg (1967), "Conditional Trend Analysis: A Breakdown by Initial Purchasing Level." *Journal of Marketing Research*, Vol. 4, 155–161.

Goodman, Leo A. (1958), "Simplified Run Tests and Likelihood Ratio Tests for Markov Chains." *Biometrika*, Vol. 45, No. 2, p. 181.

Grahn, G. L. (1969), "The Negative Binomial Distribution Model of Repeat-Purchase Loyalty: An Empirical Investigation." *Journal of Marketing Research*, Vol. 6, pp. 72–79.

Graybill, F. A. (1961), *An Introduction to Linear Statistical Models*, New York: McGraw-Hill Book Company, Inc.

Greenwood, M., and G. U. Yule (1920), "An Inquiry into the Nature of Frequency Distributions Representative of Multiple Happenings, with Particular Reference to the Occurrence of Multiple Attacks of Disease or of Repeated Accidents." *Journal of the Royal Statistical Society*, Vol. 83, p. 255.

Griliches, Zvi (1957), "Hybrid Corn, An Exploration in the Economics of Technological Change." *Econometrica*, Vol. 25, No. 4, pp. 501–522.

Haines, G. H., Jr. (1963), "A Study of Innovation on Non-Durable Goods." Unpublished Ph.D. Thesis at the Graduate School of Industrial Administration, Carnegie Institute of Technology.

Haines, G. H., Jr. (1964), "A Theory of Market Behavior After Innovation." *Management Science*, Vol. X, No. 4, pp. 634–658.

Harary, F. and B. Lipstein (1962), "The Dynamics of Brand Loyalty: A Markov Approach," *Operations Research*, Vol. X, 1, pp. 19–40.

Harter, H. L., and A. H. Moore (1966), "Local Maximum-Likelihood Estimation of Parameters of Three-Parameter Lognormal Populations from Complete and Censored Samples." *Journal of the American Statistical Association*, Vol. 61, pp. 842–851.

Herniter, Jerome D. (1965), "Stochastic Market Models and the Analysis of Consumer Panel Data." Presented at the Twenty-Seventh National Meeting of the Operations Research Society of America, Boston, Massachusetts, May 6–7, 1965.

Herniter, Jerome D., and Ronald A. Howard (1964), "Stochastic Marketing Models." Chapter 3 in Hertz and O'Donnell (eds.), *Progress in Operations Research*, Vol. II, New York: John Wiley & Sons, Inc.

Herniter, Jerome D., and John Magee (1961), "Customer Behavior as a Markov Process." *Operations Research*, IX, pp. 105–22.

Hoag, R. V., and A. T. Craig (1959), *Introduction to Mathematical Statistics*, New York: The Macmillan Company.

Holland, P. (1966)," A Variation on the Minimum Chi-Square Test," unpublished Ph.D. Dissertation, Department of Statistics, Stanford University.

Holland, P. (1967), "A Variation on the Minimum Chi-Square Test." *Journal of Mathematical Psychology*, Vol. 4, pp. 377–413.

Howard, Ronald A. (1963), "Stochastic Process Models of Consumer Behavior." *Journal of Advertising Research*, Vol. 3, No. 3 (September), pp. 35–42.

Howard, Ronald A. (1965), "Dynamic Inference." *Journal of the Operations Research Society of America*, Vol. 13, No. 2, Sept., pp. 712–33.

Indow, Tarow (1970a), "Models for Responses of Customers with a Constant Rate." Unpublished paper of the Department of Psychology, Keio University, Tokyo, Japan.

Indow, Tarow (1970b), "Models for Response of Customers with a Varying Rate." Unpublished paper of the Department of Psychology, Keio University, Tokyo, Japan.

Johnston, J. (1963), *Econometric Methods*, New York: McGraw-Hill Book Company, Inc.

Jones, J. Morgan (1969), "A Non-Stationary Probability Diffusion Model of Consumer Brand Choice Behavior." Unpublished Doctoral Dissertation in the Department of Operations Research, Stanford University, and Working Paper 146, Operations Research Division, Western Management Science Institute, University of California, Los Angeles.

Karlin, S., and J. McGregor (1959), "A Characterization of Birth and Death Processes." *Proceedings of the National Academy of Sciences*, Vol. XLV, pp. 375–379.

Karlin, S., and J. McGregor (1962), "On a Genetics Model of Moran." *Proceedings of the Cambridge Philosophical Society*, Vol. LVIII, pp. 299–311.

Karlin, S., and J. McGregor (1964), "On Some Stochastic Models in Genetics." in *Stochastic Models in Medicine and Biology*, J. Garland (ed.), Madison, Wisconsin: University of Wisconsin Press, pp. 245–279.

Kemeny, J. G., and J. L. Snell (1959), *Finite Markov Chains*. Princeton, N.J.: D. Van Nostrand Company.

Kendall, M. G., and A. Stuart (1958), *The Advanced Theory of Statistics*, Vol. I, New York: Hafner Publishing Co., Inc.

Kendall, M. G., and A. Stuart (1961), *The Advanced Theory of Statistics*, Vol. II, New York: Hafner Publishing Co., Inc.

Klein, L. R. (1953), *A Textbook of Econometrics*, Evanston, Illinois: Row, Peterson, & Company.

Kuehn, A. A. (1958), "An Analysis of the Dynamics of Consumer Behavior and its Implications for Marketing Management," unpublished Ph.D. dissertation, Graduate School of Industrial Administration, Carnegie Institute of Technology.

Kuehn, A. A. (1962), "Consumer Brand Choice — A Learning Process?" *Journal of Advertising Research*, Vol. II, pp. 10–17.

Kuehn, Alfred A., and Albert C. Rohloff (1965), "New Dimensions in Analysis of Brand Switching." Presented at the Twenty-Seventh National Meeting of the Operations Research Society of America, Boston, Massachusetts, May 7.

Kuehn, Alfred A., and Albert C. Rohloff (1967), "Consumer Response to Promotions." In Partick J. Robinson et al., *Promotional Decisions Using Mathematical Models*, Boston: Allyn and Bacon, Inc.

Lazarsfeld, P. (ed.) (1954), *Mathematical Thinking in the Social Sciences*, New York: The Free Press of Glencoe.

Lipstein, B. (1959), "The Dynamics of Brand Loyalty and Brand Switching," in *Better Measurements of Advertising Effectiveness: The Challenge of the 1960's*, Proceedings of the Fifth Annual Conference of the Advertising Research Foundation, New York.

Lipstein, Benjamin (1965), "A Mathematical Model of Consumer Behavior." *Journal of Marketing Research*, Vol. 2, pp. 259–265.

Lipstein, Benjamin (1968), "Test Marketing: A Perturbation in the Market Place." *Management Science*, Vol. 14, No. 8, pp. B437–B448.

Maffei, Richard B. (1961), "Advertising Effectiveness, Brand Switching and Market Dynamics." *The Journal of Industrial Economics*, Vol. 9, No. 2, pp. 119–131.

Massy, W. F. (1960), "Innovation and Market Penetration," unpublished Ph.D. Thesis, Department of Economics, Massachusetts Institute of Technology.

Massy, W. F. (1965), "Estimation of Parameters for Linear Learning Models," Working Paper No. 78, Graduate School of Business, Stanford University.

Massy, William F. (1966), "Order and Homogeneity of Family Specific Brand-Switching Processes." *Journal of Marketing Research*, Vol. III, No. 1, pp. 48–54.

Massy, William F. (1967), "A Stochastic Evolutionary Model for Evaluating New Products." Presented at the American Meeting of the Institute of Management Sciences, Boston, Massachusetts, April 5–7.

Massy, William F. (1969), "Forecasting the Demand for a New Convenience Product." *Journal of Marketing Research*, Vol. VI, No. 4, pp. 405–413.

Massy, William F., and Ronald E. Frank (1964), "The Study of Consumer Purchase Sequences Using Factor Analysis and Simulation," *Proceedings of the Business and Economics Section of the American Statistical Association*, December.

McConnell, Douglas (1968), "Repeat-Purchase Estimation and the Linear Learning Model." *Journal of Marketing Research*, Vol. V, pp. 304–6.

Miller, G. A., and F. C. Frick (1949), "Statistical Behavioristics and Sequences of Responses." *Psychological Review*, Vol. 56, pp. 311–24.

Montgomery, D. B. (1966), "A Probability Diffusion Model of Dynamic Market Behavior," Working Paper No. 205–66, Alfred P. Sloan School of Management, Massachusetts Institute of Technology, May.

Montgomery, D. B. (1967), "Stochastic Modeling of the Consumer." *Industrial Management Review* (Spring), pp. 31–42.

Montgomery, D. B. (1968a), "The Continuous Limit of the 'Contagious' Binomial Distribution," Working Paper 312–68, Alfred P. Sloan School of Management, Massachusetts Institute of Technology, March.

Montgomery, D. B. (1968b), "Stochastic Consumer Models: Some Comparative Results," in R. King (ed.), *Marketing and the New Science of Planning*, Chicago, Illinois: American Marketing Association.

Montgomery, D. B. (1969), "A Stochastic Response Model with Application to Brand Choice." *Management Science: Theory*, Vol. XV, No. 7, March.

Montgomery, D. B., and G. L. Urban (1969), *Management Science in Marketing*, Englewood Cliffs, New Jersey: Prentice-Hall, Inc.

Mood, A. M. (1950), *Introduction to the Theory of Statistics*, New York: McGraw-Hill Book Company, Inc.

Moran, P. A. P. (1958a), "Random Processes in Genetics," *Proceedings of the Cambridge Philosophical Society*, Vol. LIV, pp. 60–71.

Moran, P. A. P. (1958b), "The Distribution of Gene Frequency in a Bisexual Diploid Population," *Proceedings of the Cambridge Philosophical Society*, Vol. LIV, pp. 468–474.

Morrison, Donald G. (1965a), "Stochastic Models for Time Series with Applications in Marketing," Technical Report No. 8, Program in Operations Research, Stanford University.

Morrison, D. G. (1965b), "New Models of Consumer Behavior: Aids in Setting and Evaluating Marketing Plans," *Proceedings:* Fall Conference of the American Marketing Association, September 1–3, Washington, D.C.

Morrison, Donald G. (1966a), "Interpurchase Time and Brand Loyalty." *Journal of Marketing Research*, Vol. III, pp. 289–91.

Morrison, Donald G. (1966b), "Testing Brand-Switching Models." *Journal of Marketing Research*, Vol. III, pp. 401–409.

Morrison, Donald G. (1968), "Approximate Methods for Calculating the Power of Certain Goodness of Fit Tests." *The New York Statistician*, Vol. 19, No. 3, Jan.-Feb., pp. 5–7.

Neyman, J. (1949), "Contribution to the Theory of the X^2 Test," in *First Berkeley Symposium on Probability and Statistics*, Berkeley, California: University of California Press, pp. 239–273.

Orcutt, Guy H., Martin Greenberger, John Korbel, and Alice M. Rivlin (1961), *Microanalysis of Socioeconomic Systems: A Simulation Study*, New York: Harper & Bros.

Parfitt, J. H. and B. J. K. Collins (1968), "The Use of Consumer Panels for Brand Share Prediction." *Journal of Marketing Research*, Vol. V, No. 2, pp. 131–146.

Parzen, Emanuel (1960), *Modern Probability Theory and Its Applications*, New York: John Wiley & Sons, Inc.

Parzen, Emanuel (1962), *Stochastic Processes*, San Francisco: Holden-Day, Inc.

Pearson, Karl (1934), *Tables of the Incomplete Beta Function.* Cambridge, England: Cambridge University Press. (Published by the Proprietors of *Biometrika*.)

Pratt, John W., Howard Raiffa, and Robert Schlaifer (1965), *Introduction to Statistical Decision Theory*, New York: McGraw-Hill Book Company, Inc.

Raiffa, H., and R. Schlaifer (1961), *Applied Statistical Decision Theory.* Boston: Division of Research, Graduate School of Business Administration, Harvard University.

Rao. C. R. (1961), "Asymptotic Efficiency and Limiting Information," *Proceedings of the Fourth Berkeley Symposium on Mathematical Statistics and Probability*, Vol. 1, pp. 531–546.

Rao, C. R. (1963), "Criteria of Estimation in Large Samples," *Sankyā*, Vol. 25, pp. 189–206.

Rao, C. R. (1965), *Linear Statistical Inference and Its Applications*, New York: John Wiley & Sons, Inc.

Rice, W. T. (1962), "Measurement of Consumer Loyalty: Factor Analysis as a Market Research Tool," unpublished M.S. Thesis submitted to the Alfred P. Sloan School of Management, Massachusetts Institute of Technology.

Richmond, Samuel B. (1964), *Statistical Analysis*, Second Edition, New York: The Ronald Press Company.

Rogers, E. M. (1962), *Diffusion of Innovations*, New York: Free Press of Glencoe.

Roos, C. F., and V. von Szeliski (1939), *Factors Governing Changes in Automobile Demand.* New York: General Motors Corporation.

Savage, L. J. et al. (1952), *The Foundations of Statistical Inference*, New York: John Wiley & Sons, Inc.

Siegel, Sidney (1956), *Nonparametric Statistics*, New York: McGraw-Hill Book Company, Inc.

Styan, G. P. H., and H. Smith, Jr. (1964), "Markov Chains Applied to Marketing." *Journal of Marketing Research*, Vol. I, pp. 50–55.

Suppes, Patrick and Joseph L. Zinnes (1963), "Basic Measurement Theory," Chapter I in Luce, Bush, and Galanter (eds.), *Handbook of Mathematical Psychology*, Vol. I, New York: John Wiley & Sons, Inc.

Telser, Lester (1963), "Least Square Estimates of Transition Probabilities," in *Measurement in Economics*, Christ et al., Stanford, California: Stanford University Press, pp. 270–292.

Wilde, Douglas J. (1964), *Optimum Seeking Methods*, Englewood Cliffs, New Jersey: Prentice-Hall, Inc.

Wilks, Samuel S. (1962), *Mathematical Statistics*, New York: John Wiley & Sons, Inc.

Wold, H., and L. Jureen (1953), *Demand Analysis*, New York: John Wiley & Sons, Inc.

Woodlock, J. W. (1963), "A Model for New Product Decision." Presented to the Chicago Chapter of the American Marketing Association, Nov. 22.

Yance, J. (1955), "Investment Behavior in the Railroad Industry," unpublished Ph.D. Thesis, Department of Economics, Harvard University.

Yule, G. Udny, and M. G. Kendall (1945), *An Introduction to the Theory of Statistics*, London: Charles Griffin & Company, Ltd.

INDEX

Abrams, I. J., 256
Aggregation, 230
Anderson, T. W., 84, 86, 87, 90, 91, 117
Anscombe, F. J., 17, 286, 295, 297, 324, 337, 339, 384
Arbous, A. G., 143, 289, 336
Association, 196
Atkinson, Richard C., 36, 37, 141, 195, 196, 201
Attwood group, in United Kingdom, 6

Barlow, R. E., 285, 348
Bates, G. E., 143, 289, 336
Bayes theorem, 63, 358, 359, 422
Bernoulli model, 16, 18, 47, 52, 59, 60, 73, 77, 167, 168, 199
Beta distribution, 60
Bharucha-Reid, A. T., 229
Bhattacharya, S. K., 289
Billingsley, Patrick, 86
Binomial random variable, 41
Bliven, B., Jr., 264
Blueman, I., 92
Bower, G. H., 36, 37, 195, 196, 201
Boyd, H. W., Jr., 117, 254
Brand loyalty, 52, 100
Brown, George, 52, 53
Bush, Robert R., 10, 15, 141, 145, 151

Carman, James M., 144, 182, 183, 184
Central limit theorem, 71, 238
Charfield, C., 290, 337, 338
Chebyshev's inequality, 44
Chernoff, H., 446
Chicago Tribune, 170
Chi square, 31, 33–36, 42, 47, 72, 249, 267, 287
  additivity property, 72, 74

minimum, 29, 30, 36, 38, 47, 121, 163–165, 233, 247, 260, 375
  variant of minimum, 247
Cohesive element specification, 214
Coleman, James S., 16, 193, 196, 197, 205, 215, 217, 221, 223, 234, 300
Combining of classes, 145
Comparing models, 35, 36, 197
  empirical results for four stochastic models, 267–271
Conditional model probabilities, 64, 95, 101
Conjugate distributions, 63
Contagion, 55, 336
Copson, E. T., 220
Craig, A. T., 27, 32
Cramer, Harold, 24, 25, 26, 30, 34, 72, 74, 121, 238, 248
Crest toothpaste case 171, 179, 254, 265
Crockett, J., 446
Crothers, E. J., 36, 195, 196, 201
Cunningham, R. M., 52, 53

Darling, D. A., 86
Dernberg, R. L., 300, 306, 308, 309
DeWolff, P., 300, 306
Diffusion process, 229
Duesenberry, James S., 300
Duhammel, William F., 9, 87
Dynamic inference model, 77, 156, 177

Edwards, C. B., 289
Ehrenberg, A. S. C., 14, 286, 288, 290, 324, 329, 337, 338, 416
Estes, W., 141, 142, 196
Estimates and estimation, 21, 29
  asymptotically normal, 24, 32, 238–239

461